D1426901

Jack
the
Ripper

Also by Paul Begg:

Into Thin Air: People Who Disappear
The Scotland Yard Files: 150 Years of the CID, 1842–1992
(with Keith Skinner)
The Jack the Ripper A–Z (with Martin Fido & Keith Skinner)
Great Crimes and Trials of the Twentieth Century (with Martin Fido)
Jack the Ripper: The Definitive History

Jack the Ripper

THE FACTS

Paul Begg

First published in Great Britain in 2004 by Robson Books,
The Chrysalis Building, Bramley Road, London W10 6SP

An imprint of Chrysalis Books Group

British Library Cataloguing in Publication Data
A catalogue record for this title is available from the British Library.

ISBN 1 86105 687 7

Typeset by SX Composing DTP, Rayleigh, Essex
Printed by Creative Print & Design (Wales), Ebbw Vale

All pictures from the author's own collection unless credited otherwise.

For Siobán Begg

with love and respect

'I look upon this series of murders as unique in the history of our country . . .'

Contents

Acknowledgements

Since this book was first published I have had the good fortune to meet and exchange correspondence with some amazing people, many of whom I am lucky now to number among my friends. Rather than acknowledge them all, and inevitably forget to mention some important ones, I have just mentioned a few who answered specific questions, provided assistance or, sometimes unknowingly, gave support and encouragement during the writing of this new edition.

My thanks go to: Andy and Claudia Aliffe, Margaret Bird, Alex Chisholm, L Perry Curtis, Christopher-Michael DiGrazia, Christopher George, Mark Madden (for information about Joseph Barnett), Chris Scott (whose trawling through newspaper files has unearthed some gems), Stephen Ryder, Keith Skinner, Matthew Sturgis, Adam Wood, Peter Wood and Eduardo Zinna.

Throughout this book in the notes I have cited Home Office papers and Scotland Yard papers on the case, noted as HO and MEPO respectively. Although the original documents can be examined on microfilm at the Public Record Office, they are quoted in an invaluable book, *The Ultimate Jack the Ripper Sourcebook* (titled *The Ultimate Jack the Ripper Casebook* in the USA) by Stewart P Evans and Keith Skinner.

I would also like to thank Andrew Armitage for copy-editing the book; my editor at Robson Books, Jennifer Lansbury, for the patience she has shown; and Jeremy Robson for his hands-on publishing and for taking on the original title and this rewrite.

Introduction

In the East End of London in the autumn of 1888 at least five women were murdered, and in all but one case horribly mutilated, by a man known to posterity as Jack the Ripper. The crimes were reported around the world and the nickname bestowed on the murderer passed into the public consciousness to represent the ultimate evil.

No murderer had before or has since caused such a sensation, passed so quickly into folklore or gained an image – top hat, cape and Gladstone bag –' that is truly iconic: as instantly recognisable as Sherlock Holmes's deerstalker and meerschaum pipe, and as capable of conveying a meaning understood around the world – even by people who know nothing about the Ripper or what he did, or that he, unlike Holmes, actually existed.

We can probably safely be certain that, like most serial killers, Jack the Ripper was a sordid man, empty in soul and spirit, of no particular merit or distinction, and driven by perverse demons that caused him to commit hideous crimes for no discernible motive beyond the desire to kill and mutilate. Like all such people who step beyond the norm and are therefore interesting, he would probably be worth a book or two, but the sensation he caused and the reasons for it are unique and fascinating, and the Ripper has passed into folklore. The iconic Ripper is an inspiration for stories, novels, musicals – even an opera.

This book is a thoroughly revised and completely rewritten edition of *Jack the Ripper: The Uncensored Facts*, published in 1988. It is in every sense a new book. It had to be. So much has happened that is new. In 1988, while there were a number of texts exploring the crimes and their aftermath fairly thoroughly, there hadn't been a book that restricted itself to a blow-by-blow account of the crimes and their investigation. This was a gap my original edition intended to fill, but I was conscious that many casual readers might pluck the book from the shelf with a sigh and say, 'Not another book about Jack the Ripper! Surely everything there is to say has been said many times already.' So conscious was I of that instinctive reaction that I began that book's introduction with those very words. I am even more conscious of it now, and yet am also aware with hindsight of just how much in 1988 had not been said.

Back then a small shelf was big enough to hold my entire collection of well-thumbed nonfiction Ripper books; today they require two long shelves. There are 85 and most of them were published since 1988 – and that's not including reissues and revised editions, those with a chapter on the Ripper, books about the East End or biographies that mention him, assorted magazines, pamphlets and other printed matter, or the fiction. Even at the time of writing I am aware of at least six or seven titles scheduled for publication (and not simply those in preparation or looking for a publisher), and subscription magazines such as *Ripperologist* and its US counterpart *Ripper Notes* publish lengthy and often detailed articles. Meanwhile, the Cloak and Dagger Club meets six times a year in the crowded and smoky upstairs room of an East End pub to hear a guest speaker, and to exchange and buy Ripper books and collectables; and annual conferences attracting hundreds of people are alternately held in Britain and the USA.

Numerous Internet sites are devoted to or include Jack the Ripper, dominated by *Casebook: Jack the Ripper* (www.casebook.org), where there are hundreds of pages devoted to every aspect of the case, a unique library of newspaper reports, and active discussion groups where minutiae are thrashed out in open forum. Almost every facet of the Ripper and his ethos is fully discussed and debated. This book attempts to put all this information into a detailed, step-by-step account of what happened back in 1888, and to do so with the absolute minimum of speculation and theorising.

CHAPTER ONE

A Background to the Whitechapel Murders

Rip your brothers' vices open,
strip your own foul passions bare.

At 3.20 a.m. on 31 August 1888 Charles A Cross left his home to walk to work. His route took him through Buck's Row, a short, narrow street located behind Whitechapel Station. Towards the end of the street he could see something lying in a gateway and went to investigate. He didn't know it, but at that moment Charles Cross ensured his immortality within the pages of history books. He had stumbled across the first victim of a murderer who would be known to posterity by the chilling sobriquet Jack the Ripper.

Jack the Ripper is generally credited with the murder of five women of the poorest and most degenerate class in the slums of London's East End. He was never caught and the mystery of who he was has exercised the imagination of armchair detectives for over a century.

The Ripper's crimes were extraordinarily brutal and marked by extreme and increasing mutilation, but they were not especially noteworthy in the violent back alleys, dark courts, and grimy gang-ridden streets of the East End, and the murder of a down-and-out Whitechapel prostitute would not have aroused any public interest. Only a few weeks before Charles Cross made his discovery in Buck's Row, a prostitute named Emma Smith had died following a horrendous and apparently unprovoked attack by a gang of men. Her death hardly received any press coverage or public comment, yet the murder of Mary Ann Nichols (that was the name of the woman found by Cross) began what would be a panic that gripped the East End, spread far

1

beyond, and made such an impact on the Victorian consciousness that it continues to reverberate and fascinate to this day.

One of the reasons why Jack the Ripper achieved such notoriety at the time is that he killed in the right place at the right time. Indeed, had he killed in the West End of London or elsewhere in the country, or chosen his victims from another class of woman, it is possible that he would have been forgotten.

Winston Churchill described the 1880s as the end of an epoch[1] and it was indeed a decade of remarkable change that caused many people to feel anxious and some even frightened, and for various reasons the East End was the focus of those anxieties and fears. The middle classes were alarmed by social problems such as prostitution, vice and crime, and fearful of the growth of socialism and unionisation. These and other manifestations of the poor and unemployed flexing their muscles caused some people to think of France, revolution and the Paris Commune of 1871, when, after a week of fierce fighting, 20,000 insurrectionists were killed. Writing of the 1886 and 1887 winter demonstrations by the unemployed in London, Friedrich Engels observed,

> Each succeeding winter brings up afresh that great question 'what to do with the unemployed?' But while the number of unemployed keeps swelling from year to year there is nobody to answer the question; and we can almost calculate the moment when the unemployed, losing patience, will take their fate into their own hands.[2]

Eighteen eighty had dawned with little regret for the decade past. The mind of the nation seemed to be reflected by the weather, depressed and gloomy, a fog without parallel having descended over London in November and remained almost without a break until February.[3] The leader writer of *The Times* observed with an almost palpable sigh of relief, 'We leave behind us in 1879 a year which has combined more circumstances of misfortune and depression than any within general experience . . .' The same sentiment was less wordily expressed a few days later in the Liberal weekly *Reynolds' Newspaper*: 'Eighteen seventy-nine is gone, and we have all reason to be thankful . . .'[4]

Among the problems besetting society, *The Times* cited war on two continents, stagnant commerce, appalling harvests, economic problems and squabbles in politics reaching levels of 'bitterness which the most experienced politicians confess to exceed anything within their remembrance'.[5]

Apart from the problems abroad and the political squabbles, the problems that beset Britain at this time, though many and varied, can loosely be brought under the heading 'urbanisation' – a word that until the 1880s was familiarly used to mean 'make urbane' (refined or good mannered) rather than 'to be of a city'.[6] At the time of Queen Victoria's accession in 1837, the national economy was largely based on agriculture and the majority of the population of England and Wales, which numbered about 14 million, lived in towns, villages and hamlets. By the time of the census in 1851 that had changed: the economy was dependent on the produce of machines rather than the land and more people lived in cities than in rural communities. Victorian England had become the first urbanised and industrialised society on earth. Thirty years later, in 1881, the population had increased to nearly 26 million, nearly three-quarters of whom lived in cities. No other country would approach this situation until after 1900.

London was by far Britain's largest city. Its population in 1831 was 1,474,069, but by 1881 it had increased to 3,830,000, and by 1901 would be 6,586,000 – one-fifth of the total population of England and Wales. It was the biggest city on earth, eighteen miles across and covering nearly seventy square miles. It was, furthermore, the heart and brain of the greatest empire in world history, an empire covering 8 million square miles and consisting of 268 million people – almost a quarter of the earth's surface and a third of the population. It was enormously wealthy. The concentration of personal wealth within the Square Mile was without parallel in the world and its bankers, financiers, insurers, merchants and industrialists were among the richest. Britain produced half the world's iron, half its cotton cloth and two-thirds of its coal. It wasn't dominant in all things, of course, but its foreign trade was about £700,000,000 annually, twice that of Germany and the United States, her leading competitors.

For thousands of people social improvements by the 1880s had made life better than it ever had been. There was better sanitation, mortality rates had declined (except infant deaths[7]), the average life span was longer (making old-age pensions into a major political issue[8]), and cholera and typhus had been eliminated as endemic threats. Individual earnings rose steadily and prices fell (meaning that the value of wages was actually higher than appeared); the number of people in receipt of Poor Law relief fell (0.77 per cent of the population received indoor relief in 1850, 0.69 per cent in 1895). People were eating better – meat consumption per head had increased from 101.4 lb in

1870 to 130.6 lb in 1896, and refrigeration made it possible to import cheap meat and dairy produce from as far afield as Australia and New Zealand.[9] Tea consumption almost doubled between 1860 and 1900, and sugar consumption nearly trebled, as did that of butter and margarine. Business boomed and the appearance of department stores such as Harrods, Marshall and Snelgrove, Peter Robinson and John Lewis, and the expansion of multiples – the newsagents W H Smith and the chemist Boots – show that the 1880s and 1890s were a period of maximum growth. That people had spare money among the middle classes is also apparent from the growing importance of leisure: holidays and excursions, entertainments such as the music hall,[10] and sporting activities such as lawn tennis,[11] cycling,[12] and football.[13]

However, in the midst of this extraordinary wealth there was abject poverty, extensive overcrowded and unfit housing and rampant vice and crime. The masses were mercilessly exploited by the wealthy and generally landed few – the class 'who toil not, neither do they spin', as it was expressed by the radical politician Joseph Chamberlain[14] in 1883. Fewer than 7,000 people owned four-fifths of the land in the United Kingdom and the land provided those people with their wealth. Indeed, the great landowners were phenomenally wealthy and at least seventeen landowners in the 1880s enjoyed annual incomes of in excess of £5 million in today's money. But urbanisation was even hitting the traditional land-owning elite, the agricultural depression diminishing their earning power as the source of wealth shifted from owning land to financing and banking and industry. It was to a degree the decline in agriculture that caused what until the 1930s was known as 'the Great Depression'. It began in 1873 and lasted for two decades, but statistical analysis has shown it to be something of a myth created by an articulate minority consisting of landowners, farmers and the upper classes, who were hit by the fall in profits, interest rates and prices, rather than an economic decline overall.[15]

'The Great Depression' more accurately reflected the mood of the nation, full of doubts, self-questioning and disenchantment. There was also a considerable amount of labour unrest, which was in many respects the dominant feature of the period, relations between employers and employees becoming increasingly bitter and antagonistic, and a remarkably rapid growth of unions. This mood focused attention on workers, who as a general rule were unhappy with their lot.

The problem of unemployment and its attendant poverty in the 1880s was chronic. 'Unemployed' as a noun was first used in 1882 and the economist William Marshall introduced the term 'unemployment' to the study of economics in 1888.[16] For tens of thousands of Victorian Londoners life was a barely tolerable hand-to-mouth existence and the debilitating fear of unemployment was for many faced on a daily basis. It is difficult today to appreciate fully how debilitating unemployment was, because it does not now carry the awful social stigma it did in the 1880s. Apart from the physical hardships there were moral ones: hard work was a fundamental principle of religious and political thought; work meant solvency and solvency was seen as God's favour. No work therefore not only meant insolvency but also implied moral deficiency and the absence of religious sanctity. To be without the means of physical support was bad enough, but to be perceived as morally deficient was horrifying, and heroic struggles were made to keep up appearances and preserve decency. The ultimate degradation was the workhouse, which was a bricks-and-mortar testament to the widespread belief that the individual was responsible for his or her own poverty. Technological change, however, put that erroneous concept into context, because it threw a lot of people out of work, making it increasingly clear that 'conditions' contributed to unemployment.

On 19 March 1887, 29,451 working men in London were questioned and 27 per cent claimed to be out of work that day; 30 per cent said they had been out of work for more than twelve weeks in the previous twenty.[17] Although some workers enjoyed year-round employment, most were in jobs that were subject to countless vagaries: a whole slew of London trades and services, from those involved in the various clothing trades through to catering, depended on the social season, which lasted roughly from February to July. When 'the season' came to an end, and people stopped buying the clothes and requiring the staff, catering and so on, there was a slump until business picked up for the winter – for example, more than 60 per cent of the Court dressmakers became unemployed between June and August. The 1880 season was marked by a shrunken list of entertainments, due to the economic slump and bad weather.

Other workers – building workers, coal and market porters, carters, bakers and, most famously, dockworkers – were among the most vulnerable because they obtained work on a casual day-to-day basis, often waiting hours outside the yard gates in the hope of being chosen for work by the foreman, and, if unlucky, tramping from one place of employment to another. Will Crooks, who would become mayor of Poplar, recalled his desperate days of unemployment:

I first went down to the riverside at Shadwell. No work to be had.
Then I called at another place in Limehouse. No hands wanted. So I
looked in at home and got two slices of bread in paper and walked eight
miles to a cooper's yard in Tottenham. All in vain. I dragged myself
back to Clerkenwell. Still no luck. Then I turned homewards in
despair. By the time I reached Stepney I was dead beat.[18]

These workers were also the most vulnerable to bad weather. Bad
winters could put up to a third of the male workforce out of work. In
February 1855, 50,000 men were put out of work when the Thames froze
and the docks closed. The closure led to widespread unemployment and
the consequent anger, resentment and frustration caused riots and attacks
on bakers' shops in Whitechapel Road and Commercial Street. There was
a repetition of the riots in 1861, when freezing weather put large numbers
out of work, and, as John Hollingshed commented in a book published that
year, 'the distress and suffering that prevail in the metropolis, particularly
among the dock labourers, bricklayers, masons, and labouring classes at the
East End, are truly horrible.'[19] More riots took place in 1867 and the very
harsh winter of 1878–9 saw gangs of unemployed workers roaming London
begging for money.

This was the coldest winter for thirty years. On 8 February a rally was
organised in Trafalgar Square by the antisocialist Free Trade Movement,
and about 20,000 unemployed people attended. In response, the Marxist
Social Democratic Federation announced that it too would hold a meeting
there. That there would be trouble was anticipated, but the police were
completely unprepared for it and most policemen were completely unaware
of it when at some point the two groups clashed. In what seems to have been
a spontaneous decision a large number of SDF supporters left Trafalgar
Square for Hyde Park. There was some minor trouble along the way when
a wine merchant's was broken into, but the general consensus of opinion is
that the real violence began when a member of the Carlton Club,[20] a
Conservative establishment, made a derisory gesture as the procession
passed. The infuriated crowd began to hurl whatever came to hand and
continued to throw stones and smash windows as it moved along St James's
Street and Piccadilly. Some of the rioters also began to loot the shops. Half
the men followed their leader into Hyde Park, but the remainder, estimated
at between four hundred and a thousand, continued to loot and smash
windows until they were confronted by Inspector Cuthbert and fifteen

police constables from Marylebone Police Station. After a small scuffle the rioters dispersed. Damage was estimated as high as £50,000.

Queen Victoria wrote to Gladstone on 11 February,

> The Queen cannot sufficiently express her indignation at the monstrous riot . . . a momentary triumph of socialism and disgrace to the capital. If steps, and very strong ones, are not specially taken to put these proceedings down with a high hand, to punish severely the REAL ringleaders . . . the Government will suffer severely. The effect abroad is already very humiliating to this country . . . The police seem to be greatly to blame.[21]

Gladstone replied on 12 February that in his view the riot had 'stained the reputation of the country in the eyes of the civilised world'. And the whole debacle was hugely embarrassing for the police, most of whom were unaware that anything had happened until it was over, and the commissioner, Sir Edmund Henderson, resigned.

In 1886 Alfred Tennyson published a sequel to his earlier heroic and chivalrous poem 'Loxley Hall'. 'Loxley Hall Sixty Years After' was a scathing satire on Victorian England and the horrible conditions of the poor. Gladstone turned on Tennyson and accused him of marring the happiness of Queen Victoria's Jubilee celebrations. In the journal *Nineteenth Century* in January 1887, Gladstone catalogued a half-century of reforms that had ameliorated the lot of the people, and with 'that boundless, bracing optimism helped make Gladstone the supreme representative of an age of shallow-rooted thought . . .'.[22] He said he could see no grounds for disquiet at all. Gladstone was correct, up to a point. Whereas people in the past would have accepted the social evils as facts of life, they now found them intolerable and wanted to do something about them – 136 new charitable foundations were created between 1880 and 1890, for example – and this alone was a measure of how far civilisation had improved. This truth, however, did not mask the fact that behind the improvements there existed a sewer of abject poverty and vice. And the poor, the unemployed and the working classes were growing increasingly restless.

Large numbers of homeless and unemployed people had been using Trafalgar Square as a place to sleep and the famous fountains there as a place to wash themselves and their clothes. Among those who slept there was Mary Anne Nichols, whose body Charles Cross would discover the following year.

Throughout the year the socialists used it to hold meetings, demonstrations, and assorted spectacles, including a march by 2,000 people, which went from there to the Mansion House on 14 October. The crowds were addressed by numerous luminaries, including William Morris, George Bernard Shaw, Annie Besant and the Russian anarchists Kropotkin and Stepniak.

In 1887, Jubilee year, there was another demonstration in Trafalgar Square. Queen Victoria had in 1886 told Gladstone to take 'very strong' steps and to put down such events 'with a high hand'. The demonstration of 1887 was dealt with so brutally that it was thereafter known as 'Bloody Sunday'.

The new Metropolitan Police commissioner, Sir Charles Warren, believed that the activities of the socialists and the unemployed were potentially very dangerous and on 17 October 1887 he declared a temporary but unconditional ban on all meetings in Trafalgar Square. Unfortunately, there was some doubt about the legality of the ban and on 19 October the new home secretary, Henry Matthews, reversed the ban pending legal opinion.

Sir Charles Warren was a remarkable man who has passed into the history books as a bad commissioner and an even worse military commander, yet his career up to 1887 was successful, albeit not exceptionally distinguished or remarkable. Appointed by the home secretary, Hugh Childers,[23] 'never a figure of great popularity or charm',[24] Sir Charles Warren was born on 7 February 1840 in Bangor, North Wales, the fifth of six children born to Major-General Charles Warren, and educated in Shropshire and at Cheltenham College, Sandhurst and the Royal Military Academy, Woolwich. In 1857 he was commissioned and served with the Royal Engineers. He had several military postings, distinguished himself in Palestine when he undertook a reconnaissance of Philistia, the Jordan valley and Gilead, and also excavated extensively in Jerusalem on behalf of the Palestine Exploration Fund, shedding considerable light on the topography of ancient Jerusalem and the archaeology of the Temple Mount/Haram al-Sherif.[25] He saw action in the Kafir War 1877–8, when he commanded the Diamond Fields Horse, being severely wounded at Perie Bush, and in 1882 he most notably succeeded in discovering the fate of the orientalist Edward Henry Palmer.[26] In 1885 he stood as the Liberal candidate for the Hallam Division of Sheffield, but was narrowly beaten by the Conservative candidate C B Stuart-Wortley and returned to army work, being posted in January 1886 to Sudan, but was very soon afterwards recalled to serve as commissioner of the Metropolitan Police.

In the years to come Warren's tenure of office would be seen as an unmitigated disaster, largely due to the heavy hand he took with the Trafalgar Square demonstrators, and this opinion has become so ingrained that even otherwise sober commentators repeat it,[27] but at the time of his appointment it was generally recognised, particularly after the riots of 1886, that the police needed discipline, and Warren was seen as an excellent choice. *The Times* observed:

> In many essential respects, Sir Charles Warren is precisely the man whom sensible Londoners would have chosen to preside over the Police Force of the Metropolis. Though he is in the prime of life (he is only forty-six), there are few officials in Her Majesty's service who have had more varied experience. He is at once a man of science and a man of action; and for nearly twenty years he has been engaged in work of the kind most likely to develop the administrative faculties.[28]

Warren would not stay in office very long: he would resign amid extensive public criticism shortly before the last accredited Ripper murder and resume his military career, eventually to be dealt another body blow by fate. At the outbreak of war in South Africa, Warren was put in command of the 5th Division and joined Sir Redvers Buller in Natal on 21 December 1899. Here, on 24 January 1900, he commanded a disastrous assault on a hill called Spion Kop, where the British forces were massacred. He has been described as 'arguably the most incompetent British commander of the whole Second Boer War of 1899–1902',[29] but the judgement is probably overharsh because, although he cannot be absolved of responsibility,[30] many officers at the time were rather more critical of General Sir Redvers Buller.[31] Warren was promoted to general in 1904, and colonel commandant of the Royal Engineers in 1905, before retiring in 1906 to spend his final years writing extensively about religious matters, producing a volume of reminiscences called *On the Veldt in the Seventies* and devoting considerable time to Masonic research. He died at Weston-super-Mare on 21 January 1927.

Henry Matthews, the newly appointed home secretary, who would stand beside Warren during the Ripper crimes and share as much if not more odium, was born in 1826 in Ceylon (now Sri Lanka), and educated at the University of Paris and London University. Called to the bar at Lincoln's Inn, he was a skilled and successful cross-examiner who played a part in some notable trials.[32] In 1886 he won the marginal seat of East Birmingham and was appointed home secretary by the prime minister, Lord Salisbury.[33] It was a serious mistake. Matthews managed to be unpopular with almost everyone. He was, as A J Balfour put it, 'the member of the Govt. whom everyone wishes to turn out!'[34] His 'Ministerial career was a complete failure'[35] and it has been said that 'He did more, perhaps, to render the government unpopular than any other minister.'[36] During the Ripper murders Queen Victoria wrote to Salisbury complaining that the home secretary's 'general want of sympathy with the feelings of the *people* [is] doing the *Government* harm'. Salisbury replied with an admission that 'There is an innocence of the ways of the world which no one could have expected to find in a criminal lawyer of sixty.'[37] As it happened, Salisbury couldn't think of a way to get rid of Matthews, and in fact was desperate to keep him in the government,[38] but as soon as possible elevated him to Viscount Llandaff, after which Matthews played little part in public life and died in 1913.[39]

Relations between these two men would deteriorate very badly. Some have placed the blame with Sir Charles Warren – 'Warren was a man noted for his tactlessness and peppery temper; there was a stiff pride about Sir Charles too which made it difficult for him to act in a subordinate capacity . . .'[40] – but other voices laid the blame elsewhere. Evelyn Ruggles Brise, private secretary to four home secretaries, said that Matthews was 'quite incapable of dealing with men; he was a regular Gallio in his attitude to Warren's complaints. Later on he quarrelled with Bradford, and if you couldn't get on with Bradford you could get on with nobody'.[41] Sir Robert Anderson, head of the CID, thought the blame lay with Godfrey Lushington, Matthews's secretary, whose personality he described as an irritant 'blister' when a 'plaister' was needed.[42] Anderson was probably correct.[43]

The hostility between the two men can be observed in their dithering about Trafalgar Square. As they waited for a legal pronouncement on the closure of the Square to demonstrations, Warren became increasingly concerned, telling Matthews,

> . . . the mob, which at first was disorganized, is now beginning to obtain a certain amount of cohesion . . . I think it more than probable that they will get out of hand in a very short time if they are not dispersed . . . they appear to be able to get together now to the number of 2 or 3,000 in two or three minutes . . .[44]

The authorities did not tell the public – and the would-be demonstrators – the reasons for this on/off closure of the square, and the great historian Sir Robert Ensor echoed the opinion of many when he argued that this contributed to the irritation and anger of the demonstrators.[45] Delegates from various clubs met and decided to march to Trafalgar Square and formally protest 'against the illegal interference' in public meetings and then break up the gathering. Meanwhile, Warren, concerned that the socialists planned seriously to disrupt the Lord Mayor's Parade day in November 1887, found a loophole in the law that enabled him to order a ban on all meetings in Trafalgar Square because it was Crown property. As it happened it poured with rain on the day and the Lord Mayor's Parade passed without incident. The peace did not last long. On Friday, 11 November, the Metropolitan Radical Association announced plans to stage a mammoth demonstration the following Sunday. Other groups, including the Social Democratic Federation, the Socialist League, the Home Rule Union and assorted anarchist and radical clubs, groups and organisations joined in. Sir Charles Warren put 5,000 constables on duty, 2,000 in and around Trafalgar Square, and a battalion of Grenadier Guards and a regiment of Life Guards were put on standby. The socialists marched. *The Times* estimated the size of the crowd by mid-afternoon at 20,000; the police estimated the numbers at 40,000 to 50,000 – an estimated 5,000 men had marched from East London alone. The police and the soldiers responded with a very heavy hand. As Annie Besant remarked, 'The soldiers were ready to fire, the people unarmed; it would have been but a massacre.'[46]

In the course of the afternoon two men died, a hundred people were sent with injuries to hospital, 77 constables were injured, 40 rioters were arrested and received sentences of up to eight months with hard labour, and 75 charges of brutality were lodged against the police. W T Stead, the campaigning editor of the *Pall Mall Gazette*, told Gladstone the police were

... characterized by a brutality which I have never before seen in the whole of my life; and the sentences of three and six months, which have been passed upon men who, provoked beyond endurance, struck back at their lawless assailants in uniform are simply infamous.

Later that month, on 28 November, there was a minor conflict with the police and a man named Alfred Linnell suffered injuries from which several days later he died. His funeral on 18 December was huge, matched for size only by that of the Duke of Wellington, and the procession stretched a mile and a half. Annie Besant recorded that 'at Aldgate the procession took three-quarters of an hour to pass one spot'.[47] As Sir Robert Ensor remarks, 'Bitter memories of it [Bloody Sunday] lasted in the working-class districts for over twenty years. Much odium fell on Warren, who was indeed largely to blame; and much on the home secretary, Matthews, who was already unpopular in parliament.'[48]

Although Sir Charles Warren was blamed, his successor's more repressive policies have passed generally unremarked. James Monro banned almost all demonstrations and Home Secretary Matthews had to overrule him so frequently that it strained their relations. When Monro banned a Friendly Societies parade in May 1890, Matthews wrote,

> These men are the pick of the working classes, perfectly orderly, with an excellent object in view. It would be disastrous to get the police into collision with them. Processions are not necessarily illegal . . . I am quite aware how troublesome to the police these demonstrations are, but it will not do to go beyond the law in dealing with them. In the case of Trafalgar Square the law was strained to the utmost; but public safety and public opinion supported the action of the Police. That would not be so in this instance.[49]

Bloody Sunday 'ended in such a decisive victory for the authorities that it marked the end of revolutionary heroics based on the plight of the East End poor'.[50] It was a defeat for socialism, and Lord Salisbury observed that 'by October 1892 socialist quackeries will either have been dropped or they will have been exposed by experience'. As one biographer wryly observed, 'It is fortunate for Lord Salisbury that history judges him for his governance rather than his sooth-saying.'[51] On the other hand, some saw it as the start of something bigger and more disturbing: '. . . men and their families are hovering on the brink of starvation, and there is grave reason to fear that a social revolution is impending.'[52]

In the 1830s and 1840s there was widespread concern about the slum districts – not, one feels, a concern for the plight of the people who lived there, but anxiety about what would happen if they ever spilled beyond the confines of their ramshackle and squalid tenements, to spread dirt, disease, immorality and crime into respectable society. It was widely accepted that the slums, or rookeries as they were commonly known in those days, were the home and refuge of criminals. Whether or not they were is uncertain.

There appears to have been little reported crime in the rookeries themselves, but that probably means nothing, since the rookeries would have been self-policing and the denizens unlikely to possess much of value that had been obtained legally and could therefore be reported 'lost'. The whole point of concern, though, was that the rookeries were the homes of and bred criminals, not that they were places where crimes were committed. The most notorious rookery was an area called St Giles, depicted by Hogarth in *Gin Lane, The First Stage of Cruelty, A Harlot's Progress* and *The Idle Apprentice*. It is said that 54,000 people lived there in 1851. In his *Sketches by Boz* in the 1830s, Charles Dickens, who had a curious love of slums and descended into the depths of Whitechapel when the opportunity presented itself, described St Giles as

> Wretched houses with broken windows patched with rags and paper; every room let out to a different family, and in many instances to two or even three – fruit and 'sweetstuff' manufacturers in the cellars, barbers and red-herring vendors in the front parlours, cobblers in the back; a bird-fancier in the first floor, three families on the second, starvation in the attics, Irishmen in the passage, a musician in the front kitchen, a charwoman and five hungry children in the back one – filth everywhere – a gutter before the houses, and a drain behind – clothes drying, and slops emptying from the windows; . . . men and women, in every variety of scanty and dirty apparel, lounging, scolding, drinking, smoking, squabbling, fighting, and swearing.

After St Giles the most notorious rookery was Saffron Hill, where Fagin lived in *Oliver Twist* (1838). Bill Sikes lived in Bethnal Green and Dickens portrays Fagin as moving through the heart of future Ripper territory to visit him:

> The house to which Oliver had been conveyed, was in the neighbourhood of Whitechapel. The Jew stopped for an instant at the corner of the street; and, glancing suspiciously round, crossed the road, and struck off in the direction of Spitalfields.

Concerns about the plight of the labouring classes led to enquiries and investigations by select committees, royal commissions, statistical societies, local bodies and other groups. Reports were produced and Acts passed by

Parliament, among them the City Sewers Acts (1848, 1851), Sanitary Act (1866) and the Torrens Act (1868). And large areas of slum dwellings were destroyed for new roads and commercial premises, railways, docks and assorted public and private buildings. St Giles vanished under New Oxford Street in 1846–7, Saffron Hill under Farringdon Street, and some of the Whitechapel and Spitalfields rookeries vanished with the building of Commercial Street.[53] Nobody paid much interest in the welfare of the estimated 100,000 people[54] who were unceremoniously evicted, and public concern about the poor waned considerably. Their concern was reawakened in the 1880s and from 1883 there was a succession of articles and pamphlets from writers and campaigners such as Henry Mayhew, George Godwin, George Augustus Sala, James Greenwood, Richard Rowe and Walter Besant, and notably a series of illustrated articles in *Pictorial World* by the popular journalist and playwright George Sims in which he compared the slum districts and their denizens to unexplored lands and the savage tribes who lived there. According to William Booth, founder of the Salvation Army, the slums were 'a dark continent that is within easy walking distance' and full of 'nameless abominations' and 'the last Alsatias where lawlessness still reigns supreme'.[55]

Surprisingly Sims's series made little impression, but the moment was right for the Reverend Andrew Mearns, secretary of the London Congregational Union, who drew on Sims and other writers to produce a twenty-page penny pamphlet called *The Bitter Cry of Outcast London*, which described in vivid detail 'rotten and reeking tenements', gross overcrowding, sweated occupations, drunkenness, brutality and sex and crimes, claiming to a horrified and aghast readership that 'incest is common'.[56] The success of Mearns's pamphlet was undoubtedly due to its being taken up by W T Stead, editor of the ever-campaigning and circulation-hungry *Pall Mall Gazette*,[57] who reprinted it and darkly warned of popular unrest and even socialism. He caused it to grab the public conscience and sense of alarm by the throat and shake it vigorously.[58]

In 1886 a shipping-line owner named Charles Booth began a survey of poverty in London, beginning with the East End and ultimately covering the whole of the metropolis. Born in Liverpool on 30 March 1840, the third son of a wealthy corn merchant, he inherited £20,000 and invested it in the construction of two steamships, *Augustine* and *Jerome*, thus founding the Booth Steamship Company, of which he remained chairman until 1912. From this elevated position Booth was an unlikely figure to be concerned with the plight of the poor, but in 1865 he had stood for election as the Liberal parliamentary candidate and in the course of his house-to-house canvassing he visited the slums of Toxteth and had been horrified by conditions of poverty and squalor that he otherwise wouldn't have believed existed. With the revival of interest in poverty and the housing of the poor in the 1880s, Booth was angered and moved by the contradictory claims and counterclaims of various groups who disputed the extent of pauperism and, indeed, its causes. Booth had always applied statistics in his business dealings and now determined to use statistical methods to study the extent of pauperism in London, to which he and his family had moved in 1875. The results of his investigations were published in seventeen volumes between 1889 and 1903 entitled *Life and Labour of the People in London*. The survey, which *The Times* called 'the grimmest book of its generation', revealed that 35.7 per cent of East Londoners and 30.7 per cent of all Londoners were living in abject poverty. Booth also showed that poverty was not a consequence of fecklessness, idleness, improvidence or drink, but was in the main caused by low pay and the casual and irregular nature of much employment. A successive enquiry by Seebohm Rowntree in York produced similar conclusions. He wrote,

That in this land of abounding wealth, during a time of perhaps unexampled prosperity, probably more than one-fourth of the population are living in poverty, is a fact which may well cause great searchings of heart. There is surely need for a greater concentration of thought by the nation upon the well-being of its own people, for no civilization can be sound or stable which has at its base this mass of stunted human life.

Charles Booth, along with his unrelated namesake William Booth of the Salvation Army, Canon Samuel A Barnett, vicar of St Jude's in Spitalfields and founder of Toynbee Hall, and the socialist politician H M Hyndman, among other notable figures, shared the opinion that there existed a 'residuum' of hopeless and irretrievable people who corrupted and debased respectable workers, and for whose eradication various solutions were suggested, ranging from enforced confinement and retraining in rural labour colonies to compulsory sterilisation.[59]

Booth showed that there were areas of greater poverty than the East End, among them parts of Southwark and riverside Westminster, but by the time he had begun his survey East London had a reputation as a place not just of exceptional hardship but also of menace. This reputation had grown throughout the 1870s and 1880s, and is reflected in the work of popular novelists, the trend being kicked off by Walter Besant's *All Sorts and Conditions of Men*, published in 1882, Arthur Morrison's East End trilogy *Tales of Mean Streets*, *A Child of the Jago* and *To London Town*, and Israel Zangwill's wonderful novels of the Jewish East End.

1888

Eighteen eighty-eight was a very dull year. Most history books don't mention it at all, or mention it in passing. There was no cause for anxiety abroad, so Britain practically spent the whole year absorbed with its own affairs. Politically there was little happening and Lord Salisbury, 'a political philistine', was not a Gladstone or a Disraeli in terms of impressing himself upon the public conscience, although he provided a type of stolid security. The most important political achievement of the year, and to some extent of the period in general, was the Local Government Act, which set up elected county councils in England. There was a singular lull in the world of labour affairs, better trade conditions probably absorbing large numbers of the unemployed who had made headlines with their marches and demonstrations in previous years. Housing reform continued to arouse popular interest and in January a Board of Trade report for the first time revealed the horrors of sweated labour. There was little action, but a lot of talk, much of it following obscure diversionary side paths.

At the same time there was a report by a private committee investigating the conditions of women's industry, and women themselves began to campaign for rights of their own, notably the workers at the large Bryant and May match-making factory in Fairfield Road, Bow. In June 1888 Clementina Black[60] had given a speech on female labour during the course of which she cited the bad conditions endured by the workers at Bryant and May. The indomitable Annie Besant, who was a member of the audience, was so horrified that she personally interviewed several of the workers herself and wrote about her investigations in the newspaper *The Link* under the arresting title WHITE SLAVERY IN LONDON. She wrote about how the women worked fourteen hours a day, earned less than 5 shillings a week, and were subject to fines ranging from 3 pence to 1 shilling imposed by the management for sins such as dropping matches, going to the toilet without permission or arriving late for work. She also pointed out that the job done by these women was dangerous because Bryant and May used white/yellow phosphorus, which was banned in other countries because it led to a form of bone cancer nicknamed phossy jaw, which could cause the jawbones to rot and glow greenish-white in the dark. Phossy jaw was sometimes immediately fatal, but could be resolved by the agonising and disfiguring surgical removal of the jawbone.

In response, Bryant and May tried to force its workers to sign statements denying the claims made in the article, and threatened to sue Besant and *The Link*. When a group of women refused to sign and their organisers were immediately sacked, the workers went on strike, Annie Besant won the support of W T Stead, Henry Hyde Champion, Catherine Booth and George Bernard Shaw, and called for the public to boycott Bryant and May matches. Despite *The Times*' blaming of Annie Besant and her supporters for the dispute,[61] after three weeks the company caved in and agreed to re-employ the dismissed women and end the fines system.[62] The strike made national news, was a widespread talking point and inspired the formation of unions all over the country. It also focused attention on the East End.

Lord Sydney Godolphin Osborne[63] sarcastically observed that 'at last people were finding out about the awful conditions of the East End and the horrors that existed in the slums of England, whilst £500,000 was raised annually for foreign missions and even larger amounts were spent on lavish buildings such as the Church House at Westminster, and its time on a Pan-Anglican conference of bishops from all over the world'.

The 'crisis of faith' of this period is marked by a number of novels, the most popular being the extraordinarily long and massive bestseller *Robert Elsmere*[64] by Mrs Humphry Ward,[65] published in April by the London firm of Smith, Elder. It caused a widespread and often heated controversy and provoked Gladstone to write an article ' "Robert Elsmere" and the Battle of Belief'.[66] Ward's loss-of-faith novel was about a hard-working country vicar who loses his belief in miracles and resigns his living, going to live in the East End, where he founds a New Brotherhood of Christ, preaching a blend of Christianity, Positivism and the social gospel. The novel was a book of its time. For most people religious belief was the aggressive evangelical sort so typified by Victorian hymns such as the Reverend Augustus Toplady's beloved 'Rock of Ages', which accepted that the Bible was literally true: that the world had been created 6,000 years ago, that everyone was descended from Adam and Eve and that Noah and his family were the only survivors of a universal flood. During the 1880s and the 1890s there was widespread doubt and even attacks on evangelical religion, the roots of which were in the controversy surrounding the evolutionary theories of Charles Darwin – revived by his death in 1882. Other books took the same theme, among them *The Christian* by Hall Caine,[67] about a clergyman torn between his celibate vows and love for his childhood sweetheart, who becomes a slum priest in the East End. *The Christian* sold 50,000 copies in a month and, with *Robert Elsmere* and several other titles, brought the East End to further public attention.

In the arts, the musical passion of 1888 was for coster songs, working-class ditties with titles such as ''E's All Right When You Know 'Im, But You've Got to Know 'Im Furst'. They reflect the widespread popularity among all classes of the music hall and coster performers, who included Little Titch, Pimlico-born Gus Elen,[68] who began as a street busker with a barrel organ in the Strand in the 1880s and who achieved such popularity that by 1900 he could command £250 a week (over half a million a year in modern money), and Harry Champion, a near-contemporary of Elen's, whose songs 'Any Old Iron', 'I'm Henery the Eighth, I Am', and 'Boiled Beef and Carrots' are still well known more than a century later. Others were Albert Chevalier,[69] perhaps the most famous coster performer of them all, and Dan Leno, possibly the most famous entertainer of his time, who in 1888 began the first of fifteen seasons at the Theatre Royal, Drury Lane. The popularity of these Cockney songs and their performers also served to direct attention to the East End, although ironically the famous Wilton's Music Hall in the East End closed in 1888 and was turned into a mission hall.

The other 'crazes' of 1888 were football and parachuting. The Football League was founded in that year, its creation announced at a meeting at Anderton's Hotel in Fleet Street on 22 March and the first game kicking off on 8 September. Among the players was Arthur Wharton, the first black professional footballer, who from 1886 to 1888 was known as the fastest man in Britain (he broke the 100-yards world record) and for reasons that seemingly defy explanation played numerous games for Preston North End and Rotherham in goal.[70] As for parachuting, an American aeronaut, Captain Thomas Scott Baldwin,[71] who apparently called himself, or became known as, 'Professor Baldwin', arrived in England in the summer of 1888 and gave a number of exhibitions at Alexandra Palace using a (for the time) sophisticated parachute of his own invention – a silk device with a vent. Witnesses were both astonished and terrified by the great distance Professor Baldwin fell before he opened his parachute, but this was a deception caused when the balloon he had jumped from sprang upwards once its load had been lightened by the professor's exit.[72] Professor Baldwin exhibited elsewhere, including a goose fair in Nottingham, where he joined the world champion trick cyclist W G Hurst (who did fifty tricks on a Beeston Humber bike) as one of the entertainments. By chance, one of the policemen prominently involved in the Ripper enquiry, Detective Reid, was a balloonist.[73] Apart from coster songs, football, parachuting and trick cycling, novelties such as electric lighting and phonographs using wax instead of tinfoil cylinders[74] managed to attract widespread attention in 1888.

Other highlights of the year were the tercentenary celebrations of the Armada, complete with a re-enactment of a game of bowls on Plymouth Hoe; the launch of *The Star* newspaper, which would probably give more publicity to the Ripper crimes than any other; and in May the amalgamation in South Africa of De Beers and the Kimberley Central Diamond Mining company, which thus became a virtual monopoly and was in a position to fix diamond prices to this day.

Politics was dull. Nothing happened that caught the public imagination except the dirty and government-assisted campaign by *The Times* to smear the Irish Home Rule champion Charles Stewart Parnell. A participant, although only on a small scale as far as is known, was Robert Anderson, head of the CID at the time of the Ripper murders, and in 1910 his activities at this time regarding 'Parnellism' would land him in very hot water and almost cause him to lose his pension.

Overall, then, 1888 was a fairly dull year, but much of the interest of the time, as indeed is true of the decade thus far, concerned social problems, which in turn put the East End even more in the spotlight. Indeed, as Peter Ackroyd perceptively remarks in his *London: The Biography*, 'All the anxiety about the City in general then became attached to the East End in particular, as if in some peculiar sense it had become a microcosm of London's own dark life.'

The late Victorians lived through dramatically and rapidly changing times. Their economy had changed from land-based to manufacturing-based, and the established social order had changed and was changing still. These changes generated very real fears and anxieties, even apprehension of revolution, and they were fed by the social ills of London: the slums, the poverty and the immorality and crime. The East End came to represent all the ills of London as a whole, and as a result all fears and anxieties about the changing times; and Jack the Ripper came to represent the East End, as he inadvertently embodied the preoccupations of his times in a perhaps unique way: he was all the fears and anxieties wrapped in a human form, a flesh-and-blood embodiment of all that was wrong with London and with society as a whole. This lurker in the shadows, secret and silent, represented the uncertain future against which there was no defence.

Although Jack the Ripper has little historical importance, he focused national and international attention on the East End and indirectly forced slum landlords to sell their properties for redevelopment. As Jerry White noted in his history of one such redevelopment, the barrack-like tenement-block Rothschild Dwellings, 'Within six years, then, Jack the Ripper had done more to destroy the Flower and Dean St rookery than fifty years of road building, slum clearance and unabated pressure from police, Poor Law Guardians, vestries and sanitary officers.'

He impacted on and in turn became part of the public consciousness. In this respect Jack the Ripper most certainly did make a mark on history, and his crimes and times are certainly worthy of study.

CHAPTER TWO

The Beginning

The murders committed by the creature known disturbingly to posterity as 'Jack the Ripper' were characterised by extensive mutilation of the victim, the womb being the target of his attacks. It is generally accepted that he killed only five women, the characteristic mutilations being absent in one instance, possibly because the murderer was disturbed. However, it is doubtful that Jack the Ripper began his career with a full-blown murder and mutilation. He probably began with acts of lesser violence that bore none of his hallmarks: there were a number of violent attacks and murders in Whitechapel, some of which may have been the Ripper's work. Whether they were or not, they primed both the press and the public to react with outrage and horror when the 'first' Ripper murder took place.

Fairy Fay

The earliest of these attacks was on 'Fairy Fay', or so several contemporary newspapers reported, but there is no evidence that such a person ever existed. The story is interesting, however, as an example of how a tale is woven without substance. It also introduces one of the many extraordinary people wandering the streets of London in the latter years of the Victorian period.

The story of Fairy Fay has its origins with a journalist named Terence Robertson and an article in *Reynolds' Newspaper*. According to Robertson,

On the cold Boxing Night of 1887, she decided to take a short cut home from a pub in Mitre Square. This decision, which took her through the dim alleyways behind Commercial Road, cost her her life.

Two hours after she set out, a constable, on beat, shone his flickering oil lamp into a darkened doorway. At the inquest he said his lamp revealed a sight which sickened him.

21

In its ray was all that was left of 'Fairy Fay.'

Inspector Reid of Commercial Road police station took charge. His detectives questioned dozens of people who lived in the drab house overlooking the scene of the crime.

After a few weeks of vain inquiries, Inspector Reid informed his chief at Metropolitan Police Headquarters, New Scotland Yard, that the case had been shelved.

Only brief reports of the murder appeared in the Press, and by February the case was forgotten.[1]

The story was picked up by the writer Tom Cullen in his book *Autumn of Terror*. He told pretty much the same story, but says that the murdered woman was unidentified, 'Fairy Fay' being a name bestowed upon her, and specifically stating that she had been mutilated, which Robertson implied with the words 'all that was left of . . .'

Contemporary newspapers mention a murder at Christmas 1887:

The first of the series of murders was committed so far back as last Christmas, when the body of a woman was discovered with a stick or iron instrument thrust into her body as if she had been interred under the law until recently applicable to suicides, which required a person found guilty of *felo de se* [suicide] to be buried at the four cross-roads with a stake driven through the chest. In this case the woman was never identified, and no particular sensation was caused, the death being generally assumed to be the result of a drunken freak on the part of the nameless ruffians who swarm about Whitechapel. The second noticeable tragedy occurred on Aug. 7 last, when a woman named Martha Turner, aged thirty-five, a hawker, was discovered lying dead on the first floor landing of some model dwellings . . .[2]

Researchers have not been able to trace a record of any crime such as that described and the general opinion is that the crime and victim were an invention born out of confusion, its genesis being with the later murder of Emma Elizabeth Smith, who as we shall see was brutally attacked by a gang of men and an object was rammed into her vagina. She was left for dead, but was able to return to her lodging and be assisted from there to the London Hospital, where she later died from her injuries. Emma Smith differs from the Christmas 1887 victim in that she died in hospital rather than in the street, and the stake was not driven into her chest. But the method of killing bears such a close parallel that it is difficult not to conclude that they were one and the same.

Another newspaper also indicates that the earlier victim was never identified, or that poor Emma Smith's name was forgotten:

> And then other stories began to be told – not by the people, but by the police themselves, and founded only too well upon facts. They showed how high the public passion was against the murderer of Annie Chapman, Polly Nicholls, Martha Tabram, and the poor unfortunate of Osborn-street – for all four were laid at the door of the one man.[3]

I have not found a list of victims ascribed to the Ripper that includes both the Christmas 1887 victim and Emma Smith, and it is noticeable that Robertson likewise omitted the murder of Emma Smith. That they were one and the same is ultimately confirmed by a Parliamentary exchange reported in the *Manchester Guardian*, where an MP made reference to 'the case of the first murder, committed last Christmas, according to the dying testimony of the woman, several persons were concerned.'[4] That the victim of the Christmas assault lived long enough to say that she had been attacked by several persons makes the identification almost certain.

Where the date came from is an altogether different question. It has been suggested that it was supplied by a 54-year-old widow called Margaret Hayes.[5] Most newspaper reports of the murder of Emma Smith carried Hayes's claim to have been attacked in the same location as Smith shortly before Christmas 1887. Hayes, who actually lived in the same lodging house as Emma Smith, had been so brutally attacked that she remained from 8 December until 28 December 1887 in the Whitechapel infirmary.[6] It is not known whether the attack on Margaret Hayes provided the date of the mythic attack at Christmas 1887, but it seems possible.

The name 'Fairy Fay' cannot be traced beyond Terence Robertson's article in *Reynolds' Newspaper* and it is assumed to be his invention. The authors Nicholas Connell and Stewart Evans suggest that perhaps it was in part derived from a *Reynolds'* report of the appearance at Marlborough Street Court of a notorious woman known as Tottie or Tot Fay: '. . . Lillie Herbert alias Tot Fay, Lillian Rothschild, Florence St John, Mabel Gray, Lilly Cohen, Amy Sinclair, Lillian Rose, Amy Violet, Florence Le Grand, and a score of other fictitious names . . .'[7]

Tot Fay seems to have been a colourful character and at the time of her appearance at the magistrates' court, *Reynolds' Newspaper* called her 'one of the most notorious women in London' and said that 'Wherever she is charged she gives a different name, and always talks about her mamma and her relations . . .' No doubt extremely difficult and irritating, she nevertheless caused a few smiles. When she was arrested for accosting a man in Bury Street, the newspaper reported that she pleaded in court the next day:

'On my soul, I never spoke to a soul, except a friend with whom I had a cup of coffee. I walked with him to his chambers, and he was just raising his hat to say good-bye when that wicked man [pointing to the constable] came up and dragged me off like a felon. I give you my word as a lady that I never spoke to anyone else all the evening. Indeed, I would not lower myself to speak to a gentleman unless he first saluted me. I have had a great deal of trouble since I lost my dear mamma, and I only yesterday got over a serious misfortune. It is a cruel shame that I should be exposed to such degradation as this at the hands of a vulgar policeman. Really, sir, it is not safe for a young lady to walk in the streets by herself.'

   Sergeant Brewer: 'The serious misfortune to which she refers was a sentence of fourteen days' imprisonment she had at Bow Street.'

As late as 1891 she was still being hauled before the magistrates, pleading innocence and claiming that her troubles were the result of wicked policemen. *Lloyd's Weekly News* reported in November that year that she had tried to occupy a room in a man's house, claiming that she had missed her last bus, lost her latch key and 'did not want to disturb her poor ma'. In court the next day she declared to the magistrate:

'Oh, sir, kind sir, I am an unfortunate young lady – most unfortunate – and these wicked policemen – Well, there, they club together to ruin me. I was really interfered with by that man last night owing to the French shoes I was wearing. I could – really I couldn't – hardly walk, and was carrying a costume box. This man accosted me, when I had thoroughly made up my mind to pull myself together . . .'

The exchange went on along these lines for some time until the magistrate sent her to prison for three months. Tot Fay rounded on the policemen: 'Ho! Look at the wicked lies you have told. I'll have you for this. Oh, my God! Three months! Well!'[8]

Tottie or Tot Fay is even mentioned with just a hint of nostalgia by the journalist George R Sims in his book *Glances Back*:

> And in those days we had Tottie Fay, who was constantly appearing at the police court in a mud-stained opera cloak and ragged ball dress, explaining to the magistrate that though she had been overcome by liquor she was 'a perfect lady'.[9]

Tot Fay may have ended her days in Broadmoor, where she was committed in February 1894 suffering from maniacal fits.

There was also an actress named Tottie Fay whom I've come across in Robert Graves's powerful autobiography *Goodbye to All That* (1929). Describing a field punishment suffered by his servant, Private Fahy, Graves says he was 'known as "Tottie Fay" after the actress'.

Although 'Tot Fay' was the most famous of her numerous aliases, it is nevertheless difficult to believe that it suggested the name 'Fairy Fay' to Robertson. Perhaps a simpler explanation is that Terence Robertson simply took 'Fairy Fay' from the song 'Polly Wolly Doodle', where it is repeated throughout in the chorus, as in:

> *Fare thee well, fare thee well,*
> *Fare thee well my fairy fay*
> *For I'm going to Lou'siana for to see my Susyanna*
> *Sing Polly wolly doodle all the day.*

Annie Millwood

Thirty-eight-year-old Annie Millwood, the widow of a soldier named Richard Millwood, was first advanced as a possible victim by Philip Sugden in 1994.[10] She lived at 8 White's Row, Spitalfields, and on 25 February 1888 she was admitted to the Whitechapel Workhouse Infirmary. According to a brief report in the *Eastern Post* she was

> suffering from numerous stabs in the legs and lower part of the body. She stated that she had been attacked by a man who she did not know,

and who stabbed her with a clasp knife which he took from his pocket. No one appears to have seen the attack, and as far as at present is ascertained there is only the woman's statement to bear out the allegations of an attack, though that she had been stabbed cannot be denied. After her admission to the infirmary deceased progressed favourably, and was sent to the [Whitechapel Union Workhouse] South Grove . . .[11]

She was admitted to the workhouse on 21 March and on 31 March she was engaged in conversation with Richard Sage, the workhouse messenger, when he had to attend to someone else. He returned after about three minutes to find her lying on the floor. Thomas Badcock, the master of the workhouse, immediately telephoned to the infirmary for assistance from Dr Arthur, but, realising that this was a case of extreme emergency, sought assistance from a Dr Wheeler of Mile End Road. The doctor pronounced life extinct and the body was removed to the mortuary.[12]

The East Middlesex coroner, Wynne E Baxter, of whom we shall hear a great deal more, held an inquest. Death was attributed to 'sudden effusion into the pericardium from the rupture of the left pulmonary artery through ulceration'.[13] The jury returned a verdict of death from natural causes.[14]

It has been noted that Annie Millwood's injuries were similar to those suffered by Martha Tabram, a later victim of a brutal and fatal attack, and that she may have been assaulted by the same person. There is no real reason to suppose that this was the case, however, or that she was a victim of Jack the Ripper, and the *Eastern Post*'s comment that 'there is only the woman's statement to bear out the allegations of an attack' may hint at suspicions that the injuries, though severe, were self-inflicted.

Ada Wilson

At 12.30 a.m. on Wednesday, 28 March 1888, a man knocked at 19 Maidman Street, Bow, 'a small thoroughfare lying midway between the East India Dock and Bow roads',[15] the home of a young[16] dressmaker named Ada Wilson, who answered the door. A man she did not know stood there. She later described him as aged about thirty, five foot six in height, with a sunburned face and fair moustache, and dressed in dark coat, light trousers and wide-awake hat. The man demanded money, threatened to kill her if she did not produce any, and when she refused took out a clasp knife and stabbed her twice in the throat. Screams for help were heard and two young women rushed up to two constables, 232K and 539K, who were on duty outside the Royal Hotel. They went immediately to the house in Maidman Street and found Ada Wilson lying in the passage, bleeding profusely from a wound in the throat. They immediately sent for a Dr Wheeler of Mile End Road who attended to the wounds, then sent her to hospital. The police, led by Detective Inspectors Wildey and Dillworth, began a search for the man. Ada Wilson recovered enough to give an account of what had happened and provide the description of the man,[17] and, against early predictions that she would not recover, got better and was discharged on 27 April.

Some possibly interesting insights were provided by Rose Bierman, described as a 'young Jewess' by the *Eastern Post*, which also described the story of an attack by a man knocking on the door as 'alleged'. She said,

'Ada Wilson, the injured woman, is the occupier of the house, but at the time of the outrage she was under notice to quit. I knew Mrs. Wilson as a married woman, although I had never seen her husband. Last evening she came into the house accompanied by a male companion, but whether he was her husband or not I could not say. She has often had visitors to see her, but I have rarely seen them myself, as Mrs. Wilson lives in the front room, her bedroom being just at the back, adjoining the parlour. My mother and I occupy two rooms upstairs. Well, I don't know who the young man was, but about midnight I heard the most terrible screams one can imagine. Running downstairs I saw Mrs. Wilson, partially dressed, wringing her hands and crying, "Stop that man for cutting my throat! He has stabbed me!" She then fell fainting in the passage. I saw all that as I was coming downstairs, but as soon as I commenced to descend I noticed a young fair man rush to the front door and let himself out. He did not seem somehow to unfasten the catch as if he had been accustomed to do so before. He had a light coat on, I believe. I don't know what kind of wound Mrs. Wilson has received, but it must have been deep, I should say, from the quantity of blood in the passage. I do not know what I shall do myself. I am now "keeping the feast," and how can I do so with what has occurred here? I am now going to remove to other lodgings.'[18]

Ada Wilson was first mentioned as a possible Ripper victim in 1987 by Martin Fido,[19] who noted that the description of the attacker was similar to those later given of a man or men seen with a victim shortly before they were found dead. Other authorities have demurred, Philip Sugden in 1994 arguing that the attack was too far east of the Ripper's known hunting ground and that Ada Wilson's own account indicated that she was the victim of an attempted robbery that went horribly wrong.[20] However, it must be said that the robbery story seems implausible: would a robber knock on the door of a strange house and demand money from whoever opened the door? Rose Bierman said the front door was closed and the 'young fair man' was in the house. It therefore seems possible that Ada Wilson, who 'often had visitors', was a prostitute and that she was attacked by a client, the man with whom she had returned home. Was he the Ripper? Nobody will ever know, but the use of a knife and targeting the throat may fit his MO.

Emma Smith

Emma Elizabeth Smith was 45 years old, five foot two, of fair complexion, with light-brown hair and an identifying scar on her right temple. She claimed to have been a country girl, but apparently hadn't returned home for ten years or more. The widowed[21] mother of two children, a boy and a girl who at the time of her death were living in the Finsbury Park area, she had for some eighteen months been living in a common lodging house at 18 George Street, paying 4d for her bed. She was noted for leaving the house between 6 p.m. and 7 p.m. and returning at various times, usually drunk.

She evidently didn't hold her drink well Mrs Mary Russell, deputy keeper at the lodging house in George Street, said that she had known the dead woman for about two years. She said that, when Emma had had drink, she acted like a madwoman, had often come home with black eyes given to her by men and had on one occasion returned home saying she had been thrown out of a window.[22]

Walter Dew, who would achieve fame as the detective who raced across the Atlantic in time to arrest Dr Crippen[23] for the murder of his wife Belle Elmore, was assigned to Whitechapel at the time of the Ripper crimes. In his autobiography, he wrote,

Emma, a woman of more than forty, was something of a mystery. Her past was a closed book even to her most intimate friends. All that she had ever told anyone about herself was that she was a widow who more than ten years before had left her husband and broken away from all her early associations.

There was something about Emma Smith which suggested that there had been a time when the comforts of life had not been denied her. There was a touch of culture in her speech unusual in her class.

Once when Emma was asked why she had broken away so completely from her old life she replied, a little wistfully: 'They would not understand now any more than they understood then. I must live somehow.'[24]

On the night of Easter Monday, 3 April, she seems to have stuck to her routine. She was seen by 54-year-old Margaret Hayes,[25] a fellow lodger at 18 George Street, at 12.15 a.m. near Farrant Street, Burdett Road, talking to a man dressed in dark clothes and a white scarf. Hayes had seen Smith while fleeing the neighbourhood, where she said 'there had been some rough work that night' and where only a few minutes earlier she had been assaulted by two men, one of whom had stopped her by asking her the time and the other had struck her on the mouth before both had run away. Hayes also said that she had been hurt by men just before Christmas 1887[26] and had been two weeks in the infirmary. Hayes's stories are testimony to the roughness of the area, but her observation that 'there had been some rough work that night' might indicate that some gangs were on the warpath the night Emma Smith was murdered.

An hour and a quarter later, Emma Smith was making her way down Whitechapel Road. Ahead of her, near Whitechapel Church, were two or three men, one of them looking like a youth aged about nineteen. She crossed the road to avoid them – Emma Smith didn't say why she did this or what had alarmed her – but they followed and as she turned into Osborne Street, and opposite 10 Brick Lane, about 300 yards from her home at 18 George Street, the men assaulted her, robbed her of all the money she had, and rammed an object into her vagina. Somehow she managed to get back to her lodgings – the reports suggest that she returned there between 4 p.m. and 5 p.m., which if true means that she took two hours or more to cover 300 yards. Either she had been in considerable pain, or she'd been unconscious for some of that time (or the attack was later than she thought). At the

lodging house she saw several lodgers, among them Margaret Hayes and
Annie Lee, as well as Mary Russell, the deputy. Russell and Lee saw that
Emma Smith's face was bleeding, that her ear was cut and that she was in
distress, and took her to the London Hospital in Whitechapel Road, about
half a mile away. Emma reportedly went to the hospital reluctantly. The
locals feared the hospital, as they did the workhouse, as Frederick Treves,
an intern there in 1888, explained:

> The hospital in the days of which I speak was anathema. The poor
> people hated it. They dreaded it. They looked upon it primarily as a
> place where people died. It was a matter of difficulty to induce a
> patient to enter the wards. They feared an operation and with good
> cause, for an operation then was a dubious matter. There were stories
> afloat of things that happened in the hospital, and it could not be
> gainsaid that certain of these stories were true.[27]

The three women walked the half-mile to the hospital and en route Smith
pointed out the spot close to Taylor Bros cocoa factory where she had been
assaulted. Mary Russell said Smith had seemed unwilling to go into details
and this may have been because of the pain she was in, but Inspector
Edmund Reid noted in his report, 'She would have passed a number of PC's
en route but none was informed of the incident or asked to render assistance.' Perhaps this reluctance to involve the police was because she knew
her assailants and knew the punishment they would later exact if she talked.

At the London Hospital she was attended by a doctor.[28] She was able to
talk about what had happened to her and, although the doctor thought she
had been drinking, she was sober and aware of what was happening, but
there was little that could be done. Peritonitis set in, from which Emma
Smith died at 9 a.m. on 4 April.

The first the police knew of the attack was on Friday, 6 April, when the
office of the coroner for East Middlesex, Wynne E Baxter, reported that the
inquest would be held the next day at the London Hospital. Police attended.
The verdict was 'wilful murder'.

Only Walter Dew ever seems to have believed that Emma Smith was a
victim of Jack the Ripper. In his autobiography he wrote, 'I have always held
that Emma Smith was the first to meet her death at the hands of Jack the
Ripper',[29] but Dew's memory of the crime is clearly in error over detail and
it is otherwise quite clear that she was the victim of a brutal attack by several

men. It was with her murder, however, that the police opened the Whitechapel Murders file, a file that remained open until completion of the investigation into the murder of Frances Coles in February 1891. The file embraced the Jack the Ripper murders, but not all the murders were attributed to the Ripper and there was and is a degree of disagreement about which were and which were not his work. Emma Smith, though, was clearly the victim of a brutal assault, just one of what we can assume to have been several on the streets that night.

That said, we have only Emma Smith's word that she was attacked by a group of men. There is no plausible reason why she would have lied on this point, but she seems to have taken a long time to reach her lodgings, was reluctant to go to the hospital (where she would have to explain her injuries), didn't want to talk about the incident to her lodging-house companions and didn't approach any of the policemen she passed on the way to the hospital. All of this can be explained, but it does open the possibility, remote though it may be, that Walter Dew was correct in thinking she was killed by just one man.

CHAPTER THREE

Martha Tabram

Born on 10 May 1849 at 17 Marshall Street, London Road, Southwark, Martha Tabram was the youngest of five children born to warehouseman Charles Samuel White and his wife Elizabeth (née Dowsett). Her siblings were Henry (twelve years older than Martha), Esther (ten years older), Stephen (eight years older) and Mary Ann (three years older). Charles and Elizabeth, Martha's parents, separated about 1865 and Charles died later that year.[1]

By 1869, Martha was living with a man named Henry Samuel Tabram in Pleasant Place and they married at Trinity Church in St Mary's Parish, Newington, on Christmas Day 1869. At the time of his wife's death Samuel was described as a short, well-dressed man with iron-grey hair, moustache and imperial beard, employed as a foreman packer by a furniture warehouse in Deptford. At some point they moved to 20 Marshall Street, where in February 1871 Martha gave birth to their first child, a boy whom they named Frederick John. In December the following year their second son, Charles Henry, was born.

The marriage was troubled by Martha's heavy drinking and in 1875 Henry Tabram finally refused to live with Martha. He gave her an allowance of 12s. 0d. a week for three years, but, when she began accosting him in the street and pestering him for money, he reduced it to 2s. 6d. Martha responded by having a warrant taken out against him and he was locked up. When he learned about 1879[2] that Martha was living with another man, he flatly refused to support her any further. He saw her on and off after that, the last time being about eighteen months before her death, when he saw her in Whitechapel Road. She was then drunk.

Her new partner was William Turner (some sources say Henry), a sometime carpenter who at the time of the murder was hawking cheap trinkets, menthol cones and needles and pins. Described as short, dirty and dressed in a slovenly manner, he had a pale face sporting a light moustache and

imperial beard. Martha had begun living with him in 1879. Their relationship was also troubled by Martha's excessive drinking, which was the cause
of frequent separations. Turner told the inquest into Martha's death, 'Since
she has been living with me, her character for sobriety was not good. If I give
her money she generally spent it in drink. In fact, it was always drink.'[3]

She frequently went out at night and generally did not return home until
late. Sometimes she stayed out all night, which she generally explained by
claiming to have suffered a hysterical fit and been taken to the police station.
Turner said he had witnessed these fits and that they usually happened
because she was drunk. They finally separated some three weeks before her
death. The couple had been living at 4 Star Street, off the Commercial
Road, a common lodging house run by Mary Bousfield, the wife of a
woodcutter named William Bousfield. Mary Bousfield said Martha wasn't a
perpetual drunk but was a woman who would 'rather have a glass of ale than
a cup of tea'. When Turner left her, Tabram absconded owing her rent. A
perhaps touching insight into Martha's character is that one night she
returned to the lodgings and without seeing anyone left the key.

William Turner took lodgings at the Victoria Working Man's Home on
Commercial Street. He last saw Martha alive on 4 August in Leadenhall
Street, near Aldgate Pump, when he gave her 1s. 6d. to buy trinkets for trade.

Martha lived in a common lodging house at 19 George Street, Spitalfields,
using the name 'Emma' and trying to earn a living through selling trinkets
and prostitution. She was five foot three, with dark hair and a dark
complexion,[4] and was known to the police, having once been sentenced to
seven days' hard labour for having consistently annoyed the widowed sister
of Henry Tabram, Ann Morris, described as a 'very respectable woman'.[5]
Ann Morris lived at 23 Lisbon Street, Cambridge Heath Road, and Martha
thought she had encouraged her brother to leave her. Mrs Morris said she
had brought charges against Martha for annoyance on three occasions, once
after she had broken Mrs Morris's windows. Martha had served her seven
days and since then the annoyances had stopped.[6]

Monday, 6 August, was a bank holiday. The weather was poor, gloomy
grey skies threatening rain. Nobody knows what Martha Tabram did with her
day, but perhaps between 7 p.m. and 8 p.m. she may have gone out drinking.
Ann Morris saw Tabram outside or entering a pub she thought was the White
Swan in Whitechapel Road.[7] Tabram, she said, 'was then quite alone'.[8]

At 10 p.m. Martha entered the Two Brewers pub at 154 Brick Lane with
two soldiers – a corporal and a private – and a friend named Mary Ann

Connelly, known as 'Pearly Poll', a tall, masculine-looking woman[9] whose face was 'reddened and soddened by drink'[10] and who was a prostitute. The two women had known each other for four or five months. For the previous two nights Connelly had been living in Crossingham's lodging house in Dorset Street.[11]

Between 10 and 11.45 p.m. Martha, Connelly and the two soldiers visited various pubs in and around Whitechapel, drinking ale and rum.[12] Then, at 11.45 p.m. Martha Tabram and Mary Connelly separated with their respective soldier clients. Connelly took her customer, the corporal, up Angel Alley. Martha and the private appeared to go off towards Whitechapel. Connelly's business soon concluded, she left the corporal at the corner of George Yard at 12.15 a.m. She headed towards Whitechapel and the corporal went in the opposite direction towards Aldgate.

At 1.40 a.m. Joseph Mahoney, a carman, and his wife Elizabeth, who worked at a match factory in Stratford, returned to their home at 47 George Yard Buildings, described as 'a block of model dwellings, inhabited by people of the poorest description, and situated just off the Whitechapel-road'.[13] George Yard Buildings were in the northeast corner of George Yard, backing onto Toynbee Hall. George Yard itself is a narrow alley running north–south and entered from Whitechapel High Street via a covered archway next to the White Hart (which still exists). In 1888 the archway led 'into a number of courts and alleys in which some of the poorest of the poor, together with thieves and roughs and prostitutes, find protection and shelter in the miserable hovels bearing the name of houses.'[14]

Mrs Mahoney, a young woman aged 25 or 26, returned down the stairs some five minutes later to get some supper from the chandler's shop (selling groceries and general supplies) in Thrawl Street. She returned within ten minutes. The staircase was unlit and she did not notice anything suspicious on the stairs, nor did she hear any unusual sounds during the rest of the night.

At 2 a.m. PC Thomas Barrett, 226H, saw a soldier, a Grenadier, in Wentworth Street. He described the man as aged between 22 and 26, five foot six, of fair complexion with dark hair and a small brown moustache turned up at the ends. He had one good-conduct badge and no medals. PC Barrett asked the man why he was loitering in the street and the soldier replied that he was 'waiting for a mate who had gone with a girl'.[15]

At 3.30 a.m. Alfred George Crow, aged 23 or 24, with closely cropped hair and a beardless, intelligent face, who was a cab driver (cab number 6.600) and lived at 35 George Yard Buildings, went up the same steps as

Mahoney and noticed a body lying on the first-floor landing. Since it was not uncommon to see people asleep or drunk on the landing, he did not pay any attention.[16]

At 4.50 a.m.[17] John Saunders Reeves, a waterside labourer, 'a short man, with a slight dark beard and moustache, a pale and a contracted face . . . and wearing earrings',[18] left his room at 37 George Yard Buildings to go to work. On the first-floor landing he saw the body of Martha Tabram lying in a pool of blood. Without bothering to examine the body, he ran for a policeman and returned with PC Barrett 226H. Barrett immediately summoned another constable and sent him for Dr Timothy Robert Keleene of 68 Brick Lane.

It was 5.30 a.m. when Keleene examined the body and estimated that death had occurred about three hours earlier (about 2.30 a.m.). Martha Tabram had been stabbed 39 times. Among the wounds there were five in the left lung, two in the right lung, one in the heart, five in the liver, two in the spleen and six in the stomach. The breasts, stomach, abdomen and vagina had been the target of the wounding. With one possible exception, all the wounds had been made by a right-handed man,[19] and all but one of the wounds could have been inflicted with an ordinary penknife. The exception was a wound on the chest bone, which appeared to have been made with a stronger-bladed weapon such as a dagger or sword bayonet.

Dr Keleene also said that the stomach contained food in the process of digestion and 'stated positively that there were no signs of there having been recent connexion'.[20] However, there was a deal of blood between the legs, which were separated.[21]

A photograph of the corpse was taken on 8 August 1888, and her description was circulated in 116 infirmaries.[22]

The only real clue was Pearly Poll's statement that Martha Tabram had parted from her company and gone off with a soldier at 11.45 p.m., presumably for the purpose of sex.[23] However, the doctor was certain sexual intercourse had not taken place. This need not be suspicious, since most prostitutes devise ways to simulate intercourse without actual penetration, but it could lead one to suspect that the soldier went off with Martha with murder rather than sex in mind, or possibly cause one to wonder whether Martha was indeed in the company of Pearly Poll and two soldiers that night. It was at 2 a.m., some two and a quarter hours later, that PC Barrett spoke to a Grenadier guardsman who was loitering in Winthrop Street waiting for a companion who had gone off with a girl. It's doubtful that this can have been the same man, unless Connelly's timings were completely awry. However, the time does tie in with the estimated time of Martha Tabram's death.

Over the next few days Detective Inspector Edmund Reid personally supervised several line-ups of soldiers. The first, on 7 August, was at the Tower of London, where several Grenadier guards were brought before PC Barrett in the guardroom, but he failed to recognise any as the man he had seen in Wentworth Street. The following day, 8 August, Detective Inspector Reid and PC Barrett returned to the Tower and those Grenadier guards who had been on leave on the night of the murder were again paraded before the junior policeman, who picked out two men. Both were taken to the orderly room, where Barrett immediately said that he was mistaken about the first man, who was allowed to leave without having his name taken. The second man, whose name was John Leary, proved able to give an account of himself on the night of the murder and his alibi was independently confirmed by a private named Law and satisfied the police.[24] While the police were there a Corporal Benjamin, who had been absent without leave since 6 August, returned to barracks. His clothing and bayonet were examined, but no marks of blood were found on them and he was able to satisfy the police that he had been staying with his father, the landlord of the Canbury Arms,[25] Kingston-on-Thames, at the time of the murder.

The Metropolitan Police files also refer to a Mrs Jane Gilbank and her daughter, residing at 23 Catherine Wheel Alley, Aldgate, who claimed to have seen Tabram with a private of the Guards on the night of her murder. They were brought to the Tower by Sergeants Leach and Caunter,[26] and were sent one at a time along the rank, but failed to pick out anyone. It was subsequently realised that the woman they thought had been murdered and had seen was a Mrs Withers, who was afterwards found alive.[27]

Mary Ann Connelly turned up at Commercial Street Police Station on 9 August and told her story, agreeing to attend a line-up at the Tower of London the following day, but she did not turn up. She was eventually located by Sergeant Caunter on 12 August at the home of her cousin, Mrs Shean, 4 Fuller's Court, Drury Lane.[28] She would tell the inquest that she was unaware that she was twice wanted for identification parades and there was also some comment about her having threatened to drown herself, but the threat, she said, was 'a lark'. The identity parade eventually took place on 13 August. 'Can you see here either of the men you saw with the woman now dead?' she was asked, and 'in no way embarrassed, placed her arms akimbo, glanced at the men with the air of an inspecting officer, and shook her head . . .' She was patiently asked again if she could identify anyone, and 'exclaimed, with a good deal of feminine emphasis, "He ain't here." '[29] She then explained that the soldiers who had been with her had had white bands around their caps, which identified them as Coldstream Guards at Wellington Barracks. On 15 August those who had been on leave on the night of the murder were paraded before Connelly and she unhesitatingly identified two men, Private George and Private Skipper, the former having two good-conduct stripes, which could have led to his being mistaken for a corporal. Both had alibis that were verified, one being at home at 120 Hammersmith Road with his wife (or a woman supposed to be his wife), and the other in barracks.[30] In his memoirs Walter Dew said that Connelly picked out the two men 'in a fit of pique'.[31]

The inquest was opened on the afternoon of 9 August 1888, in the lecture room and library at the Working Lads' Institute, Whitechapel Road. It was described in one newspaper as a 'well and prettily furnished' room, the walls displaying portraits of the royal family and landscape pictures, one particularly magnificent portrait of the Princess of Wales by Herr Louis Fleischmann hanging above the seat occupied by the coroner, who on this occasion was George Collier, the deputy coroner of the South-Eastern Division of Middlesex, the coroner, Wynne E Baxter, being on holiday. On the left of the coroner sat the jury; on his right Dr Keeling sat with Inspector Reid, the latter described as 'a smart looking man, dressed in blue serge, who, without taking so much as a note, seemed to be absorbing all the material points'. Before the coroner sat a woman in a blue dress and black hat, and with a white checked blue handkerchief round her neck. She had a baby in her arms, and 'was accompanied by another woman – evidently her mother – dressed in an old, brown figured pompadour'.[32] She had been taken by Mr Banks, the coroner's officer, to view the body at the mortuary, and had identified it as Martha Turner, but two other women had also identified the body and supplied different names. The inquest was quickly adjourned in the hope that the police would confirm the identity of the deceased. It was reopened after two weeks, a small group of people gathering outside the Working Lads' Institute to watch the arrival of the witnesses and functionaries. More evidence was heard, and the jury, after some excited talk, returned a verdict of wilful murder against some person or persons unknown. They also asked that the stairs in 37 George Yard and similar properties be lighted until after eleven o'clock at night.

Public interest in the case overall was minimal, hardly anyone but the authorities and witnesses being present, 'the public being conspicuous by their absence,' remarked the *East London Advertiser*,[33] which also observed that the police 'are very reticent upon the matter generally, and are not disposed to assist in the publication of details'. Walter Dew confirms that the police kept 'the Press at arms length' and thought this policy – 'the policy of those in high places' – a mistake insofar as it 'flouted a great potential ally, and indeed might have turned that ally into an enemy'. A number of rumours circulated, some of them very contradictory, but most proved to be without foundation. Even before the inquest had been concluded, however, a journalist for the *East London Advertiser* felt it necessary to rebut opinions that the East End was a den of vice and iniquity:

'. . . some fearful-minded persons think the inhabitants of particular parts of our district are all ruffians and viragoes, who acquired a taste for thieving and violence in their mother's arms. The finger of scorn is only too frequently held up to us by those whose sense of justice and even common honesty should tell them how undeserved is this wholesale condemnation. Such opinions and sentiments are so ridiculous that were it not for the harm they do it would not be worth while to notice them. What are the facts? The statistics or returns of criminal offences show that, in proportion, there is really no more crime, either of a greater or lesser degree, in East London than in any other part of the metropolis, or, for the matter of that, in Great Britain.[34]

And so it was that the investigation into the death of Martha Tabram slowly fizzled out, the only clue to her murderer being Connelly's story about the soldiers, but that led nowhere. Her murder was frenzied and horrendous, her sexual organs a particular focus, as in the case of Emma Smith. However, unlike those of the later victims commonly attributed to Jack the Ripper, her throat was not cut and she was not eviscerated, which is why she has commonly been dismissed as a Ripper victim. Nevertheless, unlike Emma Smith, whose story about being attacked by a group of men seems to have been accepted by almost everyone, Walter Dew excepted,[35] Tabram was considered a Ripper victim by Frederick Abberline, Sir Robert Anderson, Edmund Reid, and Dew. She should, perhaps, be placed in the canon.

CHAPTER FOUR

Mary Ann Nichols

On 31 August 1888, in the predawn darkness of a narrow East End street called Buck's Row, Charles Cross[1] saw what at first he thought was a piece of tarpaulin. Crossing the road to investigate, he discovered that it was the body of a woman who would later be identified as Mary Ann Nichols, sometimes known by the nickname 'Polly'. The daughter of a locksmith and later blacksmith named Edward Walker[2] and his wife, a laundress, Caroline (née Webb), Mary Ann was born on 26 August 1845[3] at Dawes Court, Shoe Lane, off Fleet Street, the second of three children. The eldest was Edward, born in 1843 and the youngest, Frederick, was born in 1849. We know next to nothing of her early life, but on 16 January 1864 Mary Anne married an Oxford-born printer named William Nichols at St Bride's Parish Church, Fleet Street.[4] They had five children, Edward John, born 1866; Percy George, 1868; Alice Esther, 1870; Eliza Sarah, 1877; and Henry Alfred, 1879.

They lodged briefly at 30–31 Bouverie Street,[5] then moved in with her father at 131 Trafalgar Street, off Walworth Road, for about ten years, during which time they were witnesses at the marriage of her brother Edward Walker, an engineer, to Mary Anne Ward on Christmas Day 1869 at St Peter's Church, Walworth. On 6 September 1880 they finally got a home of their own at 6 D-Block, Peabody Buildings, Stamford Street, Blackfriars Road,[6] where they paid a rent of 5s. 9d. per week.[7] Edward Walker at this time went to live with his son at Guilford Street, Walworth.

All was not well in the Nichols family home and the marriage was marked by a series of separations[8] that led in 1880 to its breaking up for good. When Mary Ann left the family home, William Nichols later claimed that the marital troubles had been caused by Mary Ann's heavy drinking. Her father, while acknowledging that she drank heavily,[9] alleged that William Nichols had taken up with the woman who had nursed Mary Ann through her last confinement. Nichols did not deny the affair, but denied that Mary Ann had left him over it:

'I did not leave my wife during her confinement and go away with a nurse-girl. The dead woman deserted me four or five times, if not six. The last time she left me without any home, and with five children, the youngest one year and four months. I kept myself with the children where I was living for two and a half years before I took on with anybody, and not till after it was proved at Lambeth Police-court that she had misconducted herself.'[10]

Whatever the truth about the cause, there was obvious disharmony in the family and the eldest son would have nothing to do with his father at his mother's funeral.

We know a surprising amount about Mary Ann Nichols's movements in the years that followed, including her brief attempt at rehabilitation when she took a job as a domestic servant. Mary Ann moved out of the family home in September 1880 and went to Lambeth Workhouse, perhaps an indication of her desperation, since the workhouse was generally detested and avoided at all costs. They would feature prominently in what remained of Mary Ann's life:

6 September 1880–31 May 1881: Lambeth Workhouse, described herself as a charwoman.

31 May 1881–24 April 1882: Not known. William discontinued supporting his estranged wife and when the parish authorities tried to collect maintenance money he explained she had deserted him, left the children in his care and was living with another man. The man was not Thomas Drew, a blacksmith with whom she took up later.[11] William later discovered she had taken to earning a living as a prostitute. He won his case. At the time of her death, he had not seen his wife in three years.

24 April 1882–18 January 1883: Lambeth Workhouse.

18–20 January 1883: Lambeth Infirmary.

20 January–24 March 1883: Lambeth Workhouse.

24 March–21 May 1883: 131 Trafalgar Street, Walworth. This would most probably be the time when her father said that she was living with him. He said that he had not found her to be a sober woman, though she was not in the habit of staying out late at night. Her drinking had nevertheless caused friction. They had had words one night and she had left of her own volition the following morning.

21 May–2 June 1883: Lambeth Workhouse.

2 June 1883–24 October 1887: No record. This would correspond with the time when she was said to have been living with a man named Thomas Stuart Drew, a widower from 1884, when his wife had died leaving him with three children. He was a blacksmith with a shop at 15 York Street, Walworth. In June 1886, respectably dressed, Mary Ann Nichols had attended the funeral of her brother, who had been burned to death when a paraffin lamp exploded.[12]

25 October 1887: St Giles Workhouse, Endell Street.

26 October–2 December 1887: Strand Workhouse, Edmonton.

2–19 December 1887: No record. It was revealed that at this time she was in the habit of sleeping in Trafalgar Square. When a clearance of the area was made, it was discovered that she was destitute and had no means of subsistence, and she was admitted as an inmate of Lambeth Workhouse.

19–29 December 1887: Lambeth Workhouse.

29 December 1887–4 January 1888: Not known.

4 January–16 April 1888: Mitcham Workhouse (Holborn) and Holborn Infirmary (Archway Hospital).[13]

16 April–12 July 1888: Mrs Fielder, the matron of Lambeth Workhouse, found Mary Ann employment as a domestic servant with Mr and Mrs Cowdry in Wandsworth. She began work on 12 May 1888[14] and wrote to her father, 'I just write to say you will be glad to know that I am settled in my new place, and going on all right up to now. My people went out yesterday, and have not returned, so I am in charge. It is a grand place inside, with trees and gardens back and front. All has been newly done up. They are teetotallers, and religious, so I ought to get on. They are very nice people, and I have not too much to do. I hope you are all right and the boy has work. So goodbye for the present. From yours truly, "Polly". Answer me soon please, and let me know how you are. "Ingleside", Rose Hill.' Mr Walker had replied to this letter, but did not hear from his daughter again. On 12 July 1888, however, he received a postcard from Mrs Sarah Cowdry saying that Mary Ann had stolen clothing worth in excess of £3 10s.[15] from her employers and absconded.

12 July–1 Aug 1888: Not known.

1–2 August 1888: Gray's Inn Temporary Workhouse.

2–24 August 1888: 18 Thrawl Street. She shared a room with three other women and her bed with Emily Holland.

24–30 August 1888: The 'White House', 56 Flower and Dean Street, 'a doss house where men and women were permitted to sleep together'.[16]

Mary Ann Nichols was described as five foot two, with a dark complexion, brown eyes, brown hair turning grey,[17] with small and delicate features, and high cheekbones. Her teeth were a little discoloured,[18] with five missing.[19] Her friend Emily Holland, 'an elderly woman with a naturally pale face',[20] described her as 'a very clean woman'[21] 'who talked very little about her affairs' and who 'always seemed very melancholy, as though some trouble was weighing upon her mind'.[22] She always seemed to 'keep herself to herself'.[23] Nichols was almost certainly an alcoholic, two men having left her because of her drinking habits. She must nevertheless have been an attractive woman with her high cheekbones, and somehow she had managed to preserve a youthful appearance throughout the privations she had endured. A reporter for the *East London Observer* guessed her age as between 30 and 35.[24] At her inquest her father stated that 'she was nearly 44 years of age, but it must be owned that she looked ten years younger'.[25]

The night on which Mary Ann Nichols was to die, 30 August, there was a storm, sharp and frequent rain accompanied by peals of thunder and flashes of lightning dramatically splitting the night sky. Mary Ann Nichols was seen at 11 p.m. walking in Whitechapel Road. She went drinking in the Frying Pan public house in Brick Lane, which she left at 12.30 a.m., and at 1.20 a.m. she was in the kitchen of the common lodging house at 18 Thrawl

Street, where she was seen by the deputy lodging house keeper, who asked her for 4d. for her bed. Nichols replied that she did not have the money and the deputy turned her out. Nichols was unconcerned and, laughing, said, 'I'll soon get my doss money. See what a jolly bonnet I've got now.' She indicated a little black bonnet which nobody had seen before.[26]

At 2.30 a.m. Nichols was seen by Mrs Emily Holland,[27] who was returning from going to see a docks fire at Ratcliffe.[28] She had shared a room with Nichols at 18 Thrawl Street for about six weeks, until about eight to ten days earlier, when Nichols left and went to live at what Holland thought was 'The White House' in Flower and Dean Street, 'where men and women were allowed to sleep together'. Holland saw Nichols coming down Osborne Street alone. She was drunk, staggered a bit when she walked and at the corner of Osborne Street, opposite Whitechapel Church, she slumped against the wall of a grocer's shop. Holland went to her and they talked for about seven or eight minutes, and while they were talking the Whitechapel church clock struck 2.30. Holland tried to persuade her to return to Thrawl Street, but Mary Ann refused, saying, 'I have had my lodging money three times today, and I have spent it.' She seemed to have little anxiety about quickly earning enough money for her bed. Holland left Nichols, who headed off up Whitechapel Road.

Buck's Row, today named Durward Street, is a nondescript little street running between Brady Street and Vallance Road. It was entered from Brady Street, and on the right hand side ran the high walls of some warehouses that ended in a narrow building with ESSEX WHARF written ornately in red bricks along its side. On the left-hand side there was a corner pub called the Roebuck and a row of cottages that ended in a building called New Cottage, which, as the name implies, was a recently built dwelling.[29] Next to New Cottage there were some gates about nine to ten feet in height that led into stables owned by a Mr Brown. Next to the stables was the large and imposing Victorian Board School.

Writing in 1929, Leonard Matters described the street as it was at that time:

Buck's Row cannot have changed much in character since its name was altered. It is a narrow, cobbled, mean street, having on one side the same houses – possibly tenanted by the same people – which stood there in 1888. They are shabby, dirty little houses of two storeys, and only a three-feet pavement separates them from the road, which is no more than twenty feet from wall to wall.

On the opposite sides are the high walls of warehouses which at night would shadow the dirty street in a far deeper gloom than its own character in broad daylight suggests. All Durward Street is not so drab and mean, for by some accident in the planning of the locality – if ever it was planned – quite two-thirds of the thoroughfare is very wide and open.

The street lies east and west along the London and North Eastern Railway line. It is approached from the west from Vallance Street, formerly Baker's Row. On the left are fine modern tall warehouses. I was interested to note that one of them belongs to Messrs Kearley and Tonge, Ltd, in front of whose other premises in Mitre Square a murder was committed on September 30th. On the left side of the street is a small wall guarding the railway line, which lies at a depth of some twenty feet below the ground level. Two narrow bridge roads lead across the railway into Whitechapel Road. The first was called Thomas Street in 1888, but is now Fulbourne Street. The other is Court Street. By either of these little lanes, no more than two hundred and fifty yards long, the busy main artery of the Whitechapel area can be reached from the relatively secluded Buck's Row.

Going still further east, an abandoned London County Council school building breaks the wide and open Durward Street into two narrow lanes or alleys. The left hand land retains the name of Durward Street, 'late Buck's Row', and the other is Winthrop Street. Both are equally dirty and seemingly disreputable . . .[30]

Despite the appearance of the cottages in Buck's Row when Matters wrote in 1929, the street was described in *The Times* in 1888 as 'tenanted all down one side by a respectable class of people, superior to many of the surrounding streets'.[31]

In New Cottage there lived a widow, Mrs Emma Green, her two sons and a daughter. That night, 31 August, one of the sons went to bed at 9 p.m., the other son followed at 9.45, and Mrs Green and her daughter, who shared a room on the first floor at the front of the house, went to bed at 11. Mrs Green, who claimed to be a light sleeper, said that she slept undisturbed by any unusual sounds until she was woken by the police some five hours later.

Opposite New Cottage in Essex Wharf lived Walter Purkiss, the manager of the wharf, with his wife, children and servant. He and his wife, whose bedroom was on the second floor and fronted the street, went to bed between 11 and 11.15 p.m. Both claimed to have been awake at various times during the night and neither heard anything unusual.

In Winthrop Street, which ran parallel to Buck's Row, there was a slaughterhouse called Barber's Yard because it was owned by a Mr Barber. At 12.20 a.m. Henry Tomkins, 'a rough looking man',[32] and a fellow worker named Charles Britten left Barber's Yard for a stroll to Wood's Buildings[33] – a passage that led from Winthrop Street to Whitechapel Road – returning about 1 a.m. If they were gone for over half an hour then they presumably either walked further than the end of the street or they stopped for a smoke and a chat, or perhaps nipped to a pub for a drink. *The Times* reported that at night he and his mates generally went out to have a drink.[34] Neither of them saw or heard anything unusual and they returned to their work. No one left the yard after that. The gates of the slaughterhouse were open all night, so that anyone could walk into the place. Later, during the grim proceedings of the inquest, Tomkins caused some (presumably unintentional) levity when the coroner asked if women ever came to the slaughter yard. 'Oh, I don't know anything about them. I don't like them,' he replied, and there was an outburst of laughter. The coroner somewhat testily asked, 'Never mind whether you like them or not. Were there any about that night?' Tomkins replied that 'in Whitechapel Road there are all sorts and sizes. It's a rough neighbourhood, I can tell you.' He was greeted with another burst of laughter.[35] The upshot was that they saw no one pass by and didn't hear any unusual noises. No vehicle passed by and he was certain he would have heard it if one had done so.

Walter Purkiss in Essex Wharf woke up about 1 a.m. and heard nothing. Buck's Row, he said, was unusually quiet.

This said, there were early reports in several newspapers of a disturbance shortly after midnight: 'Several persons in the neighbourhood state that an affray occurred shortly after midnight, but no screams were heard, nor anything beyond what might have been considered evidence of an ordinary brawl.'[36] The *New York Times* shifted the time of the incident to about 3 a.m. and described a serious disturbance:

The victim was a woman, who, at 3 o'clock, was knocked down by some man, unknown, and attacked with a knife. She attempted to get up, and ran a hundred yards, her cries for help being heard by several persons in the adjacent houses. No attention was paid to her cries, however, and when found at daybreak she was lying dead in another street, several hundred yards from the scene of the attack.[37]

This story may have originated with a Mrs Colwell[38] or Colville[39] who lived in the charmingly named Honey's Mews, off Brady Street, some 120 yards from the murder scene. She was reported in *The Star* as saying that at 'about the time the murder was said to have been committed she heard a woman running up the street shrieking "Murder; Police." "She was running away from somebody," said Mrs. Colwell, "who, from the way she screamed, was hurting her as she ran. And it struck me as very strange that I did not hear the sound of any footsteps whatever except hers." '[40] A more sober report in the *Daily Telegraph* said she was awakened by her children, who said someone was trying to get into the house and she 'heard a woman screaming "Murder, Police!" five or six times. The voice faded away, as though the woman was going in the direction of Buck's-row, and all became quiet. She only heard the steps of one person.'[41] It remains possible that the newspapers reported an actual incident. We wouldn't necessarily know whether the woman attacked came forward and identified herself; this may not have been reported in the press or been mentioned in the severely depleted police case papers. But the more widely reported time of midnight makes it unlikely that the woman was Nichols, whose body was still warm when found and who cannot have long been dead.

At 3.15 a.m. PC John Thain, 96J, passed the entrance to Buck's Row on his beat and PC John Neil, 97J, passed the slaughterhouse in Winthrop Street, where he saw Harry Tomkins and another horse slaughterer named James Mumford at work. PC Neil passed on and walked into and down Buck's Row. He did not see anything unusual or suspicious. About the same time Sergeant Kirby also passed down Buck's Row. He, too, saw nothing to arouse his suspicions.[42]

At 3.20 a.m. Charles Andrew Cross, who for twenty years had worked for the haulier Pickford and Co. in Broad Street, left his home at 22 Doveton Street, Bethnal Green, and set off for work. A little while later, Robert Paul, who lived at 30 Foster Street, left his home and headed for his workplace in Corbett's Court, off Hanbury Street, Whitechapel. Both men took a route through Buck's Row. At 3.45 a.m. Charles Cross was the first to enter the little street. He was walking along the Essex Wharf side when he saw something lying against the gates leading to the stables next to New Cottage. A street lamp was shining at the end of the row, but it did not shed sufficient light for him to recognise the shape immediately. He later told the inquest, 'I could not tell in the dark what it was at first; it looked to me like a tarpaulin sheet, but stepping into the road, I saw that it was the body of a woman. Just then I heard a man about 40 yards off approaching from the direction that I myself had come from. I waited for the man, who started to one side as if afraid that I meant to knock him down. I said, "Come and look over here, there's a woman." '

The other man was Robert Paul. He went with Cross but it was too dark to see that the woman had been brutally murdered or to see any blood. The woman's clothes were raised almost to her stomach, her bonnet was off, but close to her head. Cross felt her hands, which were cold and limp. 'I believe she's dead,' said Cross, but Paul, having felt her face and found it warm, felt for a heartbeat and thought he detected a faint movement. 'I think she's breathing, but it's very little if she is.' He wanted to move the body, but Cross said he wasn't going to touch her. The two men, who were by now running late for work, decided to try to find a policeman.

Cross and Paul must have left Buck's Row perhaps only seconds before PC Neil turned into it from Brady Street on his beat. Walking up the right-hand side, he noticed a figure lying against the gates leading to the stables. He walked across and shone his lamp. Open eyes, unseeing and glassy in death, stared back. Mary Ann Nichols was lying on her back with her clothes disarranged. She lay with her head towards Brady Street, her arms at her side, her left hand touching the gate. Close by her left hand was the bonnet of which she had been so proud only a few hours before. Blood was oozing from a wound in her throat. PC Neil felt her arm, which was quite warm from the joints upwards.

Within four or five minutes of leaving the body Cross and Paul met PC Jonas Mizen,[43] 56H, at the corner of Hanbury Street and Baker's Row, 300 yards from Buck's Row. Mizen was engaged in knocking people up. They told him there was a woman lying on her back on the ground in Buck's Row. Cross said he believed she was dead or drunk (at the time he did not think she had been murdered), while Paul said he thought her dead. PC Mizen replied, 'All right.'[44] Cross and Paul continued on their way to work and parted company at the corner of Hanbury Street, Paul turning into Corbett's Court, leaving Cross to walk on alone to Broad Street, which he claimed to have reached at 4 a.m. Neither man had known the other prior to their meeting in Buck's Row over the corpse of Mary Ann Nichols. PC Mizen finished knocking at the place where he was, giving two or three knocks,[45] then went to Buck's Row.

At 3.47 a.m. PC Thain, on his beat along Brady Street and walking away from Whitechapel Road, passed the entrance of Buck's Row again and was

heard by PC Neil, who signalled with his lamp. PC Thain went down
Buck's Row. 'For God's sake, Jack, go fetch a doctor,' said PC Neil.'[46] PC
Thain went into Winthrop Street and collected his cape from the horse
slaughterer's, mentioning the discovery of the body to Harry Tomkins, then
went at once to the surgery of Dr Rees Ralph Llewellyn at 152 Whitechapel
Road, about 300 yards from Buck's Row.'[47]

PC Mizen arrived in Buck's Row, finding PC Neil alone with the body,
and PC Neil sent him to fetch an ambulance.

PC Neil now went across to Essex Wharf and rang the bell. Mr Purkiss
flung open the upstairs window and Neil asked him if he'd heard any
disturbance. Purkiss said 'no'. Sergeant Kirby arrived, knocked at the door
of New Cottage and Mrs Green answered from an upper window, also
saying that she had heard nothing unusual. Neil took the opportunity to
examine the ground and specifically looked for blood trails. He saw none.
He also examined the road, but could not see any marks of wheels.[48]

At 4.20 a.m. Harry Tomkins and James Mumford left the slaughterhouse
in Winthrop Street and went to view the body. They were later joined by
Charles Britten. The men remained there until the body was taken away.
Before Britten arrived, PC Thain returned with Dr Llewellyn, who made a
very cursory examination and, according to PC Neil, said, 'Move the
woman to the mortuary; she is dead. I will make a further examination of
her.' The doctor then presumably returned home until he was needed at the
mortuary. PC Mizen had by now returned with the ambulance – basically a
handcart – and helped PC Neil and PC Thain put the body aboard. It was
then taken to the mortuary in Old Montague Street. Moving the body
revealed a spot of congealed blood about six inches in diameter, which had
run towards the gutter. PC Thain also noticed a lot of blood on the back of
the body and assumed that this had run down from the neck. He got a lot of
blood on his hands when lifting the body into the ambulance.

It was roughly about this time that Patrick Mulshaw, a night porter
watching some sewage works, was told by a passing man, 'Watchman, old
man. I believe somebody is murdered down the street.' Mulshaw immediately went round the corner into Buck's Row, where he saw Nichols lying
on the ground, surrounded by some workmen and the police.[49]

At 4.30 a.m. Inspector John Spratling of J Division, 'a keen-eyed man
with iron-grey hair and beard',[50] was in the Hackney Road when he received
news of the murder. He went to Buck's Row and found two constables there
but the body had already been removed to the mortuary. PC Thain, who

was still at the murder scene, pointed out the spot where the body had been found. A carman named Green, who worked at the stables against whose gate the body was found, had cleared away much of the blood, but Inspector Spratling could see some stains between the stones. Spratling then went to the mortuary accompanied by PC Thain and there found the body still on the ambulance in the yard because the keys to the mortuary, which had been sent for, had not yet arrived. While waiting for the mortuary keeper, Spratling took a description of the dead woman, but at that time did not notice any wounds on the body. A pauper inmate of the Whitechapel Workhouse named Robert Mann arrived with the keys between 5 and 5.20 a.m. and the body was moved into the mortuary, where it was placed on a slab on the floor. Spratling made a more careful examination, discovered the injuries to the abdomen, and at once sent for Dr Llewellyn. Between five and six o'clock the same morning he told PC Cartwright to examine the neighbourhood where the body was found, including the walls, yards and adjoining railway.

At 6.30 a.m. James Hatfield, another inmate of the Whitechapel Work-house, arrived at the mortuary and, despite instructions from Detective Sergeant Enright (who had arrived there earlier) that the body of Nichols was not to be touched, Hatfield and Robert Mann stripped and washed it. At 6.45 a.m. Inspector Helson of J Division received news of the murder and went directly to the mortuary, arriving as the body was being stripped. From the mortuary he went to the murder scene.

At 10 a.m. on Saturday, 1 September, Dr Llewellyn and his assistant undertook a full postmortem examination. On the right side of the face there was a bruise, which looked as if it had been made either by a fist or by the pressure of a thumb. There was also a circular bruise on the left side of the face, which was also probably caused by a fist or a thumb. There was a small bruise on the left side of the neck and an abrasion on the right. All the bruises appeared to have been caused at the same time and were evidently recent. There were two cuts in the throat. One was four inches long and the other eight. Both cuts reached through to the vertebrae. There were no other injuries on the body apart from bruising until the lower part of the abdomen. Here, two or three inches from the left side, there was a jagged wound, very deep, having cut through the tissues. Several incisions ran across the abdomen, and on the right side there were three or four cuts running downward. All the wounds had been inflicted with a sharp knife and appeared to have been made by a left-handed man. In Llewellyn's opinion the injuries had taken about four to five minutes to inflict and were the work of a person with some rough anatomical knowledge, for he had attacked all the vital parts. *The Times* reported that 'no part of the viscera was missing'.[51] Not mentioned by Dr Llewellyn but widely reported in the press on 1 September was that one of Mary Ann Nichols's fingers bore the impression of a ring. There were no marks on the finger to suggest that it had been wrenched off and it is not known whether Nichols was wearing the ring on the night of her murder. However, it is known that the next victim of the Whitechapel murderer, Annie Chapman, was wearing two cheap brass rings on the night she was killed and that these appeared to have been forcibly removed from her finger.

In summary, Llewellyn thought Mary Ann Nichols had been murdered about half an hour before he had arrived at the scene, perhaps about 3.50 a.m., and that the murderer had needed no more than four or five minutes to perform the mutilations. He believed that Nichols had not been seized from behind, that the murderer had faced her, held his right hand across her mouth and cut her throat with a knife held in his left hand. This was deduced from bruising on the face. The weapon used would have been a pointed weapon with a stout back, such as a cork-cutter's or shoemaker's knife, and was not an exceptionally long-bladed weapon. The murderer, said Dr Llewellyn, must have had some anatomical knowledge.

About the same time as Dr Llewellyn was performing the autopsy, Inspector Spratling examined Buck's Row and Brady Street, but found no blood marks anywhere. Subsequently, in company with Sergeant Godley, he examined the East London and District railway lines and embankments, and also the Great Eastern railway yard, which was about 50 yards from the spot where the body was found. He had questioned the constable on duty there, but he had heard nothing. The search failed to find anything.

At about midday Inspector Spratling returned to the mortuary and found Nichols's clothes lying in a heap in the yard.

A journalist working for *The Star* newspaper was allowed into the mortuary to view the body and at 11.30 a.m. filed a story:

The body appeared to be that of a woman of 35. It was 5ft. 3in. in height and fairly plump. The eyes were brown, the hair brown, and the two centre upper front teeth missing, those on either side being widely separated. This peculiarity may serve to identify deceased, of whom at present writing nothing is known. Her clothing consisted of a well-worn brown ulster, a brown linsey skirt, and jacket, a grey linsey petticoat, a flannel petticoat, dark-blue ribbed stockings, braid garters, and side-spring shoes. Her bonnet was black and rusty, and faced with black velvet. Her whole outfit was that of a person in poor circumstances, and this appearance was borne out by the mark 'LAMBETH WORKHOUSE, P. R.,' which was found on the petticoat bands. The two marks were cut off and sent to the Lambeth institution to discover if possible the identity of deceased. The brutality of the murder is beyond conception and beyond description. The throat is cut in two gashes, the instrument having been a sharp one, but used in a most ferocious and reckless way. There is a gash under the left ear, reaching nearly to the centre of the throat. Along half its length, however, it is accompanied by another one which reaches around under the other ear, making a wide and horrible hole, and nearly severing the head from the body.[52]

Another journalist gave the following account:

The Whitechapel Mortuary is a little brick building situated to the right of the large yard used by the Board of Works for the storage of their material. Accompanied by Mr. Edmunds, the keeper, our reporter visited the temporary resting place of the victim on Friday morning. The first evidence seen of the tragedy on arriving in the yard was a bundle of what were little more than rags, of which the woman had been divested, and which were lying on the flagstones just outside the mortuary. They consisted of a dull red cloak already mentioned, together with a dark bodice and brown skirt, a check flannel petticoat which bore the mark of the Lambeth Workhouse, a pair of dark stockings, and an old pair of dilapidated-looking spring-side boots, together with the little and sadly battered black straw bonnet, minus either ribbons or trimmings. Contrary to anticipation, beyond the flannel petticoat, and with the exception of a few bloodstains on the cloak, the other clothing was scarcely marked. The petticoat, however, was completely saturated with blood, and altogether presented a sickening spectacle. Entering the deadhouse, with its rows of black coffins, the keeper turned to the one immediately to the right of the door, and lying parallel with the wall. Opening the lid, he exposed the face of the poor victim. The features were apparently those of a woman of about thirty or thirty-five years, whose hair was still dark. The features were small and delicate, the cheek-bones high, the eyes grey, and the partly opened mouth disclosed a set of teeth which were a little discoloured. The expression on the face was a deeply painful one, and was evidently the result of an agonizing death. The gash across the neck was situated very slightly above the breastbone; it was at least six inches in length, over an inch in width, and was clean cut. The hands were still tightly clenched. The lower portion of the body, however, presented the most sickening spectacle of all. Commencing from the lower portion of the abdomen, a terrible gash extended nearly as far as the diaphragm – a gash from which the bowels protruded . . . The body, with the exception of the face, was covered with a white sheet and a blanket.[53]

Apart from the small bundle of clothing, Mary Ann Nichols's only other possessions were a comb and a piece of a mirror found in her pockets.[54]

The petticoats were marked with 'Lambeth Workhouse P.R.', indicating the notorious[55] workhouse at Princess Road. For some years the main Lambeth Workhouse had been based at Renfrew Road. However, in 1887–8, Princess Road was used as a new 'test' workhouse. The aged and infirm were left at Renfrew Road, but the able-bodied, some 200 men and 150 women, were moved to Princess Road, where there was a particularly strict regime and inmates had to do hard work such as stone-breaking and oakum-picking in order to receive relief.

The workhouse matron was brought to view the body but didn't recognise it, and, as the day wore on and news of the murder spread, numerous people visited the mortuary to view the body. A coffee stall owner said that at 3 a.m. a woman had had a coffee at his stall on the corner of Whitechapel Road and Cambridge Road, and that the man with her had seemed fidgety and uneasy, grumbling and telling her to hurry, but on viewing the body he said he didn't think it was the same woman. And a Mr Scorer, an assistant salesman at Smithfield Market, thought the woman might be his wife, from whom he'd separated eleven years earlier and who had been an inmate of Lambeth Workhouse. By a remarkable coincidence he said she had a friend named Polly Nichols, whom he knew by sight, but after viewing the body he said it was neither his wife nor her friend Nichols. The body was eventually recognised as that of a woman who had lodged at 18 Thrawl Street and was known as Polly. People from the lodging house were summoned and among those who turned up was Emily Holland, who told about her meeting with 'Polly' at 2.30 a.m. It was not until 7.30 p.m., however, that Mary Ann Monk, an inmate of Lambeth Workhouse, and at the later inquest described as 'a young woman with a flushed face and a haughty air', came to the mortuary and identified the body as that of Mary Ann Nichols, otherwise known as Polly.

Speculation during that Friday gave rise to two theories. One, initially a police opinion, was that both Tabram and Nichols had been murdered by members of one of the gangs who were known to extort money from the Whitechapel prostitutes.[56] The theory did not survive long and the following day it was reported in the press that the police gave it no credence. The other theory was that Nichols had not been murdered in Buck's Row, but somewhere else, from where she had been taken and dumped where she was found. As *The Times* expressed it: 'Viewing the spot where the body was found, it seems difficult to believe that the woman received her death wounds there . . . if the woman was murdered on the spot where the body was found, it is almost impossible to believe that she would not have aroused the neighbourhood by her screams.'[57] This theory was revived in 1976 in Stephen Knight's highly imaginative bestselling book *Jack the Ripper: The Final Solution*, but a report by Inspector Helson states that there was no doubt but that the murder was committed where the body was found.

CHAPTER FIVE

Theories Abound, But Facts Are Scarce[1]

In the early afternoon of Saturday, 1 September, William Nichols was taken with one of his sons to view his wife in the mortuary. It was reported that he was greatly upset by the sight and told her, 'I forgive you, as you are, for what you have been to me.'

In the afternoon the inquest into Mary Ann Nichols's death was opened by the coroner for the southeastern division of Middlesex, Wynne E Baxter, who had just returned from a trip to Scandinavia and turned up at the Working Lads' Institute resplendently dressed in a pair of black and white checked trousers, a dazzling white waistcoat, crimson scarf and dark coat.[2] The library where the inquest was held was almost full with jurymen, police, reporters and interested observers. The jury was sworn, a Mr Horey being appointed foreman, then Mr Banks, the coroner's assistant, took them to view the body, which was lying stretched out at full length with the hands by the side in a black coffin at the mortuary in Pavilion Yard. The jury then returned to the library. Wynne Baxter took his seat at the head of a long table and placed a roll of paper before him on which to enter the depositions. The jury settled themselves to his left – chairs to his right being reserved for the family of Nichols. Detective Inspectors Abberline and Helson and Sergeants Enright and Godley settled themselves into their seats, and in front sat a miscellaneous collection of reporters, telegraph boys, messengers and penny-a-liners – journalists paid a penny a line. Mr Banks called the first witness. There was time only to hear testimony from Edward Walker, PC John Neil and Dr Llewellyn, before Wynne Baxter adjourned the inquest until 3 September.

An alleged attack on a woman that night caused a minor flurry of press excitement. It was reported that a woman leaving the Forester's Music Hall in Cambridge Heath Road, where she had spent the evening with a sea captain, was accosted by a well-dressed man who asked her to accompany him a short distance to meet a friend. They were not far from Buck's Row when the man violently seized the woman by the throat and dragged her down a court, where he was immediately joined by a gang of women and men, who robbed the woman of her necklace, earrings, brooch and purse, then brutally assaulted her. She tried to shout for assistance, but one of the gang laid a large knife across her throat, remarking, 'We will serve you as we did the others.' The police were said to be investigating, but in due course the *East London Observer* said that 'Inquiries made into the accuracy of the story have proved it to be absolutely false and groundless'; and the *Daily Telegraph* stated that the manager of the Forester's Music Hall had written to say 'that the police have informed him that no such outrage has been brought to their notice'. The *Eastern Argus* attributed the whole story to another incident altogether, claiming that it originated with a savage assault on a young woman named Eliza Smith by a 32-year-old labourer, John Hummerstone, at 11 Key Street, Hoxton, on 2 September. Hummerstone had returned home drunk and started a fight, and when Eliza fled into the rear yard he had knocked her down and kicked her. Then he had sat across her and drawn a large-bladed table knife across her throat and said that he meant making a second 'Buck's Row murder' of it. Neighbours who witnessed part of the assault were able to rescue her. Hummerstone was sentenced to six months' imprisonment with hard labour. But why the *Eastern Argus* thought this outrage gave birth to the story of an attack on a woman leaving the music hall is a mystery to me.[3]

That Saturday also saw the start of the long saga of whether or not a reward should have been sanctioned by the home secretary. Messrs Walter and Son, of 11–13 Church Street, Spitalfields, were among the very first to write to Henry Matthews on the subject, receiving a reply a few days later to the effect that the practice of offering rewards had been discontinued. It was a decision that Henry Matthews would have cause to regret (see Chapter Eleven).

Sir Charles Warren also came in for attack. As already stated, Warren had earned the enmity of the Radical press as a consequence of the Trafalgar Square riots in 1887, and the recently launched Radical newspaper *The Star* vilified Warren, alleging that there was widespread dissatisfaction with him within the force. As early as 1 September it seized on the murders and used them in a rather disgraceful manner to continue its unmerciful attack, reporting that its 'reporters have only got to talk to the first policeman they chance to meet on his beat in order to get his opinion of his chief, often expressed with that tropical luxuriance of phrase for which the force is famous'. It went on to comment apropos of the murders in the East End that 'The murderer must be a Man Monster, and when Sir Charles has done quarrelling with his detective service he will perhaps help the citizens of East London to catch him.'[4]

The Star was incorrect in its assertion that the uniformed police were unhappy with Sir Charles Warren. They most certainly *had* been, and, as a later head of the CID would note, 'there is no doubt that sedition was smouldering throughout the Force', but Warren's stalwart defence of his men when they were pilloried for their heavy-handed response to the Trafalgar Square 'rioters' had won their support and secured his popularity.[5] His relations with the detective force were another matter altogether. Warren believed that he had been appointed with full authority over the whole of the police force, and he also believed that the primary function of the force was to prevent crime, not to catch the perpetrator after a crime had been committed.[6] This not unnaturally brought him into conflict with Assistant Commissioner James Monro, who headed the 'detective service' (the CID – Criminal Investigation Department). Born in Edinburgh in 1838, Monro, who was lame as a result of infantile paralysis and often walked with the aid of a stick, had entered the Bengal Civil Service in 1857, served as an assistant magistrate, district judge and inspector-general of the police in Bengal – at which time he met and became friends with Melville Macnaghten, who would later become assistant commissioner of the CID – and finally commissioner of the Presidency Division (Bombay). He was blessed 'with the instinct of a born detective [and] his name became a word of terror to the subtlest native conspirators'.[7] His reputation was such that when he applied for the vacant position of assistant commissioner, CID, in 1884, he got the job.

Monro almost immediately fell out with a man named Edward Jenkinson, who headed a department at the Home Office gathering intelligence about Fenian terrorist activities in mainland Britain. As with Warren, Jenkinson had been promised a free hand but quickly discovered that he had no real authority and was obliged to hand his information over to the Metropolitan Police. He had quickly decided that the Met was grossly inefficient, indiscreet and corrupt to the point that in 1885 he would write, 'There is hardly a man among them who does not take money', for which reasons he proved very reluctant to share with them any information he possessed. Furthermore, according to Monro, Jenkinson '. . . not only collected intelligence regarding London, but he acted upon it, without any reference to the London police, by means of a number of Irish police who he had, without any authority whatever, stationed in London . . .'[8]

This enraged Monro – whom Jenkinson thought 'a very good man in his way', but with 'little energy or originality' and who was 'a real old Scotland Yardite' – and by mid-May 1885 the hostility was so great that Monro tendered his resignation. But, wrote Monro,

> 'In the Autumn of '86 I was sent for by Mr Matthews, the new Secretary of State, and had an interview with him which lasted for more than three hours. I laid the whole of the circumstances before him and told him very plainly that I could not consent any longer to work with Mr Jenkinson. He had constantly interfered with police action and to me personally on more than one occasion he had lied in such a disgraceful manner that I declined to have any dealings with him.
>
> Briefly the end was, after a short time, that Mr Jenkinson was dismissed. [9]

According to Monro, after replacements had been considered and rejected, 'at the urgent request of the Government, I consented to act as Chief of the Secret Department as regards intelligence, and at the same time retain my office as Asst. Commissioner'.

Thus it was that James Monro became head of the so-called Secret Department, known as 'Section D', the forerunner of the modern Special Branch.[10] It was financed out of imperial funds, not Metropolitan Police funds, and its brief was to keep covert surveillance on all subversives (groups such as anarchists, Fenians and assorted revolutionaries). Although the detectives[11] working for the Secret Department were not to be outwardly distinguished from other detectives, they and the department were not under the authority of the commissioner but were directly responsible to Henry Matthews, the home secretary.

This caused friction with Sir Charles Warren, who found himself with a subordinate officer engaged in police work over whom and partly over which he had no authority or influence and about which he was not even consulted.

What is surprising is that Monro, who had been in Warren's position with Jenkinson, did not exercise understanding and tact in his relationship with Warren. In fact he seems to have been extraordinarily insensitive. In November 1887 Monro complained to Warren that he and other senior

officers were overworked and requested that the strain be relieved by the
creation of a new post of assistant chief constable.[12] Warren suggested that
Monro shed some of his responsibilities – clearly meaning the Secret
Department work, arguing

> that the Assistant Commissioner should be allowed to devote his time
> and energy to his legitimate work, and that he should not be burdened
> with the care and anxiety of duties which previously occupied the
> whole of the attention of an officer of undoubted experience and
> ability at a very high salary.

Monro rather lamely replied that the Secret Department work never
detracted from his CID work because the secret work always took second
place to his CID work – 'If there is pressure the special work suffers first'.
This can't have pleased the home secretary.[13] Eventually it was agreed that Sir
Melville Macnaghten be appointed assistant chief constable, Monro being
very enthusiastic, writing, 'I saw his way of managing men when I was an
official in India and was struck by it, for he had a most turbulent set of natives
to deal with, and he dealt with them firmly and justly.'[14] Warren, however,
learned that Macnaghten had so badly mishandled some relatively peaceful
natives that they had attacked him. As Warren expressed it, Macnaghten was
'the one man in India who has been beaten by Hindoos'. This time Henry
Matthews agreed with Warren that there were better-qualified men for the
job and Macnaghten was turned down.[15] As *The Star*[16] would report, 'Matters
reached a crisis early in July [1888], when the Chief Commissioner and Mr
Monro went to the Home Office and had a long interview with the Secretary
of State, at which it was decided that Mr Monro should immediately take leave
of absence, with a view to his subsequent resignation.'[17]

It was not altogether a successful victory for Sir Charles Warren, because,
although Monro was replaced as head of the CID, he was retained as an
adviser to the Home Office, and Monro's departure was seen in some
quarters as further evidence of 'gross mismanagement at Scotland Yard',
one newspaper reporting that if the force had been well managed 'the public
would not have been deprived of the services of such able and experienced
officials as Mr. Monro and Mr. Jenkinson.' And it added,

> Mr. Monro's retirement seems to have thrown the detective depart-
> ment into confusion. Sir Charles Warren is an able man, but he is a

military man, and military ideas of organisation are quite unfitted for detective work. If a detective has no margin for discretion, if he is obliged to conform to some narrow standard of military red-tape, his usefulness must be enormously impaired.[18]

Warren had in fact also tendered his resignation from the £1,500-a-year job as commissioner, as *The Star* reported as early as 4 September 1888, speculating that his replacement was likely to be Malcolm Wood, the chief constable of Manchester. He would in fact leave at the end of the year (see Chapter Fifteen) and be replaced by Monro, who would himself clash with Henry Matthews and in 1890 tender his resignation and return to India, where he founded the Ranaghat Medical Mission before finally retiring to Cheltenham in 1905. He died there in 1920.

When James Monro vacated the seat of assistant commissioner, CID, he was replaced by Robert Anderson, who would take up his role on 1 September 1888. He later wrote,

I may here say at once that, though I was warned by many, including officers who had served under him in South Africa, that 'I could never get on with Warren,' my relations with Sir Charles were always easy and pleasant . . . I always found him perfectly frank and open, and he treated me as a colleague, leaving me quite unfettered in the control of my department; and when his imperious temper could no longer brook the nagging Home Office ways of that period, and he decided to resign his office, I felt sincere regret at his going.[19]

However, although, as Anderson would later relate, Warren had 'secured the loyal support of the Force generally', the treatment of Monro had demoralised the officers of the CID and Superintendent Williamson was on the verge of sending in his resignation. Sinister rumours about Monro's replacement circulated and according to Anderson:

If the announcement had been made that, on his official retirement on the 31st of August, I should succeed to the office, things might have settled down. For all the principal officers knew and trusted me. But for some occult reason the matter was kept secret, and I was enjoined not to make my appointment known.[20]

All of this may seem far removed from the lives of five East End prostitutes, but the difference of opinion about the role of the police, as illustrated by the dispute between Warren and Monro, was, as Bernard Porter observed in his book *The Origins of the Vigilant State*, 'really a hoary old dilemma of the British police since its earliest days: how to reconcile purity with results. Warren and Monro represented Scylla and Charybdis between which the Metropolitan force had tried to steer for years. In the 1880s it steered on to both of them; with the result that several poor women in Whitechapel got drowned.'[21]

The new head of the CID was Dr Robert Anderson, an Irishman, anti-Fenian, staunch evangelical Christian and millennialist who would author many theological books, some of which continue to enjoy considerable respect.

Born in Dublin, the son of the Crown solicitor, Robert Anderson was educated at Trinity College, Dublin, took his BA in 1862 and in 1863 was called to the Bar at King's Inn, Dublin. In 1866 his elder brother Samuel, solicitor-general in the vice-regal administration, secured him work at Dublin Castle providing the secretary-general Lord Mayo[22] with a précis of known Fenian activity. His services were again requested by the attorney general following 'the Fenian Rising' in March 1867, and for a third time in the autumn of 1867. It was in December 1867 that an attempt was made to free a prominent Irish-American Fenian named Richard O'Sullivan Burke from Clerkenwell Prison in London. The Irish police got wind of the plan and informed the British police. On 12 December a policeman saw some men insert and try to light a fuse in a barrel by the prison wall, but the damp fuse refused to light and the men took the barrel away. They returned the next day and, again watched by the police, lit the fuse. The explosion destroyed about sixty yards of prison wall and several houses opposite, shattered windows over a large area and killed a dozen people and injured 120 others, mainly women and children. The official explanation/excuse as related to the House of Commons by the home secretary on 9 March 1868 was that the police had not acted because the wording of the warning from the Irish police had led them to believe that the prison wall 'would probably be blown up from underneath, and [they] had no conception that it would be blown down . . .' If true, this explanation reveals breathtaking incompetence. The Cabinet decided to create a temporary anti-Fenian Secret Service Department attached to the Home Office and Colonel the Hon. William Fielding was appointed to head it, with Robert Anderson as his assistant. This brought Anderson to London, where he took up his new duties on 19 December 1867. Three months later the department would be closed, Fielding went on to other things and Anderson stayed on with the Home Office with the title Home Office adviser on political crime, a position he retained until May 1883, when he was for uncertain reasons relieved entirely of all his responsibilities and duties relative to Fenianism in London and was appointed to the Royal Commission on Loss of Life at Sea. He remained 'out in the cold' until Jenkinson resigned in January 1887, when his replacement, Monro, appointed Robert Anderson as his assistant at a salary of £400 per annum, despite objections raised by the under-secretary, Godfrey Lushington.[23]

He was opinionated – 'very unwilling to give up an opinion once he had formed it. He was self-satisfied, and at times, in his theological and penological ideas, original to the point of eccentricity',[24] – and 'inclined (as pious people are) to maintain that an action was morally justified because his principles debarred him from committing an immoral one',[25] he was also 'a man who set great store by moral probity'.[26] He was in fact a man of contradictions. Accused by one source of being garrulous – he 'could not keep quiet about his secret work'[27] – Anderson was described by his friend Major Arthur Griffiths as 'the most discreet, the most silent and reserved of all public functionaries. Someone once said he was a mystery even to himself. This to him inestimable quality of reticence is not unaided by a slight but perhaps convenient deafness . . .' Henri Le Caron, the spy who would work only for Anderson, declared that for 21 years Anderson 'never wavered or grew lax in his care . . . ever watchful'.[28] Anderson is therefore a difficult man to assess, and to attempt to do so demands care and caution.

Anderson took charge of the CID on 1 September 1888, the day on which Mary Ann Nichols was found murdered. A week later he would leave England. As Anderson says,

> I was at that time physically unfit to enter on the duties of my new post. For some time past I had not had an adequate holiday, and the strain of long and anxious work was telling on me . . . Dr Gilbart Smith, of Harley Street, insisted that I must have two months' complete rest, and he added that he would probably give me a certificate for a further two months' 'sick leave'. This, of course, was out of the question. But I told Mr Matthews, greatly to his distress, that I could not take up my new duties until I had had a month's holiday in Switzerland. And so, after one week at Scotland Yard, I crossed the Channel.

But this was not all. The second of the crimes known as the Whitechapel murders was committed the night before I took office, and the third occurred the night of the day on which I left London.[29]

It so happened that Sir Charles Warren was also on holiday, taking some quiet time in the South of France; Adolphus Williamson was ill with heart trouble; and Superintendent John Shore was otherwise preoccupied. Scotland Yard was dangerously close to being full of Indians and no chiefs. Fortunately, the Indians were competent and capable men.

As the uniformed and detective branches of the police engaged in their internal squabbles, journalists allowed their pens to run full with purple prose: 'Was it a maniac, some creature mad with thirst of blood, escaped from a lunatic asylum, who did to death the "unfortunate" . . . a murderous lunatic concealed in the slums of Whitechapel, who issues forth at night like another Hyde, to prey upon the defenceless women of the "unfortunate" class?' asked one newspaper.[30] Another decided that the Ripper was a 'ghoul-like creature who stalks through the streets of London, stalking down his victim like a Pawnee Indian . . . simply drunk with blood, and he will have more . . .'[31]

A third, rather more prosaically and with a large measure of truth, stated, 'Never, since the murder of Harriet Lane, now several years ago, has such excitement existed in Whitechapel.'[32] It was reported that the murder scene was daily visited by hundreds of people who speculated about the identity of the murderer and the probability of the police catching him, that hundreds more went to the mortuary in Montague Street, where, as a newspaper observed, there was nothing to see except the green gates, which nevertheless 'were the objects of an awesome curiosity'. A large number of artists and writers visited the spot, and there were amateur detectives making enquiries of their own. The three horse slaughterers who worked in Winthrop Street became the focus of particular attention, people continually chalking on the doorposts, 'This is where the murder was done.'[33] One newspaper reported that the police had made enquiries 'amongst the employees of a slaughter-house close at hand [but] nothing, however, seems to have come of it.'[34]

On Monday, 3 September 1888, the Nichols inquest resumed and heard testimony from eight witnesses. It was then adjourned until Monday, 17 September 1888. The newspapers expressed satisfaction with the 'energetic way' the coroner 'has thrown himself into the inquiry'.[35]

The newspapers reported that the police thought that the three crimes – Smith, Tabram and Nichols – were the work of one individual. They also reported that 'there is a strong belief current that there is more than one person concerned in the outrage',[36] and on the evening of 4 September claimed the police had revealed 'they have a clue to the perpetrators of the crime, and that certain persons are being kept under surveillance. No arrest, however, is expected to be made until after the coroner's adjourned inquiry, unless the suspected persons attempt to leave the district.'[37] It was soon apparent, however, that the police investigation had pretty much ground to a halt, perhaps unsurprisingly given the paucity of clues. The locals were reportedly eager to talk to the authorities and tell them what they knew, but this only confused matters. There were numerous stories circulating, some evident fantasy – or, as the newspaper put it, 'spontaneously generated by frantic terror' – and others, though credible, so contradictory that they were a waste of time discussing.[38] As one weekly would observe at the end of that first week of investigation, 'The mystery of the Whitechapel murders becomes more mysterious as time goes on. Theories abound, but facts are scarce',[39] words as true then as they are today.

As the days passed, criticism of the police increased. Across the Atlantic the *New York Times* was melodramatic and highly critical of the British police:

> Whitechapel has a murder mystery which transcends anything known in the annals of the horrible. It is Poe's *Murders in the Rue Morgue* and *The Mystery of Marie Roget*[40] rolled into one story. It is nothing less than a midnight murderer, whose step is noiseless, whose strike is deadly, and whose cunning is so great that he leaves no trace of his work and no clue to his identity. He has just slaughtered his third victim, and all the women in Whitechapel are terrified, while the stupidest detectives in the civilized world stand aghast and say they have no clue.[41]

At home the ever knocking *Star* claimed, 'Whitechapel is loud in its indignation over the inefficiency of the detectives.'[42] It reported that the police in Whitechapel had little knowledge of the area and didn't know the criminal haunts of the neighbourhood, whereas it said that in New York the local police knew 'almost every brick in every den in the district, and every felon or would-be felon who skulks behind it'. This ignorance it blamed on 'the centralised non-efficient military system which Sir Charles Warren has brought to perfection'. *The Star* argued that the

> people of the East-end must become their own police. They must form themselves at once into Vigilance Committees . . . to volunteer patrol work at night, as well as to general detective service . . . We do not think that the police will put any obstacle in the way of this volunteer assistance. They will probably be only too glad to have their efforts supplemented by the spontaneous action of the inhabitants. But in any case, London must rouse itself. No woman is safe while this ghoul is abroad. Up, citizens, then, and do your own police work![43]

The newspaper was quickly informed that a meeting of seventy men had in fact taken place after the murder of Martha Tabram and 'a committee of twelve was appointed to act as watchers'.[44] The St Jude's Vigilance Association, as it was called, was composed of working men assisted by some of the members of Toynbee Hall and its operations were confined to the immediate neighbourhood, where a member of the committee reported that brawls were frequent and policemen hard to find.[45] By 12 September the Whitechapel Vigilance Committee would be created, of which more later.

Mary Ann Nichols was buried during the afternoon of Thursday, 6 September. The body was placed in a polished elm coffin bearing a brass plate with the inscription, 'Mary Ann Nichols, aged 42; died August 31, 1888', and was taken to Ilford Cemetery in a hearse supplied by Mr H Smith, an undertaker, of Hanbury Street, drawn by two horses. The mourners – Edward Walker, William Nichols and Edward John Nichols (a grandson), plus two of Mary Ann's children – followed in two mourning coaches. All along the route the houses had the blinds drawn and a crowd numbering thousands watched the hearse pass by. A body of police under Inspector Allisdon of H Division surrounded the hearse to prevent the crowd from getting too close, but much sympathy was expressed for the relatives. The cortège passed the corner of Buck's Row into Whitechapel Road, with police stationed every few yards, and eventually reached the City of London Cemetery, being laid to rest in grave 49500, square 318.[46]

CHAPTER SIX

Annie Chapman

Annie Chapman was born Annie Eliza Smith in or about September 1840 or 1841 to George Smith and Ruth Chapman, who were not married at the time of the birth – they married on 22 February 1842 at St James Church, Paddington, giving their respective addresses at that time as Harrow Road and Market Street. George Smith was a soldier, having enlisted in the Second Regiment of Life Guards[1] on 11 December 1834.

A second child, Emily Latitia, was born in 1844 at 4 Rutland Terrace, Knightsbridge, but by the time the child was christened at Holy Trinity Church, Brompton, the family had moved to 3 Montpelier Place, Knightsbridge. By 1856 the family had moved to 12 Keppel Terrace in the parish of Clewer, Berkshire, and here two more children were born, Georgina on 1 April 1856 and Miriam Ruth on 27 October 1858. George Smith was pensioned at his own request in July 1860 at Horse Guards. He was living at 6 Middle Row North, Knightsbridge, on 25 February 1861, when a son, Fountain Hamilton,[2] was born. George took a job as a valet and the family, without Annie, moved very soon afterwards back to Clewer, where the 1861 census shows them living at 7 Keppel Terrace. George died sometime between 1862 and 1864, and the widowed Ruth Chapman took the family back to Knightsbridge, where she was living at 29 Montpelier Place.

Annie, who was about 21 when George left the army, did not accompany her parents to Clewer, but seems to have remained in London and perhaps obtained work of some sort, probably as a domestic. On 1 May 1869 she married a coachman named John Chapman, a relative of her mother,[3] at the Anglican parish church of All Saints, Ennismore Gardens, Knightsbridge.[4] The marriage was witnessed by Annie's sister, Emily Latitia, and a man named George White, described as a gentleman's coachman. For a while Annie and John lived with White and his wife at 1 Brooks Mews North, Bayswater. It isn't certain how long they were living there, but Annie went to stay with her mother at 29 Montpelier Place to give birth to her first child, Emily Ruth, on 25 June 1870, and Annie and John were there at the time of the census the following year.

John got a job working for a nobleman in Bond Street and when his second daughter, Annie Georgina,[5] was born on 5 June 1873 he and Annie were living at 17 South Bruton Mews, off Berkeley Square, Mayfair. Bruton Mews was in an area that provided stables and coach houses for the great houses in Berkeley Square and neighbourhood.

Sometime before 1880, John had got a job as a coachman/domestic servant and moved his family to Clewer, where they lived in the attic rooms of St Leonard's Hill Farm Cottage,[6] the home of a farm bailiff, Josiah Weeks, and his family. Weeks is reported to have been something of a local philanthropist. It was while here that Annie had her last child, a boy, John Alfred, who was actually born at Water Oakley, Bray, Berkshire.[7] Annie was by now drinking heavily, 'was often seen wandering about the country like a common tramp',[8] and was sometimes held by the police for drunkenness, although it was reported that she was never brought before the magistrates. Eventually, her dissolute habits caused their separation[9] in or about 1882.

Annie went to London, receiving a weekly allowance of 10s.[10] from her husband. John Chapman remained at Clewer with the children, who received good educations. Both daughters attended school, one being educated at a very respectable ladies' school in Windsor. An aunt paid for her tuition. The boy, John Alfred, was said to be a cripple who was for some time treated in a London hospital.[11] Emily Ruth, who suffered from epileptic fits, died of meningitis on 21 November 1882, aged twelve.

In 1886 John Chapman resigned his job in Clewer because of ill health and went to live at 1 Richmond Villas, Grove Road, New Windsor. John Chapman died on Christmas Day 1886 of cirrhosis of the liver, ascites (accumulation of fluid in the peritoneal cavity) and dropsy. The 10s. he sent to his wife stopped. Annie seems to have tramped to Clewer to find out what had happened, staying overnight at a lodging house in Colnbrook. People later recalled that a tramplike woman called at the Merry Wives of Windsor pub in Spital Road, Clewer.

Annie Georgina had been living with her father, but on his death she is said to have either been placed in a French institution or become a member of a performing troupe that travelled with a circus company in France. Either alternative seems unlikely and, indeed, both are dismissed as myths by descendants.[12] John Alfred was supposedly placed in a charitable school outside Windsor and would from time to time be visited by his mother. By 1891, however, he was certainly living with his grandmother and sister at 29 Montpelier Place. Ruth Smith died in 1893 and her two daughters, Georgina and Miriam Ruth, Annie's sister, both of whom remained spinsters, lived there until moving in 1927 to 17 Radnor Walk, Chelsea. Miriam Ruth died at St Luke's Hospital of 'cerebral thrombosis' aged 81. Her sister died only a month later of 'haemorrhage from a chronic gastric ulcer' on 13 February 1940.[13]

In later years, the Rev. James Paterson, described as 'Presbyterian minister, Chelsea', received a letter from a member of his congregation requesting that unfermented wine be used at services and explaining how alcoholism had been the dreadful ruin of his sister. The relevant part of the long letter read,

Just before I was six years old, my father cut his throat, leaving my mother with five children, three girls older, and one younger than myself. My eldest sister took to drink when she was quite young. Fourteen years ago I was converted. Twelve years ago I heard a sermon on 'Christians and Total Abstinence.' I signed the pledge with two of my sisters and we tried to persuade the one given to drink to give it up. She was married and in a good position. Over and over again she signed the pledge and tried to keep it. Over and over again she was tempted and fell. At last, of her own accord, she went into a home for the cure of the intemperate, her husband paid 12d. per week and she stayed one year. She came out a changed woman – a sober wife and mother, and things went on very happily for a few months. Then her husband had a severe cold, but his duty compelled him to go out, so to fortify himself against the cold, he took a glass of hot whiskey. He was careful enough not to have it in her presence for fear it should be a temptation. He drank it and came to kiss her before starting. In that kiss the fumes of alcohol were transmitted and all the old cravings came back. She went out soon after her husband and in less than an hour was a drunken mad woman. Poor thing! She never tried again, she said it was no use, no one knew the fearful struggle, and that unless she could keep out of sight or smell, she could never be free. For years we wrestled with God in prayer for her, never doubting that he would give the needed strength some day. She could not keep sober, so she left her husband and two children, one a dreadful cripple through her drink. She has had eight children, six of these have been victims to the curse. Her husband allowed her enough to live on while he lived, but he died two years after she left him. A white-haired, broken hearted man only forty five. We never knew where she lived, she used to come to us at home now and then, we gave her clothes and tried in every way to win her back, for she was a mere beggar. She said she would always keep out of our way, but she must and would have the drink. I need not follow her history for if you read the life of 'Annie Chapman', one of the worst victims in the terrible Whitechapel murders, you read the end of my sister's life.[14]

The letter writer went on to say that 'my sister's end after all our prayers, shook my faith to its very foundation' and that 'all through that terrible time I sat unknown in Halkin St. Church on Sundays',[15] but went on to say that his brother, who he said had identified Annie Chapman and was aged 28, was also an alcoholic. One month after her death he lost his job as a manager in a city warehouse for drinking and using money not his own. Some friends obtained for him a situation in Oxford Street but within a month he was drinking and then he absconded with some money. He later gave himself up and was tried at Marlborough Street Police Court, receiving a sentence of three months hard labour at Millbank Prison, which he was serving at the time the letter was written.

This letter seems factually accurate as far as the family details are concerned, although that George Smith cut his throat, that Annie Chapman had two brothers and that Fountain Smith, who was the brother who identified Annie's body, was an alcoholic, if all true, is new information and a tragic and revealing insight into the background of Annie Chapman.

Annie Chapman was five foot tall, had dark-brown wavy hair, blue eyes and a thick, flat nose. She was stout and well proportioned. Several news-papers reported that she had two or more front teeth missing,[16] but the police report[17] states that she had two teeth missing in the lower jaw, but not from the front, and the doctor who examined Chapman's body and gave evidence at the inquest stated that she was not missing any front teeth; the front teeth were perfect as far as the first molar and were very fine teeth indeed.

On separating from her husband, she went to London, and a friend, Amelia Farmer,[18] said she had principally resided in common lodging houses in Whitechapel and Spitalfields, in 1886 taking up with a man who made iron sieves, for which reason she was known to some people as Annie

Sievey, and gone to live at a common lodging house at 30 Dorset Street. This man was in fact named Jack Sivvey and eventually he left Annie to live in Notting Hill.[19] She then formed a relationship with a bricklayer's labourer named Edward Stanley, who was 47,[20] but was described in several newspapers as 'elderly'[21] and was apparently nicknamed 'The Pensioner', although there was some dispute about whether or not he was the man known by that nickname. He said he'd known Annie for about two years and had known her when she lived in Windsor, but they didn't live together. Stanley would spend weekends with her, infrequently at 35 Dorset Street, but at other places in the area.

Amelia Farmer, who said she had known Annie Chapman for five years,[22] had been a fellow lodger and also 'been in the habit of writing letters' for her, described Chapman as 'very industrious when sober, and was a very clever little woman',[23] 'very respectable . . . and never used bad language',[24] who had made antimacassars to sell and sometimes bought flowers and matches, which she would sell on the streets. Every Friday she went to Stratford to sell anything she had.[25] Farmer said that Chapman had not as 'a regular means of livelihood . . . been in the habit of frequenting the streets'[26] but added that she didn't think she was 'very particular what she did to earn a living and at times used to remain out very late at night.' Timothy Donovan also told the inquest that Annie Chapman 'had brought other men to the lodginghouse'.[27]

As for her drinking, somehow Annie Chapman seemed to be able to keep this under control. Farmer, who knew that Chapman had a taste for rum and acknowledged that Chapman 'was addicted to drink',[28] nevertheless described her as 'a sober, steady-going sort of woman, and one who seldom took any drink'. She said she had seen her the worse for drink, but that she couldn't drink much without becoming drunk.[29] The deputy of the lodging house at 30 Dorset Street, where Chapman had lived with Jack Sivvey, said that in his experience Chapman had not been given to drinking and that he was surprised to hear that she had reputedly been drinking to excess on the night of her murder,[30] and Timothy Donovan, the keeper of Crossingham's lodging house, where Chapman was living at the time of her death, said she was always very friendly with the other lodgers, that he had never had any trouble with her, and that, although she used to get drunk on Saturday nights, she was sober the rest of the week.

Annie Chapman, then, was a long-time alcoholic whose drinking caused her separation from her husband. She had received 10s. a week from her husband, on which she could have supported herself reasonably well, depending on how much she spent on alcohol. According to Amelia Farmer, Chapman does not appear to have resorted to prostitution prior to the death of her husband on 25 December 1886, but after that time she had tried to sustain herself through doing crochet work or by selling flowers and matches, but had become increasingly dissolute in her habits. She principally got drunk on Saturday nights, perhaps because she had the money to do so after her Friday at Stratford Market. What Annie Chapman probably did not know was that she was dying – a disease of the lungs and the membranes of the brain was quite far advanced.

Shortly before her death Annie Chapman, who was also known as Dark Annie and as Emily Annie,[31] was involved in a fight with a fellow lodger. The details are confused and confusing. According to Amelia Farmer, Chapman had told her that during the afternoon of Saturday, 1 September, she had been in the 'Ringers', a pub so named after the landlords Mr and Mrs Walter Ringer (the real name of the pub was the Britannia), at the corner of Dorset Street and Commercial Street. She was in the company of Ted Stanley (according to some accounts), a woman named Eliza Cooper and a man with the Runyonesque name 'Harry the Hawker', who was drunk. Chapman said that she had seen Cooper palm one of Harry's coins and replace it with a penny. She had mentioned this to Harry or otherwise drawn attention to Cooper's deceit and Cooper had struck her, blacking Chapman's eye and bruising her breast.

Edward Stanley, who had been on duty as a Volunteer (the predecessor of the modern Territorial Army) with the 2nd Brigade, Southern Division, Hants Militia, at Fort Elson, Gosport,[32] from 6 August to 1 September, returned to London and met Chapman at the corner of Brushfield Street that night.[33] According to Eliza Cooper, the couple came to 32 Dorset Street, Stanley gave Chapman 2s., and she paid for the bed for two nights. Chapman borrowed a piece of soap from Cooper and handed it to Stanley, who went and washed himself. Chapman didn't return the soap, but said, 'I will see you by and by.' If Amelia Farmer is to be believed, later that night Eliza Cooper, Chapman, Stanley and Harry the Hawker were in the Ringers, when Chapman stopped or otherwise drew attention to Cooper's attempt to switch a penny for Harry the Hawker's two-shilling piece. Later and elsewhere Cooper is supposed to have met Chapman and struck her in the face and chest.[34] This, though, conflicts with Cooper's story that she didn't see Chapman again that night.

Edward Stanley and Chapman slept at 35 Dorset Street Saturday night and left Chapman between 1 p.m. and 3 p.m. on Sunday – at which time she certainly had a black eye, and spoke to him about it.[35]

On Monday, 3 September, Amelia Farmer saw Chapman standing in the road opposite 35 Dorset Street. Chapman complained of feeling unwell, had a bruise on one of her temples, possibly the right,[36] and she opened her dress[37] to show Farmer another bruise on her chest. She said, 'You know the woman,' and mentioned a name Palmer couldn't recall, but knew to be that of a woman 'who carried out books for sale'.[38] Chapman said she intended to visit her sister. 'If I can get a pair of boots from my sister I shall go hop-picking,' she said.

On Tuesday, 4 September, Farmer saw Chapman walking at the side of Spitalfields Church. Chapman again complained of feeling unwell and said she thought she would go to the casual ward for a day or two. She mentioned that she had had nothing to eat or drink that day, not even a cup of tea, and Farmer gave her 2d., cautioning her not to spend it on rum.

It was on either Tuesday or Wednesday, the 4th or 5th, according to Eliza Cooper, that she and Chapman had their fight, but her testimony is almost certainly wrong. There can be little doubt that Chapman went into the casual ward as she was seen a couple of days later with bottle of medicine, a bottle of lotion and a box with two pills.[39]

Between two and three o'clock on Friday, 7 September,[40] Donovan got up and was coming out of his office, which faced the front door, when Chapman came in and asked if she could go down to the kitchen. Donovan said yes and asked her where she had been all the week. Chapman replied that she had been in the infirmary, but did not say which one. Chapman then went down to the kitchen.[41]

Chapman left the lodging house that afternoon and was later overheard by the night watchman, John Evans, to say that she had been to her sister's in Vauxhall.[42] At about 5 p.m. she was met by Amelia Palmer in Dorset Street. She seemed perfectly sober. Farmer said, 'Aren't you going to Stratford to-day?' She said she had been in the casual ward, but said, 'I feel too ill to do anything.' 'I saw her again about ten minutes afterwards on the same spot. She said, "It's no use my giving way. I must pull myself together and go and get some money, or I shall have no lodgings." '[43]

She returned to the lodging house soon after midnight and sent one of the lodgers to fetch her a pint of beer. This may have been William Stevens, a painter who lived at 35 Dorset Street. He said that at 12.12 a.m. he saw

Chapman in the kitchen of the lodging house and at 12.30 a.m. drank a pint of beer with her. She was not very well, he said, and said she had been in the casual ward of the Whitechapel Infirmary from Wednesday night till Friday morning.[44] She had 'a bottle of medicine, a bottle of lotion and a box containing two pills, he said, but as she was handling the box it came to pieces and she then took the pills out, picked up a piece of paper from the kitchen floor near the fireplace, and wrapped the pills up in it.'[45] The paper was a piece of envelope which he noticed had a red postmark on it. She put the piece of envelope in her pocket and he was sure it was the same piece of envelope that bore the crest of the Sussex Regiment that was found on her body.[46]

Chapman then went out again, probably to the Britannia pub on the corner of Dorset Street. She returned about 1.45 p.m.[47] Donovan saw Chapman come in and go down to the kitchen and asked the night watch-man's wife, who was in the office with him, to ask her husband to get the money from Chapman for her bed – bed No. 29, a double that 'as a rule' Chapman occupied by herself and for which she paid 8d. a night. Chapman came upstairs from the kitchen to the office and said, 'I have not sufficient money for my bed. Don't let it. I shan't be long before I am in.' Donovan said to her, 'You can find money for your beer, and you can't find money for your bed.' She said she'd only been to the Ringers at the top of the street. She was eating potatoes as she went out. She stood in the door two or three minutes, then repeated, 'Never mind, Tim: I shall soon be back. Don't let the bed.'

She was drunk but walked straight. Donovan didn't see her leave the house[48] but recalled that she was wearing a handkerchief three-corner-wise round her neck, tied in front in a knot and with a black woollen sort of scarf underneath. She'd bought the handkerchief from a lodger a week or a fortnight earlier.[49] John Evans, the night watchman, had followed Chapman up from the basement kitchen and walked to the street door as she left, seeing her enter Paternoster Row, walk to Brushfield Street and turn towards Spitalfields Church. That was the last time that Annie Chapman was definitely seen alive.

The next possible – but unlikely – sighting of Annie Chapman, and one the police were unable to substantiate, was a report that she was seen in the company of a man drinking together in the Bells in Brick Lane, later corrected to be the Ten Bells on the corner of Fournier Street and Commercial Road, a pub that opened early for the night workers opposite at Spitalfields Market. According to one of the people who worked there, a woman called into the pub about five o'clock, middle-aged and poorly dressed, and had something to drink. A man popped his head in the door and called her out. He had no coat and wore a little skull cap.[50]

Annie Chapman would be found dead in Hanbury Street. It was probably built about 1648, when it was called Lolesworth Lane, but very soon became known as Brown's Lane after William Brown, who owned a cow house and pasturage in the area, and by which name it was still known in 1888. It was described as a particularly poor area occupied 'for the most part' by Jews.[51] The entertainer Bud Flanagan (whose real name was Chiam Reeven), once a big star with the Crazy Gang but today perhaps best known for singing the theme tune to the popular television series *Dad's Army*, was born in Hanbury Street in 1896 and recalled it as

a patchwork of small shops, pubs, church halls, Salvation Army hostels, doss houses, cap factories and sweat shops where tailors with red-rimmed eyes sewed by gas-mantle light. It was typical of the Jewish quarter in the '90s. The houses were clean inside, but the exteriors were shoddy. The street was narrow and ill-lit.[52]

Sarah Cooney, who kept the Weavers Arms on the corner of Hanbury Street and Wilkes Street and was a great friend of the music hall star Marie Lloyd, 'stood out like a tree in a desert of Jews'. The Sugar Loaf pub in Hanbury Street was a regular meeting place of radicals and anarchists, many Jewish, where great names of anarchism such as Rudolph Rocker[53] spoke, and which was the forerunner of the famous Jubilee Club[54] (the successor to the Berner Street Club – see Chapter Nine).

Chapman was found in the rear yard of 29 Hanbury Street, a house that even by the architectural standards of the street was an uninspiring single-fronted dwelling, three storeys high and two rooms deep. It had probably been built around 1740 by a carpenter named Daniel Marsillat, who had leased the land from the owner, Granville Wheler.[55] It enjoyed life for quite some time as a silk-weaver's cottage, but the Spitalfields weavers, famous in their day, were gone and their properties had fallen into decay. No. 29 Hanbury Street's eight rooms were now home to seventeen people – actually less overcrowded than many of the hovels in the area. There was a single door opening from the street to a passage, 25 feet long and 3 feet wide, bare floorboards that creaked, giving access to the stairs and leading the length of the house to a plain, board-framed rear door with no lock on it

opening onto a yard. A notice board above the doorway that led into the yard
bore the legend in straggling white letters, MRS. A. RICHARDSON, ROUGH
PACKING-CASE MANUFACTURER.[56] Neither the front door nor the yard
door was kept locked (or, indeed, could be locked), especially as the
occupants of the house left for and returned from work at various hours of
the night and day. The yard, which was about two feet below the level of the
passage and reached by two or three stone steps, was 13–14 feet square and
roughly and irregularly paved with stones of all sizes and shapes. A five-
foot-six[57] fence, old and rotten, separated it from the yards either side. At
the bottom of the yard, on the left-hand side to anyone standing in the
doorway, there was a shed. On the right was a lavatory. There was no exit
from the yard except through the passage and back onto the street. Between
the steps and the fence there was a recess about three feet wide. The recess
was obscured when the yard door was opened, and it was here that the body
of Annie Chapman was found.[58]

In the ground-floor front room facing the street lived a 49-year-old
widow named Harriet Hardiman,[59] a medium-sized, well-proportioned
woman, with a very pale face and a curiously rounded chin, and her son,
William, aged sixteen. She had another son who did not at that time live
with her, James, aged 28. They both lived and slept in the room, which
doubled as a small shop used for selling cat meat.[60]

The ground-floor rear room was used by Amelia[61] Richardson, the
widow of Thomas Richardson, elderly,[62] short – 'a somewhat undersized
woman', as the *East London Observer* put it – pale-faced, and with dark
hair beginning to be streaked with grey. She had rented the house for
fifteen years, subletting most of the rooms, some of her tenants having
been with her for twelve years.[63] She was evidently a capable woman,
having continued to run her deceased husband's business and taken on the
responsibility of caring for her grandson, fourteen-year-old Thomas
Richardson, and this was evident at the inquest, where she impressed
several journalists with her clear and precise testimony, 'neither excited,
nor rambling'.[64] She ran a packing-case-making business with her son and
a workman named Francis Tyler.[65] She was also religious, and held weekly
prayer meetings in the downstairs back room.[66] She cared for an old
woman, Mrs Cox, whom she allowed to live in an attic room rent-free. She
occupied the ground-floor back room, which she used for cooking and the
prayer meetings, and the first-floor front room, where she and her
grandson slept. The rear room was occupied by an old man named

Walker, who lived there with his son, Alfred Walker,[67] who was weak-minded, but very inoffensive.

On the second floor lived Robert Thompson, a carman employed by Goodson's in Brick Lane, his wife and an adopted little girl. The rear room was occupied by two young women named Cooksley[68] or Cooksly, one of them named Eliza,[69] both employed as cigar makers.[70]

On the third floor, the front room was occupied by John Davis, 56, and his wife, Mary, 50, together with their three sons, James, 23, Benjamin, 20, and David, 18. They had been living there for only two weeks.[71] Davis was a carman employed at Leadenhall Market and described 'as an elderly man, with a decided stoop'[72] – he was in fact only 56 or 57 years old. An old woman named Sarah Cox occupied the back room on the third floor, supported by Mrs Richardson 'out of charity'.

Mrs Richardson and her grandson went to bed about 9.30 p.m., locking the downstairs back room she used for cooking and taking the key upstairs with her. It was still locked when she came downstairs in the morning. John Davis, on the top floor overlooking the street, went to bed about 8 p.m., his wife following about half an hour later and his sons coming in at different times, the last about 10.45 p.m. At 12.30 Misses Cooksly finished talking to two young men in the passage and went to bed, and it was believed that they were the last occupants of the house to retire.[73]

Mrs Richardson did not sleep very well. She woke at 3 a.m. and then dozed, hearing no noise during the night, but at nearly 4 a.m. she heard Mr Thompson leave the house for work, and she called 'Good morning' to him as he left.

At 4.40–4.45 a.m. John Richardson, a tall, stout man aged 35 with dark-brown hair, a brown moustache and a very pale face,[74] went to 29 Hanbury Street to see whether the place was properly secured. Some months earlier it had been broken into, two saws and two hammers being stolen,[75] and since then it had been his habit to go there at that time on market mornings. The front door was closed and he lifted the latch, opened the door and walked through the passage to the yard door, which was also closed. He pushed it open. He did not go into the yard but stood at the top of the steps, from where he could see the padlock securely fastened on the cellar door. One of his boots had been hurting his toe, and he now sat on the second step to cut off an offending bit of leather with a rusty little table knife without a handle that he'd used to cut up a carrot for the rabbit. He then tied up his boot, absent-mindedly put the knife in his pocket and went out of the house, leaving the yard door to close itself. He was sure he closed the front door. He was not more than three minutes in the house and it was not quite light at that time, but there was enough light for him to see and he felt that he would have seen Annie Chapman if she had been lying there.[76]

Albert Cadosch,[77] a carpenter who lived next door at 27 Hanbury Street, got up at about 5.15 a.m.[78] and went to the rear of the yard. On returning to the house, he heard talking as he passed the fence but could not distinguish any words except one, when a woman said, 'No.' He went into the house, and returned to the yard three or four minutes afterwards – he would explain to the inquest that he did not go into the yard twice out of curiosity, but because he had had an operation at the hospital[79] (he presumably went into the yard to use the outside lavatory, so the operation may have left him with a bladder problem) – when he heard a sort of a fall against the fence. He did not look to see what it was. He did not hear any other noise. He returned into the house and left by the front door to go to work. He did not see anybody as he left the house. As he passed Spitalfields Church he noticed the time: 5.32 a.m.

Elizabeth Long, who lived at 198 Church Row, Whitechapel,[80] and was the wife of a park keeper named James Long, was walking down Hanbury Street from her home and heading for Spitalfields Market, where she worked as a cart minder. The brewers' clock had just struck 5.30 when she passed 29 Hanbury Street, on the same side of the road. Outside she passed a man and woman on the pavement who were talking, standing close against the shutters or a few feet away, the man facing away from her. They were talking loudly and she overheard him say, 'Will you?' and the woman reply, 'Yes.' Mrs Long then passed them, and she went on to her work without looking back. She had visited the mortuary and seen Annie Chapman there and was sure she was the woman she had seen in the street. She was unable to describe the man, whose face she hardly saw (perhaps only in slight profile), except to say that he was dark and in her opinion looked like a foreigner (generally a euphemism for a Jew). He wore a brown deerstalker hat, and she thought a dark coat, but was not quite certain of that, and overall had a shabby genteel appearance. He appeared to be a little taller than the woman – which if the woman was Chapman would make him between five foot and five foot five – but Mrs Long could not say what age he was, except that he looked to be over forty.[81]

John Davis had slept a little, but been awake from about 3 a.m. until 5 a.m., when he had fallen back to sleep. At 5.45 a.m. the chimes of the clock on Spitalfields Church striking the quarter-hour woke him and he got up. He had a cup of tea and went downstairs. The front street door was wide open and thrown back against the wall, which didn't surprise him, as it was frequently left open all night. The rear door was closed. He opened the door and stepped out to the yard. He saw Annie Chapman lying between the steps and the fence, her head towards the house, 'her clothing up to her knees, and her face covered with blood'. He would later express with horror, 'What was lying beside her I cannot describe – it was part of her body. I did not examine the woman, I was too frightened at the dreadful sight.'

Having found the body, Davis ran back along the passage to the front door and went out into the street. Henry John Holland, a thin, sickly-looking youth with straw-coloured hair,[82] who lived at 4 Aden Yard off the Mile End Road, was on his way to work in Chiswell Street when he was summoned by Davis, who said, 'Come and look in the back yard!' Davis then spotted two men waiting outside the Black Swan,[83] a pub three doors away at 23 Hanbury Street and on the same side of the street, in the yard of which Joseph and Thomas Bayley ran a packing-case-making business. Employees of the Bayleys, they were standing outside the workshop waiting for their co-workers to arrive. Davis didn't know their names, but knew them by sight. They were James Kent,[84] a youngish-looking man with a bullet head, closely cropped hair and a sandy close-cut moustache,[85] who lived at 20 B Block, King David Lane, Shadwell, and James Green of 26 Acland Street, off Burdett Road. Davis shouted, 'Men, come here. Here's a sight. A woman must have been murdered!' Kent and Green followed Davis and Holland to the house and through the passage to the yard. Neither man went into the yard, but viewed the body from the top step.[86] Unlike the others, Holland went into the yard, but did not touch the body.

The events are now somewhat confused. James Kent went for a policeman but got as far as a pub and, not having seen a policemen, went inside for a brandy, which he probably needed – all the men who found the body said they were extremely frightened by the discovery. He then went to fetch a piece of canvas with which to cover up the body. James Green appears to have returned directly to the workshop at 23a Hanbury Street, and there waited, possibly in shock. Holland went for a policeman and found one in Spitalfields Market. He told him that a woman had been found murdered and that it was a similar case to that of Buck's Row, but the constable said he could not come and told Holland that he would find two constables outside the market. (Inspector Helson would later explain that constables on duty in the market were under strict instructions not to move from their posts.) Holland went out of the market but was unable to find any other policeman and went back to the house. He was angered or upset enough by this to report the constable's conduct at the Commercial Street Police Station that afternoon.[87]

The time was now shortly after 6 a.m. Mrs Richardson heard noises in the passage and thought the place was on fire. Her grandson, Thomas, went to investigate and soon returned, saying, 'Oh, grandmother, there is a woman murdered!' Mrs Richardson went down immediately, the police and several others were in the passage but there was no one in the yard and she was able to view the body. Realising that she was not properly attired, she went back to her room and dressed herself.

Meanwhile, Davis had gone to Commercial Street Police Station, where he reported his discovery, but by this time, shortly after 6.10 a.m.[88] it would seem, Inspector Joseph Chandler of H Division was already on his way to Hanbury Street, having seen some men running, one of whom told him, 'Another woman has been murdered.' Chandler immediately followed the man to 29 Hanbury Street. It was now about 6.20 a.m. and Holland, frustrated, returned to Hanbury Street in time to see Chandler, accompanied by a young man, run into the house. A crowd had gathered by now and there were plenty of people in the passage, but none in the yard.

Inspector Chandler sent for Dr George Bagster Phillips, whose surgery was at 2 Spital Square, and to Commercial Street Police Station for the ambulance and further assistance. Constables duly arrived and Chandler cleared all bystanders from the passage. From a neighbour he acquired some sacking with which he covered the body of Annie Chapman. Dr Phillips arrived at 29 Hanbury Street at 6.30 a.m. For 23 years the divisional police surgeon, Phillips was described as 'a character' by Walter Dew, who claimed to know him well. 'An elderly man, he was ultra-old-fashioned both in his personal appearance and his dress. He used to look for all the world as though he had stepped out of a century-old painting. His manners were charming; he was immensely popular both with the police and the public, and he was highly skilled.'[89]

Annie Chapman was lying on her back, on the left-hand side of the steps leading from the passage into the yard. Her head was about six inches in front of the bottom step, her left arm was placed across the left breast, her legs were drawn up, the feet resting on the ground, and the knees turned outwards. Her swollen face was turned on its right, 'looking' away from the fence. The swollen face and tongue, which protruded between the front teeth, but not beyond the lips, indicated suffocation – indeed, as the *Lancet* observed, 'There could be little doubt that he first strangled or suffocated his victim, for not only were no cries heard, but the face, lips and hands were livid as in asphyxia, and not blanched as they would be from loss of blood.'[90] There were recent abrasions or scratches on the left side of the neck, on the lower jaw an inch and a half to two inches below the lobe of the ear, and going in a contrary direction to the incision in the throat, and on the left side there was a more marked bruise that corresponded with that on the right. These suggested that the woman was seized by the chin to expose her throat, which was then severed with one long and deep incision from left to right. 'Almost all the blood from her body would have drained out of the divided vessels, accounting for the almost bloodless effect of the subsequent incisions in the abdomen and pelvis',[91] enabling the murderer to make almost blood-free incisions and mutilation of the abdomen.

Dr Phillips was thus able to state with certainty that Chapman had entered the yard alive and been killed where found. There was no evidence of a struggle 'about the body', but Dr Phillips reminded the coroner that the fence near Chapman's head had been smeared with blood – these smears were fourteen inches from the ground and immediately above where blood had flowed from Chapman's neck. (If Chapman had been strangled or suffocated before the incision was made then she would have been in no position to make the marks and one must assume they were made by the murderer, although Chapman may have been rendered insensible and laid on the ground, then revived slightly as her throat was cut.) Dr Phillips concluded, 'From these appearances I am of opinion that the breathing was interfered with previous to death, and that death arose from syncope, or failure of the heart's action, in consequence of the loss of blood.'

The throat had been cut through to the spine, the incisions through the skin being jagged, made from the left side of the neck on a line with the angle of the jaw. They had been carried entirely round, and again in front of the neck, and ending at a point about midway between the jaw and the sternum (breast bone) on the right side. There were two distinct cuts on the body of the vertebrae on the left side of the spine. They were parallel to each other, and separated about half an inch. It looked as if an attempt had been made to separate the bones of the neck – as though the murderer had attempted to cut through the spine to remove the head – and some commentators speculated that the handkerchief found tied around Chapman's neck had been placed there by the murderer to keep her head attached to the trunk,[92] but Dr Phillips would tell the inquest that he didn't think it had been tied on after the throat had been cut[93] and we know from other testimony that she was wearing it that night.

Dr Phillips noticed some old bruising, evidently the marks of the fight Annie Chapman had had with Eliza Cooper, and an abrasion over the bend of the first joint of the ring finger, where there were distinct markings of a ring or rings. In other words, there were ring marks on her fingers and abrasions that looked as if they'd been made when the rings were wrenched off. All witnesses said that Chapman wore rings, and Eliza Cooper in particular said that Chapman wore on the third finger of the left hand three brass rings that she'd bought from a black man.

The stomach contained food, presumably the potato she had been eating when last seen by Timothy Donovan, but curiously there were no signs of her having indulged in alcohol, and Phillips was convinced that for some hours before her death she had not taken any strong drink. Given that she was drunk when she left the lodging house at 35 Hanbury Street, this is curious, although she said that she had drunk only beer – not a 'strong alcohol', which usually means spirit – and it had been said that she got drunk very quickly, so perhaps she hadn't drunk much.

Overall, Chapman was described as 'fatty', but it was clear that she was poorly fed. The internal organs showed that she was far advanced in a longstanding disease of the lungs and the membranes of the brain were opaque, the veins and tissues coated with blood of a dark character.

A portion of the small intestines and of the abdomen was lying on the ground over the right shoulder, but still attached to the body. Two other parts of the wall of the stomach were lying in a pool of blood above the left shoulder. From the pelvis the uterus and its appendages, with the upper portion of the vagina and the posterior two-thirds of the bladder, had been entirely removed. The incisions were cleanly cut, avoiding the rectum, and dividing the vagina low enough to avoid injury to the cervix uteri. The mode in which these portions were extracted showed some anatomical knowledge. Indeed, Dr Phillips believed that there would have been greater evidence of anatomical knowledge if the murderer hadn't been acting in great haste. As the *Lancet* observed, 'obviously the work was that of an expert – of one, at least, who had such knowledge of anatomical or pathological examinations as to be enabled to secure the pelvic organs with one sweep of a knife'. When asked how long it would have taken to perform the mutilations, Dr Phillips replied, 'I myself could not have performed all the injuries I saw on that woman, even without a struggle, under a quarter of an hour. If I had done it in the deliberate manner usual with a surgeon, it would probably have taken me the best part of an hour.'

The organs had been removed and as far as was known were missing, presumably taken away by the murderer. Dr Phillips said, 'The conclusion I came to was that the whole object of the operation was to obtain possession of a certain portion of the body. Coroner Wynne Baxter would later fuel this theory. That organs were missing (i.e. removed *and taken away* by the murderer) is almost writ on stone, but Dr Phillips said that, although he had 'carefully closed up the clothes of the woman' before leaving the murder scene, he was not present when the body was moved to the mortuary and acknowledged that the body parts 'might have been lost'.

In Dr Phillips's opinion the same knife had 'very probably' been used to cut the throat and mutilate the abdomen; a very sharp knife, probably with a thin narrow blade, at least six to eight inches long, probably longer. The knife could have been of the sort a doctor would use when performing a postmortem, although he doubted that the ordinary postmortem case would contain such a knife, and a well-ground slaughterer's knife was also a possibility. He did not think the wounds had been caused by a bayonet or a sword-bayonet, and thought a knife of the sort used in the leather trade would not be long enough.

On the crucial question of time of death, when Dr Phillips first examined the body he thought that Chapman had been dead at least two hours 'and probably more', but he acknowledged that it was a fairly cold morning and the body would probably have cooled more rapidly because so much blood had been lost. Dr Phillips's original estimate would place death at or before 4.30 a.m., which effectively eliminates the worth of the testimony of Albert Cadosch and Elizabeth Long, and raises the question why John Richardson didn't see the body when he was cutting the offending leather from his shoe between 4.45 a.m. and 4.50 a.m. Coroner Baxter, though not a medical man – he was a solicitor – attached greater weight to the testimony of Albert Cadosch and, especially, Mrs Long, and felt inclined to dismiss Dr Phillips's estimate of Chapman's time of death because Dr Phillips had 'admitted that the coldness of the morning and the great loss of blood might affect his opinion'. On the other hand, the police seem to have dismissed Mrs Long's testimony and, perhaps unsurprisingly, placed faith in Dr

Phillips, whose opinion as an experienced police surgeon deserved (and deserves) respect.[94]

However, it is difficult to believe that John Richardson would not have seen Annie Chapman when he visited 29 Hanbury Street that morning. Inspector Chandler was initially prepared to believe it, because he didn't know that Richardson had sat on the middle step to cut an offending bit of leather from his shoe. Chandler therefore thought that Richardson probably pushed open the yard door and glanced to his right, saw the padlock to the cellar was secure, then turned and left, never looking to his left. But Richardson had sat on the second step down, his feet on the yard floor, and it's very hard to believe that he could have failed to see Chapman. In fact, Richardson himself was certain that he would have seen Annie Chapman's body. 'It was getting light, but I could see all over the place . . . I could not have failed to notice the deceased had she been lying there . . . I must have seen her,' he told the inquest. Unless one has an overriding reason for doing so, it is tempting to think, as Wynne Baxter clearly did, that Dr Phillips 'miscalculated the effect' of the coldness of the morning and the loss of blood.

However, the timings of Mrs Long and Albert Cadosch present problems of their own. Basically, if Cadosch heard Annie Chapman and her murderer in the yard of 29 Hanbury Street *before* 5.30 a.m., as he claimed, then Mrs Long can't have seen them outside or near 29 Hanbury Street *after* 5.30 a.m. or later still. This wouldn't be a real problem because the difference seems only to be a matter of minutes and both witnesses were estimating the time and basing their estimates on different clocks, Mr Cadosch on the one on Spitalfields Church and Mrs Long on the brewery clock in Brick Lane. Clocks being clocks, they are not likely to have given the precise time. However, Albert Cadosch's own timings cause one to raise an eyebrow. He reckoned that he had come into the yard at 5.25, used the lavatory and returned indoors, then gone outside again at 5.29, used the lavatory again, then gone back indoors and out into Hanbury Street, coming into sight of the Spitalfields Church clock by 5.32. To have achieved that timing he would have to have been speedy in the lavatory and sprinted along Hanbury Street. Furthermore, he'd almost certainly have seen Mrs Long and the couple she saw in the street. He saw neither. The discrepancy can be cleared up with one small assumption: that Mrs Long heard the brewery clock strike the quarter-hour instead of the half-hour, in which case she could have seen the couple outside Hanbury Street *before* Cadosch entered the yard (whatever the time was when he entered it).

Having viewed the body and made a preliminary examination, Dr Phillips ordered that it be taken to the mortuary in Old Montague Street, at the corner of Eagle Street, a cul-de-sac, which ended in the green doors of the mortuary. The body was conducted there by Sergeant Edmund Berry, 31H,[95] in the same shell (a makeshift coffin used to take a body to the mortuary) as was used to convey the body of Mary Ann Nichols. News of the murder had spread quickly and when the body was brought through the passage of the house to the street it was greeted by a very excitable crowd estimated to number several hundred.

At 7 a.m. Robert Mann, the pauper inmate of the Whitechapel Union who had charge of the mortuary and who received the body of Nichols, now received the body of Annie Chapman. Inspector Chandler arrived at the mortuary at about the same time. The body was lying on the ambulance and did not appear to have been disturbed. Chandler left, but told PC Barnes, 376H, to take charge. Mary Elizabeth Simonds, a resident nurse at the Whitechapel Infirmary, and Frances Wright, a senior colleague, were instructed to go to the mortuary, where they found the body lying on the ambulance. Nurse Simonds said that she was directed by Inspector Chandler to undress the corpse – which Chandler denied and which the coroner's officer said had in fact been done on the order of the clerk of the Guardians – which she did, placing the woman's clothes in a corner of the shed, but leaving the handkerchief round the neck. They then washed the blood off the body. Robert Mann had left the mortuary while this was done.

After the removal of the body, Inspector Chandler searched the yard. He found a piece of coarse muslin, a small pocket hair comb, a screwed-up piece of paper containing two pills, and a portion of envelope which on one side had the letter 'M' in a man's handwriting and a post office stamp: 'London, 28 August 1888'. On the reverse was the seal of the Sussex Regiment. It is uncertain where the piece of envelope was found.

One police report refers to 'the portion of an envelope found *near the body* of Annie Chapman (and which contained two pills)'[96] (my italics), whereas another report read '*On person* portion of an envelope stamped "Sussex Regiment" dated 23rd August. 1888'[97] (my italics). This confusion was reflected in the press. *The Star*, whose reporter had interviewed Chief Inspector West and Inspector Chandler, reported 'nothing was found in her pockets except part of an envelope . . .'[98] Two days later, however, *The Star* put most of the discoveries of the yard into Chapman's pocket and also introduced a longstanding dispute to the Ripper story, when it reported, 'In the pockets there were a handkerchief, two small combs, and an envelope with the seal of the Sussex Regiment. There were also found two farthings polished brightly, and, according to some, these coins had been passed off as half-sovereigns upon the deceased by her murderer.'[99]

The Times has the envelope being discovered during a minute search of the yard. It is 'stained with blood' and the date on it is 'London, August 20', and 'In addition, two pills were also picked up.'[100] (The date, it will be noticed, is different from that given in the police report.) *The Times* later reported Inspector Chandler as telling the inquest that 'A portion of an envelope was found lying near where her head had been, and a piece of paper containing two pills . . . On the other side of the envelope was the letter "M" in a man's handwriting. There was also a post-office stamp, "London, 28 Aug., 1888." '[101] So we now have yet another date, a piece of envelope, *and* a piece of paper containing two pills, but this may be a result of mishearing or not paying attention to the testimony, as the *East London Advertiser* reported Inspector Chandler as saying, 'A small piece of paper, a portion of an envelope, had also been lying near the head, that containing two pills . . .'[102] So, the envelope was found in Chapman's pocket or on the floor near where her head had been, it bore the date 3 August,[103] 20 August, 23 August[104] or 28 August.[105] Trying to establish the facts is a minefield for the unwary. And the wary can come a cropper too.

On 14 September, Inspector Chandler made enquiries of the 1st Battalion of the Sussex Regiment at the North Camp, Farnborough, and learned that stationery bearing the regimental seal was on sale in the canteen and used by most of the men. Enquiries among the men failed to produce anyone who admitted to knowing or writing to anyone in Whitechapel. The pay books were also scrutinised, but none of the signatures matched the writing on the portion of envelope. Inspector Chandler then spoke to Messrs Summer and Thirkettle, postmasters at Lynchford Road Post Office. They told him that the letter had been posted there, but they did not know by whom. They told him that writing paper and envelopes bearing the regimental stamp were on sale to the public at the post office, so the letter could have been posted by anyone in the district. The following day, 15 September, William Stevens visited the Commercial Street Police Station and told the police how he had seen Chapman in the kitchen with a box of pills that fell apart and Chapman 'picked up a piece of paper from the kitchen floor near the fireplace, and wrapped the pills up in it'. The envelope, it would seem, was not Chapman's.

Meanwhile, Detective Sergeant William Thicke, Sergeant Leach and other detective officers had arrived in Hanbury Street, and a telegram had been sent to Inspector Abberline at Scotland Yard. Sergeant Thicke went to the mortuary and took a description of the body, which was later circulated, and Inspector Abberline consulted with Inspector Helson of J Division, and Acting Superintendent West, who was in charge of H Division. They agreed that Annie Chapman had been murdered by the man who had killed Mary Ann Nichols.

CHAPTER SEVEN

Leather Apron

The focus of attention during the early days of the Ripper enquiry was centred on a mysterious individual nicknamed Leather Apron. He was first mentioned in *The Star*, which featured him far more prominently than any other newspapers and may even have invented him.

On 4 September the newspaper reported almost in passing,

> With regard to the man who goes by the *sobriquet* of 'Leather Apron,' he has not, it is stated, been seen in the neighbourhood much for the past few nights, but this may mean nothing, as the women street wanderers declare that he is known as well in certain quarters of the West End as he is in Whitechapel.[1]

The following day it carried a major story about Leather Apron with several headlines and subheads, including:

THE ONLY NAME LINKED WITH
THE WHITECHAPEL MURDERS

A NOISELESS MIDNIGHT TERROR
The Strange Character who Prowls About Whitechapel After
Midnight, Universal Fear Among the Women
Slippered Feet and a Sharp Leather-knife

The story was dramatic:

> He has ranged Whitechapel for a long time. He exercises over the unfortunates who ply their trade after twelve o'clock at night, a sway that is based on universal terror. He has kicked, injured, bruised, and terrified a hundred of them who are ready to testify to the outrages. He

has made a certain threat, his favourite threat, to any number of them, and each of the three dead bodies represents that threat carried out. He carries a razor-like knife, and two weeks ago drew it on a woman called 'Widow Annie' as she was crossing the square near London Hospital, threatening at the same time, with his ugly grin and his malignant eyes, to 'rip her up.' He is a character so much like the invention of a story writer that the accounts of him given by all the street-walkers of the Whitechapel district seem like romances. The remarkable thing is, however, that they all agree in every particular . . .

About 50 of the unfortunates in the Whitechapel district gave a description of 'Leather-Apron' to a *Star* reporter between midnight and three o'clock this morning. The descriptions all agreed, and most of them added to it a personal experience with the man during the last two years in which they were more or less injured. From all accounts he is five feet four or five inches in height and wears a dark, close-fitting cap. He is thickset, and has an unusually thick neck. His hair is black, and closely clipped, his age being about 38 or 40. He has a small, black moustache. The distinguishing feature of his costume is a leather apron, which he always wears, and from which he gets his nickname. His expression is sinister, and seems to be full of terror for the women who describe it. His eyes are small and glittering. His lips are usually parted in a grin which is not only not reassuring, but excessively repellent. He is a slipper maker by trade, but does not work. His business is blackmailing women late at night. A number of men in Whitechapel follow this interesting profession. He has never cut anybody so far as known, but always carries a leather-knife, presumably as sharp as leather-knives are wont to be. This knife a number of the women have seen. His name nobody knows, but all are united in the belief that he is a Jew or of Jewish parentage, his face being of a marked Hebrew type. But the most singular characteristic of the man, and one which tends to identify him closely with last Friday night's work, is the universal statement that in moving about he never makes any noise . . .

When two of the Philpott-street women directed the *Star* reporter to Commercial-street, opposite the Princess Alice Tavern, as the most likely place to find him, she added that it would be necessary to look into all the shadows, as if he was there he would surely be out of sight. This locality, it may be remarked, is but a few steps from the model dwelling house in George's-Yard, where the murdered woman of four weeks ago was found.

'Leather-Apron' never by any chance attacks a man. He runs away on the slightest appearance of rescue. One woman whom he assailed some time ago boldly prosecuted him for it, and he was sent up for seven days. He has no settled place of residence, but has slept oftenest in a fourpenny lodging-house of the lowest kind in a disreputable lane leading from Brick-lane. The people at this lodging-house denied that he had been there, and appeared disposed to shield him. 'Leather-Apron's' pal, 'Micheldy Joe', was in the house at the time, and his presence doubtless had something to do with the unwillingness to give information. 'Leather-Apron' was last at this house some weeks ago, though this account may be untrue. He ranges all over London, and rarely assails the same woman twice. He has lately been seen in Leather-lane, which is in the Holborn district.[2]

The next day *The Star* carried another long piece, quoting the owner of a women's lodging house in Thrawl Street – 'one of the darkest and most terrible-looking spots in Whitechapel' – who told some gruesome stories about Leather Apron, saying that night after night women had come into the lodging almost fainting from the terror of an encounter with the fiend.

The story about Leather Apron quickly crossed the Atlantic, being reported as far afield as Austin, Texas, where Leather Apron was described as:

a short, thickset, half crazy creature, with fiendish black eyes [who] frequented the dark alleys, and like a veritable imp haunted the gloom of the halls and passage ways of Whitechapel, and lived by robbing the female Arabs who roamed the streets after nightfall. Of powerful muscle, carrying a knife which he brandished over his victims, the London murder fiend was too terrible an assailant for the victim that cowered beneath the glitter of cold steel. [His] identity is supposed to have been established by reports of women whom he had robbed, but not murdered.[3]

The impact of Leather Apron on the public conscience was tremendous. A 48-year-old labourer named William Marchant, who was taken to the Chelsea Infirmary after tumbling from a parapet overlooking the Thames in Cheyne Walk and falling thirty feet into the water, was said by the house surgeon, a man named Moore, to have recovered consciousness but from time to time elapsed into a delirium in which he would cry out that he was not Leather Apron.[4] In another story a young girl named Duffy was sent to fetch home the cows from a field in Newry and was terrified when a partially dressed man leaped out of a hedge and chased her, saying that he was Leather Apron and the Whitechapel murderer. Duffy apparently wasn't the only victim and it was reported that 'so great is the panic amongst the female portion of the community that not one of them can be induced to go out on the Newry-road after dark, and the police, who had been unable to find the man, said they thought he was a half-crazy individual'.[5] Adding a note of levity to the story, a constable (57V) found himself in an embarrassing situation when he came across an old woman named Mary Cassidy drunk and asleep in a doorway and woke her to get her to move on. On opening her bleary eyes, Cassidy had exclaimed, 'You are "Leather Apron" – go away!' and screamed 'Murder!'[6]

In a similar case, another drunk, a cabinet maker named Thomas Mills, was found by a constable in Shoreditch, drunk and surrounded by an angry crowd who claimed he was Leather Apron and were threatening to lynch him. Brought before the magistrate at Worship Street Police Court, Mills explained that he looked like the portrait of Leather Apron published in the *Police News* and that whenever he went out people accused him. He couldn't get work because of it, he said, and when he got a drop to drink he got angry about it. It was said that Mills had been before the court many times for drunkenness, the last time being the previous Tuesday. The magistrate told Mills that if he kept sober people would not take any notice of him or see a likeness to a picture, and fined him 2s. 6d.[7]

A month later Leather Apron was still offered up as the terror of the local prostitutes. A journalist who visited the St George's-in-the-East Infirmary to see the conditions in which the patients were kept was given a tour of the wards by the recently appointed medical superintendent, Dr Saunders, and commented on a ward specially set apart for women who hadn't been admitted to the Lock Hospital (a special hospital for the treatment of venereal diseases). Saunders told the women that the journalist was looking over the infirmary and had not come to question them about the Ripper, but that they were welcome to tell him anything they knew. A 'very bright-eyed wicked-looking girl of about 22 years of age, who seemed to be of a somewhat superior type to those met with in the East End of London', called a fellow patient called Jenny,

. . . 'just tell this gentlemen what you know.'

Jenny proceeded to do so, and, at some length, dwelt upon the fact that a certain individual, about 40 years of age – a stout-built, fair-complexioned, and somewhat stout man – had been constantly seen in the neighbourhood of Whitechapel, and that he could be easily recognised by most of the inmates in that particular ward.

In reply to this the question was asked: 'Why have you not given information to the police?'

The Woman: 'Why, sir, we have done so time after time. What has been the result? Poor unfortunate women have been beaten nearly to death.'

'But do you know for a fact that a man of this description is going about and now cannot be found?'

The Woman: 'Yes, sir. We all know that we have been most brutally ill-treated, and that the wretch is the very man whom I have described.'

Dr Saunders seemed to think the statement made was strictly accurate, and said, 'They know all about Leather Apron.'[8]

Despite the widespread public acceptance that Leather Apron was a real and terrifying figure, several newspapers began to express doubts, not only that Leather Apron was Jack the Ripper but that he even existed. The *Leytonstone Express* mildly wondered whether Leather Apron was 'a mythical outgrowth of the reporter's fancy'.[9] The *Manchester Guardian* was more direct:

a theory exists that 'Leather Apron' is more or less a mythical personage, and that he is not responsible for the terrible crimes with which his name has been associated. All the same, the details of his appearance have been widely circulated with a view to his early apprehension, and all the police in the vicinity are on the look-out for him.[10]

The *Yorkshire Post* attributed this view to the police:

It is true that they possess a description of the man who is known as 'Leather Apron' and will arrest him if he can be found, but their theory is that 'Leather Apron' is more or less a mythical personage, and that he is not responsible for the terrible crimes with which his name has been associated.[11]

The *Manchester Guardian*, reporting a story from the Central News agency, stated that, among the various groups of people huddled on the pavements during the weekend of Annie Chapman's murder,

> The words most frequently heard in conversation are 'Leather Apron'. The term has become a by-word of pavement and gutter, and one more often hears it accompanied by a guffaw than whispered in a tone which would indicate any fear of the mysterious individual who is supposed to live under that soubriquet. Whilst a large number of persons – including many members of the police force – firmly believe in the existence and almost certain guilt of the aproned one, the talk of the footways indicates that a large number of the inhabitants of the East End are sceptical as to his personality. [12]

In a typically bloated piece of heavy-handed humorous prose in *The Referee*, the distinguished wordsmith George R Sims observed that no matter what extraordinary events took place – among them 'Professor Baldwin' (whom we met in Chapter One) being carried aloft by a halfpenny kite and descending from an extraordinary altitude – 'Leather Apron would remain the hero of the hour.' He went on,

> Up to a few days ago the mere mention of Leather Apron's name was sufficient to cause a panic. All England was murmuring his name with bated breath . . . Now that the first wild excitement has died down, and common sense is having a peep in, most people are beginning to see that Leather Apron has probably as much to do with the Whitechapel murders as the Archbishop of Canterbury or the Baroness Burdett-Coutts. It is astonishing how eagerly the Press seized upon the mere mention of a person with this ordinary nickname, and worked it up into a blood-curdling sensation. The name of Leather Apron has been flashed from pole to pole. It is to-day as much a byword on Greenland's icy mountains and on India's coral strand as it is in Whitechapel and Scotland-yard. And why? Primarily because there was something in the sound which suggested a big catch-on.[13]

The Star, however, seems to have had no trouble finding people who knew and could describe him: 'Mike —, a grocer in George Yard said he'd known Leather Apron very well for six years and that "the man is unquestionably mad, and that anybody who met him face to face would know it. That his eyes are never still, but are always shifting uneasily, and he never looks anybody in the eye." '[14] Timothy Donovan, deputy at a lodging house at 35 Dorset Street, from which a Ripper victim, Annie Chapman, was ejected on the night of her death, when asked if he knew Leather Apron told a *Star* reporter, 'Yes, I ought to . . . I chucked him down the stairs; he tried to murder a woman here.'[15]

The newspaper also reported that few policemen had ever seen or even heard of Leather Apron, or were even aware of his existence apart from what the newspapers had reported. This certainly wasn't the case. The police appear to have known exactly who Leather Apron was. A report to Scotland Yard dated 7 September 1888 by the local inspector of J Division, Joseph Helson, stated,

> The inquiry has revealed the fact that a man named Jack Pizer, alias Leather Apron, has, for some considerable period been in the habit of ill-using prostitutes in this, and other parts of the Metropolis, and careful search has been, and is continued to be made to find this man in order that his movements may be accounted for on the night in question, although at present there is no evidence whatsoever against him.[16]

Another report of the same date was sent to the assistant commissioner of CID by Acting Superintendent W Davis. It said pretty much the same thing, evidently being based on Helson's report:

> A man named 'Pizer' alias Leather Apron has been in the habit of ill-using prostitutes in various parts of the Metropolis for some time past, and careful enquiries have been made to trace him, but without success. There is no evidence against him at present. Enquiries are being continued.[17]

John Pizer was a Polish Jew, the son of Israel Pizer of 22 Mulberry Street. John's mother was dead, but his father had subsequently married one August Cohen. She and John's married brother and sister continued to live at Mulberry Street, but John Pizer seems to have lived in various common lodging houses. It is possible that he had a police record. We know that a man named 'John Pozer' attacked and stabbed in the hand a boot-finisher named John Willis in Morgan Street, St George's, in July 1887, for which he received six months' hard labour. This 'John Pozer' was the same age and had the same occupation as Pizer. A John Pizer also appears to have been charged with indecent assault at the Thames Magistrates' Court on 4 August 1888, but was discharged.

John Pizer was described as about five foot four, thickset, with a florid complexion, dark, almost black hair, a moustache and side whiskers. The *East London Observer* found little right with him and published a graphic description. It said his face

> was not altogether pleasant to look upon by reason of the grizzly black strips of hair, nearly an inch in length, which almost covered the face. The thin lips, too, had a cruel, sardonic kind of look, which was increased, if anything, by the drooping, dark moustache and side whiskers. His hair was short, smooth and dark, intermingled with grey, and his head was slightly bald on the top. The head was large, and was fixed to the body by a thick, heavy-looking neck . . . he appeared somewhat splay-footed . . . spoke with a thick, guttural foreign accent.[18]

It remains to be seen how accurate this description was, and the only known illustration of Pizer was dismissed by Pizer himself as bearing no more resemblance to him than it did to the Man in the Moon.[19] Other newspapers commented on his intelligence and command of English: 'For a man of his class he displays more than an ordinary amount of intelligence,' reported *The Star*.[20]

Shortly after 8 a.m. on Monday, 10 September, Sergeant Thicke and two or three other officers went to 22 Mulberry Street. They knocked on the door, which was opened by Pizer. 'You are just the man I want,' said Sergeant Thicke. 'What for?' asked Pizer. Thicke replied, 'You know what for. You know you are "Leather Apron". You will have to come with me.' Pizer said he replied, 'Very well, sir. I'll go down to the station with you with the greatest of pleasure.' Pizer would tell a Press Association reporter, 'Up to that moment I did not know that I was called by that name. I have been in the habit of wearing an apron. I have worn it coming from my employment, but not recently. I was quite surprised when Sergeant Thicke called me by the name of Leather Apron.'

This denial that he was known as Leather Apron cannot be accepted, and neither is his claim to have been surprised when Sergeant Thicke addressed him by that nickname. As we shall see, Pizer had been addressed as Leather Apron in the street and possibly even been chased by a mob, and he had gone into hiding at his home, so it is beyond question that he knew when Sergeant Thicke called that he was nicknamed Leather Apron. The denial also seems contradicted by his admission at the inquest that he was known as Leather Apron, as was reported by almost every newspaper,[21] and by Sergeant Thicke's assertion that he had known Pizer for eighteen years and that when people in the neighbourhood spoke of 'Leather Apron' they meant John Pizer.

Detective Sergeant William Thicke of H Division was born on 20 November 1845 at Salisbury, Wiltshire. He had joined the Metropolitan Police on 6 March 1868 and been appointed to H Division. He had a few brief months on B (Chelsea) Division, but had spent most of his career – from 1872 until 1886 – on P (Camberwell), before being transferred back to H Division on 3 May 1886, remaining there until he resigned on 24 April 1893, by which time he had become something of an institution on that manor. He was five foot eight and had dark hair and grey eyes. A newspaper at the time described him as a smart-looking officer, fresh-coloured, youngish-looking, with a heavy, drooping brown moustache and dark hair, 'flashily' attired in a suit of loud checks.[22] As the newspapers reported, he was known as 'Johnny Upright'. Walter Dew wrote that Thicke 'was a holy terror to the local law-breakers, was known as "Johnny Upright" because he was very upright both in his walk and in his methods.'[23]

In 1902 the celebrated American author Jack London came to London and decided to write about the poverty of the East End by living, eating and sleeping with the people of the area, but he wanted a haven 'into which I could run now and again to assure myself that good clothes and cleanliness still existed'. He was advised to seek a recommendation from 'Johnny Upright', 'A detective of thirty-odd years' continuous service in the East End, known far and wide by a name given him by a convicted felon in the dock'. At first dismissed when mistaken for a beggar seeking work, he returned better dressed the following day and arrived by hansom cab. Thicke invited him amid much humour and banter to take tea with his wife and daughters:

> 'We are humble here,' he said, 'not given to the flesh, and you must take us for what we are, in our humble way.'

The girls were flushed and embarrassed at greeting me, while he did not make it any the easier for them.

'Ha! ha!' he roared heartily, slapping the table with his open hand till the dishes rang. 'The girls thought yesterday you had come to ask for a piece of bread! Ha! ha! ho! ho! ho!'

And then, while I ate bread and marmalade, proceeded a play at cross purposes, the daughters deeming it an insult to me that I should have been mistaken for a beggar, and the father considering it as the highest compliment to my cleverness to succeed in being so mistaken. All of which I enjoyed, and the bread, the marmalade, and the tea, till the time came for Johnny Upright to find me a lodging, which he did, not half-a-dozen doors away, in his own respectable and opulent street, in a house as like to his own as a pea to its mate.[24]

Sergeant Thicke took Pizer to the police station, where he was searched, but nothing incriminating was found in his possession. Pizer said, 'Thank God . . . I know of no crime, I have been connected with no crime, and my character will bear the strictest investigation, both by my co-religionists, and Gentiles whom I have worked for.'[25] Indeed, it was reported that he was well known to several East End Liberals, and was an active worker on their behalf.

Pizer was able to account for his movements on the murder nights and provided a cast-iron alibi. On the night Nichols was murdered he had stayed at Crossman's lodging house in Holloway Road, commonly known as the 'Round-house', and had eaten his supper there at 11 p.m. He had then gone out for a walk and had seen the reflection of the great docks fire (see Chapter Four). He saw two constables talking with the keeper of Crossman's and asked them where the fire was. They told him and he went to see it. It was then about 1.30 a.m. He had got as far as Highbury railway station when the idea of watching the fire lost its appeal and he turned back, reaching Crossman's at 2.15 a.m. Although Pizer had already paid 4d. for a bed, the lodging house rules were that the money would be forfeited if the bed was not occupied by 11.30 p.m. Pizer had to pay 4d. for another bed, which he did. Before going to bed he had sat on a bench in the kitchen for a time and smoked a clay pipe. He slept through until 11 a.m., when the day attendant woke him and told him to get up as he wanted to make the bed. Pizer dressed and went down into the kitchen, and shortly afterwards saw a placard in the street reporting the murder in Whitechapel. This account of his movements was confirmed by the police.

There is a curious story that also sheds doubt on whether or not John Pizer was wholly innocent of the charges of terrorising and extorting money from the local prostitutes. According to Gabrial Pizer, John Pizer's brother, on Sunday, 2 September 1888, 'Some women had identified him [John Pizer] as "Leather Apron," and pointed him out to a policeman, but the officer had refused to take him in charge and Pizer had been pursued by a howling crowd, which not unsurprisingly frightened him considerably.'[26] John Pizer was probably alluding to this incident when he claimed at the inquest into Annie Chapman's death that he had stayed indoors over the murder weekend because he knew he would be torn apart if he went outside. It may also be the same incident as reported in *The Star*, which said that two unnamed policemen, Constables 43 and 173 of J Division, had arrested Leather Apron during the afternoon of Sunday, 2 September, but had let him go. *The Star* reported that on 5 September these policemen had accompanied Sergeant Patrick Enright in a search of all the places where 'the crazy Jew' was likely to be found.[27] This again was almost certainly the same incident as described by Sergeant Thicke in *The Star* after Pizer had been arrested:

> 'He's been in hiding safe enough, and it's my opinion his friends have been screening him. He has not been in lodging houses; he is too well known there and the people who frequent them would have been ready to lynch him. Why the other day a woman told me plainly that if she saw him she would kill him, and I could do what I liked with her afterwards. No,' keen Johnny Upright continued, ' "Leather Apron" has not been into a lodging-house since the Sunday the woman denounced him in Whitechapel and the police were bamboozled into letting him go.'[28]

Pizer also seems to have given a version of the story. *The Star* reported that Pizer said he had been accosted 'last Sunday week' in Church Street, by two women, one of whom asked him ' " 'Are you the man?' I said, 'God forbid, my good woman.' A stalwart man then came up and said, 'Come in, man, and treat me to half a pint.' I went on." '[29] This seems a pretty meaningless story, which makes any sense only if seen in context with the other snippets.

The only other titbit that might shed a little light on what happened is an odd story told by a woman named Lyons, who said that at 3 p.m. that

Sunday she had met a strange man in Flower and Dean Street who asked her to meet him at 6.30 p.m. for a drink in the Queen's Head. She promised that she would and turned up at the pub on time. The man was there and they began talking. She noticed that he had a large knife in his trouser pocket. The man said, 'You are about the same style of woman as the one that's murdered.' 'What do you know about her?' asked the woman, to which the man replied, 'You are beginning to smell a rat. Foxes hunt geese, but they don't always find them.' He then left, followed by Lyons as far as Spitalfields Church, when he noticed that he was followed and swiftly ran into Church Street. The newspapers, evidently using press agency copy, because their stories matched, reported, 'One noteworthy fact in this story is that the description of the man's appearance is in all material points identical with the published description of the up to the present undiscovered "Leather Apron." '[30] This appears to have been no idle tale, because Mrs Lyons was taken to Commercial Street Police Station to identify a suspect there.[31]

That Pizer had something to hide is further indicated by his behaviour when he returned to Mulberry Street. He'd spent Wednesday night in a common lodging house in Peter Street, Westminster, and had returned to Mulberry Street on Thursday, 6 September, arriving there about 10.45 p.m. 'I knocked at the door. My sister opened it. She was rather surprised to see me, but it is usual at Jewish holiday times to pay visits to friends. My sister's young man was present. I shook hands with him. We had some conversation about work. My sister first went to bed and put the bolt in the latch. Anybody that goes out of the house after the door is latched cannot get in again.'[32] His brother then advised Pizer to remain indoors as he was the object of a false suspicion. Pizer, believing he'd have been torn to pieces if he'd gone out, followed the advice and did not leave the house except to go into the yard – he said he was seen several times going into the yard by a next door neighbour – until arrested.

If John Pizer wasn't suspected of any criminal activity and wasn't known as Leather Apron, why would his brother have warned him to stay indoors rather than advise him to go to the police? Whether or not he was Leather Apron, and there really seems no reason for supposing that he wasn't, Pizer was not Jack the Ripper, although he did face one unusual and sticky moment. A man named Emanuel Delbast Violenia, described as half Spaniard and half Bulgarian, visited the police and claimed that he and his wife and two children had walked from Manchester to London, intending to emigrate from there to

Australia. They had arrived in London and moved into a lodging house in Hanbury Street. He said he had been walking along Hanbury Street early on the morning of the murder and had seen a man and woman quarrelling, and had heard the man threaten to stab the woman to death.

Sergeant Thicke, assisted by Inspector Canaby, placed about a dozen men, mostly Jews, in the yard of the Leman Street Police Station, among them Pizer. Violenia was then brought out and at once unhesitatingly pointed out Pizer as the man he had seen. Violenia was then taken to the Whitechapel mortuary to view the body of Chapman, and, while the result was not announced to the press, it was believed that he was unable to identify her. Subsequently, the police discredited Violenia's testimony.[33] It's quite likely that Violenia, who was described as 'a stout, stalwart man, of negro caste', knew Pizer, who told *The Star* that he knew him to be a boot finisher.[34] As far as one can make out, Violenia concocted his story simply so that he could get to see Chapman's dead body. John Pizer was released from custody and returned to Mulberry Street, where he was enthusiastically welcomed by his family and friends. *The Star* said that among those who welcomed him and offered their sympathies for the ordeal he had been through were some East End Liberals for whom he had been an active worker and to whom he was well known.

His arrest was treated as a police blunder, and a book published the following year co-authored by a noted journalist of the day named J Hall Richardson held the Pizer fiasco responsible for the subsequent reticence of the police to disclose details of the crimes:

> The man was detained for inquiries for two days, the police making no charge. 'Leather Apron' was perfectly innocent, but the police by their reticence were really responsible for the deductions that were drawn from their conduct. Henceforward, under pain of dismissal, the detectives refused information even to the accredited representatives of London papers.[35]

What appeared not to be cleared up was whether or not John Pizer was indeed 'the terror of Whitechapel unfortunates', and *The Star* drew attention to this, pointing out that the failure of the police to confront him with any of the women who claimed to know Leather Apron and who could identify him had left Pizer unfairly tainted.[36] Pizer told *The Star*, 'I shall see if I cannot legally proceed against those who have made statements about me. The charges made against me have quite broken my spirits, and I am afraid I shall have to place myself under medical treatment for some time.'[37]

Apparently, John Pizer did take legal action against the press and stories circulated about the large sums of money he obtained from various newspapers.[38] These stories were denied:

> The story that 'Leather Apron,' *alias* Mr. Piser, is getting large sums from his libel actions is untrue. More than one of them has been compromised, and for moderate amounts. Two or three of them, however, are still outstanding. The report that he has already received £5,000 is preposterously wide of the mark. £500 would, I should say, be a serious exaggeration.[39]

However, we do know that Pizer received money from *The Star*. In a book of reminiscences published in 1924 a famous journalist of the time named Lincoln Springfield explained the background to the whole story. An American journalist named Harry Dam worked with him on *The Star* covering the Whitechapel murders. Dam created a sensation by developing a theory of the authorship of these grisly crimes:

> They were, he proceeded to demonstrate, the work of a miscreant known as 'Leather Apron', and so known in consequence of the attire he wore at his everyday trade of tanning, or slipper making, or whatever it was. Day after day Dam gave the public all the thrills it wanted along these lines. But unfortunately there actually was in existence a man known to the nobility and gentry of the Mile End Road as 'Leather Apron', and he was an honest, hard-working fellow, as innocent of the series of Whitechapel murders, or any one of them, as you or I.[40]

Faced with the prospect of a major libel action, the editor, Ernest Parke,[41] sent 'minions' to Whitechapel:

> 'Leather Apron' was secured, he was brought to Stonecutter Street, and he was reasoned with sweetly, before he could get the opportunity of consulting a lawyer, or, shall I say before a lawyer could get the chance of indicating to him what wealth beyond the dreams of avarice might be his by the simple process of issuing a writ for libel. And while 'Leather

Apron' was thus cozened, a small pile of golden sovereigns was arrayed within his vision, and jingled within his hearing; with the result that he took away with him £10 in gold, and left behind him, in consideration thereof, a stamped receipt for the amount in full settlement of any claims he might have against the paper in respect of the deplorable theory of the ingenious but misguided Harry Dam. *The Star* has, since those days, had to pay various sums to aggrieved litigants for undeserved notoriety thrust upon them, and in some cases the damages have been unfairly awarded against the paper: but in averaging their libel liabilities, the directors of the paper must always have looked back with satisfaction to a transaction in which they unjustly accused a blameless citizen of seven or eight bloody murders, and got out of the mess for £10, being little more than a pound a murder.

The reputation attached to Pizer lingered. In October a woman accosted him in the street, called him 'Old Leather Apron', insulted him in other ways, and struck him three times in the face. He made a formal complaint at the Thames Police Court before Mr Lushington and was told he could issue a summons against the woman.[42]

John Pizer was innocent of the Whitechapel murders and Lincoln Springfield acknowledged that this was the case, but he did not deny that Pizer was known as Leather Apron, and the official files state very clearly that police enquiries had revealed that numerous prostitutes were afraid of a man called Leather Apron and that John Pizer became suspected because he 'has been in the habit of ill-using prostitutes in various parts of the Metropolis for some time past'. We know, too, that John Pizer had been identified as Leather Apron by 'some women' and been 'pursued by a howling crowd' – and that this happened *before* the newspapers broke the Leather Apron story. There seems little reason to doubt that John Pizer was Leather Apron and that he did terrorise the local prostitutes. What was unfortunate for him was that *The Star* – and, if Lincoln Springfield is believed, the flowery pen of Harry Dam – threw suspicion on him as being the Whitechapel murderer. (For more about Harry Dam and his supposed authorship of the 'Dear Boss' letter, see Chapter Twelve.)

CHAPTER EIGHT

Suspects

There isn't much to talk about –
We live in dullish times;
The only things the newsboys shout
Are these Whitechapel crimes.

George R Sims[1]

As the investigation into the death of Annie Chapman slowly shifted into gear, the new head of the CID, Robert Anderson, slipped away for a month's rest in Switzerland. Commentators then and particularly since have been critical of Anderson for being absent at such a crucial time, but Anderson had a throat infection and the necessary break was recommended by his doctor. Furthermore, the timing wasn't Anderson's choice, but was that of Sir Charles Warren, who was himself on holiday and had written to Anderson on 28 August[2] from the arrondissement of Lannion on the Côtes-du-Nord (today renamed the Côtes-d'Armor) in northwest France, saying that he expected to return to London about 7 September and, alluding to Bloody Sunday of the previous year, said he expected trouble with the unemployed during the winter and indicated that he wanted Anderson securely in office by October. In other words, Anderson was told to take a month's break in September, and nobody can have known as Anderson set off on that Saturday morning that the Whitechapel murders would assume the magnitude they did.

Holidays were having effects in other ways, too. Inspector Reid was on holiday and Chief Inspector West, who was acting superintendent and temporarily in charge of H Division, reported to Scotland Yard,

Every possible enquiry is being made with a view to tracing the murderer, but up to the present without success. Local Inspector Reid

101

being on his annual leave, the enquiries have been entrusted to
Inspector Chandler and Police Sergeants Thicke and Leach CI Dept.
I would respectfully suggest that Inspector Abberline, Central, who is
well-acquainted with H Division, be deputed to take up this enquiry
as I believe he is already engaged in the case of the Buck's Row murder
which would appear to have been committed by the same person as the
one in Hanbury Street.'[3]

Inspector Frederick George Abberline was directed to take charge of
the Chapman murder inquiry on 8 September 1888. He was a very distinguished policeman whose career embraced the Fenian bombing scares, the
Jack the Ripper investigation and the Cleveland Street scandal of 1889, a
case requiring a tactful investigation because it involved a male brothel used
by many distinguished young men. In recent years he has become even
better known, being portrayed in movies by Michael Caine and Johnny
Depp, albeit that the former portrayed him as a drunk and the latter, losing
touch with historical reality altogether, as a drug-addicted psychic.[4] Both
actors also portrayed him as something of a Cockney, but Abberline had
been born in Blandford, Dorset, and had worked as a clocksmith before
joining the Metropolitan Police in 1863. His rise through the ranks was
steady. Promoted to sergeant in 1865, by 1873 he had distinguished himself
sufficiently to be promoted to inspector. He was transferred to H Division,
Whitechapel, where he would remain for the next fourteen years, being
promoted to local inspector – head of H Division – in 1878. In 1887 he was
finally transferred to Scotland Yard and in 1888 was promoted to inspector,
first-class. Abberline would be promoted to chief inspector in 1890 and
retire in 1892 to become a private investigator, eventually becoming the
European representative of Allan Pinkerton's famous detective agency,
during which time he served three seasons policing the gaming rooms at
Monte Carlo. He finally gave up police work altogether and retired to
Bournemouth, settling in 1911 at Holdenhurst Road. Sir Melville Macnaghten
remembered Abberline at this time, recalling that he 'knew the East End of
London as few men have since known it. He is still hale and hearty and as
successful in his gardening operations in Bournemouth as he was in turning
the crooks out of the rooms at Monte Carlo when he was given a free hand
by the authorities in Monaco some sixteen years ago.'[5] Abberline died in
Bournemouth in 1929. A plaque was erected by Bournemouth Council on
his house in 2000, perhaps making him the only policeman to have been so

honoured. Abberline remains something of a mystery, however, and we don't even have a photograph of him. A collection of his press cuttings discovered a few years ago are annotated by a few personal observations, including a comment that a drawing of the dynamitards[6] Burton and Cunningham in *The Penny Pictorial*[7] was 'a very good likeness'. On the same page there was a drawing of Abberline and, if that of the dynamitards is a good likeness, it is probably fair to infer that it was a good likeness of Abberline too.

Years later Abberline would recall the hunt for the Ripper:

My interest in the Ripper cases was especially deep. I had for fourteen years previously been an inspector of police in Whitechapel, but when the murders began I was at the Central Office at Scotland Yard. On the application of Superintendent Arnold I went back to the East End just before Annie Chapman was found mutilated, and as chief of the detective corps I gave myself up to the study of the cases. Many a time, even after we had carried our inquiries as far as we could – and we made out no fewer than 1,600 sets of papers respecting our investigations – instead of going home when I was off duty, I used to patrol the district until four or five o'clock in the morning, and, while keeping my eyes wide open for clues of any kind, have many and many a time given those wretched, homeless women, who were Jack the Ripper's special prey, fourpence or sixpence for a shelter to get them away from the streets and out of harm's way.[8]

It is said that Inspector Abberline came to believe that Jack the Ripper was a man named Severin Klosowski, otherwise known as George Chapman, who had qualified as a surgeon in Poland and come to England in June 1887 and between 1895 and 1901 poisoned three successive wives. He was arrested for the murders in January 1903 by Detective Inspector George Godley (1858–1941), who as a detective sergeant in 1888 had served in Whitechapel on the Ripper investigation and whose knowledge of the crimes, reported *The Police Review* on his retirement, 'is perhaps as complete as that of any officer concerned'. In 1930 in the introduction to his *Trial of George Chapman* in the Notable British Trials series, H L Adam, who in the acknowledgements had credited Godley's assistance, wrote that 'when Godley arrested Chapman Abberline said to his conferrer "You've got Jack-the-Ripper at last." ' Adam also reported that 'Abberline closely questioned the Polish woman Lucy Baderski [Klosowski's first wife], about Chapman's nightly habits at the time of the murders. She said he was often out until three or four o'clock in the morning, but she could throw little light on the absences.'

While it is difficult to doubt that Godley told Adam something along the lines that Adam reported, we know that Adam's story isn't true. Abberline did not say, 'You've got Jack-the-Ripper at last' after Godley arrested Chapman because in March 1903 Abberline told a journalist for the *Pall Mall Gazette*, 'I have been so struck with the remarkable coincidences in the two series of murders that I have not been able to think of anything else for several days past – not, in fact, since the Attorney-General made his opening statement at the recent trial, and traced the antecedents of Chapman before he came to this country in 1888.' In other words, Abberline's suspicions about Klosowski were aroused by the opening statements made by the attorney-general, Sir Edward Carson, on the first day of the trial, Monday, 16 March 1903, and he accordingly could not have said two months earlier anything to Godley of the kind Adam alleges. Furthermore, Abberline had retired in 1892 and would have had no right to question Lucy Baderski about anything, but that point is irrelevant because there is no evidence that Klosowski knew Baderski before December 1888, therefore there would have been no point in questioning her about his movements during the murder year.

Abberline's theory caused a brief tussle between the *Pall Mall Gazette* and G R Sims in *The Referee*. The *Gazette* printed Abberline's 'theory' and Sims rejected it, pointing out that the Ripper was a madman who butchered his victims, while Klosowski was a poisoner, not a butcher, and sensibly asked, 'How could a man in the mental condition of "Jack" have suddenly settled down into a cool, calculating poisoner?'

The *Pall Mall* returned to Abberline who countered,

As to the question of the dissimilarity of character in the crimes which one hears so much about . . . I cannot see why one man should not have done both, provided he had the professional knowledge, and this is admitted in Chapman's case. A man who could watch his wives being slowly tortured to death by poison, as he did, was capable of anything . . .

George Sims replied that 'it is an absolute absurdity to argue that a cool, calculating poisoner like Klosowski could have lived with half a dozen women and put them quietly out of the way by a slow and calculated process after being in 1888 a man so maniacal in his homicidal fury that he committed the foul and fiendish horror of Miller's-court. A furious madman does not suddenly become a slow poisoner."[9]

And so we know that Abberline was persuaded by similarities between Klosowski and Jack the Ripper, but we do not know how seriously he held that belief or for how long, and on the face of it George R Sims's objection to the whole idea seems sensible and fair.[10] But all this was in the future and the police in September 1888 were doing all they could to find some sort of clue to work with. According to a police report they searched the rooms and questioned the residents of 29 Hanbury Street and their neighbours, enquired at all the common lodging houses about any bloodstained or otherwise suspicious-looking individuals, made enquiries among pawnbrokers and jewellers in search of Chapman's missing rings, investigated all people who behaved suspiciously in the street or were the subject of letters received from members of the public and made enquiries at the local pubs and among the prostitutes. The report concluded,

Up to the present the combined result of those enquiries did not supply the police with the slightest clue to the murderer. The only indication of the direction to find the murderer lay in the evidence of Dr. Phillips, which was in substance that the individual possessed some skill and anatomical knowledge, and that the instrument with which the injuries were inflicted was probably a small amputating knife, or a well ground butchers knife, narrow and thin, sharp with a blade from six to eight inches long.

Perhaps the most interesting item in the report is, 'Enquiries were also made to trace three insane students who had attended London Hospital. Result two traced, one gone abroad.'[11]

There are other documents in the files relating to these medical students. A memorandum in the Home Office files dated 25 October 1888 concerning a letter received from Sir Charles Warren contains notes and queries from a variety of people, including one to Charles Murdoch[12] from someone who initialled himself WTB:

Please see Mr Wortley's[13] pencil memo on Sir C. Warren's letter. Shall the police be asked at the same time for reports as to what has become

the 3rd insane medical student from the London Hosp.? About whom
under the name of Dr.   there is a good deal of gossip in circulation.

Frustratingly the name after 'Dr.' isn't given.

A draft copy of a letter dated 29 October 1888 to Warren refers to the
same question:

> Another question has arisen on the report forwarded by the Commis-
> sioner. Reference is made to three insane medical students, and it is
> stated two have been traced and that one has gone abroad. Mr
> Matthews would be glad to be informed of the date when the third
> student went abroad and whether any further inquiry has been made
> about him.

A reply to this query, a letter dated 1 November 1888 from Inspector
Abberline to Sir Charles Warren, is in the Scotland Yard files:

> With regard to the latter portion of your letter I have to state that
> searching enquiries were made by an officer in Aberdeen Place, St
> John's Wood, the last known address of the insane medical student
> named 'John Sanders', but the only information that could be
> obtained was that a lady named Sanders did reside with her son at
> number 20, but left that address to go abroad about two years ago.

What is particularly interesting and instructive about this exchange of
memoranda and letters is that they refer to three suspects about whom we
know absolutely nothing. There are no papers in the files indicating how the
police found out about these men, why they found out about them, why they
were suspected, or how seriously they were suspected. We would know
absolutely nothing about them were it not for what amounts to a few passing
remarks among Home Office mandarins leading to a question that was asked
of the police. And yet we are told that there was 'a good deal of gossip in
circulation' about one of the medical students. Not a tittle of that gossip has
reached us and the salutary lesson is that one should be wary of basing
conclusions on what is or is not in the files, or, indeed, may have leaked to the
press. Over the years case papers have been lost, destroyed, stolen, and 'gone
missing', and even documents known to have been in the files twenty or so
years ago have now disappeared. The files tell us very little indeed and, if our

ignorance about the three suspected medical students is anything to go by, they almost certainly contained information that we don't even suspect.

We know nothing of the two insane medical students who were traced, although one of them may have been a medical student at the London Hospital who appeared in court in April charged with attempting to rape a religious girl named Emily Bean.[14] The student who couldn't be traced was John William Smith Sanders. Born in Milton, Kent, in 1862, the son of Henry Shearly Sanders, a surgeon in the 49th Regiment of Foot,[15] and his wife, Laura Tucker Sanders,[16] he had lived with his mother at 20 Abercorn Place, Maida Vale,[17] not 20 Aberdeen Place, St John's Wood, as stated in Abberline's report, and was one of six children, four girls and two boys. He entered London Hospital as a student on 22 April 1879, but soon afterwards developed mental problems and a note in the records reads, 'Became ill and was placed in an Asylum'. A barely legible pencil entry seems to read, 'Away with Dr Swete for several months in 1882'. The only Dr Swete in the medical directories of the period is Dr Horatio Walter Swete of Baskerville House, Worcester.[18]

Medical certificates show that Sanders's condition deteriorated and by February 1887 had worsened to the point that he was violent, attacked friends without provocation and tyrannised his household. He was placed in Holloway Asylum, Virginia Water,[19] probably in 1887, transferred to West Malling[20] in 1896, and Heavitree Asylum, Exeter, on 30 May 1899, aged 37, and died there on 31 March 1901.

What there was about this young man that could have warranted 'a good deal of gossip' at a fairly high level of the Home Office is not known.

At 7 a.m. on 7 September, a man went into the Prince Albert, better known as the 'Clean House', at the corner of 21 Brushfield Street, on the corner of Brushfield and Stewart Street, and alarmed the landlady, Mrs Fiddymont.[21] She was talking to a friend named Mrs Mary Chappell,[22] who lived at 28 Stewart Street, in the first compartment of the bar when a man came into the middle compartment and asked for half a pint of four ale.[23] He was wearing a brown stiff hat pulled down over his eyes, a dark coat and no waistcoat. She also noticed that his light-blue check shirt was torn (rags in fact, on the right shoulder), there was a narrow streak of blood under his right ear, blood spots on the back of his right hand and dried blood between the fingers. She drew the ale, looking at him through the mirror at the back of the bar, and she noticed that he turned his back as soon as he realised he was being watched. He swallowed his ale at a gulp and went out. Mrs

Chappell went outside and saw the man head towards Bishopsgate Street. She drew the attention of a man named Joseph Taylor to him and Taylor followed him, actually managing to come alongside him. The man glanced at him, and Taylor later told a journalist, 'His eyes were as wild as a hawk's.' The man was rather thin and about five foot eight with a ginger-coloured moustache and short sandy hair. He was aged between forty and fifty. He had a shabby genteel look, pepper-and-salt trousers, which fitted badly, and dark coat, which as he walked he held together at the top. The man crossed Brushfield Street three times between leaving the Prince Albert and reaching Bishopsgate, where he stood at the corner and looked up and down the street undecided, then turned left. Taylor stopped following the man, but watched him walk as far as Dirty Dick's in Halfmoon Street. The man, said Taylor, clearly did not know where he was going and looked bewildered. On the other hand, we could observe that being in a strange neighbourhood and scrutinised and followed by the locals would have bewildered anyone. The police, perhaps for want of any other clues, took the story seriously and for some time Mrs Fiddymont's stranger seems to have dominated the investigations.

All sorts of stories would circulate about odd happenings that Saturday morning. A man was said to have changed his clothes in a lavatory of the City News Rooms in Ludgate Circus, departing hurriedly and leaving a shirt, a pair of trousers and socks. The lavatory attendant apparently deposited the discarded clothes in a bin and they were taken away on the following Monday. The matter didn't receive widespread publicity, and didn't even get the little it did get until the middle of the month, and as *The Times* commented, 'It is obviously difficult to conceive why the murderer, having possessed himself of a change of clothes, should pass from Whitechapel to Ludgate-circus and change his dress in a quasi-public place such as the City News Rooms.'[24]

Much later in September a reporter for the Press Association called on the proprietor of the newsrooms, a Mr Walker, who said that he hadn't attached any importance to the matter at the time and had no reason to do so since. Nevertheless, the police apparently visited the News Rooms three times. They were trying to find the man's clothes, and the man himself, who was described as being of respectable appearance, aged about thirty, with a dark moustache. And as one newspaper remarked, '. . . the police are very reticent about the matter, and decline to give any information on the subject. They evidently attach some importance to the affair . . .'[25]

At 10 a.m., Amelia Farmer, Chapman's friend, having read a description of the murdered woman in a newspaper, went to the police station and said that she thought she knew her. At 11.30 a.m. she was taken to the mortuary and made a positive identification. At about the same time as she gazed down at the mortal remains of her friend, the teams for a cricket match turned out on the Rectory Field, Blackheath. It was the seventh annual match in which Blackheath Cricket Club pitted their skills against the Brothers Christopherson, and among those playing for Blackheath was a young barrister/teacher named Montague John Druitt, whose short life had merely a few months to run and who would in the years to come assume prime importance as a leading contender for the mantle of Jack the Ripper.

During the afternoon of that first Saturday thousands of people gathered outside the police stations in Leman Street, Commercial Street and Bethnal Green, and 'shouted and hooted for the murderer of Annie Chapman'. The mood was ugly, the cries for vengeance were not idle threats[26] and as the afternoon wore on the crowds who had assembled in the streets began to assume a very threatening attitude towards the Jewish population. It was repeatedly asserted that no Englishman could have perpetrated such horrible crimes and that they must have been committed by a Jew. According to the *East London Observer* it was only the presence of the large number of police in the streets that prevented a riot.[27]

Newspapers sold like hot cakes. The *East London Observer* reported,

Every newsagent within two miles of the scene of the tragedy concurs in saying that never, in the whole of his experience, has there been such a run on the evening papers. Crowds waited outside the shops until fresh supplies had been brought in, while around those who were successful in obtaining copies gathered yet other crowds, who read with many a muttered exclamation of indignation, the revolting details of the murder. And as the evening wore on, and others who had just closed work were made acquainted with the news, the excitement increased apace. Rumours of other murders were set afloat, and gained no small amount of credence, until East London became panic-stricken – for there is no other term to describe the aimless, frightened way in which people paraded the crowded thoroughfares.[28]

For Mrs Mary Burridge the newspaper reports were too much. A dealer in floorcloths, she was standing at the door of her home at 132 Blackfriars

Road reading *The Star*'s account of the Whitechapel murder, when she was
taken unwell. She went indoors and collapsed in her kitchen with a fit, from
which she died the following Tuesday.[29]

Already penny dreadfuls describing the murders were being hawked on
the streets, accounts of the murder of Nichols quickly and cleverly amended
to include Annie Chapman, and the proprietor of a small waxworks in
Whitechapel Road daubed some old, much-used waxwork dummies with
streaks of red paint and was luridly advertising them in the window of his
premises as models of the Whitechapel victims. Several hundred people
surrendered a penny to view inside until a police inspector closed him down.
The proprietor apparently then luridly described the parentage of the police
in general and the inspector in particular. And as people today blame the
movies and television for violence, the *Eastern Argus* suggested that the
blame for the crimes rested with

> the picture of murders and assassinations with which the walls of the
> parish have been covered of late . . . inflaming the minds of the weak
> and passionate men . . . Not long ago there were pictures of a woman
> jumping into water to drown herself, and their appearance was
> followed by almost a score of suicides and attempted suicides.[30]

Others firmly laid the blame on serials in cheap magazines:

> It is only those whose duties cause them to be mixed up with the lower
> and criminal classes who can really appreciate how great is the evil
> influence of this pernicious literature . . . It is, to my mind, quite
> possible that the Whitechapel murders may be the fruit of such
> pernicious seed falling upon a morbid and deranged mind.[31]

As night closed in and the shops shut, people reportedly stampeded to
the well-lit main roads or sought the protection of their homes. By
12.30 a.m. few people were on the streets. One man who *was* on the street
was found in Buck's Row, where Nichols had been murdered. Shortly after
1 a.m. he was found, apparently in hiding, by a constable, and ran off at top
speed. After a hard-fought race, during which time the constable raised the
alarm, the man was caught, but put up stiff resistance until more policemen
arrived and subdued him. Described as 'a villainous-looking fellow, with
long hair and shaggy beard, dressed only in a pair of ragged blue serge

trousers, and an old dirty shirt', he was taken to Bethnal Green Police Station. Apparently there were hopes that he was the man seen by Mrs Fiddymont – one of many – but he gave an account of himself that proved to be true and he was released.[32]

Another man was arrested in Gloucester Street. He was aged about forty and had the look of a seafarer, but again was able to give a satisfactory account of himself and after a few hours of kicking his heels in the Commercial Street Police Station he was released.[33]

Across the Atlantic the *New York Times* briefly but luridly recounted the new sensation, in the process calling the London police and detective force 'probably the stupidest in the world':

London, Sept. 8. – Not even during the riots and fog of February 1886, have I seen London so thoroughly excited as it is tonight. The White-chapel fiend murdered his fourth victim this morning and still continues undetected, unseen, unknown. There is a panic in Whitechapel.

The murder in all its details was inhuman to the last degree, and, like the others, could have been the work only of a bloodthirsty beast in human shape.

All day long Whitechapel has been wild with excitement . . . The London police and detective force is probably the stupidest in the world.

Such a series of murders has not been known in London for a hundred years . . . The murders are certainly the most ghastly and mysterious known to English police history. What adds to the weird effect they exert on the London mind is the fact that they occur while everybody is talking about Mansfield's 'Jekyll and Hyde' at the Lyceum.

Aside from this local sensation Europe's little budget of trivial happenings seems hardly worth relating this week to a people who have such a genuine topic of interest as a Presidential campaign of their own.[34]

In London, newspaper readers opened their *Referee* that Sunday morning to find the columnist 'Dagonet', G R Sims, observe, not without truth, that the Whitechapel murders had 'come to the relief of newspaper editors in search of a sensation',[35] but in fairness the sensation was not the creation of the newspaper editors. The sensation on the streets was real enough. The greatest excitement, we are told, prevailed in Whitechapel, and crowds thronged Hanbury Street and the adjoining thoroughfares.[36] No lesser personage than Chief Constable Colonel Bolton Monsell[37] visited Hanbury Street in the early morning and afterwards viewed Chapman's body in the mortuary.[38] Another newspaper reported that two prominent peers (whom it didn't name) also visited the scene of the murders.[39]

The police were not forthcoming with information and several newspapers remarked on this. The *Yorkshire Post* reported,

> The police, who give information very unwillingly, and who do not accept the theory that the crime has been committed by the man designated 'Leather Apron', are indisposed to believe that the person seen by Mrs Fiddymont had any connection with the crime. They are unwilling, indeed, to accept any assistance or suggestion from any private source and work upon a plan of their own, which consists of frequent visits to common lodging-houses of the neighbourhood and a strict watch at night in all the streets in the vicinity.[40]

Contrary to this newspaper report, the official records suggest that the police were actually very interested in and seem to have seriously suspected the man who entered Mrs Fiddymont's pub. However, the unwillingness of the police to give information to the press was a common and frequent complaint, recalled the following year by the authors of *Police!*, who, as we have seen, remarked that the coroner and the police

> distrusted the newspapers. The police had especial reason to resent the publicity given by the press, which unhesitatingly exposed their shortcomings, whilst at the same time they hampered the detectives . . . under pain of dismissal, the detectives refused information even to the accredited representatives of London papers. But there was a suspicion that there was favouritism exercised.

Meanwhile, throughout that Sunday, large numbers of well-dressed people – newspapers spoke of thousands – turned up in Hanbury Street and costermongers had set up stands and were enjoying a brisk trade selling fruit and refreshments. Sometimes the road became so crowded that the police had to charge at the spectators. Throughout Saturday and Sunday the people living either side of No. 29 did business by making a small charge to view the yard where the murder had taken place or simply to view the crowds. People also visited the house in Dorset Street where Chapman had lodged. But as darkness fell the streets emptied, one newspaper noting that 'the streets again wore an unusually and unnaturally deserted aspect' and adding with considerable melodrama, 'Truly, it was a reign of terror unprecedented in the history of East London.'[41]

At 4 p.m. in Gravesend a man named William Henry Pigott approached four young men and asked them where he could get a drink of water. They told him, but instead of following their instructions he jumped on a tramcar. At this time he was carrying a black bag. He was next seen by a Mrs Beitchteller, who kept a fish shop. He did not now have the black bag, but instead carried a paper parcel which he left at the shop and which was later recovered by Sergeant Berry of the local police, who found it contained two shirts, both marked with blood. Pigott told Mrs Beitchteller that he was going across the water to Tilbury, but instead he went to the Pope's Head tavern. Here his conversation, which apparently concerned his great hatred of women, attracted attention. He was reported to the police and a PC Vollensworth was sent to investigate. He found Pigott in a dazed state, unable to give a satisfactory account of himself, and having a wounded hand, which he refused to explain. Pigott was duly arrested.

At the police station Pigott made a rambling statement to the effect that on Friday night he had wandered the streets of the East End and at 4 a.m. on Saturday, while walking down Brick Lane, he had seen a woman fall in a fit. While trying to pick her up he had been bitten on the hand by the woman and, angered by the pain, he had struck her. He had then seen two policemen approaching and had run off.

The divisional surgeon, Dr Whitcombe, was summoned and he examined the two shirts, which had now been recovered from the fish shop. He pronounced that these were stained with blood and gave it as his opinion that blood had recently been wiped from Pigott's shoes.

Inspector Abberline was summoned to Gravesend on Monday morning and returned to London with Pigott. A large crowd had gathered at Gravesend Railway Station to see Abberline and his prisoner depart, but since news of the arrest had not reached London their arrival at London Bridge passed almost unnoticed and they had a relatively quiet journey by four-wheeled cab to Commercial Street Police Station, where they arrived at 12.48 p.m.

At 2.30 p.m. Pigott was one of seventeen men placed in an identity parade before Mrs Fiddymont and other witnesses, who unanimously declared that Pigott was not the man they had seen. The police nevertheless decided to

detain him and after a couple of hours his behaviour became so strange that
Dr Phillips was summoned. He reported that Pigott's behaviour was not
inconsistent with the onset of homicidal mania. Pigott was removed to the
workhouse lunatic yard preparatory to being committed to an asylum.

Pigott was described as 52 years old, the son of a man who some years
earlier had held a position with the Royal Liver Society. He had earlier been
a publican, having paid some £8,000 for a pub in Hoxton. His movements
at the time of the murders were eventually accounted for, but his ultimate
fate is not recorded. Pigott is a fairly typical example of the kind of person
wandering around the streets at that time.

That night the police issued a curious description of a man seen to enter
the passage of 29 Hanbury Street with a prostitute. Unfortunately, no
reference to this man is made in the surviving files and the press reported
the circular differently. The *Daily Telegraph* reported,

Commercial-street, 8.20 p.m.
   Description of a man wanted, who entered the passage of a house at
which the murder was committed with a prostitute at 2 a.m., the 8th –
Age 37; height, 5ft. 7in.; rather dark, beard and moustache; dress,
short dark jacket, dark vest and trousers, black scarf, and black felt hat;
spoke with a foreign accent.'[42]

The Times' report is slightly different:

Description of a man who entered a passage of the house at which
the murder was committed of a prostitute at 2 a.m. on the 8th. – Age
37; height, 5ft. 7in.; rather dark beard and moustache. Dress–shirt,
dark vest and trousers, black scarf, and black felt hat. Spoke with a
foreign accent.[43]

The Star was rather more specific and used quotation marks to indicate
what the police circular said:

At eight o'clock last night the Scotland-yard authorities circulated a
description of a man who, they say, 'entered the passage of the house,
29, Hanbury-street, at which the murder was committed with a
prostitute, at two a.m., the 8th.' They give his age as 37, height 5ft.
7in., and add that he is rather dark, had a beard and moustache; was

dressed in a short dark jacket, dark vest and trousers, black scarf and black felt hat; and spoke with a foreign accent.[44]

The principal difference is that the *Daily Telegraph* and *The Star* say the man entered the passage *with* a prostitute at 2 a.m., whereas *The Times*, which was frequently in error, does not associate the man with either the time or a prostitute, but merely that he was seen to enter the passage.[45] That the man *was* seen to enter the passage *with* a woman is made clear by *The Star* of 12 September, in what is a very tantalising report:

The Exchange Telegraph Company learns that the police have full knowledge of the whereabouts of the man whose description has been circulated as that of the alleged Whitechapel murderer, and his identity is spoken to by several witnesses. Although not actually under arrest he is carefully watched, and his arrest is said to be only a question of time. The belief is steadily gaining ground that the man who was seen in a passage with a woman who is supposed to have been Mary Ann Nicholls on the morning of 8 Aug., and who spoke with a foreign accent, is the murderer of both Mary Ann Nicholls and Annie Chapman; and in the event of his arrest strong *prima facie* evidence will be forthcoming to connect him with the crimes. The police have keenly followed up the clue which was given them about this man.[46]

As with the medical students, we have no idea who this man was and whatever clue the police possessed it presumably fizzled out.

Sir Charles Warren returned to London on Monday, 10 September, to find that a degree of calm had descended after the intense excitement of the weekend. The 'Red Terror' as one newspaper dubbed the murderer,[47] had not struck again and people were actively seeking some evidence that would restore their confidence in the authorities. A large crowd had gathered in Hanbury Street at an early hour, along with a smaller crowd at the mortuary in Montague Street. Nobody seemed to know for certain when the inquest would begin, so the streets outside the Working Lads' Institute were relatively peaceful until some policemen and a few pressmen arrived there shortly after 9 a.m., apparently interfering with the work of a few charwomen who were sweeping out the hall. By 9.30 a.m. the jurymen arrived in twos and threes and took their seats at the back of the hall, and were soon followed by various witnesses, who a reporter noted were 'clean and as neatly dressed as their positions in life and means enabled them'.

News of these arrivals brought crowds of people to the Institute and policemen on duty could be continually heard shouting, 'Move on, please.' Mr Banks, the coroner's officer, arrived, followed by George Collier, the deputy coroner, and then Wynne Baxter. Baxter dealt with the preliminaries in a quick and businesslike fashion, had the jurymen[48] seated in the right-hand corner of the room, and the police officials – Detective Inspectors Abberline, Helson and Chandler and Detective Sergeants Thicke and Leach – were present on the other side facing them. The coroner and his deputy then accompanied the jurymen to view the body of Chapman, which the press reported was lying in the shell (makeshift coffin) that Nichols had occupied. On the return journey they were followed by a large crowd, which had to be dispersed by the police. Later in the day Wynne Baxter displayed irritation and annoyance when the police failed to produce a plan of the locality to assist him.[49]

On the streets numerous stories began to circulate and it became increasingly dangerous for anyone who even remotely resembled published descriptions of men such as the one seen by Mrs Fiddymont. Such men were 'unmercifully chased and hounded through the streets until they sought the protection of the police, or satisfied the crowds of their innocence,' reported the *East London Observer*.[50]

Meanwhile, other people penned letters to the press offering assorted suggestions for catching the murderer. It was suggested that bloodhounds be used.[51] Another suggestion was that the pupils of the murdered woman's eyes should be photographed, it being believed that the retina retained an image of the last thing seen in life.[52] 'I would suggest that the police should at once find out the whereabouts of all cases of "homicidal mania" which may have been discharged as "cured" from metropolitan asylums during the last two years,' wrote someone who signed himself 'A Country Doctor'.[53] The police appear to have taken this course of action and Commissioner Sir Charles Warren wrote to Evelyn Ruggles Brise at the Home Office that they were looking for a man called Puckridge, who 'was released from an asylum on 4 August. He was educated as a Surgeon – has threatened to rip people up with a long knife. He is being looked for but cannot be found as yet.'[54] This man was Oswald Puckridge and it isn't known whether the police ever found and questioned him.[55]

The *Lancet* was less than sure that the murderer was a lunatic and cautioned, 'It is most unusual for a lunatic to plan any complicated crime of this kind. Neither, as a rule, does a lunatic take precautions to escape from the consequences of his act; which data are most conspicuous in these now two celebrated cases.' A correspondent, Henry Sutherland MD, agreed, writing that it was 'most emphatically' his opinion 'that these murders were committed by some person or persons who were perfectly sane'. His opinion seems based in the main on the belief that an insane murderer would have attempted suicide after the crime, and he said that, since there had been no suicides in Whitechapel lately, the murderer was sane.[56]

While some newspapers found it impossible to comprehend motiveless murder and thought the crimes 'so distinctly outside the ordinary range of human experience that it has created a kind of stupor . . . unique in the annals of crime',[57] other writers described motiveless killings, and someone calling him- or herself 'S' volunteered information about the concept (often thought to be modern) of lust murderers or joy killers, recording that seven years earlier in the area of Bochum in Westphalia a man apparently lassoed women and killed them. The police, he said, had arrested a gypsy, who was in due course found guilty and beheaded, only for the crimes to recommence a few days later. The papers, he said, had described the crimes with 'the expressive term of lustmord (pleasure murder)'.[58]

The most famous contributor of letters to the press asserting that the Ripper was a lunatic was the formidably well qualified Lyttleton Stewart Forbes Winslow (1844–1913 – 'Forbes' was an addition of later life, it having been his father's forename), a noted and distinguished medical man with considerable experience of the insane. He claimed to have spoken with the police at Scotland Yard on the matter, and expressed publicly the opinion that all the murders had been committed by the same person, a lunatic ('not of the class of which "Leather Apron" belongs, but is of the upper class of society'[59]) recently discharged or escaped from an asylum. This early notion that the murderer was a toff, which in time would be the instantly recognisable iconic image of the top-hatted and caped figure we know today, was echoed elsewhere. *The Times* expressed utter astonishment at how the murderer could have escaped Hanbury Street 'reeking with blood . . . in almost broad daylight along streets comparatively well frequented' and reported that many people had concluded that the murderer was not a resident of the common lodging houses but 'a man lodging in a comparatively decent house in the district, to which he would be able to retire quickly, and in which, once it was reached, he would be able at his leisure to remove from his person all traces of his hideous crime'. The paper urged the police not to confine their attentions to the poor and penniless. Having thus attributed the crimes to someone who did not frequent the lodging houses, *The Times* went on to contradict itself, saying that it was not uncommon for men to request accommodation at a common lodging house as early (or late) as 3 a.m. and to be admitted along dark stairways into poorly lit rooms, where they could wash away the worst signs of their guilt and leave unnoticed and unremarked a few hours later.[60] Such contradictions were not uncommon because newspapers often cobbled their stories together from several sources such as the news agencies and their own reporters, and some simply published two accounts of the same incident, replete with contradictions and errors.

But even the police were beginning to doubt that the Ripper was local, or at least Sergeant William Thicke had apparently formed that opinion. The local criminals had assured him that they would unhesitatingly hand such a fiend as the murderer over to the police, and so fervently were their assurances delivered that Thicke was reportedly convinced that the murderer wasn't among 'the regular thieves or desperadoes at the East-end.'[61]

Criticism of the authorities began to mount. The *Daily Telegraph* attacked the home secretary, Henry Matthews, and *The Star* described Matthews very unflatteringly as 'a feeble, forcible red-tapeist, with the mind of a dancing master and the statesmanship of an attorney's clerk'.[62] It also called him 'a feeble mountebank, who would pose and simper over the brink of a volcano'.[63] The paper thought that a strong hand at the tiller of Scotland Yard would have prevented a home secretary from doing harm. *The Star* was dogmatically anti-Warren and its arguments were not altogether good ones. But as far afield as Canada it was being reported that the police were completely at a loss: 'The detectives are losing their heads completely under the attacks of the newspapers and the ridicule of the populace, and appear to be further from the truth than ever,' reported the *Daily Colonist*.[64]

Across the district meetings were held at various working men's clubs and other political and social organisations[65] and men formed themselves into groups to patrol the streets and raise subscriptions so that a reward could be offered. Among them were a group of Spitalfields and Whitechapel tradesmen who met at a pub to discuss their reaction to the crimes and concluded by creating what would become the best known of the vigilance organisations, the Whitechapel Vigilance Committee.[66] It consisted of sixteen men with Joseph Aarons elected secretary. Others named were

Cohen, Houghton, H A Harris, Laughton, Lord, Isaacs, Rogers, Mitchell, Barnett, Hodgins, Lindsay, Reeves and Jacobs. The *Daily Telegraph* reported on 5 October 1888 that the leaders of the Vigilance Committee were 'drawn principally from the trading class, and include a builder, a cigar-manufacturer, a tailor, a picture-frame maker, a licensed victualler, and "an actor." ' The 'actor' was probably 'Reeves', the entertainer Charles Reeves, father of the music hall star Ada Reeves, who recalled in her autobiography:

My father was one of the original Vigilance Committee set up to patrol the streets during the time of these murders . . . and how nervous my mother used to be when he went out night after night, with only a stick and a whistle for protection.[67]

At the end of the meeting they issued a notice offering a substantial reward for the capture or for information leading to the capture of the murderer.

At about 10.30 p.m. a young woman named Lloyd told a journalist that her daughter had been frightened by a man who had stared into her face and had held a half-concealed knife. A neighbour described what may have been the same incident, saying the man was short, had a sandy beard and wore a cloth cap. He had been pursued some short distance by some men, but had disappeared up a side road.[68] Mrs Lloyd later told a *Star* reporter that the incident as she had described it 'had been very much exaggerated'. The man had been chased up the street by some boys, had crossed the street and looked at her daughter as he passed by. He had said nothing, had not threatened her, and she didn't know whether he had a knife or not.[69] Although a wholly unimportant incident, it serves to illustrate how the press could magnify incidents and why care should be taken when dealing with press reports.

On Tuesday, 11 September, two doctors, one named Cowen and the other named Crabb, visited Holloway Police Station and reported that a man named Joseph Issenschmidt, who was then lodging at 60 Milford Road and was known to them as a lunatic, was probably the perpetrator of the murders. The police went to the address given by the doctors and there spoke to a George Tyler. He said that he had met Issenschmidt on 5 September and had provided him with accommodation. Issenschmidt left the house frequently over the next few days and was absent during the night

on which Annie Chapman was murdered. The police then went to 97
Duncombe Road, Upper Holloway, where they spoke to Mrs Issenschmidt.
During this and a subsequent interview they learned that she and
Issenschmidt had been married for 21 years; that Issenschmidt was a
journeyman butcher whose business at 59 Elthorne Road had failed; that as
a result of this he had become very depressed, habitually stayed away from
home, and had eventually spent ten weeks at Colney Hatch Asylum, being
released in the middle of December 1887 as cured. He had obtained a job,
but left it at Whitsun 1888. By 17 September Issenschmidt was confined at
the asylum at Bow. Sergeant Thicke visited the medical superintendent
there and ascertained that Issenschmidt admitted to having told various
women in Holloway that he was 'Leather Apron'. He claimed that he had
only been teasing them, and he assumed his present predicament was caused
by one of them having reported him to the police. He had also explained his
frequent absences from his lodgings by saying that he was often at market to
collect sheep's heads, feet and kidneys, which he dressed and sold to
restaurants and coffee shops in the West End. He said that he had left his
wife after an argument. On 18 September Abberline wrote,[70]

> He has been previously confined in an asylum, and is said to be at times
> very violent. Although at present we are unable to procure any evidence
> to connect him with the murders he appears to be the most likely
> person that has come under our notice to have committed the crimes.

On 19 September Abberline submitted a report:

> I beg to add that the man Issenschmidt who was detained at Holloway
> on 12 inst., and handed over to the parochial authorities as a lunatic, is
> identical with the man seen in the Prince Albert, Brushfield Street, at
> 7 a.m. on the morning of the murder of Annie Chapman, by Mrs
> Fiddymont and other persons. This house is only about 400 yards from
> the scene of the murder . . . He is now confined in the Bow Infirmary
> Asylum, Fairfield Road, Bow, and Dr Mickle has been seen with a view
> to arrange for Mrs Fiddymont and other witnesses to see him, but the
> doctor thinks this cannot be done at present with safety to his patient.
> As time is of the greatest importance in this case, not only with regard
> to the question of identity, but also for the purpose of allaying the
> strong public feeling that exists, I would respectfully suggest that either

the Chief Surgeon or one of the Divisional Surgeons may be requested to see Dr Mickle, the resident medical officer, to make if possible some arrangements for the witnesses to see Issenschmidt.

It was reported in the press that Issenschmidt was released as a harmless lunatic, though some years later he was readmitted to Colney Hatch and a photograph taken of him at that time shows him as very ferocious-looking. There is no mention in the files of whether or not he was the man seen by Mrs Fiddymont. However, Abberline's report testifies to the interest taken up to that time by the police in Mrs Fiddymont's testimony. Thereafter, however, the interest diminished and she is not mentioned again in the police files, from which it seems reasonable to conclude that the man she saw probably was Issenschmidt. And that he was not the Whitechapel murderer.

While the police were pursuing their enquiries into the mad pork butcher, a little girl named Laura Sickings[71] noticed some peculiar marks on the ground and on the wall in the yard of 25 Hanbury Street, the house next but one to the murder scene. Inspector Chandler had just called at the house to make a plan of the back premises of the three houses for the coroner at the inquest and she drew his attention to the marks. The whole of the yard was carefully examined, revealing a bloody trail leading to the back door of the house. The evidence seemed to suggest that the murderer had climbed over the fence from No. 29 into the yard of No. 27 and then into No. 25, where there were marks on a wall that indicated that the murderer had knocked his blood-soaked coat against it. Abutting the end of the yard of No. 25 was the yard used by Messrs Bailey. In an out-of-the-way corner the police found some bloodstained paper which, according to *The Times* of 12 September 1888, it was thought the murderer had found in the yard of No. 25, wiped his hands on it and flung it over the fence into Bailey's yard. *The Star* very cheerfully reported that the story was pie-in-the-sky, its reporter having called on Inspector Chandler, who nearly laughed when told of the theory built around the marks. The discoloration was not blood, but a trail of urine, and no bloodstained bricks or paper had been found.

In the morning, the local tradesmen who had formed the Vigilance Committee published a notice:

Finding that, in spite of murders being committed in our midst our police force is inadequate to discover the author or authors of the late atrocities, we the undersigned have formed ourselves into a committee

and intend offering a substantial reward to any one, citizens or otherwise, who shall give such information as will be the means of bringing
the murderer or murderers to justice.

The names of a large number of tradesmen were appended to the notice.

The Times also revealed that Samuel Montagu, MP for Whitechapel, had
offered a reward of £100 for the capture of the authors of the outrage.[72]
Having read about the murders in the newspapers, Montagu had gone to
Leman Street Police Station and asked an inspector whether the government
intended to offer a reward. The inspector said that he did not know, and
Montagu said that as he believed the home secretary was away from London
and that there might therefore be a delay in his authorising a reward, and he
asked that the police offer a reward of £100, which he would donate. The
inspector said that he would submit the proposal to the commissioner.

In the absence of Sir Charles Warren, assistant commissioner, Sir
Alexander C Bruce informed the Home Office. Attached to his letter there
is a memorandum on which a Home Office official noted:

> The Home Office rule is against offering rewards . . . It is generally
> agreed that the Whitechapel murderer has no accomplices who could
> betray him. Any person, other than an accomplice, who possesses
> information, would be certain, in the present state of public feeling, to
> give it without prospect of a reward. On the other hand the offer of a
> reward would be almost certain to produce *false* information.

On 13 September E Leigh Pemberton wrote to Warren stating that the
practice of offering rewards had been discontinued and that, had it been
thought necessary to make an exception in this case, the secretary of state
would have offered one on behalf of the government. Warren accordingly
wrote to Montagu on 17 September, but by this time Montagu's offer was
public knowledge and it was too late for it to be withdrawn.

While this was going on, two police constables visited Timothy Donovan
and showed him two rings discovered at a pawnbroker's, but Donovan did
not recognise them as the rings Annie Chapman had worn[73] and it must
have been increasingly apparent that the usual procedures for investigating
murder were coming up cold. To add to their troubles, the police were
inundated with hundreds of letters from people all over the country offering
suggestions and advice, or their services as private detectives.[74] Ripper-

related cases began cropping up in the courts, some of which provided some evident light relief. At Worship Street Police Court, a 34-year-old tinker named Joseph Carter was charged with being drunk and disorderly after creating a disturbance when he was refused entry to see a murder suspect and was sent to prison for five days.[75] A Whitechapel woman appeared before Mr Saunders at the same court seeking protection from her husband, who, she said, had threatened to cut her heart out as the Whitechapel murderer had done and burn it. With a condescending flippancy Mr Saunders had replied, 'But he would not do that. It would be no use to him.' The woman insisted, 'But he says he will', and Saunders said he'd send an officer to caution the husband.[76]

The criticism mounted on Wednesday, 12 September 1888, and the following day no less an august journal than *The Times* observed, 'It is now beginning to be admitted that the detectives are once more at fault.'[77] However, several newspapers were beginning to speak in defence of the authorities. Commenting on a statement in an unnamed newspaper to the effect that a police official (also unnamed) had admitted that the murderer could not be caught, and that nothing further could be done until his homicidal mania wore off or wore him out, the Manchester-based *Alderley and Wilmslow Advertiser* reflected that 'it may be safely assumed that the police authorities are doing their utmost to find the author of the ghastly murders, and it is a pity that they should be hampered by the vapid nonsense indulged in by writers who seem ever ready to turn their pen in whichever direction the tide turns'.[78] The *East London Advertiser* likewise reassured its readers: 'The police and detective force are really doing their utmost to trace the guilty person. There is no ground for the suspicion that the police are lukewarm in the matter.'[79]

Interest in the ongoing inquest diminished:

Up to the time fixed for the resumption of the inquiry there were only a handful of loiterers around the entrance to the institute, and even when the proceedings had been commenced, there were only a few persons present in addition to the coroner and jury, the usual officials, and the representatives of the press . . .[80]

The *Jewish Chronicle* reported that the East End Jewish population had come in for a lot of trouble during the week following the murder, and offered justifiable criticism of Mr Saunders of the Worship Police Court, whose flippancy I have already noted and who also displayed anti-Semitic or anti-immigrant opinions. When confronted with a man making an application on behalf of a Polish tailor for a summons for wages, he had asked why the man did not make the application himself. When told it was because he was a Pole, Saunders said, 'Well, then let him go to Poland . . . The Pole has no business in this country. He is taking the bread out of the mouths of Englishmen. You may have a summons, but I hope you won't succeed.'[81]

On Thursday, 13 September, the principal officers investigating the murders were summoned to Scotland Yard and later in the day Assistant Commissioner Bruce and Chief Constable Monsell visited the murder area, without notifying the local officials of their intention to do so, and went to Buck's Row and Hanbury Street.[82] The following day Annie Chapman was buried. The undertaker was Mr Hawes of Hunt Street, Mile End. Amid profound secrecy, the hearse was sent to the mortuary in Montague Street at 7 a.m. and the body quietly removed by the undertaker's men. The coffin was black-covered elm with a plate bearing the words ANNIE CHAPMAN, DIED SEPTEMBER 8TH, AGED 48 YEARS. The hearse took the body to the undertaker's in Hunt Street, and at 9 a.m. started for Manor Park Cemetery. It was not followed by any mourners because the relatives and friends had by prior arrangement agreed to meet at the cemetery.[83]

In the evening at about ten o'clock a man passed through the Tower subway from the Surrey to the Middlesex side, and said to the caretaker, 'Have you caught any of the Whitechapel murderers yet?' He then produced a knife, about a foot in length, with a curved blade, and remarked, 'This will do for them.' He then ran away, pulling off and discarding false whiskers as he went, and disappeared from sight somewhere along Tooley Street. He was described as about thirty and five foot three tall, with a fair complexion, dark hair and a moustache, and wearing a new black diagonal suit, light dustcoat and dark cloth double-peak hat.[84] He was probably one of the many practical jokers who seemed to appear every day, and wouldn't otherwise merit mention except that Patricia Cornwell suggested that he was the artist Walter Sickert.[85]

Another character who attracted attention was handed over to a constable on duty in or near Flower and Dean Street. His name was Edward McKenna, who gave his address as 15 Brick Lane, Whitechapel. He was taken to Commercial Street Police Station, where he was questioned and searched. His pockets were found to contain a heap of rags, two women's purses, two or three pocket handkerchiefs, two small tin boxes, a small cardboard box, a small leather strap and a spring onion. He was slightly built, about five foot seven or eight, shabbily dressed and careworn. He had sandy hair and beard and wore a skullcap.[86] He said he peddled laces and other small articles for a living and had 'been on tramp in Kent', only just having arrived back in London. The police did not attach any importance to the arrest, but detained him for enquiries, and he matched the description of the man seen by Mrs Lyons in Heath Street[87] – who was confronted with him but was unable to say whether he was the man or not – and possibly the man who reportedly called a woman thought by some to have been Annie Chapman from the Ten Bells shortly before she was found murdered, as well as the man seen in Mrs Fiddymont's pub. McKenna was in due course liberated when he was found to have an alibi,[88] but the frequency with which Jews were arrested supports the *Jewish Chronicle*'s contention that Jews were in danger.

The Star, ever dramatic, asked, 'Every new turn of this bewildering labyrinth reveals some fresh depth of social blackness, some strange and repulsive curiosity of human nature. What are we to do? Where are we to turn?'[89]

On 15 September 1888 Chief Inspector Donald Sutherland Swanson was appointed to take complete charge of the Ripper investigation at Scotland Yard. A rough handwritten memo from Sir Charles Warren was preserved among Swanson's personal papers.

I am convinced that the Whitechapel Murder case is one which can be successfully grappled with if it is systematically taken in hand. I go so far as to say that I could myself in a few days unravel the mystery provided I could spare the time & give individual attention to it. I feel therefore the utmost importance to be attached to putting the whole Central Office work in this case in the hands of one man who will have nothing else to concern himself with. Neither you or I or Mr Williamson can do this, I therefore put it in the hands of Chief Inspr. Swanson who must be acquainted with <u>every detail</u>. I look upon him for the time being as the eyes & ears of the Commr. in this particular case.

He must have a room to himself, & every paper, every document, every report every telegram must pass through his hands. He must be consulted on every subject. I would not send any directions anywhere on the subject of the murder without consulting him. I give him the whole responsibility. On the other hand he should consult Mr

Williamson, you, or myself on every important particular before any action unless there is some extreme urgency.

I find that a most important letter was sent to Divn. yesterday without his seeing it. This is quite an error & should not occur again. All the papers in Central Office on the subject of the murder must be kept in his room & plans of the positions &c.

I must have this matter at once put on a proper footing so as to be a guide for the future in cases of importance.

Everything depends upon a careful compliance with these directions.

This letter, for a long time mistakenly attributed to Robert Anderson but identified[90] as being from Sir Charles Warren, perhaps reveals either Warren's arrogance or misapprehension of how difficult it would be to catch a random, motiveless murderer, but it shows that the police were treating the crimes seriously.

Donald Swanson was born in 1848 in Geise, now pretty much a part of Thurso in Caithness in the Highlands of Scotland and distinguished as the most northerly town on mainland Britain. He was the son of a brewer named John Swanson and educated at the Miller Institution on Sinclair Street in Thurso, built for the Reverend Alexander Miller and today Thurso Public Library. He was described as 'a brilliant student' and was a Greek and Latin scholar. He planned to be a teacher and for a brief time he did teach, but the job and perhaps the quiet of Thurso lacked the sort of future he wanted for himself and he left for London. He worked as a clerk for several months for James Meikle of 8 Catherine Court, Seething Lane, who had known him since 1862, but as his employer was due to give up business he needed another job and on 20 March 1868 he saw an advertisement in the *Daily Telegraph* offering careers in the police and immediately wrote a letter of application, offering excellent credentials and concluding, '[I] do not so much desire a large salary as a good opening at a moderate one.' He joined the Metropolitan Police on 27 April 1868. He was five foot eight and a half inches tall and dark-complexioned, with hazel eyes and dark-brown hair.

There were elements in his character that seem to suggest fun. He was fined a few times, once for receiving a shilling from a prisoner after procuring him bail, for which he was cautioned and made to refund the money. In 1870 he was twenty minutes late for roll call and climbed over the railing of the section house in an attempt to avoid detection, for which he was fined two shillings. In 1874, for being outside the Lion in Carlton Square with his armband off, he was fined five shillings.

By 1888 he had reached the rank of chief inspector and would become superintendent before retiring in 1903 after a career in which he received numerous rewards and commendations, among them £5 for 'energy and zeal' in the arrest of the railway murderer Percy Lefroy Mapleton in 1881. He was married with five children – three sons and two daughters. He died on 24 November 1924 at 3 Presburg Road, New Malden, Surrey.

Swanson had a remarkable career. He was involved with the investigation of numerous crimes, including the theft of the Countess of Dysart's jewels, a crackdown on homosexual prostitution, the aforementioned arrest of Percy Lefroy Mapleton, suppressing Fenianism and helping prevent the Jameson Raid in South Africa from sparking an Afrikaner war. His contemporaries spoke highly of him. John Sweeney called him 'one of the better class of officers . . .' and Sir Melville Macnaghten said he was 'a very capable officer with a synthetical turn of mind'. He was also a great friend of Robert Anderson, with whom he exchanged Christmas cards until the latter's death, and from whom he received in 1910 a presentation copy of Anderson's memoirs, *The Lighter Side of My Official Life* into which he would pencil some notes about the Ripper's identity.[91]

Some of the hyperbole was by now beginning to irritate other sections of the press. The weekly *East London Observer* was becoming hypersensitive to the criticism heaped on the East End, for example, and complained of the 'exaggerated and distorted descriptions of its institutions and inhabitants', citing as an example an unnamed newspaper that had called the East End 'a plague spot on our civilisation.'[92]

The streets of the East End were nevertheless exciting and frightening. A man suddenly attacked a woman in Spitalfields Market, striking her and knocking her to the ground before pulling a knife. Several women gathered in the vicinity and began shrieking and crying 'murder', and an immense crowd gathered, many people being brought from Hanbury Street by the noise. The man had by this time been restrained by some men in the crowd, but the man with the knife, his ill temper having presumably put him beyond rational thought, threw off those restraining him and managed to stab the woman several times, cutting her forehead, neck and fingers before he was again pulled off. The crowd were by now shouting 'murder' and other people began crying 'lynch him', but the police arrived and were able to take the man and woman to the police station, where she was examined by the divisional surgeon.[93] These were clearly extraordinary days, the streets peopled by some very odd and dangerous individuals.

A meeting of the Whitechapel Vigilance Committee was held on Saturday night at the Crown Tavern, Mile End Road, Joseph Aarons taking the chair. He claimed that the committee was not antagonistic to the police, who were doing their best, but that the reward they were raising might assist in bringing the murderer to justice. He specifically referred to £5 donated by Spencer Charrington of the nearby brewery and £5 received from a local builder named George Lusk – who was president of the committee and would achieve notoriety himself in due course. Others who contributed were F Wootton Issacson, MP, £10, and Mrs Sarah Lane, of the Britannia Theatre, £3 3s. Both Aarons and a committee member named Rogers complained about the government's refusal to give a reward, and said that normally charitable friends had declined to contribute to the Vigilance Committee's fund because they felt it was the responsibility of the home secretary to provide a reward.[94] Funds in fact trickled in very slowly and by the end of the month would amount to £60 or £70, enabling them to offer a preliminary reward of £50.[95] At one meeting, with George Lusk in the chair, the secretary, B Harris, landlord of the Crown, said that he had approached the home secretary about a reward and had that day received a letter dated 17 September in reply, which he read out:

Sir, – I am directed by the Secretary of State to acknowledge the receipt of your letter with reference to the question of the offer of a reward for the discovery of the perpetrators of the recent murders in Whitechapel, and I am to inform you that, had the Secretary of State considered the case a proper one for the offer of a reward, he would at once have offered one on behalf of the Government, but that the practice of offering rewards for the discovery of criminals was discontinued some years ago, because experience showed that such offers of reward tended to produce more harm than good, and the Secretary of State is satisfied that there is nothing in the circumstances of the present case to justify a departure from this rule. – I am, sir, your obedient servant,

E. Leigh Pemberton.

'Jewish Socialists and Freethinkers' held a banquet at the International Working Men's Club at 40 Berner Street 'to protest against the Jewish religion and the Day of Atonement'. The banquet, reportedly unprecedented in Jewish history, had been announced in the radical socialist newspaper *Arbeter Fraint (Worker's Friend)*, and had caused a lot of anger among orthodox Jews. Trouble was expected, but members of the working men's club had said they were prepared for it and would have no need to call upon the police.[96] Little did any of them imagine how soon there would be far more notoriety than perhaps they could ever have wished for as a result of Jack the Ripper.

On Tuesday, 18 September, *The Times* published a long letter from someone who signed himself 'SGO' – in fact Sidney Godolphin Osborne – in which he commented, 'The tilled garden is fast producing the crop sown . . .' and went on in vivid prose to place responsibility for the crimes on the failure of society to clean up the squalid slums where 'tens of thousands of our fellow creatures [are] begotten and reared in an atmosphere of godless brutality, a species of human sewage, the very drainage of the vilest production of ordinary vice . . .' and warned, darkly hinting at social unrest and revolution, that 'Sewer gas will sometimes explode . . .'

The Times followed SGO's unpleasant comparison of the denizens of the East End with social refuse, and claimed that, as neglected rubbish breeds vermin, so 'neglected human refuse as inevitably breeds crime' and went on to say that, while the first duty was to catch and punish the perpetrator of the crimes, 'We have to consider how far our social organization is responsible for the preparation of the soil and atmosphere in which such crimes are produced . . . and of its well-nigh unlimited capacity to bring forth fruits of almost unimaginable evil.'

Canon Samuel A Barnett of St Jude's vicarage added his voice to this issue, claiming that 'the murders were, it may almost be said, bound to come' and arguing, with a truth as valid today as it was then, that the 'Whitechapel horrors will not be in vain if "at last" the public conscience awakes to consider the life which these horrors reveal.' He pointed out that the greater part of Whitechapel was orderly and probably more moral than 'that of many whose vices are hidden by greater wealth', but that within its boundaries were areas of concentrated evils. He asserted that there was inadequate policing of these areas, inadequate lighting and cleaning.

Barnett wrote of animals that were slaughtered in the midst of Whitechapel, bloodstained butchers familiar on the streets and brutalising sights common and frequent, and landlords who behaved irresponsibly, their properties left to fall into ruin. The rents were collected by agents, he said, who in all probability encouraged vice as a means of *paying* the rents, such monies eventually supporting the landlord. Those comfortably off people who owned the slum houses and stood to be revealed as profiting from vice probably read their morning *Times* with a trembling hand after Canon Barnett's letter.

SGO's letter inspired one of the most famous illustrations associated with the Ripper scare when *Punch* published a drawing and rhyme called 'The Nemesis of Neglect', which concluded:

> *Dank roofs, dark entries, closely-clustered walls,*
> *Murder-inviting nooks, death-reeking gutters,*
> *A boding voice from your foul chaos calls,*
> *When will men heed the warning that it utters?*
> *There floats a phantom on the slum's foul air,*
> *Shaping, to eyes which have the gift of seeing,*
> *Into the Spectre of that loathly lair.*
> *Face it – for vain is fleeing!*
> *Red-handed, ruthless, furtive, unerect,*
> *'Tis murderous Crime – the Nemesis of Neglect!*[97]

On the Tuesday that SGO's inspiring and disturbing letter appeared, a man named Charles Ludwig was charged at Thames Police Court with being drunk and threatening to stab a man named Alexander Finlay. Ludwig, who was about forty and five foot six, with a grizzled beard and moustache, had arrived in London from Hamburg some fifteen months earlier. He had attended a German club in Houndsditch and there met a hairdresser, C A Partridge, who had a shop at 1 Minories and gave him a job. Ludwig later secured lodgings with a German tailor named Johannes in Church Street, Minories, but his behaviour and habits made him unwelcome and he moved to a hotel in Finsbury, where he continued to behave in such an odd fashion – on one occasion producing several razors – that he alarmed several of the residents and on the day of the Chapman murder he was seen to wash blood from his hands.

Early on the morning of 18 September, PC John Johnson, 866 City, was on duty in the Minories when he heard a cry of 'murder' come from Three Kings Court, which was only a few yards away from the hairdressing shop where Ludwig worked for Partridge. PC Johnson responded to the cry and found Ludwig with a one-armed prostitute named Elizabeth Burns of 55 Flower and Dean Street, who, *The Star* reported, appeared to be very frightened and said, 'Oh, policeman, do take me out of this.' PC Johnson sent the man off and escorted Elizabeth Burns to the end of his beat, when she said, 'He frightened me very much when he pulled a big knife out.'[98]

'Why didn't you tell me that at the time?' retorted PC Johnson. Burns replied that she had been much too frightened at the time. Johnson then made every effort to find the man, alerting other policemen as he met them.

Ludwig had in fact gone no further than a coffee stall in Whitechapel High Street. Already there was an eighteen-year-old Pole named Alexander Freinberg, who had anglicised his name to Alexander Finlay. Ludwig thought Freinberg was looking at him and said, 'What you looking at?' Freinberg apologised. 'Oh, you want something,' replied Ludwig, obviously seeking trouble, and pulled out a long penknife.[99] Freinberg grabbed a dish from the coffee stall and prepared to throw it at Ludwig's head. Ludwig backed off and Freinberg summoned PC Gallagher, 221H, who arrested Ludwig and took him to the police station. On the way there Ludwig dropped a long-bladed penknife. On his appearance at the Thames Police Court later that morning Ludwig was remanded at the request of Inspector Abberline. After two weeks in custody, Ludwig was released, having accounted for his whereabouts at the time of the murders.[100] However, *The Star* in mid-October reported that Ludwig had again been seen brandishing a knife and that he was being kept under surveillance by the police.

Considering that the likes of Pigott, Issenschmidt and Ludwig were wandering the streets of the East End – and they were by no means the only people picked up by the police who were violent and/or unstable – clearly weakens the theories that the Whitechapel murderer was someone like J K Stephen (a cousin of Virginia Woolf advanced as a suspect by Michael Harrison) or Frank Miles (a friend of Oscar Wilde, briefly advanced by Colin Wilson in his introduction to Donald Rumbelow's book, *The Complete Jack the Ripper*), for why seek the murderer among celebrities when there were any number of forgotten lunatics actually living in Whitechapel who are far more likely?

Apart from drunks and lunatics, the police had to contend with people who wanted to confess and with prostitutes who tried to extort money from intended clients by threatening to have them arrested as the Whitechapel murderer – the name 'Jack the Ripper' not yet being on the public tongue.

A man named John Fitzgerald, a plasterer or bricklayer's labourer, admitted to the murder of Annie Chapman after either surrendering himself at Wandsworth Police Station or being taken there after being arrested in a common lodging house. It was subsequently reported that his story was incoherent and that apparently he had been drinking heavily for several days, and he was duly discharged.[101] Meanwhile an American named James Johnson was arrested after a notorious prostitute named Elizabeth Hudson had begun screaming when he rejected her propositions and when the police arrived accused him of assaulting her, throwing her to the ground and producing a knife with which he threatened to stab her. Brought before the magistrates' court, he denied the charges and proved himself to be highly respectable, while the police described Hudson as 'the worst and most troublesome prostitute in the neighbourhood'. Johnson was discharged, but his experience added another dimension to the troubles on the streets.[102]

On Saturday, 22 September, Wynne Baxter held the final day of the inquest into Mary Ann Nichols's death and passed a verdict of 'wilful murder against some person or persons unknown'. Baxter was starting to come in for criticism. It was suggested that he was exceeding his responsibilities, which were to ascertain the cause of death, and was instead engaging in an attempt to discover the murderer.[103] He took the opportunity during the afternoon of Wednesday, 26 September 1888, when he concluded the inquest into Annie Chapman's death,[104] to defend his actions, making it clear that the witnesses had provided evidence under oath that was preserved in the records of the court and could be used if the murderer was ever tried, even if the witnesses were unavailable at that time.[105]

He then went on to echo the opinions of many – still valid – that the enquiry had given people a glimpse of life 'sufficient to make them feel there was much in the 19th century civilization of which they had small reason to be proud; [a] sad tale of starvation, or semi-starvation, of misery, immorality, and wickedness . . .'[106] Perhaps because he was persuaded by a theory that he would in due course elucidate, Baxter emphasised that

> the injuries had been made by someone who had considerable anatomical skill and knowledge. There were no meaningless cuts. The organ had been taken by one who knew where to find it, what difficulties he would have to contend against, and how he should use his knife so as to abstract the organ without injury to it. No unskilled

person could have known where to find it or have recognized it when it was found.[107]

The *Lancet* agreed that the murderer had shown anatomical knowledge and skill, the uterus and its appendages, with the 'upper portion of the vagina and the posterior two-thirds of the bladder, having been entirely removed . . . the incisions were cleanly cut, avoiding the rectum, and dividing the vagina low enough to avoid injury to the cervix uteri. Obviously the work was that of an expert – of one, at least, who had such knowledge of anatomical or pathological examinations as to be enabled to secure the pelvic organs with one sweep of a knife . . .' The speed with which the killer worked also 'pointed to the improbability of anyone but an expert performing the mutilations described in so apparently skilful a manner.'[108]

Not everyone shared that opinion, however. A 'mania specialist' with the unfortunate name of Dr Savage, in an article called 'Homicidal Mania' in the *Fortnightly Review*, wrote, 'To suppose the murders to be the work of a medical man is, to my thinking, going too far' – and he postulated instead that the crimes were more likely the work of a butcher.[109]

Of lasting interest, and causing something of a sensation at the time, was a revelation by the coroner that the evidence indicated that the murderer had wanted the organ in question and that the crime had been committed with the express purpose of obtaining it. He then went on to explain that, a few hours after the publication in the press of the medical testimony, he had received a communication from 'the subcurator of the Pathological Museum' that some months ago an American had called on him and asked him to procure a number of specimens of the organ that was missing in the deceased. He wished them preserved, not in spirits of wine, the usual medium, but glycerine, in order to preserve them in a flaccid condition, and he wished them sent to America direct. He offered £20 for each specimen and said that he wanted them so that he could issue one each with a copy of a publication on which he was then engaged. He was told that his request was impossible, but was known to have made the request elsewhere.[110]

Baxter did not suggest that the doctor in question was the murderer – and it is important to remember this because it has sometimes been thought that he did – but that somebody might have heard of the offer and been inspired by it to commit the murders. Indeed, Inspector Abberline's theory that Severin Klosowski was the murderer was underpinned by his theory that Klosowski, a trained surgeon, had been inspired by the offer.

Wynne Baxter's 'theory' caused a lot of public interest. 'Nothing [else] was talked about in the East End on Wednesday . . .' reported the *East London Advertiser*, which also observed that 'Inquiries at the London Hospital, the nearest medical institution to the scene of the murder, have elicited the fact that no applications of the kind referred to by the coroner have recently been made to the warden or curator of the pathological museum attached to it.'[111] The *Lancet* thought such a request perfectly normal and acceptable, but balked at the idea that a doctor would pay £20 per specimen and that anyone would give a specimen of the uterus away with each copy of a publication, describing the idea as 'too grotesque and horrible to be for a moment entertained'. It also doubted that an American doctor would seek to purchase the organs in England, and concluded that the actual facts of the case must have been exaggerated in transmission.[112]

The weekend came round again and the talk in the pubs in Whitechapel was about the murders and whether another murder would be committed or not, and suspicions were roused by anyone who asked questions. At 11.53 that Saturday night, Albert Bachert, who lived at 13 Newnham Street and pops up frequently throughout the Ripper story, went into the Three Nuns Hotel in Aldgate. An elderly and shabbily dressed woman came in and moved from customer to customer trying to sell matches. She asked Bachert, who turned her away with a refusal, and shortly afterwards she left the pub. A man standing next to Bachert remarked that such people – presumably hawkers – were a nuisance and Bachert agreed, then the man asked if Bachert knew how old some of the women were who were in the habit of soliciting outside. Bachert guessed they were from 25 to over 35, and the man asked whether Bachert thought one of them would go with him down Northumberland Alley, a dark and lonely court off Fenchurch Street, and Bachert said he supposed they would.

The man then went outside, spoke to the match seller and gave her something. He returned to the pub, but Bachert was leaving and bade the man goodnight. It was by then about 12.10 a.m. The man, he said, was dark, about 38 and approximately five foot six or seven. He wore a black felt hat, a dark morning coat and a black tie, and a carried a black shiny bag.[113]

A little earlier a similarly aged man had gone into a pub in Batty Street, Whitechapel, where the customers were discussing the murders. For some reason the man said that he knew the Whitechapel murderer, and that they would hear about him in the morning. The man then left.[114] This story may not have been true, just one of the many tales told by people eager to get a free drink from a journalist, or to get their names in the newspaper, or maybe even by a penny-a-liner spinning out a yarn for some extra cash. But, if this actually happened, and it was just a guess, then it was a very prophetic guess.

If it was a guess.

Just a few streets away and hopefully enjoying what she had no idea were the last few hours of her life, was a woman named Elizabeth Stride.

CHAPTER NINE

Elizabeth Stride

Elizabeth Stride – also known as Long Liz,[1] Epileptic Annie,[2] Annie Fitzgerald,[3] Hippy Lip Annie[4] and Mother Gum[5] – was born on 27 November 1843 on a small farm near the village of Stora Tumlehead in the parish of Hisingen, north of the seaport of Gothenburg on the west coast of Sweden, and was found murdered on Sunday, 30 September 1888.

Elizabeth was the second of four children born to a farmer named Gustaf Ericson[6] and his wife Beata (née Carlsdotter). She had an elder sister named Anna Christina (b. 15 October 1840) and two brothers named Carl Bernhard (b. 4 January 1848) and Svante (b. 22 July 1851). Elizabeth was baptised in nearby Torslanda on 5 December.

The childhood and early years of Elizabeth are a blank, except for 1845, 1848, 1851 and 1854 parish catechetical meeting protocol (that is, records of her religious instruction), until the record of her confirmation at the church at Torslanda in 1859. The records state that her biblical knowledge at that time was very good. The following year Elizabeth applied to move to Gothenburg and was granted permission on 25 October, the official document stating that her behaviour was good and her religious knowledge extensive.

Her whereabouts between 25 October and February 1861 are not known, but during February she secured a job as a maid to Lars Fredrik Olofsson, his wife Johanna and their three children, in the parish of Majorna.[7] She stayed there until February 1864, after which her life seems to have begun to fall apart. On 25 August her mother died; the following month she discovered that she was pregnant; on 4 April 1865 she visited Kurhuset (which was probably a hospital specially for prostitutes or for the treatment of venereal diseases) and was diagnosed with condyloma (genital warts), a very common and largely incurable venereal disease; and on 21 April she gave birth to a stillborn girl. She was released from Kurhuset on 13 May, but was sent back again on 30 August diagnosed with chancre, the highly

136

contagious ulcer that forms in the first or primary stage of syphilis. The treatment took about three weeks and she was released on 23 September.

On 17 October she is found in the police records for the first time. She is described as slender, with blue eyes and brown hair, a straight nose and an oval face – and is sent to Kurhuset for another round of treatment, being released on 1 November. The police records for 3, 7, 10 and 14 November show that she was given a clean bill of health and was discharged from the police record as a professional prostitute.

Being discharged from the record was not an easy thing to achieve and required employment or marriage, and four days before being released she had managed to obtain employment as a maid with a woman named Maria Wejsner, in Husargatan 42 in Haga. Wejsner seems to have employed a large number of maids and the author Birgita Leufstadius has suggested that Maria Wejsner may have been a brothel keeper with some influence. On the other hand, she may have set about helping women who genuinely wanted to get off the streets.[8]

In December 1866 or January 1867 Elizabeth inherited 65 Swedish krona from her mother's estate. A respectable sum of money, it was enough to enable her to emigrate to London. She made a request to emigrate, which was granted on 2 February, and she left Sweden on Wednesday, 7 February 1866. According to Charles Preston, who was living at the same lodging house as Elizabeth Stride at the time of her death, she had once said that she had come to Britain in the service of a foreign gentleman,[9] and Michael Kidney, with whom she lived on and off until shortly before her death, said he believed Stride had relatives on her mother's side in Britain, and that she had come to Britain as the servant to a family living near Hyde Park.[10] By 10 July 1866 she was registered with the Swedish Church, Princess Square, St George's-in-the-East.[11]

The next couple of years are blank and we don't encounter Elizabeth again until 7 March 1869, when she married John Thomas Stride,[12] a carpenter, at the parish church of St Giles-in-the-Fields. He was living at 21 Munster Street, Regent's Park, and Elizabeth gave her address as 67 Gower Street, a lodging house run by a 64-year-old widow, Elizabeth Bond. The witnesses to the marriage were W Taylor, sexton of the church, and Daniel Fryatt, who owned a coffee shop at 6 Munster Street.

John and Elizabeth Stride opened a coffee shop at Upper North Street, Poplar, and a year or two later they moved their establishment to 178 Poplar High Street. They did not live on the premises, but a few doors away at 172.

Elizabeth Stride shows up in the records of the Thames Magistrates' Court on 21 March 1877, where she appeared before the magistrate and was removed by the police to the Poplar Workhouse. We do not know what the reasons for this were. The records of the Swedish Church in London contain a register of all who received assistance from the church and it states that Elizabeth 'in January 1879 asked for financial help from the Church because of her husband's illness'. We do not know what John Stride was suffering from, or whether he was suffering any illness at all, for it would appear that by 1881 the couple were living at 69 Usher Road, Old Ford Road, Bow. But we know that he probably wasn't a well man. He would be admitted to Poplar Workhouse in August 1884 and be sent from there to Poplar and Stepney Sick Asylum, where he died aged 63 of heart disease on 24 October.

One story Elizabeth Stride used to tell was that her husband and two of her nine children died aboard the *Princess Alice*, a tragedy of 1878. Named after Princess Alice, Grand Duchess of Hesse-Darmstadt, Queen Victoria's third daughter, the *Princess Alice* was a paddle steamer that took passengers on pleasure cruises along the Thames from London Bridge to Sheerness. At dusk on Tuesday, 3 September 1878, as the band were packing away their instruments and the 700 passengers were gathering together their belongings and preparing to disembark, the *Princess Alice* rounded Tripcock Point into Galleons Reach, some eleven miles below London Bridge, and collided with the *Bywell Castle*, a giant steel collier,[13] and was sheared in half. Only 69 people were pulled from the Thames alive. The exact number of dead was never established and *The Times* justifiably called it 'one of the most fearful disasters of modern times'.[14]

Michael Kidney, a waterside labourer, with whom Stride lived, said, 'She told me she was a widow, and that her husband . . . was drowned on the *Princess Alice*.'[15] She told him that both she and her husband had been employed aboard the vessel, and that two of her children had been drowned with her husband. One of the children, she had said, had drowned in the father's arms. Stride had managed to survive by climbing up a rope as the vessel was sinking.

Other witnesses said that Stride claimed that an injury to her mouth, perhaps visible in the mortuary photograph, was caused when she was kicked in the face while trying to escape.[16] She had sent some of her surviving children to a country school belonging to the Swedish Church, and two had gone to live with 'some friend of her husband'.[17] She claimed that she had then sold the coffee shop and gone to live in Cannon Street Road.

Several newspapers on 8 October 1888 carried a news agency story:

With reference to the identity of Elizabeth Stride, the Woolwich news-papers of the time of the *Princess Alice* disaster have been referred to, and it has been found that a woman of that name was a witness at the inquest and identified the body of a man as her husband, and of two children then lying in Woolwich Dockyard. She said she was on board and saw them drowned, her husband picking up one of the children, and being drowned with it in his arms. She was saved by climbing the funnel, where she was accidentally kicked in the mouth by a retired arsenal police inspector, who was also clinging to the funnel. The husband and two children are buried in Woolwich Cemetery.[18]

This story has never been found in any Woolwich newspaper; John Thomas Stride was alive at the time of the accident; Elizabeth Stride had no children; and Coroner Wynne Baxter, who tried to confirm the tale so tragically told by Stride, said that a subscription fund raised to assist the relatives of those who had died in the disaster made no mention of Stride. As far as can be told, the whole tragic story was a lie.

By 1881 the marriage had collapsed irrevocably, Elizabeth's heavy drinking reportedly a predominating cause, and the couple finally separated for good. On 28 December 1881 she was admitted to Whitechapel Workhouse Infirmary suffering from bronchitis and at that time gave her address as Brick Lane. She left the infirmary on 4 January 1882 and was admitted to Whitechapel Workhouse. On 7 January she was discharged and shortly afterwards moved into a common lodging house at 32 Flower and Dean Street in Spitalfields.[19] She returned to prostitution and on 13 November 1884 was sentenced to seven days' hard labour for being drunk and disorderly and soliciting.

It was the following year that she met Michael Kidney, with whom she would have a stormy off-and-on relationship for the rest of her life. The couple lived at 33 Dorset Street but in May 1886, when Elizabeth applied for and received financial aid from the Swedish Church, she gave her address as Devonshire Street, off Commercial Road.[20] She and Kidney would often separate, Stride going off for days or weeks at a time, apparently without notice or indication, and Kidney estimated that they had been apart for five months of the three years they had lived together.[21] 'It was drink that made her go away,' he said. 'She always returned without me going after her.' Kidney seems to have strongly objected to Stride's behaviour, her drinking and prostitution, and he probably became violent on occasions. On 6 April 1887 Stride accused him of assault – Stride didn't turn up at the Thames Magistrates' Court to carry through the prosecution.

Throughout 1887 and 1888 she made regular appearances before the magistrates. She was charged on 14 February and 24 October 1887 and 14 February 1888 with being drunk and disorderly and using obscene language. On 16 July 1888 she appeared before Montagu Williams, who later wrote books in which he mentioned the crimes, on a charge of being drunk and disorderly. On 31 July 1888, 8 August 1888 and 3 September 1888 she appeared on the same charges. We also know that Elizabeth Stride twice petitioned the Swedish Church for money and on 15 January and 20 September received a shilling.[22]

During this time Elizabeth Stride may also have masqueraded as a woman named Elizabeth Watts. At the inquest into her death a much-distressed woman named Mary Malcolm declared that the murdered woman was her sister. Mrs Malcolm was married to a respectable tailor named Andrew Malcolm and lived at 50 Eagle Street, off Red Lion Square in Holborn. On the night of the murder she had been in bed, when at about 1.20 a.m. she had felt a pressure on her breast and had heard three distinct kisses. On reading about the murders in the papers the next morning she suspected that the woman who had been murdered was her sister, and presumably considered her nighttime experience to have been the kisses of her sister and thus the portents of her death. She went to the East End and viewed the body, but in the gaslight she wasn't sure whether it was that of her sister or not.

The following day she viewed the body again, this time in daylight, and was certain. It *was* Elizabeth Watts. She had been married to a man named Edward Watts, the son of a wine and spirit merchant of Walcot Street in Bath, and they had had two children, a boy and a girl. But Elizabeth Watts had become addicted to drink and about eight years earlier she had been caught by her husband with a porter. There had been a quarrel, and she had returned with the children to her mother. The little girl died a short while later and the boy went to a boarding school kept by an aunt. Mrs Malcolm said Elizabeth Watts threw fake epileptic fits when drunk, that she had been charged before the Thames police magistrate with drunkenness, that she was known as 'Long Liz', and had lived with a man who kept a coffee house at Poplar, whose name Mrs Malcolm thought was Dent and who three and a half years earlier had run away to sea and been wrecked on the Isle of St Paul. Mrs Malcolm, who was extremely distressed when she gave evidence, explained that she was in the habit of meeting her sister every Saturday at about 4 p.m. on the corner of Chancery Lane and giving her money, but that Watts had visited her at work on the previous Thursday instead of the Saturday and been given a shilling and a short jacket.

The amazing thing was that Elizabeth Watts was alive and well and the Central News Agency found her living at 5 Charles Street, Tottenham, the respectable and hard-working wife of a crippled labourer at Plowman's Brickfield. Mrs Watts's story is extraordinary. She had married three times. The first marriage was to a wine merchant of Bath named Watts. His family had not approved of their marriage, she said, and he was sent abroad, dying in America, and their children, a boy and a girl, were taken from her. She did not now know what had happened to them, which preyed on her mind. She was committed to a lunatic asylum at Fisherton House, near Salisbury, but obtained a discharge and became a domestic servant at Walmer, where she met her second husband, a Mr Speller, whom she married at Deal (remembered by Mrs Malcolm as the husband's name), who was, as Mrs Malcolm said, stranded on St Paul's Island, a mountainous island in Nova Scotia with granite cliffs hundreds of feet high and a coastline of jagged rocks. Known as the Graveyard of the Gulf (of St Lawrence), it had claimed hundreds of ships that had gone ashore and thousands of people had died, many starving to death on the rocks. Speller died, his half-pay was stopped, and Elizabeth Speller, left destitute, was committed to the Peckham Lunatic Asylum, from where she was in due course pronounced sane by the Lunacy Commissioners and discharged, still destitute and now with an impaired memory. She then met and married Mr Stokes. She said she was one of eight children, but she had not seen any of her family for years, including Mrs Malcolm, from whom she said she had never received a penny.

While Mrs Malcolm steps from the pages of the British press as a respectable and emotionally upset woman who had cared for her sister and shown her true Christian charity, a woman who signed her name 'Elise' and wrote a column from London for a New Zealand newspaper called *Te Aroha News* said that a friend had had occasion to visit the inquest and had described her as

a gin-sodden virago, and identified [Stride's] remains with ghoulish relish. From first to last this woman's transparent object was to turn the catastrophe to account somehow . . . Not a word of honest pity for the dead woman's shocking fate crossed her lips. Her own goodness and generosity to her poor sister was the never-ending theme of her discourse, or would have been, if the coroner had not cut her short.[23]

'Elise' did observe, however, that Mrs Malcolm's story otherwise seemed to fit the facts, and the press certainly accepted that Stride was Mrs Malcolm's sister. There seems to be no record of Mrs Malcolm's being confronted with Mrs Stokes, but, if these women are to be believed, Mrs Malcolm met someone once a week, many of whose details fitted Elizabeth Stride. Had Stride for many years masqueraded as Mrs Stokes to obtain money from Mrs Malcolm?

On 25 September Elizabeth Stride and Michael Kidney parted company for the last time. He claimed they had been on good terms, but a woman named Catherine Lane claimed that Stride had told her that she'd left Kidney following a row.[24] Kidney denied this and said he had expected Stride to be at home when he returned from work. Where Stride went is not known, but on Thursday, 27 September, she returned to her old lodging at 32 Flower and Dean Street. Writing to *The Times* on 6 October,[25] Dr Thomas Barnardo recalled,

> Only four days before the recent murders I visited No. 32, Flower and Dean-street, the house in which the unhappy woman Stride occasionally lodged. I had been examining many of the common lodging-houses in Bethnal-green that night, endeavouring to elicit from the inmates their opinions upon a certain aspect of the subject. In the kitchen of No. 32 there were many persons, some of them being girls and women of the same unhappy class as that to which poor Elizabeth Stride belonged. The company soon recognized me, and the conversation turned upon the previous murders. The female inmates of the kitchen seemed thoroughly frightened at the dangers to which they were presumably exposed . . . One poor creature, who had evidently been drinking, exclaimed somewhat bitterly to the following effect:- 'We're all up to no good, and no one cares what becomes of us. Perhaps some of us will be killed next!' And then she added, 'If anybody had helped the likes of us long ago we would never have come to this!' . . . I have since visited the mortuary in which were lying the remains of

the poor woman Stride, and I at once recognized her as one of those who stood around me in the kitchen of the common lodging-house on the occasion of my visit last Wednesday week.

If Dr Barnardo was correct and Stride was among the women in the kitchen then she had gone to 32 Flower and Dean Street on 26 September, but the deputy there said specifically that Stride had stayed there 'only on Thursday and Friday nights', so it remains to be seen whether Dr Barnardo was mistaken or not.[26]

The lodging house deputy, a widow named Elizabeth Tanner, who knew Stride only by the nickname 'Long Liz', described her as a very quiet woman who sometimes stayed out late at night and did cleaning work for Jews. She said Stride spoke without any trace of an accent.[27] Michael Kidney said that Stride could speak Yiddish.[28] Interestingly, but perhaps coincidentally, another Ripper victim, Catharine Eddowes, also reportedly did cleaning work for Jews.

Mrs Ann Mill, a bedmaker at the lodging house, said that Stride worked when she could get work and added that 'a better-hearted, more good-natured cleaner woman never lived'. These opinions differ markedly from the impression of Stride received from other testimony and her court appearances and it seems likely that Tanner and Mill did not want to utter a bad word about someone who had died in such horrible and tragic circumstances.

On the afternoon of Saturday, 29 September 1888, the lodging house deputy paid Elizabeth Stride 6d. to clean the rooms at 32 Flower and Dean Street. She next saw Stride at 6.30 p.m. in the Queen's Head, a public house in Commercial Street. Stride soon returned to the lodging house, where she was seen between 7 p.m. and 8 p.m. by Charles Preston and Catherine Lane. Stride was preparing to go out and she borrowed a clothes brush from Charles Preston to clean up her clothing, then gave Catherine Lane a piece of green velvet to look after until she came back.[29] Thomas Bates, the watchman at the lodging house, saw her as she left and said she looked very cheerful. Bates, it was reported, was overcome by emotion while talking about Stride. 'Lor' bless you, when she could get no work she had to do the best she could for her living, but a neater and a cleaner woman never lived.'[30]

At 11 p.m. J Best of 82 Lower Chapman Street and John Gardner of 11 Chapman Street were entering the Bricklayer's Arms in Settles Street. As they went into the pub, a woman who they felt certain was Stride was leaving with a man. 'They had been served in the public house, and went out when me and my friends came in,' said Best. 'It was raining very fast and they did not appear willing to go out. He was hugging her and kissing her, and as he seemed a respectably dressed man, we were rather astonished at the way he was going on with the woman . . .' Best and his friends chaffed the man. Eventually 'he and the woman went off like a shot soon after eleven'. The man seen by Best, Gardner and their friends was described as five foot eight and well dressed in a black morning suit and coat and a black billycock hat, with a thick, black moustache, but was otherwise clean – to the point of having no eyelashes.[31]

Matthew Packer, who sold fruit and vegetables through the open bottom half of a sash window of his home at 44 Berner Street, claimed that between 11 p.m. and midnight he sold some grapes to a man who was with a woman whom he later identified as Elizabeth Stride. Packer's story was probably an imaginative fancy, but it features prominently in some accounts of the murder and throws up some interesting titbits of information.

Some newspapers, including the *Daily Telegraph* and the *Evening News* – the latter being the primary source of the Packer story – had, along with the Vigilance Committee, hired two private detectives, Le Grand and Batchelor, of 283 Strand. After the murder of Elizabeth Stride they appear to have talked with a Mrs Rosenfield and her sister Miss Eva Harstein, who lived at 14 Berner Street. Mrs Rosenfield said that early on Sunday morning she had passed the murder scene and seen on the ground a grape stalk stained with blood. Her sister said she had also seen nearby a few small petals of a white flower. The two detectives then approached Matthew Packer and after three interviews he made a statement in writing to the effect that at about 11.45 p.m. a man and woman came to his shop window and asked for some fruit. It was a dark night, and the only light came from an oil lamp that Packer had burning inside his window. The man asked the woman whether she wanted black or white grapes and the woman said black. ' "Well, what's the price of the black grapes, old man?" he inquired. "The black are 6d. and the white 4d.," replied Packer. "Well, then, old man, give us half a pound of the black," said the man.'[32] Packer gave the man the grapes, which he handed to the woman, and the couple crossed the road, where they stood opposite the shop for more than half an hour in the pouring rain, and Packer said that he'd observed to his wife, 'What fools those people are to be standing in the rain like that!' At about 12.10 or 12.15 a.m. – Packer noted the time because the pubs had been closed – the couple had crossed the road and stood in front of the Berner Street Club, and

Packer, who had begun closing up, lost sight of them. There is some seeming support for Packer's story, several newspapers having reported on 1 October that Stride was clutching a bunch of grapes in her right hand,[33] and at least one witness was quoted as saying that Stride was clutching a bunch of grapes when her body was found;[34] and on 2 October the detectives searched the drain in the passage where the body had been found and 'amidst a heap of heterogeneous filth, they discovered a grape-stalk'.[35]

Packer described the man as middle-aged (perhaps 35), about five foot seven, stout and square built, wearing a wide-awake hat and dark clothes. He had the appearance of a clerk and spoke with a rough voice, his words uttered in 'a quick, sharp way'. The woman was middle-aged, wore a dark dress and jacket, and on her bosom had a white flower that stood out distinctly in the oil light against the dark material of her jacket. Other witnesses said Stride had a red flower pinned to her jacket and the *Evening News* explained this by saying that Packer did not say Stride had only a white flower pinned to her jacket, but that his attention was *drawn* to a white flower because it stood out against her dark jacket. The detectives tested Packer's story by trying to trick him. They took him in the belief that he was to view the body of Stride and presented him with a different corpse, but Packer said it wasn't the woman he had seen. On 4 October 1888 the private detectives took him to the mortuary, where he identified the woman to whom he had sold the grapes as Elizabeth Stride.

On 6 October the *Daily Telegraph* published a sketch of the man seen by Packer, but, despite the assurances of the newspaper that it had been 'unhesitatingly selected' by Packer,[36] Packer himself was elsewhere reported to have stated with some contempt that it bore 'no resemblance whatever to the man'.[37]

By the end of the first week of October, Packer was beginning to complain bitterly that he had wasted nearly the whole week trying to help the police, had neglected his business, and had not received the least remuneration, though promises had been made to him that his time would be paid for.[38] Packer started to elaborate on his story, claiming that he had been visited by two men who had bought 12s. worth of rabbits from him, then asked for an exact description of the man who bought the grapes. One of the men then told Packer that he thought the man who'd bought the grapes was his cousin, an Englishman who had spent many years in the United States. Packer told a *Daily Telegraph* journalist that he believed the man and the journalist passed the information to the authorities, who sent Detective

Sergeants White and Mitchell to investigate. They went with Packer to the man's house and he told them where his cousin could be found.[39] The next day, however, the newspaper reported that neither of the men who spoke to Packer had been found.[40] Finally, although some papers claimed the police believed they had found the cousin referred to and that the story was being investigated, others said that detectives doubted the veracity of the greater portion of the details and attached little importance to it.[41]

In fact, doubts about Packer's story were expressed as early as 4 October, when *The Star* reported that the police had emphatically rejected it because Packer had contradicted himself too many times,[42] because there was a complete lack of evidence that Stride had any grapes in her possession[43] and because Dr Phillips's postmortem had found no trace of grape in Elizabeth Stride's stomach.[44]

Louis Diemshutz, who would in due course discover the body of Elizabeth Stride, said she was holding grapes, but other witness testimony did not support him. Abraham Heahbury, one of the first on the scene, made no mention of Stride's holding grapes and said only that in her hand 'there was a little piece of paper containing five or six cachous'.[45] Edward Spooner, a horse keeper who lived at 26 Fairclough Street, told the inquest that Stride had only a 'piece of paper doubled up in her right hand'.[46] Dr William Frederick Blackwell, another police doctor, said that he had seen no grapes in the yard[47] and Dr Phillips said that, while the larger of two handkerchiefs found on Stride's body was stained with what he believed to be fruit, 'neither on the hands nor about the body did I find any grapes, or connection with them. I am convinced the deceased had not swallowed either the skin or seed of grape within many hours of death'.[48]

On 3 October Packer had told a journalist that although his story had been published in the newspapers he had not been visited by any policeman from Scotland Yard,[49] but this was also untrue. The official records show that Sergeant Stephen White interviewed Packer at about 9 a.m. on 30 September, the morning of the murder, and that Packer had told him, 'I saw no one standing about, neither did I see anyone go up the yard. I never saw anything suspicious or heard the slightest noise. And I knew nothing about the murder until I heard of it this morning.'[50] Packer also told most newspapers that he'd sold the grapes at 11 p.m., but the *Evening News* on 4 October twice reported that he had sold the grapes at 11.45 p.m. and other newspapers reported that he sold the grapes at midnight. However, Packer had told Sergeant White that he had not done any business because of the heavy rain and that he had closed his shop early, but the rain had begun about 9 p.m. and had stopped about 11 p.m. If Packer shut up shop because of the rain then he must have closed before 11 p.m., and in fact Packer said that the man and woman had stood in the rain for over half an hour, putting the sale of the grapes at least as early as 10.30 p.m. The rain is important in another respect, because Dr Blackwell said Stride's clothes were not wet from the rain, so, if Packer sold grapes to anyone who stood in the rain, it was not Elizabeth Stride.

Perhaps the clearest indication that the whole story is a fabrication is that the private detective named Le Grand was a crook. His real name appears to have been Christian Briscony and he may have been the son of a Danish diplomat or someone connected with the Danish diplomatic service. He had several pseudonyms, among them Nelson, Le Grand, Grant, 'French Colonel' and Captain Anderson. In 1877 he had been convicted of a series of thefts (he was an inveterate shoplifter) and was sentenced to a remarkably stiff eight years in prison. By 1888 he had reinvented himself as Le Grand and set up business in the Strand, but by June 1889 was again in trouble with the law, this time for sending threatening letters demanding money from a Harley Street surgeon named A Malcolm Morris. He received a sentence of two years with hard labour. In 1891 he was again charged, this time under the name of Charles Grant, with sending letters to various wealthy women threatening to kill them if they did not pay him substantial sums of money. It would seem that he was suffering a mental illness because he did not need money when he made the threats.[51]

In his account of the Ripper murders the late Tom Cullen claims that the grapes 'became a part of East End folklore' and says that he was told by Mrs Annie Tapper in the kitchen of her Stepney council flat how she had sold the grapes. She watched shop for Mr and Mrs Packer while they ate dinner, she said, and sold the grapes to a man who came into the shop and let her keep the change, with which she bought a halfpennyworth of red cabbage and a halfpennyworth of chips.[52]

At 11.30 p.m. William Marshall,[53] a labourer in an indigo warehouse who was aged about fifty[54] and lived at 64 Berner Street, came to the doorway of his house and stood there from about 11.30 until midnight. It was not raining during that time. At 11.45 p.m. he noticed a woman he later identified from her face and dress as Elizabeth Stride talking to a man outside No. 63. The woman was wearing a small crêpe bonnet, but was not wearing a flower in her bosom, though the witness may have missed it because his attention was directed to the man due to his behaviour. Marshall did not see the man's face clearly, but otherwise described him as of middling height,[55] middle-aged and rather stout, and he was mildly spoken, as if well educated. He had the appearance of a clerk rather than a manual worker. He was very decently dressed in a black coat and light trousers, and a round cap with a small peak of the sort a sailor would wear. The man was 'a-kissing her and cuddling her', his arms round her neck, and they remained talking for about ten minutes, Marshall overhearing the man say, 'You would say anything but your prayers.' Stride then walked away with the stranger.[56]

No. 40 Berner Street was a house converted into the International Workingmen's Educational Association, commonly referred to as the Berner Street Club,[57] and at its rear were the printing and editorial offices of the socialist newspaper *Arbeter Fraint* (*Worker's Friend*). Both the club and the newspaper had a national and international reputation, were highly controversial, and regarded by the leaders of Anglo-Jewry as distinctly dangerous.[58]

It was remembered, if slightly faultily, by one of its members, the writer Thomas B Eyges, who in his strange but fascinating little book of memories described it as

> an old wooden[59] two-storey[60] building [which had] a spacious room with a capacity of over 200 people and contained a stage. Here were performed by amateurs mostly in Russian language plays by well known Russian revolutionists – Tchaikovsky (not the famous composer), Volchovsky, Stepniak, Winchevsky, Gallop; later came Simon Kahn, Krantz, Feigenbaum, Yanovsky, and others . . . Invariably, on Saturday and Sunday evenings, there was a truly international gathering of Russian, Jewish, British, French, Italian, Czech, Polish, and radicals of other nationalities . . . Quite often the renowned radical poet, William Morris, was seen there reading his splendid verses. It may be said that there, in Berner Street, was laid the foundation for true International Brotherhood of Mankind . . . Like Faneuil Hall in Boston, Berner Street Club was the 'Cradle of Liberty', for the workers' emancipation from economic slavery, in London.[61]

At the front there was a single window and a door. The front door opened into a hallway, and halfway along a staircase led to the first floor. Three doors led off the hall, one to a front room used as a dining room, the second, a little beyond the staircase, to the rear ground-floor room used as a kitchen, and the third opening into an outdoor passage that ran from a gate to the rear of the house. On the first floor there was a single room with three windows, all looking out on the rear yard. It was used for entertainments:

> It was of medium size and held hardly more than a hundred and fifty persons. Plain benches without backs stretched through it crosswise and along the walls. Everywhere extreme poverty, but everywhere also the endeavour to overcome poverty. On the walls hung a number of portraits: Marx, Proudhon, Lassalle overthrowing the golden calf of capitalism . . . At the front the room was enclosed by a small stage . . .[62]

A third storey provided accommodation for the steward and his wife, and guests.

Along the side of the house there ran a passage, nine to twelve feet wide and entered through two large wooden gates that folded backwards from the street. Into the left one was set a small wicket door that could be used when the gate was shut. On one gate in white paint there was the legend W. HINDLEY, SACK MANUFACTURER, on the other A. DUTFIELD, VAN AND CART BUILDER. The passage ran along the full length of the house and at the end reached the rear door leading into the house, opposite which were two lavatories. The passage led into an extensive area known as Dutfield's Yard, because a man named Arthur Dutfield had until recently carried on his business as a van and cart manufacturer there, or more properly Stable Yard.[63] The yard contained a workshop used by a sack manufacturer named Walter Hindley. Next to it was an unused stable and next to that, an extension built on to the rear of the club, was *Arbeter Fraint*'s two-roomed stone office. On the left-hand side of the yard there was a single house converted into three artisans' dwellings.

Saturday, 29 September, was no different from the weekends described above. About a hundred people turned up. The chair was taken that evening by a young man named Morris Eagle, who opened the discussion, 'Why Jews Should Be Socialists', and after a typically lively evening the discussion finished close to 11.30 p.m. After saying their farewells, most people left the club by the street door. By midnight there were twenty to thirty people in the club, some of them upstairs, where they stood in little groups talking, singing and dancing, and about a dozen in the downstairs rooms.

Morris Eagle, who lived at 4 New Road, off Commercial Road, was a jewellery traveller. He left the club between 11.30 and 11.45 p.m. to take his girlfriend. He left by the front door and did not go through the side passage where Stride's body would be found.

At about 12.10 a.m. William West, who lived at 2 William Street and was overseer of the *Arbeter Fraint* printing office, left the club by the side entrance and went into the printing office to return some literature. The editor, Philip Kranz, was there reading. West returned to the club again by the side entrance and looked towards the gates, which attracted his attention because they were open. He could hear the singing from the club, but he saw nothing unusual, although the passage was unlit and he admitted to being short-sighted, saying that if the body had been there he might not have noticed it. Going into the club, he called his brother and together they went to William Street. Another member of the club, Louis Stansley, left the club at the same time and accompanied them as far as James Street. He didn't think there was anyone in Berner Street.[64]

At 12.30 a.m. Charles Letchford walked along Berner Street, where he lived at number 30, 'and everything seemed to me to be going on as usual'. He added that his sister was standing at the door at 12.55 p.m., but did not see anyone.[65]

PC William Smith, 452H, passed through Berner Street on his beat[66] between 12.30 and 12.35 a.m. and walked towards Commercial Street. He saw a man and a woman whom he later identified as Elizabeth Stride on the pavement opposite the club. The woman, he noticed, had a flower pinned to her jacket. The man was about five foot seven and wore a dark overcoat and dark trousers and was wearing a hard felt deerstalker hat. He had a newspaper parcel in his hand. He was clean-shaven and appeared respectable, and PC Smith guessed his age to be about 28.[67]

Morris Eagle returned to the club about 12.40 a.m. with the intention of having supper. He found the front door closed, so went through the gateway into the yard. He did not notice anything on the ground, but it was rather dark and he wasn't sure whether anything could have been there or not. He was also uncertain whether there had been anyone in the street. Eagle went upstairs to see a friend, whom he found singing a song in Russian. Morris joined him in the singing.[68]

A printer and photographer by trade named Joseph Lave, a Russian who had recently arrived in Britain from the United States and was temporarily living at the Berner Street Club, left the club to get a breath of fresh air and strolled for five minutes or more, going as far as the street. He said everything was very quiet and he noticed nothing wrong.[69]

At 12.45 a.m. James Brown, who lived at 35 Fairclough Street, left his home to get some supper from a chandler's shop at the corner of Berner Street and Fairclough Street. On his way back about three or four minutes later he saw a man and woman standing against the wall by the Board School in Fairclough Street. As he passed he heard the woman say, 'No, not tonight, some other night.' For some reason this made him turn around. The man had his arm up against the wall, and the woman had her back to the wall facing him. The place where they were standing was rather dark, but Brown was able to describe the man as about five foot seven and stoutish, wearing a long coat that came very nearly down to his heels. He had a hat on, but Brown couldn't describe it. He was nearly convinced that the woman was Elizabeth Stride, although he did not notice any flowers in her dress. He got home to eat about a quarter of an hour later. When he had nearly finished his food, he heard screams of 'police' and 'murder'. He opened a window, but could not see anyone and the screams ceased. Shortly afterwards he saw a policeman standing at the corner of Christian Street. He heard a man opposite call out to the constable that he was wanted and saw the policeman run along to Berner Street.

Mrs Fanny Mortimer, the wife of a carman named William Mortimer, who lived at 36 Berner Street, three doors from the club, told a reporter for the *Evening News* that she had gone outside shortly after she had 'heard the measured, heavy stamp of a policeman passing the house on his beat'. She stood at her door for no more than ten minutes, she said, and had neither seen nor heard anything unusual. The only person in the street was a young man carrying a shiny black bag who entered from Commercial Road, walked briskly down Berner Street, looked up at the club as he passed, and turned the corner by the Board School at the bottom of the street. She had returned indoors, bolted the door and prepared for bed, which was in the front room on the ground floor. About four minutes later she heard a pony and cart pass by and remarked on it to her husband.[70]

For some reason Mrs Mortimer was not called to give evidence at the inquest, which is odd because, although she didn't see anything, her testimony is crucial to estimating the time Stride was murdered. Exactly when Mrs Mortimer went to her door is uncertain. She said she had gone

outside after hearing the measured tread of what she assumed to be PC
Smith passing on his beat, which would therefore have put her outside
between 12.30 and 12.45 a.m., but if she had been outside at that time she
would have seen the couple seen by PC Smith, would have seen Charles
Letchford passing through the street at 12.30 a.m., Morris Eagle returning
to the club at 12.35 a.m., a club member named Joseph Lave taking a stroll
at or about 12.40 a.m. and an assault on a woman outside the club at 12.45
a.m. Mrs Mortimer saw none of those people and none of those people said
they saw her, all of which suggests that Mrs Mortimer did not go to her door
immediately after hearing a policeman pass by (or if she did then PC Smith
was much later than he said). We also know that the person she did see, the
man with the shiny black bag, was named Leon Goldstein, who lived at
nearby 22 Christian Street and went along to the police station after reading
about himself in the newspapers. He had left a coffee house in Spectacle
Alley and passed Berner Street shortly before 1 a.m. His bag, he said,
contained empty cigarette boxes.[71] The evidence therefore points to Mrs
Mortimer's having gone to her door about 12.45 a.m. and returned indoors
shortly before hearing a pony and cart pass by, which we know was at 1 a.m.

It is particularly interesting that in his autobiography, *I Caught Crippen*,
Walter Dew, looking back over fifty years, recalled Mrs Mortimer by name
and her story about seeing the man with the black bag, and, evidently
unaware that the man had been identified, said she was 'the only person ever
to see the Ripper in the vicinity of one of his crimes'.[72] If Dew recalled Mrs
Mortimer after fifty years, and remembered her, albeit erroneously, in an
important context, it is all the more mysterious that she was never called to
give evidence at the inquest.

However, other people didn't give evidence, either, among them the man
who witnessed an extraordinary incident. A man entered Berner Street from
Commercial Road, followed moments later by a man of strong Jewish
appearance named Israel Schwartz. A woman was standing outside the gates
of the club and on reaching her the first man stopped, exchanged some
words, then assaulted her. Schwartz thought it was a domestic dispute and
crossed the road to avoid it. He saw a second man who appeared to be
leaving a pub on the corner and busy lighting a clay pipe, for which reason
he is commonly referred to by modern researchers as 'Pipeman'. Someone
then shouted 'Lipski!', which was the name of an East End Jewish murderer
who attained notoriety the previous year; the name was briefly used as a

term of abuse to Jews. Schwartz hastened his pace and, when he thought he was followed by the second man, started running. The following day, after learning about the murder, he went to the police station in Leman Street and told his story. He was taken to view the body of Elizabeth Stride and identified it as that of the woman he had seen attacked and who fifteen minutes later would be found dead in the passage beside the club.

If Schwartz's story is true – and the police clearly believed him – then he probably saw Elizabeth Stride assaulted by the man who murdered her. It is statistically improbable that the same woman would have been assaulted in the same place twice and by different men within fifteen minutes, or that one man would have assaulted two women in the same place within fifteen minutes. The story is therefore worth examining in detail.

According to the official report:[73]

12.45 a.m. 30th Israel Schwartz of 22 Helen Street,[74] Backchurch Lane, stated that at this hour on turning into Berner Street from Commercial Street & had got as far as the gateway where the murder was committed he saw a man stop and speak to a woman, who was standing in the gateway. The man tried to pull the woman into the street, but he turned her round & threw her down on the footway & the woman screamed three times, but not very loudly. On crossing to the opposite side of the street, he saw a second man standing lighting his pipe. The man who threw the woman down called out apparently to the man on the opposite side of the road 'Lipski' & then Schwartz walked away, but finding that he was followed by the second man he ran as far as the railway arch, but the man did not follow so far. Schwartz cannot say whether the two men were together or known to each other. Upon being taken to the mortuary Schwartz identified the body as that of the woman he had seen & he thus describes the first man who threw the woman down:– age about 30 ht. 5ft 5in. comp. fair hair dark, small brown moustache, full face, broad shouldered, dress, dark jacket & trousers, black cap with peak, had nothing in his hands.

Second man age 35 ht 5ft 11in. comp. fresh, hair light brown, moustache brown, dress dark overcoat, old black hard felt hat wide brim, had a clay pipe in his hand.

Later in the report we read,

It will be observed that allowing for differences of opinion between the PC and Schwartz as to the apparent age and height of the man each saw with the woman whose body they both identified there are serious differences in the description of dress:- thus the P.C. describes the dress of the man whom he saw as black diagonal coat, hard felt hat, while Schwartz describes the dress of the man he saw as dark jacket black cap with peak, so that at least it is rendered doubtful whether they are describing the same man.

If Schwartz is to be believed, and the police report of his statement casts no doubt upon it, it follows if they are describing different men that the man Schwartz saw & described is the more probable of the two to be the murderer, for a quarter of an hour afterwards the body is found murdered. At the same time account must be taken of the fact that the throat only of the victim was cut in this instance which measured by time, considering meeting (if with a man other than Schwartz saw) the time for the agreement & the murderous action [i.e. the time for Stride to have met someone else, talked and come to a business agreement, and for the act of murder to have taken place] would I think be a question of minutes, five at least, ten at most, so I respectfully submit it is not clearly proved that the man that Schwartz saw is the murderer, although it is clearly the more probable of the two.

To this report the Home Office officials had made some marginal notes, one of the most interesting being, 'The police apparently do not suspect the second man Schwartz saw and who followed Schwartz.' The other, probably made by Home Secretary Henry Matthews, is also curious: 'The use of "Lipski" increases my belief that the murderer was a Jew.'

Either Matthews had succumbed to the utterly preposterous notion that the murders were too horrible to have been committed by a Gentile Englishman or we shall have to remain unaware of any *rational* reasons he had for holding this belief.

Oddly, the Home Office also asked for an explanation of the word 'Lipski', when it is inconceivable that anyone had forgotten the name of Israel Lipski, a *cause célèbre* of the previous year in which a convicted murderer whose guilt many disputed made a plea for clemency that caused Henry Matthews considerable anxiety,[75] and it assumed that the word had been addressed by the attacker to Pipeman and that Pipeman was therefore an accomplice. Abberline explained,

I beg to report that since a jew named Lipski was hanged for the murder of a jewess in 1887 the name has very frequently been used by persons as mere ejaculation by way of endeavouring to insult the jew to whom it has been addressed, and as Schwartz has a strong jewish appearance I am of opinion it was addressed to him as he stopped to look at the man he saw illusing the deceased woman.

I questioned Israel Schwartz very closely at the time he made the statement as to whom the man addressed when he called Lipski, but he was unable to say.

There was only one other person to be seen in the street, and that was a man on the opposite side of the road in the act of lighting a pipe.

Schwartz being a foreigner and unable to speak English became alarmed and ran away. The man whom he saw lighting his pipe also ran in the same direction as himself, but whether this man was running after him or not he could not tell, he might have been alarmed the same as himself and ran away. . . .

Inquiries have also been made in the neighbourhood but no person named Lipski could be found.[76]

Abberline thought the attacker addressed Schwartz, but concluded this *only* because Schwartz had a strong Jewish appearance.

In answer to the same question, Assistant Commissioner Anderson wrote:

With ref. to yr letter &c. I have to state that the opinion arrived at in this Dept. upon the evidence of Schwartz at the inquest in Eliz. Stride's case is that the name Lipski which he alleges was used by a man whom he saw assaulting the woman in Berner St. on the night of the murder, was not addressed to the supposed accomplice but to Schwartz himself. It appears that since the Lipski case, it has come to be used as an epithet in addressing or speaking of Jews.[77]

The important thing about this draft letter is that Anderson wrote that Schwartz had given evidence at the inquest, but no newspaper reported his appearance or his testimony, nor was his testimony cited by the coroner in his summing up. Either Anderson was wrong, or Schwartz gave evidence *in camera*, or for some reason the police withheld his testimony. On the face of it, the last two options seem highly unlikely, but it is known from the files that the police believed Schwartz's story throughout and after the period of the inquest. Why wouldn't such a material witness have been called to the inquest? And, of course, the same question can be asked of Mrs Mortimer.

Schwartz's story received scant attention in the press, the only lengthy report being in *The Star*, whose journalist seems to have been fortunate enough to be in the police station at Leman Street when Schwartz turned up to tell his story. *The Star* reported:

> Information which may be important was given to the Leman-street police late yesterday afternoon by an Hungarian concerning this murder. This foreigner was well dressed, and had the appearance of being in the theatrical line. He could not speak a word of English, but came to the police-station accompanied by a friend, who acted as an interpreter. He gave his name and address, but the police have not disclosed them. A *Star* man, however, got wind of his call, and ran him to earth in Backchurch-lane. The reporter's Hungarian was quite as imperfect as the foreigner's English, but an interpreter was at hand, and the man's story was retold just as he had given it to the police. It is, in fact, to the effect that he SAW THE WHOLE THING.
>
> It seems that he had gone out for the day, and his wife had expected to move, during his absence, from their lodgings in Berner-street to others in Backchurch-lane. When he came homewards about a quarter before one he first walked down Berner-street to see if his wife had moved. As he turned the corner from Commercial-road he noticed some distance in front of him a man walking as if partially intoxicated. He walked on behind him, and presently he noticed a woman standing in the entrance to the alley way where the body was afterwards found. The half-tipsy man halted and spoke to her. The Hungarian saw him put his hand on her shoulder and push her back into the passage, but, feeling rather timid of getting mixed up in quarrels, he crossed to the other side of the street. Before he had gone many yards, however, he heard the sound of a quarrel, and turned back to learn what was the matter, but just as he stepped from the kerb A SECOND MAN CAME OUT of the doorway of the public-house a few doors off, and shouting out some sort of warning to the man who was with the woman, rushed forward as if to attack the intruder. The Hungarian states positively that he saw a knife in this second man's hand, but he waited to see no more. He fled incontinently, to his new lodgings. He described THE MAN WITH THE WOMAN as about 30 years of

age, rather stoutly built, and wearing a brown moustache. He was dressed respectably in dark clothes and felt hat. The man who came at him with a knife he also describes, but not in detail. He says he was taller than the other, but not so stout, and that his moustaches were red. Both men seem to belong to the same grade of society. The police have arrested one man answering the description the Hungarian furnishes. This prisoner has not been charged, but is held for inquiries to be made. The truth of the man's statement is not wholly accepted.[78]

Schwartz's story reported in *The Star* differs in several important respects from that given in the police documents. According to *The Star* the man pushed Stride into the passage, whereas the police report says he threw her to the pavement outside the gates. *The Star* says Schwartz looked back on hearing a quarrel, but there is no mention of this in the police document. Most significantly, in the newspaper account the second man carried a knife, whereas to the police Schwartz said that this man had simply been lighting his pipe. And *The Star* account says it was the second man who cried out 'Lipski!' *at* the attacker, whereas in the police version it is the attacker who cried out 'Lipski!' Also noteworthy is the claim in *The Star* that 'The police have arrested one man answering the description the Hungarian furnishes. This prisoner has not been charged, but is held for inquiries to be made. The truth of the man's statement is not wholly accepted.' It isn't clear whether this man was the attacker or Pipeman, but elsewhere the newspaper referred to the incident witnessed by Schwartz and stated: 'Those who saw it thought that it was a man and his wife quarrelling, and no notice was taken of it.'

Unless 'Those' was a slip of the pen, the newspaper seems to be suggesting that more than one person witnessed the assault *and had expressed opinions about it*. The only person apart from Schwartz who witnessed the incident was Pipeman. Had the police talked to him? Is that why, as the Home Office observed, the 'police apparently do not suspect the second man'? Some evidence for this was contained in a report in *The Star* the following day:

In the matter of the Hungarian who said he saw a struggle between a man and a woman in the passage where the Stride body was afterwards found, the Leman-street police have reason to doubt the truth of the story. They arrested one man on the description thus obtained, and a

second on that furnished from another source, but they are not likely
to act further on the same information without additional facts.[79]

The report claims that the police were doubting and abandoning
Schwartz's story and, bearing in mind that Schwartz didn't appear at the
inquest, we should be wary before dismissing what *The Star* says. However,
it is flatly contradicted by the official files, which show that the police
believed Schwartz's story as late as 1 November 1888. What is important
about this snippet is that it says two arrests had been made, one based on the
description provided by 'the Hungarian' (Schwartz) and the other on a
description 'furnished from another source', and, unless bad phrasing or
some other mistake by the journalist had given the wrong impression, the
context makes it beyond doubt that both sources were describing the
assault. The other witness therefore has to be Pipeman.[80]

An interesting addition to the conundrum is a report in the far-flung *New
York Times*, which had its own correspondent in London:

The daring character of the murders is evident from the fact that two
people at least saw a man and the woman together in the Berner-
street gateway, and one saw him throw her down. He went away and
left her there, but it was half an hour before it was known that she
had been murdered.[81]

Unfortunately, this report is ambiguous because it isn't entirely clear
who 'went away', the attacker or the witness. The obvious and probably
intended inference is that it was the witness(es).

Just after 1 a.m. Louis Diemshutz, a 26-year-old Russian Jew and a
traveller in cheap jewellery who for the past six years had acted as steward
of the Berner Street Club,[82] turned his little pony-drawn cart from
Commercial Road into Berner Street. He had been to the market at Westow
Hill, near Crystal Palace, but, since the night was wet, he had returned
earlier than usual and planned to drop some goods off with his wife at the
club before taking his pony on to its stabling in George Yard, off Cable
Street. As he'd passed the clock outside a tobacco shop in Commercial Road
he'd noticed that the time was 1 a.m. or a minute or two after,[83] so it was no
later than 1.05 a.m. When he entered the passage at the side of the club his
pony shied away from the right-hand wall. Diemshutz looked down and saw
what at first he thought was a heap of dirt. He prodded it with the butt end

of his whip. Not being able to move it, he struck a match and saw that it was a woman. At first he thought it was his wife, but on entering the club by the side door further up the passage he found her in the front room on the ground floor with several club members. I told them, 'There is a woman lying in the yard, but I cannot say whether she is drunk or dead.' He then went to the concert room upstairs and told some of the members that 'there is a woman lying in the yard, and I think she is drunk.'[84] Morris Eagle, who was still in the upstairs room, and a young man named Isaac M Kozebrodsky (who was familiarly known as Isaacs) immediately accompanied Diemshutz downstairs. In the passage Eagle struck a match and to their horror they saw the body, blood trickling from the neck into the gutter and travelling almost from the gate to the club. The dance was immediately stopped and Diemshutz and Kozebrodsky ran for a policeman. Eagle followed and, on seeing Diemshutz and a man named Jacobs going for the police in the direction of Fairclough Street, Eagle turned in the opposite direction towards Commercial Road, all the time shouting, 'Police!'

Reaching the Beehive pub on the corner of Fairclough Street and Christian Street, Diemshutz and Jacobs met a man named Edward Spooner, the horse keeper we met earlier. Spooner, who had been standing there with a young woman for about 25 minutes, asked him what was going on. They told him and returned with him to the club, stopping only to talk with a Mr Harris, who had come out of his house in 'Tiger Bay' (Brunswick Street), attracted by the sound of a policeman's whistle.[85] There were about fifteen people in the yard. One of them struck a match and Spooner lifted the chin of the woman. For the first time Diemshutz saw the wound in her throat. According to Spooner, the woman had a piece of paper doubled up in her right hand, and a red and white flower pinned to her jacket.

Mrs Mortimer, preparing for bed, heard the commotion and immediately ran out, thinking that there was a row at the club. Someone told her that a dreadful murder had been committed and she went to look for herself. She saw the body, and saw Spooner touch the face and say the flesh was still warm, and she realised that the murder must have been committed while she had been standing at the door of her house.

Morris Eagle had by now reached the corner of Grove Street, where he saw two constables and told them that a woman had been murdered in Berner Street. They were PC Henry Lamb, 252H, and PC Edward Collins, 12HR. They went into the passage and Lamb flashed his light on the body. He then sent the other policeman for the nearest doctor, and Eagle to the police station to inform the inspector. He bent to examine the body, putting his hand on the face, which was still warm, and feeling for a pulse. Some of the crowd began pressing around him, but he told them to keep back as they might get some of the blood on their clothing and by that means get themselves into trouble. He then blew his whistle and ordered the gates to be shut. Spooner, who thought he had been there for about five minutes before the police arrived,[86] helped to fasten them. Lamb put a constable at the gate and told him not to let anyone in or out.

Lamb went into the club and began examining the place. Inside it was dark enough for him to need to turn his lamp on in order to look at the people and examine their hands and clothing for any marks of blood. There were fifteen to twenty people in the clubroom on the ground floor. Lamb examined every room, and in the upstairs room with the stage came across Diemshutz, who had rather coolly or perhaps abstractedly returned inside the club and gone about his duties.[87] Lamb then went outside, examined the toilets and woke the residents of the cottages looking into the yard. For PC Lamb it was the start of a very long night. He would remain there until morning, leaving only once when he started to help convey the body to the mortuary but was fetched back.[88]

PC William Smith's beat took him back into Berner Street. He saw a group of people outside the gates of No. 40, went there, saw PCs 12HR and 252H, then saw Stride.

PC Collins reached the residence of Drs Kay and Blackwell at 100 Commercial Road between 1.05 and 1.10 a.m. Dr Blackwell was asleep and the door was answered by his assistant, Edward Johnston, who immediately woke the doctor and informed him of what had happened, then accompanied the policeman to Berner Street, arriving there just as PC Smith was leaving to go to the police station for the ambulance. PC Smith went along Berner Street and turned into Fairclough Street, seeing no one as he went.[89] Meanwhile, Mr Johnston examined the woman and the wound to the throat, which appeared to have stopped bleeding. He felt the body and found it was all warm, with the exception of the hands, which were quite cold. Dr Blackwell arrived three or four minutes later and immediately checked his watch. It was precisely 1.16 a.m. Dr Blackwell estimated that Stride had been dead for twenty to thirty minutes by the time he arrived – which placed death between 12.45 and 1 a.m.[90]

Other officers and medical men began arriving at the scene in rapid succession. Chief Inspector West and Inspector Pinhorn were followed at

1.25 a.m. by Dr George Bagster Phillips. Inspector Reid arrived shortly afterwards, and was in turn followed by Superintendent Arnold.

According to the medical examination at the scene and the subsequent postmortem,[91] Stride was lying lengthways on her left side, her face completely towards the wall. There was mud on the left side of the face and matted in the hair. The face was pallid, the mouth slightly open. All the teeth on the left lower jaw were absent. The face, neck, chest and legs were quite warm, but the hands were cold. Her feet pointed towards the street and were about three yards from the gateway, her legs were drawn up and her feet almost touched the wall. Her right hand was lying across her chest and was smeared inside and out with blood. It was open. The left hand, lying on the ground, was partially closed and contained a small packet of cachous – a pill used to freshen the breath – wrapped in tissue paper. A number of the cachous were in the gutter. The pocket of the underskirt contained a padlock key, a small piece of a pencil, a pocket comb, a broken piece of a comb, a metal spoon, some buttons and a hook.

Blood was running in the gutter into a drain. There was some clotted blood just under the body, but there were no spots of blood elsewhere, although some of the blood had been trodden about near to where the body was lying. However, it was very dark at the time and Blackwell had examined the scene only by light of a policeman's lamp, so he couldn't be certain that there were no blood splashes on the wall. It was a very mild night and it was not raining at the time. There was no wet on Stride's clothing. Blackwell noted a flower pinned to her dress and her bonnet lying on the ground a few inches from the head.

There was a very clean six-inch incision in the neck, which began on the left side, two inches below the angle of the jaw, and almost in a direct line with it. It nearly severed the vessels on the left side, cut the windpipe completely in two, and terminated on the opposite side an inch below the angle of the right jaw, but without severing the vessels on that side. The windpipe being completely cut through, she was unable to make any sound, but, because the vessels on only one side had been severed, Stride would have bled to death comparatively slowly – probably a minute and a half, according to Dr Blackwell's estimate.

At the postmortem the doctors found that the stomach contained partly digested food, apparently consisting of cheese, potato and farinaceous (starchy) powder. When the body was undressed it was noted that there was a bluish discoloration over both shoulders, especially the right, and under the collarbone and in front of the chest. These marks were produced by pressure from two hands, but may not have been recent or connected with the crime. Dr Phillips believed that Stride had been seized by the shoulders and forced onto the ground, where her murderer, who was on her right side (i.e. facing the wall), had cut her throat from left to right. He thought that the murderer had 'a knowledge of where to cut the throat' and stated that he would not necessarily have been bloodstained, the commencement of the wound being away from the murderer, so the blood would have flowed away from him and into the gutter. However, Phillips's theory did not account for Stride's bloodstained hand and wrist, and he wasn't able to provide any explanation to account for it. Blackwell argued that the murderer had taken hold of the back of the check silk scarf Stride had worn around her neck – the bow or knot of which was turned to the left side and pulled tight – and used it to pull back the head. The action of grabbing the back of the scarf would have made Stride grasp the front of the scarf with her right hand, thus causing blood to get on her hand when her throat was cut. Dr Blackwell also observed that the cut exactly corresponded with the lower edge of the scarf, which was slightly frayed, as if cut by the edge of a sharp knife.

During his summing up at the inquest, Wynne Baxter pointed out that Stride had apparently made no noise, that there were no signs of a struggle, that she still gripped the cachous in her left hand, and that, from the appearance of the blood on the ground, the throat had been cut *after* she was actually on her back. From this he deduced that Stride had willingly been placed or had placed herself on her back on the ground, whereupon the murderer had quickly cut her throat.

Baxter's opinion must be treated with caution. It had been raining quite heavily and the ground was wet and muddy, so it is doubtful that Stride would have voluntarily lain down on the ground. It also didn't account for the tightened knot of the scarf, which showed that it had been used to pull back the head tightly enough for the edge to be frayed as the knife ran along it. And it didn't explain the bloodstained hand. What seems more probable is that Stride was standing, possibly facing the wall, when her killer grabbed the back of the scarf and pulled her head back, exposing the throat and at the same time causing Stride's knees to buckle. Instinctively she raised her hand to her throat, while the left hand involuntarily tightened around the cachous. She was quickly pulled to the ground, the knife simultaneously slicing the throat. The bruising on the shoulders, if not old, could have been caused by the man seen by Schwartz – who actually told *The Star* that he saw the man 'put his hand on her shoulder and push her back into the passage'. Wherever he pushed her, to the pavement or into the passage, he's likely to have grabbed her shoulders, where the bruising was found. It seems reasonable to argue, therefore, that the bruising probably proves that Stride was indeed the woman whom Schwartz saw assaulted, and it is further reasonable to suppose that the man who assaulted her was her murderer. But the body was not mutilated, which has given rise to the then (as now) common belief that the murderer was interrupted by the arrival of Louis Diemshutz, which seems likely given the testimony of Edward Spooner that blood was still flowing from the throat when he arrived there.

The problem is that the incident witnessed by Schwartz was timed by him at 12.45 a.m. Mrs Mortimer came to her door within five minutes, about 12.50 a.m., and saw nobody except Leon Goldstein hurrying past with his black bag. If Stride was already dead by 12.45 a.m., then not only is it unlikely that blood would still have been flowing from her throat when Spooner arrived at the scene at least fifteen minutes later, but it is also clear that the murderer would have had time to mutilate the body. Either the assault never happened (a suggestion for which we have no evidence), or the woman seen assaulted by Schwartz was not Stride (which seems statistically improbable and may not be supported by the bruising), or Schwartz's estimate of the time was wrong and he entered Berner Street after Mrs Mortimer had gone indoors.

In the course of the next few hours the police examined Dutfield's Yard, the club, the houses in the yard and the *Arbeter Fraint* offices. Twenty-eight people were searched and had their clothes examined. Nothing significant was found. Inspector Reid did make one curious statement at the inquest, which was reported without comment in *The Times* on 6 October 1888. He said that on searching the building in the yard he discovered that 'a door of a loft was found locked on the inside, and it was forced. The loft was searched, but no trace of the murderer could be found.' Nor, apparently, was there any trace of the person who bolted the door from the inside!

At 4.30 a.m. the body of Elizabeth Stride was removed to the mortuary. By 5 a.m. the police had concluded their initial enquiries. At 5.30 a.m. PC Collins washed away all traces of blood.

Eyewitness testimony is notoriously unreliable. People will give different accounts of the same event even when that event is closely observed. We should therefore expect significant variations in the descriptions of the man and woman seen together that night. *Prima facie*, the least reliable witnesses must be PC William Smith and James Brown, for both paid the couple scant attention and had no reason to remember them. Brown's times are estimates and he was further disadvantaged by the fact that the couple were standing in a particularly dark place and shrouded by shadows. A further problem in the evidence of James Brown is that he claimed to have seen Elizabeth Stride at the same time as Schwartz claimed to have seen her being assaulted. They obviously could not have seen Stride in two places at the same time and with different men, so one or the other was clearly mistaken about the time, though not necessarily by more than three or four minutes.

The police files do not mention Brown, from which we might infer that the police did not regard his evidence as important, although he was called to testify at the inquest, and Schwartz was not. The possibility exists that the couple seen by Brown could have been Edward Spooner and the woman he was with. On the other hand, William Marshall watched the couple for about ten minutes and Schwartz witnessed an assault that may have engraved the faces of the woman and her assailant on his memory. The descriptions of the man given by Marshall and Schwartz bear the strongest similarity. It is therefore possible – but by no means certain – that Israel Schwartz was the last person to see Stride alive and may have seen Jack the Ripper.

CHAPTER TEN

Catherine Eddowes

Catherine Eddowes, also known as Kate Kelly, was born on 14 April 1842 and found murdered on Sunday, 30 September 1888. She was born at Graisley Green, Wolverhampton, the daughter of a tinplate worker named George Eddowes, who worked at the Old Hall Works,[1] and his wife Catherine (née Evans),[2] a cook at the Peacock Hotel. In 1843 she went with her parents and brothers and sisters to London, where George Eddowes obtained employment with Perkins and Sharpus in Bell Court, off Canon Street in the City of London. The family lived at 4 Baden Place and later at 35 West Street, Bermondsey, and several more children were born. Eventually there would be twelve, although only ten survived.[3] Having spent most of her life pregnant, Catherine's mother died on 17 November 1855 at 7 Winter's Square, Bermondsey, aged 42. Two years later George Eddowes died, aged 49.

Two sisters, Harriet and Emma, had left home in 1851 and entered domestic service. Their elder sisters[4] moved across the river and the youngest Eddowes children[5] were admitted as orphans to Bermondsey Workhouse and went to the Industrial School to learn a trade. Catherine was found a position back in Wolverhampton, where, at her sister Emma's request, an aunt, Elizabeth Eddowes, managed to get her work. Aunt Elizabeth, her husband William and their three children lived at 50 Bilston Street, and Catherine worked as a tin plate stamper at the Old Hall Works.[6] She did not keep her job for long, apparently having been found stealing, and she ran away from Wolverhampton to live in Birmingham with an uncle, a one-time pugilist but now a boot- and shoemaker named Thomas Eddowes at the Brick Hill, Bagot Street. Catherine worked as a tray polisher, but after about four months she returned to Wolverhampton, where she stayed for nine months before she went back to Birmingham.

Here she met a man named Thomas Conway, who is sometimes mistakenly called an old man because he was described as a pensioner, but was in fact in his mid-twenties and drawing a small regimental pension. His real name appears to have been Thomas Quinn and he was born in County Mayo, Ireland, in 1837. In 1857 he joined the 1st Battalion, 18th Royal Irish Regiment, and served for four years, over two years in Bombay and Madras, from where he was invalided home suffering from heart disease brought on by the heat. Further illnesses led to his discharge in October 1861, when he was 24.

Catherine began living with Conway and had his initials 'TC' crudely tattooed in blue ink on her forearm. They made a living by selling chap-books[7] written by Conway, who also did labouring work when he could. They had a child,[8] then moved to London, taking good lodgings in Westminster, where a second child, Thomas, was born. Another son, Alfred George, was born in 1873. By now Catherine's heavy drinking had turned into alcoholism and this, combined with what was described as a fiery temperament, caused the relationship to deteriorate. She reportedly sometimes had black eyes and bruises,[9] from which it appears the rows were sometimes violent. Her daughter, Annie Philips, who also fell out with her mother because of her drinking, said that her father was a teetotaller and that her mother's drinking had caused rifts. She said that 'before they actually left each other she was never with him for twelve months at a time, but would go away for two or three months . . .'[10]

Eddowes's sister, Mrs Elizabeth Fisher, who lived at 33 Hackliffe Street, Greenwich, told a different story, claiming, 'My sister left Conway because he treated her badly. He did not drink regularly, but when he drew his pension they went out together, and it generally ended in his beating her . . .'[11] This may simply have been a case of Mrs Fisher's defending her sister, but on the other hand Thomas Conway was hardly likely to have admitted wife beating.

By 1880 the marriage had collapsed and Catherine left Thomas and their two sons, who were now living at 71 Lower George Street, Chelsea.

Catherine's sister, Eliza, who had married a butcher named James Gold in January 1859, had by now taken up with a man named Charles Frost and was living on the top floor of 6 Thrawl Street, Spitalfields. It is not known whether or not this encouraged Catherine to move to the East End, but by 1881 she was there, sometimes resorting to prostitution, but otherwise, like Elizabeth Stride, earning money working for the Jews in Brick Lane.

Eddowes moved into Cooney's, a lodging house at 55 Flower and Dean Street and there met John Kelly.[12] He jobbed around the markets, but for more than twelve years he had been employed fairly constantly by a fruit salesman named Lander. He was found to be a 'quiet and inoffensive' character with 'fine features' and 'sharp and intelligent eyes', but he was a sick man, having a kidney complaint and a bad cough.[13]

Eddowes was given a relatively good character by those who knew her. We know that in September 1881 she was charged at Thames Magistrates' Court with being drunk and disorderly, but she was discharged without a fine by the magistrate. Frederick William Wilkinson, the deputy of Cooney's Lodging House, where she and Kelly stayed, said that Eddowes 'was not often in drink and was a very jolly woman, often singing'. As far as he knew she was not in the habit of walking the streets; she was generally in the lodging between 9 p.m. and 10 p.m.; and he had never known or heard of her being intimate with anybody but John Kelly'.[14] John Kelly said he did not know that Eddowes ever went out for immoral purposes, but said that she sometimes drank to excess, though was not in the habit of doing so.[15] Her sister, Eliza Gold in Thrawl Street, said that Eddowes was of sober habits'.[16]

Every year, Eddowes and Kelly went to Kent for the hop-picking season. In the 1880s the acreage assigned to hops in Britain averaged 66,000 and hop picking gave a regular 'holiday' in the countryside to thousands of city dwellers. In 1890 it was estimated that between 50,000 and 60,000 people went to pick hops in a good season. In 1888, Kelly and Eddowes went to Hunton, a village about five miles from Maidstone in Kent, where once there were extensive plantations. They stopped off in Maidstone, where Eddowes purchased a pair of boots from Arthur Pash in the High Street and a jacket from Mr Edmetts's pawnbroker shop.

'We didn't get on any too well and started to hoof it home,' said Kelly. 'We came along in company with another man and woman who had worked in the same fields, but who parted with us to go to Cheltenham when we turned off towards London. The woman said to Kate, "I have got a pawn ticket for a flannel shirt. I wish you'd take it since you're going up to town. It is only for 9d, and it may fit your old man." So Kate took it and we trudged along. It was in at Jones's, Church-street, in the name of Emily Burrell. She put the ticket back in our box and we moved on. We did not have money enough to keep us going till we got to town, but we did get there and came straight to this house. Luck was dead against us . . . we were both done up for cash.'[17]

They turned back early instead of going hop picking, and reached London on the afternoon of Friday, 28 September. In London Kelly managed to earn 6d. Eddowes took 2d. and told Kelly to use the remaining 4d. to get a bed at Cooney's. Eddowes said that she would get a bed in the casual ward in Shoe Lane. In an interview given to the *East London Observer*, the superintendent of the casual ward said that Eddowes was well known there, but that this was the first occasion that she had stayed there for some time. Eddowes explained that she had been hopping in the country, but she said, ' "I have come back to earn the reward offered for the apprehension of the Whitechapel murderer. I think I know him." "Mind he doesn't murder you too," replied the superintendent jocularly. "Oh, no fear of that," was the remark made by Kate Eddowes as she left.'[18]

I have been unable to find any corroborative statement from John Kelly, to whom Eddowes would surely have confided that she knew or had any suspicions about the identity of Jack the Ripper, and I am inclined to believe that either she was joking or that this statement was invented by the casual ward superintendent or the journalist involved.

The next day, Saturday, 29 September, Eddowes returned to 55 Flower and Dean Street at 8 a.m., having been turned out of the casual ward because of some unspecified trouble there. They were 'done up for cash', as Kelly put it, but Kelly pawned his boots, Eddowes taking them to a broker named Smith, who had premises in Church Street, where she pledged them in the name of 'Jane Kelly', giving her address as 6 Dorset Street,[19] for 2s. 6d. With this money Kelly and Eddowes bought some food, tea and sugar, and between 10 a.m. and 11 a.m. they ate breakfast in the lodging house kitchen, being seen there by Wilkinson, the lodging house deputy.

By the afternoon, they were again without money and Eddowes said she would see if she could get some money from her daughter in Bermondsey. She parted with Kelly in Houndsditch at 2 p.m., promising to be back no later than 4 p.m. According to Kelly, he begged her to be back early because they had been talking about the Whitechapel murders, but, according to *The Star*, ' "Don't you fear for me," said she, "I'll take care of myself, and I shan't fall into his hands." "I never knew if she went to her daughter's at all," said Kelly. "I only wish to God she had, for we had lived together for a long while, and never had a quarrel." '[20]

Eddowes's statement is slightly odd because her daughter, Annie Philips, stated that her mother was such a persistent scrounger that she had kept her address from her, and we know that during 1887 she moved from

Bermondsey first to 15 Anchor Street, off the Southwark Park Road, and then to nearby Dilston Grove. If Eddowes was such a persistent scrounger, surely she would have tried to get money from Annie before and would have known that she no longer lived in Bermondsey. So did Eddowes sincerely intend to go to Bermondsey, or did she have reasons of her own for being away from Kelly for a few hours? Did she really have an idea about the identity of Jack the Ripper?

Catherine Eddowes left Kelly and went off goodness knows where. She was wearing a black jacket edged with imitation fur around the collar and cuffs, the pockets trimmed with black silk braid and imitation fur. Underneath was a brown linsey bodice, with a black velvet collar and brown metal buttons down the front. She wore a chintz skirt, buttoned at the waist, and on her head was a black straw bonnet trimmed with green and black velvet and black beads, which tied with strings under the chin. She had a pair of men's lace-up boots on her feet and a piece of red silk gauze as a scarf around her neck.

The next few hours of Catharine Eddowes's life are a blank. We know she got some money from somewhere and that she spent it drinking, because at 8.30 p.m. PC Louis Frederick Robinson, 31 City, noticed a small group of people gathered outside No. 29 Aldgate High Street. On going over he found the object of their interest to be Catharine Eddowes, drunk and crumpled in a heap on the pavement.[21] He asked if anybody knew her, but nobody did. He heaved her to her feet and leaned her against the shutters of No. 29, but she slipped sideways. PC Robinson then summoned the assistance of PC George Simmons, 959 City, and together they took Eddowes to the Bishopsgate Police Station.

On arriving at the police station, Eddowes was asked her name, but she said, 'Nothing.' She was placed in a cell by the station sergeant, James Byfield. At 8.50 p.m. PC Robinson looked in on her. She was asleep and smelled strongly of drink. At 9.45 p.m. PC George Henry Hutt, 968 City, took charge of the prisoners. He visited them several times during the course of the night.

At 12.55 a.m. Sergeant Byfield instructed PC Hutt to see if any of the prisoners were fit to be released. Eddowes was found to be sober and was brought from the cells. On being asked her name, she said, 'Mary Ann Kelly' and gave her address as 6 Fashion Street. She asked the time and Hutt answered, 'Too late for you to get any more drink.' She said, 'Well, what time is it?' Hutt replied, 'Just on one.' Thereupon she said, 'I shall get a fine hiding when I get home, then.' Hutt said, 'Serve you right; you have no right to get drunk.' At precisely 1 a.m. – just before Elizabeth Stride's body was discovered – Catharine Eddowes left the station. PC Hutt pushed open the swing-door leading to the passage, and said, 'This way, missus.' She passed along the passage to the outer door. Hutt said, 'Please, pull it to.' She replied, 'All right. Good night, old cock.' She pulled the door to within a foot of being closed, and Hutt saw her turn to the left towards Houndsditch, which led back to Aldgate High Street and was in the opposite direction to her quickest route back to Flower and Dean Street.

Houndsditch is a road that connects Bishopsgate with Aldgate, joining Aldgate at its junction with Fenchurch Street. Running almost parallel with Houndsditch was Duke Street, and parallel with Duke Street was Mitre Street. Between Duke Street and Mitre Street was a small square called Mitre Square. It was about 77 by 80 feet and the primary entrance was a road about 25–30 feet wide from Mitre Street. Two passages at the far end of the square also provided entrance. On the right was a short piece of roadway and pavement known as Church Passage, 85 feet long and 6 feet wide, leading into Duke Street. On the left – the northeastern side – an archway led into a passage 55 feet long and 5 feet wide, which led into a little open market called St James's Place. Just through the northeastern passage was a fire brigade station. No one on duty that night would see or hear anything unusual, and in St James's Place some street improvements were taking place and a watchman named James Blenkingsop was there. He saw nobody except a respectably dressed man who at about 1.30 a.m. asked him if he'd seen a man and a woman go through the passage.[22]

On entering Mitre Square from Mitre Street, one would see on the left a large warehouse fronting Mitre Street owned by Williams and Co. Next to it were two old houses, one unoccupied and the other (No. 3) occupied by a policeman named Richard Pearce and his wife. Next to the houses was another large warehouse, this one belonging to Kearley and Tonge[23] – near whose warehouse in Buck's Row Mary Nichols had been found murdered.

On the right were four shops facing Mitre Street, No. 9 on the corner belonging to a picture-frame maker, C Taylor and Co., which was empty at night. The rear of Taylor's shop and the unoccupied premises next door actually backed onto the square, and it was at the rear of the unoccupied premises that Eddowes's body would be found. A short passage led to the rear of the houses that completed the row. The area was poorly lit because the gas lamp was not functioning properly. Next to the passage was a yard and then a warehouse belonging to Horner and Co. At the far end was another large warehouse belonging to Kearley and Tonge.

Eddowes seems to have walked past Houndsditch and turned into the parallel street that became Duke Street. It was estimated that it would have taken Eddowes no longer than about eight minutes to reach Mitre Square, but it seems to have taken her over half an hour to get there. It is not known what she was doing during that time.

At 1.30 a.m. PC Edward Watkins, 881 City, reportedly a very conscientious officer and spoken of very highly by his inspector, passed through Mitre Square on his beat. The night after the murder he was accompanied on his beat by a journalist from *The Star* and explained,

'I was working left-handed last night . . . sometimes I go into Mitre-square through the Church Passage, but last night I entered from Mitre Street. It was just half-past one when I turned out of Aldgate and passed round the next corner into the square. At that time there was nothing unusual to be seen. I looked carefully in all the corners, as I always do, turning my lantern light in every direction. I am positive there was nothing wrong at that time.'[24]

At 1.35 a.m. Joseph Lawende, a commercial traveller in the cigarette trade who lived at 45 Norfolk Road, Dalston, and who had business premises in St Mary Axe, left the Imperial Club at 16–17 Duke Street in the company of Joseph Hyam Levy and Harry Harris. They had been delayed because it was raining and he glanced at the club clock as he went out and checked the time against his own watch. The distance between the club and Church Passage was about nine or ten yards. He walked a little ahead of his companions. Levy had at some time said that Mitre Square ought to be watched, and Lawende therefore gave a little more than passing notice to the couple standing at the entrance to the passage. The woman was standing facing the man and Lawende could not see her face, but she was wearing a black jacket and bonnet and he would later believe that they were the same as those worn by Eddowes. The man was taller than Eddowes, and he was wearing a cloth cap with a peak, but Lawende told the inquest that he doubted that he'd recognise the man again. He saw her put her hand on the man's chest, but in a friendly way, not as if to push him away. Lawende then walked past and did not look back.[25]

Joseph Hyam Levy, a butcher who lived at 1 Hutchinson Street, Aldgate, said he was on the opposite pavement to the couple, that he noticed them but they didn't seem suspicious in any way and he didn't take any notice of them.[26] There is an inescapable feeling that Levy was being evasive. Lawende said that Levy had said the Square ought to be watched and Levy told the coroner that on leaving the Imperial Club he had observed the couple and said to Harry Harris, 'I don't like going home by myself when I see these sorts of characters about. I'm off.' At the inquest he was asked if there was anything terrible in their appearance, and replied, 'I did not say that.' Asked if he felt frightened by the couple, he said, 'Not exactly.' It may simply have been that he didn't like being out late at night – he said he was usually at home at eleven – but equally it is difficult to escape the impression that he was being evasive. The couple were merely talking together on the opposite pavement, and were doing nothing to cause alarm, but Levy looked upon them with distaste and yet he claimed to have walked on by without taking any notice of them at all. Perhaps he was simply offended by what he supposed they were doing, but it is a pity it wasn't clarified at the inquest.

Harry Harris, a furniture dealer of Castle Street, Whitechapel, apparently saw nothing.

At the inquest on 5 October Mr Crawford, the city solicitor, intervened during the questioning of Lawende, saying, 'Unless the jury wish it I have a special reason why no further description of this man should be given now.' The jury accepted and no description was given. Curiously, the police had already issued a brief description of the man and it was published in numerous newspapers. *The Times* reported that 'He was described as of shabby appearance, about 30 years of age and 5ft 9ins. in height, of fair complexion, having a small fair moustache and a cap with a peak.' The Home Office files contain a fuller description. He was aged thirty, five foot seven or eight, of fair complexion, with a fair moustache, of medium build, wearing a pepper-and-salt-coloured loose jacket, a grey cloth cap with peak of the same colour, and a reddish handkerchief tied in a knot round the neck, and having the appearance of a sailor. Major Henry Smith, acting commissioner of the City of London Police, recalled Joseph Lawende in his autobiography, calling him 'a sort of hybrid German . . . a strange mixture, honest apparently, and intelligent also', who, Smith thought, spoke the truth, because he could not 'lead' him in any way, and who made it clear that he had only a short look at the man and wouldn't recognise him again. Smith believed the man and woman seen by Lawende were, 'without doubt, the murderer and his victim', and Smith described the man seen as 'young, about the middle height, with a small fair moustache, dressed in something like navy serge, and with a deerstalker's cap – that is, a cap with a peak both fore and aft.'[27]

There was something unusual going on after the murders of Elizabeth Stride and Catherine Eddowes. On 1 October the *Evening News* reported, 'The police are extraordinarily reticent with reference to the Mitre Square tragedy.' The *Yorkshire Post* on the same date said, 'The police apparently have strict orders to close all channels of information to members of the press.' Even the *New York Times* on 1 October was moved to complain of the police that 'they devote their entire energies to preventing the press from getting at the facts. They deny to reporters a sight of the scene or bodies, and give them no information whatever.'

Then, on 2 October, the *Manchester Guardian* reported,

The barrier of reticence which has been set up on all occasions when the representatives of the newspaper press have been brought into contact with the police authorities for the purpose of obtaining information for the use of the public has been suddenly withdrawn, and instead of the customary stereotyped negatives and disclaimers of the officials, there has ensued a marked disposition to afford all necessary facilities for the publication of details and an increased courtesy towards the members of the press concerned.

It is possible that the police opened channels of communication both to direct attention away from areas that they regarded as sensitive, and because they had those sensitive areas reasonably secured. This is suggested by the fact that the press, apart from *The Star*, never got close to Israel Schwartz and also by a very interesting statement in the *Evening News* of 9 October. Referring to Lawende and Levy, the paper says,

They [the police] have no doubt themselves that this was the murdered woman and her murderer. And on the first blush of it the fact is borne out by the police having taken exclusive care of Mr Joseph Levander [*sic*], to a certain extent having sequestrated him and having imposed a pledge on him of secrecy. They are paying all his expenses, and one if not two detectives are taking him about. One of the two detectives is Foster. Mr Henry Harris [*sic*], of the two gentlemen our representative interviewed, is the more communicative. He is of the opinion that neither Mr Levander nor Mr Levy saw anything more than he did,

and that was only the back of the man. Mr Joseph Levy is absolutely
obstinate and refuses to give the slightest information. He leaves one
to infer that he knows something, but he is afraid to be called on the
inquest. Hence he assumes a knowing air.

Five minutes after Lawende, Levy and Harris passed the man and
woman at the entrance to Church Passage, PC James Harvey passed down
Duke Street and went down Church Passage as far as the entrance of Mitre
Square. 'I saw no one. I heard no cry or noise,' he told the inquest. 'I was at
the end of Church Passage about 18 or 19 minutes to 2.' He was certain of
the time because he had checked the post office clock.

Constable James Harvey, 964 City, had gone on his beat that evening,
which took him down Mitre Street to Aldgate, where he checked the time
by the post office clock – it was almost 1.30 a.m. – and turned into Duke
Street. He reached Church Passage and walked to the end. He neither saw
nor heard anything suspicious and returned on his beat back down Duke
Street towards Aldgate.

PC Watkins completed the circuit of his beat, and having met no one
during his rounds, nor heard any sounds except the echo of his own
footsteps, he found himself back at Mitre Square at about 1.45 a.m. He
stopped at the entrance to the square to look up and down Mitre Street, then
turned into the square, passing a shop owned by a picture frame maker
named Taylor. At the rear of the shop he flashed his light into a corner – and
there, by the gates leading into a factory yard, lay Catherine Eddowes. He
later told a journalist for *The Star*: 'I can tell you it didn't take me a moment
to see that the Whitechapel murderer had been our way . . . she was ripped
up like a pig in the market . . . I have been in the force a long while, but I
never saw such a sight.'[28] He went straight across the road to get help from
George Morris, the watchman at Kearley and Tonge's wholesale grocery.

Morris[29] had begun work at 7 p.m. and had been busy cleaning the offices
and checking the warehouse. He was sweeping a corridor when PC Watkins
knocked at his door, which was slightly ajar. Morris opened it wide. Watkins
said, 'For God's sake mate come to my assistance.' Morris said, 'Stop till I
get my lamp,' and the two men then went across to the body, Morris asking
what the matter was and Watkins telling him. Morris shone his light on the
body, then ran up Mitre Street into Aldgate, blowing his whistle. PC
Harvey had now come down Duke Street to Aldgate, heard the whistle and
saw Morris with a lamp. He asked Morris what was wrong, Morris said that

a woman had been ripped up, and PC Harvey, now joined by PC Holland, 814 City, who had been across the street, went to Mitre Square. Morris returned to his premises, while Harvey and Holland viewed the body, PC Holland leaving almost immediately to fetch Dr George William Sequeira at 34 Jewry Street, Aldgate, who arrived at 1.45 a.m.

According to Major Henry Smith,

In August, 1888, when I was desperately keen to lay my hands on the murderer, I made such arrangements as I thought would insure success. I put nearly a third of the force into plain clothes, with instructions to do everything which, under ordinary circumstances, a constable should not do. It was subversive of discipline; but I had them well supervised by senior officers. The weather was lovely, and I have little doubt they thoroughly enjoyed themselves, sitting on door-steps, smoking their pipes, hanging about public-houses, and gossiping with all and sundry.

Given that the accepted sequence of murders began at the end of August 1888, Smith's claim to have been desperately anxious during that month to catch the killer has been taken by some as an example of his unreliability, but there is confirmation in a report written to the Home Office in October 1888 in which Inspector James McWilliam stated,

acting upon stringent orders issued by the Commissioner with a view to preventing if possible a repetition of the murders which had previously been committed in Whitechapel and to keep close observation upon all Prostitutes frequenting public-houses and walking the streets, extra men in plain clothes have been employed by this department since August last to patrol the Eastern portion of the City.[30]

Three of those plain-clothes policemen were Detective Constables Halse, Marriott and Outram and they were in the area of the murder searching the passages of houses. They heard about the murder at 1.55 a.m. and at once headed for Mitre Square.[31] About the same time as Halse and his colleagues heard about the murder, Inspector Edward Collard, on duty at Bishopsgate Police Station, received the same news. He at once sent telegraphs to his superiors, which brought them to Mitre Square in quick succession, sent a constable to fetch the police surgeon, Dr Frederick

Gordon Brown, and then headed for Mitre Square himself. He timed his arrival at 2.03 a.m. and he took immediate steps to have the neighbourhood searched. Dr Gordon Brown arrived a few minutes later, followed by Superintendent McWilliam, chief of the Detective Department, and Superintendent Foster. McWilliam sent Halse and his colleagues off to search in all directions, both in the streets and in the lodging houses, and several men were stopped and searched. Halse went to Middlesex Street, then to Wentworth Street, and returned to Mitre Square via Goulston Street. He saw nothing unusual. Collard searched Mitre Square for any trace of bloody footprints but found none, and searched the backs of the empty adjoining houses, but nothing was found.[32]

Dr Gordon Brown reached Mitre Square about 2.18 a.m. Major Henry Smith recalled in his memoirs,

> The night of Saturday, September 29, found me tossing about in my bed at Cloak Lane Station, close to the river and adjoining Southwark Bridge. There was a railway goods depot in front, and a furrier's premises behind my rooms; the lane was causewayed, heavy vans were going constantly in and out, and the sickening smell from the furrier's skins was always present. You could not open the windows, and to sleep was an impossibility. Suddenly the bell at my head rang violently. 'What is it?' I asked, putting my ear to tube.
>
> 'Another murder, sir, this time in the City.' Jumping up, I was dressed and in the street in a couple of minutes. A hansom – to me a detestable vehicle – was at the door, and into it I jumped, as time was of the utmost consequence. This invention of the devil claims to be safe. It is neither safe nor pleasant. In winter you are frozen; in summer you are broiled. When the glass is let down your hat is generally smashed, your fingers caught between the doors, or half your front teeth loosened. Licensed to carry two, it did not take me long to discover that a 15-stone Superintendent inside with me, and three detectives hanging on behind, added neither to its comfort nor to its safety.
>
> Although we rolled like a 'seventy-four' in a gale, we got to our destination – Mitre Square – without an upset, where I found a small group of my men standing round the mutilated remains of a woman.

Catherine Eddowes had been attacked with calculated ferocity. She was on her back, her head resting on a coal hole and turned towards the left shoulder, arms by the side of the body, both palms upwards, the fingers slightly bent. The hands and arms were bronzed as if by sunburning. The left hand had a small bruise, recent and red, on the back between the thumb and first finger. Near the right hand there was a thimble. At the back of the head was Eddowes's black straw bonnet, the back lying in a pool of blood, which had run from the neck. There was a quantity of clotted blood on the pavement on the left side of the neck, round the shoulder and upper part of arm. Several buttons were found in the clotted blood after the body was removed. The left leg was extended straight down, in a line with the body, and the right leg was bent at the thigh and knee. The throat was cut, the wound extending about six or seven inches from the left ear to about three inches below the lobe of the right ear. The sterno–cleido mastoid muscle had been cut through, the cricoid cartilage below the vocal cords was severed through the middle and the large vessels on the left side of the neck had been cut through to the bone, the knife marking the intervertebral cartilage. The left carotid artery had been cut, causing almost instantaneous death. On the right side the sheath of the vessels was just open, the carotid artery suffering a pinhole opening, and the internal jugular vein was open to the extent of an inch and a half but was not cut through.

After death, the murderer had mutilated the abdomen and face of poor Catherine Eddowes. The intestines had been pulled out and placed over the right shoulder, and a piece of the intestines about two feet long had been completely detached and placed between the body and left arm. Dr Gordon Brown thought the murderer had done this deliberately. There had not been any appreciable bleeding from the vessels to get on the hands of the murderer. The murderer had carefully removed the left kidney and the uterus was cut away with the exception of a small portion, both organs being absent, presumably taken away by the murderer.

The police surgeon believed the mutilation of the face was deliberate. It included nicks to the lower eyelids and two inverted Vs on the cheeks below the eyes. The murderer had taken the time to do this and Gordon Brown therefore didn't think he had been disturbed. The lobe and auricle of the right ear was cut obliquely through and when the body was undressed at the mortuary the severed portion of the ear fell from the clothing. The tip of the nose was completely cut off.

There were no indications that Eddowes had recently had sex.

The medical opinion was that Eddowes had been murdered very recently – Dr Gordon Brown thought no longer than 40 minutes before his arrival (i.e. after 1.40 a.m.) – and that she had been on the ground when the fatal wound was inflicted. All the injuries were probably done in a hurry but could not have been inflicted in less than five minutes, and a sharp pointed knife at least six inches long had been used. The surgeon thought the murderer possessed 'a good deal of knowledge as to the position of the organs in the abdominal cavity and the way of removing them' and he felt that it 'would require a great deal of knowledge as to its position' to have removed the kidney, as it is covered by a membrane and is easily overlooked. A butcher would have possessed the necessary knowledge.

Dr George Bagster Phillips, who was invited to attend the autopsy, apparently agreed with Gordon Brown. A report by Detective Chief Inspector Donald Swanson states that Drs Gordon Brown and Phillips were of the opinion that

> the mutilation so far gave no evidence of anatomical knowledge in the sense that it evidenced the hand of a qualified surgeon, so that the Police could narrow their enquiries into certain classes of persons. On the other hand as in the Metropolitan Police cases, the medical evidence shewed that the murder could have been committed by a person who had been a hunter, a butcher, a slaughterman, as well as a student in surgery or a properly qualified surgeon.[33]

Dr Phillips said that the parts removed would have had no use for surgical purposes and he could not suggest a reason why they had been taken away, and Dr Gordon Brown observed that the murderer would not have been covered in blood.[34]

On the left side of the body were three small black buttons generally used for women's boots, a small metal button, a common metal thimble and a small mustard tin containing two pawn tickets, one for John Kelly's boots and the other for the flannel shirt given to Eddowes by Emily Burrell when they parted company on the road back from hop picking in Kent. A Sergeant Jones picked them up and gave them to Inspector Collard.

Eddowes had an assortment of possessions on her and these were itemised in some detail by the police. Apart from her clothes, already described – black cloth jacket, brown linsey bodice, chintz skirt and black straw bonnet, silk scarf and men's boots – she wore a grey petticoat, a very old green alpaca skirt and a very old blue skirt, white calico chemise, and a man's white front-buttoned vest. Scattered about her person were

1 large white handkerchief
2 unbleached calico pockets with tape strings
1 blue-striped bed ticking pocket
1 white cotton pocket handkerchief with a red and white bird's-eye border
1 pair of brown ribbed stockings, the feet mended with white
12 pieces of white rag
1 piece of white coarse linen
1 piece of blue and white skirting
2 small blue bed ticking bags
2 short black clay pipes
1 tin box containing tea
1 tin box containing sugar
1 piece of flannel
6 pieces of soap
1 small-tooth comb
1 white-handled table knife and a metal teaspoon
1 red leather cigarette case with white metal fittings
1 empty tin matchbox
1 piece of red flannel containing pins and needles
1 ball of hemp
1 piece of old white apron

The ambulance arrived and the body was being placed aboard it when Detective Daniel Halse returned to the square. Halse, accompanied by Drs Sequeira and Gordon Brown and Inspector Collard, accompanied the body to the mortuary, where they witnessed it stripped by Mr Davis, the mortuary keeper. Halse noticed that a piece of Eddowes's apron had been torn away.

At 2.20 a.m. PC Alfred Long, 254A, who had been temporarily drafted to assist H Division, had been passing through Goulston Street on his beat. He noticed nothing to excite his attention. At 2.55 a.m., when his beat brought him back through Goulston Street, he noticed a piece of apron on the floor of the common stairs leading to 118–119 Goulston Street Buildings. The apron was stained and one corner of it was wet with blood. It was also smeared with what appeared to be faecal matter. Although he had by now heard of the murder in Mitre Square, he did not associate the piece of apron with that crime, but, perhaps with the case of Martha Tabram in mind, he thought instead that a murder had been committed on the stairs or corridors within Goulston Street Buildings. Long at once called PC 190H, who was on an adjoining beat, then searched the staircase leading to the building and six or seven internal staircases, but could find no trace of blood or any recent footmarks. He did not make any enquiry of the residents in the tenements, but his attention was drawn to some writing on the wall above where the apron lay and he noted down the wording in his pocket book. The writing was in white chalk on black bricks, which formed a kind of dado, the bricks above being white. There were three lines of writing in a good schoolchild's round hand, the capital letters being about three-quarters of an inch high and the others in proportion. PC Long did not know whether the writing was recent, but according to Detective Halse it had the appearance of being so, because he thought it would have been rubbed out by the people passing in and out if it had been done long before.

Long said the writing read, 'The Jews are the men that will not be blamed for nothing.' Halse said his wording was, 'The Juwes are not the men who will be blamed for nothing.'

The question of the spelling was to come up at the inquest later, when the city solicitor, Mr Crawford, questioned PC Long about the wording and the spelling of the word 'Jews', and PC Long was insistent that the wording was, 'The Jews are the men that will not be blamed for nothing' – although he conceded that the spelling of 'Jews' may have been 'Juwes'.

PC Long left PC 190H to make sure nobody left or entered the building, then went to the police station, arriving there between 3.05 and 3.10 a.m., where he reported his discoveries to the duty inspector. The inspector immediately returned with Long to Goulston Street and inspected the writing, then they went to Leman Street. The inspector duly handed the apron to Dr Phillips.[35]

Meanwhile, Superintendent Arnold of the Metropolitan Police visited Goulston Street and viewed the writing on the wall. He became apprehensive that, in the light of the strong anti-Jewish feeling in the area following the Leather Apron scare, the writing could cause a riot. He decided the best thing to do was to wash it off and he left an inspector in charge with a sponge to await instructions from Sir Charles Warren.[36]

Detective Halse and Major Smith had by now viewed Eddowes's body in the mortuary and together gone to Mitre Square, where they learned about the discovery of the piece of apron. Accompanied by Detective Sergeant Lawley and Detective Constable Hunt,[37] they went to Leman Street Station and from there Halse, Lawley and Hunt went to Goulston Street, saw the spot where the apron had been found and viewed the writing on the wall. Halse remained by the writing and Lawley and Hunt returned to Mitre Square.

At 3.45 a.m., Superintendent McWilliam arrived at the detectives' office and spoke to Station Sergeant Izzard, then telegraphed Scotland Yard informing the Metropolitan Police of the murder. McWilliam then went with DS Downes to Bishopsgate Police Station and from there to Mitre Square. Major Smith, Superintendent Foster, Inspector Collard and several detective officers, including DS Lawley and DC Hunt, were there, and they informed McWilliam about the apron and the writing on the wall. McWilliam ordered that the latter be photographed and told the policemen to go and search all the residences in the building. Enquiries were made at every door of every tenement, but nothing was learned.

McWilliam went to the mortuary in Golden Lane, saw the piece of apron and compared it with the one Eddowes had been wearing. The piece was of the same material and had been torn off. The two pieces matched perfectly. There was *and is* no doubt that Jack the Ripper passed through Goulston Street on his way from Mitre Square, and had taken brief refuge in the entrance to the Goulston Street buildings to wipe his hands and his knife, discarding the piece of apron. Whether or not he also took the time to write a message on the wall is debated.

McWilliam left the mortuary and went back to the detectives' office and had a description of the murdered woman and her clothing telegraphed to the divisions and Metropolitan Police.

At about 5 a.m., PC Long returned to his duty in Goulston Street, at which time Sir Charles Warren arrived at Leman Street Police Station and spoke to Superintendent Arnold about the two murders. Arnold expressed his concerns about the writing on the wall, and Warren decided that he should shoulder the responsibility for obliterating potential evidence and went to Goulston Street, arriving there as it began to get light. Soon, Middlesex Street and the surrounding streets, home of the famous Petticoat Lane Sunday Market, would be full of Jewish vendors and Gentile purchasers from all parts of London. Seeing that the writing was on the jamb of the open archway and visible to anybody in the street – and could not be covered up, since any covering would merely be torn off – Warren shared Arnold's apprehensions. There were several police around the spot when he arrived, both Metropolitan and City, and a discussion took place about what best to do, and whether the writing could be left covered up for an hour until it could be photographed. Warren decided that it would be best to remove the writing, so he took a duplicate and ordered the writing washed off. This happened at about 5.30 a.m. and was witnessed by PC Long, who later told the inquest that he had heard no objections.[38] Warren then went to Mitre Square and viewed the murder scene before heading off to the City Police HQ to explain why the writing on the wall had been obliterated.[39]

One of the news agencies would in due course state that the police attached a great deal of importance to the spelling of the word 'Jews' because 'Juwes' was the way the East End Polish Jews spelled the word. It said it was considered by the police to be 'a strong indication that the crime was committed by one of the numerous foreigners by whom the East End is infested'.[40] There was indeed discussion about the meaning of the word, notably among the Home Office mandarins who were beginning to express doubts that they were receiving the complete story from the City Police.[41] But the suggestion that 'Juwes' was the East End immigrant Jews' spelling was quickly refuted, *The Star* sending a journalist to the offices of the *Jewish Chronicle*, where he was informed by a staff member whose father was a Polish Jew that the Yiddish word for Jew was 'Yiddin'.[42] And, given the hostility of *The Star* to Sir Charles Warren, it rather surprisingly supported his decision to erase the writing, albeit grudgingly, saying that he 'acted with blundering haste and military rashness', but that 'his motive seems to have been just a trifle more creditable than usual'.

Major Henry Smith referred to the erasure in his autobiography:

Sir Charles Warren was instantly apprised of this discovery, and, coming down himself, ordered the words to be wiped out, alleging as his reason for so doing that he feared a rising against the Jews. This was, I thought, a fatal mistake, as Superintendent McWilliam plainly told Sir Charles when he called about seven o'clock, accompanied by Superintendent Arnold. It is just possible the words, if photographed, might have afforded an important clue. The assassin had evidently wiped his hands with the piece of apron. In Dorset Street, with extraordinary audacity, he washed them at a sink up a close, not more than six yards from the street. I arrived there in time to see the blood-stained water.[43]

Smith's colourful story about the bloodstained water in Dorset Street has no known factual foundation, but years later, on 7 January 1905, the *City Press* reported,

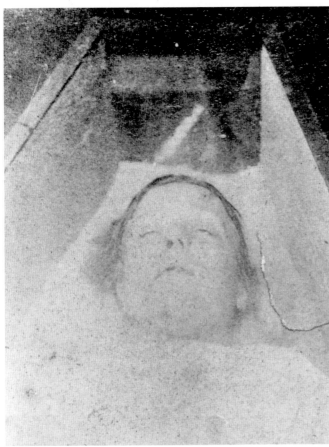

VICTIMS

Left: Mary Ann Nichols.

Below left: Annie Chapman, about the time of her marriage.

Below: Annie Chapman.

Above: Elizabeth Stride.

Right and below: Catherine Eddowes.

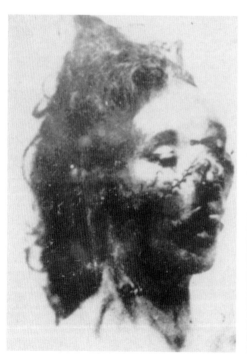

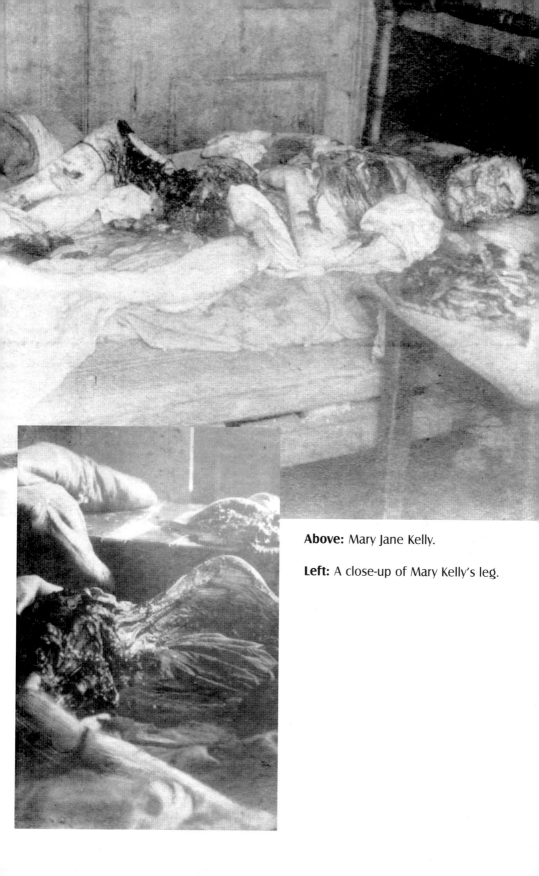

Above: Mary Jane Kelly.

Left: A close-up of Mary Kelly's leg.

MURDER SCENES & RELATED LOCATIONS

Top: Buck's Row – Mary Ann Nichols was found dead by the imposing Victorian Board School on the left of the street.

Above left: Hanbury Street, scene of the murder of Annie Chapman. © Ray Luff

Above right: The yard where Nichols's body was discovered.

Left: Hanbury Street – a contemporary illustration.

THE SCENE ON SUNDAY IN BERNER STREET

Above left: Berner Street – the wheel on the wall shows the Socialists' club, where Elizabeth Stride was murdered.

Above right: A contemporary newspaper showing the crowds gathered in Berner Street after the murder of Elizabeth Stride.

Left: Mitre Square, scene of the murder of Catherine Eddowes.

Below: Diagram and sketches relating to the Mitre Square murder, prepared for the inquest.

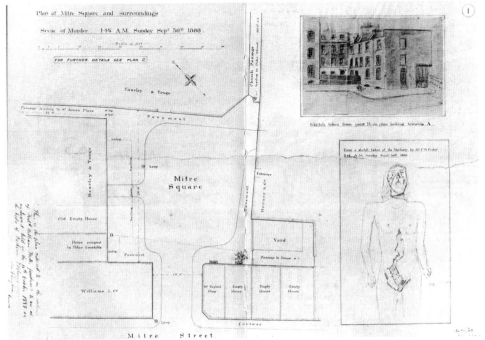

Above: Goulston Street, where a piece of Eddowes's apron was dropped. © Paul Begg

Below: Dorset Street, scene of the murder of Mary Jane Kelly.

Dorset Street, at the Commercial Street end – on the left-hand side on the corner is the Britannia, known locally as the Ringers, and in the distance on the right is the Ten Bells, where Kelly is last known to have been drinking.

Above: Entrance to Miller's Court, off Dorset Street, scene of Mary Jane Kelly's murder. To the left is John McCarthy's shop and to the right the 'shed'.

Right: The rear of Miller's Court, showing the windows of Kelly's room.

The apron belonging to the woman who was murdered in Mitre Square was thrown under a staircase in a common lodging house in Dorset Street, and someone – presumably the murderer – had written on the wall above it, 'The Jewes are not the people that will be blamed for nothing.'[44]

It is significant that the newspaper, like Major Smith, wrote 'Dorset Street'. Perhaps in both cases Goulston Street was meant, and that the sink of bloodstained water was in the latter. But, wherever it was, it is exceptionally doubtful that Major Smith was at any time close enough to the murderer to have seen bloodstained water gurgling down a plug.

In 1975 a BBC television series called *The Ripper File* and a later best-selling book by the late Stephen Knight argued that the word 'Juwes' featured at the very heart of high-level Masonic rituals, and alleged that Sir Charles Warren, a devoted and high-ranking Mason, had the writing erased because it implicated the Freemasons and perhaps showed that Jack the Ripper was a Mason. The theory argued that 'Juwes' was the collective name for Jubelo, Jubela and Jubelum, who murdered Hiram Abiff, the architect of Solomon's Temple. However, the collective name for this band of thugs in Masonic ritual, both in the United Kingdom and in the United States, was 'Ruffians'. Apparently 'Juwes' is not and never has been a Masonic word, nor has 'Juwes' or any word approximating to it ever appeared in Masonic ritual. But, whether they had or not, the inherent weakness in this argument is that the erasure did not prevent the spelling of the word becoming known, nor would it have stopped the significance of the word being revealed to the press by any disgruntled high-level Mason. The erasure therefore achieved none of the objectives of which Warren is accused.[45]

CHAPTER ELEVEN

The Matter of Rewards

The populace clamoured without in the yard
For Matthews, Home Sec., to be feathered and tarred.[1]

In response to public feeling at the time of the murders of Mary Nichols and Annie Chapman, rewards had been offered by Samuel Montagu,[2] the MP for Whitechapel, and by the Whitechapel Vigilance Committee, which had put posters around the district that read,

> Finding that, in spite of murders being committed in our midst, our police force are still inadequate to discover the author or authors of the late atrocities, we, the undersigned, have formed ourselves into a committee and intend offering a substantial reward to anyone, citizen or otherwise, who shall give such information that will bring the murderer or murderers to justice.[3]

Neither the government nor the Metropolitan Police had offered a reward – this policy had been abandoned in 1884 – and they had both come in for considerable criticism. Within hours of the discovery of Catherine Eddowes's body within the jurisdiction of the City of London Police, Sir James Fraser, the commissioner, offered a reward of £500:

> Whereas at 1.45 a.m. on Sunday, the 30th of September last, a Woman, name unknown, was found brutally murdered in Mitre-square, Aldgate, in this City, a Reward of £500 will be paid by the Commissioner of Police of the City of London to any person (other than a person belonging to a police force in the United Kingdom) who shall give such information as shall lead to the discovery and conviction of the murderer or murderers.

Information to be given to the Inspector of the Detective Department, 26, Old Jewry, or at any police-station.

James Fraser, Colonel, Commissioner.
City of London Police Office.
26, Old Jewry, 1 Oct., 1888.

It was soon after announced that the lord mayor would likewise offer on behalf of the Corporation of London an additional reward of £500. These announcements served to refocus and increase the criticism of the home secretary, Henry Matthews, and Metropolitan Police commissioner, Sir Charles Warren. *The Star* continued its merciless hounding of Warren: 'The police, of course, are helpless. We expect nothing of them. The metropolitan force is rotten to the core . . .'[4] And the *Observer* rightly remarked unfavourably on Warren's massively ill-timed instruction that the police should keep an eye on drunken people so that the publicans who served them with drink could be identified and prosecuted. Some newspapers even voiced very real fears of revolution, one widely published press agency report warning, 'With each fresh murder in the Whitechapel series public alarm has been accentuated and unless something can soon be done to restore confidence in the detective powers of the police panic will be the result.'[5]

Perhaps it was proximity to the events that prevented the London newspapers from exercising rational thought. It took traditional Northern common sense in the shape of the *Yorkshire Post* to voice a defence of the police, but the voice was too small to be heard over the baying of the press in London:

> The police then are at fault, because the circumstances transgress their experience. The criminal annals of this country offer no parallel to these hideous and apparently purposeless Whitechapel murders, and with no precedent to guide them, perhaps it is not surprising that the police are at fault.[6]

It was the home secretary, Henry Matthews, however, who increasingly came in for criticism over his failure to sanction a reward. As early as the Buck's Row murder there had been expectations that a reward would be offered, it being believed that the crimes were the work of one of the gangs who have been under the observation of the police for some time past, and it is believed that, with the prospect of a reward and a free pardon, some of them might be persuaded to turn Queen's evidence, when some startling revelations might be expected.[7]

When no offer of a reward was forthcoming *The Star* accused the government and the police of criminal folly and urged an immediate offer of £500 'for the discovery of the Man Monster or of his accomplices, if accomplices there be'.[8]

The foreman of the jury at the conclusion of the inquest into the death of Mary Nichols raised the subject of rewards, saying, '. . . if it had been a rich person that was murdered there would have been a reward of £1,000 offered; but as it was a poor unfortunate hardly any notice was taken'. He was firmly rebuked by the coroner, who stated that the government had long since abandoned the practice of offering rewards.[9] This contributed to a sense of general indignation picked up by *The Star*, which reported, 'Whitechapel was furious at the refusal to grant a reward, and was very significantly saying that if the murders had happened in Mayfair we should have had rewards fast enough.'[10]

It was a complaint echoed by George Lusk and Joseph Aarons of the Whitechapel Vigilance Committee who wrote a letter to the *Daily Telegraph* in which they remarked that the offer of a substantial reward would 'convince the poor and humble residents of our East-end that the government authorities are as much anxious to avenge the blood of these unfortunate victims as they were the assassination of Lord Cavendish and Mr Burke.'[11]

The feeling of one law for 'them' and another for 'us' was growing, and it contributed greatly to the sense of dissatisfaction felt by the increasingly rebellious poorer classes. It was a contributing factor to the unease being experienced by the new middle classes and caused the upper classes to ponder quietly on the possibility of revolution. It also caused the Ripper crimes to be remembered in the public mind for years to come.

The reaction against Matthews had from the first been caustic:

. . . Mr. Matthews, a feeble mountebank, who would pose and simper over the brink of a volcano.[12]

At the least the offer of a reward would have done something to allay panic by showing that Mr Matthews and the police were awake to their responsibilities. It will be difficult to convince anyone of that now.[13]

We have had enough of Mr Home Secretary Matthews, who knows nothing, has heard nothing, and does not intend to do anything in matters concerning which he ought to be fully informed, and prepared to act with energy and despatch. It is high time that this helpless Minister should be promoted out of the way of some more competent man . . .[14]

If Mr Matthews had read his *Star* he would have been told in time that Whitechapel was furious at the refusal to grant a reward, and was very significantly saying that if the murders had happened in Mayfair we should have had rewards fast enough.[15]

The Tory *Vanity Fair* saw the very real prospect that Matthews's continued presence in office might upset the stability of the government. It complained of his 'utter want of tact and common sense' and 'blundering', and concluded that he had 'been tried and found utterly wanting, and sooner or later he must go. And if he go not soon his Ministerial presence will undoubtedly imperil the existence of the Government.'

The *Daily Telegraph*, then regarded as 'the voice of the people', was the thorn in Matthews's side that *The Star* was in Warren's. It claimed that Matthews was deaf to the entreaties of the public: 'Mr Secretary Matthews . . . would make an admirable president of an asylum for deaf mutes, or consulting physician to a hospital for incurables, but . . . is decidedly out of place at the Home Office.'[16]

All this *before* the so-called 'Double Event'! After the Double Event the criticism intensified. The *Manchester Guardian* rather rudely observed:

It is rather hard upon Mr Matthews that he, who has never proposed legislation for the reform of the City, nor indeed done anything by personal initiation of a remarkably useful character, should now be placed in this difficulty by that unreformed Corporation he has done his best to protect. But if the £500 reward offered by the City for the apprehension of the Whitechapel murderer should be claimed, it may go hard with Mr Matthews in regard to his refusal.[17]

The *Daily Telegraph* in its leader column commented:

The fact can be no longer disguised that the Home Secretary now in office is a source of miserable weakness and discredit to the present

Administration. In the House of Commons he has been nothing more nor less than a fantastic failure. In the provinces he is scarcely known even by name; and when the provincials do become aware of him it is only to mistrust him, and to express disrespectful and indignant astonishment that a Government, otherwise so capable and so popular, should drag with it a dead weight of so much vacillation, so much ineptitude, and so many frankly naive confessions of crass ignorance concerning things of which the most common-place Home Secretary ought to be fully cognisant. That Mr Matthews does not know, that he is not aware, that he does not remember, or that he has not heard of things which to any ordinarily intelligent man should be as manifest as the sun at noonday, have been Session after Session stereotyped replies of the Home Secretary to the simplest questions. Very likely Mr Matthews is in many respects an excellent gentleman; but it is high time for him to go and excel somewhere else and in some other department than the Home Office.

Matthews had won the marginal seat of East Birmingham in 1886 and, as an inexperienced political newcomer, was surprised at his appointment as home secretary by Lord Salisbury. It has been said that it was in response to Queen Victoria's insistence that Matthews have office.[18] Matthews possessed charm and wit and a fine legal brain, but was exceedingly unpopular and 'the member of the Govt. whom everyone wishes to turn out!' as A J Balfour put it[19] – and 'he did more, perhaps, to render the government unpopular than any other minister'.[20] Lord Salisbury was very well aware of Matthews's shortcomings. He admitted to Queen Victoria, 'Mr Matthews has certainly not been as successful as was hoped. There is an innocence of the ways of the world which no one could have expected to find in a criminal lawyer of sixty.'[21] He had flirted with various ways of removing him from office, but the government had a very small majority and Lord Salisbury couldn't risk Matthews's marginal East Birmingham seat in a by-election. Salisbury and the other big political players of the party had therefore reluctantly decided that Matthews had to stay *in situ* until the general election, when he could be quietly moved from the political arena with a title in appreciation of his services.[22] This explains why Salisbury refused to accept Matthews's resignation over the Cass case in 1887 and why the mounting criticism of Matthews no doubt caused considerable alarm in the corridors of power, for had he tendered his resignation, and had public feeling forced Lord Salisbury to accept it, then Jack the Ripper could have been instrumental in bringing the government down. Even Queen Victoria recognised and was concerned by such a possibility – she was not passionate about the Liberals – and wrote to Salisbury on 28 October 1888 that Matthews's 'general want of sympathy with the feelings of the *people* are doing the *Government* harm'.[23] Few if any other serial killings have been so politically dangerous, and this must be taken as an indicator of how seriously the crimes would have been taken within government.

The reward question brought Matthews into serious conflict again with Sir Charles Warren, especially when the latter, who was perhaps more attuned to public feeling than the former, appeared to make an about-face on the question of a reward. The official files reveal a tedious but historically instructive exchange of correspondence in which each man politely bickered and manoeuvred to avoid being blamed by the other.

On 10 September Samuel Montagu, MP for Whitechapel, had written to the commissioner,

> Feeling keenly the slur cast upon my constabulary by the recent murders & the non discovery of the criminal or criminals I hereby authorise you to print & distribute at my expense posters offering £100 reward for the discovery & conviction of the murderer or murderers, which reward I will pay.[24]

Alexander Carmichael Bruce, senior assistant commissioner, had passed this over to Henry Matthews requesting the earliest possible instructions and stressing 'Mr Montagu is anxious that no time should be lost'.[25] The document passed through the hands of several officials and Charles Troup, junior clerk at the Home Office, noted at the bottom of the document that the Home Office had ceased to sanction rewards, observing,

> The HO rule is against offering rewards: and, even if exceptions to the rule are allowed, I think this case is the last in which it should be done.
>
> It is generally agreed that the Whitechapel murderer has no accomplices who could betray him.
>
> Any person, other than an accomplice, who possesses information, would be certain, in the present state of public feeling, to give it without prospect of reward.
>
> On the other hand the offer of a reward would be almost certain to produce false information.

Even if the case were a proper one for a reward, the M.P. for the district is not the proper person to offer it. Of course SofS. cannot forbid Mr. Montagu to publish the offer, but he can forbid Police to give their authority to it.

?Say that [i.e. the clerk suggests the officials ask the following], had the case been considered a proper one for the offer of a reward, SofS. would at once have offered one on behalf of the Govt., but the practice of offering rewards was discontinued some years ago because experience showed that in their general effect such offers produce more harm than good, and the SofS. thinks the present case one in which there is special risk that the offer of a reward might hinder rather than promote the ends of justice.[26]

One of the complaints levelled at Matthews was that 'he was disinclined to deal with police matters personally, and left overmuch to the discretion of subordinates, who were in the habit of issuing orders to Warren in Matthews's name but without his express command.'[27] There is no particular evidence that this was the case in this instance, but it will be seen that Matthews was not opposed to rewards or convinced by the arguments against them, and someone more in touch with the feeling of the local community might have recognised that, although a reward might have done no material good, it would have been a valuable palliative to public feeling. As it was, Charles Troup's suggested reply was sanctioned and E Leigh Pemberton accordingly wrote on 13 September on Henry Matthews's behalf to Sir Charles Warren.[28] In turn Carmichael Bruce wrote to Samuel Montagu on Warren's behalf on 15 September informing him of the decision. For reasons not entirely clear, Montagu, who claimed not to have received the letter until 17 September, was very displeased, and wrote a stiff letter to Sir Charles Warren in which he expressed the opinion that the Home Office decision was 'not in accord with the general feeling on the subject'. He claimed that Sir Charles Warren's tardy response had meant that news of the offer had already got into the press and would have to be honoured in the event that it brought information that led to the capture of the murderer.[29] Warren, justifiably irritated that Montagu should have held him responsible for delays that were not his, fired off an angry letter in reply (which in the event he thought better of and never sent):

I can only regret that you should have thought fit to impute delay to me in a matter entirely outside my control and duties. It was a matter lying entirely between you and the S. of State and if you required an immediate reply you could have telegraphed the Sec of State yourself.[30]

Warren's anger was justified. The decision had not been his, the delay had not been his and the delay had not caused Montagu's offer to get into the press. Montagu was working to his own agenda and using Warren, none too cleverly, as his whipping boy: Montagu had visited Chief Inspector John West at Leman Street Police Station on Monday, 10 September, and made his offer of a reward, and Inspector West had promised to pass it across to Scotland Yard. On Tuesday, 11 September, Inspector West visited Montagu and informed him that the proposal had been submitted to the home secretary and – according to Montagu – said he thought it would be favourably received. That afternoon the news of Montagu's offer was published in *The Star*[31] – not the following day, as Montagu told Warren – and, since news of the offer was probably leaked by Montagu himself, he seems to have acted on the opinion of Inspector West, assuming he acted on the opinion of anyone at all, and Warren later ventured, probably rightly, 'that one of the principal objects of the Reward offered by Mr Montagu was to shew to the world that the Jews were desirous of having the Hanbury Street murder cleared up, and thus to direct from them the very strong feeling which was then growing up'.[32] If this was true, and it has a ring of truth about it, then it was important to Montagu to have the offer reported, irrespective of whether it was accepted by the police or not.

This was an irritating episode for Warren, and tedious to describe, but it illustrates how both he and Matthews were manoeuvred into positions from which they would later find it impossible to escape.

The point of all this as it would develop the next month is that Charles Troup's advice had been taken by Matthews without consultation with Sir Charles Warren. Warren would later say that he had therefore assumed that the reply was one of policy on which his opinion was not required and that had it been required he would have been approached to give his opinions in writing. As it was, Warren had meetings with E Leigh Pemberton on 14 and 17 September and on 18 and 19 September with J S Sandars,[33] and on neither occasion did he intimate that he in any way favoured the offer of a reward. On 3 October Matthews had 'prolonged interviews'[34] about the murders, among them a meeting with Warren who said that a reward 'would serve as "eye-wash" for the public and nothing else', and that as rewards had already been offered by the City authorities there was no reason to make an additional offer.[35]

On 5 October Sir Charles Warren appeared to do a complete about-face and advocated offering a very substantial reward indeed of £5,000. Evelyn Ruggles Brise seems to have recognised the importance of Warren's *volte face* or perhaps he simply overreacted to it, and he immediately informed Henry Matthews. As it turned out the timing was inconvenient for Matthews, and Brise received a small flea in his ear as a consequence. There exists among the papers of J S Sandars the copy of a letter written to Evelyn Ruggles Brise by Henry Matthews that is very revealing:

> I am sure you meant well and were acting in what you believed to be my interests tonight, but I think on consideration you will see that your action was very embarrassing. Your messenger arrived here after 8 o'clock and sent in with your box a message that he had to catch a train at 9. I had to leave my guests in the middle of dinner, – to read all the papers you sent and to scribble an answer in about 20 or 25 minutes. In as much as you asked me to reverse a decision twice publicly announced a decision about which I had had a long conference with Sir C W day before yesterday and [Assistant Commissioner] Mr Monro yesterday with the result that the latter approved and that the former did not disapprove – I am not using too strong a word when I say that the appeal under such circumstances of hurry was at least embarrassing. I have never myself shared to the full extent the HO prejudice against rewards; nor have I thought Harcourt's reasoning on the subject at all conclusive. I am disposed to regret now that in the first instance I did not sacrifice to popular feeling and offer a considerable reward. But in as much as I did yield to the official view and refuse to make an offer and subsequently repeated the refusal, I feel that my hands are tied. Unhappily the first HO letter (to Montagu M.P. I think) was so worded as to make a change of front still more difficult. Sir C W on Wednesday told me he thought a reward was of no practical use; – that it would serve as 'eye-wash' for the public and nothing else; – and that after the Lord Mayor's offer it was unnecessary. He appears, on your report, to have modified his opinion to a considerable extent. He certainly the day before yesterday did not say a word to urge the offer of a reward upon

me – although I distinctly asked him what was his view. He gave not the slightest hint of the enormous reward that you suggest, quoting him.

I feel very strongly that to make such an offer now, after what has passed, so far from conciliating public opinion (and that is admittedly the only reason for the step) would cover me with ridicule and contempt – as having given way to popular pressure – with nothing to justify or call for change, which would itself be the strongest condemnation of my previous action.

There must be done something publicly. Why cannot the police apply to the magistrates for search warrants against all the houses in which they think it probable or possible that the murderer may be concealed? If warrants are refused, that would be a new circumstance. I agree with Sir C W that he cannot act on Sir J Ellis' suggestion and search houses illegally, with all the fearful consequences that might follow from resistance. Again, the police can legally search all probable hiding places without warrant – if they can get the consent of the landlord or a person having control of the premises. A house to house search (of suspicious places) with the consent of the landlord, or under warrant, would be helpful – and would give some satisfaction to the public. If it resulted in nothing (as it probably would) there would be some sort of ground for offering a reward.

You say nothing about the suggestion of my offering a free pardon to anyone not the actual perpetrator of the murders. I could do that more easily, and with less discredit, than would follow from offering a reward. Has Sir C W considered the effect of such an offer? There may be persons who conceal and harbour the murderer and who are therefore afraid to speak – I mentioned this to Pemberton, but not to Warren, on Wednesday.

Your letter does not at all enable me to grasp how and why Sir C W has changed his mind since Wednesday. I imagine that you yourself have been Out of Town and perhaps hardly know of what has taken place, and what the HO have written. At any rate your letter shows no indication of your having grasped that I have taken a certain line on grounds of principle and reason and that I shall incur more public censure by abandoning it without some very good reason, than by adhering to it. If I could without discredit satisfy public feeling I would be very glad to do so. But I have already and irretrievably incurred the odium of resisting a popular outcry for a useless measure and I should only make matters worse by yielding to it without some reason that could be defended in argument.

If Sir C W felt able to write to me officially that the police had exhausted every means at their command – that they had not only failed, but had no expectation of succeeding in tracing the murderer – and that therefore, as a last resort, he felt bound to suggest recourse to an expedient which experience proves to be unsatisfactory and even mischievous, namely the offer of a reward – I might act on such a letter – provided I might make it public. But I think it is too soon *for the credit of the police* to take such a step yet. They do not seem to have exhausted the resources of detective energy. The fear of another murder tomorrow or Sunday is really too shadowy to be grounds for action.

I have marked this letter 'private' because I intend it for you alone. Use its contents discreetly in talking with Sir C W. I could hardly act on a letter from him nakedly recommending a large reward without more. For his own credit and that of the force it is imperative that some visible evidence of effort – of ingenuity – of vigorous and intelligent exertion – should be on record. Anybody can offer a reward and it is the first idea of ignorant people. But more is expected of the CID. Sir C W will not save himself, or put himself right with the public, by merely suggesting that. This conversation with you looks as if he wanted to hedge at my expense.

I wish you had come here instead of writing – I should have preferred an interview to this long letter written late at night and very incoherently.

6 October

I have thought it best to write a note myself to Warren upon his of the 4th. Will you keep a copy and send it to him at once.

Sir Charles Strand's note. He is a barrister – was a solicitor – and has intelligence and quickness. If he can be useful, I think he is trustworthy. Anderson was to return today.

I return Sir C W's letter – keep it.

Yours etc.

H.M.[36]

The irony is that neither Matthews nor Warren was ever wholly opposed to the government's offering a reward. The decision not to offer rewards had been taken in 1884 by Sir W V Harcourt, the home secretary in Gladstone's Liberal government, and Matthews had simply followed precedent, presumably in the belief that he was supported by Warren. Although he was inclined to regret his decision and was willing to offer a reward, there was no way he could do so without losing face. Matthews's nice touch was to suggest that he would agree to offer a reward if Warren publicly declared the utter failure of the police to capture Jack the Ripper. He must have known that Warren would not – and could not – have admitted to that, even if it were true, but it firmly put the ball in Warren's court.

Warren did what he could to lob the ball back, writing on 6 October to say that from the outset his 'opinion had not been asked on this subject' and that he had accordingly assumed the decision not to offer a reward to be a matter of government policy on which his comments were not required. However, he pointed out that circumstances could change: 'if other murders of a similar nature take place shortly, and I see no reason to suppose that they will not, the omission of the offer of a reward on the part of the Government may exercise a very serious effect upon the stability of the Government itself'.

Warren was a fairly astute man who was also in a better position to gauge public feeling than was Matthews, and he clearly recognised that further murders would provoke a serious public reaction against the government. Anticipating Parliamentary questions and possibly Matthews's downfall, he realised that Matthews would publicly state that he had acted with the agreement of the commissioner – which Matthews had not initially done – and that Warren would be tarred with the same brush. He therefore wrote to Matthews that

in matters of this kind the Commissioner of Police ought to be fully consulted, unless the Secretary of State is quite prepared to state in Parliament that he acted entirely on his own views without consulting the Commissioner . . . I write this now in order that if it comes to a question in Parliament you may be enabled to say that from a Police point of view the Commissioner had no strong opinion as to the necessity for the offer of a reward at the time you authorised the letter to be written to Mr Montagu; but at the same time I wish it to be understood that as a question of policy, with which you may perhaps think I have nothing to do, I certainly think a reward should have been offered.[37]

It was a deft return that left Matthews floundering a little and there followed a tedious volley of tactfully worded letters. Matthews replied on 7 October, saying that Warren had simply forwarded Montagu's letter without any recommendation or suggestion and that it had therefore been reasonable for Matthews to have assumed that Warren saw no reason to depart from the rule, and he observed too that the meetings with E Leigh Pemberton and with Matthews himself had been for the express purpose of eliciting Warren's opinions more fully and effectually than if Warren had been consulted by letter. The full force of his reply was couched in a gentle acknowledgement that there were exceptions to every rule. It asked if Warren would confirm that the police and the CID had exhausted all the means of discovering the criminal and now had no reasonable prospect of catching him. It further asked whether there was any information that made him think there was someone who could be induced by the prospect of a reward to give information, or whether there was any special circumstance that distinguished the Whitechapel crimes from those where rewards had been rejected and which would make a reward acceptable in this case. Warren hit the ball straight back. He said that he could find only one example of a Scotland Yard opinion being that rewards did no good, that Scotland Yard's opinion always appeared to have been that rewards may possibly be of little use but could do no harm and may be productive, and that was certainly the opinion of himself, Robert Anderson and Frederick Williamson. He said that the police investigation had hardly commenced and that there was no information indicating an accomplice – an interesting observation given the Schwartz story (and perhaps additional confirmation that Pipeman had been identified). But his killer shot was that the murders were unique and not in the same category as the other crimes on which the 1884 ruling was based.

Warren had the upper hand and his letter was widely circulated among the Whitehall mandarins. Matthews's response, which barely cleared the net, was a time-wasting request on 17 October that Warren provide a list of cases that were inconsistent with the evidence on which the 1884 ruling was based.

The argument would probably have continued until the question of rewards was raised in Parliament, as it was in November 1888, but by that time there would have been another murder and Warren would have resigned.

CHAPTER TWELVE

Dear Boss

'To imagine a man deliberately murdering
and mutilating women, and then confessing
the deed on a postcard, is to turn
Mr W. S. Gilbert loose upon the Whitechapel murders at once.'[1]

On Thursday, 27 September 1888, the Central News received a letter. It had been posted that day and the envelope bore the address, 'The Boss, Central News Office, London City', and a postmark showing that it had been posted in 'London EC'. According to the date on the letter itself, it had been written on 25 September 1888.

Dear Boss.

I keep on hearing the police have caught me but they wont fix me just yet. I have laughed when they look so clever and talk about being on the right track.

That joke about Leather Apron gave me real fits. I am down on whores and I shant quit ripping them till I do get buckled. Grand work the last job was, I gave the lady no time to squeal. How can they catch me now, I love my work and want to start again. You will soon hear of me with my funny little games. I saved some of the proper red stuff in a ginger beer bottle over the last job to write with but it went thick like glue and I cant use it. Red ink is fit enough I hope ha. ha. The next job I do I shall clip the ladys ears off and send to the police officers just for jolly wouldnt you. Keep this letter back till I do a bit more work then give it out straight. My knife's so nice and sharp I want to get to work right away if I get a chance, good luck.

197

Yours truly

Jack the Ripper

Dont mind me giving the trade name.

Wasnt good enough to post this before I got all the red ink off my
hands curse it. No luck yet. They say I'm a doctor now ha ha.

The Central News treated the letter as a joke and did nothing with it for
two days, but on 29 September it was forwarded to Scotland Yard with a
short covering note: 'The editor presents his compliments to Mr
Williamson & begs to inform him the enclosed was sent the Central News
two days ago, & was treated as a joke.'[2]

On 1 October the Central News received a second communication, a
postcard addressed 'Central News Office, London City EC' and smeared
with what looked like blood. It read, seemingly reflecting knowledge only
the murderer could have known,

I wasn't codding dear old Boss when I gave you the tip. You'll hear
about saucy Jacky's work tomorrow double event this time number
one squealed a bit couldnt finish straight off. had no time to get ears
for police, thanks for keeping last letter back till I got to work again.

Jack the Ripper.[3]

The Central News very quickly released the text of the letter to the press
and the *Daily Telegraph* on the morning of 1 October quoted the letter in full
along with a statement by the agency:

The agency says: The whole of this extraordinary epistle is written in
red ink in a free, bold, clerkly hand. It was of course treated as the work
of a practical joker, but it is singular to note that the latest murders
have been committed within a few days of the receipt of the letter;
that, apparently, in the case of his last victim the murderer made an
attempt to cut off the ears; and that he actually did mutilate the face in
a manner which he has never before attempted. The letter is now in
the hands of the Scotland-yard authorities.[4]

That afternoon *The Star* quoted the content of the postcard.

Scotland Yard meanwhile had a poster showing facsimiles of the letter and postcard printed and circulated to the newspapers and divisional police stations and pasted on walls, and on 4 October the *Daily Telegraph* published both, remarking,

> The letter and the post-card were handed to the Scotland-yard authorities, and, although they do not profess to attach any great importance to them, still they thought it well to have *facsimiles* prepared, and to send them to the Press, in the possibility that the handwriting may be recognised by some one . . . The writer is probably an American or an Englishman, who has mixed with our cousins on the other side of the Atlantic. 'Boss,' 'Fix me,' 'Shan't quit,' and 'Right away' are American forms of expression.[5]

The Star was critical of the *Daily Telegraph*:

> By the way, why does our friend, the D.T., print facsimiles of the ghastly but very silly letters from 'Jack the Ripper'? We were offered them by the 'Central News,' and declined to print them. They were clearly written in red pencil, not in blood, the obvious reason being that the writer was one of those foolish but bad people who delight in an unholy notoriety. Now, the murderer is not a man of this kind. His own love of publicity is tempered by a very peculiar and remarkable desire for privacy and by a singular ability to secure what he wants. Nor is there any proof of any pre-knowledge of the Mitre-square crimes, beyond the prediction that they were going to happen, which anybody might have made. The reference to ear-clipping may be a curious coincidence, but there is nothing in the posting of the letter on Sunday. Thousands of Londoners had details of the crimes supplied in the Sunday papers.[6]

The next day, 5 October, the Central News received yet another communication. Thomas J Bulling at the agency did not send the letter to Chief Constable Frederick Williamson, but simply transcribed it:

Dear Mr Williamson,

At 5 minutes to 9 o'clock tonight we received the following letter the envelope of which I enclose by which you will see it is in the same handwriting as the previous communications.

5 Oct. 1888

Dear Friend,

In the name of God hear me I swear I did not kill the female whose body was found at Whitehall. If she was an honest woman I will hunt down and destroy her murderer. If she was a whore God will bless the hand that slew her, for the women of Moab and Midian shall die and their blood shall mingle with the dust.[7] *I never harm any others or the Divine power that protects and helps me in my grand work would quit for ever. Do as I do and the light of glory shall shine upon you. I must get to work tomorrow treble event this time yes yes three must be ripped. will send you a bit of face by post I promise this dear old Boss. The police now reckon my work a practical joke well well Jacky's a very practical joker ha ha Keep this back till three are wiped out and you can show the cold meat.*

Yours truly

Jack the Ripper

Yours truly
T. J. Bulling
A. F. Williamson Esqr.

It is not known how seriously the police took this third communication, or whether they took it seriously at all, and it was hardly remarked on in the press. *The Star* alone commented that the Central News Agency – while claiming that people who saw the Goulston Street graffito thought it was in the same hand as the letter and postcard (which *The Star* called 'a discredited rumour') – had also claimed receipt of a third communication 'which it is deemed prudent to withhold for the present'.[8]

That the handwriting may have been thought to match that of the Goulston Street graffito was perhaps not as discredited as *The Star* imagined. There exists in a file of commissioners' letters a short correspondence dated 10 October 1888 from Sir Charles Warren to Godfrey Lushington:

Thanks for memo of Mr Troup. We will look into matter at once. It is rather a difficult matter. I do not know whether the P.O. can tell in what letter boxes the letter of Jack the Ripper is posted.

At present I think the whole thing a hoax but of course we are bound to try & ascertain the writer in any case.

If I cannot send you the style of writing on the wall tonight I will send it tomorrow morning.

The word 'style' in this letter suggests that there may have been some question about whether the handwriting of the graffito and the letter matched, although the promised letter from Warren the following day discussed the idiom, Warren saying that it did not appear to him to be English, French or German, but probably Irish or Spanish or Italian.

Whether these communications were from the murderer or not, the name 'Jack the Ripper' was a stroke of genius that fired the imagination and ensured that the unknown murderer would join the pantheon of the greatest villains of fact and faction. As two contemporary observers noted:

The fame of 'Jack the Ripper' spread far and wide. It is probable that nothing would have been heard of this cognomen had it not been for the indiscretion of Scotland Yard in publishing a facsimile of sensational letters sent to a news agency, which thereby gave to these interesting documents the stamp of official authority.[9]

The fact that the self-postcard-proclaimed assassin sent his imitation blood-besmeared communication to the Central News people opens up a wide field for theory. How many among you, my dear readers, would have hit upon the idea of 'the Central News' as a receptacle for your confidence? You might have sent your joke to the *Telegraph*, the *Times*, any morning or any evening paper, but I will lay long odds that it would never have occurred to communicate with a Press agency. Curious, is it not, that this maniac makes his communication to an agency which serves the entire Press? It is an idea which might occur to a Pressman perhaps; and even then it would probably only occur to someone connected with the editorial department of a newspaper, someone who knew what the Central News was, and the place it filled in the business of news supply. This proceeding on Jack's part betrays an inner knowledge of the newspaper world which is certainly surprising. Everything therefore points to the fact that the jokist is professionally connected with the Press. And if he is telling the truth and not fooling us, then we are brought face to face with the fact that the Whitechapel murders have been committed by a practical journalist – perhaps by a real live editor! Which is absurd, and at that I think I will leave it.[10]

In later years senior policemen not only echoed Sir Charles Warren's conclusion that the letter and postcard were fakes: they also seem to have thought they had a shrewd idea who the faker was. In 1910 Robert Anderson wrote in a serialisation of his memoirs that would be published in book form later in the year, 'I will only add here that the "Jack-the-Ripper" letter which is preserved in the Police Museum at New Scotland Yard is the creation of an enterprising London journalist.' A footnote added, 'I should almost be tempted to disclose the identity of the murderer and of the pressman who wrote the letter above referred to . . .'[11]

It has been suggested that the identity of the journalist was not certain because, had it been, there would have been no reason for Anderson to have feared a libel action, but a great many things are sometimes 'known' but not provable.

At the time Anderson's autobiography put him in the news, a correspondent to the *East London Observer*, who signed himself 'A Wide-Awake East-Ender', wrote on 11 April 1910 that the letter and postcard were the work of 'an enterprising local penny-a-liner', the word 'enterprising' echoing Anderson:

SIR, In your last issue you amusingly allude to the fact that during the awful period of the Whitechapel murders the police not only fooled themselves, but were fooled by the reporters. This is quite true, and Sir Robert Anderson, who is just now so much before the public eye, may like to know that the postcards, apparently written with blood, received by the H Division of Police, were the work of an enterprising local penny-a-liner, who used his fore-knowledge to 'line' the reports of the receipt of these strange missives. At the time the daily papers seized with avidity any 'murder' news, and as the postcards were received by the police the truth of the reports could not be denied. It never occurred to the intelligent CID that they could have traced the authorship of both postcards and reports. They know better now. The same journalistic operator was probably responsible for the blood-smeared jacket found in the garden of a house in the Mile End-road, once rented by a proprietor of your paper and now in the possession of the Mile End Guardians as a scattered home. Quite a respectable sum of money was made by the 'lining' to the then daily and evening papers of this ghastly 'find.'

In 1914 Sir Melville Macnaghten, who had joined the Metropolitan Police in June 1889 as assistant chief constable, CID – Anderson's second-in-command and eventual successor – published his own memoirs, *The Days of My Years*. He didn't claim to know the identity of the letter writer, just said that he 'had shrewd suspicions as to the actual author' and that 'I have always thought I could discern the stained forefinger of the journalist' in the Ripper correspondence.[12] Macnaghten's statement is curious because, as Anderson's assistant, he would, it might be expected, have known what Anderson knew and shared Anderson's certainty, yet on the identity of the letter writer, as with their respective views about the identity of Jack the Ripper, their ideas were not identical. Anderson knew; Macnaghten only thought he knew.

An anonymous contributor to *Crime and Detection* in August 1966 recalled,

In 1931, working on an outline for a life of William Palmer, the Rugeley poisoner, a friend mentioned an ex-jockey who was living not far from my home (then Henley-on-Thames). Through several introductions, to reach this character, I finally arrived at a man named Best, an ex-journalist. He was spry and very clear-minded, though well past 70. He knew the jockey, and arranged a meeting at the house of a friend in a small place called Culham, on the Oxon–Berks border.

I met the ex-jockey, a vigorous old gentleman of, he claimed, 95. Known as Jack, or John, Faulkener, he had ridden a number of races for William Palmer, and his fund of reminiscences was large.

Returning homewards with me, Best discussed murders, the Whitechapel murders in particular. With much amplifying detail he talked of his days as a penny-a-liner on *The Star* newspaper. As a freelance he had covered the Whitechapel murders from the discovery of the woman, Tabram. He claimed that he, and a provincial colleague, were responsible for *all* the 'Ripper' letters, to 'keep the business alive . . . in those days it was far easier to get details, and facts from the police, than today.' Best did not mind me having these facts so many years later, and said a close reading of the *Star* of the time might be informative, and that an experienced graphologist with an open mind would be able to find in the original letters 'numerous earmarks' of an experienced journalist at work; the pen used was called a 'Waverley Nib' and was deliberately battered to achieve an impression of semi-illiteracy and 'National School' training! Best scoffed at the notion that the 'Ripper' had written a single word about his crimes.

Some years before this the late Edgar Wallace mentioned that in his reporting days the better informed Fleet Street men were satisfied that a newspaperman was 'behind' the letters.'[13]

Again, we need to remember that Best wasn't necessarily talking about the 'Dear Boss' letter and 'Saucy Jacky' postcard, and neither letter reflects a battered pen nib to give the impression of the 'semi–illiteracy and "National School" training' – although it does fit the Lusk letter, to be discussed shortly. The reference to *The Star* is very interesting, however, since that newspaper seems to have been determinedly against anyone being taken in by the correspondence, dismissing the author as a 'practical joker' as early as 1 October 1888. The reference to *The Star* is also interesting because it has elsewhere been suggested that one of its journalists concocted the Ripper correspondence.

The *Daily Democrat* of Woodland, California, on 5 December 1890 published the following story under the heading, 'An Idle Story':

CHICAGO, December 4th. – A special from San Francisco was published this morning saying that while Harry Dam, a New York and San Francisco journalist, was at work on the London *Star* he concocted the 'Jack the Ripper' letters which created such a sensation in London in connection with the Whitechapel murders. In reply to the inquiry as to the truth of the story, T. P. O'Connor, M.P., who was editor of *The Star* at the time, says he never heard of the story before and doesn't believe a word of it.[14]

Harry Dam is an interesting possibility, given that he was an American and the correspondence was noted for its Americanisms, and T P O'Connor, the founder and owner of *The Star*, was not likely to have admitted that one of his journalists wrote the letters that were widely regarded as having misled the police and given the name 'Jack the Ripper' to the world, especially if that same journalist had brought the newspaper perilously close to a libel action. Dam was accused of having done so by Lincoln Springfield, who alleged that Dam was responsible for the Leather Apron scare. According to Springfield,

> The office legend about Dam was that he had hitherto been private secretary to the Governor of California, and had amassed thousands of dollars by the illicit sale of pardons to murderers, felons, and other unfortunates whose lives or freedom were in the keeping of the Governor as the controller of the States prisons. At all events, Dam had arrived hastily and quietly from the States, had joined us on *The Star*, and had, like the rest of us, been put upon the job of solving the mystery of the Whitechapel murders.[15]

It is not known whether there is any truth in this story, but a strange little report in another California newspaper suggests that there may have been. In November 1890 the *Fresno Weekly Republican* reported,

> The intimation comes from Sacramento that the state is on the eve of a wholesale prison delivery, by the enlargement of the heart of the governor. Is Waterman about to emulate the example of Stoneman or does Boruck propose to profit by the light shed in his office by the illustrious Harry Dam?[16]

It helps to make sense of this story to know that 'Stoneman' is George Stoneman, the fifteenth governor of California, who was a supporter of prison reform and parole and who in the last few weeks of his term granted 260 pardons and commuted 146 death sentences. The article suggests, therefore, that the same largesse was about to be bestowed by George Whitney Waterman, the seventeenth governor of California (who was vice-governor until his predecessor, Stoneman's successor, died in office). However, it suggests that the generosity may have less to do with Waterman's views on penal reform than with his private secretary, Marcus

D Boruck, emulating Harry Dam, presumably Stoneman's secretary, which would suggest that the story told by Lincoln Springfield is true.

Henry Jackson Wells Dam (1856–1906) was born in San Francisco and moved to London, where on 27 October 1892 he married an actress named Dorothy Dorr, and had two children, both born in London – Colby Dorr Dam (born 7 August 1894) and Loring Dam (born 8 May 1896). Dam went on to enjoy considerable success as a librettist, his most famous and successful play being a musical farce called *The Shop Girl*, which opened at the Gaiety Theatre on 24 November 1894, broke all records for the theatre and ran for 546 performances.[17] Among the cast was George Grossmith Jnr, the son of a Savoyard and co-author of *The Diary of a Nobody*. Another play, *The White Silk Dress*, enjoyed 132 performances and *The Red Mouse* was adapted in 1917 into a silent movie and renamed *Her Silent Sacrifice*. He continued as a journalist and is particularly noted today for a historically interesting article he published in *The Strand Magazine* in March 1897 called THE NEW TELEGRAPHY. AN INTERVIEW WITH SIGNOR G. MARCONI. Dam and his wife returned to America in the early 1900s, and Dam died in Cuba in 1906.

Dorothy Dorr, who had appeared on the London stage in *Lights of Home* in 1892 – co-written (with Robert Buchanan[18]) by George R Sims – and *Lost Paradise* in 1892–3, appeared in a succession of Broadway plays from 1902 to 1910 and appeared in a few movies between 1924 and 1925 – *Picking Peaches* (1924), *The Hollywood Kid* (1924), the Harold Lloyd eight-reeler *Girl Shy* (1924), *Legend of Hollywood* (1924) and *Quicker'n Lightnin'* (1925).

Perhaps the most extraordinary comment of all about the correspondence was published in the Radical MP and pro-Parnellite Henry Labouchere's magazine *Truth* on 11 October 1888:

> On the doctrine of possibilities, it is long odds against the murderer having written the 'Jack the Ripper' letters. He may have, and so may many thousands of others. But there is a coincidence in respect to these letters to which attention has not yet been drawn. The handwriting is remarkably like that of the forgeries which the *Times* published, and which they ascribed to Mr Parnell and to Mr Egan. I do not go so far as to suggest that the *Times* forger is the Whitechapel murderer, although this, of course is possible; but it may be that the forger takes pride in his work, and wishes to keep his hand in.[19]

The story refers to letters supposedly written by the Irish MP Charles Stewart Parnell and published by *The Times* in a series of articles intended to discredit him. The letters were forgeries, the creation of a onetime editor, journalist and friend of Parnell named Richard Pigott, and there is no doubt that the forger's identity was known to Parnell and was probably known to Labouchere by 11 October 1888. Indeed, it has even been suggested that Robert Anderson may have met Pigott in Paris on 4 October and perhaps obtained from him a confession to the authorship of the letters. It is tempting to wonder whether Labouchere was therefore hinting at the author of 'Dear Boss', but it is probably useful to remember that the mystery of Jack the Ripper provides rich seams from which to mine tempting speculation.

Another policeman thought the writer was a journalist and thought he knew who it was. Detective Chief Inspector John George Littlechild, after he retired from the Metropolitan Police, became a private enquiry agent and is chiefly remembered today as the man hired by Charles Russell to gather evidence against Oscar Wilde on behalf of the Marquess of Queensbury. On 23 September 1913 Littlechild replied to a letter written to him by the journalist George R Sims. Littlechild wrote, regarding the Central News journalist Thomas J Bulling,

With regard to the term 'Jack the Ripper' it was generally believed at the Yard that Tom Bullen [*sic*] of the Central News was the originator, but it is probable Moore, who was his chief, was the inventor. It was a smart piece of journalistic work. No journalist of my time got such privileges from Scotland Yard as Bullen. Mr James Munro when Assistant Commissioner, and afterwards Commissioner, relied on his integrity. Poor Bullen occasionally took too much to drink, and I fail to see how he could help it knocking about so many hours and seeking favours from so many people to procure copy. One night when Bullen had taken a 'few too many' he got early information of the death of Prince Bismarck and instead of going to the office to report it sent a laconic telegram 'Bloody Bismarck is dead'. On this I believe Mr Charles Moore fired him out.

Despite what Littlechild says about the privileges allotted Bulling by Scotland Yard, Central News did not enjoy an altogether savoury reputation. In 1888 there were two primary news agencies serving the national and provincial press: the Press Association and Central News. The Press Association had been formed by a group of provincial newspaper bosses just prior to the passing of the Telegraph Act in 1868 (which nationalised the private telegraph companies who had hitherto monopolised news distribution), and, following an alliance with Paul Julius de Reuter's London-based international-news agency, soon dominated the business. Central News was older, having been created as Central Press in 1863 by William Saunders, the owner of several provincial newspapers, and his brother-in-law Edward Spender. It changed its name to the Central News Agency in 1870–1, and immediately entered bitter competition for business with the Press Association – competition that by 1887 and throughout 1888 had become a furious cost-cutting battle. The Central News had quickly developed a reputation for being fast, delivering scoops and providing stories that were overall more lively and colourful, but, as George Scott relates in his book *Reporter Anonymous: The Story of the Press Association*, some of Central News's practices were highly questionable: 'During the 1880s there was a suspicious series of incidents that caused the Press Association to fear there was an element of corruption, possibly bribery, at work.' Central News also developed a reputation for supplying unreliable stories, its overseas correspondents in particular being accused of inventing stories, or, as Scott put it, 'using their imaginations when the facts were unexciting'. As early as 1883, Central News had been accused of inventing a story about a plot to murder the new governor-general of Canada,[20] and as late as 1895 *The Times* printed a highly critical article accusing Central News of embellishments in its reports.[21]

It may be doing Central News a gross injustice to suggest from this that either Bulling or Moore was responsible for coining the name 'Jack the Ripper' and it isn't immediately clear what advantage there would have been for them to have done so. That the letter and postcard were sent to a news agency was itself immediately suspicious, as George R Sims observed at the time, and neither Bulling nor Moore could have expected to go unsuspected as the perpetrator of a hoax – and, according to Littlechild, neither did. Clearly there wasn't a unanimous opinion at Scotland Yard, but it was 'generally believed' that Bulling was the hoaxer – though Littlechild himself seems to have favoured Moore. Sadly we know too little about the career of either man to form a judgement.

The story that Bulling developed a drink problem and was ultimately fired in 1898 for sending the 'Bloody Bismarck' telegram has prompted speculation that he was the man referred to by R Thurston Hopkins in his book *Life and Death at the Old Bailey*:

> But it was in a letter, received by a well-known News Agency and forwarded to the Yard, that the name first appeared . . . It was perhaps a fortunate thing that the handwriting of this famous letter was not identified, for it would have led to the arrest of a harmless Fleet Street journalist. This poor fellow had a breakdown and became a whimsical figure in Fleet Street, only befriended by the staffs of newspapers and printing works. He would creep about the dark courts waving his hands furiously in the air, would utter stentorian 'Ha, ha, ha's,' and then, meeting some pal, would button-hole him and pour into his ear all the 'inner story' of the East End murders. Many old Fleet Streeters had very shrewd suspicions that this irresponsible fellow wrote the famous Jack the Ripper letter . . .[22]

Amid all the letters that were posted to the police, press and assorted private individuals, a great many of them signed Jack the Ripper, probably the most important and most interesting is the Lusk Letter. George Akin Lusk, a builder and decorator who specialised in music hall restoration, who was elected president of the Whitechapel Vigilance Committee, had been much in the news during September and especially the first week of October, when a letter he had written to the home secretary and to several newspapers was published. During this time, Lusk, who seems to have been a very respectable businessman, appears to have come in for some unwelcome attention.

On Thursday, 4 October, at about 4.15 in the afternoon, a man described as aged thirty to forty and about five foot nine, with a florid complexion, bushy brown beard, whiskers and moustache, went to the home of Mr Lusk and asked to speak with him. Lusk was not at home, but was at a tavern kept by his son (George Lusk Jr) and the man went there. He met Lusk and tried to persuade him to take him into a private room, but Lusk refused – the man's appearance being 'so repulsive and forbidding' – and they talked in the bar parlour instead, the man asking questions about the activities of the Vigilance Committee. The man behaved in a way that made Lusk very suspicious and, when the man asked directions to the nearest coffee and dining-rooms, Lusk directed him to a place in Mile End Road and followed him, but the man seemed deliberately to give Lusk the slip by disappearing up a court.[23]

Around 10 October 1888 a man was seen lurking about Lusk's premises. Lusk reported him to the police and a description was issued.[24] Two days later, on 12 October, Lusk received a letter bearing a Kilburn postmark and with handwriting said to resemble that of the 'Dear Boss' letter. It read,

> I write you a letter in black ink, as I have no more of the right stuff. I think you are all asleep in Scotland-yard with your bloodhounds, as I will show you to-morrow night (Saturday). I am going to do a double event, but not in Whitechapel. Got rather too warm there. Had to shift. No more till you hear me again.
>
> JACK THE RIPPER.[25]

Another communication, a postcard, addressed to 'Mr Lusk, Head Vigilance Committee, Aldeney-street, Mile-end', read:

> Say Boss –
>
> You seem rare frightened, guess I'd like to give you *fits*, but can't stop time enough to let you box of toys[26] play copper games with me, but hope to see you when I don't hurry to [sic] much
>
> Bye-bye, Boss.[27]

On 15 October, shortly after 1 a.m., a Miss Marsh was serving in her father's leather shop at 218 Jubilee Street, when a stranger dressed like a cleric came in, referred to the Vigilance Committee's reward poster, which was in the window, and asked for the address of George Lusk. Miss Marsh directed the man to the Crown, on the corner of Jubilee Street and Mile End Road, but he didn't want to go to a pub, so Miss Marsh got a newspaper that gave Lusk's address, though not the house number, and, as she read this out, the man noted it down in a pocket book. He then thanked Miss Marsh and left the shop. The man was described as about 45 and six foot tall, slim with a sallow complexion, a dark beard and moustache, and wearing a soft-felt black hat drawn over his forehead, a stand-up collar and a very long, black, single-breasted overcoat, with a Prussian or clerical collar partly turned up. He spoke with what was taken to be an Irish accent. Lusk said that nobody answering the description called on him and that he did not see anyone at all like the man in question.[28] However, on the evening of the following day, Tuesday, 16 October, Lusk received a small parcel, a cardboard box about three and a half inches square, wrapped in brown paper, which bore an indistinct London postmark. It was addressed to him, but did not have the house number, the one piece of information Emily Marsh had been unable to provide her visitor, which she noticed when eventually she read an account of Lusk's parcel. Lusk opened it and found inside a piece of offensive-smelling meat that he thought to be a portion of a kidney. Enclosed in the box was a letter:

From hell

Mr Lusk

Sir

I send you half the Kidne I took from one woman prasarved it for you. tother piece I fried and ate it was very nise. I may send you the bloody knif that took it out if you only wate a whil longer signed Catch me when you can

Mishter Lusk.

There was no doubt that the handwriting of the note was the same as that of the postcard received earlier,[29] and, although Lusk at first took it to be a practical joke, as he had the earlier communications, he was nevertheless alarmed and decided to bring it to the attention of other members of the Vigilance Committee at a meeting late the following evening, Wednesday, 17 October, at the Crown pub. At the meeting he brought up the subject of the parcel and, according to an interview with Joseph Aarons, said, 'I suppose you will laugh at what I am going to tell you, but you must know that I had a little parcel come to me on Tuesday evening, and to my surprise it contains half a kidney and a letter from Jack the Ripper.' Aarons laughed and said he thought somebody was trying to frighten him, but Lusk said he didn't find it a laughing matter and Aarons said that as it was late they'd leave the matter to the following morning, then take a look at the parcel and decide what to do.

On Thursday morning Joseph Aarons, W Harris and two members named Reeves and Lawton visited Lusk's house and inspected the parcel and the other correspondence. Lusk was clearly agitated – 'Throw it away;

I hate the sight of it,' he said – but he was convinced that it was a sheep's kidney. Aarons wasn't so sure and recommended taking it to Dr Frederick Wiles at his surgery at 56 Mile End Road. Wiles was out, but his assistant, F S Reed, examined the contents of the box and immediately expressed an opinion that the meat was half of a longitudinally divided human kidney. He thought it best to hand the kidney to Dr Openshaw of the London Hospital, where it could be microscopically examined.

According to Joseph Aarons, the committee members were left at the surgery while Reed took the kidney to Openshaw, who said it was a left kidney taken from a woman who was in the habit of drinking, the kidney showing signs of a disease associated with alcohol abuse.[30] Dr Openshaw gave an interview to *The Star* in which he said that some claims made in the newspapers were untrue – he did not know the sex of the person to whom it had belonged, nor did he know how long ago it had been removed from the body. The kidney was passed to Dr Gordon Brown, the city police surgeon, for microscopic examination, and, according to a report by Chief Inspector Swanson,

> . . . the result of the combined medical opinion they have taken upon it, is, that it is the kidney of a human adult, not charged with a fluid, as it would have been in the case of a body handed over for purposes of dissection to an hospital, but rather as it would be in a case where it was taken from the body not so destined. In other words similar kidneys might & could be obtained from any dead person upon whom a post mortem had been made from any cause by students or dissecting room porter.[31]

The Star publicly stated the same thing, that 'it may be doubted whether it has any serious bearing on the Mitre-square murder. The whole thing may possibly turn out to be a medical student's gruesome joke.'[32] The following day it announced in an odd little report headed EASY TO HOAX THE POLICE – THE KIDNEY STORY,

> As a motive for the disgusting hoax of the kidney, it is suggested that the person who sent it to its recipient desired to keep up the excitement about the crimes. We are now informed that the information of the receipt of the parcel was sold at a high figure, so that the hoax does not appear so stupid as it seemed at first.[33]

The implication of this report is clear: that a newspaper or news agency paid a large sum of money for the exclusive right to report the story, but it does not altogether make much sense and certainly the police and other records suggest that the police vigorously pursued their investigations.

There was considerable discussion about where the package was posted. The *Daily Telegraph* reported that this was being investigated by Scotland Yard. The barely legible postmark – only the letters 'ond' being decipherable – led the authorities to conclude that the parcel had been posted in London. Post Office officials suggested the Eastern or the East Central district, and, because letters and packages travelling from one district to another usually bore the postmark of both, the presence of only one postmark on the package suggested that it was dispatched from the district in which it was received, which would be the Eastern district. The package had not been dispatched via parcel post, but bore two penny stamps, showing it had been dropped into a postbox in the ordinary way. This created a problem, however, because the package was too large for ordinary postboxes, which indicated that it may have been posted in Lombard Street or Gracechurch Street, where the post offices had unusually wide postboxes. Alternatively, the sender could have handed it to the postman emptying a box.

Whether or not the Lusk kidney was that of Catherine Eddowes remains an unanswered and perhaps unanswerable question. Dr Frederick Gordon Brown appeared to give a fairly decisive answer in an interview with the *Sunday Times*, yet it appears contradictory. He began by saying, 'So far as I can form an opinion, I do not see any substantial reason why this portion of kidney should not be the portion of the one taken from the murdered woman.' Then he went on to explain that the Lusk kidney 'had not been in spirit for more than a week', and that 'as it exhibits no trace of decomposition, when we consider the length of time that has elapsed since the commission of the murder, we come to the conclusion that the probability is slight of its being a portion of the murdered woman of Mitre Square.' In other words, he was saying that, as the Lusk kidney had been preserved in spirits for no more than a week, had it been Eddowes's, it would show signs of decomposition, and, since it did not show signs of decomposition, it was unlikely to have been hers, which overall seems a substantial enough reason for saying it wasn't Eddowes's kidney.

Several newspapers, among them the *Daily Telegraph*, reported on 20 October that 'a small portion of the renal artery adheres to the kidney' and that a large portion adhered to Eddowes's body, and that the Lusk kidney exhibited signs of Bright's disease,[34] as did the kidney remaining in Eddowes's body. However, both claims were repudiated, the *Sunday Times* on 21 October saying that it had interviewed Dr Gordon Brown, who said that 'there is no portion of the renal artery adhering to it [the kidney], it having been trimmed up, so, consequently, there could be no correspondence established between the portion of the body from which it was cut'.[35] No evidence that either kidney, the one sent to Lusk or the one remaining in Eddowes, betrayed signs of advanced Bright's disease was ever given.

However, Major Henry Smith stated with little doubt that the kidney did retain renal artery and did show signs of Bright's disease:

When the body was examined by the police surgeon, Mr Gordon Brown, one kidney was found to be missing, and some days after the murder what purported to be that kidney was posted to the office of the Central News, together with a short note of rather a jocular character unfit for publication. Both kidney and note the manager at once forwarded to me. Unfortunately, as always happens, some clerk or assistant in the office was got at, and the whole affair was public property next morning. Right royally did the Solons of the metropolis enjoy themselves at the expense of my humble self and the City Police Force. 'The kidney was the kidney of a dog, anyone could see that,' wrote one. 'Evidently from the dissecting-room,' wrote another. 'Taken out of a corpse after a post-mortem,' wrote a third. 'A transparent hoax,' wrote a fourth. My readers shall judge between myself and the Solons in question.

I made over the kidney to the police surgeon, instructing him to consult with the most eminent men in the profession, and send me a report without delay. I give the substance of it. The renal artery is about three inches long. Two inches remained in the corpse, one inch was attached to the kidney. The kidney left in the corpse was in an advanced stage of Bright's Disease; the kidney sent me was in an exactly similar state. But what was of far more importance, Mr Sutton, one of the senior surgeons of the London Hospital, whom Gordon Brown asked to meet him and another practitioner in consultation, and who was one of the greatest authorities living on the kidney and its diseases, said he would pledge his reputation that the kidney submitted to them had been put in spirits within a few hours of its removal from the body – thus effectually disposing of all hoaxes in connection with it. The body of anyone done to death by violence is not taken direct to the dissecting-room, but must await an inquest, never held before the following day at the soonest.[36]

Although not noted for reliability and despite several demonstrable errors – the kidney was not sent to Central News and thence to himself – the City Police were responsible for investigating the kidney and Major Smith cites the authority of a man who was indeed 'one of the greatest authorities living on the kidney and its diseases'. This was Henry Gawen Sutton (1836–91), who was physician and lecturer in pathological anatomy at London Hospital but is perhaps best known for publishing with Dr William Withey Gull, later to feature prominently in the Ripper story, a revolutionary paper of particular relevance to what Major Smith has written, 'On the pathology of the morbid state commonly called chronic Bright's disease with contracted kidney ("arterio-capillary fibrosis")' in *Medico-Chirurgical Transactions* (London, 1872, Vol. 55, pp. 273–326), which led Gull and Sutton to give their names to Gull–Sutton syndrome – arteriosclerotic fibrosis of the kidney.

Sutton was a very distinguished physician – quiet, studious, shy and not particularly ambitious – and as a consequence was overshadowed by others, particularly Gull. It is remarked in a book about great doctors of the nineteenth century,

> The world outside knew little of him, neither the *Lancet* nor the *British Medical Journal* gave an obituary notice of him, but those who were fortunate enough to know him recognized in him a profound, original thinker and a thorough physician, skilled at the bedside and in the post-mortem room.[37]

This account is wrong in one respect: an obituary of Sutton was published in both the *British Medical Journal*[38] and *Lancet*,[39] as well as *Medico-Chirurgical Transactions*.[40]

Given that Major Smith may have been talking with the backing of Henry Gawen Sutton, one must give credit to what he says and accept the possibility that the Lusk kidney had been extracted from Eddowes.

I note, however, that according to Smith, Sutton said that the kidney had been placed in spirits within hours of being removed from the body, thus it was *not* taken from a body dissected during a postmortem. This is contrary to what Chief Inspector Swanson wrote in a report of 11 November:

'. . . similar kidneys might & could be obtained from any dead person upon whom a post mortem had been made from any cause by students or dissecting room porter.' Again, though, we meet with apparent contradictions, in this case, because Swanson's report also says the kidney was 'not charged with a fluid, as it would have been in the case of a body handed over for purposes of dissection to an hospital'.

What we do know is that despite the statement by Dr Gordon Brown in the *Sunday Times* on 21 October, as late as 30 October the Home Office was still questioning whether or not the Lusk kidney belonged to Eddowes, and Swanson's report of 6 November did not dismiss the possibility, as presumably it would have done if Gordon Brown had indeed declared that it wasn't.

Dr Thomas Horrocks Openshaw, a distinguished if rather more flamboyant successor to Sutton as curator of the pathology museum at the London Hospital, received a letter himself, sent on 29 October:

Old Boss, you was rite it was the lift kidny i was goin to hopperate agin close to your ospitle just as I was goin to dror my nife along of er bloomin throte them cusses of coppers spoilt the game but i guess i will be on the job soon and will send you another bit of innerds.

Jack the Ripper

o have you seen the devle with his mikerscope and scalpul a lookin at a kidney with a slide cocked up

The crime novelist Patricia Cornwell discovered that this letter was written on paper manufactured by A Pirie and Son, a manufacturer whose paper was also used by the British artist Walter Sickert, and also that the back of the postage stamp contained a single-donor mitochondrial DNA sequence that corresponded with that found on correspondence written by Sickert. Mitochondrial DNA is far from being a DNA fingerprint (in the sense that nuclear DNA is), and it would be extremely rash to draw any conclusions from these probable coincidences.[41] However, Anna Geuzner Robins, a Sickert expert consulted by Cornwell, believes that Sickert wrote many, if not most of the 'Ripper' letters preserved in the record repositories, including 'Dear Boss' and the Lusk letter. Her reasons have yet to be published in any kind of detail and therefore cannot be properly assessed.

CHAPTER THIRTEEN

Are You One of Us?

'London this morning will talk and think of nothing else except these new proofs of the continued presence in our streets of some monster or monsters in human form.'[1]

The Double Event horrified the East End and the world beyond. Newspapers as far away as Australia and New Zealand, as well as numerous cities and towns in America, reported the crimes almost as they happened. In some cases the prose was tinged with sensationalism, sometimes it expressed genuine bafflement, while others criticised the police and government, or blamed the social and moral conditions of the East End.

> Never in the record of criminal history have the police of any country been called upon to unravel a mystery so complete . . . . Whatever the objects of these wholesale murders and whoever the murderer may be, every civilized nation waits in anxious suspense for the horrible mystery to be solved.[2]

> It is so impossible to account, on any ordinary hypothesis, for these revolting acts of blood that the mind turns as it were instinctively to some theory of occult force, and the myths of the Dark Ages rise before the imagination. Ghouls, vampires, bloodsuckers, and all the ghastly array of fables which have been accumulated throughout the course of centuries take form, and seize hold of the excited fancy. Yet the most morbid imagination can conceive nothing worse than this terrible reality; for what can be more appalling than the thought that there is a being in human shape stealthily moving about a great city, burning with the thirst for human blood, and endowed with such diabolical astuteness, as to enable him to gratify his fiendish lust with absolute impunity?[3]

The Terror of Whitechapel has walked again . . . Whitechapel is half mad with fear. The people are afraid even to talk with a stranger . . . [4]

Our Detective Department is utterly unequal to deal with criminals of more than average ingenuity . . . Our Home Secretary is a perverse and stubborn official who, having made up his mind to do nothing whatsoever that may tend towards the discovery of the Whitechapel murderer, sticks to his resolve with immovable stolidity, deaf to argument, exhortation, and persuasion. [5]

The horrible dens of vice and crime that blot the fair face of our most thriving communities, are whatever else may be said of them, crying impeachments of the indifference and carelessness with which those in responsible positions, both governmental and social, look upon their less fortunate fellowmen. [6]

As for the East End itself,

The appearance of East London early on the Sunday morning so soon as the news of the murders was known – and, indeed, all day – almost baffles description. At ten o'clock, Aldgate and Leadenhall-street, Duke-street, St. James'-place, and Houndsditch were all literally packed with human beings – packed so thick that it was a matter of utter impossibility to pass through. The Babel of tongues as each inquired of the other the latest particulars, or the exact locality of the Aldgate murder, or speculated on the character or whereabouts of the murder, was simply deafening. Every window of every inhabited room in the vicinity was thrown open, for the better view of the inmates; and seats at these windows were being openly sold and eagerly bought. [7]

They weren't the only people profiting from the crimes. Crowds of people turned out from an early hour and *The Star* remarked that by 11 a.m. Sunday morning the entire population of the East End seemed to be on the streets, their numbers added to by sightseers from other parts of London and the provinces, many brought by cabs and private carriages. To service the needs of these people were assorted costermongers selling fish, bread, fruits, sweets and almost anything else edible. Newsvendors hawked their 'special editions'; hawkers sold cheap serials, rapidly updated with little care for accuracy, to include the latest crimes. One woman did a brisk trade selling cheap but dangerous swordsticks. 'Here you are, now,' she cried, 'sixpence for a swordstick. That's the sort to do for 'em.'[8] And a pavement artist attracted an immense crowd in Whitechapel Road with drawings of the victims, that of Eddowes 'a masterpiece of sanguinary ghastliness. What it lacked in delineation and unity it made up in disgusting details.'[9]

On the other hand, the crimes also took a terrible toll on people who were physically or mentally ill equipped to handle the horror. A Mrs Sodeaux, the wife of a silk weaver, who lived on the top floor of 65 Hanbury Street, had become 'greatly agitated' since the murders and hanged herself from the banister. Her body was found by her eight-year-old daughter, who frantically sought assistance but tragically couldn't get anyone to go to the body until the police arrived.[10]

The crowds gathered outside the club in Berner Street and were moved on by the police, who reportedly swarmed in every corner of Whitechapel as 'thick as bees in a clover field',[11] but when the police had finished their investigations and the body of Elizabeth Stride was removed and the passage cleaned down, the club committee charged curiosity-hunters a small sum to be admitted to view the spot where the body was found and hear the story of its discovery. The money thus earned went into a 'propaganda fund'.[12]

At Mitre Square the entrances were cordoned off, but 'the sensation-seeking crowds seemed to gather some satisfaction from mere proximity to the spot where the curtain had last been raised on the terrible series of tragedies'.[13] Among those who gathered outside Mitre Square was John Kelly, with whom Catherine Eddowes had lived. He thought Eddowes had stayed overnight with her daughter and wasn't initially concerned by her absence. As he later explained to a journalist,

> . . . on Sunday morning I wandered round in the crowds that had been gathered by the talk about the two fresh murders. I stood and looked at the very spot where my poor old gal had laid with her body all cut to pieces and I never knew it. I never thought of her in connection with it, for I thought she was safe at her daughter's.

It wouldn't be until Monday that he would begin to worry. Then, in an account of the crimes in *The Star*, he read the name 'Emily Burrel' (who, as we saw earlier, had given Eddowes a pawn ticket for a flannel shirt) and later in the article a reference to the initials 'TC' tattooed on the victim's forearm.

In dazed horror he went to the police and so began his personal ordeal of identifying the body.[14]

The crowds around the murder sites diminished a little between 2 and 4 p.m., coinciding with various meetings that were held during the afternoon. At 3 p.m. nearly a thousand people gathered in Victoria Park to listen to several speeches in which Sir Charles Warren and Home Secretary Matthews were severely criticised. The meeting concluded with a resolution that it was high time both men should resign. Similar meetings were held at four other locations in London that day with similar resolutions being passed. One meeting of the unemployed was held in Hyde Park, one person carrying a huge placard bearing the words, THE WHITECHAPEL MURDERS. WHERE ARE THE POLICE? LOOKING AFTER THE UNEMPLOYED.[15]

Darkness came and the streets emptied. The well-lit main streets retained something of the bustle, but the side roads, alleys and courts, ill lit or in darkness, were deserted. Tradesmen were complaining that their businesses were suffering, although the omnibus business was experiencing a minor boom as people took a bus trip through Whitechapel. Prostitutes themselves were suffering from want of business. Poorly dressed, unable to find money for food or a bed or a bit of warmth in a pub, they huddled in shop doorways trying to get a little shelter from the cold wind. Eventually moved on by the police, many gathered near a church or a chapel 'as if in the belief that within the shadow of a temple of worship there was some protection even for them. The spectacle was a very sad one.'[16] Others stood under the glare of a street lamp or huddled in doorways, all discussing the murders. ' "He'll be coming through the houses and pulling us out of our beds next," says one. "Not he," says another; "he's too clever for that. He catches the late birds, he does." "Then he won't catch me," says the first. "I don't leave my doorway after dark." '[17]

As the darkness wore on, the shadowed corners and gloomy passages became deserted. Before midnight there was scarcely a woman to be seen on the streets. There were a few people to be found in Mitre Square, where *The Star* reported that a 'keen-eyed little Jew was explaining to the half-dozen women the position the body had occupied, and was pointing out some water marks as blood stains'. One woman had a crying baby in her arms. 'Does it want to see the blood, bless its heart? So it shall. Take a good look at it, my pet. You may see enough of it if this sort of thing keeps up.'

The *Star* reporter walked to Berner Street, which was deserted, and returned to Aldgate, where he passed a man muffled in a long scarf, which he also used to wrap his hands. A passing policeman observed to a companion that nobody would notice if the man's hands were covered in blood, but they didn't stop him.

The Double Event intensified the attacks in the press on Matthews and Warren, particularly because Matthews had left London to visit what *The Star* called 'pot-house Tories' in Birmingham.[18] The *Daily Telegraph* called Matthews 'Helpless, Heedless, Useless', and remarked, 'If the Home Secretary fails to wake up and do his duty Lord Salisbury will have to dismiss a minister who has not good sense enough to resign.'[19] *The Star* compared the Metropolitan Police very unfavourably with the City Police, claiming that, while its reporter had no difficulty getting information from officers of the City Police, the Metropolitan Police seemed ignorant of even the most basic facts surrounding the Berner Street murder. This may have been due less to ignorance than to strict instructions not to give information to the press, but *The Star*'s criticisms provided its readers with little reassurance.[20] Superintendent Foster of the City Police had been highly visible during the morning overseeing the measurement and drawings of Mitre Square that were being made in preparation for the inquest, and Sir Charles Warren also visited both murder scenes during the morning.

Emotions were certainly running high, and any arrests, for whatever offence, immediately produced a cry 'the Whitechapel murderer' from the people in the street, and an immense crowd gathered, hooting and jeering. Understandably, the notoriety wasn't welcomed. One unnamed man even applied at the Marylebone Police Court to bring charges against a man in Tottenham who had accused him of being Leather Apron and caused him to be arrested and held by the police for three and a half hours.[21]

Sunday passed into Monday. At about 12.30 a.m. a man named Thomas Coram, a labourer in a coconut warehouse who lived at 67 Plumber's Row, off Commercial Road, near the home of John Pizer's family, was walking home when he found a knife lying on the doorstep of a laundry belonging to Mr Christmas at 253 Whitechapel Road. A bloodstained handkerchief was wrapped around it. The blade was about ten inches long. Coram called PC Joseph Drage, 282H, who took it to Leman Street Police Station. PC Drage was not certain the knife wasn't there when he passed the doorway at 12.15, but did not believe it was there at 11.30 p.m., when he'd stood near the spot and had seen the landlady let out a woman. The knife was duly passed to Dr Phillips for examination.[22]

At a late hour a well-known character known as One-armed Liz who lived in Flower and Dean Street, accompanied Sergeant Thicke to St George's Mortuary and there identified the body of Elizabeth Stride as that of a woman she knew as 'Annie Morris'. It is unclear whether One-armed Liz had completely misidentified the body or whether 'Annie Morris' was a name used by Stride.[23] Others began coming forward too, among them Charles Preston and John Arundell, both of whom identified the body as that of Elizabeth Stride.

With the dawn and people beginning work after the weekend, the staff arrived at the post office in Aldgate High Street, only a few yards from Mitre Square, and discovered that burglars had entered from an adjoining empty house, forced the safe and stolen £70, plus stamps valued at £350 and £3.[24]

Shortly after 10 a.m. Mr McWilliam, Superintendent Foster and Inspector Collard met the city coroner[25] and a postmortem on Eddowes was conducted at the city mortuary in Golden Lane. Photographs were taken both before and after.[26] Meanwhile, Wynne E Baxter opened the inquest on Elizabeth Stride at St George's Vestry Hall in Cable Street, a large and excited crowd having gathered outside.[27] Inside, remarked the ever critical *New York Times*, sat the detectives 'listening to the sworn testimony to find out who did it'.[28]

The detectives did rather more than that. Chief Inspector Donald Swanson summarised police activity following the murders of Stride and Eddowes in a report to the Home Office on 19 October. An extensive house-to-house search was conducted. More than two thousand lodgers were questioned and examined, and some eighty thousand handbills[29] requesting information about any suspicious people were distributed:

Police Notice. – To the occupier. – On the mornings of Friday, 31st August, Saturday, 8th, and Sunday, 30th Sept., 1888, women were murdered in Whitechapel, it is supposed by someone residing in the immediate neighbourhood. Should you know of any person to whom suspicion is attached, you are earnestly requested to communicate at once with the nearest police-station. – Metropolitan Police Office, 30th Sept., 1888.[30]

The Thames Police made enquiries of sailors aboard ships in the docks or on the river; enquiries were made among Asiatics in the various opium dens in London; approximately three hundred people were questioned as a result of communications from members of the public; 76 butchers and slaughterers were questioned and 'three of the persons calling themselves Cowboys who belonged to the American Exhibition were traced and satisfactorily accounted for themselves'.[31]

These cowboys must have belonged to Buffalo Bill Cody's Wild West Show, which arrived in London as part of Queen Victoria's Golden Jubilee celebrations. The show had sailed aboard the steamship *State of Nebraska* in the spring of 1887, and returned to the United States in the spring of 1888, but some of the cowboys are known to have liked Britain and stayed behind. It is difficult to equate the London of Jack the Ripper with the age of the American Wild West, yet only seven years before the Whitechapel murders, in July 1881, Billy the Kid had been shot dead; in October of that same year Wyatt Earp and Doc Holliday fought it out with the Clantons in the gunfight at the OK Corral; and in April 1882 Bob Ford shot and killed Jesse James.

Robert Anderson, summoned back from his holiday, returned to London on 6 October. In his autobiography he wrote,

On my return I found the Jack-the-Ripper scare in full swing. When the stolid English go in for a scare they take leave of all moderation and common sense. If nonsense were solid, the nonsense that was talked and written about those murders would sink a *Dreadnought*. The subject is an unsavoury one, and I must write about it with reserve.

I spent the day of my return to town, and half the following night, in reinvestigating the whole case, and next day I had a long conference on the subject with the Secretary of State and the Chief Commissioner of Police. 'We hold you responsible to find the murderer,' was Mr Matthews's greeting to me. My answer was to decline the responsibility. 'I hold myself responsible,' I said, 'to take all legitimate means to find him.' But I went on to say that the measures I found in operation were, in my opinion, wholly indefensible and scandalous; for these wretched women were plying their trade under definite Police protection. Let the Police of that district, I urged, receive orders to arrest every known 'street woman' found on the prowl after midnight, or else let us warn them that the Police will not protect them. Though the former course would have been merciful to the very small class of woman affected by it, it was deemed too drastic, and I fell back on the second.

During that week the atmosphere in the East End continued to be excited, thousands of people visiting the scenes of crime and becoming such a disturbance that the police were forced to keep them away, especially from the largely residential Berner Street.[32] Coroner S F Langham opened the inquest into Eddowes's death at the city mortuary, the room being crowded and many more people gathered outside the building. Elizabeth Stride was buried on Friday, 6 October, in the quietest possible manner, and at the expense of the parish.[33]

An assortment of theories were advanced in the newspapers by journalists as well as members of the public, several of which have remained popular with theorists. It was suggested that the murderer may have worn woman's clothing, or may be a policeman,[34] or an ex-policeman whose motive was to bring the police into disrepute.[35] As with all such theories, then and since, the extraordinary degree of mutilation strongly indicated a murderer who didn't have such an ordinary motive. The *Daily Telegraph* would report that a belief was gaining ground that the murderer did not use common lodging houses, but probably occupied a room, or perhaps took refuge in an empty warehouse. It suggested that the murderer was believed to live somewhere between Middlesex Street and Brick Lane.[36]

Escaped lunatics made the news. Somebody called 'X' wrote to the *Daily Telegraph* about an inmate of Leavesden Asylum, near Watford in Hertfordshire, who escaped from his keepers when taking exercise, and women were warned to be vigilant, as the man was dangerous. The Leavesden Asylum Committee pointed out that the man had escaped on 16 September 1887 and while at Leavesden was 'perfectly quiet and harmless, and certainly had no homicidal tendency'.[37] A leading expert on insanity, Dr William A Hammond of New York, said the police were wrongly looking for a 'repulsive, uncouth butcher, dripping with blood', whereas the killer was probably a mild-mannered man, possibly moving in the very best circles, known among his acquaintances for his modesty, refinement and humanity, and who may even have an effeminate horror of bloodshed and strife. He said that when the killer was caught 'the law should shield its eyes while society hangs the maniac'.[38]

Displaying an equally cavalier attitude towards life as Dr Hammond did to the insane and the law, Inspector Byrnes of the New York police suggested that fifty women be deployed across Whitechapel and watched by a force of disguised policemen. The killer would soon fall into the trap, said Byrnes, adding that even if one of the women fell a victim 'I should get the murderer'.[39]

Roderick McDonald, the coroner for northeast Middlesex, who had just returned from holiday and would be plunged into the heart of the mystery, was called upon to preside over a later victim of Jack the Ripper, and wrote to the newspapers suggesting that the murderer quietened or silenced his victims by first drugging them with rum or brandy laced with an opiate such as morphine.[40] An idea that to many at the time must have seemed completely off the wall was suggested by Fred W P Jago,[41] who observed in *The Times* that 'the surface markings on no two thumbs are alike' and that it should be possible to match the bloody thumbprint to the person who made it.[42] This was a remarkable observation for 1888 and possibly one of the most sensible bits of advice to come from anywhere, but fingerprinting was still very much in its infancy.[43]

A Mr Forbes, apparently a noted war correspondent, wrote to the *Daily News* suggesting that the murderer was a medical student who was committing the crimes to punish prostitutes from one of whom he had contracted a disease (later to be suggested in a slightly modified form by Leonard Matters in one of the earliest full-length accounts of the crimes.[44] A correspondent who called himself 'Observer' wrote to the *Daily Telegraph* suggesting that 'lines drawn through the spots where the murders were committed assume the exact form of a dagger', and modern theorists have noted that they form an arrow pointing to the Houses of Parliament and a black magic symbol.[45] That the murderer was a black magician occurred to several contemporaries, a newspaper reporting that an eminent engineer in London had likened the murderer, who he suggested was a medical maniac, to the witches in *Macbeth*, bent 'over a bubbling caldron of the hellbroth' made from the victim's body parts in the search for an elixir of life, and it was reported that the police had made enquiries among various dealers in herbs in Whitechapel to find out if anyone had recently purchased any unusual compounds. The newspaper commented that if the police were spending time investigating 'wild theories like this' it showed that clues were utterly absent.[46] Similar ideas have been advanced several times in recent years.[47]

The Star claimed that the uterus and other organs were extracted from female corpses for the purpose of making thieves' candles, which, according to superstition, caused those upon whom the light fell to go to sleep. At the trial of a notorious German robber named Theodor Unger, nicknamed 'the handsome Charley', who was executed at Magdeburg in 1810, it was shown that gangs of thieves had established a factory for the production of such candles. Such candles also featured in the trials of robber bands at Odenwald and in Westphalia, in the years 1812 and 1841 respectively, and most recently in a trial at Biala, in Galicia, in 1875, in which a woman had been mutilated in a way reminiscent of the Ripper. It was even suggested that they had played a part in the Ritter case.[48]

In 1884 a Galician Jew named Moses Ritter was accused of having outraged a Christian girl named Frances Mnich in a village near Krakow and then hired a Christian Pole named Stochlinski to murder and mutilate her. Some claimed that the crime had been committed to obtain organs to make a thieves' candle, but Jew haters claimed that certain fanatical Jews believed that they could atone for sins committed with a Christian woman by killing and mutilating her, and numerous supportive passages from the Talmud were quoted to support the claim. Ritter had been tried three times at Rzezow in Galicia, each time found guilty and sentenced to death, and each time had the sentence revoked, the last time permanently – it was said because Stochlinski, the actual murderer and accuser, had died in prison. When the story appeared in *The Times* it provoked an immediate response from Hermann Adler, the chief rabbi, and M Gaster, chief rabbi of the Spanish and Portuguese Jews' Congregations of England. Hermann Adler stated unequivocally that 'in no Jewish book is such a barbarity even hinted at. Nor is there any record in the criminal annals of any country of a Jew having been convicted of such a terrible atrocity'. This was true. A Professor Delitzsch and Dr Josef S Bloch, members of the Austrian Parliament, had repeatedly demonstrated this at Ritter's trial, and M Gaster, at greater length and with less precision, wrote that the accusations against Ritter 'were clumsy fabrications' and that the core of the tale had been disproved time and again.[49]

It can't be said that *The Times* tried to induce anti-Jewish feeling, but some newspapers came close to it, although whether by design or careless reporting isn't clear. The *East London Observer* quoted the Reverend Dr Tyler as saying at a special meeting on 8 October of the Young Men's Christian Association, the subject of which was 'The Recent Fiendish Atrocities in Our Midst', that, while 'crime was decidedly on the decrease [it] was largely brought about by the wholesale importation of the scum of other countries'. He had in fact said 'the importation of the scum and depraved characters from all parts of this and other countries'; therefore the report that he said only 'the scum of other countries' made his remarks more contentious than they actually were, especially as he referred to Russians and Poles not as scum but only as people coming to Britain 'very largely to escape conscription'.[50] There were many anti-Jewish stories in circulation, however, and some bigoted and extraordinarily stupid people around. A man named Edward Dillon Lewis wrote a letter to *The Times* in which he argued that the murderer had to be a foreigner because that type of murder was unknown as having been committed by an Englishman, and because the celerity with which the crimes had been committed was inconsistent with 'ordinary English phlegmatic nature'.

In marked contrast to Stride's funeral, Catherine Eddowes, during the afternoon of 8 October, was given a fine and traditional East End send-off. Crowds gathered outside the city mortuary in Golden Lane and there were spectators at the windows and even on the roofs of adjoining buildings. The coffin was of polished elm, with oak mouldings, and bore a plate inscribed with gold letters, saying, CATHERINE EDDOWES, DIED SEPT. 30, 1888, AGED 43 YEARS. One of Eddowes's sisters laid a beautiful wreath on the coffin as it was placed in the hearse, and at 1.30 p.m. the cortège set off. It consisted of an open glass hearse drawn by a pair of horses, a mourning coach (containing sisters Harriet Jones, Emma Eddowes, Eliza Gold and Elizabeth Fisher, along with two nieces, Emma and Harriet Jones, and John Kelly, all dressed smartly in black, the women weeping) and a brougham conveying representatives of the press. Thousands of people followed the procession along Golden Lane, Old Street, Great Eastern Street, Commercial Street, Whitechapel Road – where a large crowd had gathered outside St Mary's – Mile End Road, through Stratford to Ilford, the police maintaining order under Superintendent Foster and Inspector Woollett, and beyond the City boundaries under Superintendent Hunt and Inspector Burnham. The cortège reached Ilford at 3.30 p.m., where about five hundred people were waiting, men and women of all ages, many of the latter carrying infants in their arms, gathered round the grave. A wreath of marguerites was added to the coffin by another relative of Eddowes, and the remains were interred in the Church of England portion of the cemetery. The service was conducted by the chaplain, the Reverend Mr Dunscombe. The costs of the funeral were met by G C Hawkes, an undertaker, of 41a, Berner Street, who was a vestryman of St Luke's, and the City authorities, to whom the burial ground belonged, remitted the charges.[51]

Throughout October the police presence on the streets was highly visible and varied. It was reported that detectives patrolled Commercial Road in pairs. Some policemen adopted disguises that were apparently clumsy, obvious and unconvincing – those dressed up as dock labourers receiving special comment – and were noticeable because they were always followed at a small distance by a uniformed policeman.[52] The Vigilance Committee held regular meetings at 9 p.m. in the Crown in Mile End Road, and, whenever other commitments permitted, its members – 'citizen detectives' – took to the streets, following assigned beats and wearing, so it was reported, noiseless boots, and they had reportedly hired the services of two private detectives – presumably Le Grand and Batchelor, whom we met in Chapter Nine – and a number of 'physically capable' men from the ranks of the unemployed as bodyguards.[53] In addition, a private firm of detectives had women decoys out on the streets in order to try to catch the murderer[54] and there were assorted journalists and numerous private individuals playing Sherlock Holmes. It evidently became quite confusing to know who was who.

About midnight one night a reporter from Bow dressed himself in women's clothing and began prowling around Whitechapel. His masculine stride attracted the attention of PC Ludwig, who said, 'Stop. Are you not a man? I can see that you are.' The journalist said, 'Yes.' PC Ludwig then quietly asked, 'Are you one of us?' The journalist said he wasn't and admitted to being a journalist. PC Ludwig took him to Leman Street, where he was held for an hour and a half.[55]

Although there had been a house-to-house enquiry on 3 October 1888 and the distribution of some eighty thousand handbills, a specific search of Jewish premises was reported by *The Star* on 17 October. A pea-souper fog had descended over London that morning and become thicker as the hours passed – 'the lights of London show through the opaque atmosphere with Whistlerian dimness', *The Star* remarked, almost poetically – and at 10 a.m. the police began a house-to-house search among the East End Jews. They apparently demanded admission to every room and the search was very thorough: they 'look underneath the beds, and peer into the smallest cupboards', examined knives, and specifically asked about any friends, relatives and lodgers, past and present, and how respectable they were.[56] The following day, 18 October, the house-to-house was reportedly complete, and Sir Charles Warren issued a statement, saying that 'acknowledgement is due on all sides for the cordial co-operation of the inhabitants, and he is much gratified that the police officers have carried out so delicate a duty with the marked goodwill of all those with whom they have come in contact'. Warren included all classes and creeds.[57] Curiously,

Robert Anderson, the head of the CID, who was still out of the country when the house-to-house began, claimed in his autobiography,

> During my absence abroad the Police had made a house-to-house search for him, investigating the case of every man in the district whose circumstances were such that he could go and come and get rid of his blood-stains in secret. And the conclusion we came to was that he and his people were certain low-class Polish Jews; for it is a remarkable fact that people of that class in the East End will not give up one of their number to Gentile justice.[58]

The *Daily Telegraph* had in fact reported on 3 October that the police were specifically searching unoccupied houses,[59] which may bear Anderson out, and this story in *The Star* of a specific search of Jewish premises seems like possible confirmation of his claim that the house-to-house enquiry directed attention at the Jews. What is clear, however, is that it did not direct attention at anyone in particular,[60] although a Swedish newspaper did report that 'the prime suspect is now a foreigner who was living not far from Berner Street'. It added that he had been reported to the police by a woman with whom he had been living and was at present under close surveillance.[61] This is a reference to 'the Batty Street Lodger', who was the subject of a burst of excitement in some newspapers mid-month. The *Daily News* gave a fullish account:

> According to a Correspondent, the police are watching with great anxiety a house at the East-end which is strongly suspected to have been the actual lodging, or a house made use of by someone connected with the East-end murders. Statements made by the neighbours in the district point to the fact that the landlady had a lodger, who since the Sunday morning of the last Whitechapel murders has been missing. The lodger, it is stated, returned home early on the Sunday morning, and the landlady was disturbed by his moving about. She got up very early, and noticed that her lodger had changed some of his clothes. He told her he was going away for a little time, and he asked her to wash the shirt which he had taken off, and get it ready for him by the time he came back. As he had been in the habit of going away now and then, she did not think much at the time, and soon afterwards he went out. On looking at his shirt she was astonished to find the wristbands and

part of the sleeves saturated with wet blood. The appearance struck her as very strange, and when she heard of the murders her suspicions were aroused. Acting on the advice of some of her neighbours, she gave information to the police and showed them the bloodstained shirt. They took possession of it, and obtained from her a full description of her missing lodger. During the last fortnight she has been under the impression that he would return, and was sanguine that he would probably come back on Saturday or Sunday night, or perhaps Monday evening. The general opinion, however, among the neighbours is that he will never return. On finding out the house and visiting it, a reporter found it tenanted by a stout, middle-aged German woman, who speaks very bad English, and who was not inclined to give much information further than the fact that her lodger had not returned yet, and she could not say where he had gone or when he would be back. The neighbours state that ever since the information has been given two detectives and two policemen have been in the house day and night. The house is approached by a court, and as there are alleys running through it into different streets, there are different ways of approach and exit. It is believed from the information obtained concerning the lodger's former movements and his general appearance, together with the fact that numbers of people have seen this same man about the neighbourhood, that the police have in their possession a series of most important clues, and that his ultimate capture is only a question of time.[62]

On the following day both the *Daily Telegraph* and the *Manchester Guardian* briefly recounted the basic facts, the *Telegraph* concluding, 'Inquiry was instituted, with the result that the incidents mentioned are said to have been "satisfactorily accounted for." '[63] The *Guardian* reported, 'The hope that this might lead to the mystery being cleared up seems, however, to be of a very slender nature, as a telegram received last night states that the lodger clue was investigated by the police some days ago, and that the explanations given in the case were quite satisfactory.'[64] The following day, 17 October, the *East Anglian Daily Times* carried a report in which it said that the police had taken exceptional precautions to keep a lid on the story and on Monday afternoon had categorically denied the truth of it, but, said the newspaper, 'there is no doubt that a man was taken into custody on suspicion of being the missing lodger from 22 Batty Street, and that he was afterwards set at liberty.'

A Central News story, somewhat garbled in that it said the landlady was a laundress and the lodger just a customer, said the man returned to the house the previous Saturday – 13 October – was arrested, taken to Leman Street Police Station and released within an hour or two. Although the story was never a big one in the press, which may reflect its contemporary importance, it would seem to have been well enough known by November to be the butt of some of George R Sims's humour in his 'Dagonet' column in *The Referee*:

> But perhaps the most remarkable piece of evidence is that of a laundress, who forwards a pair of cuffs, and says:- 'Sir Charles Warren. – Sir, – These cuffs come in the washin from Mr ~ (name and address given). There is a stain on them which looks like blood. He is a queer-looking man, my dorter says, as she has seen him when calling for the bill, and is wife is a inverlid. If he is not the Whitechapel murderer, please return, as I do not want to be mix up in the affair. P.S. – If the rewarde is pade, I hope I shall have my rites.'[65]

The story of the Batty Street lodger has assumed some importance in recent years, it being argued that he was an American and possibly identified with an American suspect named Francis Tumblety (see Chapter Fourteen), but the sparse reports about the lodger don't refer to his nationality, except in the case of both Central News and the Swedish newspaper, where he is referred to as a 'foreigner', a term often applied to the East European immigrants entering the country. That the lodger was such a person might gain credence from the landlady, who was described as a German with a bad command of English, yet seems to have understood her lodger well enough.

Numerous people were arrested, often simply for looking suspicious, as in the case of an unnamed man arrested early one morning in Commercial Street and detained at Leman Street Police Station until his name and address were verified,[66] or the man arrested in Norwood because he had scratches on his face, which proved to have been received 'domestically'.[67] Others were arrested for claiming to be the murderer or to know him or to have private information about the killings. Some were drunks or drug addicts. A man in a restaurant in Milk Street, Cheapside, ordered and drank a glass of beer, then injected himself with morphine. He began rambling about lending his overcoat to someone and its being worth £100 if it could talk. He was arrested and held by the City Police for two days.[68]

William Bull, the son of very respectable parents who lived in Stannard Road, Dalston, who claimed to be a medical student of the London Hospital, but proved to be unknown there, turned up at Bishopsgate Police Station and confessed to the crimes. Taken seriously – he confessed in front of Major Smith – he later claimed that he'd been 'mad drunk' and duly signed the pledge.[69] The pledge was also signed by 'J. Duncan', who also claimed to be a doctor. He was seen by Thomas Ryan, who was in charge of a cabmen's reading room and shelter in Westbourne Grove, who thought him half perished with cold and cooked him a chop. Several cabmen were in the shelter at the time, talking of the murders, and the man told Ryan, 'Don't you know who committed the murders? I did them. I've had a lot of trouble lately. I came back from India and got into trouble at once. I lost my watch and chain and £10.' The man appeared to be drunk and had a bottle of brandy on him, but he willingly signed a temperance pledge – putting his name down as 'J. Duncan; doctor'. The man ate his chop and went out. It is perhaps testament to the thoroughness of the police – and to the coincidences that can befog an investigation – that the police received information from the governor of Newcastle Prison that the man was John George Donkin, who had been imprisoned there in January and again in December 1881 for assaulting a woman. By the time this information reached the police, however, they had already traced the man of the cabmen's shelter, who had identified himself as John Davidson and satisfactorily accounted for himself.[70]

CHAPTER FOURTEEN

Francis Tumblety

During October suspicion fell on an Irish-American named Francis Tumblety. We don't know for certain why suspicion fell on him, although it is possible that it had something to do with the Lusk letter, for Scotland Yard apparently put out a request for handwriting samples and on 29 October received a cable from the chief of police in San Francisco, Patrick Crowley, offering to send them samples of Tumblety's handwriting. Scotland Yard replied, asking that the samples be sent at once.[1] Tumblety managed to evade the police and fled under an assumed name back to the United States, followed by a Scotland Yard detective who for an unspecified time kept him under surveillance, it being freely and extensively reported in American newspapers that Tumblety was suspected of being the murderer or being involved with the Whitechapel crimes. Tumblety was not brought to trial, however, and died in 1903 a very wealthy but mysterious man. On 23 September 1913 Detective Chief Inspector John George Littlechild wrote a letter to the journalist George R Sims, who had written to Littlechild asking him if he had ever heard of a 'Dr D.' in relation to the Ripper crimes. Littlechild replied:

> I never heard of a Dr D. in connection with the Whitechapel murders but amongst the suspects, and to my mind a very likely one, was a Dr T. (which sounds much like D.) He was an American quack named Tumblety and was at one time a frequent visitor to London and on these occasions constantly brought under the notice of police, there being a large dossier concerning him at Scotland Yard. Although a 'Sycopathia Sexualis' subject he was not known as a 'Sadist' (which the murderer unquestionably was) but his feelings toward women were remarkable and bitter in the extreme, a fact on record. Tumblety was arrested at the time of the murders in connection with unnatural offences and charged at Marlborough Street, remanded on bail, jumped his bail, and got away

to Boulogne. He shortly left Boulogne and was never heard of afterwards. It was believed he committed suicide but certain it is that from this time the 'Ripper' murders came to an end.

Francis J Tumblety was born to James and Margaret Tumblety[2] about 1831 in Ireland.[3] He was the youngest of eleven children, there being two brothers named Patrick and Lawrence, and eight sisters named Jane and Bridget (twins), Alice, Margaret, Ann, Julia, Elizabeth and Mary. The family lived in Rochester, New York, and according to Captain W C Streeter, a canal boat owner who recalled Tumblety as a youth, the family lived about a mile south of the centre of Rochester on Sophia Street (later renamed Plymouth Avenue).[4] Edward Haywood, who worked at the Bureau of Accounts in the State Department, and who had known Tumblety in boyhood,[5] recalled in the Rochester *Democrat and Republican* that 'he used to run about the canal in Rochester, a dirty, awkward, ignorant, uncared-for, good-for-nothing boy. He was utterly devoid of education.' According to Captain Streeter, by the age of fifteen, Tumblety, who apparently had no regular friends, was selling largely pornographic books and papers on the Erie canal boats. He disappeared about 1850, said Streeter, who didn't see him again for about a decade.[6] Captain Streeter's memory of Tumblety's selling pornographic literature agrees with the 1851–2 Rochester City Directory, the last record of his living in Rochester, and lists him as Franklin Tumilty, giving his occupation as peddler. Tumblety's father, James, died on 7 May 1851, aged 74, and this is probably when Tumblety left town.

Whether or not Tumblety at any time gained any medical experience in Rochester is uncertain. Edward Haywood said Tumblety did jobs for 'a "Doctor" Lispenard, who carried on a medical business of a disreputable kind' from a little drug store at the back of a grand shopping area called Reynolds Arcade in Rochester.[7] Captain Streeter said that one of Tumblety's brothers worked as a steward for a prominent local physician named Dr Fitzhugh,[8] but this lacks any kind of supportive evidence, and there is also a report that he worked for an H J Lyons, an 'Indian Herb Doctor', who had an office over the post office.[9] Another early report also claimed that Tumblety once had an office in Smith's Block, where he went by the name of Philip Sternberg, and treated a certain class of diseases.[10]

Tumblety seems to have drifted into acting, for there is a record of him in his days before he dispensed medicines visiting Toronto 'with a strolling company of concert or menagerie folks'.[11] But by 1855 he was peddling herbal remedies. Edward Haywood, having travelled west about 1855, said he was in Detroit when Tumblety turned up there posing as a doctor.[12]

In 1857 he was in Montreal and about to have one of his first brushes with the law. He was arrested on 23 September for allegedly selling a local prostitute named Philomene Dumas a bottle of pills and a liquid that he said would abort her pregnancy. He appeared before a Grand Jury, but was released on 1 October and the charges against him were dropped on 25 October. One newspaper clearly felt that Tumblety had 'escaped the penalty of the law, despite the serious facts proved against him in the inquiry conducted before the police magistrate, because of the specialised nature of the accusation . . .'[13]

Within a month or two of being cleared Tumblety had published in the local newspapers an advertisement announcing his intention *not* to stand for election to the Colonial Parliament. Here we perhaps catch sight of one of the tricks Tumblety used to generate publicity. The elections were the big news of the day, so Tumblety grabbed a little of the reflected limelight for himself by announcing that, despite being urged by many key political figures to stand in opposition to Thomas Darcy McGee,[14] he did not at that time intend to contest the election, but believed that were he to do so he would have been successful.[15] It was a clever and simple con. Claiming not to be able to do something, even though one had been urged by many unnamed society figures, bestowed respectability and generated publicity, it wasn't easily denied, and, in the event that the claim was disputed, it only generated further publicity. It was a ploy frequently used by Tumblety over the years, who time and time again would be connected – or would cleverly connect himself – with major events of the day, including the assassination of President Lincoln.

In 1857 he arrived in Toronto and opened an office on King Street. He claimed to be an American Indian or to have learned his medicine from one, and in front of his office he displayed a large pair of buck horns, which he claimed were presented to him by an Indian chief named Sundown. Selling herbal cures, he apparently did very good business.[16] A Mr Smythe of Hibernia Bank of Toronto was able to recall him years later.[17] C S Gurnet, who had recalled Tumblety in Toronto as part of a company of strolling players, said that he had on one occasion in Toronto been accused of extorting a watch from a farmer under false pretences and sent for trial. He was also tried and convicted of practising medicine without a licence, and fined C$100,[18] but he appealed and produced some kind of certificate that enabled him to reverse the judgement and resume his practice.[19]

Tumblety may have had a brief flirtation with Brooklyn, New York, in 1860, it being reported that in that year he 'burst upon the people of Brooklyn as a sort of modern Count of Monte Cristo, and cut a wide swath in the affections of certain susceptible women. After a few months he dropped out of sight as suddenly as he had appeared . . .'[20] He seems to have gone to St John, New Brunswick, where he took lodgings at the leading hotel, and claimed to be 'an eclectic physician of international reputation'.[21] Loudly dressed, mounted on a white horse and followed by one or more hounds, he made quite a sensation when going through the streets on his way to his patients.[22] As usual, he ran foul of the licensed doctors, but things went badly wrong for him on Monday, 17 September 1860, when James Portmore, a carpenter well known and liked in St John, attracted by Tumblety's advertisements to be able to cure all ills, visited him and was given a bottle of 'medicine'. He took it, but after a little while vomited and became very ill. His wife called Tumblety to her home and accused him of poisoning her husband and pointed to the bottles of medicine he had prescribed, but Tumblety told her to apply hot-water fomentations over her husband's kidneys, which she did. Tumblety then went away, and a minute or two later she noticed that the bottles of medicine were missing. She then summoned a Dr Humphreys and afterwards a Dr Botsford, who advised her to call the police. It was by now the evening of Wednesday, 26 September 1860. The police were called and found James Portmore dying, and he died soon after the visit. The following day an inquest was held, and Dr Tumblety was cross-examined. Drs Humphreys and Botsford had made a postmortem examination and swore positively that the immediate cause of death was acute inflammation of the stomach; they also maintained that inflammation of the stomach was not attributable to natural causes, but was always the result of a powerful irritant, such as an acid. According to the newspaper report, however, 'they would not swear that it could not possibly be otherwise, and they could find no such substance in the stomach'. Despite this, it was clear that the case had not gone well against Dr Tumblety and, indeed, the jury found a verdict of manslaughter against him, but by then he had fled. Leaving St John between ten and eleven o'clock that Thursday night, astride a white horse and followed by a faithful hound,[23] he fled across the border to Calais, Maine. In October there appeared in a Maine newspaper, the *Eastport Sentinel*, an article, possibly written by Tumblety, in which it was claimed that Tumblety had administered a decoction of parsley tea, which Portmore thought was doing him some good, but his doctors prevailed upon him to retake the medicine they had prescribed, which he did, and died. One of the doctors was a bitter enemy of Dr Tumblety and, despite the fact that the postmortem examination had shown no traces of poison or 'the slightest indication of any deleterious drug' in Mr Portmore's stomach, the coroner had directed the jury to bring in a verdict of manslaughter. Dr Tumblety was away, said the article, but would return to stand trial as soon as the Circuit Court opened. He never did return.[24]

It has to be said that from the brief report in the *Morning Freeman* no evidence seems to have been forthcoming that the acute inflammation of the stomach was caused by Dr Tumblety's medicine and no trace of such an irritant was found, although this may be accounted for by Portmore's acute vomiting before death.

From St John it is said that Tumblety fled to Boston – though he clearly stayed a while in Eastport, Maine – where he was again seen riding a magnificent white horse followed by a dog or dogs, and dressed extravagantly, but now he represented himself as the inventor of a cure for pimples. His business apparently did very well and he opened a branch office in New York and also visited numerous cities as far south as San Francisco.[25]

The *Brandon Mail*, a Canadian newspaper, reported years later[26] that Tumblety had practised in Nova Scotia, where he was accused of malpractice, having nearly killed a patient by administering the wrong medicines, and had fled to the States to escape prosecution. This may be a version of the Portmore story, but it is interesting because the newspaper claimed that he was known by the name Sullivan. In March 1861, when Tumblety was in New York, he complained that his name had been forged on two cheques and money falsely withdrawn from his account with the Chemical Bank. The bank claimed that the cheques were genuine and John Q Jones of the bank instituted official enquiries to establish Tumblety's character, alleging that it had already been shown that his real name was Sullivan,[27] that he was a menial servant of Dr Tumblety who had died and whose name and talents he had assumed.[28]

In New York Tumblety apparently called himself Dr Blackburn, and he had an office in Washington Street, boarding nearby with a Mrs Foster at 95 Fulton Street. He used to ride down Fulton Street in Brooklyn dressed in a hunting coat covered with gold braid and followed by several valuable hunting dogs. The boys used to mock him and call him 'Humpty Dumpty', which name seemed to please him.[29] Detective Cornelius Mahoney, of the

Brooklyn Central Office, later recalled the 'Doctor' as a 'peculiarly dressed man who used to scatter money for the boys to pick up'. It was an advertising scheme.[30] The *New York Times* would later recall that Tumblety was

> of striking personal appearance, being considerably over six feet in height, of graceful and powerful build, with strongly marked features, beautifully clear complexion, a sweeping mustache, and jet-black hair. He went dashing about the streets mounted on a handsome light chestnut horse, and dressed in the costliest and most elaborate riding costumes . . . In these rides he was invariably accompanied by a valet as handsomely apparelled and horsed as himself, and a brace of superb English greyhounds.

It was also reported that he 'cut a wide swath in the affections of the feminine lodgers',[31] which is in marked contrast with his later hatred of women, and at this time his pimple banisher was mainly sold to fashionable ladies who 'were in constant attendance at his office'.[32]

In 1861 Tumblety went to Washington. An unnamed naval officer would later recall meeting Tumblety there. The officer was looking at a mechanical toy in the window of a toy store, when Tumblety came to stand beside him and began to talk about it. He invited the man to his room to view a similar contraption that was supposed to show the circulation of the blood. He thought Tumblety was a decided crank who knew almost nothing about anatomy, although an ointment for skin diseases seemed to have some merit. 'He rode a magnificent horse – a bay, with white spots – and used to dash up the avenue. At certain points boys would run from the curb, with notes for him, thus giving folks the impression that he was doing a driving business.'[33]

Edward Haywood recalled that in Washington Tumblety wore a military fatigue costume and told him he was senior surgeon on the staff of General George McClellan (1826–85) who on 1 November 1861 was appointed general-in-chief commanding the Union armies in the Civil War – and who was an utter failure, being required to relinquish command on 9 November 1862. According to Haywood, a Lieutenant Larry Sullivan, who belonged to a Rochester regiment and was familiar with McClellan's staff, plainly told Tumblety he was a liar.[34] It was later reported that Tumblety denied having claimed to be in McClellan's service and explained how the falsehood had come about.[35] Haywood said that Tumblety remained in Washington during the Civil War, but his practice was restricted to selling an ointment to women, the Tumblety Pimple Destroyer, and at one time large posters advertising the cream adorned the walls of Washington. Tumblety made money, said Haywood, spent it lavishly and lived in the most extravagant elegance.

Colonel C A Dunham also knew Tumblety in Washington, where he said he met him a few days after the battle of Bull Run – which was fought on 21 July 1861, putting Tumblety in the capital earlier than Haywood suggests. Tumblety would dress in a richly embroidered coat, with medals pinned to his chest, a semi-military peaked cap perched on his head and wearing cavalry trousers with the brightest of yellow stripes down the sides, along with riding boots and spurs. With a dignified manner and what was described as a 'rather stagy gait', he used to hang around the hotels, the war department and the navy yard, trying to impress and curry favour with the officers by claiming to have diplomas from medical colleges in Europe and America, to have gained extensive experience at hospitals in Europe, and at much financial loss to himself, having accepted the appointment of brigade surgeon, which, fortunately for his private patients, would not be taking him from Washington in the foreseeable future.

One day Colonel Dunham and his lieutenant-colonel accepted an invitation to dine with Tumblety at his very cosy and tastefully arranged quarters consisting of three rooms on H Street. There were eight guests, the meal was provided by one of Washington's best caterers, and afterwards they played poker and whist. When Tumblety was asked why no women had been invited, his face

instantly became as black as a thunder cloud. He had a pack of cards in his hand, but he laid them down and said, almost savagely: 'No, Colonel, I don't know any such cattle, and if I did I would, as your friend, sooner give you a dose of quick poison than take you into such danger.' He then broke into a homily on the sin and folly of dissipation, fiercely denounced all woman and especially fallen women.

Then he invited us into his office where he illustrated his lecture, so to speak. One side of this room was entirely occupied with cases, outwardly resembling wardrobes. When the doors were opened quite a museum was revealed – tiers of shelves with glass jars and cases, some round and others square, filled with all sorts of anatomical specimens. The 'doctor' placed on a table a dozen or more jars containing, as he said, the matrices (uteri) of every class of women. Nearly a half of one of these cases was occupied exclusively with these specimens.[36]

According to Dunham, Tumblety explained that when he was a young man he had fallen in love with and married a pretty but somewhat older woman, who he noticed had a habit of flirting with other men and whom he one day saw enter a house with a man. On making enquiries he discovered that she had been a prostitute before the marriage and had remained one after.

Tumblety's extreme hatred for women would be increasingly commented on, as would his taste for the company of young men, and there is one incident recalled by a correspondent to the *Evening Star* that is potentially disturbing (if true). When Tumblety was in Washington he became very friendly with a young boy named Isaac Golladay, the nephew of ex-Congressmen Jacob Shall Golladay and Edward Isaac Golladay[37] of Kentucky. The lad's father, Frederick Golladay, who ran a boarding house in Washington, formed a bad opinion of Tumblety and tried to break up the friendship. The boy then left the boarding house one night and was not seen again. Dr Tumblety left Washington shortly afterwards. It was hoped that Golladay had gone to Europe with Tumblety and might possibly return. It is not known whether he did so.[38]

Colonel Dunham also told a story in the *Evening Star* that there was what he called 'a free, or it may have been 10-cent, concert saloon known as the Canterbury Music Hall', where an actor looking in every way like Tumblety burlesqued him. Tumblety was outraged and sued the Canterbury's management for libel. Then one night a powerful man sprang from the auditorium to the stage, shouted that Dr Tumblety was a friend of his and that he wouldn't see him insulted in such a manner, and tugged at the actor's moustache – which remained firmly in place and revealed the 'actor' to be Tumblety himself. It remains to be seen how true this story is: a contemporary newspaper report indicated that the burlesque was never staged, Tumblety having gone to court in March 1862 claiming that, on 7 March and on numerous occasions prior to that, George Percival of the Canterbury Music Hall 'did utter and publish a false and malicious libel, to the great injury and detriment of his reputation as an authorised physician'. Percival, it seems, had published a programme of forthcoming amusements, among them a farce 'proposed to be performed' and entitled *Doctor Tumblety's First Patient*. Tumblety objected to his name being used, had requested that it be withdrawn, and produced for the court a diploma and other things to prove that he was an authorised physician. The newspaper observed that Tumblety's 'skill as a physician, however, is undoubted, his practice in Washington being very extensive, and among the higher classes of society'.[39] In fact, as early as December 1861 advertisements had appeared in the newspapers promoting Tumblety at the Canterbury Hall:

CANTERBURY HALL

(Formerly the Washington Assembly Rooms)

Louisiana Avenue, near corner of 6th Street in the rear
of the National and Brown's Hotels,

OPEN EVERY NIGHT!

With the first talent in America.

ENTIRE CHANGE OF PROGRAMME.

Reappearance of MISS JULIA HUDSON

The Beautiful Songstress

New Songs, New Dances, and New Plays

TONIGHT

THE BEAUTIFUL BALLET

LA MONDOLINA

LA MONDOLINA

LA MONDOLINA

TUMBLETY OUTDONE.[40]

Tumblety proved to be a great traveller who moved around the country and travelled abroad. In 1863 he was in St Louis, where he claimed he took rooms at the prestigious Lindell Hotel, but where he was soon arrested for wearing a military uniform with medals he did not deserve. He would later complain in a pamphlet that he was constantly persecuted by jealous medical rivals. From St Louis he went to Carondelet, Missouri, where he was arrested and incarcerated for two days apparently, he believed, simply on the grounds of his military garb and ostentatious style. In early May 1864, back in New York, an asthmatic named Fenton Scully was attracted by Dr Tumblety's claim to cure all ills and in return for $14 received an asthma cure. It didn't work; in fact the asthma became worse, and in due course he revisited Tumblety and demanded his money back. Tumblety, said Scully, ordered him from the premises and, when Scully proved as obstinate as his asthma and refused to go, Tumblety booted him out – literally. Tumblety was arrested by Officer Riggs of the 41st Precinct, and subsequently, in court, was represented by a Mr Parmenter, 'once a legal luminary in the Police Court'. Tumblety produced two witnesses who swore that Tumblety never touched Scully, and as Scully had no means of proving otherwise, his charges were thrown out.[41]

In 1865 Tumblety was arrested in St Louis on suspicion of complicity in the assassination of President Lincoln. On Monday, 1 May, a detective in Brooklyn arrested a fifteen-year-old boy on suspicion of being connected with the assassination plot, having for some months allegedly been employed as a messenger by John Wilkes Booth. The boy apparently alleged that David E Herold, the companion of Booth, had been the agent and companion of a man known as the 'Indian Herb Doctor' – clearly Tumblety. The boy added that Tumblety had also been acquainted with Booth in Washington.[42]

Abraham Lincoln was shot by John Wilkes Booth on 14 April 1865. After the assassination the government arrested several hundred people, most of whom were quickly released due to lack of evidence, but eight people were tried for conspiring with Booth, among them Herold, who was with Booth when the latter surrendered at Garrett's farm, Virginia, two weeks after the assassination. Herold was hanged on 7 July 1865.

Although he had briefly studied pharmacy at Georgetown University, Herold, the sixth of eleven children born to the chief clerk at the Navy Store at the Washington Navy Yard, was a poor-witted youth, aged about 22 but with the mind of an 11-year-old. He had quickly abandoned college on his father's death and for almost a year before the assassination he had worked as a druggist's clerk. It was claimed that Herold had been Tumblety's servant sometime in the past, and initial reports, as in the *New York Tribune*, found the claim reasonable, saying that published descriptions of Herold perfectly matched the appearance of Tumblety's companion.[43] Herold does not appear to have been the same person as Tumblety's companion, as attested years later by Colonel Dunham, who claimed to have known Tumblety's companion quite well.[44]

Tumblety was arrested at his office on Third Street, St Louis, on 6 May 1865,[45] loudly proclaiming his innocence, and he was imprisoned in Washington on 10 May, to remain there until 26 May. Unfortunately for Tumblety, he had formerly used as an alias the name 'J H Blackburn' and this caused him to be confused with a Dr Blackburn who was at that time the subject of hysteria-producing articles in the Northern press in which he was accused of practising germ warfare. In April 1864 in Bermuda there had been an outbreak of yellow fever – a viral infection transmitted by a biting mosquito but in the mid-1800s thought to be transmitted through contact with infected persons or their personal possessions. Dr Luke Pryor Blackburn (1816–87), one of America's leading authorities on the disease, who had been a Confederate agent in Canada during the war, volunteered his services and stayed there until the disease abated in late October, receiving hearty praise from the British authorities.

But in April 1865 Charles M Allen, the US consul to Bermuda, claimed that Blackburn had gone to Bermuda at the behest of the Confederate government in order to gather infected clothing that would then be shipped as second-hand clothing to Northern cities and army camps. In May, Godfrey Joseph Hyams, a Union informer, claimed that he had helped Blackburn pack several trunks of infected clothes and had taken them to several cities, including, he would say, New Bern, North Carolina, where a yellow fever epidemic broke out in the summer of 1864, killing more than two thousand soldiers and civilians. The Northern press was full of scaremongering stories that portrayed Blackburn as a monster, and he was arrested in Canada and in October 1865 put on trial, being acquitted for lack of evidence. Whether Blackburn was guilty or not is unknown, but the charges do not seem consistent with his humanitarianism – his tombstone is inscribed LUKE PRYOR BLACKBURN – THE GOOD SAMARITAN – and his only recorded comment regarding the charges was 'too preposterous for intelligent gentlemen to believe'. After the war he resumed his practice in Kentucky, fought a yellow fever outbreak there in 1878, and became state governor.[46]

There exists a report by Colonel John P Baker, provost marshal general of Missouri, to Charles Dana, assistant war secretary:

I have the honour to forward herewith, in compliance with your telegram of this date, Dr Tumblety, alias Blackburn. All his papers had been carefully examined previous to the arrival of your order, but nothing was found in them tending to implicate him with the assassination.

Tumblety's papers and his own admissions show that he has tramped the continent from Quebec to New Orleans, in the character of an 'Indian Herb Doctor'; has gained an extensive notoriety as an impostor and quack; has been compelled to leave several towns and cities in Canada for his rascality and trickery, and is being continually importuned and threatened by those he has deluded and swindled.

Tumblety's principal associates in Saint Louis have been one J. W. Blackburn, his assistant in the 'medical profession', and one Oregon Wilson, an artist. There appears to be nothing against them, except they belong to a class of adventurers that encumber and prey upon society.[47]

When Tumblety was released he wrote to several newspapers announcing the calumny done to him, among them the *New York Times*:

Kirkwood House
Washington, D.C.,

Monday, June 5, 1865

To the Editor of the *New-York Times*:

After three weeks' imprisonment in the Old Capitol Prison in this city, I have been unconditionally and honorably released from confinement by direction of the Honorable Secretary of War, there being no evidence whatever to connect me with the yellow fever or assassination plot with which some of the Northern journals charged me of having some knowledge.

My arrest appears to have grown out of a statement made in a low licentious sheet published in New-York to the effect that the Dr Blackburn, who has figured so unenviably in the hellish yellow fever plot, was no other person than myself. In reply to this absurd statement, I would most respectfully say to an ever-generous public that I do not even know this fiend in human form named Dr Blackburn, nor have I ever seen him in my life. For the truth of this assertion I can bring hundreds of distinguished persons throughout the United States to vouch for my integrity, and, if necessary, can produce certificates from an innumerable number of gentlemen occupying high official positions.

While in imprisonment I noticed in some of the New-York and other Northern papers, a paragraph setting forth that the villain Herrold [sic], who now stands charged with being one of the leading conspirators in the assassination plot, was at one time in my employ. This, too, is false in every particular, and I am at a loss to see how it originated, or to trace it to its origin. For the past five years I have had but one man in my employment, and he is yet with me, his character being beyond reproach. I never saw Herrold, to my knowledge, and I have no desire to see him.

Another paper has gone so far as to inform the public that I was an intimate acquaintance of Booth's; but this, too, is news to me, as I never spoke to Booth in my life, or any of his family.

I do hope that the papers which so industriously circulated these reports connecting me with these damnable deeds, to the very great injury of my name and position, will do me the justice to publish my release, and the fact of my having been entirely exonerated by the authorities here, who, after a diligent investigation, could obtain no evidence that would in the least tarnish my fair reputation.

I feel it but due to the authorities here to state that, while in the Old Capitol, I was treated with the utmost kindness and consideration, and was placed in the same quarters assigned to Gov. Brown, Gov. Vance, Hon. Mr Lamar, and others of note.

With these few remarks in justice to myself, I will close by submitting them to the public.

Respectfully,

DR F. TUMBLETY[48]

Tumblety also wrote a book – more of a short pamphlet – of his life up till his arrest in St Louis, *Kidnapping of Dr Tumblety. By Order of the Secretary of War of the US*, which he had published in Cincinnati in 1866.

Some were not charitably inclined to accept that an injustice had been done to Tumblety, but thought instead that he had seized the opportunity to associate himself with a national news story and engineered his arrest for the publicity. The *Evening Times* of Hamilton, Ontario, was under no illusion, reporting,

> It is now stated that the arrest of Blackburn, alias Dr. Tumblety, is nothing but a smart advertising dodge on his part by which his 'infallible cures' will be better known. He has bamboozled Stanton into putting him into the Old Capitol, from which, of course, he will soon emerge innocent, a hero, and the demand for his nostrums will be increased at least a hundred fold.[49]

Years later Colonel Dunham concurred:

> It is perfectly clear that Tumblety purposely brought about his own arrest by sending anonymous letters to the federal authorities to the effect that Blackburn and himself were identical. His object, of course, was notoriety. He knew he was too well known in Washington, whither he felt certain he would be sent, to be kept long in custody.[50]

Tumblety travelled. The naval officer who met Tumblety outside the toy shop in Washington met him again in San Francisco in 1869, where 'he was doing very poorly', and Mr Smythe of the Hibernia Bank met Tumblety at the Occidental Hotel in San Francisco. Tumblety was renting an office at 20 Montgomery Street and apparently remained there until September 1870.[51] He then returned to New York, where late in 1870 a man named Clement R Bennett, a stenographer of the Circuit Court, saw Tumblety carrying a jockey riding whip, the head of which appeared resplendent with jewels, in company with a flashily dressed man. He had a very well-appointed suite of rooms at the Northern Hotel on Cortland Street, and, according to Bennett,

> cordially invited any young men whom he fancied, wherever he met them, in the parks, squares or stores, to call upon him at this hotel, where he was wont to say he would show them 'an easy road to fortune.' By his suavity he was successful beyond comprehension in enlisting and securing the attendance, at certain hours of the day and evening, of good-looking young men and boys, greenhorns, to 'walk into my parlor.' He pretended to be a 'specialist' and to have a cure for some of the ills which flesh is heir to.[52]

It was about 1870 that Tumblety went to London. A Chicago lawyer, Colonel James L Sothern, met him there. According to Tumblety's own and typically boastful account,

> I visited London where I was induced to prolong my stay beyond the anticipated period, through the request of parties who were anxious for me to prescribe for them. It was at this time that I had the gratification of an introduction to Charles Dickens, the immortal 'Boz', and my brief acquaintance with this eminent writer constitutes one of the most pleasant episodes of my life. During my sojourn in London I was the recipient of marked courtesies from many of England's most illustrious men and women.

He spent two weeks in Berlin, then returned to London for a short while before travelling to Liverpool, from where he embarked for New York. Tumblety later claimed that he was attached to the ambulance service of France during the siege of Paris in 1870–1, being presented with the Brittany cross and a diploma.[53] Back in New York in 1872 he discovered that his time in Nova Scotia had been exposed in *Frank Leslie's Illustrated Newspaper*, an innovative publication founded by Ipswich-born Henry Carter (1821–80), and inspired by the pioneering *Illustrated London News*. Carter, who had adopted the pseudonym 'Frank Leslie', had gone to New York in 1848 and launched his newspaper in 1855. He quickly realised the value of in-your-face spice and sensationalism – his motto was 'never shoot over the heads of the people' – and reported the murder cases and sensationalism with full gusto.[54] Tumblety was furious and when he encountered the newspaper's editor, Ralston, in the bar of the Fifth Avenue Hotel, he began a fight. Tumblety, who was almost universally dismissed as a coward, apparently got the worse of it and was then arrested by Detective T J Golden for assault, but Ralston declined to make any complaint. Tumblety then challenged Ralston to a duel, but Ralston told him he was not really worth fighting with.[55]

Tumblety briefly visited Montreal in 1875,[56] and then returned to England, where he advertised his services in the Liverpool press and attracted the attention of the journalist Hall Caine (1835–1931), who would become an extraordinarily famous and popular writer of sensational romances but is today forgotten except for his reminiscences of Dante Gabriel Rossetti and for being the dedicatee of Bram Stoker's *Dracula*.

According to Hall Caine's biographer, Vivien Allen, in Liverpool Tumblety 'soon gathered a coterie of young men around him and was generally thought to be homosexual'. According to the biography,

> By the beginning of 1875 the American doctor had made Liverpool too hot to hold him and he went to London. The Liverpool papers attacked him and he replied vigorously. He used Caine to write a pamphlet in his defence and tried to involve him in various odd schemes, some of them very odd indeed.

Caine apparently visited Tumblety in London several times during 1875, but Tumblety appears to have been looking to him for money. He wrote to Hall Caine to say he was thinking of starting a business in London manufacturing 'better pills than Holloway's'[57] and causing a sensation by giving away £10 worth of them free. He wanted a partner to share in the profits, and, as Vivien Allen observes, no doubt the costs. By 4 August, when Tumblety wrote from the Midland Hotel in Birmingham, Caine was being begged for money. At the end of the month Tumblety returned to New York. He would write Hall Caine several more letters, twice from New York, then once from San Francisco: 'It gives me great pleasure to hear from you and I should dearly love to see your sweet face and spend an entire night in your company.'

On 31 March 1876 he wrote from St Louis. It was the last letter and included a cutting from a newspaper reporting that Tumblety was in prison.

It was about this time, 1877–8, that Tumblety formed a relationship with a young man named Lyons. According to a New York lawyer named William P Burr,[58]

> The lad had just come from college and was a fine looking young man. He was out of employment. Tumblety greeted him and soon had him under complete control. He made him a sort of secretary in the management of his bonds, of which he had about $100,000 worth, mostly in governments, locked up in a downtown safe-deposit company. He employed the youth as an amanuensis, as he personally was most illiterate.[59]

On 23 April 1878 Tumblety sailed for Europe on the *Montana*,[60] a relatively new steamer built in 1874 and owned by the Guion Line, which operated a service between New York and Liverpool, leaving Lyons to act as his power of attorney.

As far as one can tell, Tumblety didn't return to America until 1880, when he discovered that the young man had disappeared along with some South Carolina railroad bonds worth about $7,000. Tumblety, who had a herb store at 77 East Tenth Street, had the man's mother charged with taking the bonds and she was arrested. Burr was enlisted to represent her and under cross-examination Tumblety's case against her collapsed, there being one memorable scene in court when Burr pressed Tumblety to identify the institution from which he had graduated a doctor. Tumblety looked furious, almost ready to leap upon Burr and strike him, but refused to answer and caused something of a commotion in court. When the case was thrown out, the son returned and charged Tumblety with atrocious assault. According to Burr, 'the evidence collected in this case was of the most disgusting sort' and a copy of the *Police Gazette* was produced in which there was a portrait of Tumblety and several columns of biography. The youth didn't go further with the charges, but Tumblety brought a suit against a broker named William P O'Connor, who had sold the bonds. Apparently, O'Connor was defended by a firm called Boardman & Boardman, who, with the assistance of two Brooklyn detectives named Charles Frost and Charles Chambers, gathered a lot of evidence against Tumblety, who seems not to have furthered the case.[61]

This whole story, which seems very well attested, throws some doubt on the story told by Clement R Bennett that he met Tumblety in 1879 in San Francisco, at which time, according to Bennett, Tumblety was 'looking shabby, careworn, lame, appeared to be living a dissolute and dissipated life, and was begging for a night's lodging'.[62]

William P Burr reiterated to a newspaper journalist that Tumblety was almost illiterate, and showed him an example:

I had a big batch of letters sent by him to the young man Lyon [*sic*], and they were the most amusing farrago of illiterate nonsense. Here is one written from the West. He never failed to warn his correspondence against lewd women, and in doing it used the most shocking language.

According to Burr, Tumblety 'had a seeming mania for the company of young men and grown-up youths' and was often to be seen 'hovering about the old post-office building, where there were many clerks'. He was 'a coward physically, though he looked like a giant', but 'once he had a young man under his control he seemed to be able to do anything with the victim'.[63]

In New York in 1880 it was reported that he was often seen at the Fifth Avenue Hotel with Charles Julius Guiteau, the notorious and probably chronically insane attorney who at that time was a familiar figure stationed outside Republican headquarters on Fifth Avenue. The following year, on 2 July 1881, he assassinated President James Abram Garfield as he was about to depart for a vacation from the Baltimore and Potomac Railroad Station. Although widely agreed today to have been insane, Charles Guiteau was hanged at the District of Columbia jail on 30 June 1882.[64]

In July 1882 Martin H McGarry applied for work at 7 University Place. Tumblety was outside – 'a big fine-looking man . . . He had on a braided English smoking jacket, black striped trousers, Oxford ties and a peaked cap'[65] – who said there was no work in the house but offered him a job as a travelling companion. McGarry related the succession of travels – strolling around New York, a trip to Niagara Falls, Rochester, Saratoga, back to New York for the winter. Then off to Boston, New Haven, Philadelphia, back to New York. Then Tumblety decided to visit Glasgow, where McGarry did not want to go, and Tumblety went on his own, returning after a month to lodge at a Mrs McNamara's, 79 East Tenth Street. Then McGarry accompanied Tumblety to Queenstown, Dublin and for a week at Inniskillen Falls. On returning from this trip McGarry's uncle told him he would have to live henceforth at home with his sisters, so he became a shipping clerk and in due course, through money earned from Tumblety, was able to buy his own business. As for Tumblety's attitude towards women, McGarry said, 'He always disliked women very much. He used to say to me, "Martin, no women for me." He could not bear to have them near him. He thought all women were impostors, and he often said that all the trouble in this world was caused by women.'[66]

Tumblety was not unknown to the British police and Chief Inspector Littlechild told G R Sims that Tumblety was 'constantly brought under the notice of police, there being a large dossier concerning him at Scotland Yard'. For unknown but easily deduced reasons – he had a publicly stated hatred of women and especially prostitutes – suspicion fell on him in connection with the Whitechapel murders. He was arrested, but no charges could be brought against him and he was charged instead with committing an act of gross indecency with John Doughty (on 27 July 1888), Arthur Brice (on 31 August 1888), Albert Fisher (14 October 1888) and James Crowley (2 November 1888). The calendar of prisoners for the Central Criminal Court session commencing 10 December 1888 records that Francis Tumblety was received into custody on 7 November, that the date of the warrant was 14 November, and that he was bailed on 16 November, and that recognisances of defendant (the bail money) were estreated (forfeited to the court).

The charges were brought according to what was known as the Labouchere Amendment to the Criminal Law Amendment Act of 1885 which read,

> 48&49 Vict. c.69, 11: Any male person who, in public or private, commits or is party to the commission of, or procures or attempts to procure the commission by any male person of any act of gross indecency with another male person, shall be guilty of a misdemeanour, and being convicted thereof shall be liable at the discretion of the Court to be imprisoned for any term not exceeding two years, with or without hard labour.

The charge was a misdemeanour, which at common law in England was a crime which was neither a treason nor a felony, but misdemeanours included serious offences such as conspiracy, riot and assault, and the sentences were stiff.

An objection to his being Jack the Ripper is that the last generally accepted victim, Mary Jane Kelly, was murdered on the night of 8–9 November. There is no doubt that Tumblety was in custody on 7 November and he could have been in custody at the time of the murder. One might also notice that he was otherwise engaged with Arthur Brice on 31 August, when Nichols was murdered. However, it has been argued that without a court appearance within 24 hours Tumblety would have been bailed to reappear in seven days, 14 November, which was the date of the warrant, and he was bailed again on 16 November against a surety of $1,500 given by two men who acted as bondsmen, neither of whom had known Tumblety for more than a few days prior to his arrest.[67]

On 20 November 1888 a hearing was held at the Old Bailey and the trial was postponed until 10 December. On 23 November 1888, according to the *New York Times*, Chief Crowley of San Francisco police received a request from

Scotland Yard that he send samples of Tumblety's handwriting. Tumblety had by now fled to Boulogne, then gone to Le Havre, where on 24 November 1888 he boarded the French Transatlantic Line steamer *La Bretagne* under the alias 'Frank Townsend'. He remained in his cabin feigning sickness until the liner docked in New York at 1.30 in the afternoon on Sunday, 4 December 1888. The New York police were expecting him and two New York policemen, Detectives Crowle and Hickey, positioned themselves either side of the gangplank and impatiently glanced at the passengers as they walked down. As the *New York World* reported, eventually Tumblety appeared:

> a big, fine-looking man . . . with a heavy, fierce-looking mustache, waxed at the ends; his face was pale and he looked hurried and excited. He wore a dark blue ulster, with the belt buttoned. He carried under his arm two canes and an umbrella fastened together with a strap.[68]

He hurried to a cab, had a small steamer trunk placed on the box, gave directions in a low voice and was driven away. The two detectives jumped into another cab and followed him.[69] He went to 79 East Tenth Street, the home of Mrs McNamara, with whom Tumblety had lodged frequently in the past – his own business being located at No. 77.

In due course an English detective arrived.

> He was a little man with enormous red side whiskers and a smoothly shaven chin. He was dressed in an English tweed suit and wore an enormous pair of boots with soles an inch thick . . . From his little billycock hat, alternately set jauntily on the side of his head and pulled loweringly over his eyes, down to the very bottom of his thick boots, he was the typical English detective. If he had been put on the stage just as he paraded up and down Fourth Avenue and Tenth Street yesterday afternoon he would have been called a caricature.[70]

He took up surveillance in a bar across the road and actually told the barkeeper over a drink that he was an English detective out 'to get the chap that did' the Whitechapel murders, and asked questions about Tumblety. Unless the *New York World* was grossly exaggerating, the detective behaved oddly, to say the least, and one can only assume that his strange and conspicuous manner was intended to draw attention to himself rather than the reverse.

Mrs McNamara said of Tumblety that he 'would not harm a child. He is a perfect gentleman and always paid me punctually. He wouldn't hurt anybody. He once followed me up three flights of stairs to pay me a dollar he owed me.'[71] She was not host to him for very long. The *New York World* reported that it appeared that Tumblety had fled 79 East Tenth Street, probably early in the morning on 5 December 1888.[72] A workman living opposite said that he'd seen Tumblety outside the house and that he showed a great deal of nervousness, glancing over his shoulder constantly, finally walking to Fourth Avenue and taking an uptown car. A *New York World* reporter managed to get into the boarding house and into Tumblety's room. There was a half-open valise on a chair near the window and a big pair of boots of the English cavalry regulation pattern, but nothing else.

Thomas Byrnes,[73] the celebrated and corrupt chief inspector of the New York Police Department, who had reportedly known Tumblety for over twenty years, and always regarded him as a suspicious and mysterious individual,[74] was said to have laughed at the suggestion that Tumblety was involved in the Whitechapel murders, that the crime for which he was under bond in London was not extraditable and that he had no charge against him, but was keeping him under observation[75] so that 'if they think in London that they need him and he turns out to be guilty our men will probably have an idea where he can be found'.

On or about 10 December 1888 Inspector Andrews arrived in Toronto with Roland Gideon Israel Barnet, who was charged with having contributed to the failure in 1887 of the Central Bank of Toronto. On 20 December he went to Montreal, where he had an interview with Chief of Police Hughes. Newspapermen collared him and questioned him about the Whitechapel murders. He reportedly said that 'there were 23 detectives, 2 clerks and 1 inspector employed on the Whitechapel murders case and that the police were without a jot of evidence upon which to arrest anybody' – this apparently related to the detectives in London, not in Canada – and it was announced at police headquarters on 21 December that Andrews and two other Scotland Yard men were to investigate the Ripper in Canada.[76] Andrews went to New York and it was reported in several newspapers, including the *Pall Mall Gazette*, that he was there in connection with the Whitechapel murders investigation.[77]

Detective Inspector Walter Andrews is mentioned by Walter Dew,[78] who called him 'a jovial, gentlemanly man, with a fine personality and a sound knowledge of his job', as being one of the three main Ripper hunters, along with Chief Inspector Moore and Inspector Abberline, but he is not mentioned in any of the surviving police or Home Office reports on the case, from which some writers have concluded that 'he had been given the task of investigating Tumblety as a suspect from an early stage.'[79]

The *New York Herald*, no friend of Charles Stewart Parnell, on 23 December 1888 gave Inspector Andrews's visit a different purpose. Citing a telegraph received from Montreal the previous day, it said that 'ever since his arrival in the country and his subsequent lengthy stay in Toronto rumours have been current to the effect that he was one of many men in the employ of the British government . . . in the search for the least evidence that will seemingly injure the Parnellites'. This was all to do with a major political scandal in Britain in which *The Times* was trying to link the Irish Nationalist leader, Charles Stewart Parnell, with Fenian and other terrorist outrages in London. Andrews apparently denied that that was his mission, but the newspaper reported that 'on the eve of his departure for home the emissary of Scotland Yard admitted that he could not deny the charge and practically acknowledged that that was his mission'.

Andrews apparently stated that the British government operated a highly organised detective system in Canada and the United States, and that there were informers occupying high positions in Irish societies, so that the British authorities were aware of every move almost as quickly as the Nationalists themselves. Henry J Cloran, president of the National League, said that he was aware of Inspector Andrews's journey even before he had left London, and that he had been watched ever since he had landed at Halifax.

This is an extraordinary report, but not beyond possibility. The Parnell story rears its head more fully in a later chapter, but we know of several claims that the police were seeking evidence to support *The Times*. William Henry Joyce, an IRC man who in 1888 became a resident magistrate, was allegedly told to drop some cases he was investigating because they had 'been got up by *agents provocateur*' working for the British authorities and that the police had planted bombs as evidence to justify arrests.[80] Andrews's mission in Canada and America therefore could have had more to do with Parnell than with the Ripper investigations, as, indeed, could Tumblety – a Brooklyn newspaper, the *Daily Eagle*, reporting on 27 April 1890 that a couple of years earlier 'he was under suspicion on account of his supposed connection with the advanced branch of the Irish national party'. And Tumblety curiously refers to himself and Parnell in his second booklet, *Dr Francis Tumblety – Sketch of the Life of the Gifted, Eccentric and World Famed Physician*, published in 1889:

Now let me say a word about the attacks which certain American news-papers recently made on me, attacks that were as unfounded as the onslaught made on the great Irish leader. While I was not in a position to defend myself, these papers continued their foul slanders, but my friends will readily see, from the foregoing pages and from the testimonials, how utterly base and wholly groundless these aspersions were. Like Parnell, I have emerged from the battle totally unscathed with my social and professional standing unimpaired. It is gratifying to recall the pleasure with which my friends welcomed me to my native land. I treasure these tributes among the dearest things in my possession.

Tumblety turned up in Brooklyn about 18 January 1889 under the name of Smith at the boarding house of Mrs Helen Lamb, at 204 Washington Street. Towards the end of the month (possibly 27 January), a young man called at the house during a heavy rainstorm and Tumblety paid his bill from a big roll of banknotes, packed his trunks, and had them loaded on a truck, which the young man had summoned, and drove off into the rain, disappearing as silently and as mysteriously as he had appeared.[81]

Tumblety almost vanished from the pages of history until he is heard of in Washington, where he was arrested on 18 November 1890 on the charge of being a suspicious character. No account is given of what he was doing to attract the attention of the police, specifically a Detective Horne, but Judge Millar said there was strong circumstantial evidence of his recent suspicious conduct to show that the suspicions were justified, and that although, compelled to dismiss the case, he did so with reluctance, and it was reported that the police would keep Tumblety under surveillance during his stay in Washington.[82]

Tumblety's connection with the Whitechapel crimes is a strange one. Americans became a focus of suspicion in the press and among the public following Wynne Baxter's story about the American surgeon paying for uteri, and especially after receipt of the Dear Boss letter and Saucy Jacky postcard with their use of Americanisms. The arrests of several Americans were reported in the press, and others were questioned, including three cowboys who had come to Britain the previous year with Buffalo Bill's celebrated Wild West Show for Queen Victoria's Jubilee.[83] While we know from the Littlechild letter that Tumblety *was* suspected of being the Jack the Ripper, we have no idea why suspicion fell on him beyond what appears to be his openly declared hatred of women and especially of prostitutes. However, there is no report or newspaper story that so much as puts Tumblety in the East End, let alone connects him with the prostitutes there, and no newspaper report records the arrest of someone who could be Tumblety.

There have been efforts to connect him with the Batty Street lodger (see Chapter Thirteen), but the links are tenuous, to say the least. There was a report in *The Globe* on 10 October 1888 that a detective from the CID at Scotland Yard had recently travelled to Liverpool and traced the movements there of a man who had travelled to London, taken rooms in a well-known first-class West End hotel and then disappeared leaving his bill unpaid. In his room was a black leather bag containing documents, clothing, chequebooks, letters and prints of an obscene description. The newspaper reported that the hotel management had placed an advertisement in *The Times* giving the man's name and stating that unless the bag and contents were claimed – and by inference the bill paid – they would be sold by auction under the Innkeepers' Act. This was duly done in September by a well-known auctioneer in London, some of the contents having meanwhile been handed to the police. The newspaper said that the owner of the bag was in the habit of 'slumming' in the East End, and said it had been suggested that he had come to Liverpool from America,[84] but apart from his being in the habit of slumming, which was not an uncommon pastime, nothing connected the man with Tumblety or the Batty Street lodger and the newspaper emphasised that it was only suggested that the man was an American.

Liverpool, of course, was understandably subject to surveillance and newspapers testify that this was the case,[85] some claiming that the police thought the Ripper would try to make his escape via the city.[86]

Perhaps the closest description yet found that could put Tumblety in the East End is an extraordinary story told by a man named John Lardy and most fully reported in the *Daily News* on Friday, 19 October. At 10.30 p.m. on Wednesday, 17 October, Lardy and a friend were outside a pub called the Grave Maurice, almost opposite London Hospital. He saw a man cross the road, peer through the window into the pub as if looking for somebody, then go inside for a minute or two. He looked up and down the street, crossed the road, spoke to two women who Lardy thought were prostitutes and who shook their heads as if saying no. The man then went to a shop and bought a newspaper. Lardy and his friend followed, but the man did nothing more than walk to a narrow passage called King Street near the Tower. He went into a house there and emerged 25 minutes later, going off towards Whitechapel Road, Lardy and his friend losing sight of him in the fog.

The only reason for connecting this man with Tumblety is the description provided by Lardy, who said he was between 40 and 45 and six foot tall with black hair and a moustache, which attracted Lardy's attention, though not, as far as can be told, for its remarkable and distinctive size, but because it looked like a false one, one end pointing upward and the other towards the ground. He also had the appearance of an American.

The next we hear of the man is that he was behaving suspiciously in Bermondsey and was arrested. There seems to have been some confusion about who arrested the man, the newspapers reporting that he had been arrested by the City Police, but this was denied to the Central News,[87] probably correctly, as Bermondsey was in Metropolitan Police jurisdiction and anyone attracting attention by behaving suspiciously there would have been arrested by the Metropolitan Police. With that the man disappears from the newspapers, although an almost identical story appeared in the *Daily Telegraph* a month later when it reported that early in the morning on 22 November the police arrested a man in Bermondsey whose movements had been watched for some days. The prisoner was taken to the Commercial Street Police Station, but was released after satisfying the police of his innocence of the Whitechapel crimes.[88] There is no reason beyond Bermondsey to connect this man with Lardy's, although the police could have kept Lardy's man under surveillance and eventually made an arrest. If it was Lardy's man, he wasn't Tumblety.

The remainder of Tumblety's life seems to have been spent in relative obscurity. From about 1893 until his death in 1903 he lived during the summer in Rochester, New York, at the home of an elderly niece named Alice FitzSimons, using her house as both home and office, and during the winter he lived in St Louis. He developed a heart condition and during the afternoon of 26 April 1903 he was admitted to St John's Hospital at 307 South Euclid Avenue, St Louis, a charitable institution run by the Sisters of Mercy, an order of nuns established in Dublin. He used the name 'Townsend' again. Following a walk on Monday, 25 May, he collapsed, falling and breaking his nose. On Thursday, 28 May 1903, he died. His body was transported to Rochester, where he was buried at the Holy Sepulchre Cemetery, 2461 Lake Avenue, Rochester, in a family grave. The memorial reads:

REQUIESCAT IN PACE
DR FRANCIS TUMUELTY[89]
DIED
MAY 28, 1903
AGED 70 YEARS

Tumblety left a staggering $138,000 in cash with the banking firm of Henry Clews and Co., and in his will he left $10,000 to Cardinal Gibbons, and $10,000 to Archbishop Ireland, this money to be used for charitable purposes, and some $20,000 was distributed among family. The rest of the money was unattributed and led to a prolonged legal dispute, a curious feature of which was a claim by Joseph R Kemp of Baltimore, Maryland, acting on behalf of the Home for Fallen Women in Baltimore, which claimed that by a will of 3 October 1901 it had been left $1,000 plus jewellery. The petition was rejected.

Although a surprisingly large amount of information about Tumblety is known, there is a lot that we don't know and it is foolish to try to draw hard and fast conclusions. On the face of it, he is an unlikely Ripper. Littlechild never said he was, and arguably wouldn't have mentioned him at all if G R Sims hadn't recalled him to mind by asking about a 'Dr D.' Littlechild's remark (which we saw earlier in his letter to Sims) was that Dr T(umblety) was 'amongst the suspects, and to my mind a very likely one'. This has sometimes been interpreted as meaning that among the suspects Tumblety was a very likely one to have been the Ripper, but Littlechild meant only that most of the suspects had been arrested for flimsy reasons, such as looking or behaving suspiciously, making claims when drunk, and so on, whereas Tumblety's claim to be a doctor and his open hatred of women in general and prostitutes in particular made him a more likely suspect than they were. Later in the letter Littlechild also wrote that Tumblety 'was not known as a "Sadist" (which the murderer unquestionably was)'. Whether or not Jack the Ripper was in reality a sadist is immaterial. Littlechild evidently believed he was and presumably therefore would have discounted Tumblety on the grounds that he was not one. The only observation that seems to contradict these conclusions is his statement, 'certain it is that from this time [Tumblety's flight to America] the "Ripper" murders came to an end', but this is probably meant as no more than an explanation why somebody might have thought Tumblety to be the Ripper, G R Sims having written to Littlechild about a suspect, 'Dr D.', against whom somebody clearly did entertain suspicions.

Despite occasional claims that Tumblety could be moved to violence, as was the case when he assaulted the editor of *Frank Leslie's Illustrated Paper*, Tumblety was generally dismissed as a coward. And while he seemed to associate with young men – and it was occasionally remarked that he hung around places such as the post office, where there were young clerks – there is no reference to his associating in later life with prostitutes or with any women, except Mrs McNamara. But more than the lack of violence in his character or any record that he associated with prostitutes, it is chiefly Tumblety's appearance that doesn't tally, as his marked physical description doesn't fit that of anyone seen with any victim or in the area of any of the crimes. In 1890 Tumblety was described as

> an enormous man, over six feet in height, with broad shoulders. His hair is black, tinged with gray, and his skin is red and coarse. His moustache is a rather large affair, evidently dyed black, and extends around the corners of his mouth. His eyes are steely blue . . . he spoke in a weak, effeminate voice.[90]

That distinctive moustache – highly distinctive if it is accurately represented by the picture of Tumblety – was there in 1888, as evidenced by the description of him as he left the ship at New York after his flight from Le Havre: 'a big, fine-looking man . . . with a heavy, fierce-looking mustache, waxed at the ends . . .' The moustache was always there. Tumblety was a 'very tall, muscular man, with a huge black mustache', reported the Brooklyn *Daily Eagle* on 4 May 1865; his 'black mustache was of such huge proportions and singular cut that it would have attracted attention anywhere', said the *Olean Democrat* on 8 August 1889. From these descriptions Tumblety would have been as conspicuous in the East End as a brass band at a funeral.

CHAPTER FIFTEEN

Sir Charles Warren Resigns

Sir Charles at last throws up the sponge,
He yields to Matthews' latest lunge;
The latter says, with angry spite,
Sir Charles did wrong when he did write.[1]

Sir Charles Warren resigned on 8 November 1888. Henry Matthews informed Queen Victoria in a letter headed 'Whitehall, 10th Nov. 1888':

Mr Henry Matthews with his humble duty to your Majesty begs to inform your Majesty that the Cabinet have to-day decided to accept the resignation of Sir Charles Warren. It arose in this way. Sir Charles Warren wrote an article in the last number of *Murray's Magazine* in which he discusses the whole subject of the administration of the police force, makes suggestions as to the discharge of their duties, and gives an historical review of the subject. The article would probably not have attracted much attention if it had not contained some passages which appear to convey personal criticism of public men. It is contrary to the usages of the Civil Service officials to publish articles about the department to which they belong; and in the Home Department there has been since 1879 a rule prohibiting any officer of the department from publishing any work relating to the department without sanction of the Secretary of State. I thought it my duty to call Sir C. Warren's attention to this rule, and to request his compliance with it in future. He had not sought for any sanction before publishing the article. In his reply to my communication Sir C. Warren contended that the Secretary of State has not the power of issuing orders for the police force; he informed me that he would not have accepted the post of Commissioner of Police if he had been told the

Home Office rule applied to that post; he declined to accept the instructions which had been sent to him, and placed his resignation in the hands of the Government.

It is not the first time that Sir C claimed to be in a position of independence which was wholly inconsistent with the authority and responsibility of the Secretary of State. The Cabinet took the matter into consideration to-day and decided that the resignation must be accepted.

Mr Henry Matthews thinks that your Majesty may probably be glad to have the earliest possible information of the fact, and to receive a brief account of the circumstances.[2]

Queen Victoria was clearly sorry to see Sir Charles Warren go, as is evident from her reply to Matthews dated 13 November 1888:

The Queen has received with sincere regret Mr. Matthews's letter of the 10th, in which he reports the resignation of Sir Charles Warren.

It would of course be impossible to recognise Sir Charles Warren's contention that he was not under the orders of the Secretary of State, but the Queen fears this resignation will have a bad effect in encouraging the law-breakers to defy the police, who, under Sir Charles Warren, have always done their duty admirably.

At the same time the Queen fears that the detective department is not so efficient as it might be. No doubt the recent murders in Whitechapel were committed in circumstances which made detection very difficult; still, the Queen thinks that, in the small area where these horrible crimes have been perpetrated, a great number of detectives might be employed, and that every possible suggestion might be carefully examined and, if practicable, followed.

Have the cattle boats and passenger boats been examined?

Has any investigation been made as to the number of single men occupying rooms to themselves?

The murderer's clothes must be saturated with blood and must be kept somewhere.

Is there sufficient surveillance at night?

These are some of the questions that occur to the Queen on reading the accounts of this horrible crime.[3]

It was widely thought at the time that Sir Charles Warren had resigned because of criticism resulting from the Whitechapel murders, but this was not the case. The precise cause had been an article he wrote for the November 1888 issue of *Murray's Magazine*. In writing the article, he had breached a Home Office rule that forbade him from writing material for publication. On 8 November 1888, with a typical lack of tact, 'instead of dealing with the matter in a courteous and moderate spirit, as might be expected with an official of the importance of the Chief Commissioner, [Matthews] instructed one of the clerks in the department to send him a curt letter, calling his attention to the regulations':[4]

> Sir, – Mr Secretary Matthews directs me to state that his attention has been called to an article signed by you in this month's number of Murray's Magazine, relating to the management and discipline of the Metropolitan Police Force. He desires me to forward to you the enclosed copy of a Home Office circular which was duly communicated to the Commissioner of Police in 1879, and to state that the directions in that circular were intended to apply to the Metropolitan Police and to every officer in the force from the Commissioner downwards. I am accordingly to request that, in the future, the terms of this order may be strictly complied with.

The attached minute read,

> The Secretary of State, having had his attention called to the question of allowing private publication, by officers attached to the department, of books on matters relating to the department, is of opinion that the practice may lead to embarrassment and should in future be discontinued. He desires, therefore, that it should be considered a rule of the Home Department that no officer should publish any work relating to the department unless the sanction of the Secretary of State has been previously obtained for the purpose.

Warren replied on the same day:

> Sir, – I have just received a pressing and confidential letter, stating that a Home Office circular of May 27, 1879, is intended to apply to the Metropolitan Police Force. I have to point out that, had I been told

that such a circular was to be in force, I should not have accepted the post of Commissioner of Police. I have to point out that my duties and those of the Metropolitan Police are governed by statute, and that the Secretary of State for the Home Department has not the power under the statute of issuing orders for the police force. This circular, if put in force, would practically enable every one anonymously to attack the police force without in any way permitting the Commissioner to correct false statements, which I have been in the habit of doing, whenever I found necessary, for nearly three years past. I desire to say that I entirely decline to accept these instructions with regard to the Commissioner of Police, and I have again (Lord R. Churchill and other members, – 'Again!') to place my resignation in the hands of Her Majesty's Government.

Matthews replied on 10 November:

Sir, – I beg to acknowledge your letter of the 8th inst. In that letter, after contending that the Secretary of State has not the power under statute of issuing orders for the Metropolitan Police, you decline to accept his instructions that the Commissioner and all officers of the force should comply with the Home Office minute of May 27, 1879, by which officers attached to the Home Department were enjoined not to publish any work relating to the department without the previous sanction of the Secretary of State, and you place your resignation in the hands of Her Majesty's Government. In my judgment the claim thus put forward by you as Commissioner of Police, to disregard the instructions of the Secretary of State, is altogether inadmissible, and accordingly, I have only to accept your resignation. At the same time, I am glad to acknowledge the services which you have rendered to Her Majesty's Government during the course of your administration of the police force.

Matthews confirmed to Parliament that the resignation of Sir Charles Warren had been accepted only because he had refused to comply with the Home Office minute of 27 May 1879, and had nothing to do with the 'failure of the police to discover recent crimes in the metropolis' – an obvious reference to the Whitechapel murders – or with differences of opinion between Warren and Assistant Commissioner Monro, on which point he stated that Monro had 'not interfered in any way with the conduct of the business of the Criminal Investigation Department, nor has he been consulted by myself or by any one else, to my knowledge, on that subject. The advice which I have sought from Mr Monro was confined to the general question of the organisation proper for the department in the abstract, without any reference whatever to the daily current business of the department.'

Sir Charles Warren thought otherwise. Shortly after his resignation he was interviewed by the London correspondent of the *New York Herald*, who wrote, 'Instead of the military martinet which he is represented to be in some quarters, I found a gentleman of courteous manner and amiable disposition, with much dignity.' He was a 'military man, looking little over forty and considerably bronzed. He wears a mustache suggestive of silence and his features are regular and handsome.' Asked if he had resigned because of the last Whitechapel murder,

Sir Charles adjusted his glasses and smiled.

'No,' he resumed, emphatically: 'no, I sent in my resignation before the Kelly murder, on the 8th of this month, and immediately after Mr Matthews' statement in the House of Commons in reference to my article in *Murray's Magazine*. The resignation was accepted yesterday. That article was perfectly innocuous and could not do any harm.'

In a nutshell, what happened was that Warren appreciated that the Home Office was responsible for policy decisions affecting the police – such as whether or not rewards should be offered – but he did not believe Matthews had any authority regarding the day-to-day running of the force and could not, for example, issue orders to officers subordinate to the commissioner. As Warren said,

A curious feature of the whole business was that the government, represented by Mr Matthews, held me personally responsible for all the crime in London and yet they made communications to my subordinates. It was first Assistant Commissioner Munro, now it is Mr Anderson.

The final straw, according to Warren, was Matthews having what amounted to a rebuke written by a clerk.[5]

In the end it was acknowledged that Matthews had right on his side, but the judgement of several newspapers – and in the long run probably also of history – was that Matthews took the opportunity to rid himself of Warren. At least one contemporary newspaper observed that 'while his friends cannot deny that he made a grand tactical blunder in claiming a position practically independent of the Cabinet and of Parliament itself, they must regard him as the victim of the pure hostility of Mr Matthews'.[6] *The Times* put it slightly differently: 'The reproof administered to Sir Charles Warren by the Home Secretary for defending himself in the pages of a magazine was merely the accident which determined a resignation sooner or later inevitable.'

Newspapers also thought the Whitechapel murders had been to a degree responsible for the resignation:

For the beginning of discord we should probably have to go back to the Trafalgar-square riots, when SIR CHARLES WARREN clearly knew his own mind, and how to carry out a definite policy, while MR. MATTHEWS as evidently did not know his own mind and showed no capacity for action. A rupture might, however, have been avoided had nothing occurred to throw an exceptional strain upon the department. But the series of brutal and mysterious murders in Whitechapel concentrated public attention upon the constitution and management of the police and detective forces. The defects of a faulty organization were dragged into daylight, and the men responsible for the time being came in for the severe criticism which ought in justice to have been bestowed upon their predecessors and upon the public which had long acquiesced in what is now unsparingly condemned. SIR CHARLES WARREN in particular was held responsible for the failures of the Criminal Investigation Department, which he did not construct and which he found himself powerless to reorganize. That department is largely, if not exclusively, manned by the ordinary police, but appears to be, nevertheless, provided with a chief who has direct relations with the Home Office, behind the back of the man actually responsible for the discipline, organization, and efficiency of the whole police force. In such circumstances friction is inevitable as soon as the Chief Commissioner, either from choice or necessity, makes any sort of energetic and thoroughgoing effort after efficiency.[7]

During the morning of 12 November Sir Charles Warren's books and papers were removed from his office. Warren was gone.

*

On 24 November 1888 Henry Matthews informed Queen Victoria that the Cabinet had selected James Monro as the best candidate for the post of commissioner, pointing out that he had 'considerable experience of police duties both in India and in the Metropolis' and observed that he believed the appointment 'would give satisfaction to the general body of the Metropolitan police'. His remarks were somewhat tempered, however, by the concluding observation that 'there are few qualified for the office who would be willing to accept it.' [8]

CHAPTER SIXTEEN

Mary Jane Kelly

Mary Jane Kelly – who was also known as Marie Jeanette Kelly, Fair Emma,[1] Ginger[2] and Black Mary[3] – was born in Ireland and was found murdered on Friday, 9 November 1888.

Kelly was about 25, five foot seven and stout. She had blue eyes, a fair complexion and her hair colour is variously given as blonde,[4] ginger,[5] light[6] and dark.[7] The *Daily Telegraph* reported that Kelly 'was of a fair complexion, with light hair, and possessing rather attractive features, dressed pretty well. Usually she wore a black silk dress, and often a black jacket, looking shabby genteel in her attire, but generally neat and clean.'[8]

Walter Dew claimed to know Kelly quite well by sight. He said he had often seen her parading along a stretch of Commercial Street between Flower and Dean Street and Aldgate, or along Whitechapel Road, usually in the company of two or three other women, always fairly neatly dressed, invariably wearing a clean white apron, but never a hat. He described her as 'quite attractive' and 'a pretty, buxom girl'.[9] Sir Melville Macnaghten, who never saw her in the flesh, had heard it said that she was 'possessed of considerable personal attractions'.[10]

Her background is a mystery and is pieced together from what she told her lover Joseph Barnett or other associates. All or none of it could be true, or just bits and pieces here and there.

She said she had been born in Limerick, Ireland, but it is not clear whether she meant County Limerick or Limerick town. Her father was named John Kelly and she had six or seven brothers and one sister. As a child she had moved with her family to Wales, where her father got a job as a foreman in an ironworks in either Caernarvonshire or Carmarthenshire – more likely the latter (in West Wales), where there were several substantial ironworks. When she was about sixteen, Kelly married a collier named Davis or Davies, but two or three years later he was killed in a mine explosion. Without any means of support, Kelly went to Cardiff, where she lived with a cousin, who introduced her to prostitution – Chief Constable Hemingway of Cardiff would later say that he had no recollection that any woman answering Kelly's description had come to the attention of the police[11] – and, according to Barnett, she also spent eight or nine months in an infirmary in Cardiff.

The late Stephen Knight, in his highly controversial and bestselling *Jack the Ripper: The Final Solution*,[12] claimed that in about 1884 Kelly moved from Cardiff to London, found employment as a domestic servant and received board and lodging at the Providence Row Women's Refuge in Crispin Street, Spitalfields, and the following year was found a permanent position at a tobacconist's in Cleveland Street in Fitzrovia. Despite what appears to have been a longstanding tradition among the nuns of the refuge that Kelly was resident there,[13] the rest of the story lacks supportive evidence and conflicts with Kelly's own, independently attested account of her life.

Reconstructing Kelly's life from various sources, it seems that on arrival in London she made the acquaintance of a French woman in the neighbourhood of Knightsbridge and worked for her in a high-class West End bordello. She had dressed well, been driven about in a carriage and generally led the life of a 'lady'. She had made several trips to France and told Barnett that she had accompanied a gentleman to Paris but had not liked it there and had returned after about two weeks. It all sounds very unlikely, but Kelly certainly adopted the French spelling of her name, calling herself 'Marie Jeannete', and otherwise it is within the bounds of possibility.

In the early 1880s it was widely believed that large numbers of young English women and girls were lured or even abducted abroad and forcibly detained in legalised Continental brothels. The evidence shows that the involuntary prostitution of young British women was nowhere near as widespread as some people imagined, but it was certainly true that procurers for foreign brothels kept an eye open for young and pretty prostitutes and would-be prostitutes. One such man was a Brussels brothel owner named Edouard Roger, who frequently visited London to recruit girls. With false promises of more money, a more luxurious lifestyle, better living conditions or prospects of marrying a well-off man or even an aristocrat, he persuaded them to register with the foreign police as a prostitute. They would then be 'sold' to a brothel, where they quickly discovered that all the promises were untrue and where they were virtual slaves. Before going abroad the girls were generally treated with care and lived in a degree of luxury, and Kelly's story sounds as if she had fallen into the hands of a procurer.

We next hear of Mary Kelly when she was living with a Mrs Buki[14] in St George's Street (otherwise Ratcliffe Highway), just north of the London Docks North Quay, who apparently accompanied Kelly to the home of the French lady in Knightsbridge and demanded the return of a box of expensive dresses.[15] This information, turned up by journalists after Kelly was dead would if true seem to be independent confirmation of the details Kelly gave to Barnett, and also suggests that Kelly's descent into the East End was extraordinarily rapid. This could be explained by the fact that the procurers invested money and time in 'conning' their girls and may even have taken advance payment from the foreign brothel keeper, so if at the last moment the girl refused to register as a prostitute with the foreign police, or otherwise managed to slip back to Britain, the procurer might be very anxious to extract his own pound of flesh. Kelly could have fled to the crowded East End to avoid the West End, where she may have been known. It may also be significant that Kelly apparently started drinking heavily during this time. Eventually it made her unwelcome with Mrs Buki and Kelly moved on.

She moved to live with Mr and Mrs McCarthy[16] at Breezer's Hill, off Pennington Street, St George's-in-the-East. On 10 November 1888, after Kelly's death, Mrs Elizabeth Phoenix of 157 Bow Common Lane, Bow, visited Leman Street Police Station and said that, from the description in the newspapers, she felt sure that Kelly had resided at her brother-in-law's house in Breezer's Hill about three years before.[17] This was almost certainly John and Mary Ann Jane McCarthy[18] (no known relation to Kelly's future landlord), who lived at 1 Breezer's Hill. The couple had married on 2 June 1884 and must have moved to Breezer's Hill soon after. They are still listed there in the 1891 census, and it may have been a brothel.[19] Mrs Phoenix said Kelly was about five foot seven and rather stout with blue eyes, and hair reaching almost to her waist. She said that Kelly had claimed that her parents had discarded her.[20] The press investigated and Mrs McCarthy said that Kelly had left her house eighteen months to two years earlier – late 1886 or early 1887 – and had gone to 'live with a man who was apparently in the building trade' and who Mrs McCarthy believed would have married Kelly, but some time later she had been awakened at two o'clock in the morning by Kelly, who asked for a bed for the night, and in their conversation said she wasn't with that man any more. Mrs McCarthy said she hadn't seen Kelly since.[21]

This man was probably Joseph Fleming, Barnett having said that Kelly had lived with two men before him, a man named Morganstern, who lived opposite or in the vicinity of Stepney gasworks, and Fleming, who had lived in Bethnal Green. Barnett said Kelly seemed very fond of him and that he still visited her. A neighbour of Kelly's, Julia Venturney, said that Kelly was fond of a man other than Barnett, whose name was also Joe, who she thought was a costermonger and who sometimes visited and gave money to Kelly, who had remarked that he often 'ill-used her' because she lived with Barnett.[22]

By 1886 Mary Jane Kelly was living at Cooley's Lodging House in Thrawl Street, Spitalfields, and, according to an unnamed prostitute, was living there when she met Joseph Barnett[23] in Commercial Street on 8 April 1887, Good Friday. Barnett, a porter at Billingsgate Market and sometime fruit hawker, took Kelly for a drink and they arranged to meet the following day. It was at this second meeting that they decided to live together.[24]

Kelly seems to have had little contact with her family and there are hints of a troubled relationship with her parents and a lot of resentment. Apart from Mrs Phoenix's observation that Kelly said her family had discarded her, Barnett said that her father had once come to London to look for her and that she had hidden from him.[25] Her sister, said Barnett, was very fond of her and was very respectable, travelling from marketplace to marketplace. The six brothers lived in London, except one, possibly named Henry, who was serving with the 2nd Battalion of the Scots Guards, which Barnett believed was stationed in Ireland. He was known among his comrades by the nickname Jonto or Johnto.[26] This brother had once visited her in London.[27]

Barnett said that Kelly never had any correspondence with her family, but her landlord, John McCarthy (not the one in Breezer's Hill), said that Kelly sometimes received letters from Ireland, he thought from her mother[28] (but he could have said brother and been misheard). The army lists record that the 2nd Battalion of the Scots Guards transferred from Chelsea Barracks in London to Dublin in August 1888 and then to the Curragh in County Kildare, where they stayed until returning to Chelsea in June 1889. Unless Barnett had a particular interest in troop movements or was otherwise interested in the 2nd Battalion, his knowledge of its current location suggests that Kelly's having a brother in the 2nd Battalion is authentic, and perhaps the best clue to establishing her true past.

Apart from immediate family, there was a cousin in Cardiff who Kelly claimed had introduced her to prostitution, and a friend named Lizzie Albrook said that Kelly had spoken of a relative who was on the stage in London.[29] Kelly also visited the Elephant and Castle district occasionally to visit a friend[30] and had gone frequently to a pub in Fish Street Hill, where the Monument stands. Enquiries by a Sergeant Bradshaw revealed that she had not been there for upwards of a month.[31]

Barnett described Kelly's family as 'fairly well off'[32] and Mrs McCarthy said they were 'well-to-do people'.[33] Kelly was said to have been 'an excellent scholar and an artist of no mean degree',[34] while a friend, Maria Harvey, described her as 'much superior to that of most persons in her position in life'.[35] An unnamed woman who claimed to have lived at Cooley's Lodging House at the same time as Kelly said that she was a fluent Welsh speaker.[36]

Tom Cullen, when researching his 1965 book on the murders, advertised for people with memories of the crimes and spoke with Dennis Barrett, who claimed that as a boy he knew Kelly by sight. He called her 'Black Mary' and Cullen described Kelly as a 'mythomaniac . . . incapable of stating a fact without embroidering upon it'. According to Barrett, Kelly was 'a bit of a terror' who had her pitch outside the Ten Bells pub – 'and woe to any woman who tried to poach her territory . . . such a woman was likely to have her hair pulled out in fistfuls'. Cullen also says Kelly was given to robbing drunken sailors in the Britannia.[37]

Nothing that Cullen said can be shown to be untrue, but it is largely inconsistent with other accounts of Kelly, the only support found so far being a report by the London correspondent of the Philadelphia *Press* who spoke to a woman with a daughter called Kate and who lived opposite Kelly's room. 'She had not always been on peaceable terms with the murdered woman, but they were good friends, though quarrelsome . . . she would fight and did not care what sort of place she lived in.'[38] Others who knew her reported her differently. Joseph Barnett said that he had 'always found her of sober habits'; her landlord John McCarthy said that 'when in liquor she was very noisy; otherwise she was a very quiet woman'.[39]

Whether or not Kelly was an alcoholic is uncertain. Walter Dew indicated that she was not accustomed to heavy drinking, but newspapers reported that she was somewhat addicted to drink and that her drinking had increased lately, Kelly rapidly going from bad to worse.[40] Otherwise, a neighbour, Caroline Maxwell, said that Kelly 'was not a notorious character'[41] and another neighbour, Catherine Pickett, said 'She was a good, quiet, pleasant girl, and was well liked by all of us.'

Joseph Barnett was born on 25 May 1858 at 4 Hairbrain Court,[42] near the Mint in London, the fourth of five children of Irish-born John and Catherine Barnett. John Barnett died in July 1864 of pleurisy and his wife is not mentioned in the 1871 or 1881 Census and may have died as well or possibly deserted her family. Raising the children – Daniel (b. 1851), Catherine (b. 1851), Joseph and John (b. 1860) – seems to have fallen to the eldest, Dennis (b. 1849). They lived at various addresses over the next few years and all became porters at Billingsgate Fish Market. Joseph's porter's licence (No. 853) shows that he was five foot seven and fair complexioned with blue eyes and a moustache.[43] He may have suffered from a speech impediment called echolalia, which caused him to repeat the last words spoken to him when replying to a question.

After deciding to live with Barnett, Kelly moved out of Cooley's Lodging House in Thrawl Street and the couple took lodgings in George Street, off Commercial Street, moving to Little Paternoster Row off Dorset Street – from where they were evicted for not paying the rent and for getting drunk – and Brick Lane, one of the most notorious areas of the East End. From Brick Lane they moved to a small and shabby room known as 13 Miller's Court, which was actually the back room of 26 Dorset Street, which Kelly took in her own name at a weekly rent of 4s. 6d.[44]

Dorset Street is a turning off Commercial Street and it still exists, although all the houses are gone and it is now an unnamed road between the rear of some buildings on one side and a multistorey car park on the other. It runs between Commercial Street and Crispin Street, the entrance almost opposite Christchurch churchyard at one end and at the other facing the Providence Row Night Refuge and Convent, a large building built in the 1860s where nuns of the Order of Sisters of Mercy ran a night refuge for homeless women and children. It had been built in the mid-1600s, when the surrounding land was open fields and was originally called Datchet Street. Narrow and about 130 yards long, by 1888 it was lined with decaying houses. The name was corrupted to Dorset Street and it was widely known as Dosset or Dossers Street because there were a lot of common lodging houses there. Two of the largest were owned by William Crossingham, both somewhat confusingly referred to as 'Crossingham's', one opposite Miller's Court, at No. 17 Dorset Street, said to be of a somewhat superior character, the other at No. 35, already distinguished as Annie Chapman's lodging. At the Commercial Street end of Dorset Street was the Britannia, the large beer house where Annie Chapman had been drinking the night she died. At the other end of the street was the Horn of Plenty, and in the middle was the Blue Coat Boy.

Though short and narrow, Dorset Street was notorious. It was shaded black on Charles Booth's poverty maps, meaning that it was the worst type of street, classified as vicious and semicriminal. Booth's police guide spoke of Dorset Street as the worst street in London, full of poverty, misery, vice, a cesspool into which the foulest and most degraded had sunk, full of 'thieves, prostitutes, bullies', and women, dirty, unkempt, their skirts and clothing torn. Booth also noted, perhaps for its comic value, perhaps in disgust or perhaps simply out of sorrow, 'one very fat lady at a window. She has sat there for years. She is now too fat to get out of the door.'

According to Booth, Dorset Street was frequented by the 'lowest of all prostitutes' and some common lodging houses there 'were merely another name for brothels'. On a visit in 1898 Booth noted that there had been three stabbing cases and one murder in the street in the past three months. Canon Samuel A Barnett of St Jude's vicarage called Dorset Street 'the centre of evil' and referred to 'the hells of Dorset Street', and the police told a reporter for the *Daily Telegraph* that Dorset Street was 'hardly safe for any respectable person by day and certainly not at night'. The newspaper said that authorities had described Dorset Street and Paternoster Row, which ran off it, as 'whirlpools, and the poor and the wretched are dragged into them'.

An arched passage about a third of the way along Dorset Street from the Britannia, between Nos 26 and 27, led into Miller's Court. In 1929 Leonard Matters visited Dorset Street, by then renamed Duval Street, and described Miller's Court in his book *The Mystery of Jack the Ripper*:

At the time of my first visit to the neighbourhood most of the houses on the left-hand side of the street were unoccupied, and some were being demolished. The house in which Kelly was murdered was closed, save for one front room still occupied by a dreadful looking slattern who came out of Miller's Court into the sunlight and blinked at me.

When she saw me focus my camera to get a picture of the front of the house, the old hag swore at me, and shuffled away down the passage.

I took what is probably the last photograph of the house to be secured by anybody, for three days later Miller's Court and the dilapidated buildings on either side of it were nothing but a heap of bricks and mortar. The housebreakers had completely demolished the crumbling wreck of the slum dwelling in which 'Jack the Ripper' committed his last crime!

Miller's Court, when I saw it, was nothing but a stone flagged passage between two houses, the upper stories of which united and so formed an arch over the entrance. Over this arch there was an iron plate bearing the legend, 'Miller's Court.' The passage was three feet wide and about twenty feet long, and at the end of it there was a small paved yard, about fifteen feet square. Abutting on this yard, or 'court', was the small back room in which the woman Kelly was killed – a dirty, damp and dismal hovel, with boarded-up windows and a padlocked door as though the place had not been occupied since the crime was committed.

But the strange thing was that nobody in the neighbourhood seemed to know the history of Miller's Court.

I asked a very old man on the opposite side of the street how long he had been living there.

'Over forty year,' he answered.

Then he told me that a murder had taken place when he was a young man.

'That's the house,' he said, pointing to one lower down the street. 'They say it's 'aunted, but I never seen nobody comin' out of it at nights.'[45]

The Whitechapel Board of Works Annual Report for 1878 described the passage as entered through an arched covered entrance and was 26 feet 4 inches long and 2 feet 10 inches wide. It did not run the full length of the houses either side, but finished a few feet short of the end, just before coming to a door on the right-hand side, which led into Mary Kelly's room. Beyond was the Court, 50 feet long, 7 feet 10 inches wide at Kelly's end and narrowing to 5 feet 6 inches. Six small houses, three either side, had been built here, probably in the 1840s: one up, one down, and numbered consecutively – the first house on the right-hand side was No. 1 downstairs, No. 2 upstairs, the next was No. 3 down and No. 4 up, and so on. The rooms were small, 12 by 12 by 8 feet, but according to the census in 1881 they were home to thirty people. All the houses were whitewashed at ground-floor level and provided with green shutters.[46] At one end of the court there were three public toilets, and at the other a public dustbin. There was also probably a gas lamp on the wall opposite Kelly's door.

Mary Kelly's room was about 12 feet square and a thin and flimsy partition separated it from the rest of the house.[47] Opposite the door was a fireplace; on the left of the door were two windows looking out into the Court, in the smaller one of which there were two panes of broken glass; a man's coat was put across these to keep out the draught. The window was near enough to the door for someone to reach through and bolt or unbolt the door. To the right of the door there was a bedside table – or a disused marble-topped washstand[48] – so close that the door would bang against it when swung open. Next to the table there was a bed, its head against the door wall, its side against the right-hand wall. Underneath the bed was a tin bath. Some sources mention a table close to the larger window and a chair, and a cheap print titled *The Fisherman's Widow*[49] hanging over the fireplace. The only illumination, apart from the fire, when lit, was the candle Kelly had bought from McCarthy, which she had placed on top of a broken wine glass.

The front room of 26 Dorset Street was a shop, unoccupied at the time and used by McCarthy as a storeroom for barrows and other such articles.[50] The *Evening Express* reported that the room 'was formerly left open, and poor people often took shelter there for the night; but when the Whitechapel murders caused so much alarm the police thought the place offered too much temptation to the murderer, and so the front was securely boarded up.'

In October the *Daily Telegraph* reported that six women and a man had been taken by the police to view the body of Catharine Eddowes and that two of the women had identified her as a woman whose name they did not know but who had frequently been without money and had slept in a shed off Dorset Street – 'the nightly refuge of some ten to twenty houseless creatures who are without the means of paying for their beds'.[51] The *Daily Telegraph* later identified this 'shed' as the front room of 26 Dorset Street,[52] and Elizabeth Prater, who occupied an upstairs room of 26 Dorset Street, referred to the downstairs front room as 'the shed'.[53] It would be a remarkable and astonishing coincidence if Catherine Eddowes did sometimes sleep in the front room of 26 Dorset Street, and it cannot pass unobserved that Eddowes pawned John Kelly's boots in the name of Jane Kelly of 6 Dorset Street – a mistranscription of 26 perhaps?

It has often been observed that all roads lead to Dorset Street: Nichols seems to have had no known connection, but Chapman had lodged at 30 Dorset Street and was living at Crossingham's at No. 35 when murdered; Stride lived at 38 Dorset Street, and Eddowes may have used No. 26.

Nos 26 and 27 Dorset Street and the houses in Miller's Court were owned by John McCarthy, who lived at and ran a chandler's shop (which sold groceries and general supplies) from the ground-floor room of No. 27. Walter Dew had nothing to say about McCarthy's character, beyond that he 'was well known to us as a common lodging-house proprietor', but Arthur Harding, a minor villain of the next generation, said McCarthy, whom he called 'McCarty', had been an old clothes dealer who then went in for furnished rooms. 'Those Irish blokes who came over here set up little businesses like that, they got it [their money] out of swindling the poor people out of small sums.'[54] Curiously, McCarthy wasn't Irish, but came from a family born and bred in the East End and was himself born in Dieppe, France. More interestingly, Harding said,

> McCarthy owned all the furnished rooms down there. He was an Irishman, a bully, a tough guy.
> Marie Lloyd used to see him, because there was a pub round the corner she used to go to. All his daughters were in show business on account of Marie Lloyd. They had plenty of money.[55]

Harding referred to McCarthy as a 'bully' and he may only have meant that McCarthy was the sort of person who maliciously intimidates and terrorises, but in the East End argot of the day a 'bully' was a pimp, and a brothel owner was known as a 'bully boss'. Charles Booth used 'bully' in this context when he said that Dorset Street was full of 'thieves, prostitutes, bullies'. Add to this that several of the women living in McCarthy's rooms were prostitutes and that at the time of her death Kelly had accumulated surprisingly substantial arrears of 29 shillings,[56] it isn't unreasonable to conclude that McCarthy may have been a pimp.[57]

The newspapers reported that McCarthy 'emphatically disowns any knowledge of his tenement having been used for improper purposes', and McCarthy did indeed deny knowledge of anything immoral, such as the fact that Kelly and Barnett were not married. However, on his death in 1935 the *East London Observer* recorded that he was 'held in the highest esteem by a large circle of East Londoners . . . was a kind-hearted man and a generous subscriber to local charities. He was a life governor of several hospitals . . . In fact he was always giving a helping hand to somebody.'

As Arthur Harding says, John McCarthy was a friend of Hoxton-born Marie Lloyd,[58] perhaps the most popular of all the music hall entertainers. Marie Lloyd never lost her East End roots and drank in several East End pubs, notably the Sugar Loaf, run by John Cooney in Hanbury Street, and the Seven Stars and the Flower Pot in Brick Lane. It is not known whether she assisted the stage careers of McCarthy's children, but McCarthy's son, John Joseph McCarthy, who used the stage name Steve McCarthy, was a very popular entertainer who married the major music hall star Marie Kendall[59] and was the grandfather of the elegant actress Kay Kendall

(1926–59, whose full name was Justine Kay Kendall-McCarthy), wife of Hollywood star Rex Harrison and possibly best remembered today as the 'plumpet' playing Rosalind Peters in the 1954 movie *Genevieve*.[60]

Kelly and Joe Barnett seem to have lived together happily enough until Barnett lost his job, probably around July or August 1888 – he would tell the inquest he had been out of work for three or four months[61] – and Kelly returned to prostitution, which caused arguments, during which one of the panes of glass in the window nearer the door may have been broken.[62] Barnett later modified his story slightly, claiming that he had left Kelly because she had allowed a prostitute named Julia to share their room, and afterwards let a Mrs Harvey stay there. Barnett told a reporter, 'She would never have gone wrong again, and I shouldn't have left her if it had not been for the prostitutes stopping at the house. She only let them because she was good-hearted and did not like to refuse them shelter on cold bitter nights.' Whatever the exact cause, between 5 p.m. and 6 p.m. on 30 October Barnett left Kelly and went to live at Mr Buller's Boarding House, otherwise a common lodging house at 24–25 New Street, on the corner of Bishopsgate Street and almost opposite Bishopsgate Police Station.[63]

We don't know who Julia was. Barnett's statement in the *Daily Telegraph* on 12 November clearly distinguishes between Julia and Mrs Harvey, but *The Times* on the same day reported that 'a woman, who is known by the name of Julia and who was in the habit of continually visiting Kelly's room, states she knew that she had two cotton shirts there'. This is unquestionably Maria Harvey, who on 9 November made a statement to the police in which she said that she had left 'two dirty cotton shirts' in Kelly's room. If 'Julia' was another name for Maria Harvey, one can only assume that the Mrs Harvey referred to by the *Daily Telegraph* was a mistake for Mr Harvey. However, we don't know that Maria Harvey, who at the inquest described herself as a laundress,[64] was a prostitute. It barely matters, however, but several people said they saw Mary Kelly after the time when medical opinion was certain she was dead. If Kelly allowed other women to use her room, and if witnesses mistakenly thought that one of them was Kelly, this could explain why otherwise reliable people rigidly stuck to their stories that they had seen Kelly after we know she was dead. Alternatively, it has been suggested that it was Mary Kelly who was seen and that the victim of Miller's Court was one of the women she allowed to use her room. This intriguing possibility was offered up in the movie *From Hell* (Albert Hughes, Allen Hughes, 2001), but the idea has many inherent problems and is probably as likely as the conclusion to that film, in which Kelly ran off to live happily ever after with Inspector Abberline.

We know a little of Mary Kelly's movements during the week she died. Maria Harvey, described as a 'young woman',[65] spent Monday and Tuesday nights with Kelly, then took a room at 3 New Court, off Dorset Street.

On Wednesday Kelly bought a halfpenny candle from John McCarthy's shop, and it would later be found, half used, atop a broken wine glass in Kelly's room.[66] Later Kelly was seen with a rather smart-looking man in Miller's Court by Thomas Bowyer, a pensioned soldier nicknamed 'Indian Harry',[67] who was employed by McCarthy.

> Harry Bowyer states that on Wednesday night he saw a man speaking to Kelly who resembled the description given by the fruiterer of the supposed Berner Street murderer. He was, perhaps, 27 or 28 and had a dark moustache and very peculiar eyes. His appearance was rather smart and attention was drawn to him by showing very white cuffs and a rather long white collar, the ends of which came down in front over a black coat. He did not carry a bag.[68]

It would not have been in the least remarkable for a respectably dressed man to have been seen on the main thoroughfares of Whitechapel, and, given the number of 'tourists' attracted to the area by the crimes, perhaps not overly remarkable to see one down a side street, even one such as Dorset Street, even though the *Daily Telegraph* thought it 'dangerous even in daylight'. But finding one in Miller's Court, a cul-de-sac down which no stranger would have had cause to venture, must be remarked unusual. He may have been a client, of course, or a relative, or someone visiting one of the other rooms, or a man on official business, or a policeman.

That Wednesday night Kelly spent some time in her room with a woman named Elizabeth Foster. Foster told a Press Association reporter:

> I have known Mary Jane Kelly for the last eighteen months, and we were good friends. She used to tell me she came from Limerick. She was as nice a woman as one could find, and, although an unfortunate, I don't think she went on the streets whilst she lived with Barnett.[69]

Maria Harvey claimed to have spent time with Kelly on the Thursday. There is one report that Harvey and Kelly spent the afternoon in Harvey's room in New Court, and that after drinking together they parted company at 7.30 p.m., but at the inquest she said they had spent the afternoon in Miller's Court, leaving only when Barnett arrived at about 7.05 p.m. The latter story is almost certainly wrong. Barnett didn't visit Kelly on Thursday until 7.30 p.m. or later, and when he arrived he found Kelly with 'a female who lives in the same court', which, even if we didn't already know that the woman was named Lizzie Albrook, is unlikely to have been how Barnett would have described Maria Harvey, whom he knew and on whose account he had left Kelly. Whether Maria Harvey was with Kelly on the Thursday at all is open to question.

In the early evening, Mary Kelly had a drink with Elizabeth Foster in the Ten Bells[70] on the corner of Commercial Road and Fournier Street. Kelly left about 7.05 p.m.[71] She seems to have returned to Miller's Court and to have met there Lizzie Albrook, whose statement to journalists not only throws doubt on Maria Harvey's claims but is valuable for the insight it provides into Kelly's character:

> I knew Mary Jane Kelly very well, as we were near neighbours. The last time I saw her was on Thursday night about 8.00, when I left her in her room with Joe Barnett, who had been living with her. About the last thing she said was, 'Whatever you do don't you do wrong and turn out as I have.' She had often spoken to me in this way and warned me against going on the streets as she had done. She told me, too, that she was heartily sick of the life she was leading and wished she had money enough to go back to Ireland where her people lived. I don't believe she would have gone out as she did if she had not been obliged to do so to keep herself from starvation. She had talked to me about her friends several times and on one occasion told me she had a female relation in London who was on the stage.[72]

Barnett was uncertain of the time he arrived, placing it between 7.30 p.m. and 7.45 p.m., and Albrook thought she left about 8 p.m. Barnett didn't stay for long, but simply apologised for having no money to give her, chatted a little and left. Kelly was sober, they'd had nothing to drink together, and had parted on good terms. Barnett had returned to his lodgings, where he had played whist until 12.30 a.m., and had then gone to bed. In recent years it has been suggested that Joseph Barnett could have been the murderer, the crimes being committed to frighten Kelly off the streets, but the theory is too improbable. The police would almost certainly have suspected Barnett and closely questioned him and confirmed his alibi, but the motive attributed to Barnett isn't persuasive: people can and do kill to achieve something, but the frenzied mutilation of Kelly is beyond such a prosaic motive.

Mary Jane Kelly's movements from the time when Joseph Barnett left her in the room in Miller's Court until 11.45 p.m. are unknown.

Julia Venturney,[73] a German[74] widow working as a charwoman and living with a man named Harry Owen at 1 Miller's Court, opposite Kelly's room, returned home at 8 p.m. and went straight to bed. She claimed at the inquest that she had been unable to sleep and had lain awake in bed throughout the night, but had heard no sounds and no singing. She must have been asleep, however, because there seems little doubt that later that night Kelly was heard singing for some considerable length of time.[75]

Maurice Lewis, a tailor living in Dorset Street, who said he'd known Mary Kelly for the past five years and described her as about five foot three, stout and dark, said he saw her between 10 and 11 p.m. in the Horn of Plenty in Dorset Street, drinking with some women, one of them known as Julia, and a man named Dan, who sold oranges in Billingsgate and Spitalfields markets and with whom she had been living until recently. He said she'd left with a respectably dressed man, but did not know whether the man had stayed with her all night or not.

'Dan' was clearly Barnett, the man with whom she had been living, and the mysterious Julia is correctly named too, but Barnett was at his lodgings, and he'd have been foolish to have lied about that if he had spent the night in the corner pub, where he was undoubtedly known and would have been seen. Lewis also claimed to have known Mary Kelly longer than she appears to have been living in the East End and described a woman who was considerably shorter than she was. All of this adds up to Lewis's getting the night wrong *and* thinking that Kelly was someone else. Unfortunately, John McCarthy repeated the same story – although he was probably repeating something he'd been told rather than had personally witnessed, or may have been misreported or misattributed, saying, 'At eleven o'clock last night (Thursday) she was in the Britannia public-house, at the corner of this thoroughfare (Dorset Street). She was then intoxicated. The young man in her company appeared to be very respectable, and was well dressed.'[76]

The first reliable report of Mary Kelly after 8 p.m. was by a widow named Mary Ann Cox, who lived at 5 Miller's Court, the last house on the left-hand side of the Court. She was a prostitute and said she had known

Kelly for about eight months. At 11.45 p.m. she turned from Commercial Street into Dorset Street. Walking a short distance ahead were Kelly and a man. The couple turned into Miller's Court and, as Cox entered the passage, Kelly and the man were going into Kelly's room. Mrs Cox said, 'Goodnight, Mary Jane.' Kelly said, 'I am going to have a song.' Kelly was barely able to speak and Mrs Cox realised she was very drunk. The man banged the door shut.

Cox went on to her own room and heard Kelly start to sing 'A Violet I Plucked From My Mother's Grave When A Boy'. Kelly, said Cox, was wearing a linsey frock and a red knitted crossover (a shawl) pulled around her shoulders. She was bare-headed. The man was aged about 36, was stout and had a fresh complexion but had blotches on his face, small side whiskers and a thick carroty moustache. He was dressed in shabby dark clothes, a long dark overcoat and black felt billycock hat, and was carrying a quart can of beer.[77]

Walter Dew in *I Caught Crippen*[78] gave a very accurate account of the exchange between Mrs Cox and Mary Kelly, but he said the man had a beard, which 'gave us for the first time something really tangible to work upon. We knew what the man we were after looked like. We knew the kind of clothes he wore and, most important of all, we knew that he was bearded.' This is the only mention of his having a beard, and there seems no reason why the detail should otherwise be omitted from the descriptions of the man given by Mrs Cox. On the other hand, Dew was there and was fairly accurate in his retelling of Mrs Cox's story, so it's odd that he should have been so emphatic about it.

Another problem with Mrs Cox's story is caused by a passing comment in the *Daily Telegraph* on 12 November 1888, which stated that enquiries had failed to discover any publican who served Kelly or her companion with beer that night.[79] This statement, if true, throws into doubt Mrs Cox's story, throws doubt on her claim that Kelly was singing – although a woman named Catherine Picket claimed it too – and throws doubt on Kelly's being drunk. The problem is that it was claimed that Kelly had been drinking about 8 a.m. the next day and enquiries were made to see if anyone remembered serving her at that time. Nobody did. The newspaper may have thought that the result of that enquiry applied to an enquiry regarding the blotchy-faced man.

Mrs Cox went out again shortly after midnight.

At 12.30 a.m. a flower seller named Catherine Picket heard Kelly singing: 'I heard her singing Friday morning about half past twelve. She was singing "I plucked a violet from my mother's grave", rest her soul in Heaven, poor dear. Rest her poor dear soul.' In fact Picket was irritated by Kelly's singing and decided to complain, but was stopped by her husband. 'If it hadn't been for my Dave – that's my old man you must know – I should have come out of my room and caught the whitelivered villain! But Dave says to me, you just leave the woman alone so I stopped where I was – worse luck for the poor dear soul! – and goes to bed . . .'[80] The hapless Dave probably spent the rest of his life being told that Jack the Ripper would have been caught but for him!

It started to rain. Mary Ann Cox returned to her room and warmed her hands by her fire. Kelly was still singing. Mrs Cox went out shortly after 1 a.m. and did not return until 3 a.m.

Elizabeth Prater, who had been deserted by her boot machinist husband William Prater about five years earlier, now earned her living as a prostitute[81] and lived in Room 20 Miller's Court, an upstairs room in 26 Dorset Street. She had gone out at 5 p.m. and had 'been having a deal to drink that night'. She returned home at about 1 a.m. and stood at the entrance to Miller's Court for about half an hour, waiting for the man with whom she now lived, but he did not turn up. She then chatted in McCarthy's shop for about ten minutes and went up to her room. She put two chairs in front of her door, and without bothering to undress she lay on her bed and immediately fell into a drunken sleep. During the time she had been outside she had seen no one enter or leave Miller's Court and had heard no singing.[82]

At some unstated time during the night, twenty-year-old Sarah Roney and two friends met a man in Brushfield Street, the next street along from Dorset Street. He was wearing a black coat and a tall hat and he carried a black bag. The man asked, 'Will you come with me?' The girls refused and enquired about the contents of his bag. 'Something the girls don't like,' he replied, then walked away. This same man may have been seen by a Mrs Paumier[83] on the day following the murder of Kelly.[84]

At 2 a.m. George Hutchinson, a man of military appearance who was an unemployed labourer and former groom,[85] was walking along Commercial Street. At the corner of Thrawl Street he passed a man, but paid him scant attention and walked on to Flower and Dean Street, where he met Mary Kelly, who he claimed he had known for about three years, to whom he had sometimes given a few shillings and in whose company he had been a number of times.[86] She approached him and said, 'Mr Hutchinson, can you lend me sixpence?'

'I can't,' said Hutchinson. 'I've spent all my money going down to Romford.'

Kelly said, 'Good morning. I must go and find some money.' She did not seem to be drunk, 'but was a little bit spreeish',[87] and Hutchinson watched her walk off towards Thrawl Street. She walked past the man whom Hutchinson had passed earlier and as she did so he placed his hand on her shoulder and said something that Hutchinson did not hear. Kelly and the man laughed. Kelly said, 'All right.' The man said, 'You will be all right for what I have told you.' And he put his right arm around Kelly's shoulders. Hutchinson noticed that he was holding a pair of kid gloves in his hand, and that in his left hand he had a small parcel about eight inches long wrapped in American cloth with a strap round it.[88]

They began to walk back towards Dorset Street and Hutchinson leaned against the lamp outside the Queen's Head public house, 74 Commercial Street, where Elizabeth Stride had a drink the night she died. As Kelly and the man walked past, the man 'hid down his head with his hat over his eyes'.[89] Hutchinson stooped and looked him in the face, and in response the man gave what Hutchinson described as a stern look. Kelly and the man then turned into Dorset Street. Hutchinson followed. They stood at the corner of Miller's Court for about three minutes. The man said something to Kelly, who said 'Alright my dear, come along. You will be comfortable.'[90] He then placed his arm on her shoulder and gave her a kiss. Kelly incongruously said she had lost her handkerchief, and the man pulled out a red handkerchief and gave it to her. They both then went up the Court together. Hutchinson followed them into the Court, but could see nothing.

Hutchinson described the man as being of Jewish appearance, aged about 34 or 35, five foot six tall, very surly and pale-complexioned, with dark hair and eyes and a slight moustache curled up at each end. He was wearing a dark felt hat turned down in the middle, a long dark coat, the collar and cuffs trimmed with astrakhan, a dark jacket underneath and a light waistcoat, across which a very thick gold chain with a large seal and a red stone was visible.[91] He had on a shirt with a white linen collar, and a black tie to which a horseshoe pin was affixed. His trousers were dark and button boots and gaiters with white buttons completed the ensemble.[92]

Hutchinson hung around for three-quarters of an hour to see if they came out, but there was no sign of them. During the time he stood there he said that one policeman went by the Commercial Street end of Dorset Street and one man came out of a lodging house, then returned inside. Hutchinson was certain that no one came down Dorset Street at all. Hutchinson wandered away at 3 a.m., just as a clock struck the hour, and wandered the streets for the rest of the night.[93]

The police believed Hutchinson. Inspector Abberline described Hutchinson's statement as 'important', and said that, having interrogated him, he was 'of opinion his statement is true'. According to Abberline, he had watched them because he had been surprised to see a man so well dressed in her company.[94]

A young woman named Sarah Lewis,[95] a laundress living at 34 Great Pearl Street, Spitalfields, had an argument with her husband and went to stay the night with her parents, Mr and Mrs Keyler, who lived at 2 Miller's Court. She passed Spitalfields Church, the clock striking 2.30 a.m., and noticed near the Britannia two or three[96] people. One, a respectably dressed young man with a dark moustache, was talking to a woman. They both appeared to be drunk. Standing close by was another woman, poorly dressed and hatless. Lewis heard the man say, 'Are you coming?' and saw the woman turn away, as if to go in the opposite direction. Lewis walked on. She would later elaborate this story, saying that the man looked very much like a man she had chaffed on Wednesday when in the vicinity of Bethnal Green Road with her sister. This man had accosted them and asked them to accompany him to a lonely spot. They had refused, had become alarmed and had run off. The man was of average height with a pale face and a black moustache. He was wearing a long brown overcoat over a short black jacket, pepper-and-salt trousers and an unusually high round hat. The black bag he carried was about nine inches long.

Lewis passed the trio outside the Britannia and turned into Dorset Street. Opposite Miller's Court there was a man. She paid him scant attention, but was able to describe him as stout-looking and not very tall, and wearing a black wide-awake hat. He was looking up the Court as if waiting or looking for someone. Further on were a man and a woman, the latter drunk. There was nobody in the Court and she went into Mrs Keyler's, where she dozed in a chair.[97]

At 3 a.m. Mary Cox returned to her room. It was raining hard. There was no noise or light coming from Kelly's room and Mrs Cox went to bed and tried to get some sleep.

Sarah Lewis woke and heard the clock strike 3.30. She sat awake and shortly before 4 a.m. she heard 'a scream like that of a young woman, which seemed to be not far away. The voice screamed out "murder" '. There was only one scream.

Elizabeth Prater, in the room above Kelly's, was awakened by her little black kitten Diddles[98] walking across her neck. She thought the time was between 3.30 and 4 a.m. and she heard a cry of 'Oh! Murder!' in a faint voice. She took no notice because she said it was common to hear cries of murder. She fell back asleep, then woke at 5 a.m. and went to the Ten Bells for a glass of rum. The only people in the street were two or three men harnessing some horses.

At 5.45 a.m. Mrs Cox heard what she thought was a man's footsteps leaving Miller's Court.

At 7.30 a.m. Catherine Picket woke and half an hour later left her room to go to the market to buy some flowers. It was chilly and raining and she thought she would borrow Kelly's shawl. She went to Kelly's room and knocked on the door, but there was no reply. Thinking that Kelly was asleep, she went off.

At 8 a.m. Maurice Lewis, the tailor who lived in Dorset Street and said he'd seen Kelly in the Britannia that evening, was reported as claiming to have seen her leave her room, then return to it a few moments later.[99]

At 8.30 a.m. Mrs Caroline Maxwell left Crossingham's Lodging House opposite Miller's Court. She lived with her husband Henry Maxwell at 14 Dorset Street. He was the night watchman at Crossingham's and she assisted him. They had worked through the night and Mrs Maxwell was leaving the lodging house, going home with her lantern and other things. She had some errands to run, then she was going to go to bed. She saw Kelly standing at the entrance to Miller's Court. She had known Kelly for about four months and knew her well enough to be on speaking terms with her. She had not seen Kelly for about three weeks, and, as it was unusual to see her early in the morning, she spoke to her. According to her inquest testimony, 'I said to her, what brings you up so early? She said, I have the horrors of drink upon me, as I have been drinking for some days past. I said why don't you go to Mrs. Ringers (meaning the Public House at the corner of Dorset Street called the Britannia) and have a pint of beer. She said I have been there and had it, but I have brought it all up again.' At the same time Kelly pointed to some vomit in the roadway.[100]

Mrs Maxwell then went to Bishopsgate to get her husband's breakfast and was away about half an hour, returning to Dorset Street about 9 a.m. She noticed Kelly outside the Britannia, talking to a man aged about thirty who was approximately five foot five tall and stout, and was dressed as a market porter. Kelly had on a dark dress with a black velvet body, and a scarf of some sort around her neck. Mrs Maxwell didn't pay any attention, but went to bed and knew nothing more until she awoke late that afternoon.

Mrs Maxwell's story conflicted with the later medical opinion that Kelly had been dead for several hours by 8.30 a.m., and enquiries at the Britannia and at other pubs in the area indicated that Kelly was nowhere served with beer on the morning of her death. Indeed, the landlady of the Britannia said that the pub hadn't been busy that morning and she was therefore certain that Kelly hadn't been there. But, as the *Daily Telegraph* reported, Mrs Maxwell was 'severely cross-examined' and remained 'very positive' that it was Kelly she had seen. The paper clearly struggled to equate Mrs Maxwell's obvious sincerity and the utter failure of her story to conform with the known facts. 'It is not obvious what motive she could have for making a false representation,' it observed, and the possibility that she was confused about the day, it said, was dismissed by Mrs Maxwell, who said that there were circumstances 'connected with her own work that enabled her to fix it as Friday morning without any doubt or misgiving whatever'.[101]

According to *The Times*, Mrs Maxwell had gone that morning to the milk shop and recalled it because she had not been there for some time. Enquiries supported what she said.[102] Even at the inquest Mrs Maxwell stuck to her story, even when cautioned by the coroner, 'You must be very careful about your evidence, because it is different to other people's.'[103] Recalling the events years later, Walter Dew was equally baffled as the *Daily* Telegraph, writing: 'If Mrs Maxwell had been a sensation-seeker – one of those women who live for the limelight – it would have been easy to discredit her story. She was not. She seemed a sane and sensible woman, and her reputation was excellent.' And he added, 'In one way at least her version fitted into the facts as known. We knew that Marie had been drinking the previous night, and, as this was not a habit of hers, illness the next morning was just what might have been expected.'[104]

At 10 a.m. Maurice Lewis said that he was playing pitch and toss in 'McCarthy's Court'. He and his companions then went to 'the Ringers'. He was positive that on going in he saw Kelly drinking with some other people. He was not sure whether there was a man among them.[105]

Sometime before 10.30 a.m.,[106] John McCarthy called for his assistant, Thomas 'Indian Harry' Bowyer, and told him to go to No. 13 and try to get some rent. Bowyer hurried from the shop and went down the passage to Kelly's room. He knocked at the door, but did not get a reply. He tried the door, but it was locked. He knocked again. He looked through the keyhole, but could not see Kelly. He went into the Court, reached through the broken pane of glass in the window of Room 13 and plucked back the muslin curtain. The first thing he saw was two lumps of flesh on the bedside table. He then looked at the bed – the horribly butchered mess that lay there was barely recognisable as a human being.

Bowyer rushed back to McCarthy. 'Guv'nor! I knocked at the door and could not make anyone answer. I looked through the window and saw a lot of blood.'

'Good God! Harry, you don't mean to say that . . .'

McCarthy, with Bowyer following, rushed round to Room 13 and looked through the window. 'The sight we saw I cannot drive away from my mind,' McCarthy said later. 'It looked more like the work of a devil than of a man. I had heard a great deal about the Whitechapel murders, but I declare to God I had never expected to see such a sight as this. The whole scene is more than I can describe. I hope I may never see such a sight as this again.'[107]

McCarthy told Bowyer not to tell anyone, but to go to the police station and fetch someone. Bowyer hurried off. McCarthy took care of the shop, then hurried after him. They went to the Commercial Street Police Station and asked for either Inspector Reid or Inspector Abberline. Neither was available. They spoke instead to Inspector Beck. Walter Dew was there:

And now I approach a phase of the Ripper story which I would give a great deal even now to have expunged from my memory.

As my thoughts go back to Miller's Court, and what happened there, the old nausea, indignation and horror overwhelm me still.

The thing of which I am about to write happened nearly fifty years ago. Yet my mental picture of it remains as shockingly clear as though it were but yesterday.

It is all before me now. Jack the Ripper at his most devilish. No savage could have been more barbaric. No wild animal could have done anything so horrifying.

If I remember rightly it was between ten and eleven o'clock in the morning that I looked in at Commercial Street police station to get into touch with my superiors. I was chatting with Inspector Beck, who was in charge of the station, when a young fellow, his eyes bulging out of his head, came panting into the police station. The poor fellow was so frightened that for a time he was unable to utter a single intelligible word.

At last he managed to stammer out something about 'Another one. Jack the Ripper. Awful. Jack McCarthy sent me.'

Mr McCarthy was well-known to us as a common lodging-house proprietor.

'Come along, Dew,' said Inspector Beck, and gathering from the terrorized messenger that Dorset Street was the scene of whatever had happened, we made him our pilot, as we rushed in that direction, collecting as many constables as we could on the way.[108]

Dew went to Miller's Court:

The room was pointed out to me. I tried the door. It would not yield. So I moved to the window, over which, on the inside, an old coat was hanging to act as a curtain and to block the draught from the hole in the glass.

Inspector Beck pushed the coat to one side and peered through the aperture. A moment later he staggered back with his face as white as a sheet.

'For God's sake, Dew,' he cried. 'Don't look.'

I ignored the order, and took my place at the window.

When my eyes had become accustomed to the dim light I saw a sight which I shall never forget to my dying day.

The whole horror of that room will only be known to those of us whose duty it was to enter it. The full details are unprintable.

There was a table just beneath the window. On the bed, which was drawn obliquely across the small room, was all that remained of a good-looking and buxom young woman.

There was little left of her, not much more than a skeleton. Her face was terribly scarred and mutilated.

All this was horrifying enough, but the mental picture of that sight which remains most vividly with me is the poor woman's eyes. They were wide open, and seemed to be staring straight at me with a look of terror.

Inspector Beck quickly recovered from his shock and sent messages to the chief station by quick-running constables. From there the messages were promptly relayed by telegraph to Scotland Yard.[109]

The precise sequence of events now becomes hazy because the police seem to have imposed a blanket of silence about the murder and newspaper reporters were forced to gather snippets of information from wherever they could. Much of their information was wrong, some of it was wildly inaccurate and many early reports were almost *completely* wrong.[110]

One of the most enduring myths to arise during this time of utter confusion was that Mary Kelly had a child. The story had its origins with a Press Association report that a young woman, who is either unnamed in the newspapers or called Margaret, said that she had met Kelly in Dorset Street about 10.30 p.m. on the night of the murder, and that Kelly had threatened to kill herself if she could not get any money. Soon afterwards Kelly met a respectably dressed man and took him to her second-floor room.[111] Her little boy, who was asleep there, was sent to a neighbour's house and didn't go back until the next morning, when he did not see his mother but was sent on an errand by the man.[112] Some early reports, particularly in America and Canada, all apparently citing the same source, gave the woman's name as 'Lizzie Fisher'. This may indeed have been the woman's name.

The woman wasn't Mary Kelly: she didn't live in a second-floor room and Joseph Barnett specifically stated that she didn't[113] have any children. Eventually some newspapers offered a correction:

> The pathetic story told in many papers of the murdered woman's solicitude for her little son is entirely without foundation. Kelly had no child. The only boy of whom anything is known belonged to a woman with whom she was very friendly, and who stayed with her on several occasions.[114]

The woman who had stayed with Kelly and who had a child was evidently Mrs Maria Harvey, because among the items she said she left in Kelly's room, which were probably burned in the fire, was 'a little boy's shirt'.[115]

Inspector Walter Beck arranged for news of the murder to be telegraphed to Scotland Yard and other police stations, and requested bloodhounds.[116] He sent for the doctor, and organised a search. Fortunately, forty extra constables had been sent to the Commercial Street Police Station in anticipation of Socialist disturbances in connection with the lord mayor's show, and Inspector Beck was able to use these men to clear idlers away and cordon off each end of Dorset Street. He posted two burly constables at the entrance to Miller's Court with strict instructions to prevent access and egress. A man who lived at 3 Miller's Court and who worked as a market porter left his rooms to buy some milk – having heard nothing during the night – and was immediately stopped by the police.[117]

At 11 a.m. Dr George Bagster Phillips received a call to go to Miller's Court and set off almost immediately, arriving at 11.15 a.m. He looked through the lower of the broken panes in the smaller window and satisfied himself that there was nobody in the room in need of his assistance. In the course of the afternoon Dr Phillips would be joined by Dr Bond, Dr Gordon Brown, and a Dr J R Gabe, who later told journalists that he had seen a great deal in dissecting rooms, but he had never witnessed such a horrible sight. Inspector Frederick G Abberline arrived at Miller's Court about 11.30 a.m. Inspector Beck informed him that bloodhounds had been sent for and it was understood that they were on the way, and Dr Phillips advised against forcing the door to Kelly's room until the dogs arrived, so no attempt would be made to enter the room.[118]

At midday Mrs Paumier, a roasted-chestnut seller on the corner of Widegate Street, about two minutes' walk from Miller's Court, was approached by a man who said, 'I suppose you have heard about the murder in Dorset Street?' Mrs Paumier replied that she had. The man grinned. 'I know more about it than you,' he said and walked off. He was dressed like a gentleman and wore a black coat, speckled trousers and a black silk hat. He was about five foot six, had a black moustache and carried a black shiny bag. Mrs Paumier thought that he was the man who had accosted Sarah Roney and her friend.

Shortly after midday Scotland Yard telegraphed various police stations with a terse message: 'Found at 10.30 a.m., a woman cut to pieces in a room on the ground floor at 26, Dorset-street, Spitalfields.'[119] The news of a new murder spread rapidly through the streets. It was reported that women who appeared more like fiends than human beings rushed about the streets telling their neighbours the news, and shouting in angry voices their rage and indignation. Crowds gathered at either end of Dorset Street, their numbers estimated at over a thousand, and the police had great difficulty controlling them. One constable apparently struck an onlooker and the crowd mobbed and hooted him, and he was forced to flee to the Commercial Street Police Station followed by a huge mob.[120] At Dorset Street the police searched all the adjacent houses for suspicious characters, questioned the residents and inmates of the common lodging houses, and generally looked for any clues.

At 1.30 a.m. Inspector Arnold arrived with the news that the order for the bloodhounds had been countermanded and that the door to Kelly's room was to be forced open. McCarthy took a pickaxe to the door jamb and the door swung open, knocking against the bedside table. The locked door is something of a mystery. It appears to have had an automatic or spring lock[121] – the sort that locks when the door is closed and can be opened only with a key from the outside or by turning a knob or pulling a catch from inside. Joseph Barnett said that they had lost the key some time ago and that he and Kelly would bolt and unbolt the door by reaching through the broken window. It isn't clear whether he literally meant that the door had a bolt separate from the spring lock, or whether by 'bolt' he meant operate the spring lock itself. Whether or not a bolt could have been manipulated through the broken window is unknown, but, by whatever means Barnett and Kelly locked and unlocked the door, it is surprising that the police did not realise that they could enter the room by the same method.

That McCarthy had to force the door open with a pickaxe is also odd. It must have been very common for tenants to abscond, so one would assume that McCarthy would have possessed a set of spare keys so that he could gain access to his property without having to incur the cost of replacing locks and repairing door frames. Presumably he did not take this elementary precaution.

After considerable delay and difficulty a photographer was brought to the scene and photographs were taken of the interior and exterior of 13 Miller's Court. A slight drizzling rain was falling and it was so overcast that it was almost dark. In the conditions and with the equipment available, the photographer did a remarkable job. The photographs still exist. They convey far better than words ever could the sheer barbarity of Jack the Ripper.

Within a very short time, cabs began arriving in Dorset Street. They had already brought Inspectors Abberline and Reid and several other detectives. Robert Anderson arrived at 1.50 p.m. and remained at the murder scene for some time.[122] Dr Bond arrived at about the same time and began his examination of the body at 2 p.m. Among others who arrived that afternoon were Chief Constables Monsell, Howard and Roberts. The *Manchester Guardian* reported that 'never before had so many men been despatched to the scene of a murder from Whitehall'.[123] Joseph Barnett was indoors when he heard that a woman had been murdered in Dorset Street, but he did not know at first that the victim was Mary Jane Kelly. When he discovered that it was, he went to the police. He appears to have been very closely questioned about his whereabouts and the police investigated his account of his movements and satisfied themselves that they were correct.[124]

The doctors began their examination of the body at about 2 p.m. The mutilated remains of Mary Kelly were in the middle of the bed, inclined to be nearer the doorside edge of the bed. Both Dr Phillips and Dr Bond believed the body had been moved into that position by the murderer and that Kelly had been lying on the right side of the bed, the side nearer the wooden partition, her head and neck in the top right-hand corner. This conclusion was indicated by the large quantity of blood under the bedstead and the saturated condition of the palliasse, pillow and sheet at the top corner of the bedstead. Dr Bond observed that the corner of the sheet to the right of Kelly's head was cut and saturated with blood, from which he concluded that her face had been covered with the sheet at the time of the attack. Dr Phillips thought that severance of the right carotid artery was the immediate cause of death.

According to a report by Dr Bond, which makes disturbing and gruesome reading, Kelly was lying in the middle of the bed, her body inclined to the left, her head resting on the left cheek. The bed clothing at the right corner was covered in blood, and on the floor beneath was a pool of blood covering about two feet square. The wall by the right side of the bed and in a line with the neck was marked by blood, which had struck it in a number of separate splashes. The face was hacked beyond recognition, gashed in all directions, the nose, cheeks, eyebrows and ears partly removed. The lips were blanched and cut by several incisions running obliquely down to the chin. The neck was severed all round down to the bone, the fifth and sixth vertebrae being deeply notched. The skin cuts in the front of the neck showed distinct ecchymosis (bleeding into surrounding tissue caused by bruising). The air passage was cut through at the lower part of the larynx through the cricoid cartilage. The left arm was close to the body with the forearm lying across the abdomen, the right arm resting on the mattress, the elbow bent and the forearm supine with the fingers clenched. The arms were mutilated by several jagged wounds and the right thumb showed a small superficial incision about an inch long, with extravasation of blood in the skin, and there were several abrasions on the back of the hand showing the same condition.

The breasts were cut off. One breast was found under the head, the other by the right foot. The breasts had been removed by more or less circular incisions, the muscles down to the ribs being attached to the breasts. The intercostals between the fourth, fifth and sixth ribs were cut through and the contents of the thorax were visible through the openings. On opening the thorax it was found that the right lung was minimally adherent by old firm adhesions, the lower part of the lung broken and torn away. The left lung was intact, adherent at the apex with a few adhesions over the side. In the substances of the lung were several nodules of consolidation. The pericardium was open and the heart was absent. Dr Bond seems to have meant that the heart had been taken from the place where it should have been, not that it was absent from the room (i.e., taken away by the killer).

In the abdominal cavity was some partly digested food of fish and potatoes, and similar food was found in the remains of the stomach attached to the intestines. The skin and tissues of the abdomen from the costal arch to the pubes were removed in three large flaps. The legs were wide apart, the left thigh at right angles to the trunk and the right forming an obtuse angle with the pubes. The whole of the surface of the abdomen and thighs was removed and the abdominal cavity emptied of its viscera, which were found distributed around the body: the uterus and kidneys under the head with one of the breasts, the liver between the feet, the intestines by the right side and the spleen by the left side. The flaps removed from the abdomen and thighs were on the bedside table. The front of the right thigh was entirely stripped of skin, and the left thigh was stripped of skin, fascia and muscles as far as the knee. The left calf had been slashed through to the deep muscles.

Apart from Dr Bond's reference to the absence of the heart (meaning removed from the body), no mention was made of any part of Kelly's body being missing and the *Daily Telegraph* reported that the Central News claimed 'upon what is described as indisputable authority, that no portion of the murdered woman's body was taken away by the murderer'. *The Times* said that 'the post-mortem examination was of the most exhaustive character, and surgeons did not quit their work until every organ had been accounted for and placed as closely as possible in its natural position'.

Nevertheless, that organs had been removed from the body was a persistent rumour and on 13 November *The Times* explained, 'At the first examination, which was only of a cursory character, it was thought that a portion of the body had gone, but this is not the case.'

However, on the same day the *Daily Telegraph* assured its readers, 'We are enabled to state, on good authority, that notwithstanding all that has been said to the contrary, a portion of the bodily organs was missing.' One can only assume that the organ in question was the heart. Whether or not it was really missing is not known.[125]

At 2 p.m., when Bond began his examination, the body was comparatively cold and rigor mortis had set in and increased during the progress of the examination. Bond believed that rigor had begun between six and twelve hours after death, from which he calculated that death could have taken place between 2 a.m. and 8 a.m. However, he also found the remains of a meal, possibly fish and chips, in the stomach and scattered about over the intestines. Since digestion ceases immediately on death and a typical meal takes about two to four hours to pass out of the stomach, the fact that Kelly's last meal had partly passed into the intestines indicated that death had taken place about three or four hours after she had eaten. This led Bond to conclude that Kelly had died about 1 or 2 a.m., but it was based on the (reasonable) assumption that the food in Kelly's stomach and intestines was the remains of a meal eaten the night before, possibly between 10 and 11 p.m.

The food in the stomach essentially rules out the possibility that the woman seen by Mrs Maxwell at 8.30 a.m. was the murdered woman. Had it been, she would have had to have eaten at the improbably early time of 4.30 a.m. or later, and, even allowing for the vagaries of stomach emptying, not appreciably close to 8.30 a.m. Whoever Mrs Maxwell saw at 8.30 a.m. almost certainly wasn't the woman whose mutilated remains were found in 13 Miller's Court. Either Mrs Maxwell saw somebody else, or she was mistaken about the day. Or, as some have speculated, the body was not that of Mary Jane Kelly.

From the medical and some other information, it was seen that Kelly had taken off her clothes and laid them down in an ordinary manner, as if preparing to sleep.[126] She was in bed when murdered and Dr Bond thought the fact that the sheet had been pulled up over her neck indicated that she had been asleep when attacked (although the superficial incision on the thumb might be consistent with an attempt by Kelly to defend herself, perhaps when the cry of 'murder' was heard). Her body had been close to the partition, which could mean either that she simply favoured that side of the bed or that she was sharing the bed.

Dr Bond also provided the police with an early offender profile, suggesting that the police were very well aware of what are today often thought of as modern investigative techniques. Contrary to other medical opinion, Bond did not think the murderer possessed scientific or anatomical knowledge, and went so far as to say, 'In my opinion he does not even possess the technical knowledge of a butcher or horse slaughterer or any person accustomed to cut up dead animals.' Bond believed that all five murders from Nichols to Kelly were 'no doubt' committed by the same person, that a knife at least six inches long, very sharp, pointed and about an inch in width had been used, possibly a clasp knife, butcher's knife or a surgeon's knife. Bond considered that the killer's hands and arms and parts of his clothing must have been smeared with blood, from which he reasoned that the killer was in the habit of wearing a cloak or overcoat to hide the bloodstains – which fits Hutchinson's description of a man who wore an overcoat and gloves. He was a man of physical strength and of great coolness and daring, but in appearance was likely to be quiet, inoffensive-looking, probably middle-aged and neatly and respectably dressed. He thought it possible but unlikely that the murderer was inspired by revenge or religious mania, preferring what Bond called 'homicidal or erotic mania', suggesting that the killer was in a sexual state he called 'satyriasis'.[127] Bond thought the killer was without regular employment or otherwise had a small regular income or a pension. He was probably solitary and eccentric in his habits, possibly lived among respectable persons who knew his character and habits and entertained suspicions they were unwilling to communicate to the police for fear of trouble or notoriety.

At 3.50 p.m. a one-horse carrier's cart with an ordinary tarpaulin cover was driven into Dorset Street and halted opposite Miller's Court. A long shell, or coffin, dirty and scratched with constant use, was taken from the cart into Room 13 and the remains of Mary Kelly were placed inside. The news that the body was about to be removed caused a great rush of people from the courts running out of Dorset Street, and there was a determined effort to break the police cordon at the Commercial Street end. Shortly after 4 p.m. the shell, covered with a ragged-looking cloth, was brought from Kelly's room and placed in the cart. The crowd pressed round and 'ragged caps were doffed and slatternly-looking women shed tears' as the cart moved off to the mortuary adjoining Shoreditch Church to await the inquest at the Shoreditch Town Hall. No. 13 Miller's Court was then closed, the window boarded up and the door padlocked.[128]

There are problems fixing the time of death based on witness testimony because it is uncertain which witnesses we can believe, and whether the witnesses were recalling the correct time or correct day. Mrs Maxwell's testimony is the most extreme and extraordinary example, but Mary Ann Cox, a very important witness, is also open to question. She saw Kelly with a blotchy-faced man who was carrying a pail of beer, but at least one newspaper reported (perhaps mistakenly) that nobody could be found who had served either Kelly or the man with beer. She also said that Kelly was singing for a considerable period of time, but nobody except Catherine Picket claimed to have heard her; also, Picket's story wasn't widely reported and she didn't give evidence at the inquest, so some doubt is cast on its reliability. Kelly had been singing for a long time and presumably entertaining her blotchy-faced companion until shortly before 1 a.m., but the only means of light in Kelly's room was the candle she'd recently bought from McCarthy, and that was barely half used.

Elizabeth Prater, who had arrived home about 1 a.m. and saw nobody leave Miller's Court, told the inquest that the partition with Kelly's room was very thin and that she could hear Kelly walk about in the room and see a glimmer of light through gaps in the partition, but had heard no sound and seen no light. Indeed, if Prater's testimony is to be believed, it would seem that by the time Prater went to her room, Kelly had either left her room about 1 a.m., between the departure of Mrs Cox and Prater's arrival, or gone to bed. Mrs Cox also said that Kelly was incoherently, falling-down drunk, but Kelly's clothes had been taken off and folded as if she had undressed normally for bed, which suggests that she wasn't falling-down drunk (Elizabeth Prater didn't bother to undress, let alone place her clothes folded for the next day). That Kelly had undressed normally for bed is possibly supported by the likelihood that she was asleep when murdered – would she have taken off and folded her clothes if she were entertaining a client or planning to go out again when business was concluded? Also, Kelly's being falling-down drunk doesn't rest easy with her meeting Hutchinson two hours later, at which time Hutchinson described her as only 'spreeish'. Could Kelly have sobered up in a couple of hours?

On the other hand, Mary Ann Cox's story holds together reasonably well. Kelly returned drunk with the blotchy-faced man, she sang drunkenly and probably intermittently for an hour, undressed at some point and folded her clothes, and went to bed about 1 a.m., either alone or with her companion, and fell asleep. All was quiet when Elizabeth Prater returned home.

It is George Hutchinson's story that creates problems with this scenario – but it creates other problems too. The police believed George Hutchinson's story, Abberline writing on 12 November, 'I have interrogated him this evening and I am of the opinion his statement is true';[129] but such comments were made at the time Hutchinson told his story and we do not know how long this faith in Hutchinson persisted. To modern commentators the extraordinary detail of Hutchinson's story is suspicious, and it has been questioned whether such a well-dressed man would have ventured into such a notorious area, valuables such as the tiepin and watch chain so obviously on display.

That his story was true is possibly supported by Sarah Lewis/Mrs Kennedy, who came down Dorset Street at 2.30 a.m. and saw a man standing opposite Miller's Court. Sarah Lewis gave her testimony at the inquest before George Hutchinson came forward with his story, so she knew nothing about him, and, while it is difficult to believe that the man she saw wasn't Hutchinson, Hutchinson never mentioned seeing Sarah Lewis. In fact he said that he had seen nobody in Dorset Street except a man who briefly left a lodging house and a policeman who passed at the Commercial Street end. Lewis described the man she saw as 'a stout-looking man, and not very tall'. We have no description of Hutchinson, except that he was 'of a military appearance', and some may doubt that a short, stout-looking man would impress anyone as a man of military-looking appearance. And, while Hutchinson's story throws doubt on Mrs Cox's, it is equally true that Mrs Cox's throws doubt on Hutchinson's. Mrs Cox's claim that she saw a very drunk Kelly is seemingly supported by Kelly's lengthy singing of the same song, independently attested by Catherine Picket (if we choose to believe her); yet Hutchinson claimed Kelly was little more than cheerily tipsy.

One final observation: the evidence suggested that Kelly had been sleeping close up against the partition when she was murdered and that her body had been moved more to the middle of the bed after death, and the cuts on the bed sheet suggested that she had it pulled up over her neck, which indicated to Dr Bond that she was asleep. Unless she had fallen into a drunken sleep, that she was asleep suggests that she was comfortable with and unafraid of the man in bed with her. The *Evening News* had earlier observed, 'As women of this sort are now on the alert in Whitechapel, we may infer that the assassin must appeal to them in some way that disarms suspicion. In other words, he cannot suggest by his appearance that he is a bloodthirsty miscreant.'

This reasoning must surely apply to Mary Jane Kelly more than most. She was a young and apparently physically attractive young woman, so she probably found it easier to attract customers than some of the women patrolling the streets. She was heavily in arrears, but for the moment she had a room and wasn't desperate for 4d. just so she could get a bed for the night, so she had fewer reasons to take risks. There is also the possibility that her killer appeared normal and harmless, and may even have been known to her. This is especially true when we take into account that at the inquest Joseph Barnett was asked if Kelly had ever expressed fear of anyone.

CORONER: Have you heard her speak of being afraid of anyone?

BARNETT: Yes; several times. I bought newspapers, and I read to her everything about the murders, which she asked me about.

CORONER: Did she express fear of any particular individual?

BARNETT: No, sir.

Walter Dew wrote, without elaboration, 'There was no woman in the whole of Whitechapel more frightened of Jack the Ripper than Marie Kelly.'[130]

Of whom was Mary Kelly afraid? Was it the other 'Joe' in her life, or friends of the French lady in Knightsbridge? Did she have more than the usual and obvious reasons to be interested in and perhaps fear Jack the Ripper? And would someone who was scared, as Kelly was scared, if these sources are believed, have shared her bed and fallen asleep with someone other than a man she knew and trusted?

As ever, the Ripper crimes provide ample food for speculation, but one should avoid overindulgence.

That night about three thousand poor inhabitants of Whitechapel gathered at the Great Assembly Hall, Mile End Road, and were treated to a meat tea and miscellaneous entertainment. This was part of the next day's Lord Mayor's Day celebrations and the cost was defrayed by the lord mayor. Across London, in the House of Commons, Dr George Bagster Phillips had a conference with Mr Stuart-Wortley, the undersecretary of the Home Office. Meanwhile, in the chamber, Mr Conybeare asked the home secretary whether he had seen an account in the evening papers of another terrible murder in the East End of London, and whether he did not think it time to replace Sir Charles Warren with someone who would investigate the crimes. This was greeted with cries of 'Oh!' and the speaker's shouts of 'Order!' Sir Charles Warren, of course, was already gone, although this was not generally known at the time.[131]

In Spitalfields, Dorset Street was patrolled by the police all night, no one being allowed to loiter near the place. Elsewhere, the streets were alive with people, thousands of idlers attracted through curiosity to the area, where there was something of the feel of a fair.[132] A young, respectably dressed clerk visited Dorset Street and asked all sorts of questions about the murder, thereby attracting considerable attention to himself, and on leaving the street he found himself followed, at first by three men, then by more and more people until the mob had grown to such proportions that he fled to the police for protection. Another man was arrested near Dorset Street because he carried a black bag. The arrest attracted the attention of a howling mob, which followed the man and arresting officer to Commercial Street Police Station.

On Saturday a murder pardon was issued:

The Commissioner of Police

Metropolitan Police

Murder Pardon

Whereas on November the 8th or 9th in Millers Court Dorset Street Spitalfields, Mary Janet Kelly was murdered by some person or persons unknown, the Secretary of State will advise the grant of Her Majesty's Gracious pardon to any accomplice not being a person who contrived or actually committed the murder who shall give such information and evidence as shall lead to the discovery and conviction of the person or persons who committed the murder.

(Sd) Charles Warren

Commissioner of Police of the Metropolis
Metropolitan Police Office
4 Whitehall Place
SW
10 November 1888

The pardon applied only in the case of Mary Kelly and, on 23 November 1888, Mr Hunter, the MP for Aberdeen North, raised a question in Parliament, asking Henry Matthews 'Whether he is prepared, in the case of

the Whitechapel murders, other than that of the woman Kelly, to offer a free
pardon to any person not being the actual perpetrator of the crimes?'
Matthews replied, 'I should be quite prepared to offer a pardon in the earlier
Whitechapel murders if the information before me had suggested that such
an offer would assist in the detection of the murderer. In the case of Kelly
there were certain circumstances which were wanting in the earlier cases,
and which made it more probable that there were other persons who, at any
rate after the crime, had assisted the murderer.'

Matthews had in fact considered offering a pardon back in October and
had discussed and written about the possibility to Evelyn Ruggles Brise at
the Home Office:

> You say nothing about the suggestion of my offering a free pardon to
> anyone not the actual perpetrator of the murders. I could do that more
> easily, and with less discredit, than would follow from offering a
> reward. Has Sir C W considered the effect of such an offer? There may
> be persons who conceal and harbour the murderer and who are
> therefore afraid to speak – I mentioned this to Pemberton, but not to
> Warren, on Wednesday.[133]

Robert Anderson also writes in his autobiography, 'One did not need to be
a Sherlock Holmes to discover that the criminal . . . if he was not living
absolutely alone, his people knew of his guilt, and refused to give him up to
justice.'[134] And Dr Bond in his report had also commented along the same
lines, saying that the killer 'was probably solitary and eccentric in his habits,
possibly lived among respectable persons who knew his character and habits
and entertained suspicions they were unwilling to communicate to the Police
for fear of trouble or notoriety'. It therefore seems highly probable that
nothing distinguished the Kelly murder from the preceding ones, except that
official opinion was that the murderer's people, friends or family, were afraid
of handing him over for fear of being arrested themselves.

The newspapers were full of the usual criticism of the police and the
home secretary, although it was more muted than before, perhaps because
the newspapers had already said all they could say, perhaps because they
finally appreciated that the crimes were beyond the ordinary and that the
authorities could not really be blamed, or perhaps because it was realised
that it was wrong to use the murders to score political points. The *Daily
Telegraph* was particularly respectful to the rank and file of the police:

They are not highly paid, and they are not drawn from a class generally educated to the exercise of authority, of patience, or of discipline; yet, as a body, they have for years past displayed all these qualities in ample measure, and have thereby earned the respect – we might almost say the friendship – of the people.

The newspaper even acknowledged that Warren was 'an upright, conscientious, zealous, and fearless officer, who has devoted his energies without stint to the work confided to him, and has performed it to the best of his lights'. But, as ever, the home secretary came in for attack, albeit restrained: 'the helpless and heedless ineptitude of the Home Secretary'.[135]

It has to be observed that press interest in the murders – or at least press coverage – showed a remarkable decline. In his excellent book *Jack the Ripper & The London Press*, Professor L Perry Curtis provides a graph based on an analysis of the total column inches devoted to Ripper coverage in the daily newspapers, which shows that after an initial peak following the discovery of Kelly, and a brief increase at the time of the inquest, the coverage of the crimes declined almost to what it was before Nichols was murdered.[136]

The new murder had quickly attracted the attention of Queen Victoria, who was at Balmoral in Scotland and telegrammed Lord Salisbury:

This new most ghastly murder shows the absolute necessity for some very decided action. All these courts must be lit, & our detectives improved. They are not what they shld be. You promised, when the 1st murders took place to consult with your colleagues about it.[137]

At 7.30 a.m. on Saturday, Dr Phillips, assisted by Dr Bond, Dr Gordon Brown, Dr William P Dukes (the H Division police surgeon) and Dr Phillips's assistant, began an exhaustive two-and-a-half-hour-long (or six-and-a-half-hour-long, depending on the source) autopsy.[138] The press also reported that East End coroners Dr Roderick Macdonald and Wynne Baxter visited Dorset Street, each maintaining that the murder had occurred in his district and that the enquiry was his responsibility (the murder had occurred in Baxter's district but the body had been removed to Macdonald's). Macdonald would specifically deny that he had spoken to Baxter about it.[139] During the afternoon Dr Macdonald did visit 13 Miller's Court with Dr Phillips while the police made a thorough search and paid particular attention to the ashes in the grate, which were passed through a sieve and examined by the doctors. This suggests that possibly an organ was missing, perhaps thought burned, hence the presence of doctors. Nothing, apparently, was found.

A crowd was still gathered in front of Miller's Court, but it was not as large as it had been. A columnist for the *East and West Ham Gazette* reported that an acquaintance who had visited the scene that Saturday evening had remarked on the number of carriages that had brought morbidly curious owners to view the murder site. 'That is slumming with a vengeance,' observed the writer.[140] Among the crowds were tradesmen, some selling pamphlets describing the Whitechapel crimes and shouting in shrill voices the lurid detail promised within, their cries mingling with those of vendors of fruit and assorted other edibles, all of whom seemed to be doing a lively business. There was also a large number and variety of evangelistic services available to the locals: 'Commercial Street appeared to be singularly favoured in the matter of moral agencies,' remarked the *Daily Telegraph*.

The lodging houses were apparently regularly visited by small bands of men and women who sometimes took with them a harmonium or other musical instrument to make their gatherings more attractive, and these were augmented by open-air preachers on street corners, a 'worship hour' after the ordinary service at St Jude's Church, a well-attended service at Spitalfields Church, and at Toynbee Hall a discussion entitled 'Pleasure and Pain as the Basis of Ethical Systems'. The last of these, led by Mr Cunninghame, secretary of the Parnell Commission, did little for the local population, but was earnestly listened to by a group of intelligent-looking young men.[141]

Saturday became Sunday and perhaps because a lot of people had a day off work the crowds in Spitalfields grew greater. There was a brief flurry of excitement following a report that a woman had been found murdered in Jubilee Street, but the report was false,[142] and another burst of excitement occurred shortly before 10 p.m., when a powerful-looking man wearing large spectacles and who had blackened his face confronted a woman named Humphreys near George Yard. She asked what he wanted, but in reply he only laughed and the woman started shouting 'Murder!' The man was then seized by two young men, one of them the well-known pugilist and later contender for the world heavyweight championship, Wolf Bendoff.[143] A crowd gathered and there were cries of 'Lynch him', sticks were brandished and the man was assaulted. Not too much damage was done before the police arrived and took him to Leman Street Police Station, although it took eight men to keep the crowd at bay. At first he refused to give any name, but later said that he was William Holt, a doctor at St George's Hospital, and that he lived in Willesden and had for some time played at being a detective and had been out in various disguises for the last few nights.

Described as about 35, five foot seven and dark-complexioned with a dark moustache and spectacles, he would feature in a story that gained almost mythic proportions in later years.[144] In his autobiography Sir Melville Macnaghten referred to a Ripper suspect (see Chapter Nineteen) who had drowned in the Thames 'after he had knocked out a Commissioner of Police and very nearly settled the hash of one of Her Majesty's principal Secretaries of State'. Macnaghten was referring to the resignation of Warren and the press condemnation of Henry Matthews. But, to a writer named Edwin T Woodhall, the black-faced man – whose visage under the writer's pen came to include white-painted circles around the eyes and a white-painted nose, moustache and mouth – became someone who savagely attacked two government officials. According to Woodhall's eager imagination the black-faced man was later found drowned in the Thames.

On Monday, 12 November 1888, Dr Roderick Macdonald, the coroner for the northeastern district of Middlesex, assisted by the deputy coroner, Mr Hodgkinson, opened his enquiry into the death of Mary Kelly at the Shoreditch Town Hall. The jury answered to their names, then one of them voiced the opinion of many when he said, 'I do not see why we should have the inquest thrown upon our shoulders, when the murder did not happen in our district, but in Whitechapel.' The coroner's officer, a Mr Hammond, replied, 'It did not happen in Whitechapel.' The coroner, taking on an unpleasant air of superiority, severely rebuked the juror, saying, 'Do you think that we do not know what we are doing here, and that we do not know our own district? The jury are summoned in the ordinary way, and they have no business to object. If they persist in their objection I shall know how to deal with them. Does any juror persist in objecting?' The juror bravely persisted, 'We are summoned for the Shoreditch district. This affair happened in Spitalfields.' The coroner replied, with what can only have baffled all concerned, 'It happened within my district.'

Then another juror bravely interjected, 'This is not my district. I come from Whitechapel, and Mr Baxter is my coroner.' Macdonald again adopted an overbearing attitude: 'I am not going to discuss the subject with jurymen at all. If any juryman says he distinctly objects, let him say so.' Macdonald paused, then said, 'I may tell the jurymen that jurisdiction lies where the body lies, not where it was found.' And that put an end to the matter, at least as far as the jury were prepared to question Macdonald's authority.

The jury were duly sworn and then taken by Inspector Abberline to view the body at the mortuary adjoining Shoreditch Church. They then went to Miller's Court and viewed the room. They were absent nearly an hour. Returning to Shoreditch Town Hall, the jury heard testimony from Joseph Barnett, Thomas Bowyer, John McCarthy, Mary Ann Cox, Elizabeth Prater, Caroline Maxwell, Sarah Lewis, Dr George Bagster Phillips, Julia Venturney, Maria Harvey, Inspector Beck and Inspector Abberline. Then the coroner addressed the jury: 'The question is whether you will adjourn for further evidence. My own opinion is that it is very unnecessary for two courts to deal with these cases, and go through the same evidence time after time, which only causes expense and trouble. If the coroner's jury can come to a decision as to the cause of death, then that is all that they have to do. They have nothing to do with prosecuting a man and saying what amount of penalty he is to get. It is quite sufficient if they find out what the cause of death was. It is for the police authorities to deal with the case and satisfy themselves as to any person who may be suspected later on. I do not want to take it out of your hands. It is for you to say whether at an adjournment you will hear minutiae of the evidence, or whether you will think it is a matter to be dealt with in the police-courts later on, and that, this woman having met with her death by the carotid artery having been cut, you will be satisfied to return a verdict to that effect. From what I learn the police are content to take the future conduct of the case. It is for you to say whether you will close the inquiry to-day; if not, we shall adjourn for a week or fortnight, to hear the evidence that you may desire.'

Macdonald's wishes were clear and the foreman, having consulted with his fellow jurors, said that they had sufficient evidence to give a verdict.

'What is the verdict?' asked Macdonald.

'Wilful murder against some person or persons unknown,' replied the foreman.[145]

The Times wryly observed, 'Some surprise was created among those present at the inquest in Shoreditch Town-hall by the abrupt termination of the inquiry, as it was well known that further evidence would be forthcoming.' The *Daily Telegraph* commented, 'Comparatively little that was new was elicited by the coroner's inquiry into the death of Marie Jeanette Kelly' and would also point out that the inquest was terminated before Kelly's relatives had had an opportunity to identify the body. The *Daily Telegraph* also contradicted Dr Macdonald's claim that the only responsibility of the inquest was to ascertain the cause of death, saying that since the reign of King Edward I common law had decreed that

> 'all the injuries of the body, also all wounds, ought to be viewed; and the length, breadth, and deepness, with what weapon, and in what part of the body the wound or hurt is; and how many be culpable, and how many wounds there be, and who gave the wounds – all which things must be enrolled in the roll of the coroner's.' No question was put as to any of these points; the doctor was not asked about the nature of the weapon that had been used to cause the injuries. It has been held that a coroner is bound to accept all evidence tendered, and to take down in writing the material parts. Dr. Macdonald interrogated the witnesses, but it was Mr. Hodgkinson who committed their testimony to writing. It is in the power of the Attorney-General to apply to the High Court of Justice to hold a new inquest, if he is satisfied that there has been rejection of evidence, irregularity of proceedings or insufficiency of inquiry. This course is improbable, as it is stated that Mr. Phillips, the divisional surgeon of police, with whom the coroner consulted in private, has had a commission from the Home Office for some time, and he does not consider himself a 'free agent'; but it is pointed out that by hurriedly closing the inquest the opportunity has been lost of putting on record statements made on oath, and when the memory of witnesses is fresh. It is not improbable that a long interval may elapse before a prisoner is charged at the police–court.[146]

Rowland Adams Williams, the former deputy coroner of Crickhowell, wrote to *The Times* on 26 September 1888, that the object of the inquest was not merely to establish the cause of death, as Macdonald had claimed, but to give a full description of the injuries – which in the case of Kelly was not done – to establish the identity of the deceased, and to establish as far as was possible the time of death. It was with regard to the last point that Baxter had repeatedly adjourned the inquests that he conducted so that the police could locate and bring forward witnesses. Had Macdonald done as it seems he should have done, Hutchinson could have been examined under oath and his testimony would have been admissible in a court of law in the event that he was unavailable if somebody stood trial at a later date.

Even Macdonald's claim that the inquest was the responsibility of the coroner in whose district was located the mortuary where the body lay seems to have been incorrect. The law apparently didn't allow a body to be removed to a mortuary that was not in the district where the murder was committed. The *Pall Mall Gazette* of 27 December 1889 carried a story about a man who had died in a common lodging house in Heneage Street, Spitalfields, and whose body was left for three days perched on the side of a kitchen table because there was at that time no mortuary to which he could be taken 'and as the law stood it would not allow a body to be removed' to a mortuary in a neighbouring district. Macdonald was therefore wrong, and the removal of the body to a mortuary in his district was itself illegal.

The inquest was extraordinary and it is difficult to avoid the conclusion that the body was taken to Macdonald's district to avoid the protracted and detailed enquiries conducted by Wynne Baxter, to say nothing of all the attendant publicity and the opportunity this afforded the press to castigate the law and the government.

During the days that followed, a lot of people gave information to the police and a large clerical staff was fully occupied at Leman Street Police Station dealing with the resulting accumulation of case papers. The crowds dwindled at Dorset Street but were still there in sufficient numbers to make it dangerous for a respectably dressed man to loiter. Anyone behaving in the least way suspiciously was also in danger of being detained for an hour or two by the police.

During a thorough search of casual wards and other places of a similar character, the attention of the police was drawn at the Holborn casual ward to a man named Thomas Murphy, who was searched by the police and found to possess a formidable-looking knife with a blade about ten inches long. He was detained while the account he gave of himself was verified.[147] A German who was unable to speak a word of English had a terrifying experience in the Whitechapel Road when he gazed at a woman in some way that alarmed her and she screamed out that he was Jack the Ripper. The man was immediately surrounded by a crowd of people and a strong police escort was needed to get him to Commercial Street Police Station safely. *The Times* reported that he was followed by 'an enormous mob of men and women, shouting and screaming at him in the most extraordinary manner'. At the police station the man explained through an interpreter that he had arrived in London from Germany the day before and was to leave for America that day.[148] And a City constable in plain clothes attracted the attention of some people in Commercial Road, who called out that he was Jack the Ripper. Within a few seconds some hundreds of people surrounded the constable, who quickened his pace, only to find that the mob quickened theirs and surrounded him. Fortunately, some H Division policemen came to his aid.[149]

In the afternoon of 17 November 1888 Birmingham police informed Scotland Yard that a man suspected of being concerned in the Whitechapel murders had left there by train for London. The man, it was said, was a doctor who some years earlier had practised in London with another gentleman of some repute, but who currently lived in a common lodging house, and it was believed that he may have travelled to London to commit the crimes and almost immediately left London for Birmingham on an early train. Detectives Leach and White went to Willesden Junction and Euston and at the latter Inspector White arrested the man, who was duly questioned and, after establishing his whereabouts at the time of the murders, was released. *The Times* reported that Birmingham police had kept the man under surveillance for five days and had asked the Metropolitan Police to watch him, not arrest him, and that they felt the action of the London police had 'stupidly warned the man that he was suspected'.[150]

Among the more comical arrests was that of Sir George Arthur, a captain in the Royal Horse Guards and an amateur actor (although I'm not sure if he ever achieved a more mobile role than that of a corpse in the production of a play called *Theodora*). He went play-acting in Whitechapel, dressing himself in an old shooting coat and a slouch hat, where he attracted the attention of two policemen and was arrested when he approached a known prostitute. At the police station he was able to send a cable to Brook's Club and prove his identity and was released with profuse apologies. The story was eagerly printed abroad, but was kept out of the British press, and Sir George went to Monte Carlo for a few weeks to recover from the ordeal.[151]

Two names that have attracted some interest in recent years emerged in the days following the murders. One was Nicolas Wassili, the son of wealthy parents who was born in 1847 in Tiraspol, in the province of Kherson, Russia, and educated in Tiraspol and at the University of Odessa. He became a fanatical member of a religious sect, which the contemporary press called the Shorn – otherwise called the Skoptsy, a cult that emerged in the second half of the eighteenth century and blossomed in St Petersburg and Moscow under the leadership of Kondratly Selivanov. It came to be considered the most dangerous of all sects and membership was declared illegal by the orthodox church of Russia. Members fled the country, among them Wassili, who fled to Paris. He took lodgings in a poor area called the Rue Mouffetard (on the Left Bank, south of the Seine, one of the oldest and until recently most disreputable streets in Paris), spent his days studying and his nights prowling the streets trying to reform prostitutes. When lectures did no good, he offered money, but increasingly began threatening the women with a knife.

Then he met a young orphan named Madeleine who was prostituting herself in the Rue Richelieu (which runs from Montmartre to the Louvre). He got her lodgings in Rue Serrurier with a Mme Guidard, and a job in a lacemaking business, and within a short time he urged her to embrace the beliefs of the Shorn and marry him. Madeleine was horrified at the idea and seized the opportunity to flee, leaving a note:

> I thank you a thousand times for all your kindness. I respect but cannot love you. I am grateful, but why should I sacrifice all my life to my gratitude? That which brought us together separates us. You saved me, but you ought not to ask me as a reward. I cannot reconcile your roles of gutter preacher and lover. Forgive me and forget me.

Eight weeks later, Madeleine was found dead and Wassili had disappeared. Further prostitute murders followed: a dead woman was found in a quiet side street of the Faubourg St Germain; a third body was found three days later in the Rue Mouffetard; five more victims were found butchered in the Arrondissement des Panthéon between the Boulevards St Michel and de l'Hôpital. Then, in the Rue de Lyon, an attack was made on a street girl, who had the chance to cry for help before she was strangled and the police caught Wassili. He was tried, but his lawyer, Jules Glaunier, declared him insane and the jury agreed. After a short stay in a private asylum in Bayonne, Wassili was sent back to Tiraspol, and was released in January 1888. He was on his way to London when last seen.

Despite the wealth of detail, much of it accurate, especially the geographical locations in Paris, the story has not been substantiated. No record of a Vassiliev can be found in the records of the University of Odessa and no murders corresponding with those of Wassili in Paris have been identified. In early October 1888 the *Daily Telegraph* had carried a couple of reports about the interest taken in the Whitechapel murders in Paris, and it discussed similar crimes committed in the French capital but did not mention Wassili. On 17 November *The Star* published a report of an interview with M Mace, a former chief of the Sûreté, who said that 'no such person committed murders in Paris in 1872'.

On that day in Russia a newspaper called *Novosti* published the Wassili story, but it was a reprint of a foreign article. Curiously, on 28 November 1888, the *Pall Mall Gazette*, *The Star* and the *Daily Telegraph* carried a story about Wassili, which they attributed to *Novosti*, but which claimed, as *Novosti* did not, that he was a fanatical anarchist who on release from the asylum 'went to London, and there lodged with different compatriot refugees until the first woman was assassinated in Whitechapel, since which time his friends have not seen him'. In an excellent article in *Ripperologist*, Stepan Poberowski has suggested that the story was 'planted' in the newspapers by the tsarist secret police, the Okhrana. Apparently the Okhrana wanted to convince the French public and authorities that Russian radicals posed serious dangers. Paying journalists to 'plant' stories unfavourable to Russian radicals was among the 'tricks' employed, particularly by Pyotr Rachowski, the head of the Foreign Bureau based in Paris. The suggestion is that the Wassili story was invented or appropriated by the Okhrana following the Stride murder in the passage of the Berner Street Club in the hope that it would encourage Scotland Yard to interrogate Russian immigrants in London and thereby collect valuable information that Okhrana agents known to have worked in Scotland Yard could have passed to Paris.

Poberowski's theory may be the origin of an exaggerated claim made years later by a journalist who covered the Whitechapel murders named William Le Queux. In his book *Things I Know* Le Queux claimed to have seen a manuscript written in French by Rasputin in which it was stated that the Ripper was a mad Russian doctor named Alexander Pedachenko, sent to London to commit the crimes to confuse Scotland Yard. A later writer, Donald McCormick, used Le Queux as the foundation for his own fanciful story about the Ripper.[152]

The second of the two names that have aroused interest was that of a 27-year-old Swede, Nikaner A Benelius, who was living at 90 Great Eastern Street, Shoreditch, and had been arrested in connection with the murder of Elizabeth Stride, but had been released. He had continued to live in the neighbourhood, staying in a German lodging house run by a man to whom Benelius was apparently 25s. in arrears. At 10.30 a.m. on Saturday, 17 November, he had entered the house of Harriet Rowe, a married woman living in Buxton Street, Mile End. He said nothing to Mrs Rowe, but grinned, then left the house. Mrs Rowe had followed at a discreet distance, and on seeing a constable, PC Imhoff, 211H, she ran to him and told him what had happened. Benelius said that he had only intended to ask the way to Fenchurch Street. Two men, one of whom was believed to be Benelius's landlord, told the police that Benelius had at times been preaching in the street and had of late been acting very strangely. His movements were enquired into and he was released when it was established that he could have played no part in the murders.[153]

Mary Kelly was buried on Monday, 19 November 1888, at the expense of Mr H Wilton, for fifty years the parish clerk and keeper of the Shoreditch mortuary, along with any contributions received from elsewhere. This act of generosity prevented a second inquest being conducted, as Wynne Baxter reportedly stated would have had to happen if the body had been removed from Shoreditch to Whitechapel for burial.[154] Mr Wilton's generosity did cause him to receive some publicity, which in turn led to his being visited by an elderly woman who offered a large sum of money for a lock of Mary Kelly's hair. She explained that she knew a woman spiritualist, blind since the age of three, who the elderly visitor felt sure would be able to give an accurate description of Kelly's killer if only she could have a lock of Kelly's hair to hold. Wilton declined to comply with the woman's wishes and she left, expressing her disappointment.[155]

Several thousand people had gathered outside Shoreditch Church and shortly after 12.30 p.m. they saw Mary Jane Kelly's polished elm and oak coffin, with metal mounts and bearing a plate on which was engraved, MARIE JEANNETTE KELLY, DIED NOVEMBER 9, 1888, AGED 25 YEARS, brought on the shoulders of four men from the mortuary and placed on an open hearse drawn by two horses. Three large wreaths were on the coffin, two crowns of artificial flowers and a cross made up of heartsease. The wreaths on the coffin bore cards inscribed with remembrances from friends who used the same pubs as Kelly. Attached to the cross was a large card bearing the words, 'A last tribute of respect to Mary Kelly. May she rest in peace, and may her murderer be brought to justice.'

The very emotional crowd gathered around the hearse and men and women struggled desperately to touch the coffin. Women with faces streaming with tears cried out, 'God forgive her!' and every man's head was bared. The newspapers reported that 'the sight was quite remarkable, and the emotion natural and unconstrained'.[156] The hearse was followed by two mourning coaches, one containing three people and the other containing five. Among them were Joseph Barnett, someone representing John McCarthy, and the six women who had given evidence at the inquest: Mary Ann Cox, Elizabeth Prater, Caroline Maxwell, Sarah Lewis, Julia Venturney and Maria Harvey.

The cortège went to the Roman Catholic Cemetery at Leytonstone by way of Hackney Road to Cambridge Heath Road, Whitechapel Road and Stratford, a distance of about six miles, but progress was very slow because hundreds of men and women escorted the coffin for a good distance. The cemetery was finally reached at two o'clock. The Reverend Father Columban, with two acolytes and a cross-bearer, met the body at the door of the little chapel at St Patrick, and the coffin was carried at once to a grave in the northeastern corner. Barnett and the poor women who had accompanied the funeral knelt on the clay by the side of the grave, while the service was read. The coffin was incensed, lowered and then sprinkled with holy water, and the simple ceremony ended. The floral ornaments were afterwards raised to be placed upon the grave, and the filling-up was completed in a few moments, watched by a small crowd of people.[157]

A morbid touch to the whole proceedings was added by a story recited by an unnamed columnist of the *East London Observer* who reported on good authority that a showman had offered John McCarthy £25 for a month's use of Mary Kelly's room, and that another had tried to hire or buy Kelly's bed. To McCarthy's credit, both offers were rejected.[158]

Press interest in the murder of Mary Kelly diminished considerably. There were some bursts of interest, as when a rumour spread on Wednesday, 21 November, that another murder had been committed. In fact a woman named Annie Farmer had been attacked but not killed, and the police ventured with some certainty the opinion that the attacker was not the Ripper, this judgement being based on the superficiality of the wounds, the absence of any skill in the cuts and the assailant's use of what appeared to be a blunt knife. The attack happened in 19 George Street, a short road that connected Thrawl Street with Flower and Dean Street. No. 19 was a common lodging house in the charge of a deputy and a watchman, described as 'a mulatto, known as "Darkie" '.[159] 'Darkie' said that a dark man and a woman came to the lodging house at 6.30 a.m. and the man paid 8d. for a double bed. The couple were given one of the partitioned-off boxes on the first floor. Ellen Marks, a tailoress, stated that between 9.30 and 10 a.m. she was standing outside 18 George Street with a woman named Mary Callaghan, who lived at 7 Thrawl Street, and a man named Frank Ruffle. A man came downstairs at No. 19 and ran into the street. He made 'use of a common expression' and said, 'Look at what she has done.' There was blood on his mouth and a scratch, and his hands had blood upon them. Almost as soon as he made off, a woman screamed 'He has cut my throat.'[160]

Callaghan said Annie Farmer was respectably connected, but had been reduced to her present impoverished condition through drink. She was to be seen nightly round the railings at Spitalfields Church, and used to sleep in odd corners whenever she failed to find someone to pay her for the price of a bed in a common lodging house. It was believed that Farmer was married to a respectable tradesman in City Road who allowed her 10s. a week, and that 'Farmer' was her maiden name. She was reasonably well educated and reportedly had three children. She was a known prostitute and had several nicknames, including 'Flossie', 'Tillie', 'Dark Sarah,' 'Laughing Liz' and 'Singing Liz', the last because she formerly obtained a livelihood by singing in the streets. Her attacker was never caught and Farmer recovered.[161]

Another flurry of interest occurred in December and it perhaps has a pertinence to comments made by Robert Anderson in his 1910 auto-biography *The Lighter Side of My Official Life*. Following Kelly's murder the police made a house-to-house enquiry in Dorset Street and the surrounding neighbourhood and a woman named Mary Cusins – the deputy of a lodging house in Paternoster Row – and a lodger named Cornelius Oakes told them that a Polish Jew, a thirty-year-old cigar maker named Joseph Isaacs, had lodged at her house for three or four days before the murder and during that time had behaved strangely: he used to change his clothing frequently and was heard to threaten violence to all women above seventeen years of age. He had disappeared soon after the murder.

On Wednesday, 5 December, Isaacs returned to the lodging for a violin bow, which he had left there. When he left the house Cusins followed him to a pawn shop, where Isaacs asked the owner, Levenson, to repair the bow. With Levenson distracted on this job, Isaacs grabbed a watch and bolted from the shop. Cusins informed the police, who kept a lookout for the man and on Thursday, 6 December, Isaacs was arrested near Drury Lane and taken to Bow Street Police Station. What is curious is that Inspector Abberline was summoned 'and subsequently brought away the prisoner in a cab, which was strongly escorted ... Great reticence is observed regarding the affair, and at Commercial Street Station the officials deny any knowledge of the arrest, although the man is understood to be detained there.'

Isaacs was charged on Friday, 7 December, at Worship Street Police Court, Detective Record asking for a remand, which was granted. As far as is known Isaacs merely behaved oddly and was a petty thief, but the fact that Inspector Abberline was summoned and that Isaacs was taken to Commercial Street Police Station under heavy escort suggests that he was suspected of far more than that, and one suspects that he was suspected, and perhaps *strongly* suspected, of being Jack the Ripper. We don't know why, but it is tempting to speculate that something emerged after the murder of Kelly that focused attention on Polish Jews.[162]

CHAPTER SEVENTEEN

Murders After Mary Kelly

'Jack the Ripper' was a name very quickly picked up around the world and applied to similar crimes both before and after the Ripper series in 1888, and in some cases it was actually suggested that the murderer *was* Jack the Ripper. The police dossier on the crimes included murders other than the canonical five that were for a while suspected but not certainly known to have been committed by the Ripper. The files were closed in 1892, either because the police knew who the Ripper was or *didn't* know who he was but reasonably assumed he was dead or at least no longer active, or possibly because a file has to be closed sometime.

Rose Mylett

Rose Mylett (1862–88) was also known as Catherine Millett, Drunken Lizzie Davis, and Fair Alice Downey. On the night of 19–20 December 1888 she was seen in the company of two men, first at about 7.55 p.m. by an infirmary night attendant who possessed the distinctly unusual name of Charles Ptolomay (or Ptolomey), who saw her speaking to two sailors near Clarke's Yard, between 184 and 186 Poplar High Street, and heard her say, 'No, no, no!' And about 2.30 a.m. she was seen with two men by a woman named Alice Graves outside the George pub in Commercial Road. At 4.15 a.m. she was found dead in Clarke's Yard by PC Robert Goulding. The throat had not been cut and the body had not been mutilated, faint markings around her neck suggesting that she had been strangled. None of this was indicative of the Ripper.

Curiously, Robert Anderson later asserted that Mylett had not been murdered, and even in 1910 asserted in *The Lighter Side of My Official Life* that Mylett's was a 'death from natural causes, and but for the "Jack the Ripper" scare, no one would have thought of suggesting that it was a homicide'. He was supported by Dr Bond, but Wynne Baxter, the coroner, dismissed the idea as 'nonsense'. Nobody was ever caught or convicted of the crime.

Alice McKenzie

Alice McKenzie, also known as Alice Bryant and more famously as Clay Pipe Alice after the clay pipe she habitually smoked, is a bit of a mystery woman prior to taking up with an Irishman named John McCormack, who also called himself Bryant, about 1883. They lived together in numerous lodging houses and by 1889 they were living at the splendidly Dickensian-sounding Mr Tenpenny's lodging house in Gun Street, McCormack being employed as a porter by Jewish tailors in Hanbury Street and McKenzie working as a washerwoman and charwoman for some Jews, and known as an occasional prostitute.

At 11.40 p.m. on 16 July 1889 Alice McKenzie was seen by a friend named Margaret Franklin hurriedly walking in Flower and Dean Street. Franklin shouted out hello and McKenzie replied, 'All right. I can't stop now.' At 12.50 a.m. PC Walter Andrews entered Castle Alley, which ran off Whitechapel High Street, and found the body of McKenzie lying on the pavement. Blood had flowed from two stabs in the left side of her neck. Her abdomen had been superficially mutilated.

Dr George Bagster Phillips did not think the murder had been committed by Jack the Ripper. Dr Bond disagreed and thought the murderer *was* the Ripper, and this opinion was shared, albeit only initially, by Commissioner Monro, who noted, 'I need not say that every effort will be made by the police to discover the murderer, who, I am inclined to believe, is identical with the notorious Jack the Ripper of last year.'[1]

Monro must have changed his mind. Robert Anderson, who had a singular gift of being on holiday when a murder was committed in Whitechapel, and was on holiday when McKenzie was murdered, wrote in 1910[2] that he assumed the murder to have been 'by another hand. I was absent from London when it occurred, but the Chief Commissioner investigated the case on the spot and decided it was an ordinary murder, and not the work of a sexual maniac.'

The Pinchin Street murder

At 5.15 a.m. on 10 September 1889, PC William Pennett was drawn by the smell to the decomposing remains of a woman, missing both the head and legs, that had been dumped under a railway arch in Pinchin Street and covered by an old chemise. The woman's abdomen was badly mutilated in a fashion reminiscent of the Ripper, but Swanson noted that, unlike the Ripper, the murderer had left the genitals alone, and the crime wasn't attributed to the Ripper. The body was never identified.

Frances Coles

Frances Coles, a.k.a. Frances Coleman, Frances Hawkins and 'Carrotty Nell', was born in 1865 to James William Coles, a bootmaker. She had worked for a while for a wholesale chemist in a street called Minories in the East End (named after the nuns who once had a convent there), but in her late teens something happened and she became a casual prostitute. She tried to maintain her former appearances to her father and sister, visiting the former every Sunday and attending church with him, claiming still to work for the chemist and to be living with a respectable elderly lady in Richard Street, off Commercial Road.

On 11 February 1891, Frances Coles was in the Princess Alice, a pub in Commercial Street that won brief notoriety in the Ripper story for being used or being in the vicinity of places frequented by Leather Apron. It still exists, although it is now called the City Darts. Thomas Sadler, a 53-year-old fireman aboard the SS *Fez* who had that day returned from a voyage and been discharged, had made his way into the East End and eventually to the Princess Alice. He'd been a client of Frances Coles before, and they quickly settled into a night of drinking before booking in to a common lodging house at 8 White's Row, Spitalfields.

The next day, 12 February, they enjoyed a pub crawl, but sometime between 9 and 11 p.m. they had an argument and separated. Sadler was later attacked by a woman and two male accomplices in Thrawl Street and robbed of his watch and money. Penniless, he made his way to the previous night's lodgings in White's Row, where Coles was in a drunken stupor at a kitchen table. Charles Guiver, the night watchman, helped Sadler clean himself up the best he could, but Sadler had to leave because he had no money.

Coles later woke up and also left the lodging house. At 1.30 a.m. she purchased some bread and mutton from a shop called Shuttleworth's in Wentworth Street and ate it. A short time later, in a slightly belligerent mood and escorted from the shop, she headed off towards Commercial Street, where she met a friend and fellow prostitute named Ellen Callagher, who warned her to give a wide berth to a man nearby whom she knew to be violent. Coles ignored the warning, propositioned the man and went off with him.

That night was a big night for PC Ernest Thompson, a new recruit, as it was his first unsupervised night on the beat. At 2.15 a.m. he was in Chamber Street, near Leman Street Police Station, and approaching Swallow Gardens. He heard the sound of some footsteps in the distance, and in a few seconds he was in Swallow Gardens, where he found Frances Coles, blood pouring from a wound in her throat. She was still alive and Thompson stayed with her, as police regulations dictated, and was thereafter to be known as the man who let the Ripper escape. In 1900 Thompson would be stabbed to death in a brawl by Barnett Abrahams.

Sadler was charged with the murder of Frances Coles on 16 February, but witness testimony and good legal representation by the Seamen's Union showed that by the time of the murder he had been in several brawls, possessed only an extremely blunt knife and was incapably drunk. Charges against Sadler were eventually dropped on 2 March and Sadler left the Thames Police Court to welcoming cheers from the public, who had shrewdly judged that the police were trying to fit him up. The police genuinely seem to have believed he was the murderer, but whether or not he was Jack the Ripper is open to question and to be doubted.

CHAPTER EIGHTEEN

The Macnaghten Memorandum

As already remarked, in his autobiography published in 1910 Sir Robert Anderson stated that the Ripper's identity was known. As head of the CID, Anderson was in an ideal position to know, but his claim was never properly investigated and until relatively recent years it was dismissed as an error. That the identity of Jack the Ripper might have been known to the police therefore wasn't treated seriously until 1959, when the late television presenter Daniel Farson was making an episode of his television series *Farson's Guide to the British* with Lady Christabel Aberconway, the daughter of Sir Melville Macnaghten, and was shown some of her father's papers, which included the draft of a memorandum Macnaghten had written in 1894 in which he named three suspects: Montague John Druitt, a Russian named Michael Ostrog and a Polish Jew named Kosminski.

Macnaghten had joined the Metropolitan Police as chief constable, CID, in June 1889 and in February 1894 had written a report denying the claim made in a series of articles in the *Sun* newspaper that a young man named Thomas Cutbush was Jack the Ripper. Cutbush had been arrested in March 1891 and arraigned in April of that year on a charge of maliciously wounding Florence Grace Johnson and attempting to wound Isabella Fraser Anderson. It is not known whether the report was intended for anyone in particular, though it seems likely that it was meant as a guide for the home secretary in the event that questions might be asked in Parliament. The report is headed 'confidential' and dated '23 February 1894'.

There are two versions of the report, an official version preserved in the Scotland Yard files on the Whitechapel murders and distinguished as the 'Macnaghten Report',[1] and the draft now in the possession of Sir Melville Macnaghten's descendants and distinguished as the 'Aberconway version'.[2] The Aberconway version is not an original document, but a copy typewritten by Lady Aberconway's secretary with two pages handwritten by Lady Aberconway herself naming the three suspects. The whereabouts of the original document are unknown. It had been inherited, with other papers, by Lady Aberconway's elder sister, Julia Donner, on their mother's death. They passed from Julia Donner to her son Gerald Melville Donner and it is believed that he took them to India when he went to live there. He died in India in November 1968 and the papers disappeared, possibly destroyed.

This third set of papers would be of largely academic interest because there is no reason to suppose that they differed in any way from the copy made by Lady Aberconway, but in the early 1950s an old friend of Gerald Donner's from Harrow named Philip Loftus spent Christmas with him and was shown Sir Melville's papers. Loftus's memory of the content of what he saw differs from either of the extant versions. In a letter to Lady Aberconway in August 1972, Philip Loftus described the suspects as 'Michael John Druitt', 'a feeble-minded man (probably Thomas Cutbush)', and 'a Polish-Jew cobbler nicknamed Leather Apron'.[3] In October 1972, in a review of Daniel Farson's book *Jack the Ripper* in the *Guardian*, Loftus omitted the names of Cutbush and the nickname 'Leather Apron', but added that the material he had seen was 'in Sir Melville's handwriting on official paper, rather untidy and in the nature of rough jottings'.[4]

The official version and the Aberconway draft both mention a Polish Jew, Kosminski, who could be the man identified by Loftus as the 'Polish-Jew cobbler nicknamed Leather Apron', but nowhere in the extant versions is it stated that 'Kosminski' was a cobbler or that he was nicknamed 'Leather Apron'. Loftus therefore saw a version different from the Aberconway version, perhaps an early draft, or Lady Aberconway did not make a faithful transcription of the original.

A third possibility is that Loftus's memory was at fault, and this gains some support from his remembering that one of the suspects was Thomas Cutbush, the very person whom Macnaghten wrote the report to exonerate. We know that Loftus had read Tom Cullen's book *Autumn of Terror*, in which there is an account of the arrest of John Pizer, and it is therefore possible that Loftus made an erroneous connection between the Polish Jew Kosminski and the Polish Jew cobbler Pizer. The 'Donner Papers' may therefore be the lost original of the report transcribed by Lady Aberconway, misremembered by Loftus, and not a variant.

Analysis of the two sets of papers makes it abundantly clear that Macnaghten was relying on his memory and not working from written sources such as police reports. On Page 5 of the Aberconway Papers he stated that Elizabeth Stride's murderer had been disturbed when 'three Jews drove up to an Anarchist Club in Berners [*sic*] Street' (the street's name was 'Berner'). In fact the murderer was disturbed – if he was disturbed at all – by the arrival of one man, Louis Diemshutz, in his pony and cart. Macnaghten also refers to a suspect bearing a resemblance to a man seen by a City PC in the vicinity of Mitre Square, and it seems clear that Macnaghten has confused details of the murders of Stride and Eddowes and that the 'City PC' was in fact PC William Smith of the Metropolitan Police, who saw in Berner Street a man in the company of a woman whom he later identified as Elizabeth Stride, and the three Jews who supposedly disturbed Stride's killer were Lawende, Levy and Harris, who in fact saw a woman who may have been Eddowes at the entrance to Mitre Square.

The most obvious difference is that Macnaghten deleted from the report almost every personal comment. The result is that the report reads like informed police opinion, whereas from the notes it is clear that much of it was Macnaghten's own. Possibly the most important deletion is the claim in the notes that against the three named men 'the police held very strong suspicion'. In the report Macnaghten merely says that any one of the three men was 'more likely than Cutbush to be the killer'. This deletion poses the question whether or not the police did have strong suspicions – or any suspicions at all – about the three men.

A related argument suggests that Macnaghten did not intend that any special significance should be attached to the three men; that they were merely three names randomly selected from a list of any number of suspects and intended only to illustrate the characteristics of the type of man – a type 'more likely than Cutbush' – to have committed the Whitechapel murders. It must be understood that there is no apparent foundation for this conjecture. In the first place, if they had been randomly selected, there would have been no need for Macnaghten to exonerate two of them in favour of Druitt. Secondly, if, as seems probable, Sir Robert Anderson's unnamed Polish Jew was Kosminski, it is clear that Kosminski was also a primary candidate. That two of those named can be shown to have been favoured by senior officers suggests that those named were serious suspects and not just names plucked at random from a list.

If the police ever knew or ever thought they knew the identity of Jack the Ripper, it seems probable that he would be one of those named: Druitt, Ostrog or Kosminski. I will deal with each in turn in the next three chapters.

CHAPTER NINETEEN

Montague John Druitt

In the Aberconway Papers – his draft report – Sir Melville Macnaghten says,

Mr M J Druitt, a doctor of about 41 years of age and of good family, who disappeared at the time of the Miller's Court murder, and whose body was found floating in the Thames on 31 Dec: i.e. 7 weeks after the said murder. The body was said to have been in the water for a month, *or more* [Macnaghten's emphasis] – on it was found a season ticket between Blackheath and London. From private information I have little doubt but that his own family suspected this man of being the Whitechapel murderer; it was *alleged* that he was sexually insane.

In the final report he says,

A Mr M J Druitt, said to be a doctor and of good family, who disappeared at the time of the Miller's Court murder, and whose body (which was said to have been upwards of a month in the water) was found in the Thames on 31 Dec. – or about 7 weeks after that murder. He was sexually insane and from private info. I have little doubt but that his own family believed him to have been the murderer.

In his autobiography, *Days of My Years*, Macnaghten wrote,

Although, as I shall endeavour to show in this chapter, the Whitechapel murderer, in all probability, put an end to himself soon after the Dorset Street affair in November 1888, certain facts, pointing to the conclusion, were not in possession of the police until some years after I became a detective officer [p. 54] . . .

There can be no doubt that in the room at Miller's Court the madman found ample scope for the opportunities he had all along been seeking, and the probability is that, after his awful glut on this occasion, his brain gave way altogether and he committed suicide; otherwise the murders would not have ceased [p. 61]. . . .

I do not think there was anything of religious mania about the real 'Simon Pure' nor do I believe that he had ever been detained in an asylum, nor lived in lodgings. I incline to the belief that the individual who held up London in terror resided with his own people; that he absented himself from home at certain times, and that he committed suicide on or about the 10 November 1888, after he had knocked out a Commissioner of Police and very nearly settled the hash of one of Her Majesty's principal Secretaries of State [p. 62].

Montague John Druitt was born on 15 August 1857 to William and Ann (née Harvey) Druitt at Westfield, an imposing house in Wimborne, Dorset. The family would have seven children, the last born in 1870, the year Montague won a scholarship to Winchester and Ann Druitt's health began to fail. Montague's father's health had also deteriorated and in 1876, the year Montague won a scholarship to New College, Oxford, he took early retirement, aged 56. In 1880 Montague graduated with a third-class honours degree in classics and took a teaching job at a school at 9 Eliot Place, Blackheath, owned by George Valentine, who was headmaster.

Born in Bombay, Valentine had purchased the establishment in 1873 from the Reverend Thomas Jackson Nunns, who had bought a school in Maidenhead called St Piran's, which still exists. Valentine's school, which was a completely new establishment and probably opened in September 1873, was a boarding school preparing boys for the universities, the army and the professions, and many of its pupils achieved distinction in later life. Valentine appears to have been widely respected and the school was well staffed with graduate teachers and servants. In a report of Valentine's death, the school was described as 'a highly successful educational establishment'.[1]

Montague soon began to enjoy the social life at Blackheath. In 1881 he began playing for the Morden Cricket Club, Blackheath, and was soon appointed club treasurer. The records of the Blackheath Hockey Club show that at this time George Valentine proposed and Assistant Master Frederick Henry Lacey seconded Montague for membership, and he continued to pay his 10s. 6d. annual dues until his death.[2]

In 1882 Montague was admitted to the Inner Temple, the certificate being signed by J B Maule, presumably a member of the treasurer's office staff.

On 14 July 1883 Druitt was nominated for membership of the MCC by two nominees of the highest repute[3] and he was elected on 26 May 1884. An 1893 article by Malcolm Christopherson described Druitt as being among the best players in the history of the Blackheath Club and indicated that he was of county standard.[4]

In 1885, Morden Cricket Club merged with the Blackheath Cricket, Football and Lawn Tennis Company Ltd, and Druitt became a director, being appointed treasurer and company secretary. On 29 April he was called to the Bar of the Inner Temple[5] and the Law Lists of 1886–7 record that he had chambers at 9 Kings Bench Walk and was of the Western Circuit and of the Winchester Sessions. The entry for 1887 records that he was a special pleader for the Western Circuit and Hampshire, Portsmouth and Southampton Assizes. A special pleader was a legal practitioner who devoted his attention to the drawing of common-law pleadings, and the term generally described a class of lawyers who were students at the Inns of Court and who were enlisted to practise as counsel under the Bar by virtue of stamped certificates issued by the Inland Revenue. These pleaders confined themselves to what is known as chamber practice, namely pleading in civil proceedings, advising in cases, attending summonses in judges' chambers and teaching pupils.

It was almost unanimously accepted that Druitt's legal career did not flourish and he is often described as a 'failed barrister'. This was an assumption based on the erroneous belief that he took the teaching job after he had been admitted to the Inner Temple. It was thus reasonable to conclude that he resorted to teaching because his legal career had proved unsuccessful. Had his career been unsuccessful, if he never obtained a single brief, as some people have commented, then he would have been politely but firmly 'advised' to vacate his chambers. But we know that Druitt practised, we know of some cases in which he appeared, and as far as can be told his legal career was successful.

When he died, Druitt left an estate valued at £2,600. He did not own property, so the bulk of his estate was cash.[6] Druitt had borrowed money from his father in the form of an advance deducted from a legacy of £500 contained in a codicil of his father's will. This money had been used to finance his legal education. He did not further inherit from his father's estate. He evidently had no money of his own at that time. The sum of £1,083 of Druitt's estate was posthumously inherited from his mother, leaving a balance of £1,517. Even if the whole £500 of his father's bequest is deducted from this sum, leaving £1,017, Druitt would have left more money than he could have earned as a teacher. Teaching salaries were beginning to increase – a certified principal and assistant teacher could earn £119 (men) and £72 (women), on average in 1883[7] – but even if Druitt had been earning above this figure, say £200 per annum, almost double the average, his total earnings would only have been £1,400. In view of the quite considerable expenses that he would have had to meet – chambers fees, travelling costs, moving with the Blackheath social elite – it is clear that Druitt's estate far exceeded his earnings as a teacher. He must have had a secondary income and it seems safe to assume that it was the law.

It is of course unusual that Druitt should have been a special pleader, since such people have not usually been called to the Bar, as had Druitt, but rules at the Inns of Court were less strict in the 1880s than they are today and it is possible that Druitt did not have a flair in the courtroom and consequently took on chambers practice, offering legal advice to barristers, clients and others. This work was and is lucrative, and cannot be interpreted as a sign of a failed career.

On 27 September 1885 Druitt's father died of a heart attack and his mother's mental health began to deteriorate. She became delusional and melancholic (defined at the time as a form of clinical depression accompanied by strong suicidal urges). She attempted to take her life with an overdose of laudanum (tincture of opium) and in July 1888 she was sent to the Brook Asylum in Clapton, London, where she was placed under care of Dr Frederick William Pavy. Two months later she was sent on leave of absence to an establishment in Brighton, where she was looked after by Dr Joseph Raymond Gasquet. She remained there until 31 May 1890, when she was sent to the Manor House Asylum, Chiswick. She died there from heart failure on 15 December 1890.

Mental instability was an inherited trait in Mrs Druitt's family, her sister suffering a bout of mental illness and their mother having committed suicide while insane. Mrs Druitt's mental condition took the form of delusions – that she was being electrocuted, for example – an unreasonable refusal to spend money, and the rejection of food. If Druitt inherited this trait he could have become depressed and suicidal as a result of any significant disappointment (such as the loss of his job).[8]

We know some of Druitt's movements during 1888. On 1 September, the day after Nichols was murdered, Druitt was playing cricket for Canford against Wimborne at Canford in the West Country; he apparently bowled well.[9] At 11 a.m. on 8 September 1888, the morning on which Chapman was murdered, Druitt played cricket at the Rectory Field, Blackheath, for Blackheath against the Brothers Christopherson. On 19 September he defended a clerk named Christopher Power at the Central Criminal Court against an accusation of maliciously wounding with intent to murder Peter Black, the outcome being that Power had committed the act while insane.

On 19 November, ten days after the murder of Mary Kelly, he was present at a board meeting of the cricket club, where he 'proposed that an acre of land be taken behind the Grand Stand at a similar proportionate rent to that paid for the present land. The proposal to be referred to a Committee to report.' On 22 November he represented the family business in an appeal held before Lord Chief Justice Coleridge and Justices Manisty and Hawkins – which he won.[10] That Druitt continued to carry out his responsibilities – and in the case of the legal appeal carried them out with great success – destroys the suggestion that his brain gave way immediately or soon after the murder in Miller's Court, as Macnaghten asserted, showing that he was wrong or at the very least should not be interpreted literally.

On or about Friday, 30 November 1888, Montague John Druitt was dismissed from Eliot Place for 'a serious offence'. It is often assumed that Druitt was summarily dismissed – that he committed the offence and almost simultaneously left the school – but it is significant that 30 November seems to have been the end of term, so the offence may have been committed weeks before and Druitt may have worked out his employment under notice of dismissal. We do not know what the offence was, but it has been accepted, and is today given as if it were a fact that Druitt was a homosexual and that the offence was possibly that of molesting boys. Had this been the case then it is likely that Druitt would have been dismissed immediately and not worked out his term of employment.

Montague John Druitt was last seen alive on 3 December 1888. On 11 December 1888 his eldest brother, William Harvey Druitt, who lived in Bournemouth and was part of the firm of J and W H Druitt, solicitors of Borough Chambers, learned from a friend that Montague had not been seen at his chambers for over a week. William investigated and learned that his brother had been dismissed from Eliot Place. Among Druitt's possessions he discovered a suicide note. On 21 December the minutes of the Blackheath Cricket, Football and Lawn Tennis Company record, 'The Honorary Secretary and Treasurer, Mr M J Druitt, having gone abroad, it was resolved that he be and he is hereby removed from the post of Honorary Secretary and Treasurer.'

Had Druitt really expressed his intention of leaving the country? Was emigrating just an excuse he had given? Or was 'gone abroad' a euphemism?

On 31 December Druitt's body was pulled from the Thames near Chiswick. The inquest into his death was held at the Lamb Tap, Chiswick, on 2 January 1889. The coroner was Dr Thomas Diplock and accounts of the inquest were given in several newspapers (the original inquest records do not appear to have survived). The fullest account is to be found in the *Acton, Chiswick and Turnham Green Gazette,* 5 January 1889:

FOUND DROWNED. – Shortly after midday on Monday, a water-man named Winslade, of Chiswick, found the body of a man, well-dressed, floating in the Thames off Thorneycroft's. He at once informed a constable, and without delay the body was at once conveyed to the mortuary. On Wednesday afternoon, Dr Diplock, coroner, held the inquest at the Lamb Tap, when the following evidence was adduced:- William H Druitt said he lived at Bournemouth, and that he was a solicitor. The deceased was his brother, who was 31 last birthday. He was a barrister-at-law, and an assistant master at a school in Blackheath. He had stayed with witness at Bournemouth for a night towards the end of October. Witness heard from a friend on 11 December that deceased had not been heard of at his chambers for more than a week. Witness then went to London to make inquiries, and at Blackheath he found that deceased had got into serious trouble at the school, and had been dismissed. That was on 30 December.[11] Witness had deceased's things searched where he resided, and found a paper addressed to him (produced). The coroner read this letter, which was to the effect:- 'Since Friday I felt that I was going to be like mother, and the best thing for me was to die.' Witness continuing, said deceased had never made any attempt on his life before. His mother became insane in July last. He had no other relative. Henry Winslade was the next witness. He said that he lived at No. 4, Shore Street, Paxton Road, and that he was a waterman. About one o'clock on Monday he was on the river in a boat, when he saw the body floating. The tide was at half flood running up. He brought the body ashore and gave information to the police. PC George Moulson, 216 T, said he searched the body, which was fully dressed, excepting the hat and collar. He found four large stones in each pocket in the top coat; £2.10s. in gold, 7s. in silver, 2d. in bronze, two cheques on the London and Provincial Bank (one for £50 and the other for £16), a first-class season ticket from Blackheath to London (South Western Railway), a second-half return Hammersmith to Charing Cross (dated 1 December), a silver watch, gold chain with silver guinea attached, a pair of kid gloves, and a white handkerchief. There were no papers or letters of any kind. There were no marks of injury on the body, but it was rather decomposed. A verdict of suicide whilst in unsound mind was returned.

Unfortunately, this report bears the hallmarks of an inexperienced and probably junior journalist, and it is remarkable that it passed the attention of the subeditors and made it into print. Most significantly it does not name Druitt, the subject of the inquest, or any medical testimony, and it contains several errors. It says that 'there were no papers or letters of any kind found on the body', whereas both the *County of Middlesex Independent* of 2 January 1889 and the *West London Observer* of 5 January 1889 refer to the authorities having contacted Bournemouth as a consequence of papers being found on the body.

Of some importance is the suicide note. We don't know what it actually said: the *Acton, Chiswick and Turnham Green Gazette* makes clear that the words 'Since Friday I felt I was going to be like mother, and the best thing for me was to die' were *not* a direct quote but the gist of the letter as a whole, and the *Richmond and Twickenham Gazette* of 5 January 1889 described the letter as 'to the effect that "what he intended to do was best for all parties" '. Assuming that the letter was written shortly before he committed suicide, it makes it difficult to believe that Druitt was Jack the Ripper. A man who had murdered and mutilated five women is not likely to have given as his reason for committing suicide that he had feared some mental instability *since Friday*. Of course, there is absolutely no reason why the letter could not have been written weeks before Druitt killed himself, written long before his homicidal urges – assuming that he ever had any – had taken control. But if the letter *was* written shortly before his suicide, and if the Friday mentioned in the suicide letter *was* 30 November, the day he was dismissed from Eliot

Place, it would seem that his doubts about his mental condition had a direct relationship with his dismissal. Since the school seems to have been connected with the most enjoyable and perhaps important aspects of Druitt's social life, perhaps the loss of his job and any shame about the cause may have depressed him to the extent that he realised that he was suffering from the same symptoms of melancholia as had reduced his mother to a deluded and pitiful woman. This alone could explain why Druitt killed himself.

On 7 February at a board meeting of the Blackheath Cricket Club, 'It was resolved that the Directors had heard with much regret of the death of Mr M J Druitt who had zealously fulfilled the duties of Honorary Secretary and Treasurer for three years.' Ann Druitt died on 15 December 1890, and, on 24 July 1891, William Druitt inherited Montague's estate.

Turning to Sir Melville Macnaghten, almost everything he has to say about Druitt is wrong. He says that Druitt was 'said to be a doctor'. Setting aside the question of who it was who said this, Druitt was in fact a barrister/teacher. It has been suggested that Druitt may have had a brief flirtation with medicine between graduation and his application to the Inns of Court, but this would not have made him a doctor or given anyone any cause to refer to him as one. Whatever the source of this information, it was wrong. But the highly significant point is that the mistake shows that neither Macnaghten nor his source could have been acquainted with the evidence given at the inquest into Druitt's death, where Druitt's occupation was clearly stated.

Analysis of Macnaghten's writing suggests that his source of information about Montague Druitt was PC Moulson's report about finding the body in the Thames. Macnaghten knew about the season ticket from Blackheath to London, which was found on Druitt's body, and this knowledge shows that Macnaghten had information postdating Druitt's suicide. But inaccurate biographical and other information shows that he had no knowledge of the evidence given at the inquest. Macnaghten's source must therefore date between the discovery of the body and the inquest, and is likely to be the report submitted by PC Moulson, who pulled Druitt's body from the Thames.

Further evidence for this conclusion is contained in a statement in Macnaghten's autobiography, in which he states his belief that Druitt 'resided with his own people' and 'absented himself at certain times'. Neither is true, as would have been perfectly clear from the evidence given at the inquest. However, the *West London Observer* reported that papers found on Druitt's body 'indicated that he was a resident of Bournemouth'.

Druitt's brother lived in Bournemouth, but the papers found on Druitt's body indicated that Druitt lived there too.

In the Aberconway Papers, Macnaghten stated that Druitt was 'about 41 years of age'. Druitt was 31. However, both the *County of Middlesex Independent* and the *West London Observer* reported that when the body was pulled from the Thames it looked like that of a man aged about 40. The age given by Macnaghten could have been based on the estimated age of the body when pulled from the Thames, although it must be deemed unlikely that Macnaghten would have been so pedantic as to estimate the age of a decomposing corpse as 41 years (although we might care to note that Macnaghten seems to have been sufficiently pedantic to write 'about 41 . . .'), and it would be more reasonable to suppose that Macnaghten wrote '41' when he meant '31', but this would mean that he possessed accurate biographical information about Druitt, which otherwise we have no reason to suppose he possessed. It seems best to assume therefore that something among the papers found on Druitt's body suggested that he was 41.

Macnaghten says that 'Druitt disappeared at the time of the Miller's Court murder' and in his autobiography he is even more precise, saying that Druitt 'committed suicide on or about 10 of November 1888'. The former statement carries an unwarranted implication, while the latter is wrong. There seems to be no question but that Macnaghten assumed that Druitt's mental stability completely collapsed after the murder of Mary Jane Kelly and that he committed suicide within days. Neither assumption is true: Druitt continued to teach at the school in Blackheath until perhaps as late as 30 November; he appears to have successfully carried out his legal work (he evidently regularly visited his chambers until about the same date, otherwise his week-long absence would not have warranted comment); and he continued to fulfil his responsibilities with the cricket club. He would seem to have conducted his life in the way to which he was accustomed until at least the end of November.

Macnaghten says that Druitt was 'alleged' to be sexually insane. It is clear from page 109 of his autobiography, where he refers to the murderer Neill Cream as a 'sexual maniac', that Macnaghten defined this term as a person who derived pleasure from killing. However, the point is that Macnaghten *did not know* that Druitt was sexually insane. Macnaghten is unlikely to have obtained this information from a member of Druitt's family because the person concerned would surely have provided Macnaghten with accurate biographical information. It was therefore obtained at second hand, from someone who did not know much about Druitt.

The most damning evidence against Druitt must be the suspicion or belief of the family that he was responsible for the Whitechapel murders, although the Scotland Yard and Home Office files provided ample testimony that many people were suspected by their family and friends, so the suspicion itself may not be all that significant. The point, though, is that, if Macnaghten had received this information from the family, it is reasonable to assume that he would have possessed accurate biographical information. The absence of such information indicates that the source was not a member of the family and that whatever the family believed or was supposed to believe was heresy.

Finally there is what might be called 'negative' evidence – that is inferences drawn from what was *not* said. In contrast to what he had to say about Kosminski and Ostrog – they were homicidal and had a great hatred of women, which are very good reasons why suspicion fell on them – Macnaghten has nothing of this kind to say about Druitt beyond unsubstantiated allegations about Druitt's mental state and the opinion of his family.

From Macnaghten's writings it is abundantly clear that he did not know for certain that Montague John Druitt was Jack the Ripper. From the foregoing analysis it is difficult to avoid the conclusion that Macnaghten knew nothing whatsoever about Druitt (other than hearsay about his mental state and the opinion of his family) except what was contained in PC Moulson's report concerning the discovery of Druitt's body in the Thames. The important and perhaps unanswerable questions are, therefore: when and why did suspicion ever fall on Druitt? and why was Macnaghten inclined to favour Druitt above any other suspect?

I believe that part of the answer is provided by a sentence in Macnaghten's autobiography,[12] the significance of which seems to have been generally overlooked. He wrote,

Although, as I shall endeavour to show in this chapter, the Whitechapel Murderer, in all probability, put an end to himself soon after the Dorset Street affair in November 1888, certain facts, pointing to this conclusion, were not in possession of the police till some years after I became a detective officer.

Here again the words 'in all probability' suggest an absence of certainty that Druitt was the Whitechapel murderer, but the crucially important statement is that 'certain facts pointing to this conclusion' – otherwise the information suggesting that Druitt was the murderer – were not received by the police until 'some years after' June 1889 when Macnaghten joined the Metropolitan Police as chief constable, CID. However, if the allegations against Druitt were taken seriously by the police and investigated, a report would have been produced. Such a report would have contained accurate biographical information, which Macnaghten clearly did not possess. The report was therefore withheld from him, which seems improbable, or no report was produced, in which case the allegations against Druitt could not have been taken seriously, forcing us to wonder why Macnaghten therefore favoured him.

The only realistic conclusion that seems to emerge from this conundrum is that, some years after June 1889, Macnaghten received information to the effect that the family of an unnamed man who committed suicide in the Thames at the end of 1888 believed him to have been Jack the Ripper, that Macnaghten checked the files and pulled PC Moulson's report about Druitt and assumed that Druitt was the man whose family suspected him. It seems unreasonable to suppose that Sir Melville Macnaghten was so irresponsible as to base an accusation on such a flimsy connection as the mere fact that Druitt committed suicide several weeks after the murder of Mary Jane Kelly.

In 1903 Inspector Abberline gave an interview to the *Pall Mall Gazette* in which he responded to a claim made in a Sunday newspaper[13] that the Whitechapel murderer 'was a young medical student who was found drowned in the Thames'. Abberline is reported to have replied,

'Yes,' said Mr Abberline, 'I know all about that story. But what does it amount to? Simply this. Soon after the last murder in Whitechapel the body of a young doctor was found in the Thames, but there is nothing beyond the fact that he was found at that time to incriminate him. A report was made to the Home Office about the matter, but that it was "considered final and conclusive" is going altogether beyond the truth. Seeing that the same kind of murders began in America afterwards, there is much more reason to think the man emigrated. Then again, the fact that several months after December, 1888, when the student's body was found, the detectives were told still to hold themselves in readiness for further investigations seems to point to the conclusion that Scotland Yard did not in any way consider the evidence as final.'[14]

Macnaghten referred to a doctor aged about 41; the Sunday newspaper referred to a 'young medical student'; Abberline talked about a young doctor whom he also referred to as a student. They would *not* appear to have been talking about the same person, and none of them appear to have been referring to Druitt, who was 31, was not a student and was not a doctor. However, all three sources *were* talking about someone pulled from the Thames in late November or early December 1888, and we know of only one person who was pulled from the Thames at that time: Montague Druitt.

It is therefore assumed, probably correctly but by no means with absolute certainty, that Druitt was the Thames suicidee in late 1888. This being the case, that he was dismissed as a valid suspect by a source as respected and informed as Inspector Abberline has been remarkably influential in knocking Druitt down the totem pole of suspects, but the evidence indicates that he was not aware of the evidence possessed by Macnaghten and that his conclusion was therefore invalid. Sir Melville Macnaghten clearly states that the 'certain facts' pointing to the conclusion that Druitt was the murderer came to the attention of the police only some *years* after he joined the Metropolitan Police in June 1889. However, Abberline is clearly referring to and basing his judgement on a report made *at the time the body was pulled from the Thames*. Furthermore, Abberline clearly states that there was nothing to incriminate him except the coincidence that his body was pulled from the Thames at the end of 1888. The report to the Home Office was therefore probably a routine report about a death in suspicious circumstances.

In other words, all Abberline knew was that Druitt's death had been routinely investigated by the police at the end of 1888 or early 1889, and nothing was found to incriminate him with the murders. But Macnaghten had information received some years after June 1889 (probably after Abberline's retirement in 1892), which implicated a late-1888 Thames suicide. Macnaghten appears to have lacked biographical detail, from which it must be concluded that he assumed the suicide in question was Montague Druitt, presumably because there was no other late-1888 Thames suicide.

Of course, we have no idea what the information was that the police received after 1889, although nothing we know about Sir Melville

Macnaghten suggests that he would have accepted someone's guilt on flimsy evidence, so we can reasonably do no more than assume that the evidence must have been compelling. Whether it related to Druitt or not, we don't know.

CHAPTER TWENTY

Michael Ostrog

Michael Ostrog was also known as Bertrand Ashley, Dr Barker, Claude Cayton or Clayton, John Evest, Max Grief Gosslar, Max Kaife Gosslar, Dr Grant, 'Grand Guidon', Stanislas Lublinski, Ashley Nabokoff, Orlof, Henry Ray, Max Sobieski and Count Sobieski.

Sir Melville Macnaghten gave few details about Ostrog. In his draft he wrote,

> Michael Ostrog, a mad Russian doctor and a convict and un-questionably a homicidal maniac. This man was said to have been habitually cruel to women, and for a long time was known to have carried about with him surgical knives and other instruments; his antecedents were of the very worst and his whereabouts at the time of the Whitechapel murders could never be satisfactorily accounted for. He is still alive.

In the official report:

> Michael Ostrog, a Russian doctor, and a convict, who was subse-quently detained in a lunatic asylum as a homicidal maniac. This man's antecedents were of the worst possible type, and his where-abouts at the time of the murders could never be ascertained.

Anderson's friend Major Arthur Griffiths refers to Ostrog in his book *Mysteries of Police and Crime*, although he does not name him:

> The second possible criminal was a Russian doctor, also insane, who had been a convict both in England and in Russia. This man was in the habit of carrying about surgical knives and instruments in his pockets; his antecedents were of the very worst, and at the time of the

Whitechapel murders he was in hiding, or, at least his whereabouts were never exactly known.

Sir Basil Thompson obliquely refers to Ostrog in *The Story of Scotland Yard*,[1] although he appears to combine Ostrog and Druitt: 'The belief of CID officers at the time was that [the murders] were the work of an insane Russian doctor and that the man escaped arrest by committing suicide at the end of 1888.'

George R Sims in 1907 wrote,

The second man was a Russian doctor, a man of vile character, who had been in various prisons in his own country and ours. The Russian doctor who at the time of the murders was in Whitechapel, but in hiding as it afterwards transpired, was in the habit of carrying surgical knives about with him. He suffered from a dangerous form of insanity, and when inquiries were afterwards set on foot he was found to be in a criminal lunatic asylum abroad. He was a vile and terrible person, capable of any atrocity.

Both these men [the other was the Polish Jew] were capable of the Ripper crimes, but there is one thing that makes the case against each of them weak.

They were both alive long after the horrors had ceased, and though both were in an asylum, there had been a considerable time after the cessation of the Ripper crimes during which they were at liberty and passing about among their fellow men.[2]

Nothing is known about Michael Ostrog himself. There is a French police record in which he claimed to have been born in Warsaw in 1835. He may have come from a good family, is said in a British document to have received a superior education, and he certainly seems to have possessed the manners and bearing to be accepted into society. He may once have been married, and he was a Jew, although one document gives his religion as Greek Orthodox. He claimed to have been a surgeon, and this seems likely. He also claimed to have served two years with the Russian army and five years with the Russian navy, which is less likely given that his first appearance in Britain was when he was 27. By profession he was a sneak thief. He appears to have been well known and notorious in the early part of his career, but later seems to have been a failure and spent most of his life in prison. Perhaps he was happy there. But, whatever else he was, he was *not* Jack the Ripper. The mystery is why anyone ever thought he might have been.

The earliest account of Michael Ostrog so far traced is in 1863 when he passed himself off as a 27-year-old student named Max Grief Gosslar or Max Kaife Gosslar and stole an opera glass and case from Charles Levi at Oriel College, Oxford, and other property from George Frederick Price at New College, Oxford. He was caught and sentenced to ten months in prison.[3]

In 1864 he visited Bishop's Stortford, where he claimed to be an illustrious Pole, a count or a prince, who had been hunted from place to place and survived by living wild in the woods. 'Genteel in appearance, affable in speech, and most interesting and engaging in manners, his troubles had cast a halo of semi-martyrdom around him' and many people took him into their homes. He then went to Cambridge, where he used the name Max Sobieski and came a cropper when he was found in a college in the process of committing a crime, and was convicted of being a rogue and a vagabond, being sentenced to three months in prison.[4]

In July 1864 he was in Tunbridge Wells and calling himself Count Sobieski, the exiled son of the king of Poland.

His appearance was much in his favour, being young and tall, and his expression of melancholy and the recital he made of his supposed wrongs and sufferings in the cause of his country procured for him a great deal of sympathy. It was his custom to walk on the Parade, and get the Parade Band to play the Polish national anthem, and he would wander gloomily along, as though absorbed in his melancholy reflections.

He ingratiated himself with many respectable people, including a number of young women, from whom he obtained money and property, but soon decamped.[5] He went from Tunbridge Wells to Exeter, where in December he was sentenced to eight months in prison for fraud and larceny.[6]

He would have spent much of 1865 in prison and we don't hear of him again until January 1866, when he was acquitted on charges of fraud at Gloucester Quarter Sessions.[7] He went from Gloucester to Maidstone in Kent, where on 19 March he stole a gold watch and other articles from the home of Mrs Esther Carpenter. She lived at the Palace in Maidstone and left a gold watch, gold lockets and other trinkets on a table. Ostrog apparently rang the bell at the front door and asked to see the curate, and in the absence of the maid slipped into the house and stole the items.

From Maidstone he went to Chatham, where, on 20 March, he took lodgings at the Globe Inn. He became friends with an unnamed medical man of great respectability who introduced him to a number of people in local society, among them Thomas White, who was connected with the military staff at Chatham, and from whom he would be accused (and acquitted) of stealing a gold cross on 13 April, which the next day he gave to Esther Brenchley, apparently a barmaid at the Bull Hotel in nearby Rochester.[8] On 26 April he stole two books from James Burch, the landlord of the Globe Inn in Chatham. He went to Rochester, where he arrived with a woman, took a bedroom and sitting room at the Bull Hotel, but left without settling his account. George Wilson, the landlord of the Bull, found that Ostrog had left a bag in his room and he opened it, finding inside the books stolen from James Burch.

He was confronted by the police but reportedly desperately resisted arrest and was taken into custody only after a chase. He was remanded and appeared before the Kent Summer Assizes in August, where he was charged under the name of Bertrand Ashley, alias Ashley Nabokoff, and described in the press as 'the great Russian swindler'. To his manifest astonishment the judge, Mr Justice Channell,[9] sentenced him to seven years' imprisonment.[10]

He was released on 23 May 1873 on ticket-of-leave, meaning that he had to report his whereabouts regularly to the police. Later in the month he stole a valuable silver cup, a silver soap dish, a shaving pot, a glass toothbrush dish with silver top and eleven studs worth £5 from Captain Ferdinand W Milner at Woolwich Barracks. He then went to Windsor, where he stayed from July to December at the South Western Railway Hotel. At this time he cultivated the friendship of a historian and teacher named Oscar Browning (1837–1923), then an assistant master at Eton, who had given Ostrog money and a book. He also gave him free run of the library. On 15 July 1873 Alfred Hands Cooke, a student at Eton, discovered that a silver cup, a trophy inscribed with his name and that of a previous winner, had been stolen from his rooms. The police investigated and on 4 October Superintendent Thomas Durham eventually traced the cup to Dubree's pawnshop at 73 Charlotte Street, London, where it had been pawned by Dr Watkins Robert O'Connor of Osnaburgh Terrace, Portland Road, London. Visited by the police, Dr O'Connor explained that Michael Ostrog had called on him on 27 August, seeking O'Connor's former partner, Mr Baker Brown,[11] whom he said he had known in St Petersburg. He explained that he had been a surgeon with the Russian Imperial Guard, but had been forced to flee the country in consequence of fighting a duel in which he had killed a man, and wished to ask Baker Brown for assistance.

Ostrog and O'Connor became friendly, and the former paid O'Connor several visits, turning up in September with some books and a cup – he claimed that he had won the cup in a boat race on the Neva but had removed the inscription in case it led the Russian detectives to him. He left the cup and books with Dr O'Connor, and towards the end of November instructed him to sell them, which he did. He pawned the cup with Mr Dubree and sold the books to a second-hand-book dealer, Walter Brown of Great Portland Street, London, and sent Ostrog the money.

The books O'Connor had sold for Ostrog had been stolen by him from Eton on two occasions, on 4 and 25 August, after he had convinced a college servant named George Finey that Oscar Browning had given him permission to borrow the books from the library. He took *Smith's Dictionary of Biography and Mythology* and *Smith's Dictionary of Geography*. Ostrog would later argue for no good purpose, as he was aware it wouldn't affect his sentence, that he was guilty of receiving property through deception, but was not guilty of actual theft because he had not personally stolen the books but had been given them.

Back in Eton yet again on 28 September, Ostrog and another man were seen to come out of the Lower School passage by one of the college servants, who became suspicious and went to investigate, discovering that the House-Singing Cup and a small tankard were missing, along with a large quantity of quality clothing. He pursued the men along Slough Road as far as Colnbrook. Meanwhile, back at Eton others had discovered the robbery and alerted the police, who undertook what by today's standards was a speedy and extensive investigation, even searching trains, but without luck.[12] By a curious coincidence Melville Macnaghten was captaining a cricket team playing against Eton, his old school, at the time.[13] Ostrog later wrote to a one-time friend that he was returning to Russia and could be contacted via a Mr Carl Swedenburg, using poste restante in Berlin, but instead he went to Burton-on-Trent.

By ways unknown, Superintendent Thomas Oswell learned that Ostrog was staying at the Fox and Goose Inn in Burton-on-Trent. Ostrog was in the dining room and Oswell, sensing that he was potentially dangerous, swept aside the cutlery before arresting him. Ostrog vehemently protested that he was a Swedish doctor visiting the breweries[14] and had to be forcibly taken to the police station, where he drew an eight-chambered revolver from his pocket and grappled with Oswell until relieved of the weapon. The next day he was taken to Slough to be identified by Superintendent Dunham of the Bucks Constabulary.[15] He was tried under the name of Bertrand Ashley at the Buckingham Quarter Sessions on 5 January 1874, defended himself and pleaded guilty, receiving a sentence of ten years in prison and a further seven years' police supervision. The newspapers reported that on receiving the sentence Ostrog 'seemed somewhat chagrined'.[16] His records at Buckinghamshire County Gaol in Aylesbury, where he was held, described him as a surgeon, aged forty with a dark complexion and dark-brown hair, and of the Greek religion. He was born in Russia, his father was dead and he was unmarried. He claimed to have served two years with the Russian army and five years with the Russian navy, and to have received a superior education. On 28 January 1874 he was sent to Pentonville Prison.[17]

Ostrog was released from prison on 28 August 1883 on ticket-of-leave. He failed to report and his description was published in the *Police Gazette*. His age was given as fifty, he was five foot eleven, dark-skinned, with dark brown eyes and grey hair. He had two moles on his right shoulder and flogging marks on his back.[18]

There is a break in the record from 1883 until 1887, but it is likely that he was in France and possibly even in prison there. It is known that he was deported by ministerial order on 9 June 1886.

In 1887 Ostrog, dressed in a flannel cricket suit, dark jacket and straw hat, boldly walked past the gatekeeper of the Royal Military Academy, Woolwich, who thought he was an officer, and entered Room 79, 2nd Division, the room of Cadet George Bigge, where he put into his black bag a metal pint tankard Bigge had won as second prize in the high jump. Bigge was unwell and was on the bed, unseen by Ostrog until he jumped up and tried to prevent the theft. Bigge, though lame, gamely pursued Ostrog and even managed to knock him to the ground, but Ostrog ran off. Other cadets came to Bigge's assistance and on learning what had happened ran after Ostrog, who despite having a good head start and being a decent runner himself, was caught and grabbed by a cadet named Fisher and very quickly surrounded. He was taken back to the academy and handed over to the police. Ostrog claimed to be a Belgian doctor named Bonge and on the way to the police station took a quantity of nux vomica from his pocket and swallowed it. At the police station he refused to take an emetic, but he was moved to the Miller Memorial Hospital at Greenwich, where one was administered. In July he appeared in court and in explanation of the crime 'said he was going to play cricket but got sunstroke, and felt an irresistible urge to run a race, and thought he was doing so when the cadets were following him . . . His wife had been unfaithful to him.'[19]

He was held in prison and reappeared in court in August. After hearing the evidence of the police, Ostrog feigned insanity by picking up his overcoat, which he had draped over the rail of the dock, and calmly announcing, 'I am going to France.' He had to be forcibly restrained from leaving the dock. Later Superintendent Dunham described Ostrog as 'among the most desperate criminals who ever lived'.[20] He was convicted under the name Claude Clayton at the Central Criminal Court on 12 September 1887 and sentenced to six months' imprisonment.[21] He was sent to Wandsworth Prison, but removed from there on 30 September 1887 to the Surrey Pauper Lunatic Asylum. The Register of Male Admissions records Ostrog's presence there under the name Claude Cayton or Clayton, gives his age as fifty and states that he was Jewish, a surgeon and married. He was suffering from mania,[22] the supposed cause of which was not known. He was discharged on 10 March 1888.[23]

This is now the crucial period as far as our main interest in Ostrog is concerned and it would appear that he was in France. We possess little in the way of detail, but it would seem that he was well known in the country under various aliases, including Stanislas Lublinski and 'Grand Guidon', under which names he was arrested by the French police on 26 July for the theft of a microscope. He was held in custody until brought to trial on 18 November 1888, when he was sentenced to two years in prison in Paris.

In the meantime, he had failed to report to the British police and his description had once again appeared in the *Police Gazette*:

3. – Convict Supervision Office. – MICHAEL OSTROG, alias BERETRAND ASHLEY, CLAUDE CLAYTON and Dr GRANT, Office No. 22550, whose apprehension is sought for failing to report – age 55, height 5ft 11ins, complexion dark, hair dark brown, eyes grey, scars right thumb and right chin, two large moles right shoulder and one back of neck, corporal punishment marks, generally dressed in semi–clerical suit. Polish Jew. Was sentenced 5th January 1874 at Aylesbury to ten years penal servitude and seven years Police supervision for larceny. Liberated on licence 25 August 1883. Again sentenced at the Central Criminal Court 14 September 1887, to six months hard labour for larceny. On 10 March 1888 he was liberated

from Surrey County Lunatic Asylum and failed to report.

Warrant issued.

Special attention is called to this dangerous man.[24]

Curiously, on 13 May 1889, three watches and chains were stolen from Mr Betjeman, a watchmaker and jeweller of Eton. According to Frederick Rowell, a man had visited the jeweller's claiming to be from Windsor Castle and wanting to see some watches and chains for Prince Teck. The jeweller had none good enough, but Frederick Rowell, the sales assistant, said that he could get some from London. Rowell duly went to London to get the watches and the customer returned to the shop during the afternoon, this time wearing a mortar board earlier acquired from a hosier named Samuel Lingwood, and said he wished to take the watches away. Rowell insisted on accompanying the customer, who took him to Eton, where the boys assumed he was a don or an outside tutor and saluted him. Rowell's suspicions were thus allayed and he allowed the customer to take the watches into another room unaccompanied. The customer absconded. He went to Windsor, then got a lift to Staines with a man named Edward Edwin Merridew, in whose cab he left his mortar board, visited a pawnshop in Staines and then went to Richmond. Ostrog would be accused of this crime and stand trial in 1894.[25]

On 9 August 1889 the *Police Gazette* again listed Ostrog as wanted for not having reported to the police. The report requested enquiry 'at hospitals, infirmaries, workhouses, etc.', and as before referred to Ostrog as a 'dangerous man'. It may be coincidence, but the 1888 and 1889 appeals in the *Police Gazette* correspond with Whitechapel murders.

On 17 April 1891 Ostrog was apprehended for failing to report while under police supervision. He was charged at Bow Street, remanded, again brought up and remanded, and on 1 May sent to St Giles Workhouse, Endall Street, where he was examined by Dr William C Sheard and certified insane. Ostrog apparently claimed to have 20,000 houses and 500,000 francs – and on 7 May 1891 he was sent to Banstead Lunatic Asylum.[26] A report attached to his medical documents by Frederick Wright, the relieving officer of the Strand Poor Law Union, claimed that Ostrog was suicidal but not a danger to others. On that same day Melville Macnaghten wrote to the medical officer at Banstead requesting that the Convict Supervision Office at Scotland Yard be informed if Ostrog was discharged. He was detained at Banstead from 1891 until 1893.

On 20 June 1893 he was arrested for robbery at Canterbury. At that time he feigned insanity, and was being taken to Dover in order to be transferred over the Channel, when he escaped and committed a robbery at Maidstone (which Ostrog denied).[27]

On 6 November 1893 Ostrog stole two books and a silver cup from John Hay Brooks at Eton College and early the next year he was arrested – apparently behaving very violently – and charged not only with that crime but also with the theft in 1889 of the watches and chains from the jeweller's in Eton. Ostrog told the court he was a professor of bacteria and a French Republican who had £80 million in the Bank of England, and he vehemently denied that he was at Eton in 1889, claiming at first to have been in Banstead asylum[28] at the time and later changing this to a government asylum in France until 1890, when he had returned to England to sell the British Navy a life belt that could enable someone to swim around the world. He implored the court to write to the asylum and seek confirmation. He was not believed and was convicted. About twelve weeks later the French authorities confirmed Ostrog's claim to have been in a French asylum and he was released with £10 in compensation.

In 1898 he was back at the Royal Military Academy in Woolwich, where he was seen to enter the room of one of the cadets. Books were then found to be missing and Ostrog was quickly apprehended, convicted the following day under the name Henry Ray at the Woolwich Magistrates' Court and sentenced to six weeks' hard labour.

Finally, in August 1900, Ostrog stole a microscope belonging to Colonel James Mulroney of the Indian Medical Service from the London Hospital in Whitechapel and quickly pawned it at a shop owned by John Arnold in Lewisham High Street. Ostrog foolishly stayed in the area and was seen by Arnold, who had been informed by the police that the microscope was stolen. He arrested him and called the police. Ostrog was brought to trial under the name John Evest in December 1900 and was sentenced to five years in prison, but was assured that because of his partial paralysis he would not be required to do any work he could not do. He was imprisoned first at Wormwood Scrubs and afterwards at Parkhurst, and was released on licence on 17 September 1904. He gave his address as 29 Brooke Street, Holborn. He then entered St Giles Christian Mission, Holborn. We hear nothing further about him.[29]

Michael Ostrog was a small time opportunist thief who began his career as a con man, relying upon his appearance to gain entry to places from where he could steal whatever came to hand. He could be violent when arrested, and it is interesting that Superintendent Oswell in Burton-on-Trent swept aside the table cutlery before confronting him. Ostrog was also reportedly suicidal and on one occasion when he tried to throw himself under a train, he almost took with him the police guard hand-cuffed to him. Nothing in his police record suggests that he was otherwise violent or a danger to others, and one report states that he was not. Nothing suggests that he was Jack the Ripper or suggests why anyone might have thought that he could be.

We know that the police in 1888 requested that lunatic asylums provide them with the names of all recently released patients. Ostrog was released from the Surrey Pauper Lunatic Asylum in March and his name was probably thrown up at that time. Macnaghten states that Ostrog was 'unquestionably a homicidal maniac', that he was 'habitually cruel to women' and that he 'carried about with him surgical knives'. If this was true then it is clear why suspicion would have fallen on him,

Nothing in his known criminal activities or record supports these claims. He was dangerous but there is little or no evidence that he was actually homicidal, and there is nothing in his known criminal activities or record to suggest that he was cruel to women (although wife beating and even a hatred of women don't reveal themselves in one's occupation, even when that occupation is thievery). One might observe that Tumblety professed a great hatred of women, yet most of his fortune appears to have been made from dealing *with* women, to whom he sold a pimple cream. On top of this, there is absolutely no reason why Macnaghten should have invented these details, especially for a police report, although we should note that he dropped them from the official report and they are not repeated in any Macnaghten-based sources such as G R Sims, so perhaps Macnaghten was uncertain about it or realised it was untrue.

Overall, though, does the exoneration of Ostrog throw doubt on the value of Macnaghten's report? Perhaps it does, but it probably doesn't. Michael Ostrog was real; somebody thought he could have been Jack the Ripper and must have had their reasons; and, since these people were not inexperienced idiots, the reasons were probably good ones. And *if* Ostrog carried surgical knives, hated women and had expressed violence towards them, then they were indeed good reasons. But the Macnaghten memorandum only reflects Macnaghten's thinking in February 1894. Later in 1894, after Ostrog had vehemently protested his innocence of the theft of watches and chains in

1889 and it was shown that he had been detained in a French lunatic asylum, it was established that he could not have committed the Ripper murders. We don't know whether Sir Melville Macnaghten knew this, but it is probable that he did and certainly his friend George R Sims was able to write in 1907 that 'when inquiries were afterwards set on foot he was found to be in a criminal lunatic asylum abroad'. Suspicion about Ostrog may have lasted no more than four years.[30]

CHAPTER TWENTY-ONE

Kosminski

Unlike Montague Druitt and Michael Ostrog, who are identified beyond question, we do not know the identity of 'Kosminski', who is named in two sources by his surname only. The discussion is also made more complex and important because a third source, Robert Anderson – who was head of the CID at the time of the murders and may be regarded as being in a position to know the facts – stated several times that Jack the Ripper *was* a Polish Jew, but he did not name him; Chief Inspector Swanson identified Anderson's suspect as 'Kosminski'. The examination of 'Kosminski' is therefore complicated by (1) the need to discuss Aaron Kosminski, the man identified as 'Kosminski', (2) what the sources say about Polish Jew suspects and how closely they fit Aaron Kosminski and (3) whether Robert Anderson should be treated seriously or dismissed as a liar, geriatric wishful thinker, or otherwise unreliable.

In his draft memorandum Sir Melville Macnaghten described his second suspect:

No. 2 Kosminski, a Polish Jew, who lived in the very heart of the district where the murders were committed. He had become insane owing to many years indulgence in solitary vices. He had a great hatred of women, with strong homicidal tendencies. He was (and I believe still is) detained in a lunatic asylum about March 1889. This man in appearance strongly resembled the individual seen by the City P.C. near Mitre Square.

In his report he wrote,

(2) Kosminski, a Polish Jew & resident in Whitechapel. This man became insane owing to many years indulgence in solitary vices. He had a great hatred of women, specially of the prostitute class, & had

strong homicidal tendencies: he was removed to a lunatic asylum
about March 1889. There were many circumstances connected with
this man which made him a strong 'suspect'.[1]

Macnaghten provides some information that is unique to him, chiefly the
date, March 1889, which as far as is known does not correspond with Aaron
Kosminski, who was committed to an asylum in February 1892. One should be
wary of attributing an error to a source unless there are strong reasons for doing
so, which in this case there aren't, but in the absence of any other suspect who
fits the criteria of the sources and who was committed in March 1889, there is
little choice but to assume that either there is a gap in our knowledge about
Aaron Kosminski or Macnaghten wrote 1889 when he meant 1892. There is
also nothing in Aaron Kosminski's medical record to suggest that he had a great
hatred of women in general or prostitutes in particular, and the record states
that he was not dangerous to others, which contradicts Macnaghten's claim
that he had strong homicidal tendencies. But the medical record is sparse,
describes Aaron Kosminski in 1892 and after, so is useless as evidence of him
before that date, and consists almost entirely of terse, twice-yearly notes about
his physical health and general wellbeing. Aaron Kosminski therefore could
have had a hatred of women and prostitutes and it wouldn't have been mentioned in the case papers, and his homicidal tendencies – he did once threaten
his sister with a knife – may not have manifested themselves in the asylum,
where he may have lacked the necessary stimuli. Otherwise Aaron Kosminski
fits what few details remain: he was a Polish Jew, he lived in the murder district,
he was committed to an asylum and – probably establishing the identification
conclusively – the cause of his insanity was euphemistically given as self-abuse,
otherwise masturbation, which is what Macnaghten meant by solitary vices.[2]

Robert Anderson also referred to a Polish Jew suspect in his 1910
autobiography *The Lighter Side of My Official Life*, and startlingly and
uniquely among senior police officers he claimed that the man *was* Jack the
Ripper. As with the Macnaghten memorandum, there are two versions of
Anderson's memoirs, a serialised version published over several weeks in
Blackwood's Magazine, and a version published a couple of months later as
a book. They are almost identical, but differ in a couple of significant
respects. The magazine serialisation read,

One did not need to be a Sherlock Holmes to discover that the criminal
was a sexual maniac of a virulent type; that he was living in the

immediate vicinity of the scenes of the murders; and that, if he was not living absolutely alone, his people knew of his guilt, and refused to give him up to justice. During my absence abroad the Police had made a house-to-house search for him, investigating the case of every man in the district whose circumstances were such that he could go and come and get rid of his blood-stains in secret. And the conclusion we came to was that he and his people were low-class Jews, for it is a remarkable fact that people of that class in the East End will not give up one of their number to Gentile justice. And the result proved that our diagnosis was right on every point. For I may say at once that 'undiscovered murders' are rare in London, and the 'Jack-the-Ripper' crimes are not within that category. And if the Police here had powers such as the French Police possess, the murderer would have been brought to justice. Scotland Yard can boast that not even the sub-ordinate officers of the department will tell tales out of school, and it would ill become me to violate the unwritten rule of the service. The subject will come up again, and I will only add here that the 'Jack-the-Ripper' letter which is preserved in the Police Museum at New Scotland Yard is the creation of an enterprising London journalist.

In a footnote he added:

Having regard to the interest attaching to this case, I should almost be tempted to disclose the identity of the murderer and of the pressman who wrote the letter above referred to, provided that the publishers would accept all responsibility in view of a possible libel action. But no public benefit would result from such a course, and the traditions of my old department would suffer. I will only add that when the individual whom we suspected was caged in an asylum, the only person who had ever had a good view of the murderer at once identified him, but when he learned that the suspect was a fellow-Jew he declined to swear to him.

In the volume edition he wrote:

One did not need to be a Sherlock Holmes to discover that the criminal was a sexual maniac of a virulent type; that he was living in the immediate vicinity of the scenes of the murders; and that, if he was not living absolutely alone, his people knew of his guilt, and refused to give him up to justice. During my absence abroad the Police had made a house-to-house search for him, investigating the case of every man in the district whose circumstances were such that he could go and come and get rid of his blood-stains in secret. And the conclusion we came to was that he and his people were certain low-class Polish Jews; for it is a remarkable fact that people of that class in the East End will not give up one of their number to Gentile justice.

And the result proved that our diagnosis was right on every point. For I may say at once that 'undiscovered murders' are rare in London, and the 'Jack-the-Ripper' crimes are not within that category. And if the Police here had powers such as the French Police possess, the murderer would have been brought to justice. Scotland Yard can boast that not even the subordinate officers of the department will tell tales out of school, and it would ill become me to violate the unwritten rule of the service. So I will only add here that the 'Jack-the-Ripper' letter which is preserved in the Police Museum at New Scotland Yard is the creation of an enterprising London journalist.

Having regard to the interest attaching to this case, I am almost tempted to disclose the identity of the murderer and of the pressman who wrote the letter above referred to. But no public benefit would result from such a course, and the traditions of my old department would suffer. I will merely add that the only person who had ever had a good view of the murderer unhesitatingly identified the suspect the instant he was confronted with him; but he refused to give evidence against him.

In saying that he was a Polish Jew I am merely stating a definitely ascertained fact. And my words are meant to specify race, not religion. For it would outrage all religious sentiment to talk of the religion of a loathsome creature whose utterly unmentionable vices reduced him to a lower level than that of the brute.

The important differences between these statements are as follows:

- In the serialisation Anderson wrote 'low-class Jews', but in the volume edition he specified that they were 'low-class Polish Jews' and thereby clearly indicated recently arrived immigrant Jews who were at that time flooding the East End of London.
- He omitted from the volume edition the reference to the publisher's acceptance of liability for libel.

- He omitted from the volume edition the reference to the identification having taken place when the suspect was caged in an asylum.
- He changed 'declined to swear to him' to the harder 'refused to give evidence against him'.
- And he added to the volume edition the last three sentences in which he stated (a) that it was 'a definitely ascertained fact' that Jack the Ripper was a Polish Jew,[3] (b) that he was specifying race, not religion, and that to have discussed the religion of the Ripper would have been an outrage to all religious sentiment, which again emphasised that he was talking about the immigrant East European Jews, and (c) he said that the suspect had engaged in 'utterly unmentionable vices' that had reduced him to a level lower than that of the brute.

Anderson's comments on Ripper

Sir Robert Anderson hinted and stated on a number of occasions from 1901 onwards that the Ripper had been identified, and as discussed in the main text he very probably held the belief as early as 1895, so it is probably safe to assume that Anderson believed the suspect to be the Ripper from the day of the eyewitness identification until his death.

'Or, again, take a notorious case of a different kind, "the Whitechapel murders" of the autumn of 1888. At that time the sensation-mongers of the newspaper press fostered the belief that life in London was no longer safe, and that no woman ought to venture abroad in the streets after nightfall. And one enterprising journalist went so far as to impersonate the cause of all this terror as "Jack the Ripper," a name by which he will probably go down to history. But all such silly hysterics could not alter the fact that these crimes were a cause of danger only to a particular section of a small and definite class of women, in a limited district of the East End; and that the inhabitants of the metropolis generally were just as secure during the weeks the fiend was on the prowl as they were before the mania seized him, or after he had been safely caged in an asylum.' (Anderson (1901), 'Punishing Crime', *The Nineteenth Century*, February)

'Or, again, take a notorious case of a different kind, "the Whitechapel murders" of the autumn of 1888. At that time the sensation-mongers of the newspaper press fostered the belief that life in London was no longer safe, and that no woman ought to venture abroad in the streets after nightfall. And one enterprising journalist went so far as to impersonate the cause of all this terror as "Jack the Ripper," a name by which he will probably go down to history. But all such silly hysterics could not alter the fact that these crimes were a cause of danger only to a particular section of a small and definite class of women, in a limited district of the East End; and that the inhabitants of the metropolis generally were just as secure during the weeks the fiend was on the prowl as they were before the mania seized him, or after he had been safely caged in an asylum.' (Anderson (1907), *Criminals and Crime: Some Facts and Suggestions* (London: Nisbet), pp. 3–4)

'Detractors of the work of our British Police in bringing criminals to justice generally ignore the important distinction between moral proof and legal evidence of guilt. In not a few cases that are popularly classed with "unsolved mysteries of crime", the offender is known, but evidence is wanting. If, for example, in a recent murder case of special notoriety and interest (Crippen), certain human remains had not been found in a cellar, a great crime would have been catalogued among "Police failures"; and yet, even without the evidence which sent the murderer to the gallows, the moral proof of his guilt would have been full and clear. So again with the Whitechapel murders of 1888. Despite the lucubrations of many an amateur "Sherlock Holmes", there was no doubt whatever as to the identity of the criminal, and if our London "detectives" possessed the powers, and might have recourse to the methods, of Foreign Police Forces, he would have been brought to justice.' (Anderson, Preface to H L Adam (1911), *The Police Encyclopedia*, Vol. 1 (London: Routledge)

Robt. Anderson has assured the writer that the assassin was well known to the police, but unfortunately, in the absence of sufficient legal evidence to justify an arrest, they were unable to take him. It was a case of moral versus legal proof . . . But the question still remains, who and what was Jack the Ripper? Sir Robt. Anderson states confidently that he was a low–class Jew, being shielded by his fraternity. Sir Hy. Smith pooh-poohs this, declaring with equal confidence that he was a Gentile . . .' (Hargrave L Adam (1912), 'Scotland Yard and its Secrets', *The People*, 9 June)

*

Because Anderson's claim had been in the public domain since 1910 and largely dismissed or ignored for most of the time since then, or at best treated as one of the many inexplicable curiosities of the case, nobody really connected Anderson's Polish Jew with Macnaghten's 'Kosminski' until the 'discovery' of the Swanson marginalia in 1987 put the matter beyond question by clearly identifying them as one and the same.

The Swanson marginalia are pencilled notes on the margins and endpapers of a presentation copy of Anderson's memoirs made by Chief Inspector Donald Swanson. It was one of several books presented over the years by Anderson to his old friend; another was a copy of Anderson's *Criminals and Crime*, which he gave to Swanson as a New Year's Day gift in 1908. The books along with other materials had been passed down in Swanson's family and their existence was made public at the end of 1987 by the *Daily Telegraph*. At the bottom of page 138, where Anderson had written, 'I will merely add that the only person who had ever had a good view of the murderer unhesitatingly identified the suspect the instant he was confronted with him . . .', Swanson added, 'and after this identification which suspect knew, no other murder of this kind took place in London'.

Where Anderson had written that the witness 'refused to give evidence against him', Swanson wrote, 'because the suspect was also a Jew and also because his evidence would convict the suspect, and witness would be the means of murderer being hanged which he did not wish to be left on his mind.'

On the end-paper Swanson wrote:

Continuing from page 138, after the suspect had been identified at the Seaside Home where he had been sent by us with difficulty in order to subject him to identification, and he knew he was identified. On suspect's return to his brother's house in Whitechapel he was watched by police (City CID) by day & night. In a very short time the suspect with his hands tied behind his back, was sent to Stepney Workhouse and then to Colney Hatch and died shortly afterwards – Kosminski was the suspect – DSS

Anderson's story is relatively simple. The police, or at least some of them, had concluded that the murderer was living in the East End, either alone and able to get rid of the bloodstains unobserved, or with people who must have seen the bloodstains and known or suspected his guilt, but didn't want to hand him over to the police. They made a house-to-house investigation of every man who lived alone and could get rid of his bloodstains unobserved, and this evidently failed to turn up any suspects because the police concluded that the murderer must live with people who suspected his guilt, which in turn suggested that he was an immigrant Polish Jew because immigrant Polish Jews were reluctant to hand one of their own over to the Gentile authorities. There is nothing in what Anderson says to allow us to infer that the police had a suspect at that time. It was sometime later, months or even years, that they identified Jack the Ripper and learned that their diagnosis (today we'd probably call it a profile) was correct. Apart from this, we can milk from Anderson's account a few sparse details: the suspect was male, Polish and a Jew, he lived in the heart of the murder district, had people to protect him, indulged in 'utterly unmentionable vices' that dehumanised him (probably the same as the 'solitary vices' that according to Macnaghten were responsible for driving Kosminski insane – a phrase that was a euphemism for masturbation), and was committed to an asylum where he was identified by an eyewitness.

The story told by Swanson is slightly more complex, is littered with problems and anomalies, and is immediately in conflict with Anderson's claim in the *Blackwood's* serialisation that the identification had taken place when the suspect 'was caged in an asylum'. Swanson states the contrary, that the suspect had been identified and *afterwards* been committed to the asylum. Anderson's claim seems contextually improbable. He clearly blamed the witness for refusing to give evidence, but if the suspect had been 'caged in an asylum' he would almost certainly have been certified insane and thus been deemed unfit to plead. So no trial could or would have been possible, and the witness's willingness or otherwise to give evidence would have been irrelevant.[4] The only reason why the witness's willingness to testify would have mattered would have been if a trial could have taken place, and for that to have happened the witness could not have been certified. That Anderson realised his mistake may explain why the reference to the asylum was omitted from the volume edition of his memoirs.

Swanson's story otherwise does not disagree with the sparse details provided by Anderson, but it does tell a tale that seems to fly in the face of accepted police procedure, and this has provoked a range of doubts and questions. However, Swanson was a career policeman who rose through the ranks to a very senior position and we need have no doubts that he would have known proper police procedure – he lived it. And, since Swanson had overall responsibility for the Ripper investigation, it is reasonable to believe that he was talking from first-hand experience, either being present at the event he describes or having been party to sanctioning it. In the unlikely event that the identification happened without his knowledge, one can only suppose that he would have raised the same questions as modern commentators and been satisfied with the answers. That Swanson's story is extraordinary is important to bear in mind, but this should not cause one to disbelieve or reject it.[5]

Swanson does not tell a complicated story, but on hearing it one feels like a child who compulsively asks 'why?' of every detail. He says that a suspect was 'sent' 'with difficulty' by the Metropolitan Police to be identified at a place called 'the Seaside Home'. He was positively identified by a witness and the suspect 'knew he was identified' (we are told this twice), but the witness refused to testify because the suspect was also a Jew and because the witness did not want the execution of the suspect on his conscience. The police therefore released the suspect into the care of his brother in Whitechapel and 24-hour surveillance was maintained by the City CID. Within 'a very short time' he was taken 'with his hands tied behind his back' to Stepney Workhouse and from there to the asylum at Colney Hatch. Thereafter, says Swanson, 'no other murder of this kind took place in London' and the suspect died soon after being committed.

The whys start with the word 'sent', which implies that the suspect was taken for identification by someone else, perhaps his family. Swanson also says the police 'sent' the suspect 'with difficulty', and it is not easy to imagine why the police would have had any difficulty sending a suspect in such an important case for identification. The place of identification is also an odd one. 'The Seaside Home' is almost unquestionably the Convalescent Police Seaside Home in Hove, opened on 17 March 1890. The police had used other convalescent homes, but these were not for the exclusive use of policemen and, had Swanson meant one of them, it is likely that he would have identified the specific establishment. He also wouldn't have capitalised the 'S' and 'H' in 'Seaside Home'. When Swanson wrote in 1910 the name Seaside Home meant one place and one place only: the Convalescent Police Seaside Home.

We can only wonder at how the identification was conducted. The police usually asked people on the street to attend an identity parade, but we must assume that there were not many low-class Polish Jews strolling along the pavement outside the convalescent home from whom twelve or so volunteers could have been found for a line-up, and a low-class Polish Jew is otherwise hardly likely to have blended in with a group of recuperative policemen. The suspect could therefore have been very obvious to the witness, which must in turn devalue the worth of the identification. This may explain why Swanson twice referred to the suspect knowing he had been identified. This emphasis may suggest that it has a special significance, such as the suspect betraying recognition of the witness. Mutual recognition would certainly have convinced many observers that the suspect was the man.

That the suspect was released is extraordinary. One would have thought that the police would have used any means possible to detain a positively identified suspect, and therefore they must have had a very compelling reason for releasing him. Perhaps the most obvious reason is that they had held onto the suspect for as long as the Habeas Corpus Act allowed, this Act being the law that ensures that a person detained by the authorities is brought before a court of law within a defined time so that the legality of the detention can be examined, and Anderson in fact indicates in *The Lighter Side of My Official Life* that this was the case. He wrote, 'And if the Police here had powers such as the French Police possess, the murderer would have been brought to justice.' In *The Police Encyclopedia* in 1911 he wrote, '. . . there was no doubt whatever as to the identity of the criminal, and if our London "detectives" possessed the powers, and might have recourse to the methods, of Foreign Police Forces, he would have been brought to justice.'[6] And in *Criminals and Crime* in 1907 he had written, in more general terms,

> Great crimes are seldom 'undetected'; but of course it is one thing to discover the author of a crime, and a different matter altogether to obtain legal evidence of his guilt. And in this country the evidence must be available when an accused person is placed under arrest. Not so in countries where the police are armed with large despotic powers which enable them to seize a criminal without any evidence at all, and to build up a case against him at leisure, extracting the needed proofs, it may be, from his own unwilling lips.[7]

That the British police could not hold a suspect indefinitely was something of a favourite litany of Anderson.[8] It seems clear that the police let the suspect go because they had to.

The suspect was allowed to return to his brother's house in Whitechapel. This was within the jurisdiction of the Metropolitan Police, yet Swanson says that surveillance was maintained by the City CID, which seems improbable, as there are no easily discernible reasons why the Metropolitan

Police would have asked the City CID to maintain surveillance on a Metropolitan Police suspect within Metropolitan Police jurisdiction. Since the Metropolitan Police would not have asked the City CID to maintain surveillance, their presence must be because they were maintaining surveillance on a man suspected of having committed a crime in the City, which in turn suggests that they maintained surveillance after the identification because they had been maintaining surveillance before it. The question is: did the City CID know that the suspect had been taken for identification? Major Smith's reaction to the publication of Sir Robert Anderson's memoirs would suggest that they did not, in which case we are presented with the unlikely image of the Metropolitan Police sneaking a suspect away from under the noses of the City CID, then returning him. Again, though, unlikely as this seems, it would explain why they had 'difficulty' sending the suspect for identification and why such an out-of-the-way place as the Convalescent Police Seaside Home was used.

The suspect returned to his brother's house and 'a very short time' afterwards was taken 'with his hands tied behind his back' to the workhouse and thence to the asylum. There is nothing in what Swanson says that allows us to infer that any great time elapsed between the suspect's return to his brother's house and his being taken to the workhouse. We could probably allow for a week at the most, but probably no more than a matter of days, and we may reasonably speculate that the form of restraint – hands tied behind his back – indicates that he was taken for committal by his family, not by the police, who would have used more formal restraint such as handcuffs.

The suspect died soon afterwards, which is not in conflict with Anderson but is in conflict with Aaron Kosminski, who did not die until much, much later.

The story these sources tell us is relatively simple – Jack the Ripper was identified by an eyewitness, but the witness refused to give evidence and the suspect had to be released, whereupon his family put him beyond the reach of the police by having him certified insane and committed to a lunatic asylum. But, while the story is simple, it is almost impossible to accept, especially after analysis has thrown up a number of anomalies and other problems, so the dominant activity among commentators has been to cast doubt on it. Some have dismissed the whole story as laughable,[9] others have credited Anderson with a poor memory,[10] credited the whole story to geriatric wishful thinking[11] or suggested that he confused the identification of the Polish Jew with another identification or vice versa. It has even been suggested that Anderson lied, unable to admit that he and the CID had been defeated by Jack the Ripper. As is clear, there is no cohesive and persuasive argument against the truth of Anderson's story, just a jumble of doubts and objections. The arguments are often poorly thought through,[12] but they boil down to Anderson's veracity, and analysis of the Kosminski story is as much an analysis of Anderson as it is an examination of the facts about the suspect.

Anderson is a complex character and no doubt subject to all the failings and foibles that beset all human beings. But after reading Anderson's secular and theological writings, and with a knowledge of the morals and mores of the time, as well as an understanding of Anderson's complicated religious beliefs and how they would have influenced his thinking and actions, the author Martin Fido completely rejected any idea that Anderson would lie in self-interest: 'Now one thing is certain about the dedicated and scrupulous Christian: he is not a vainglorious liar or boaster . . . and would never have lied about his professional life to enhance either his own or his police force's reputation . . .' Fido went on to observe:

> Not that he was as priggishly truthful as Washington with the legendary cherry tree. As an ex-Secret Serviceman, he had occasion to make his attitude to mendacity quite clear. He said in his memoirs that he perceived an obvious Christian duty never to lie to one's brothers; but he denied that murderous terrorists and subversives were brothers, entitled to hear truth they would only misuse. Still, he felt that one of his associates was wrong to have taken the Fenian oath of loyalty without intending to keep it. And Hargrave Adam tells a story which shows that he would tell half-truths to a suspected murderer.
>
> Hair-splitting? Of course. That is the nature of scrupulosity. But it is quite incompatible with publishing lies in books for a wide audience.[13]

J A Cole in *Prince of Spies*, a biography of Henri Le Caron, who spied on the Fenians for the British and attributed his longevity and life to Anderson's discretion, concluded, 'Anderson was no doubt an irritating and opinionated man, inclined – as pious people are – to maintain that an action was morally justified because his principles debarred him from committing an immoral one.[14]

Anderson also lacked a reason for lying. In his autobiography he wrote that 'kudos is not to be gained by preventing crimes, but by detecting them and successfully prosecuting the offenders',[15] and, since the Ripper wasn't prosecuted, there was no kudos. However, Anderson really didn't need any Ripper-related kudos because by the time he wrote his memoirs in 1910 the CID had achieved a solid reputation and the Ripper case was a relatively unimportant matter over two decades old.

Philip Sugden, deservedly one of the most respected commentators on the Ripper mystery, concluded that, while Anderson could not be dismissed 'as an arrant liar', during his retirement,

> He must sometimes have reflected there upon those hectic days at the Yard. And when he did it would doubtless have given him comfort to think, that whatever the world might say, he had laid the Ripper by the heels. Over the years, with the selective and faulty memory characteristic of advancing age, he came to believe it.

The 'geriatric wishful thinking' theory is hurt by Swanson's tacit support of Anderson, although Sugden gets round this by suggesting that, 'In supporting him, Swanson exhibited that same capacity for self-deception . . . Anderson and Swanson had come to inhabit a world of wish-dreams.'[16]

While one could at a push accept one geriatric wishful thinker, the idea of Anderson and Swanson as a matched pair pushes credulity too far, but it was never a theory that held water because Anderson had been writing since 1901 about the Ripper's being caged in an asylum. Indeed, he probably believed it as early as 1895, if not before. In May of that year Major Griffiths, using the pen name Alfred Aylmer, wrote of Anderson in *The Windsor Magazine*, a successful rival to *The Strand Magazine*:

> Although he has achieved greater success than any detective of his time, there will always be undiscovered crimes,[17] and just now the tale is pretty full. Much dissatisfaction was vented upon Mr Anderson at the utterly abortive efforts to discover the perpetrator of the Whitechapel murders. He has himself a perfectly plausible theory that Jack the Ripper was a homicidal maniac, temporarily at large, whose hideous career was cut short by committal to an asylum.[18]

This article shows that Anderson entertained the Polish Jew theory as early as 1895.[19] We clearly aren't looking at a man wishfully thinking he'd identified the Ripper. We're looking at a man who genuinely believed he *had* identified him.

Other people have found the basic facts of Anderson's story impossible to digest. It has been argued that one Jew would not have protected another Jew simply because he was Jewish, and Anderson's claim has been seen as a gross and serious example of anti-Semitism. It is an ugly allegation but one that has become immeasurably uglier since the Holocaust. It was an allegation levelled against Anderson at the time, and was one he vehemently denied,[20] and that may explain why he quietly changed 'low-class Jews' to 'low-class Polish Jews' and took pains to stress that he was referring to 'race, not religion'. He was also lambasted in the *Jewish Chronicle* by 'Mentor' – the pen name of the controlling editor, Leopold Jacob Greenberg[21] – for claiming that Jews 'guarded [Jack the Ripper] so that he could continue his horrible career, just because he was a Jew'. Major Henry Smith, perhaps inspired by 'Mentor', also had a go at Anderson in his own memoirs published in 1910, but completely misunderstood what Anderson had written and thought Anderson was accusing many people instead of one or two.

> Sir Robert does not tell us how many of 'his people' sheltered the murderer, but whether they were two dozen in number, or two hundred, or two thousand, he accuses them of being accessories to these crimes before and after their committal.
>
> Surely Sir Robert cannot believe that while the Jews, as he asserts, were entering into this conspiracy to defeat the ends of justice, there was no one among them with sufficient knowledge of the criminal law to warn them of the risks they were running.[22]

Anderson did not actually say that Jews 'guarded' the Ripper because he was a Jew, nor did he mean that the Ripper was guarded by the Jewish population as a whole. He simply said that the newly arrived immigrant Jews fleeing Eastern Europe were less disposed than other Jews or the population as a whole to surrender one of their number to the police. And Anderson was not alone in saying this. In an article entitled 'The Truth About the Whitechapel Murder' a former City Police detective inspector named Harry Cox wrote about the time he maintained surveillance on a Jewish suspect. He said that the local Jewish residents agreed to cooperate only because they thought the police were factory inspectors investigating 'sweating', and

POLICEMEN
Above left: Sir Charles Warren.
Below left: James Monro.

Above right: Sir Robert Anderson.
Below right: Sir Melville Macnaghten.

Left: Chief Inspector Donald Swanson.

Below: The Swanson marginalia.

My Official Life

people of that class in the East End will not give up one of their number to Gentile justice.

And the result proved that our diagnosis was right on every point. For I may say at once that "undiscovered murders" are rare in London, and the "Jack-the-Ripper" crimes are not within that category. And if the Police here had powers such as the French Police possess, the murderer would have been brought to justice. Scotland Yard can boast that not even the subordinate officers of the department will tell tales out of school, and it would ill become me to violate the unwritten rule of the service. So I will only add here that the "Jack-the-Ripper" letter which is preserved in the Police Museum at New Scotland Yard is the creation of an enterprising London journalist. *Known to Scotland Yard head officers also*

Having regard to the interest attaching to this case, I am almost tempted to disclose the identity of the murderer and of the pressman who wrote the letter above referred to. But no public benefit would result from such a course, and the traditions of my old department would suffer. I will merely add that the only person who had ever had a good view of the murderer unhesitatingly identified the suspect the instant he was confronted with him; but he refused to give evidence against him. *because the suspect was also a Jew and also because his evidence would convict the suspect, and witness would be the means of murderer being hanged which he did not wish to be left on his mind.*

after this identification which suspect knew, no other murder of this kind took place in London.

138

DSS

Continuing from page 138, after the suspect had been identified at the Seaside Home where he had been sent by us with difficulty, in order to subject him to identification, and he knew he was identified. On suspect's return to his brother's house in Whitechapel he was watched by police (City CID) by day + night. In a very short time the suspect with his hands tied behind his back, he was sent to Stepney Workhouse and then to Colney Hatch and died shortly afterwards —

Kosminski was the suspect —

DSS

ABERLINE

Left: Inspector Frederick G Abberline.

Above: H Division Criminal Investigation Department, 1889, with: (*back row, left to right*) PC Thompson, PC Cole, PC Tyson, PC Pearce, PC Payne, PC Whitbread, PC Gill, Sgt. Leach; (*middle row*): Sgt. Cumner, PC Kendall, Sgt. Smith; (*front row*): Sgt. Pearce, Sgt. Thicke, Inspector Reid, Sgt. Caunter, Sgt. Harrison and Sgt. Glenister.

Below left: Sgt. Thicke in later life with his daughters Rose, Amelia and Alice – all of whom met Jack London. © Prof. D Bryce-Smith

Below right: Chief Inspector John G Littlechild.

Above left: Home Secretary Henry Matthews.

Above right: George Lusk of the Vigilance Committee, who received half a kidney through the post.

Left: Wynne E Baxter, who conducted almost all the inquests.

SUSPECTS

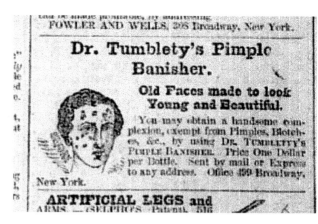

Above left: Francis Tumblety.

Above right: An advertisement for Francis Tumblety's pimple banisher cream.

Below left: Montague John Druitt.

Below right and bottom: Michael Ostrog.

·25· Sept· 1888.

Dear Boss.
 I keep on hearing the police
have caught me but they wont fix
me just yet. I have laughed when
they look so clever and talk about
being on the right track. That joke
about Leather apron gave me real
fits. I am down on whores and
I shant quit ripping them till I
do get buckled. Grand work the last
job was, I gave the lady no time to
squeal. How can they catch me
I love my work and want to st
again. You will soon hear of me
with my funny little games. I
saved some of the proper red stuff in
a ginger beer bottle over the last job
to write with but it went thick
like glue and I cant use it. Red
ink is fit enough I hope ha. ha.
The next job I do I shall clip
the ladys ears off and send to the

Above: The 'Dear Boss' letter (*continued overleaf*).

police officers just for jolly wouldnt
you. Keep this letter back till I
do a bit more work. then give
it out straight. My knife's so nice
and sharp I want to get to work
right away if I get a chance.
Good luck.

yours truly
Jack the Ripper

Dont mind me giving the trade nam

I want good [...] [...]
to post this before
I got all the red
ink off my hands
curse it
No luck yet. They
say I'm a doctor
now ha ha

Above: The 'Dear Boss' letter (*continued*).

Right: Handbills distributed by Thames Police.

POLICE NOTICE.

TO THE OCCUPIER.

On the mornings of Friday, 31st
August, Saturday 8th, and Sunday,
30th September, 1888, Women were
murdered in or near Whitechapel,
supposed by some one residing
in the immediate neighbourhood.
Should you know of any person
to whom suspicion is attached, you
are earnestly requested to communicate at once with the nearest
Police Station.

Metropolitan Police Office,
30th September, 1888.

Printed by McCorquodale & Co. Limited, "The Armoury," Southwark.

we knew well that they had no intention of helping us. Every man was as bad as another . . . I am sure they never once suspected that we were police detectives on the trail of the mysterious murderer; otherwise they would not have discussed the crimes with us as openly as they did.[23]

Frederick Porter Wensley, who served in H Division during his junior years and was the first man to rise through the ranks to the elevated position of chief constable, CID, observed in his memoirs, *Detective Days*, that the mostly immigrant victims of a gang known as the Bessarabians 'were even more loath than Britishers to call for help, or give information to the police'.[24]

Donald Rumbelow observed of the immigrant community at the much later time of the Houndsditch Murders in 1911,

But there were strong reasons of self-preservation for not going to the police. Most immigrants, particularly those from Russia and the countries under its domination, believed that there was little or no difference between the Tsarist police system, which used murder and torture and systematically carried out pogroms against a suffering population, and the English policeman. Already, by late Saturday morning, there was astonishment among the Russian immigrants that the police had not carried out a pogrom.[25]

This understandable reluctance on the part of the immigrant Jews to trust the authorities was explained by Chaim Bermant in his excellent history of East End Jewish immigration:

If the Ripper was a Jew, then one can be fairly certain that his fellows would have kept quiet about it for the simple reason that the whole community could have been held culpable for his deeds, and that the menacing mood of hostility which surrounded them would have given way to outright violence.[26]

The immigrant Jews faced a multitude of problems and suffered a catalogue of hardship that caused them to be a society unto themselves. Immigrants had come to a land of strange customs, with a strange language, strange laws and a social structure they didn't understand. They were distrustful of the authorities, scared of the native population and scared of their coreligionists. As Lloyd P Gartner put it,

Immigrant Jewry formed a society apart, with standards derived from other sources than England. In the first generation of immigrant settlement there was a great deal of mutual avoidance; even with good will on both sides, there was so little common ground between the immigrant Jew and his neighbour that it could not have been otherwise.[27]

William J Fishman likewise observed, 'Not only were immigrants open to the hostility of British workmen, they also had to endure the harsh criticism of fellow Jews long settled in the area.'[28]

Anderson's bare statement seems distasteful, but it has all the hallmarks of being true. The newly immigrant Jews had no reason to trust the British authorities, trust Anglo-Jewry or trust the British people, whose violent reaction against Jews they had already witnessed during the Leather Apron scare. On top of this, not only did 'Mentor' himself provide excellent reasons why a Jew might 'protect' one of his or her own, he even wrote that he would have done so himself:

What is more natural than the man's hesitancy to identify another as Jack the Ripper so soon as he knew he was a Jew? What is more natural than for that fact at once to cause doubts in his mind? The crimes identified with 'Jack the Ripper' were of a nature that it would be difficult for any Jew – 'low-class' or any class – to imagine the work of a Jew. Their callous brutality was foreign to Jewish nature, which, when it turns criminal, goes into quite a different channel. I confess that however sure I might have been of the identity of a person, when I was told he had been committing 'Jack the Ripper' crimes, and was a Jew, I should hesitate about the certainty of my identification . . .[29]

'Mentor' was correct in saying that 'callous brutality was foreign to Jewish nature';[30] and, in giving this as a reason why a Jew might find it hard to believe another Jew capable of murder, 'Mentor' also plausibly explained why a Jew might be reluctant to hand one of his or her own over to the law. And, if 'Mentor' would 'hesitate' before identifying a fellow Jew, even a perfect stranger, it takes little to imagine how infinitely harder it would have been for a mother to suspect a son, a brother to suspect a brother, or, in the very close-knit Jewish immigrant community, a neighbour to suspect a neighbour.

Other commentators have tried to find examples of claims by Anderson that contradicted the story of a suspect's being identified. The late Melvin Harris thought he had found derogatory comments about Anderson in the House of Commons by no less a personage than Winston Churchill, and uncovered a statement by an MP that Harris suggested shows Anderson was, in Harris's words, 'flighty with the truth . . . often enough to have it remarked on'. Concluding that the witness must have been Israel Schwartz or Joseph Lawende, this commentator shrilly protested,

> Let us spell out what this implies: on 30 September the police knew for certain that the murderer had been seen, beyond doubt. They knew, as well, that they had testimony from a person who could pick out the killer without hesitation. In short they had an invaluable clue in their hands and it only needed a face-to-face confrontation between their witness and the killer to tie the whole case up. Is this at all possible? Not on your life! Anderson's own words prove this to be absurd. Consider first of all his report to the Home Secretary of 23 October 1888. The telling part reads:
>
>> I wish to guard against its being supposed that the inquiry is now concluded. There is no reason for furnishing these reports at this moment except that they have been called for. That a crime of this kind should have been committed without any clue being supplied by the criminal, is unusual, but that five successive murders should have been committed, without our having the slightest clue of any kind is extraordinary, if not unique, in the annals of crime. The result has been to necessitate our giving attention to innumerable suggestions, such as would in any ordinary case be dismissed unnoticed, and no hint of any kind, which was not obviously absurd, has been neglected.
>
> Does it really have to be hammered home that this alone destroys the fallacy that a key witness was known? Perhaps it does need hammering, since the significance of these words seem [*sic*] to have been missed by too many people. Very well, the man is confessing without reservations that he does not have 'the slightest clue of any kind'. No witnesses; no trails leading to a hideout; no bloody clothing that can be fitted to a suspect; nothing.[31]

The imagined significance of Anderson's words is illusory and therefore nothing needed to be hammered home. Apart from having stated that
he was talking about clues 'supplied by the criminal', the context is that he
meant clues that would direct the police to the murderer, not a witness
who would hopefully be able to confirm the suspect's guilt *after* he had
been found.[32]

Finally, we must briefly look at some seriously disparaging comments I
referred to above, made about Anderson in the House of Commons,
among them the witty quip by the Irish MP Jeremiah McVeagh, which
Melvin Harris thought showed that Anderson was 'flighty with the truth .
. . often enough to have it remarked on'.[33] But first – and more importantly
– let us dwell on some comments by a youthful Winston Churchill, then
home secretary, who claimed that a statement by Anderson had been
repudiated, talking of his garrulous and inaccurate indiscretions of
advancing years and gross boastfulness. All of these were a consequence of
some blame shifting when Anderson inadvertently sparked a controversy
that swept him up in what has 'rightly been described as "the greatest
political fraud of modern times" . . . guided, directed, and controlled by
the then Unionist administration in conjunction with *The Times* and its
object was to destroy a political policy by assailing the personality of its
leaders and supporters'.[34]

In the serialisation of his memoirs Sir Robert Anderson had written,

> To the present hour I do not know whether the Home Secretary was
> then aware of my authorship of the *Times* articles of 1887 on 'Parnellism
> and Crime', for in relation to this matter I acted with strict propriety in
> dealing with Mr Monro and not with the Secretary of State.

Very briefly, in 1887 the fiercely Unionist *Times* newspaper had published a series of articles intended to ruin the reputation and the political
career and policies of Charles Stewart Parnell (1846–91), the charismatic,
paradoxical and ultimately enigmatic leader of the Irish Home Rule
movement. The articles, called 'Parnellism and Crime', began on 7 March
1887 and purported to show that Parnell approved of the terrorist
activities of extremist groups such as the Clan-Na-Gael and their
sometime bedfellows the Fenian Brotherhood. The most damaging piece
of evidence was a letter Parnell was supposed to have written in 1882 in
which he expressed regret at having to condemn the Phoenix Park

murders. Parnell sensibly refused to sue for libel and treated the accusations with contempt, but *The Times* continued the attack with a series of three far less inflammatory follow-up articles beginning on 13 May 1887 called 'Parnellism and Crime – Behind the Scenes In America'.[35] This time Parnell requested that the allegations be investigated by a House of Commons Select Committee and the hearings began on 17 September 1888. They were a barely disguised attempt to indict the Irish parliamentary party and its Liberal allies and kill in the womb any idea of home rule, and Lord Randolph Churchill described them 'a revolutionary tribunal for the trial of political opponents'.[36] The government couldn't have been in bed with *The Times* more publicly without risking indecency charges: the three presiding judges were all staunch Unionists and the attorney general acted on behalf of *The Times*. However, the manager of *The Times* was exposed under a formidable cross-examination by Herbert Asquith, a future prime minister but then a struggling barrister, to have done nothing to authenticate the letters, which had in fact been written by a man named Richard Pigott. Pigott was described with passion by Lord Randolph Churchill as 'a man, a thing, a reptile, a monster – Pigott! – the bloody, rotten, ghastly foetus – Pigott! Pigott! Pigott!' Pigott's defence collapsed under a demolishing cross-examination by Parnell's leading counsel and he privately confessed to the radical MP Henry Labouchere and George Augustus Sala before slipping away to Madrid and shooting himself at the Hotel des Ambassadeurs.[37] Parnell was cleared in February 1890, and *The Times* had to pay him £5,000 libel damages and foot a bill for legal costs of £200,000 (nearly £10 million by today's standards).

The Irish Nationalists and their Liberal allies believed that Lord Salisbury's Unionist government had actually conspired with *The Times* in the writing of the articles and with the express purpose of smearing Parnell in an effort to bring down a political opponent, but they had never been able to prove it. Anderson's admission seemingly changed all that. Here was a civil servant in the pay of the Salisbury administration admitting to having received official sanction to author the articles 'Parnellism and Crime', and they were determined to use Anderson to lever the lid off a can of worms that the Whitehall mandarins were equally determined to keep firmly shut. What hardly mattered to anyone was Anderson's protest on 12 April 1910 that he had not written 'Parnellism and Crime' – which had in fact been written by a *Times* journalist named John Woulfe Flanagan – but the largely inoffensive follow-up series 'Parnellism and Crime – Behind the Scenes in America'. In his manuscript he had written 'May 1887' and thereby clearly identified the articles, but his typist had omitted 'May' from the manuscript submitted for publication.[38]

Anderson was innocent but about to be trampled. Now we come to Jeremiah McVeagh, who, in the House of Commons on 20 April 1910, asked Winston Churchill, the home secretary, '. . . will the right hon. gentleman say why it is that Sir Robert Anderson, as a subordinate, received an increase in salary, a pension and a knighthood, while the superior official [James Monro] received neither pension nor knighthood?'[39]

The meaning was clear, but Mr Flavim, the MP for North Kerry, spelt it out with alphabet bricks: '. . . was the knighthood conferred on him for services rendered by him to the Tory Party?'

Churchill neatly parried the question by remarking, 'I am afraid I cannot give any explanation for the caprices of fortune in the world' – but it was the beginning of a major debate. Ostensibly this revolved around whether Anderson's revelations had forfeited his pension, but it was in fact a tussle over that can of worms, and as far as one can tell it was a can of nasty worms indeed.

Basically, on 26 January 1887, representatives of *The Times* showed the Pigott letters to a distinguished lawyer named Sir Henry James and were shocked to discover that he had already seen them, that he believed Pigott to be involved in authoring them and that he strongly advised against publication. Warned that the letters might be of questionable authenticity, the newspaper delayed publication and the manager of *The Times*, John Cameron Macdonald, wrote a letter to W H Smith, first lord of the Admiralty and leader of the House of Commons. If Smith did not know what was going on, then the letter's 'phraseology was such that Smith would have found it impenetrably cryptic',[40] which suggests that he and other cabinet colleagues knew what *The Times* was doing and were assisting. It is also known that Henry Matthews was supplying, or arranging for *The Times* to be supplied with, information about the Land League and for its Irish representative to receive information from a wide range of government officials.[41] As Lord Salisbury's biographer, Andrew Roberts, has observed, '*The Times* already received special concessions over other newspapers and press associations, but now the Government actually allowed the paper's solicitor privileged access to the secret files held in Dublin Castle on Irish MPs and others'.[42]

But the scandal may have gone deeper still. John Daly, a future mayor of Limerick, who was languishing in prison on what he claimed were false accusations of intending to throw several bombs from the gallery into the chamber of the House of Commons, claimed that Pigott and *The Times*'s solicitor had visited him in prison at Chatham at the time of the *Times* articles and tried to get from him information implicating Parnell. A fellow prisoner, Thomas J Clarke, claimed that he had been visited by Chief Inspector Littlechild and offered his release and a job if he gave evidence to the Parnell Commission. Even deeper and murkier waters are hinted at by William Henry Joyce, an IRC man who not only supported Daly's claim to have been fitted up, but claimed that he had been told to drop his investigation into some attempted bomb outrages because they had 'been got up by *agents provocateur* in the employ of Anderson', and that 'the bombs had been placed by the police so that the victims would be caught red-handed'.[43]

The mandarins would not have wanted Anderson revealing more of what he already knew, and they certainly didn't want him to be treated seriously by the Irish Nationalists and used to probe the past, and so they chose to diminish and discredit Anderson. In a major debate in the House of Commons, reported over two pages in *The Times*, Winston Churchill brutally tore into Anderson. He said that Anderson's claim to have received James Monro's sanction had 'been definitely repudiated by Monro', that the Parnell articles had little of importance in them, and that the Police Act of 1890 and an Act of 1906 made it clear that pensions were granted on the understanding that pensioners would not publish anything that was 'discreditable or improper', be it fact or fairy tale.

At this point the tenacious Jeremiah McVeagh linked Anderson to the great fairy tale collector Hans Christian Andersen by wittily quipping, 'I take it that the statement of Sir Robert Anderson that he had the permission of his official superior to write these articles for *The Times* may be treated as another of Anderson's Fairy Tales'. He received a satisfying round of laughter that was probably more robust than the remark deserved, but it did not mean, and never should have been interpreted as meaning, that Anderson was (as Harris said) 'flighty with the truth . . . often enough to have it remarked on'. In fact he probably wasn't flighty at all because although Monro in his letter denied that he officially sanctioned Anderson to write the articles, he admitted in a roundabout way that he may not have given Anderson that impression.[44]

Churchill went on to describe Anderson's revelations in *Blackwood's Magazine* as

> the garrulous and inaccurate indiscretion of advancing years . . . I have looked through these articles, and they seem to me to be written in a spirit of gross boastfulness – they are written, if I may say so, in the style of 'How Bill Adams won the Battle of Waterloo'. The writer seems anxious to show how important he was, how invariably he was right, and how much more he could tell if only his mouth was not, what he was pleased to call, closed.

This was greeted with laughter in the House of Commons, but it really wasn't true. The admission may have been garrulous and indiscreet, but it certainly wasn't inaccurate. Anderson did write the articles and he did have or thought he had Monro's permission – and Anderson's memoirs were no more boastful than those of any other memoirist of the period, such as Major Smith[45] – but Anderson was the scapegoat. As the Irish Nationalist MP T P O'Conner acknowledged, the Irish Nationalists were using Anderson 'to shoot at higher game' and Winston Churchill was likewise using Anderson to shield the higher game from being hit. Bobbing around helplessly like a cork on a stormy sea, Anderson was treated very shabbily, and almost lost his pension.

For all this, it is difficult to assess whether a source is telling the truth when there is no independent verification of what it says, and memoirs are notoriously unreliable because their authors are likely to present themselves in the best possible light. But a source can be tested by looking for similar statements that can be verified against known or accepted history. As we've just seen, the memoirs contain other admissions of far greater magnitude than those concerning the Ripper, one being Anderson's admission that he had authored a series of articles for *The Times* called 'Parnellism and Crime – Behind the Scenes in America' and the other being that the organiser of a plot to assassinate Queen Victoria was a British informer. And both claims were true, so it is therefore reasonable to assume on balance that the Ripper revelations were true also.

This said, it is worrying that there is no corroboration from informed sources – Swanson excepted – such as contemporary policemen like Sir Melville Macnaghten and Major Smith, or journalists and writers who had good police contacts such as G R Sims, H L Adam and Major Griffiths.

Macnaghten in particular poses a difficult problem because he was Anderson's immediate junior and one day successor, and clearly knew about Kosminski, yet flew in the face of his boss and blatantly stated his preference for Druitt.

Macnaghten's rejection of 'Kosminski' seems a crucial factor in any assessment of the tale's veracity. On the other hand, what possible advantage could Anderson have hoped to achieve by inventing a story that he *knew* his colleagues and the senior press knew to be untrue? And why didn't people like Macnaghten state with well-chosen words in their own memoirs that Anderson was lying or exaggerating or wandering in his mind? This especially applies to Swanson, who certainly held Anderson in the highest regard, but had no reason to accept uncritically such a story – let alone accept it with a tacit endorsement – in pencilled jottings intended for no eyes but his own.

Who was the suspect?

Two primary sources provide details about the suspect: Sir Robert Anderson and Chief Inspector Donald Swanson. In addition, we have Sir Melville Macnaghten's testimony and the writings of people who appear to have taken their information from him, most notably Major Arthur Griffiths and the journalist George R Sims.

Sir Robert Anderson tells us very little about the suspect except that he was male, Polish, a Jew, that he lived in the heart of the murder district, had 'people' to look after him[46] and that he was committed to an asylum. He also engaged in 'utterly unmentionable vices that reduced him to a lower level than that of the beast'.

Swanson tells us a bit more. The identification took place at 'the Seaside Home', which is almost certainly the Convalescent Police Seaside Home and means that the identification must have taken place after the establishment opened on 17 March 1890; he had a brother who lived in Whitechapel; the suspect was sent to Stepney Workhouse and from there to Colney Hatch asylum; and, crucially, his name was 'Kosminski'. This virtually confirms that Anderson's suspect was – or at least that Swanson thought Anderson's suspect was – the 'Kosminski' named in the Macnaghten memorandum.

Macnaghten says that he was Polish, a Jew, that he 'lived in the very heart of the district where the murders were committed', and that his insanity was due to 'many years indulgence in solitary vices'. This information almost follows Anderson's description, the 'solitary vices' (masturbation) corresponding with the 'utterly unmentionable vices' mentioned by Anderson.[47] Macnaghten differs from Swanson, however, by saying that 'Kosminski' was confined to an asylum 'about March 1889', which means identification could not have taken place at the Convalescent Police Seaside Home. He adds some new information, namely that 'Kosminski' had a great hatred of women – the Aberconway version has the additional information 'specially of the prostitute class' – and had homicidal tendencies.

Turning to the secondary sources, because we know that these were close to the primary sources, when they give us new information it is easy to assume that it had been received from Anderson, Swanson or Macnaghten and therefore to give credence to it. Instead we must allow for the possibility that the author has introduced elaborations of his own to expand or clarify what Anderson, Swanson or Macnaghten said. For example, in 'Scotland Yard and its Secrets' in *The People* in June 1912, Hargrave L Adam says that Sir Robert Anderson had assured him that the Ripper:

> was well known to the police, but unfortunately, in the absence of sufficient legal evidence to justify an arrest, they were unable to take him. It was a case of moral versus legal proof. The only chance the police had, apparently, was to take the miscreant red-handed.[48]

Now, this approximates to what Anderson and Swanson tell us but in saying that the only chance the police had was to take the Ripper red-handed, Adam implies that the police knew who the murderer was at the time of the crimes, which is something for which there is absolutely no evidence, and it looks and feels like H L Adam was trying to make sense of a story about which he had less information than we do.

In 1898 in *Mysteries of Police and Crime*, Major Arthur Griffiths, clearly basing his information on Sir Melville Macnaghten, with whom he served on the Committee on Identification of Habitual Criminals appointed in 1893, wrote of three police suspects: 'One was a Polish Jew, a known lunatic, who was at large in the district of Whitechapel at the time of the murders, and who, having afterwards developed homicidal tendencies, was confined in an asylum.'

According to Griffiths, the suspect was a known lunatic who displayed homicidal tendencies and was committed after the crimes had ceased.[49]

The journalist George R Sims provides us with a few important new details as well as some interesting expansion.

> The first man was a Polish Jew of curious habits and strange disposition, who was the sole occupant of certain premises in Whitechapel after night-fall. This man was in the district during the whole period covered by the Whitechapel murders, and soon after they ceased certain facts came to light which showed that it was quite possible that he might have been the Ripper. He had at one time been employed in a hospital in Poland. He was known to be a lunatic at the time of the murders, and some-time afterwards he betrayed such undoubted signs of homicidal mania that he was sent to a lunatic asylum.
>
> The policeman who got a glimpse of Jack in Mitre Court said, when some time afterwards he saw the Pole, that he was the height and build of the man he had seen on the night of the murder . . . [Sims then describes a man who appears to have been Ostrog.]
>
> Both these men were capable of the Ripper crimes, but there is one thing that makes the case against each of them weak.
>
> They were both alive long after the horrors had ceased, and though both were in an asylum, there had been a considerable time after the cessation of the Ripper crimes during which they were at liberty and passing about among their fellow men.

Sims believed the Polish Jew to have been employed in a hospital in Poland and, in Whitechapel, to have been the only occupant of 'certain premises' at night (which would seem to contradict Anderson), and shared Griffiths's belief that suspicion fell on the suspect after the crimes had ceased. Most importantly, Sims says that the man did not betray signs of homicidal mania until 'a considerable time' after the crimes ceased. Some of these details certainly agree with Anderson and Swanson: that the suspect was committed to the asylum a short time after the identification at the Seaside Home provides a date sometime after 1892, for example, that fits with Sims's assertion that the Polish Jew was at liberty for some considerable time after the cessation of the crimes (which Sims considers to have been with the murder of Mary Jane Kelly). But Sims may also have coloured his story with interpretations of his own (as is suspected of H L Adam). He goes on to describe a doctor whose body was pulled out of the Thames a month after the murder of Mary Kelly — evidently

Macnaghten's suspect, who we think was Montague John Druitt, but whom he described as:

> a doctor who lived in a suburb about six miles from Whitechapel, and who suffered from a horrible form of homicidal mania, a mania which leads the victim of it to look upon women of a certain class with frenzied hatred.
>
> The doctor had been an inmate of a lunatic asylum for some time, and had been liberated and regained his complete freedom.
>
> After the maniacal murder in Miller's-court the doctor disappeared from the place in which he had been living, and his disappearance caused inquiries to be made concerning him by his friends who had, there is reason to believe, their own suspicions about him, and these inquiries were made through the proper authorities.

Sims was an intimate of Sir Melville Macnaghten, who referred to him as a friend,[50] and Macnaghten was clearly his source for the story of the Polish Jew, as is shown by the reference to a nonexistent City PC (see page 378), but if Sims's account of Macnaghten's own favoured suspect can be so far removed from the facts as we understand them to be, it is unavoidable that we must treat what Sims says about the Polish Jew with caution.

The emergent picture, as far as it can be trusted, is that suspicion fell on a Polish Jew sometime after the cessation of the crimes. He lived in Whitechapel, had a brother and was committed to an asylum, possibly 'about March 1889', if we give credence to Macnaghten, but probably sometime after early 1890 if we believe Swanson.

A thorough search of asylum records by the author Martin Fido in 1986–7 found only one 'Kosminski', a young man named Aaron Kosminski, and no other 'Kosminski' has since been found in the records. He was born in 1865[51] in Poland and entered England in 1882 aged seventeen.[52] He had a brother named Woolf[53] and sisters.[54] He was a Jew, a hairdresser by profession,[55] and unmarried.[56] On 12 July 1890 he was admitted to the Mile End Old Town Workhouse on the instruction of his brother Woolf. His address at that time is given as 3 Sion Square, a small street located at the top of Mulberry Street (where John Pizer lived). This was the home of his brother-in-law Woolfe Abrahams, a master tailor, his wife Betsy (Aaron's sister), and three daughters.[57]

Aaron's admission to Mile End Old Town Workhouse was on the order of someone who signed himself M Whitfield and the reason for admission was given as '2 years insane' (i.e., insane since 1888).[58] We don't know why Aaron was admitted at that time, but it wasn't serious because he was discharged three days after admission, on 15 July 1890, into the care of his brother, whose address is given as 16 Greenfield Street.[59] This was in fact the home of another brother-in-law, Morris Lubnowski, his wife Matilda (Aaron's sister) and their children.

The next six months are blank, but during the afternoon[60] of 4 February 1891 Aaron Kosminski[61] was readmitted to the Mile End Old Town Workhouse from 16 Greenfield Street. The informant was again his brother and Aaron was again admitted by M Whitfield.[62] This time there was to be no release. Three days later, during the morning[63] of 7 February 1891, Aaron[64] was discharged to the Middlesex County Lunatic Asylum, Colney Hatch.[65] The Register of Admissions[66] records the following:

Order no.	11,190
Adm.	7 February 1891
Age	26
Civil State	Single
Occupation	Hairdresser
Religion	Hebrew
Education	R&W
Time Insane	6 years insane
Cause	self-abuse
Form of Disorder	Mania
Symptoms of Disorder	Incoherence
Bodily State	Fair
Discharged	19 April 1894

Another surviving document is the Male Patients Day Book, New Series, No. 20, Middlesex Asylum, Colney Hatch:

Regd. No. of Admission	11,190
Name	Aaron Kozminski
Order signed by	H. Chambers Esq., J.P.
Reception order dated	6th day of February 1891
Age	26

Parish	Mile End Old Town
Marital Status	Single
Previous Occupation	Hairdresser
Religious persuasion	Hebrew
If first attack	No
Age on first attack	25
Previous Treatment	Mile End Old Town Workhouse July 1890
Duration of existing attack	6 months [added in red: '6 years']
Supposed Cause	Unknown [added in red: 'Self-abuse']
Subject to Epilepsy	No
Suicidal	No
Dangerous to others	No
Any relative afflicted with insanity	Not known
Nearest known relative	Wolf Kozminski (brother)
	8 Lion [Sion] Square
	Commercial Rd E[67]

He declares that he is guided and his movements altogether controlled by an instinct that informs his mind, he says that he knows the movements of all mankind, he refuses food from others because he is told to do so, and he eats out of the gutter for the same reason.

Jacob Cohen, 51 Carter Lane, St Paul's EC[68] says that he goes about the streets and picks up bits of bread out of the gutter and eats them, he drinks water from the tap and he refuses food at the hands of others. He took up a knife and threatened the life of his sister. He is very dirty and will not be washed. He has not attempted any kind of work for years.

Signed E.K. Houchin
23 High St. Stepney

Form of Disorder: Mania

Observations
On admission patient is extremely deluded. As mentioned in the certificate he believes that all his actions are dominated by an 'Instinct'. This is probably aural hallucination. Answers questions fairly but is inclined to be reticent and morose. Health fair.

The case notes thereafter are biannual and relate in the main to his physical condition. They tell us nothing about his mental condition, the nature of his hallucinations, or what he said or did.

1891 Feb. 10 Is rather difficult to deal with on account of the Dominant Character of his delusions. Refused to be bathed the other day as his 'Instincts' forbade him.

1891 April 21 Incoherent, apathetic, inoccupied; still the same 'instinctive' objection to weekly bath. Health fair.

1892 Jan 9. Incoherent. At times excited & violent – a few days ago he took up a chair and attempted to strike the charge attendant: apathetic as a rule, and refuses to occupy himself in any way – Habits cleanly. Health fair.

1892 Nov 17. Quiet and well behaved. Only speaks German.[69] Does no work.

1893 Jan 18 Chronic mania. Intelligence impaired; at times noisy, excited and incoherent; unoccupied; habits cleanly; health fair.

1893 April 8 Incoherent. Quiet lately. fair health.

1893 Sept 18 employed. Indolent, but quiet and clean in habits. Never employed. Answers questions concerning himself.

1894 April 13 Demented and incoherent, health fair.

1894 April 19th Discharged. Relieved. Leavesden.[70]

On 19 April 1894 Aaron Kosminski was admitted to the Leavesden Asylum,[71] the admission order having been signed by Dr Case, medical superintendent, Leavesden. Aaron Kosminski was probably taken to Leavesden by train, arriving at Watford Junction Station and being transported from there to the asylum in a hired van pulled by a pair of horses. Among some loose papers at the Greater London Record Office is a document that gives Aaron's nearest known relative at this time as his mother, Mrs Kosminski, living at 63 New Street,[72] off New Road, Whitechapel.

The sparse case notes for Leavesden, again largely biannual comments on his physical condition, present a deteriorating case.

M.A.B. Leavesden Asylum. Case Register (Male) 12a[73]

Aaron Kosminski.

Nature of illness: dementia.

10.9.10 Faulty in his habits, he does nothing useful and cannot answer questions of a simple nature.

29.9.11 Patient is dull and vacant. Faulty and [?] in habits. Does nothing useful. Nothing can be got by questions.

15.4.12 [?]

6.9.12 No replies can be got. Dull and stupid in manner and faulty in his habits. Requires constant attention.

16.1.13 Patient is morose in manner. No sensible reply can be got by questions. He mutters incoherently. Faulty and untidy in habits.

16.7.14 Incoherent and exciteable. Troublesome at times. Hallucinations of hearing. Untidy.

17.2.15 Patient merely mutters when asked questions. He has hallucinations of sight and hearing and is very excitable at times. Does not work. Cleanly but untidy in dress.

2.2.16 Patient does not know his age or how long he has been here. He has hallucinations of sight and hearing and at times is very obstinate. Untidy but clean, does no work.

Register of Patients Leavesden [loose papers]

1894

Name: Aaron Kosminski

Date of Admission: 19th April 1894

Parish: Mile End

Religion: Jew

Age on Admission 29

Mental diagnosis: Dem Sec [Secondary dementia]

1.4.14 Patient has hallucinations of sight and hearing, is very excitable and troublesome at times, very untidy, bodily condition fair.

1.3.15 No improvement

11.11.15 Patient has cut over left eye caused by knock on tap in washhouse

8.7.16 No improvement

5.4.17 No improvement

26.5.18 Patient put to bed passing loose motions with blood and mucous

27.5.18 Transferred to 8a

3.6.18 Diarrhoea ceased. Ordered up by Dr Reese.

28.1.19 Put to bed with swollen feet

20.2.19 Put to bed with swollen feet and feeling unwell. Temp. 99°

13.3.19 Hip broken down

22.3.19 Taken little nourishment during day, but very noisy

23.3.19 Appears very low. Partaken of very little nourishment during day.

24.3.19 Died in my presence at 5.05 a.m. Marks on body, sore right hip and left leg. Signed: S Bennett, night attendant.

Weight taken on 17th May 1915: 7st 8lb 10ozs.

on 5th February 1919: 6st 12lb.

Note dated 25th March 1919 to Mr Friedlander, Undertaker of Duke Street, United Synagogue, London E. The body of Aaron Kosminski. Signed by:

H.W. Abrahams, 'The Dolphin', Whitechapel E, London, 25th March 1919.[74]

Relation to deceased: brothers [*sic*][75]

Another document, dated 30 March 1919, is from G Friedlander, sexton and officer of the Burial Society, St James Place, Aldgate EC3, to A J Freeman at Leavesden Asylum, acknowledging receipt of a certificate dated 28 March registering Aaron Kosminski's death.

Through the offices of the Burial Society of the United Synagogue, Aaron Kosminski was buried on 27 March 1919 at East Ham Cemetery at a total cost of £12 5s. Aaron Kosminski's address at this time is given as 5 Ashcroft Road, Bow.[76] This was the home of Morris Lubnowski and his now much-enlarged family of eight children, two boys and six girls. Interestingly, Morris and Matilda had come to England in 1881, probably the same time as Aaron, and lived until December 1882 at 10 Plummers Row. They moved and spent three years at nearby 10 Yalford Street and in December 1885 moved to 16 Greenfield Street. Almost immediately after Aaron was committed they moved to 63 New Street.[77] For some reason they now changed their name to Cohen or Lubnowski-Cohen and the family appear in the 1891 census as 'L Cohen'. By 1894 they had been joined by Aaron's mother, Golda. Morris began his own greengrocery business. The family moved to 64 Wellesley Street, and in the autumn of 1910 to 5 Ashcroft Road, where they remained until 1930.

Aaron's other sister, Betsy, lived with her husband Woolfe Abrahams at 3 Sion Square until they moved with their six children at the end of the century to Cheetham in Manchester, where a seventh child, Harry, would be born. Manchester's Jewish community was founded in the 1780s at the time when Manchester was developing as a centre of business and trade and the majority of immigrants drawn there were attracted by opportunities in the textile industry. By 1900, when Woolfe and his family moved there, Manchester's Jewish population had reached 35,000, making it the largest such community outside London. Most of the poorer immigrants settled along the north edges of the cities of Manchester and Salford, and the wealthiest in Crumpsall and Higher Broughton. The middle classes, to which Woolfe now evidently belonged, established themselves in Cheetham Hill, a now rundown and rather seedy district of commercial buildings, warehouses and empty streets that was once a thriving township independent of Manchester and became one of the largest Jewish communities in the country. It was in Derby Street, Cheetham, that Mr Marks and the English-born and non-Jewish Mr Spencer opened their first store. Also in Cheetham, next to a pub called the Derby Brewery Arms, was the headquarters of the Manchester School of Zionism, founded by Chaim Waizmann, whose meeting with Arthur Balfour led to the Balfour Declaration, which stated, 'His Majesty's Government looks with much favour on the establishment of a Jewish state in Palestine' – so it was here that the state of Israel was born.

There can be little doubt that Aaron Kosminski was Anderson's suspect. No other 'Kosminski' has been found in asylum records, Aaron fits all the (limited) criteria of Anderson's suspect: he was male, Polish, a Jew; he lived in the heart of the murder district and had 'people', a family, to protect him; and he was committed to an asylum. His medical records give the cause of his insanity as self-abuse (masturbation), which corresponds with the 'utterly unmentionable vices' of Anderson's suspect and the 'solitary vices' of Macnaghten's 'Kosminski'.

Aaron Kosminski also fits almost all the criteria to be Swanson's suspect. His committal in 1891 means that he could have been identified at the Convalescent Police Seaside Home, the first Annual Report of which states, 'From its opening, until March 1st, 1891, the Home has received 102 visitors – 1 ex-superintendent, 9 inspectors, 11 sergeants, and 74 constables, 5 ex-police officers, and 2 other visitors admitted by special request.'[78] It is tempting to wonder if those two 'other visitors', who clearly were not

serving or ex-policemen, could have been the suspect and the witness.
Kosminski had a brother who lived in Whitechapel, and he was committed
by his family, which could correspond with Swanson's claim that the
suspect was taken to the workhouse with his hands tied behind his back.

However, Aaron Kosminski was not sent to Stepney Workhouse but to
Mile End Old Town Workhouse; the murders did not cease with Aaron
Kosminski's committal; and he did not die soon after being committed to
Colney Hatch. It should be observed, however, that the expanding Borough
of Stepney absorbed Mile End Old Town in 1901, so, when Swanson wrote
nine years later, Mile End Old Town Workhouse *was* Stepney Workhouse.
The 'Jack the Ripper' sequence is generally regarded as having ended with
the murder of Mary Jane Kelly in 1888, but the sequence of Whitechapel
murders continued until the murder of Frances Coles in 1892. Among
Swanson's private papers was a list of victims compiled at the time of the
murder of Alice McKenzie in 1889, to which Swanson had appended the
name of Frances Coles. This paper probably indicates that Swanson
included Coles as the last murder, and one can observe that the police files
on the Whitechapel crimes were closed with the Coles case. If Swanson did
count Coles as the last murder, this ties in well with Kosminski, albeit that
Aaron Kosminski had been committed shortly before Coles was murdered.
There is no immediately explicable explanation for Swanson's belief that
the suspect died soon after committal.

Who was the witness?

Turning to the thorny problem of who the witness could have been, we
immediately encounter a conflict because Macnaghten and sources
apparently based on him suggest that the witness was a City PC, while
Anderson and Swanson say the witness was a Jew (who is unlikely to have
been a policeman because a policeman is highly unlikely to have refused to
give evidence). The problem is further complicated by the fact that we know
of no City PC who saw anyone likely to have been the murderer near the
Mitre Square murder, and because Macnaghten himself betrays evidence of
being confused about the witness himself.

But, before examining this in any greater detail, let's look at the sources.
In his draft report Sir Melville Macnaghten wrote of the suspect, 'This man
in appearance strongly resembled the individual seen by the City PC near

Mitre Square.' Elsewhere in the report he wrote, 'No one ever saw the Whitechapel murderer (unless possibly it was the City PC who was a beat [*sic*] near Mitre Square) . . .'

Major Arthur Griffiths wrote, 'This man was said to resemble the murderer by the one person who got a glimpse of him – the police constable in Mitre Square.'[79]

And George R Sims wrote, 'The policeman who got a glimpse of Jack in Mitre Court said, when some time afterwards he saw the Pole, that he was the height and build of the man he had seen on the night of the murder.'[80]

As noted, no City PC is known to have seen a man suspected of being the Ripper in or near Mitre Square. However, the surviving records are very incomplete and it is possible that a City PC saw someone and that his report has not been preserved and never made it into the press. A popular alternative to this scenario is the suggestion that Macnaghten misremembered the witness as a City PC when in fact it was Joseph Lawende, the Jewish traveller in the cigarette trade who saw a woman he thought was Eddowes at the entrance to Mitre Square. The solution has the attractiveness of retaining the location given by Macnaghten (Mitre Square), gives us a Jewish witness, as stated by Anderson and Swanson, and explains why the City CID maintained surveillance on the suspect.

Lawende was also used – or allegedly used – as a witness on one and possibly two further occasions. In February 1891 Thomas Sadler was put in a line-up to see if a witness could identify him. According to the *Daily Telegraph*,

> Probably the only trustworthy description of the assassin was that given by a gentleman who, on the night of the Mitre-square murder, noticed in Duke-street, Aldgate, a couple standing under the lamp at the corner of the passage leading into Mitre-square. The woman was identified as one victim of that night, Sept. 30, the other having been killed half an hour previously in Berner-street. The man was described as 'aged from thirty to thirty-five; height 5 ft 7 in, with brown hair and big moustache; dressed respectably. Wore pea jacket, muffler, and a cloth cap with a peak of the same material.'[81] The witness has confronted Sadler and has failed to identify him.[82]

And, according to the *Pall Mall Gazette*, the police investigated the antecedents of a sailor named William Grant Grainger, who had seriously wounded Alice Graham on 10 February 1895. The newspaper reported that

> there is one person whom the police believe to have actually seen the Whitechapel murderer with a woman a few minutes before that woman's dissected body was found in the street. That person is stated to have identified Grainger as the man he saw. But obviously identification after so cursory a glance, and after the lapse of so long an interval, could not be reliable; and the enquiries were at length pulled up in a cul-de-sac.

Neither account names Lawende, although there can be little doubt that he was the witness in question, but the use of Lawende in these cases would suggest that he was *not* Anderson's witness. The murder of Frances Coles took place two weeks after Aaron Kosminski had been committed to the asylum, and Swanson is clear that the suspect had been committed *after* the identification. In other words, if Lawende was the witness in both cases then he would have positively identified Kosminski, then been asked to identify Sadler, and we can only assume that the positive identification of Kosminski would have negated anything Lawende said about Sadler and made his testimony utterly worthless. Had the witness already positively identified the suspect, the witness would not have been reused, and since Lawende was used in the Sadler case it follows that he was not used to identify Anderson's suspect. Furthermore, if Anderson's witness had refused to testify, despite the extreme pressures we may suppose to have been brought to bear to make him do so, the police are not likely to have turned to him again, and again.

Of course, it is possible that Lawende's identification of the Polish Jew was restricted – which may explain why Macnaghten never mentioned it – but the idea that Lawende was the witness is fraught with numerous other problems. There is no clear and plausible reason why the Metropolitan Police would have been involved in taking the suspect in a City crime (the murder of Eddowes) to be identified by a City witness (Lawende). On top of which, Joseph Lawende was widely reported in the press at the time of Eddowes's murder as stating that he would not be able to recognise the man he saw again. Any defence counsel would have seriously devalued the worth of Lawende's testimony in 1888, let alone as late as 1892, as even the *Pall Mall Gazette*'s journalist was aware, and it is hard to conceive that either he or the police would have considered his testimony the linchpin on which a successful prosecution largely depended. 'It should now be clear why Lawende's identification of Kosminski cannot possibly be considered a conclusive or even persuasive piece of evidence,' one informed commentator has written.[83]

On the other hand, if we accept that Lawende was the witness we have (a) to explain why the City CID didn't have their suspect identified by their own witness, (b) to explain what unfathomable reason the Metropolitan Police had for taking a City suspect in a City crime to be identified by a City witness and (c), if Lawende was such a bad witness, to explain why Anderson, whose many faults don't appear to have included arrant stupidity, based a conclusion about the murderer's identity on ludicrously inferior evidence.

A solution to the problem is perhaps provided by Macnaghten himself. When describing the murder of Elizabeth Stride in Berner Street, Macnaghten states that the murderer was disturbed by the arrival of three Jews in a cart. We know that the murderer was in fact disturbed (if he was disturbed at all) by the arrival of one Jew in a cart, Louis Deimschutz, and, in writing 'three Jews', Macnaghten probably had in mind the three Jews of Mitre Square: Lawende, Levy and Harris. If so, if Macnaghten had mentally transferred the witnesses in Mitre Square to Berner Street, then it is probable that he transferred the Berner Street witness to Mitre Square, and that the City PC was not a City PC at all, but PC Smith in Berner Street.

This possibility does have a satisfying neatness about it. There is no need to postulate a City PC of whom we know nothing, or to suppose that Macnaghten confused a Jewish traveller in cigarettes with a City police constable. The Metropolitan Police would not have been taking a suspect to be identified by a City witness, and Anderson would not have been basing his conclusion on an unsatisfactory witness. The only difficulty is that PC Smith was not a Jew, could not have been the Jewish witness, and, if all he thought was that the suspect was the same height and build as the man he'd seen, his testimony would hardly have had the importance Anderson and Swanson clearly attached to it. In short, he wasn't and couldn't have been Anderson's witness – unless Macnaghten's witness was *not* Anderson's witness and Macnaghten did not know about the identification by the Jewish witness.

This notion is unpalatable. It seems inconceivable that Macnaghten would not have known about Anderson's Jewish witness, yet his ignorance of the witness would explain why he didn't mention him and would certainly explain why Macnaghten and those who based their accounts on him did not attach significance to Anderson's theory.

If Lawende wasn't the witness – and it should have been reasonably clear from the start that he was such a bad witness that Anderson was unlikely to have placed such credence in him – and if the Jewish witness was not PC Smith, the only alternative is Israel Schwartz. He isn't an inspiring witness, but he is certainly preferable to Lawende,[84] and Anderson himself supplies a clue that Schwartz was indeed the witness. He wrote in his memoirs that the witness was 'the only person who ever had a good view of the murderer'.

Anderson may only have meant that the witness saw the suspect with one of the victims, but many people claimed to have seen men with victims: Mrs Long saw a man with Annie Chapman in Hanbury Street; several people saw Elizabeth Stride with a man in Berner Street; Joseph Lawende saw a woman talking with Eddowes at the entrance to Mitre Square; and several people, notably George Hutchinson, saw men with Mary Kelly. And several of these people, had a good view, again notably Hutchinson. Schwartz is distinguished by the fact that he is the only known witness to have seen a woman being attacked. Neither the man nor 'Pipeman' need have been the killer, as the police observed at the time, but, as we saw in Chapter Nine, it is statistically improbable that Stride was assaulted twice in the same place on the same night within fifteen minutes by different men. If it can be fairly said of anyone that he saw the murderer, it can only be said of Israel Schwartz.

Conclusion

Aaron Kosminski fits all the criteria to be Anderson's suspect, and, with the exception of dying soon after the identification, with everything Swanson said; and the utterly 'unmentionable vices' connect him with Macnaghten's 'Kosminski'. Sir Robert Anderson appears to have been an intelligent, informed and reliable source, and from at least as early as 1895 – and probably 1892 – until his death he seems to have believed that the Ripper was committed to an asylum. Swanson did not disagree with Anderson, and, since he was writing for himself, he could have expressed himself forthrightly and honestly, so his silence is tacit agreement.

Aaron Kosminski's surviving medical records are twice yearly reports concerning his physical and mental wellbeing, and they tell us nothing specific about his mental behaviour, the nature of his visual and audio hallucinations, what he said, how he behaved, or anything else, and what they do tell us about his physical condition applies to 1892 and later. They do *not* indicate what he was like in 1888. His committal papers show that he was severely deluded with the hallucinations, and utterly unable to look after himself. The excessive and public masturbation is a symptom of hypersexuality – otherwise known as the 'satyriasis' from which Dr Bond suggested the Ripper was suffering – and has been associated with serial killers. The threat to his sister with a knife could have been homicidal. It is possible that, if Aaron Kosminski's mind lost its grip on reality after the murder of Mary Kelly and gave itself up completely to hallucinations, he would have very quickly changed from a relatively clean and respectable-looking young man into the shambling wreck we see in his committal papers in 1892.

Whether or not Aaron Kosminski was Jack the Ripper is unknown and will probably always remain so, but it appears that Sir Robert Anderson and Chief Inspector Donald Sutherland Swanson believed he was. They were there and they were in a position to know.

David Cohen

To bring this chapter to a close, it may be appropriate to mention here the David Cohen, or confusion, theory, which parallels the case against Aaron Kosminski – up to a point – and requires brief discussion. For his 1987 book *The Crimes, Detection and Death of Jack the Ripper*, Martin Fido undertook an exhaustive search of the workhouse and asylum records in search of 'Kosminski', but understandably didn't extend his search as far as 1892 and initially missed Aaron Kosminski. Assuming that Robert Anderson would not have lied, he concluded that 'Kosminski' had to be in the asylum records under a different name and the most likely Polish Jew asylum inmate he'd come across was 'David Cohen'. An unmarried tailor, aged 23, with dark-brown hair and beard and the same colour of eyes, he was picked up by the police, apparently during a brothel raid.[85] He appeared at the Thames Police Court on 7 December 1888 charged with being 'a lunatic found wandering at large' – a term defined by the Lunacy Amendment Act and applied to anyone who was, or was deemed to be, a lunatic who was not under proper care and control – and committed to

Whitechapel Workhouse,[86] where his medical record shows that he was suicidal, very violent, threatened other patients and tore down a lead pipe in the ward and the wire guard from a window.

Fourteen days later, on 21 December 1888, he was discharged to the Colney Hatch asylum, where he remained in an agitated state until he died on 20 October 1889. He was buried on 23 October 1889 and his death certificate records his last known address as 86 Leman Street, which was a Protestant Boys Club, and Martin Fido has suggested that it was a mistake for the more plausible Poor Jews Temporary Shelter at 84 Leman Street.

'David Cohen' had been arrested by the police, he had been committed to an asylum a short time after the murder of Mary Kelly, which would explain the sudden cessation of the crimes, and in the asylum he was extremely violent and dangerous to others, which Martin Fido thought reflected a Ripper-like personality. Unfortunately, 'David Cohen' didn't sound anything like 'Kosminski', but Fido's searches had thrown up a 'K[something]ski' – a young man named Nathan Kaminski, who was admitted to the Whitechapel Workhouse Infirmary on 24 March 1888 suffering from syphilis and who was discharged as cured six weeks later. There was absolutely nothing to connect him to the crimes, but he was the *only* 'K[something]ski' in the records; his address, 15 Black Lion Yard, fitted the direction the murderer probably took after dropping the apron in Goulston Street;[87] and, as Fido discovered, he didn't have a death certificate. Fido suggested that Kaminsky was Cohen, the nasality of the East End Jewish accent having caused the clerk to mishear 'Nathan Kamin' as 'David Cohen'. Fido was later told that 'David Cohen' was a John Doe name regularly applied by petty bureaucrats to Jews whose names they couldn't understand or pronounce. This is popularly believed but lacks supporting evidence and has otherwise been dismissed as a pious myth. Cohen, in any case, is a common and legitimate Jewish name.

Then Martin Fido found Aaron Kosminski, quickly concluded that he was Macnaghten's 'Kosminski' and that he was a harmless and nonviolent imbecilic lunatic who would never have been suspected of being Jack the Ripper and couldn't be Anderson's suspect. He suggested that 'Cohen' and Aaron Kosminski had become confused. He obviously didn't know how, but speculated that in 1888 the Metropolitan Police arrested a Polish Jew whose identity they did not know and who was committed as 'David Cohen', but several years later learned that the City Police had suspected a similarly aged Polish Jew named Aaron Kosminski and assumed Kosminski was the same man they had committed as 'David Cohen'. Fido thought the subsequent 'discovery' of the Swanson marginalia supported his opinion because it contained details that matched Cohen but not Kosminski. In fact only one detail matched: Kosminski did not die soon after committal, as Swanson says, but Cohen did, assuming that ten months is defined as soon.

The confusion hypothesis evolved over time as Martin Fido's ground-breaking research tried to make sense of bits of data as they emerged, but there can now be little doubt that Aaron Kosminski was Robert Anderson's suspect. The confusion hypothesis depends on the Metropolitan Police not knowing the name of 'David Cohen', but research has shown that they did know his name: he was charged at the Thames Police Court under the name Aaron Davis Cohen,[88] and the police knew enough about him to know his age, that he was unmarried and had no family, and that his occupation was that of a tailor. They also knew his last address – which, if Fido correctly identified it as the Poor Jews Temporary Shelter in Leman Street, probably means that Cohen wasn't even in the country when the murders were committed. The shelter, opened in 1885, only provided accommodation for up to two weeks after arrival in the UK,[89] which means that Cohen had been in the country since mid-November. On top of all this, there is abundant evidence that police of all ranks, including Anderson and Swanson, continued to believe that the Ripper was at large long after Cohen's committal and death.

CHAPTER TWENTY-TWO

Other Ripper Suspects

There are lots of Ripper suspects and pinning the tail on the donkey, so to speak, has for many years been something of a popular albeit dubious pastime. Suspects, some suggested seriously, others tongue-in-cheek, range from people like Joseph Barnett, Mary Kelly's boyfriend, suspected as far as one can tell simply because he was there, through the famous, such as Dr Thomas Barnardo, to the pseudonymous, such as 'Dr Stanley', whose confession was supposedly published in a South American journal or newspaper that as yet nobody has been able to find. The trawlings have also brought to light a host of fascinating minor eccentrics who peopled the stage of Victorian London, such as Roslyn Donston Stephenson, a black magician who was on the fringe of the original investigations and was claimed in later years by those who knew him to have been the Ripper.

These speculations are often persuasively written, they can make entertaining reading and they often throw up bits and pieces of new information, but otherwise they don't make good history and they can mislead people into believing things that aren't true. Most people have heard of Jack the Ripper, but, thanks to a couple of books and a few movies, an awful lot of them think he was 'something to do with the royal family', and such escapist suspects seem to be regularly discussed on TV documentaries because they are 'sexy' and most people have heard about them. In this respect the three most influential Ripper books published in the last thirty years or so – influential in the sense that they have been read by the largest number of people who in turn may have been persuaded to accept that the suspects advanced were indeed the Ripper – are Stephen Knight's *Jack the Ripper: The Final Solution*, Shirley Harrison's *The Diary of Jack the Ripper* and the bestselling crime novelist Patricia Cornwell's *Portrait of a Killer: Jack the Ripper – Case Closed.* These three books respectively introduced the Royal Conspiracy/Dr Gull theory, the confessional diary of the Liverpool cotton dealer James Maybrick, and the seemingly persuasive forensic evidence against the artist Walter Sickert.

Probably the best-known theory, wheeled out in no fewer than three movies, most recently *From Hell*, is that which in its various manifestations introduces a cast of characters that includes the royal physician Dr William Gull, Queen Victoria's grandson Prince Albert Victor and the psychic and medium Robert James Lees. The seeds of the story appear to have been planted in a tale allegedly told by a prominent London physician named Dr Howard to William Greer Harrison[1] of the Bohemian Club[2] in San Francisco, and reported in several newspapers, the earliest traced so far being the Fort Wayne *Sentinel*, 24 April 1895:[3]

MYSTERY SOLVED!

Identity of Jack the Ripper Known

The Perpetrator of the Whitechapel Murders Was a London Physician of Prominence.

San Francisco, April 24.

Dr Howard, a London physician of considerable prominence, was the guest of Wm. Greer Harrison at the Bohemian Club recently. The Englishman told a singular story to his host and vouched for its correctness in every particular. It related to the mystery of Jack the Ripper, which the physician declared was no longer a mystery among the scientific men of London, nor the detectives of Scotland Yard.

He said that the assassin was a medical man of high standing and extensive practice. He was married to a beautiful and amiable wife, and had a family. Shortly before the beginning of the Whitechapel murders, he developed a peculiar, and to his wife, an inexplicable mania, an unnatural pleasure in causing pain. She grew so alarmed that she became afraid of him and locked herself and her children up when she saw the mood coming on him. When he recovered from the paroxysms and she spoke to him about it, he laughed at her fears. Then the Whitechapel murders filled London with horror. The suspicions of the wife were aroused, and as one assassination succeeded another, she noted, with heart breaking dread, that at the periods when these murders were supposed to have been committed, her husband was invariably absent from home.

At last the suspense and fear of the wretched wife became unbearable, and she went to some of her husband's medical friends, stated the case and asked their advice and assistance. They called the Scotland Yard force to assist them, and by adding one fact to another, a chain of evidence pointing to the doctor as the author of the murders became complete.

The physicians visited the murderer and told him they wished to consult him about the remarkable case. They stated his own case in detail and asked him what should be done under the circumstances. He replied that while the unmistakeable insanity of the person who could commit these crimes would save him from the halter, he should certainly be confined in a lunatic asylum. Then they told him that he himself was the maniac who had committed these fearful acts. He declared the impossibility of the accusation, but confessed that of late years there were gaps in the twenty four hours of which he positively had no recollection. He said he had awakened in his room as if from a stupor and he found blood upon his boots and stains of blood upon his hands. He also had scratches upon his face and his amputation knives had shown signs of use, though he could not recall having assisted at any operation.

These doctors then assured him there could be no doubt of his identity with the White Chapel assassinations. They made an exhaustive search of the house, led by the accused, and found ample proofs of murder, and the unhappy man whose mind at that moment was in its nominally clear condition, begged to be removed from the world as a guilty and dangerous monster. The necessary papers were made out and the irresponsible murderer was committed to an insane asylum. In a month or two he lost all semblance to sanity and is now the most intractable and dangerous confined in the institution.

A few days later the story was retold with some elaborations in the 28 April 1895 issue *Sunday Times-Herald* of Chicago.[4] The newspaper stated that the elaborations had been provided by an unnamed 'gentleman of this city' (Chicago), also described as 'a London clubman', who was enabled to speak only because Dr Howard had already spoken. He described the physician as 'in good standing, with an extensive practice' who 'had been ever since he was a student at Guy's Hospital, an ardent and enthusiastic vivisectionist' and he said the physician had been identified as Jack the Ripper through the efforts of the spiritualist medium Robert James Lees.

The newspaper told a long, fanciful and barely factual story, which in summary was that Lees visited Scotland Yard after having a premonition of a murder, but was treated as a crank by the sergeant on duty. The following day a murder was discovered just as Lees had described and, for reasons not explained and otherwise unclear, Lees was so shocked that he immediately took his family abroad. Four more murders were committed during his absence, but Lees had received no premonition of these and he returned to England, where one day he was in an omnibus with his wife when a man got on at the top of Notting Hill and Lees immediately recognised him as the murderer in his earlier vision. According to the paper, the

> bus turned into Oxford Street and at Marble Arch the man got out, followed by Lees, who discreetly trailed him down Park Lane towards Apsley House. There the man hailed a cab and left Lees standing on the pavement. That night Lees had a premonition that another murder would be committed and that this time the murderer would attempt to sever the victim's ears. The following morning he hastened to Scotland Yard, where the police took interest because they had received a post card purporting to be from the murderer and in which he said, 'To prove that I am really Jack the Ripper, I will cut the ears off the ninth victim.'

The murder was committed and one ear was completely severed, and again Lees went abroad. This time seven murders were committed during his absence. Eventually, Lees returned to England and one day was dining at the Criterion with Roland B Shaw, a mining stockbroker of New York, and Fred C Beckwith, the financial promoter of an American syndicate in London,[5] when he was suddenly struck by another premonition, which again proved to be true. This time Lees met with a sceptical police inspector who was nevertheless prepared to accept Lees's help, and one night accompanied him as he followed a psychic trail that eventually led to the gates of a West End mansion, the residence of one of the most celebrated physicians in the West End. The doctor was questioned, his guilt was established and he was quietly taken to a private insane asylum in Islington. It was announced that the doctor had died, and a sham burial was gone through, an empty coffin being placed in the family vault in Kensal Green, and the doctor ended his days in the asylum under the name Thomas Mason, patient 124.

The originator of the story, Dr Howard, has not been certainly identified, but on 19 May 1895 *The People* ran a version of the story in which he was very loosely identified with an unnamed doctor. A Dr Benjamin Howard identified himself with this doctor and wrote a letter of complaint and protest, in which he claimed,

> . . . my name is dishonourably associated with Jack the Ripper & in such a way, as if true, renders me liable to show cause to the British Medical Council . . . there is not a single item of this startling statement concerning me which has the slightest foundation in fact . . . & at the time of the alleged public statement by me I was thousands of miles distant from San Francisco, where it is alleged I made it.[6]

This Dr Benjamin Howard (1836–1900) was an American doctor who in 1877 became a member of the Royal College of Surgeons and in 1879 a Fellow of the Royal College of Surgeons of Edinburgh. He had an East End connection, having been instrumental with a Mr Crossman, the deputy chairman of the London Hospital, in establishing an accident ambulance system in Britain, but he was principally known for his work with artificial-respiration techniques, having given his name to what became known as the Howard Method, a subject on which he lectured, delivered papers and gave demonstrations before some of the most eminent medical groups in Britain.[7]

As for Robert James Lees, he was born at Hinckley in Leicestershire in 1849, began his working life as a cabinet fitter in Birmingham and, shortly after his marriage in December 1871, joined the staff of the *Manchester Guardian*. In 1874 he moved his family to London and became advertising manager for a new monthly magazine and later a journalist. From 1879 to 1889 he was a tourist guide for visiting Americans. This was when, in 1878, he suffered a financial crisis and acquired considerable debts, lost his home and property and for ten years lived in poverty, penniless and considering suicide. How Lees returned to financial solvency is a mystery, especially as he was able in 1893 to found the People's League, an organisation in which poor people combined to make bulk purchases of necessary commodities such as coal and clothing material at discounted prices. It also provided, among other things, recreational facilities and Christmas parties with gifts for children, as well as general education, religious studies and self-help.

By 1 January 1895 it had about 1,600 members, but in that year Lees was forced by illness to close it. Curiously, this was the year when the *Sunday*

Times-Herald article appeared. He moved to St Ives in Cornwall, then to Plymouth in Devon, and finally in 1902 to Ilfracombe, where he devoted himself to writing. His wife died in 1912 and about 1928 he moved to Leicester, where he lived in a house donated by spiritualist friends, apparently now without any significant money, dying there in January 1931.

Lees is best known for the claim that as a child he acted as a medium for Queen Victoria. This was apparently around 1862–3, and, when a paragraph in *The Medium and Daybreak* reported a séance at which Lees allegedly received a message from Prince Albert. Queen Victoria sent two incognito court officials to test Lees by asking him for Albert's pet name for Victoria. Queen Victoria's distinguished biographer, Elizabeth Longford, disputes the claim and dismisses such evidence as exists as faked, pointing out the factual inaccuracies (*The Medium and Daybreak* wasn't published until 1870), doubting even that Queen Victoria had any interest, let alone belief, in spiritualism.

As for the claim that Lees identified Jack the Ripper, the *Sunday Times-Herald* story is grossly inaccurate: the number of crimes and the time over which they were committed are exaggerated and the locations are wrong. There is no mention of the incident in Lees's diary or in any of his writings, and he appears not to have made any comment on the story until close to his death. However, the *Sunday Times-Herald*'s details about Lees himself are tolerably accurate, perhaps indicating a source close to Lees or even Lees himself, and in essence the story about his visiting the police and their reaction to him is confirmed by his 1888 diary entries. He *did* visit the police and offer his services, and he *was* received with disrespect and rejection:

Tuesday, 2 September 1888: Offered services to Police to follow up East End Murders – called a fool and lunatic.
   Got trace of man from spot near Berner Street.

Wednesday, 3 September 1888: Went to City Police again – called a madman and fool.

Thursday, 4 September 1888: Went to Scotland Yard – same result, but they promised to write me.

In 1928 the *Leicester Illustrated Chronicle* published an article about Robert James Lees by Hugh Mogford, a convert to spiritualism, in which

Lees reportedly claimed that he had been instrumental in the apprehension of Jack the Ripper. The *Leicester Mercury*'s obituary on 12 January 1931 stated that Lees 'claimed to be the only surviving person who knew the identity of Jack the Ripper' and that

> some months ago, he told a *Leicester Mercury* man that he offered his services to Scotland Yard, with a view to tracing the criminal . . . His visits to the yard became so persistent, that at length, the authorities agreed to his co-operation . . . Mr Lees made the astounding statement to the *Leicester Mercury* that he actually enabled the Yard to associate with the crime, a man who died in a lunatic asylum.

The report also said, 'Miss Eva Lees told the *Leicester Mercury* that the responsibility of his knowledge of the "Ripper" had weighed more heavily on her father of late years.'[8] His devoted daughter, Eva, also gave an interview to *Le Matin*, in which she insisted that she had no knowledge of the identity of Jack the Ripper, but admitted only that her father had 'played some part'.[9]

On the negative side, also in 1931, a Mrs Brackenbury, who was working for the Society for Psychical Research, visited Scotland Yard and discussed the case with CID officials, one of whom had been keeper of the criminal records since 1901. None of them had heard of Lees or of any medium connected with the investigation. She also questioned ex-Inspector Wensley, who likewise said he'd never heard of Lees's visits to the police. In 1949 D J West also questioned Scotland Yard on the subject, receiving a reply that said there was 'no foundation for the newspaper stories that the murderer was known to the Police, and traced through the aid of a medium. I am told there is no trace record of a person named James Lees to whom you refer in your letter.'[10] One should accept, however, that if there is any truth in the Lees story it is likely that the principal participants would have been sworn to strict secrecy and accordingly facts would never have received wide circulation – and thus, of course, almost any conspiracy theory can neatly and conveniently explain the absence of verifiable details. It is also possible that Lees went to the City Police, whose Ripper records appear to have been destroyed during the Blitz in World War Two.

The royal conspiracy theory and Prince Albert Victor

Probably the most widely known theory about the identity of Jack the Ripper is that either he was Prince Albert Victor or the murders were committed to hide something the prince had done. This theory has been presented in several books and at least three films, most recently *From Hell*, but the earliest allusion to it is in *The Encyclopaedia of Murder* by Colin Wilson and Patricia Pitman, who retell the Lees story and say, 'The story connected with Lees usually goes on to add either (a) that the doctor was the Queen's physician, or (b) that Jack the Ripper was some relative of the Royal Family.'[11] The first mention of Prince Albert Victor by name is in a book by Philippe Jullian entitled *Edward and the Edwardians*, published in French in 1962 and in an English translation in 1967. Jullian wrote,

> Before he died, poor Clarence was a great anxiety to his family. He was quite characterless and would soon have fallen a prey to some intriguer or group of roués, of which his regiment was full. They indulged in every form of debauchery, and on one occasion the police discovered the Duke in a *maison de rencontre* of a particularly equivocal nature during a raid. Fifty years before, the same thing had happened to Lord Castlereagh, and he had committed suicide.[12] The young man's evil reputation soon spread. The rumour gained ground that he was Jack the Ripper . . .[13]

The *maison de rencontre* or 'house of meeting' is a reference to the Cleveland Street scandal of 1889, in which a number of prominent men, Prince Albert Victor rumoured to be among them, were discovered to be clients of a homosexual brothel,[14] and Jullian suggests that the rumours connecting the prince with the Ripper circulated *after* that scandal. No such rumours predating Jullian have been found, however, and the first to postdate him was an article, 'Jack the Ripper – A Solution?', by a distinguished doctor named Thomas Stowell published in a relatively obscure magazine called *The Criminologist*.[15]

Dr Thomas Stowell, CBE, FRCS, was a lecturer at the London School of Economics, chief medical officer to ICI, consulting surgeon with the Emergency Medical Service, honorary surgeon at the Victoria Infirmary, Northwich, and senior honorary surgeon and radiologist at the mid-Cheshire Orthopaedic Clinic, Northwich. He had been educated at St Paul's and St

Thomas's Hospital, where he was a pupil and friend of Theodore Dyke Acland (1851–1931), who was the husband of Caroline Gull, the daughter of Sir William Gull. Acland was the editor of Gull's published papers.[16] Stowell wrote that he 'knew them both intimately and often enjoyed the hospitality of their home in Bryanson Square, over many years.'

Although Stowell called his suspect 'S', his narrative clearly identified him as Prince Albert Victor, and there can be no doubt that this is who he meant because he told the author Colin Wilson.[17] Stowell speculated that 'S' had become infected with syphilis while on a world cruise when aged about sixteen – this would have been Prince Albert Victor's well-documented cruise aboard HMS *Bacchante* – and that the disease had driven him homicidally insane. He believed that 'S' was caught within an hour or two of the murder of Eddowes, had been quietly certified insane and placed under restraint in a private mental home in the Home Counties under the care of Sir William Gull, but that he escaped to murder Mary Jane Kelly. Recaptured and returned to Gull's ministrations, 'S' recovered sufficiently to take a five-month cruise in 1889 and undertake some public duties during the summer of 1890, although Stowell pointed out that his speeches contained little more than a hundred words, from which he speculated that the prince was heading towards the depression and dementia that would inevitably overtake him.

Stowell presented no hard evidence to support his story, except that he stated that Caroline Acland had told him that she had 'seen in her father's diary an entry, "informed Blank that his son was dying from syphilis of the brain". The date of the entry was November 1889 . . .'

We don't know whether the diary entry actually had a blank space where the father's name should have been or whether Stowell omitted the name from his article – presumably the latter. There is nothing improbable about Prince Albert Victor's suffering from syphilis: he was regularly attended by a young doctor named Alfred Fripp, who later became a famous surgeon, and papers discovered after his death included a prescription for the prince that Fripp's biographer has suggested indicates the prince had also suffered from a gonorrhoeal infection.[18] What we don't know and what Stowell did not explain was why he thought a syphilitic Prince Albert Victor was Jack the Ripper.

What is very curious, however, is that, while Stowell did not offer any evidence to support his contention that 'S' was Jack the Ripper, he firmly pointed the finger of guilt elsewhere:

Many false trails were laid. Some, no doubt, were intended to mislead the police, some to mollify the angry press and public and some no doubt to puff the egoism of the neurotic exhibitionist.

One of these was that the murderer must be a surgeon to have removed the kidneys and pelvic organs. This is nonsense, for in those days, before the advent of antiseptic and aseptic surgery, the abdomen was almost inaccessible to the surgeon.

To support this fantasy it was not unnatural for the rumour-mongers to pick on a most illustrious member of my profession of the time – perhaps of all time – Sir William Gull, Bt., M.D., F.R.C.P., F.R.S.

He was physician to Guy's Hospital, Physician in Ordinary to Her Majesty, Queen Victoria, to H.R.H. The Prince of Wales, and physician to a large number of aristocracy and the wealthy including, if I am right in my deductions, the family of Jack the Ripper. It is said that on more than one occasion Sir William Gull was seen in the neighbourhood of Whitechapel on the night of a murder. It would not surprise me to know that he was there for the purpose of certifying the murderer to be insane so that he might be put under restraint as were other lunatics apprehended in connection with murders.

Stowell then went on to tell the Lees story, which he said he'd read in a book by Fred Archer called *Ghost Detectives*, and speculates that the 'imposing mansion' to which Lees led the police was 74 Brook Street, Grosvenor Square, the home of Sir William Gull. Even more remarkably, he says Caroline Acland herself told him that,

at the time of the Ripper murders, her mother, Lady Gull, was greatly annoyed one night by an unappointed visit from a police officer, accompanied by a man who called himself a 'medium', and she was irritated by their impudence in asking her a number of questions which seemed to her impertinent. She answered the questions with non-committal replies such as 'I do not know,' 'I cannot tell you that,' 'I am afraid I cannot answer that question.' Later Sir William himself came down and in answer to the questions said he occasionally suffered from 'lapses of memory since he had had a slight stroke in 1887'; he said that once he had discovered blood on his shirt.

Dr Stowell made three seemingly extraordinary claims: (1) that it was rumoured that Sir William Gull was the Whitechapel murderer – we know of no such rumours; (2) that he was seen in Whitechapel at times when murders were committed – we don't know of any source that says this; and (3) that Sir William Gull was the physician to whose house Lees brought the police. Dr Stowell ostensibly mentions these things as support of the contention that 'S' was the Ripper – Gull was in the East End in search of 'S' and had a bloodstained shirt because he had attended 'S' – and he seems oblivious of the fact that he had effectively pointed the finger at Gull.

We know of no rumours linking Sir William Gull with the Whitechapel murders, although it is possible that some perceptive readers may have thought they recognised Sir William Gull as the physician in the *Sunday Times-Herald* article and stories based on it, where he was described as 'a physician in high standing, and in fact was enjoying the patronage of the best society in the west end of London', 'He had been ever since he was a student at Guy's Hospital, an ardent and enthusiastic vivisectionist . . .', and he was 'one of the most celebrated physicians in the west end . . .' Gull had been a student at Guy's Hospital; he was a physician; he enjoyed the patronage of the best society – having been appointed physician to the Prince of Wales in 1871 and subsequently physician extraordinary, and afterwards physician in ordinary to Queen Victoria – and he supported vivisection. Indeed, he took an active part in the late-nineteenth-century controversy surrounding vivisection, gave evidence to the House of Lords and wrote an article for *Nineteenth Century* in which he stated that 'physiological experiments are useful . . . [and] therefore justifiable'. He claimed that the cruelty involved was preferable to ignorance.

The only problem is that the context of Stowell's article suggests that the rumours connecting Gull with the crimes were distinct from the Lees story, which leaves open the possibility that the *Times-Herald* article really was reflecting a genuine and contemporary rumour connecting Gull to the crimes, and perhaps Dr Stowell, being close to the Aclands, had heard it. What is extraordinary, however, is that Dr Stowell says that Gull was seen in Whitechapel 'on more than one occasion . . . on the night of a murder' – which is otherwise unknown to researchers – and added what is effectively corroboration of the Lees story. A speculation advanced by Colin Kendall in *The Criminologist* was that Stowell was 'playing a very artful game' and really pointing the finger of guilt at Sir William Gull while appearing to identify someone else.[19]

Dr Thomas Stowell said, 'For nearly fifty years . . . he has kept to himself evidence about the real identity of Jack the Ripper', from which we can deduce that he came across his evidence around 1920 or a little earlier[20] when, as he told Colin Wilson, Caroline Acland asked him to help sort her father's papers. Otherwise he was 'both a liar and a fantasist', as one commentator has called him, which is no doubt the simplest solution and perhaps also the true one, but completely lacks any significant support and is also the easiest way to avoid addressing difficult questions.

Whatever Dr Thomas Eldon Stowell knew, it died with him. On 2 November 1970 he appeared on the BBC television news programme *24 Hours* and did not deny that Prince Albert Victor was his suspect, but on 4 November 1970 *The Times* published an article in which it stated that, at the time of the Double Event, the murder of Stride and Eddowes, Prince Albert Victor was in the company of Prince Henry of Battenberg and a colonel clerk at Glen Muick, and that when Mary Kelly was killed the prince was at Sandringham in Norfolk. The following day Dr Stowell wrote to *The Times*:

I have at no time associated His Royal Highness, the late Duke of Clarence, with the Whitechapel murderer or suggested that the murderer was of Royal blood.

It remains my opinion that he was a scion of a noble family.

The particulars given in *The Times* of November 4 of the activities of His Royal Highness in no way conflict with my views as to the identity of Jack the Ripper.

Yours faithfully, a loyalist and a royalist
Thomas E.A. Stowell[21]

Stowell died on 8 November 1970, before the letter was published, leaving behind a folder labelled 'Jack the Ripper'. His son, Dr T E Stowell, destroyed it:

I read just sufficient to make certain there was nothing of importance . . . The family decided that this was the right thing to do. I am not prepared to discuss our grounds for doing so.

My father left no instructions or requests on what we were to do with it. I know that he had been interested in this subject for many

years, and that it arose again recently – for what reason I don't know.
The case doesn't interest me particularly. It was before my time.[22]

Dr Stowell's revelations caused newspaper headlines around the world
and the idea that Jack the Ripper was a member of the royal family
stimulated considerable interest in the subject and may be said to have given
birth to the modern era of interest. But, whatever evidence Dr Stowell may
have possessed for his belief that Prince Albert Victor was Jack the Ripper,
the records show that the prince was not in London when any of the
canonical murders were committed. Between 29 and 31 August (Nichols) he
was in Yorkshire staying with friends; between 7 and 9 September
(Chapman) he was either at Danby Lodge in Yorkshire with Lord Downe
or at the Cavalry Barracks in York where he was stationed with the 9th
Lancers, and Queen Victoria's journal records that he lunched with her at
Balmoral on 10 September, so could not have been very far from there on
the evening of 9 September. As already observed, on 29 September (Stride
and Eddowes) he was in Scotland with Prince Henry of Battenberg and a
colonel clerk at Glen Muick, lunching with Queen Victoria the following
day at Balmoral; and on 9–10 November (Kelly) the prince was at
Sandringham in Norfolk. So, unless someone comes up with good evidence
that Prince Albert Victor was not in any of these places, it must be
concluded that Prince Albert Victor was *not* Jack the Ripper.

That is not the end of his involvement in the story however.

Prince Albert Victor

Prince Albert Victor Christian Edward was the grandson of Queen Victoria
and eldest son of Albert Edward, and was in line to succeed to the throne on
his father's death. Born prematurely on 8 January 1864 at Frogmore House,
Windsor, and privately educated, he served aboard the training ship
Britannia at Dartmouth, then accompanied his younger brother George on
a world cruise to British colonies aboard HMS *Bacchante*, a voyage
distinguished by an alleged sighting of the legendary ghost ship and its
spectral skipper, the *Flying Dutchman*.[23] Between 1882 and 1883, he
received some tuition from James Kenneth Stephen (also advanced as a Jack
the Ripper suspect[24]) and entered Trinity College, Cambridge, in October
1883, went to Aldershot in 1886, became a lieutenant in the 19th Hussars in

1886, visited Ireland in 1887, received an honorary LLD from Cambridge in 1888, went to India in 1889–90,[25] was created Earl of Athlone and Duke of Clarence and Avondale in 1890 and died from pneumonia following influenza at Sandringham on 14 January 1892.

He has been described as typical of the upper-class twit – languid, interested in nothing, showing enthusiasm for little beyond 'every form of dissipation and amusement'. He was

> certainly dear and good, kind and considerate. He was also backward and utterly listless. He was self-indulgent and not punctual. He had been given no proper education, and as a result he was interested in nothing. He was heedless and as aimless as a gleaming goldfish in a crystal-bowl.[26]

He was lazy, dull, apathetic, irresponsible, backward to the point of idiocy, and a problem waiting in the wings for those who may have looked ahead to his possible accession to the throne.

In 1973 BBC television researchers working on a six-part drama-documentary series called *Jack the Ripper* were put in touch[27] with a man named Joseph Gorman, who claimed to be the illegitimate son of the artist Walter Sickert and told an astonishing story that was subsequently investigated by a journalist named Stephen Knight and published in a bestselling book called *Jack the Ripper: The Final Solution*.

According to Gorman, Sickert had a studio in Cleveland Street that was regularly visited by Prince Albert Victor. Opposite, at 6 Cleveland Street, was a tobacconist's, where a young woman named Annie Crook worked. Prince Albert Victor fell in love with her and they were married, Annie giving birth shortly afterwards to a baby daughter. The Establishment learned of the marriage and was horrified, partly because Annie Crook was a commoner and partly because she was a Catholic. The shop was raided in April 1888. Prince Albert Victor was whisked away and in due course sent to India, while Annie Crook was committed to an asylum. However, the child had been in the care of Mary Kelly, who had witnessed the marriage and was now in fear for her life. She entrusted the child to the care of Walter Sickert and fled into the East End, where she told her story to a group of friends who urged her to blackmail the government. Lord Salisbury, the prime minister, turned to Freemason friends, who in turn enlisted the assistance of Sir William Gull. Gull and a coachman named John Netley duly murdered the women, making the crimes look like the work of a madman, and Sir Robert Anderson acted as lookout during the murders and helped to misdirect the investigation.

Stephen Knight's version differed slightly from the original story, the primary difference being that Walter Sickert and not Robert Anderson played the part of the lookout. A later Sickert-based variant on the theme identified the third man as Lord Randolph Churchill.[28]

Knight's investigations showed that William Crook (d. 1891) and Sarah Ann Crook (1839–1916) had a daughter, Annie Elizabeth Crook (1862–1920), who on 18 April 1885 gave birth at St Marylebone Workhouse to an illegitimate daughter named Alice Margaret Crook (1885–1950). Annie's address was given on the birth certificate as 6 Cleveland Street and her occupation was given as 'confectionary assistant'. Knight also identified a man named John Charles Netley (1860–1903), a carman who was killed in an accident in 1903 and had no known link with Sickert and therefore seemed persuasive evidence of the truth of the story.

Unfortunately, the story otherwise collapses through lack of support. Walter Sickert isn't known to have had a studio in Cleveland Street. No. 6 Cleveland Street was demolished in 1886, the year after Alice Margaret was born, and Annie Elizabeth Crook wasn't living there when the supposed raid took place in April 1888,[29] and, although Annie was eventually committed to the lunacy ward of Fulham Road Workhouse, she enjoyed her liberty for many years after 1888 and lived at various known addresses. She wasn't a Roman Catholic, and the secret marriage, which cannot be verified, would not have been legal under the Royal Marriages Act of 1772.

As for Mary Kelly, she had apparently been living in the East End from 1886 and had been living with Joseph Barnett since Easter 1887. She did not live in Cleveland Street, and Barnett never mentioned that she had worked in a shop there or anywhere else. Kelly therefore wouldn't have been in a position to take care of Annie's child and wouldn't thereby have possessed information with which she could blackmail the royal family.

Whether or not the story told by Joseph Gorman is a complete invention, or whether, like many such tales, there is a kernel of truth – and, if so, what that truth might be – is uncertain. It is known that Alice Margaret Crook married a man named William Gorman and had five children, among them Joseph Gorman/Sickert (1925–2003), but there is no evidence that he was other than legitimate.

However, in 1992 I met Joseph Sickert's cousin, Ellen May Lackner, who confirmed that elements of Gorman's story circulated within the family during his infancy; the story, or elements of it, were not his invention. She recalled that wealthy people sometimes visited the house, and she thought there was a connection with the birth of Alice Margaret, who she thought was the illegitimate daughter of Walter Sickert, not Prince Albert Victor, and although she vaguely remembered some mysterious and frightening connection with Jack the Ripper, she thought it was an invention to deter too much enquiry into Alice.

As a footnote to the story, one should mention *Prince Jack*, a book by the late Frank Spiering that has never been published in the United Kingdom and is basically a retelling of Dr Thomas Stowell's theory, with the added bonus of a claim to have found the material Dr Stowell first saw. Attracted by Dr Stowell's story, Frank Spiering had begun to research material for a proposed book of his own. According to Spiering, a friend who was a professor at Rutgers, the State University of New Jersey, observed that Gull was a pioneer in internal medicine and recommended that Spiering visit the Academy of Medicine Library at 2 East 103rd Street in Manhattan, New York, because it has one of the most extensive collections of writings in the field. If any institution outside the United Kingdom was to be bequeathed Gull's papers, it would have been the Library.

In the card index Spiering found a single card

S115 Acland, Theodore Dyke

See:
Gull, Sir William Withey

A collection of the public writings of . . . Edited . . . by Theodore Dyke Acland.
Medical Papers
London, New Sydenham Soc, 1894 IX2 p.3–609 p.19 p.180

This card was a reference to a published book, a collection of Sir William Gull's published writings arranged and edited by his son-in-law Theodore Dyke Acland and published in London by the New Sydenham Society in 1896. He ordered it and in due course it arrived from the basement, accompanied by a sheaf of 120 handwritten and unsigned pages in a stiff, brown leather binding. Written in black ink in Sir William Gull's hand-writing, they covered a variety of topics and about thirty pages in he read,

On 3 October I informed the Prince of Wales that his son was dying of syphilis of the brain. Under suggestion using the Nancy method[30] my patient admitted to me the details of the murders he had com-mitted in Whitechapel.

Patient related that the knife he used was taken from a horse slaughterhouse in Buck's Row.

An overwhelming ecstasy from watching butchers in Aldgate High Street caused him to add a leather apron to his accoutrements.

He tied a red bandanna around the second woman's throat which he used to half strangle her before he cut her throat back and forth until the blade touched bone. He said he felt extreme fear when he drove the knife into her chest but kept slashing until he had cut open her stomach.

Patient continued on as to how he later showed a kidney to James and James did not believe him. But James thought it would be funny to send it to the police.

Patient complained of headache over the forehead and vertex and intense pain down the back. His manner is quick and talkative with slight delirium . . .[31]

In 1994 the author Martin Fido visited the New York Academy of Medicine Library and checked the card index, finding it exactly as Frank Spiering had described, but there was no accompanying volume of hand-written notes and the library staff had no knowledge of any such volume.[32] As Mr Spiering can be shown to indulge in exaggeration elsewhere, and the notes themselves sound phoney, particularly the reference to the leather apron, they are regarded as fake.

To sum up, in 1895 a Chicago newspaper published a story that focused heavily and with factual accuracy on Robert James Lees, who, it claimed, led the police to the home of a highly influential physician whom it appeared to identify as Sir William Gull. In 1960 Dr Thomas Stowell, a pupil and friend of Sir William Gull's son-in-law, Theodore Dyke Acland, began talking about a 'theory' apparently based on documents he saw among Sir William Gull's papers showing that Prince Albert Victor was Jack the Ripper. Stowell published his 'theory' a decade later, but gave no evidence for his belief beyond claiming to have seen a document indicating that Prince

Albert Victor suffered from syphilis, a possibility suggested by the earlier biographer of the prince's doctor, and claims that Sir William Gull was seen in Whitechapel when the murders were committed and that he was visited by the police and admitted to once finding blood on his shirt for which he could offer no explanation.

In 1973 BBC television researchers were directed to Joseph Gorman/ Sickert, who claimed that the murders had been committed by Sir William Gull at the behest of the government to prevent the illegal marriage of Prince Albert Victor and a commoner from becoming common knowledge. In one version of this story the child of the prince was entrusted to the care of the artist Walter Sickert; in another Walter Sickert was an accessory to the murders. In 1990 Walter Sickert became the lone murderer.

In her book *Sickert and the Ripper Crimes*[33] Jean Overton Fuller claimed that in 1940 when her mother, Violet Overton Fuller, was collaborating on a book with Florence Pash (1862–1951), an artist who had been a friend, associate and possibly lover of Walter Sickert, Pash dribbled out her belief that Walter Sickert was the murderer.

Walter Richard Sickert

Walter Richard Sickert was born in Munich in 1860, the eldest son of the Danish painter and illustrator Oswald Adalbert Sickert. The family moved to London in 1868 and Walter received an education at University College School, Bayswater Collegiate School, and King's College School. He had a brief and unsuccessful stage career, studied for a year at the Slade School of Art under Alphonse Legros (1837–1911), a British painter chiefly noted for graphics on macabre and fantastic themes, and at James McNeill Whistler's[34] studio in Tite Street, Chelsea. Whistler influenced Sickert, as did Edgar Degas, whom he met in Paris in 1883 and whose work influenced Sickert's 1880s paintings of music halls and theatres.

In 1885 Sickert married Ellen Cobden, the daughter of a Liberal politician, Richard Cobden, who was twelve years his senior, and the marriage was not a happy one.

Between 1885 and 1922 Sickert spent part of each year in Dieppe and in 1899, following his divorce from Ellen, he lived there for seven years, apparently suffering from paranoia. On his return to England he took lodgings at 6 Mornington Crescent and his work between that time and 1914 is known as his 'Camden Town Period'. In 1907 he created an association of artists known as the Fitzroy Street Group and in 1909 produced a series of paintings, known as the *Camden Town Murders*.[35]

In 1911, the year in which the Fitzroy Street Group became the Camden Town Group and included luminaries such as Augustus John and Percy Wyndham Lewis, Sickert married Christine Drummond Angus, a student eighteen years his junior. The marriage lasted until her death in 1920, in which year Sickert moved to Dieppe, where he lived for two years. He returned to London, became an associate of the Royal Academy in 1924, and two years later married for the third time, this time to the painter Thérèse Lessore. He became a member of the Royal Academy in 1934, in which year he moved near to Margate in Kent and took a studio at 10 Cecil Square in Margate itself. He resigned from the Royal Academy in 1935 and in 1938 moved to Bathhampton, Bath, where he died on 23 January 1942.

A Sickert expert, Wendy Baron, described him as 'handsome, witty, gallant, charming, with an intuitive understanding of women, particularly women with latent artistic talents, possessed an enormous appeal for the opposite sex. Many of his pupils could not help loving him . . .' He was eccentric, particularly in his dress, and enigmatic; he developed artistic theories and techniques throughout his career, was a prolific and influential art critic, and is regarded as a pivotal figure in the development of early-twentieth-century British art. Virginia Woolf thought Sickert's paintings each told a story: 'As I remember, his show was full of pictures that might be stories . . . The figures are motionless, of course, but each has been seized in a moment of crisis; it is difficult to look at them and not to invent a plot . . .'[36] Many of Sickert's paintings, typically his most famous, *Ennui* (c. 1913), either convey a feeling of numbing, stultifying boredom on a rainy Sunday afternoon in the depths of suburbia, or inspire a sense of unease, as if one had intruded on a painful domestic dispute. Either nothing is happening, or something is about to explode. This should be a warning to everyone who sees a Ripper meaning in his paintings: it is intended that the viewer sees what he or she wants to see, and reads into it a whole novel. Sickert painted much that was sordid or on the edge of sordidity – the rather plump nude of *La Hollandaise* (1905–6) is possibly a prostitute, the title derived from the prostitute nicknamed La Belle Hollandaise in Honoré de Balzac's *Gobseck*. He was also a prolific letter writer and wrote several hundred letters to the press.

According to the story told to Violet Overton Fuller by Florence Pash, Sickert had a studio in a street where there was a male brothel (Cleveland Street). He was looking after a baby and had employed a shopgirl (Mary Kelly) as a nanny. Florence Pash came to know the girl quite well, but she soon left Sickert's employ because her pay was irregular, being dependent on his selling a picture. She drifted to the East End and prostitution, then began blackmailing Sickert, perhaps threatening to reveal his infidelities to his wife. She was soon afterwards murdered.

Sickert for some time continued to look after the baby, and once Florence Pash took it out and was hurt in an accident when a coach drove straight at them. Walter Sickert said it was a murder attempt and Florence Pash lived in fear for a long time thereafter. The crucial part of the story, however, was that Pash said Sickert had told her that he had seen the bodies of all the Ripper's victims *in situ*. She realised this would have been possible only if Sickert was himself the murderer.

The trouble with Jean Overton Fuller's account is that she is recalling a story her mother told her several decades earlier, which Jean's mother had in turn pieced together from bits and pieces of information given to her at different times by Florence Pash, and which Florence was herself piecing together from disparate bits of 'evidence'. Moreover, Jean Overton Fuller was reasonably well versed in the story of the Ripper, having first encountered it when friendly with a one-time disciple of Aleister Crowley named Victor Neuberg and done some research.[37]

Analysis is further complicated by the fact that she was demonstrably contaminated by her reading of Knight's book.[38] But, if one accepts that before she read Knight's book Fuller had a basic story, albeit an incoherent one lacking context – and there seems no reason to suppose that her claim is untrue – then there may be a factual foundation to the Sickert/Knight story. But, as already observed, it is impossible to look at the photograph of the horribly brutalised body of Mary Kelly and believe that she was killed for revenge or, as in this theory, to silence a blackmailer.

Walter Sickert has a long-time connection with the Ripper crimes. He claimed to have once been mistaken for Jack the Ripper by a group of girls, that he took rooms previously occupied by Jack the Ripper and that he thought he knew who the Ripper was.

The story of being mistaken for the Ripper by a group of girls is related by Robert Emmons in his biography of Sickert, in which Emmons records that it happened one night as Sickert was coming home through Copenhagen

Street. Another biographer, Denys Sutton, says Sickert had visited a music hall and that he returned home dressed in 'a long check coat, long to the ankles, and carried a little black bag for his drawings. A party of young girls fled from him in terror, yelling, Jack the Ripper! Jack the Ripper!'[39]

The poet, novelist and autobiographer Osbert Sitwell recalled in his introduction to a collection of Sickert's writings,[40] that Sickert was fascinated by the case of the Tichborne Claimant, an imposter who tried to gain the estates and wealth of a missing heir called Tichborne and whom Sickert believed to be genuine, and Jack the Ripper, because he thought he knew who the Ripper was.

> He told me – and, no doubt, many others – how this was . . . Some years after the murders, he had taken a room in a London suburb. An old couple looked after the house, and when he had been there some months, the woman, with whom he used often to talk, asked him one day as she was dusting the room if he knew who had occupied it before him. When he said 'No' she had waited a moment, and then replied, 'Jack the Ripper!' . . . Her story was that his predecessor had been a veterinary student. After he had been a month or two in London, this delicate-looking young man – he was consumptive – took to staying out occasionally all night. His landlord and landlady would hear him come in at about six in the morning, and then walk about in his room for an hour or two until the first edition of the morning paper was on sale, when he would creep lightly downstairs and run to the corner to buy one. Quietly he would return and go to bed; but an hour later, when the old man called him, he would notice, by the traces in the fireplace, that his lodger had burned the suit he had been wearing the previous evening. For the rest of the day, the millions of people in London would be discussing the terrible new murder, plainly belonging to the same series, that had been committed in the small hours. Only the student seemed never to mention it: but then, he knew no one and talked to no one, though he did not seem lonely . . . The old couple did not know what to make of the matter: week by week his health grew worse, and it seemed improbable that this gentle, ailing, silent youth should be responsible for such crimes. They could hardly credit their own senses – and then, before they could make up their minds whether to warn the police or not, the lodger's health had suddenly failed alarmingly, and his mother – a widow who was

devoted to him – had come to fetch him back to Bournemouth, where she lived . . . From that moment the murders had stopped . . . He died three months later.

Before leaving the subject, I may add that, while I was engaged in writing this account of Sickert, my brother reminded me that the painter had told us that when his landlady had confided in him that morning, in the course of her dusting, the name of Jack the Ripper, he had scribbled it down in pencil on the margin of a French edition of Casanova Memoirs which he happened to be reading at the time, and that subsequently he had given the book away – we thought he had said to Sir William Rothenstein. Sickert had added, 'And there it will be now, if you want to know the name.' Accordingly, I wrote to Lady Rothenstein: but neither she nor Sir William remembered the book. On my consulting Mrs Sickert, she maintained that her husband had told her that he had given the volume to Sir William's brother, Mr Albert Rutherston. And this proved to have been the case. My friend Mr Rutherston informed me that he lost the book only during the bombing of London, and that there had been several pencil notes entered in the margin, in Sickert's handwriting, always so difficult to decipher.

A sombre and rather gloomy painting titled *Jack the Ripper's Bedroom*, dating from about 1908, is generally thought to be the room at 6 Mornington Crescent, which he took on his return from his self-imposed exile in France following the break-up of his first marriage. Denys Sutton in his biography says Sickert 'painted a picture of Jack the Ripper in 1906 (so he told Keith Baynes[41])'. If so, the painting no longer exists or has an impenetrable title, or Baynes may have misunderstood Sickert, who may in fact have been referring to *Jack the Ripper's Bedroom*.

Marjorie Lilly told how Sickert would pretend to be Jack the Ripper and have Ripper 'moods', but this was simply his theatricality coming out, and a way of getting into a certain frame of mind. He also had days when he exhibited Napoleon moods, Burns moods and Byron moods.[42]

What all this actually shows is that Walter Sickert had an interest in Jack the Ripper among a lot of other things, but if something sinister is to be read into that then we are both in trouble, you for reading this book and me for writing it. But Sickert-as-the-Ripper hit the headlines in 2002 with the publication of *Portrait of a Killer: Jack the Ripper – Case Closed* by the bestselling crime novelist Patricia Cornwell.

Portrait of a Killer was a good idea badly presented and perhaps doomed to failure before it even started. Picking on a suspect and trying to make the facts fit simply isn't good history – but applying modern forensic investigative techniques to a historical problem was a very worthy experiment, and Patricia Cornwell should be applauded not only for undertaking it but for having the guts to fund the project with her own money, albeit that the risk of complete and utter failure was probably marginal as she had a legion of fans who would have bought any book she wrote. What she shouldn't have done, however, was to claim that she had solved the mystery. She hadn't. Indeed, she had come nowhere near it, and this was manifestly obvious to reviewers around the world.

In May 2001 Patricia Cornwell visited Scotland Yard and met Deputy Assistant Commissioner John Grieve, now retired, who aired some personal suspicions about Walter Sickert's being Jack the Ripper. Intrigued, Cornwell went away and casually began to find out more about Walter Sickert. 'All I did was look at his paintings and his life, and one thing led to another . . .' What it led to was a determined and perhaps obsessive crusade to prove Sickert guilty. Eighteen months later and having spent $6 million on research, she claimed she'd done it – Jack the Ripper, case closed.

The core of Cornwell's case is that Sickert's murderous rampage was a consequence of a fistula – a hole – at the base of his penis that required three operations (two were failures), which would have made erection impossible and may have required amputation. She has further found that Walter Sickert used writing paper from the same manufacturer as used by someone who in 1888 wrote a 'Ripper' letter to Dr Openshaw of the London Hospital, and she has established that some Sickert correspondence has traces of the same DNA as found on the stamp of the Openshaw letter. Couple all this with Sickert's known interest in Jack the Ripper, that he painted his own bedroom and called the picture *Jack the Ripper's Bedroom*, that he had an interest in shocking murder, enjoyed low life, strolled on the fringes of the East End and seems singularly self-centred, and you have a compelling case.

Unfortunately, the case becomes less compelling when these points are examined a little more closely. The alleged fistula of the penis was based on a chance remark by John Lessor, a non-blood descendant. While there is no reason to disbelieve him, or Cornwell's own – and admittedly not unreasonable – argument that the number of operations the young Sickert suffered suggests that the fistula was serious, the idea is not supported by assorted other details: he received treatment at St Mark's Hospital, but, as Cornwell herself points out, St Mark's 'was dedicated to' the treatment of fistulas of the anus, rectum and vagina – not the penis. Sickert, she says, was treated by Dr Alfred Cooper (whom Cornwell incorrectly calls Alfred Duff Cooper, who was Dr Cooper's son and a statesman and first Earl Norwich), whose specialities, again, as Cornwell admits, 'were the treatment of rectal and venereal diseases'. Searches of Dr Cooper's various writings have failed to unearth any mention of his treating fistulas of the penis.

Unsurprisingly, there are no specific references to the size of Walter Sickert's member, but we know that he was married three times and some sexual dysfunction may be suggested by the fact that none of the marriages produced children. However, he was believed to have had several mistresses, was cited as an adulterer by his first wife in her divorce petition and was strongly rumoured to have had a son, Maurice, by a dramatically red-haired Dieppe fishwife named Madame Villain, known as La Belle Rousse.[43] Jacques-Emile Blanche, an intimate friend, wrote in 1902 of Sickert as 'this immoralist . . . with a swarm of children of provenances which are not possible to count.'[44]

This evidence, such as it is, suggests that Walter Sickert underwent an operation for a rectal fistula and otherwise enjoyed an active and perhaps overactive sex life.

Patricia Cornwell claims that most of the letters purporting to be from Jack the Ripper preserved in the public archives were genuinely from the murderer, and as evidence claims similarities of language, or as she expresses it, 'the unique and repeated use of linguistic combinations in multiple texts'. Unfortunately, it isn't clear what 'unique . . . linguistic combinations' she is talking about. Ripper authorities dismiss this as a ludicrous contention, arguing that the grammar, spelling, tone and handwriting of the letters vary too greatly for them to be the work of a single person, and more solidly that the similarities of language are due to the writers trying to imitate the letters they had seen published in the newspapers. They also point out that we actually know about several hoax-letter writers, two or three of whom received a degree of publicity, most famously – because she made the national press – Maria Coroner of Bradford.[45]

Cornwell is on slightly stronger ground with her paper evidence because she shows that three 'Ripper' letters, one of them to Dr Openshaw of the London Hospital, and eight letters by Walter Sickert were written on paper bearing the watermark of the famous Aberdeen-based paper manufacturer

Alexander Pirie and Sons. Unfortunately, Alexander Pirie paper was very common, perhaps the equivalent of Croxley Script or Conqueror today, so this isn't in itself remarkable. Slightly more problematic is the fact that Sickert's letters, all printed with the address 54 Broadhurst Gardens, all date between 1885 and 1887. In 1888 and later his printed stationery was a paper called Joynson Superfine, manufactured by William Joynson and Sons at St Mary Cray in Kent. Walter Sickert therefore doesn't appear to have been using paper by Alexander Pirie and Sons in 1888, and the 'Ripper' letters on Pirie paper therefore did not come from him.

What may be significant is that the stamp on the letter to Dr Openshaw bears the same DNA as on a letter written by Sickert. On the face of it this looks a very exciting piece of evidence, but there are two types of DNA. Nuclear DNA (nucDNA) is inherited from both parents, is unique to the individual and is proof of identity; but mitochondrial DNA (mtDNA) is transferred only through the maternal line, which means that people with a common maternal ancestor can share mtDNA, and that common ancestor may have lived forty or sixty generations ago, perhaps even back to the dawn of man. Millions of people can therefore share mtDNA and it isn't in any sense an identifier. Unfortunately, the nucDNA on the 'Ripper' correspondence was too degraded to be of use, so the experts went for mtDNA instead and found that an mtDNA sequence of 16294-73-263 was found on (1) the stamp of the 'Ripper' letter sent to Dr Openshaw, (2) the envelope of a bloodstained 'Ripper' letter, (3) the envelope containing a letter from Ellen Sickert, (4) the envelope of a letter from Walter Sickert and (5) the stamp on a letter by Walter Sickert. Patricia Cornwell therefore demonstrated that the letter to Dr Openshaw was written by someone using the same popular brand of paper as Walter Sickert had used six months or so earlier and that the stamp was licked by Walter Sickert or any one of the thousands of people who made up the 1 per cent of the population who shared his mtDNA. This in itself was probably a remarkable enough discovery, although some evidence on its statistical probability would have been useful, but it was very far from 'case closed', and since the Openshaw letter isn't known to be from Jack the Ripper, it shows only that Walter Sickert may have sent hoax letters.

However, the problem is that Walter Sickert may not have been in England when the murders were committed. He probably left London about mid-August. On 6 September his mother wrote from St Valéry-en-Caux, westwards from Dieppe, describing how Walter and his brother Bernhard were enjoying swimming and painting; on 16 September Jacques-Emile Blanche visited Sickert; and on 21 September Ellen, Sickert's wife, wrote to her brother-in-law that Walter had been in France for some weeks. If letters supposedly from Walter Sickert were posted when he was in Normandy, then clearly they were not from him – and, even more clearly, if he was in Normandy when the murders were committed, he wasn't the murderer.

Case open. But the saga is a long way from finished.

Anna Gruetzner Robins, a reader in the history of art at the University of Reading who has published extensively on Sickert,[46] discovered a small number of Sickert letters at the Getty Research Institute in Santa Monica, California. These were examined by Peter Bower, a distinguished forensic paper historian and paper analyst who specialises in the examination and analysis of papers for purposes of dating, attribution, authentication and usage. He found that three letters written by Sickert on his mother's stationery came from the same batch of 24 sheets of stationery as two Ripper letters. All five letters bore the watermark Gurney Ivory Laid, a paper manufactured by a company called Leppard and Smith. This company made relatively small runs of paper and the sheets were roughly guillotined to size, then folded and divided into quires (24 sheets). Each quire was then hand-guillotined, which is the important point because apparently each guillotining would be unique in some way, as is the case in this instance, and it was this that enabled Peter Bower to identify the two Ripper letters as coming from the same quire as three letters known to have been written by Sickert.

In November 2003 I participated with Peter Bower and Anna Gruetzner Robins in a symposium at Tate Britain called 'The Art of Murder: Representation and Crime in Late Victorian Britain', where Robins gave a fascinating and all too short illustrated presentation in which she argued that there are visual and linguistic reasons that link the 'Jack the Ripper' letters identified by Peter Bower as having been written by Walter Sickert to a much larger group of 'Ripper' letters, perhaps numbering as many as two hundred, and in answer to a question posed by me said that she believed he was responsible for 'Dear Boss' and the Lusk letter. Robins was not the first to conclude this either. In 1993, the graphologist Marie Bernard[47] was reported as saying that she had compared Walter Sickert's handwriting with that of the 'Dear Boss' letter and was 'absolutely convinced that Walter Sickert is the man behind the Jack the Ripper letter'.[48] She was reportedly planning to publish her findings in a book in 1994, but appears not to have done so.

Anna Gruetzner Robins dismissed the idea that Walter Sickert was Jack the Ripper, maintaining that he was simply a macabre hoaxer, but if he created the name 'Jack the Ripper', agreed by most experts to be responsible in great measure for creating the Ripper myth, then his role in this story will be far more important than that of a mere hoax-letter writer, and his behaviour in this case will of necessity force a reassessment of his life and work.

It is also hugely difficult to accept that Walter Sickert could have written more than two hundred hoax letters, especially if he was in France during September 1888, and there is the serious objection to his having authored 'Dear Boss' in the face of contemporary police opinion that it was written by a journalist, whom Chief Inspector Littlechild in his letter to George R Sims identified as Tom Bulling. But Peter Bower and Anna Gruetzner Robins are two highly qualified experts whose opinions cannot and should not be lightly dismissed. Their evidence does need to be scrutinised, however, and at the time of writing it hasn't been published in the necessary detail.

The Maybrick diary

The proposition that Jack the Ripper was a Liverpool-based cotton broker named James Maybrick who died in 1889 is different from that of other suspects because it depends not on finding verification of old memories and rumours, but on the authenticity of the so-called Maybrick diary – it isn't a diary but a sort of confessional into which the supposed author wrote and perhaps exorcised thoughts and emotions that could not be uttered else-where. The researcher is not concerned with the truth or otherwise of the internal content of the diary, although it is obviously important and has, unfortunately, been the preoccupation of the authors of two books on the subject, but on whether or not the diary itself is genuine. After all, if the diary is a fake then the content hardly matters. That said, knowing the diary to be a fake still leaves open the mystery of who faked it, when they faked it and why they faked it, which in turn may not help resolve the mystery of the Ripper's identity, but would certainly have a bearing on the historiography of the Ripper case.

Born in 1838, James Maybrick was the founder of Maybrick and Company, cotton merchants, based in Liverpool with a branch office in the cotton port of Norfolk, Virginia. His wife, several years his junior, was a

Southern belle, pretty, blue-eyed, with strawberry-blonde hair, named Florence. In 1888 they lived in a large house in Liverpool called Battlecrease and gave every appearance of happy prosperity, but James was addicted to arsenic, which was thought to aid virility. It didn't, but it apparently induces a pleasant feeling of serenity and wellbeing, sometimes of strength and confidence. His business was failing and his marriage was on the rocks. Early in 1889 James fell seriously ill, perhaps, and ironically, from the effects of arsenic withdrawal, and died. Florence was accused of murdering him. Her trial was a *cause célèbre* in its day: it was presided over by a judge who was extremely biased and also going insane, and was in almost every sense a travesty. Nevertheless, Florence was convicted and condemned to hang, but fortunately her sentence was commuted to life in prison and, after fifteen years, she was released. In 1904 she published her memoirs, *My Fifteen Lost Years*, returned to America and settled in South Kent, Connecticut, where she spent her last years as a recluse surrounded by cats – she was known locally as the 'Cat Lady' – and where on 23 October 1941 she died.

A little over half a century later, on 9 March 1992, a man calling himself Michael Williams contacted Doreen Montgomery of the respected literary agency Rupert Crew Ltd. He told her that he possessed what purported to be the diary of Jack the Ripper, in which James Maybrick told the story of how he had seen his wife with her lover (unnamed) in an area of Liverpool called Whitechapel. Tormented by this knowledge, by an unreleasable anger and by a strange excitement at the thought of his wife and her lover together, he vented his emotions on a prostitute in Manchester, and afterwards on prostitutes in Whitechapel, London. The diary continued with a rambling account of the murders and concluded with a change of heart and a full confession to Florence. The diary ends by saying, 'I give my name that all know of me, so history do tell, what love can do to a gentle man born. Yours truly, Jack the Ripper. Dated this third day of May 1889.'

Doreen Montgomery realised that someone's having the diary of Jack the Ripper was unbelievable, but there was something about what he said or the way he said it that persuaded her to invite him to bring the diary to London. Williams, who would reveal that his real name was Mike Barrett (it has never been properly established why he called himself Williams), arrived with the diary at Doreen Montgomery's office on Monday, 13 April. Two of Montgomery's clients, Shirley Harrison and her research partner Sally Evemy, were also present and were invited to investigate the diary if it proved to be something more than the suspected hoax. What they were given was what looked like a hard-covered ledger, but was in fact a special book popular with the Victorians and Edwardians and designed to hold pasted-in postcards, photographs, theatre tickets, autographs and assorted mementoes. The pages had a divider between them so that the book would close flat even when thick items like postcards and visiting cards had been pasted in. The first 64 pages had been removed; there were 63 pages of handwritten text beginning mid-sentence and concluding with the signature 'Jack the Ripper'; and the last seventeen pages were blank.

The provenance or history of the diary was unknown. Mike Barrett was casually friendly with 67-year-old Tony Devereux, who in March 1991 went into hospital for a hip replacement. Barrett afterwards visited him at home and ran occasional small errands, and on one visit in May 1991 Devereux gave him a parcel wrapped in brown paper and told him to do something with it. Barrett took it home and read it, but to his disbelieving questions Devereux would say no more than that it was genuine and that nobody else living knew it existed. In August 1991 Tony Devereux died unexpectedly in Walton hospital.

Shirley Harrison took the diary to the British Museum and afterwards to Jarndyce, a highly respected antiquarian book dealer. Both cursorily examined it, said that nothing immediately indicated it was not from the late nineteenth century, and strongly recommended proper scientific analysis. Thereafter numerous and sometimes conflicting scientific tests were conducted, with generally inconclusive results.

Over the months that followed Mike Barrett's life fell apart, his marriage collapsed irrevocably and his heavy drinking increased. Confused, hurt and generally experiencing a gamut of ever-changing emotions, he believed that the diary was at the centre of his problems and thought his wife would return to him if he got rid of it. In June 1994 he duly contacted a Liverpool journalist named Harold Brough, who had been covering the story since it broke, and confessed to having forged the diary. Brough was singularly unimpressed and wrote that Barrett had been unable to answer simple questions such as where he'd bought the 'scrapbook' and the ink.

Barrett recontacted Brough and said he'd bought the diary from an auction house named Outhwaite and Litherland and the ink from an art shop in Bluecoat Chambers, Liverpool, and he would much later describe making the purchase in greater detail, giving the lot description and numbers and the sales procedure. Kevin Whay, a director of the company, checked the company's files and archives and said that 'no such description or lot number exists. Furthermore we do not and have never conducted our sales in the manner in which he describes.'

Mike Barrett would retract the confession within a short time, which set the pattern of his behaviour over the next few years as his personal demons gained an ever firmer hold on his life. He would confess and retract, then confess again, and his story changed, sometimes in a single telling, from his being the lone forger, to forging the diary with his wife, to her being the lone forger, or to their working with others. The stories provoked a kaleidoscopic confusion.

Meanwhile, his estranged wife eventually said that her father had inherited his grandmother's possessions, which included the diary, shortly before the outbreak of World War Two, that he'd seen the diary when on leave in 1943 and had finally taken possession of it in 1950. She went on to explain that she had given the diary to Devereux to give to Barrett because she was worried by Barrett's consistently heavy drinking, but knew that he aspired to be a writer and thought he would find the diary divertingly inspirational. She said that she had done this on the spur of the moment and given it very little thought because her primary concern was to give Barrett a challenge that would keep him out of the pub while making sure that he didn't pester her terminally ill father for more information. Her story was subsequently confirmed by her now deceased father.

Nothing further has since transpired about the origins or history of the diary before Mike Barrett took it to Doreen Montgomery's office. However, a new dimension was given to the story in 1993, when a charming man named Albert Johnson reported that he had recently purchased a gold watch and found scratched on the inner case the initials of the Ripper's five canonical victims, the signature 'J. Maybrick' and the words 'I am Jack'. The watch was reportedly a woman's watch made in 1846. This has caused some people to question why James Maybrick would have carried a woman's watch, the possibility that the watch could have belonged to Florence presumably being dismissed for some reason. It has subsequently been argued that the watch is in fact a gentleman's standard dress watch. Two reputable and respected examiners have concluded that the scratches are old, Dr S Turgoose, of the University of Manchester Institute of Science and Technology's Corrosions and Protection Centre, has given his opinion that the scratches are likely to be tens of years old, are compatible with a date of 1888/9 and are not likely to be recent. The results of these tests have been disputed, which seems to be the fate of practically all the tests conducted so far, but if the scratches on the watch are indeed tens of years old then the possibility exists that they and the diary were created at the same time.

When faced with a possibly forged document the most important thing is provenance: the history of the document showing ownership over time. Poor provenance or the lack of provenance altogether is highly suspicious. In fact poor provenance is alone sufficient to brand the diary a forgery. Mike Barrett's otherwise wholly unsupported claim to have been given the diary by a man who had since died and a denial by the man's family that he had ever owned it (they said that he could not have possessed the diary without their knowing about it) is therefore very worrying indeed. Furthermore, the absence of any evidence of previous ownership can also be taken as indicating the probable forger or source of the forgery.

These and other reasons have led the majority of people to conclude that the diary is a modern forgery, probably dating from 1987 or later. But if the diary really is connected with the watch, and if the scratches on the watch really are old, then credence has to be given to the story told by Ann Graham (Barrett's wife, who reverted to her maiden name). Another factor, generally overlooked, is that over the years Mike Barrett has been desperate that his claims to have forged the diary be believed, especially when he thought his admissions might restore his marriage, and at one point he even hired a private detective to help him prove his claims and sell his story to a national newspaper. What he has never done, however, is tell a clear and coherent story of how the forgery was conceived and executed. That is to say, he has never explained who had the idea, where they had it, and what it was hoped the forgery would achieve, who else was involved, what research was done and where, how the book and ink were obtained, who obtained them, who actually conceived the plot (such as it is), who wrote the story, who penned it into the diary, how they planned to sell it, and so on. If Barrett had forged the diary, one might expect that this would have been a tale he told, maybe in ever-increasing detail. But Mike Barrett hasn't done that.

Moreover, the journalist Harold Brough was singularly unimpressed with Barrett's first confession and reported that he couldn't answer simple questions such as where he'd bought the book and the ink. Efforts to corroborate the details he later provided have failed, the auction house having denied ever having a sales procedure such as described by Barrett and having no record of the auction lot. In short, he wants it believed that he is the forger but there is no evidence that he was – and, if he wasn't, who was?

For most people the probability that the diary is a forgery is all that matters, and who forged it and why and when are unimportant. But there is a wider issue involved. In 1992, the year that Mike Barrett visited Doreen Montgomery with the Maybrick diary, Bill Gates, the CEO of Microsoft, paid a jaw-droppingly massive $30.8 million for the *Codex Leicester*, a folio of scientific observations and illustrations by Leonardo da Vinci. Other manuscripts before and since have fetched millions, and even historically trivial and insignificant historical documents, such as autographed letters, often sell for anything from hundreds to thousands of pounds. It is therefore important that we develop techniques to authenticate documents, not simply to help prevent individuals and institutions being conned into spending huge sums, but to ensure that primary source material is accurate and that bogus documents don't mislead and misdirect the proper interpretation of history.

There are recognised techniques for authenticating documents and the Maybrick diary even challenges some of these. For example, the text of a questioned document can be analysed and conclusions based on the absence of new information, lack of detail, naïveté of the writing and even the inclusion of errors attributable to other sources. A small example in the case of the diary is the content. The hoax-busting author Melvin Harris has written, 'In many ways the text is hilarious . . .' whereas David Canter, professor of psychology at the University of Liverpool, where he is the director of the Centre for Investigative Psychology, sees it as 'inventive psychological writing of the highest order'.[49] When opinion can be so divergent, it clearly isn't safe to base definitive conclusions on it.[50]

Most forgeries are created relatively close to their sale (or purpose of creation) and the forger is one or two steps removed from the buyer, or in the case of the so-called Black Diaries of Roger Casement, the question is whether or not they were written by Casement or were created contemporaneously by the British security services to blacken his character. The Maybrick diary is different. We are possibly looking at an old forgery, a con that was created but never used, and the task is not merely to authenticate the document, or otherwise, but to date as closely as possible its creation.

Who was Jack the Ripper?

Who knows! I certainly don't. In all probability he was a complete nobody who like thousands of other people in the East End lived a day-to-day existence, who may have been arrested for some other crime, may have been committed to an asylum, or may even have died of natural causes in some dosshouse, his name unknown, his secret unsuspected. Sir Robert Anderson and Chief Inspector Swanson seem to have believed he was Aaron Kosminski, and while what very little we know about him doesn't make him look like a serial killer – although I confess to being uncertain about what a serial killer is supposed to look like – one can only assume that they had good reasons for suspecting him. Perhaps more important than whether or not Aaron Kosminski was Jack the Ripper is that Anderson and Swanson would have known the evidence against all the serious suspects. If they thought the evidence against Kosminski was the strongest, they either seriously misjudged the evidence against other suspects or that evidence was weaker.

But the identity of Jack the Ripper isn't really very important. It's the story of those crimes, of the women who died, and of the society and times in which they lived that matters and that holds the enduring fascination.

Notes and References

Chapter One – A Background to the Whitechapel Murders

1. Churchill, Winston Spencer (1906), *Lord Randolph Churchill*, Vol. 1 (New York, NY: Macmillan), pp. 268–9.
2. Cited in Harris, Jose (1972), *Unemployment and Politics: A Study in English Social Policy, 1886–1914* (London: Clarendon Press), p. 54.
3. These carboniferous London fogs came to be known about 1807 as a 'London Particular' and Charles Dickens, who graphically described London's fogs in many of his novels, called it such in *Bleak House* (1853) – 'This is a London particular. A fog, miss.' These impenetrable fogs were also called pea-soupers and literature is full of many wonderful descriptions, a favourite being 'a dull, wretched vapour, like the wraith of a pecunious suicide come into a fortune immediately after the fatal deed' (Zangwill, Israel, 1895, *The Big Bow Mystery*); but they were very serious. A fog in 1813 lasted almost a week, was so dense that one couldn't see from one side of a street to the other and smelled distinctly of coal tar. A fog in 1873 increased the death rate by 40 per cent above normal, and similar increases in the death rate followed the notable fogs of January 1880 and February 1882 (along with later ones in 1891, 1892, 1948 and famously in 1952, when an estimated four thousand people died, peaking at nine hundred a day). The worst-affected area of London was usually the East End, which, being low-lying, inhibited fog dispersal, and where the density of factories and domestic dwellings was greater than almost anywhere else in the capital.
4. *Reynolds' Newspaper*, 6 January 1880. George W M Reynolds (1814–79) wrote sex-and-violence novellas with cliffhanger chapter endings, among them the bestselling *The Mysteries of London* (London: George Vickers, 1845), which enabled him to launch the *Sunday Reynolds' Newspaper* in 1850. Its content reflected its founder, mixing foreign news and politics with police news, news of labour disasters (i.e. in collieries and elsewhere), and Ireland. Sidney Webb said that in the 1880s it was

419

representative of labour opinion. It cost a penny in the 1880s, usually had eight pages and had a Saturday night and Sunday morning edition. It became the *Sunday Citizen* in 1962 and ceased publication in 1967.

5. *The Times*, 1 January 1880. Benjamin Disraeli's Conservative government, in power since 1874, was described by *Reynolds' Newspaper* (6 January 1880), as 'the worst Parliament that ever sat in England since the days of Charles the First'. It would be beaten in the general election of 1880 by the Liberals and Gladstone returned as prime minister (against the wishes of Queen Victoria, who wanted Lord Hartington). The election in 1885 returned the Conservatives to power with Lord Salisbury at the helm and an unworkably small majority that resulted in Lord Salisbury's resignation, the dissolution of his government and a short-lived return by Gladstone, whose blink-of-an-eye government was judged on his Irish Home Rule policies, the then dominant presence in British politics; in 1886 Lord Salisbury returned to power.

6. In fact the first use of the word in the context of citylike is in 1888 in the *Boston Journal*, 4 February 1888 – 'It is impossible to urbanize a country'.

7. An average of 142 out of every 1,000 live births died within the first year, which was nevertheless far better than in Austria, France, Germany, Italy and Russia. See B R Mitchell (1975), *European Historical Statistics 1750–1970* (London: Macmillan), pp. 128–9.

8. Even so, only 0.5 per cent of the population were over 80 years and only 4 per cent of the male population and 5 per cent of the female population was over 65 years.

9. The first ever supply of refrigerated meat from Australia arrived in England in February 1880 aboard the steamship *Strathleven*.

10. In 1892 there were 160 music halls providing employment for 350,000 people and the 35 largest music halls in London had a nightly audience of 45,000 people. There were additionally 200 theatres, 950 concert halls, galleries, public halls, and gardens.

11. Lawn tennis was at the height of its first popularity in the 1880s. The Lawn Tennis Association was founded on 26 January 1888 at the Freemasons' Tavern, Great Queen Street, London. William Renshaw, six times Wimbledon champion, was the first president.

12. Cycling boomed during the 1880s and by 1891 there were more than 5,000 bicycle manufacturers in England.

13. A game with ancient origins of which little seems known for certain, by the twelfth century it had become a violent mob exercise with no rules – which is today adopted by those on the terraces. Clubs were formed from 1820 onwards, but there were no agreed rules and this unsatisfactory position remained until formal rules were agreed when the Football

Association was formed at a meeting at the Old Freemasons' Tavern in London in October 1863.

14. Joseph Chamberlain (1836–1914), MP for Birmingham 1876–1910, and leader of the Radicals in the late 1870s and 1880s.

15. The famous economist Alfred Marshall (1842–1924) observed to a Royal Commission enquiring into the depressed state of the economy in 1886, he could see 'a depression of prices, a depression of interest, a depression of profits . . . I cannot see any reason for believing that there is any considerable depression in any other respect' (Mathias, p. 365).

16. *Science*, Vol. XI.

17. M J Cullen (1975), 'The 1887 Survey of the London Working Class', *International Review of Social History*, I, pp. 53, 55.

18. George Haw (1907), *From Workhouse to Westminster: The Life Story of Will Crooks, M.P.* (London: Cassell and Co.).

19. John Hollingshed (1861), *Ragged London* (London: Smith, Elder & Co.).

20. The Carlton Club was founded in 1832 as a Conservative party political organisation. The Pall Mall building was destroyed in an air raid during World War Two. The secretary of the Carlton testified that the trouble actually began when a man with a red flag addressed the crowd – this man would have been Lambeth-born John Burns, who would later lead the successful dock strike in 1889 with Ben Tillett. He became MP for Battersea in 1892 and was the first working-class government minister. He later claimed that the flag was a worker's handkerchief tied to a stick – 'the workers' flag', the title of the socialist battle hymn written by James O'Connell in 1899 and sung originally to 'The White Cockade' but most familiarly to 'Tannenbaum':

> *The worker's flag is deepest red*
> *It shrouded oft our martyred dead;*
> *And ere their limbs grew stiff and cold*
> *Their life-blood dyed its every fold.*
> *Then raise the scarlet standard high!*
> *Beneath its folds we'll live and die.*
> *Though cowards flinch and traitors sneer*
> *We'll keep the red flag flying here.*

21. George Earle Buckle (ed.) (1930), *The Letters of Queen Victoria: A Selection from Her Majesty's Correspondence and Journal Between the Years 1886 and 1901*, Vol. I (London: John Murray) pp. 52–3.

22. Philip Magnus (1954), *Gladstone: A Biography* (London: John Murray), p. 363.

23. Hugh Culling Eardley Childers, 1827–96.

24. Roy Jenkins (1995; 1997), *Gladstone* (London: Macmillan; New York: Random House), p. 544.

25. He published three books on these experiences, *The Recovery of Jerusalem* (1871), *Underground Jerusalem* (1874), and *The Temple or the Tomb* (1880).

26. Edward Henry Palmer had been sent in June 1882 on a secret-service mission, but had vanished during the night of 10–11 August. Warren and two companions undertook an intricate enquiry and discovered the party had been ambushed and shot by the Arabs. Warren tracked down the murderers, who were duly executed. Warren received the KCMG and in 1883 he was created a knight of justice of the Order of St John of Jerusalem.

27. That Warren was an autocrat who wanted everything done his own way, rather than a leader brought in to enforce discipline and who then had his hands tied by a vacillating home secretary, is an image that has succeeded in obscuring the truth. Belton Cobb, a commentator who should have known better, called Warren 'an autocratic, elderly soldier who wanted to run everything his own way – the military way.' Belton Cobb (1956), *Critical Years at the Yard* (London: Faber and Faber), p. 226. Warren, at 46, was hardly elderly. At least I hope not.

28. *The Times*, 20 March 1886.

29. Saul David (1997), *Military Blunders* (London: Constable Robinson), p. 35.

30. An effort was made to do so by an anonymous author – actually Warren himself under a pseudonym, 'Defender' (1902), *Sir Charles Warren and Spion Kop: A Vindication* (London: Smith Elder & Co.).

31. '[T]he chief fault lay in the disinclination of the officer in supreme command to assert his authority and see that what he thought best was done.' Quoted in J Symons (1963), *Buller's Campaign* (London: Cresset Press), p. 568.

32. The best known today are probably *Lyon v. Home* (1868), an action brought against a spiritualist; the Tichborne case (1869), when an imposter claimed to be a wealthy missing heir; and most famously *Crawford v. Crawford and Dilke* (1886), which brought about the political downfall of Sir Charles Dilke.

33. Robert Arthur Talbot Gascoyne Cecil, 3rd Marquis of Salisbury (1830–1903), whose family had played a part in politics since William Cecil, Queen Elizabeth I's Lord Burghley.

34. R H William (1988), *The Salisbury–Balfour Correspondence 1869–1892* (Hitchin: Hertfordshire Record Society), A J Balfour to Lord Salisbury, 28 January 1889.

35. Robert Rhodes James (1959), *Lord Randolph Churchill* (London: Weidenfeld and Nicolson), p. 245. In fairness, it should be pointed out

that Matthews never asked for the office of home secretary and 'He was so flabbergasted by the offer of a secretaryship of State that he left Arlington House under the impression that he had declined, but, finding himself gazetted Home Secretary the next day, accepted his fate.' Shane Leslie (1921), 'Henry Matthews Lord Llandaff', *The Dublin Review*, vol. 168, January.

36. Sir Robert Ensor (1936), *England 1870–1914*, Oxford History of England series (Oxford: Oxford University Press).

37. Andrew Roberts (1999), *Salisbury: Victorian Titan* (London: Weidenfeld and Nicolson), pp. 506–7.

38. Matthews had won a marginal seat, which Salisbury's government could not afford to put at risk with an election, so Matthews's attempted resignations were turned down. He could not be dismissed and quiet removal would have generated all sorts of potentially damaging and definitely unwanted speculation.

39. There is an unpublished biography of Henry Matthews by W S Lilly.

40. Oliver Ransford (1969), *The Battle of Spion Kop* (London: John Murray), p. 33.

41. Watkin Wynn Williams (1941), *The Life of General Sir Charles Warren: By His Grandson* (Oxford: Blackwell), p. 220. 'Bradford' was Sir Edward Bradford, commissioner 1890–1903.

42. Sir Robert Anderson (1910), *The Lighter Side of My Official Life* (London: Hodder and Stoughton), p. 126.

43. Shane Leslie (1921), 'Henry Matthews Lord Llandaff', *The Dublin Review*, vol. 168, January, pp. 1–22, places much emphasis on how Matthews 'kept officials at a distance through his secretaries'. And George Dilnot (1930) in *The Story of Scotland Yard* (London: Geoffrey Bles), p. 97, refers to 'the friction that notoriously existed between Sir Godfrey Lushington and the high officials of the police'.

44. MEPO 2/182, Warren to Matthews, 31 October 1887.

45. Sir Robert Ensor, op. cit., p. 180: 'Warren alternately permitted and prohibited them [the meetings]; but the more the police interfered, the larger the meetings became.'

46. Annie Besant (1893), *An Autobiography* (London: T Fisher Unwin), p. 325.

47. Ibid., p. 327.

48. Sir Robert Ensor, op. cit., p. 181.

49. MEPO 2/248, Matthews to Monro, 3 May 1890.

50. A commentator quoted by Andrew Roberts (1999), *Salisbury: Victorian Titan* (London: Weidenfeld and Nicolson), p. 471.

51. Andrew Roberts, ibid., p. 471.

52. *East London Observer*, letter from RJW to editor.

53. In these cases the demolition was done to get rid of the rookeries and disperse their populations. The land cleared in the case of Farringdon Street remained unused for thirty years, becoming popularly known as 'Farringdon Waste'. The people displaced had little choice but to stay in the areas, especially if they lived close to their employment, so they simply moved into the neighbouring slum district, making it even more overcrowded.

54. See Gareth Stedman Jones (1971; 1976), *Outcast London: A Study in the Relationships between Classes in Victorian Society* (Oxford: Oxford University Press; Harmondsworth, Middlesex: Penguin Books).

55. General Booth called his book *In Darkest England: The Way Out*, imitating H M Stanley's *Into Darkest Africa*.

56. Although when he appeared before a Royal Commission on the Housing of the Working Classes he was willing only to claim of incest that 'you do meet with it and frequently meet with it, but not very frequently'.

57. In 1885, fired by genuine belief and real passion, W T Stead set out to expose in a series of articles called 'Maiden Tribute of Modern Babylon' the sins of child prostitution and white slavery. To prove how easily it could be done, he bought a young girl named Eliza Armstrong for the purpose of prostitution from her mother for £5. Stead would suffer for his act, even though he took every precaution to ensure the safety of the child, and was sent to prison for three months because legally the father had right to the child, not the mother, who was not in a position to sell her.

58. See Anthony S Wohl (ed.) (1970), *The Bitter Cry of Outcast London with leading articles from the Pall Mall Gazette of October 1883 and articles by Lord Salisbury, Joseph Chamberlain and Forster Crozier* (London: Leicester University Press).

59. Britain's narrow victory in the Boer War (1899–1902) caused poverty to be critically re-examined and many Imperialists, Liberal economists and Fabian socialists (including Bernard Shaw, Sidney Webb and H G Wells) seriously advanced schemes for the compulsory elimination of the 'idle and incompetent' (perhaps a tenth of London's population), and, had the problem not been eliminated by the First World War it is likely that William H Beveridge and Winston Churchill at the Board of Trade would have turned them into government policy.

60. In 1886 Clementina Black became a member of the Women's Trade Union League and travelled the country trying to persuade women to join trade unions. In 1889 she helped form the Women's Trade Union Association.

61. 'The pity is that the match girls have not been suffered to take their own course, but have been egged on to strike by irresponsible advisers. No effort has been spared by those posts of the modern industrial world, the Social Democrats, to bring the quarrel to a head.' *The Times*, 14 July 1888.

62. Bryant and May continued to have a hard time. Annie Besant and her followers began to campaign against the continued use of yellow phosphorus and in 1891 the Salvation Army opened a match-making factory in Old Ford, East London, using harmless red phosphorus and paid the workers almost twice as much as Bryant and May. It took until 1901 before the managing director of Bryant and May, Gilbert Bartholomew, announced the cessation of their use of yellow phosphorus.

63. A prolific letter writer to *The Times*, where he signed himself S.G.O. A long letter published on 18 September 1888 inspired one of the most famous 'Ripper' cartoons to appear in *Punch*, 'The Nemesis of Neglect', published on 29 September 1888.

64. London: Smith, Elder, 1888; New York: Macmillan, 1888.

65. Mrs Humphry Ward (1851–1920), whose real name was Mary Augusta Arnold, was the granddaughter of Dr Thomas Arnold – head of Rugby School at the time of Thomas Hughes's *Tom Brown's Schooldays* – and niece of Matthew Arnold. Born in Tasmania, she moved to England with her family in 1856. She married Thomas Humphry Ward, fellow and tutor of Brasenose College, Oxford. In 1881 he joined the staff of *The Times* and they moved to London, where she believed her religious beliefs could benefit the poor and weak. She emulated Robert Elsmere by founding a largely Unitarian settlement for the poor in London, which later became the Passmore Edwards Settlement in Tavistock Square (after John Passmore Edwards, who financed it). Curiously she was anti-suffrage and the first president of the Anti-Suffrage League in 1908.

66. In *The Nineteenth Century*, 1888.

67. Some twenty years earlier Hall Caine had formed a friendship with and had possibly briefly been the lover of Francis Tumblety, an American quack doctor who died very rich and was in 1888 suspected by Scotland Yard of being Jack the Ripper or otherwise connected with the crimes. For a biography of this now all-but-forgotten celebrity in his day, see Vivien Allen (1997), *Hall Caine: Portrait of a Victorian Romancer* (Sheffield: Sheffield Academic Press), pp. 37–40.

68. It has been claimed that among the interesting things about the surviving recordings of Gus Elen, apart from their intrinsic value, is his original Victorian cockney dialect, now literally a thing of the past.

69. His full name was Albert Onesime Britannicus Gwathveoyd Louis Chevalier. His autobiography (1901) was *Before I Forget* (London: T Fisher & Unwin).

70. Peter Vasili (1998), *The First Black Footballer: Arthur Wharton 1865–1930: An Absence of Memory* (London: Frank Cass). The Football League was the brainchild of a director at Aston Villa and the owner of a

linen draper's shop near Villa Park in Birmingham named William McGregor. It is generally accepted that Jack Gordon of Preston scored the first goal of the new competition, and North End won the FA Cup.

71. Thomas Scott Baldwin (1854–1923), made his first balloon ascent in 1875 and soon became a star attraction at county fairs all over the United States. By 1885 the novelty had begun to grow thin and when seeking another daring novelty he redesigned the rigid parachute invented a century before, made it flexible so that it was easy to pack, and took to parachuting from his balloon. He made his first parachute jump in January 1885 (some sources say on 4 July 1887). He would ascend on a small seat, then detach himself from the balloon and, when the chute had filled sufficiently to float him down, he detached himself from the seat. He has been dubbed 'the father of the modern parachute'. He died in 1923 and was buried with full military honours at Arlington National Cemetery, Virginia. The airport at Baldwin Field, Quincy, Illinois, is named after him.

72. For those interested in such things, *The Oxford English Dictionary* gives 1888 as the first recorded use of the word 'parachutist', it being used in an article in the *Weekly Scotsman* on 6 October, when it referred to 'Mr. Baldwin, the now well-known balloonist and parachutist'.

73. Reid started ballooning shortly after joining the police force and was once described as 'the most daring balloonist of the early eighties'. In the 1870s he made a parachute jump from a balloon at a height of 1,000 feet. In 1883 he was awarded a gold medal to commemorate his record ascent in the balloon *Queen of the Meadow*. He made 23 ascents from the Crystal Palace and Alexandra Palace. For a more detailed account of Reid's life see Nicholas Connell and Stewart P Evans (2000), *The Man Who Hunted Jack the Ripper: Edmund Reid and the Police Perspective* (Cambridge: Rupert Books).

74. The Edison Phonograph Company was formed on 8 October 1887. It wasn't tinfoil but strips of lead with grooves etched into them and the first wax cylinders Edison used were white and made of ceresin, beeswax, and stearic wax.

Chapter Two – The Beginning

1. *Reynolds' Newspaper*, 29 October 1950.
2. *Daily Telegraph*, 10 September 1888 (repeated verbatim in the *Woodford Times*, 14 September 1888). The *East London Advertiser*, 14 September 1888, reported, 'Since Christmas week in 1887 nine women have been

murdered in the East-end . . . An unknown woman found murdered near Osborne and Wentworth streets, Whitechapel'.

3. *East London Observer*, 15 September 1888.
4. *Manchester Guardian*, 13 November 1888.
5. Some sources give the name as Hames. *The Times*, not always the most reliable of sources, says her name was Margaret Hayes.
6. According to Nicholas Connell and Stewart P Evans (2000), *The Man Who Hunted Jack the Ripper: Edmund Reid and the Police Perspective* (Cambridge: Rupert Books).
7. Connell and Evans (ibid.), pp. 15–19; *Reynolds' Newspaper*, 15 January 1888.
8. *Lloyds Weekly News*, 11 January 1891.
9. George R Sims (1917), *Glances Back* (London: Jarrolds).
10. Philip Sugden (2002), *The Complete History of Jack the Ripper* (London: Robinson); first published in 1994.
11. *Eastern Post*, 7 April 1888.
12. *East London Advertiser*, 7 April 1888.
13. Death certificate.
14. *East London Advertiser*, 7 April 1888.
15. *East London Advertiser*, 31 March 1888.
16. Although Philip Sugden, presumably drawing on the London Hospital's patient admissions register (1888), says she was 39. See Sugden, op cit.
17. See *East London Advertiser*, *East London Observer* and *Eastern Post*, 31 March 1888, for the story.
18. *Eastern Post*, 31 March 1888.
19. Martin Fido (1987), *The Crimes, Detection and Death of Jack the Ripper* (London: Weidenfeld and Nicolson); revised edition, 1989 (London: Weidenfeld and Nicolson); 1993 (New York, NY: Barnes and Noble).
20. Sugden, op. cit.
21. The newspapers (*East London Advertiser*, 14 April 1888, for example) state that she was a widow, but the London Hospital admission registers state that she was married and give her occupation as charwoman. See London Hospital, Patient Admission Register, 1888.
22. Mary Russell's inquest testimony reported in *Walthamstow and Leyton Guardian*, 14 April 1888.
23. In 1910 Dr Hawley Harvey Crippen murdered his horrendous wife, dismembered her body and buried her in the basement of their house. He then fled across the Atlantic with his mistress, Ethel Le Neve, aboard the ocean liner *Montrose*, hotly pursued by Walter Dew of Scotland Yard aboard the *Laurentic*. The newspapers followed the chase with considerable enthusiasm, ensuring Crippen, who was caught and executed, a notoriety that far exceeded the novelty of his crime. On the outbreak of World War

One in 1914 the Admiralty requisitioned the *Laurentic* for use as an armed merchant cruiser, and on 25 January 1917 she struck a mine off the northern coast of County Donegal, Ireland. She sank with the loss of 350 lives. She was carrying about £5 million in gold bullion, later recovered.

24. Walter Dew (1938), *I Caught Crippen: Memoirs of Ex-Chief Inspector Walter Dew C.I.D.* (London: Blackie and Son), p. 92. Dew must be reciting information received at second hand because he doesn't hint that he knew Emma Smith. And it should be noted that his account is otherwise faulty, for although he recalls much that is accurate, such as the location of the assault, he incorrectly says that a man found her there lying unconscious and bleeding to death. This is not impossible because Emma Smith was somewhere for the hour or more between the attack and reaching her lodging.

25. *The Times*, 14 April 1888.

26. It has been suggested that this is the origin of the story of Fairy Fay. Terence Robinson, writing in *Reynolds' Newspaper*, 29 October 1950, gives this name to a woman who was supposedly murdered on 26 December 1887, but nothing has been found to support the story.

27. Sir Frederick Treves (1923), *The Elephant Man and Other Reminiscences* (London: Cassell), pp. 54–5; reprinted 1980 (London: Star Books).

28. He is called Mr George Haslip in Inspector Reid's report, Dr Hellier in *Lloyd's Weekly News*, Sunday, 8 April 1888 and Dr G H Hillier in the *Morning Advertiser*, Monday, 9 April 1888.

29. Dew, op. cit., p. 92.

Chapter Three – Martha Tabram

1. Philip Sugden (2002), *The Complete History of Jack the Ripper* (London: Robinson); first published in 1994.

2. William Turner, the man with whom Martha Tabram 'took up', told the inquest that he had been living with her on and off for about nine years.

3. Inquest testimony, *East London Observer*, 25 August 1888.

4. Report by Inspector E Ellisdon, 10 August 1888, MEPO 3/140, fol. 238.

5. *East London Advertiser*, 24 August 1888.

6. *Eastern Post* and *East London Advertiser*, 25 August 1888.

7. That she thought it was the White Swan was reported in the *East London Advertiser*, 25 August 1888.

8. This sighting is often placed much later, at 11 p.m., but the *Eastern Post*, 25 August 1888, gave the earlier time and quoted Mrs Morris as saying Martha was alone. Given that at 11 p.m. she was with Connelly, the earlier time seems possible.

9. *East London Advertiser*, 18 August 1888.

10. *East London Observer*, 25 August 1888.

11. *East London Advertiser*, 25 August 1888.

12. MEPO 3/140, fol. 38.

13. *East London Observer*, 11 August 1888.

14. *East London Advertiser*, 11 August 1888.

15. *East London Observer*, 18 August 1888.

16. Alfred George Crow, inquest testimony, variously reported, but see *East London Advertiser* and *East London Observer*, 11 August 1888. The physical description was given in the latter.

17. Report by Inspector E Ellisdon, 10 August 1888, MEPO 3/140, fol. 238.

18. *East London Observer*, 11 August 1888.

19. 'Then in reply to questions from the coroner as to whether he could tell whether the wounds were made by a right or left-handed person, the doctor said one of the wounds might have been made by a left-handed man, but not the others' (*East London Advertiser*, 11 August 1888).

20. *East London Advertiser*, 11 August 1888.

21. *East London Observer*, 11 August 1888.

22. MEPO 3/140, fol. 34.

23. At the inquest Pearly Poll had made an ambiguous statement to the effect that there had been an argument about money 'but not with the deceased', which suggests that it was either between the soldiers or between one or both the soldiers and Poll. It may have been an argument about the charge for her 'services'.

24. He said that he had spent that night drinking in Brixton with a Private Law, but Law had wandered off while Leary was relieving himself behind a building. Leary had then headed to the Strand, where at 4.30 a.m. he met Law and together they went for a drink in a pub near Billingsgate, returning to the barracks at 6 a.m. Law independently corroborated Leary's story. See MEPO 3/140, fol. 40.

25. Which at the time of writing still exists and is an attractive community pub, but how long it will last amid the redevelopment in Kingston remains to be seen. See *Kingston Borough Guardian*, 6 December 2002.

26. Eli Caunter, whose nickname was 'Tommy Roundhead', according to Frederick Porter Wensley (1931), *Detective Days* (London: Cassell), p. 13.

27. MEPO 3/140, fol. 54.

28. Ibid., fol. 45.

29. Variously reported, but see *East London Observer*, 18 August 1888.

30. MEPO 3/140, fol. 42.

31. Walter Dew (1938), *I Caught Crippen: Memoirs of Ex-Chief Inspector Walter Dew C.I.D.* (London: Blackie and Son), p. 103.

32. *East London Observer*, 11 August 1888.
33. *East London Advertiser*, 11 August 1888.
34. Ibid., 25 August 1888.
35. 'Whatever may be said about the death of Emma Smith there can be no doubt that the August Bank Holiday murder, which took place in George Yard Buildings, less than a hundred yards from the spot where the first victim died, was the handiwork of the dread Ripper.' Dew, op. cit., p. 97.

Chapter Four – Mary Ann Nichols

1. Variously called 'George Cross' (which is a medal) by *The Times*, and he is so named by several authors who understandably accepted the authority of that newspaper.
2. His address at the time of his daughter's murder was 16 Maidswood Road, Camberwell.
3. In 1887 she lied to the Strand Board of Guardians, describing her father as her stepfather and saying she'd lived with him for about three years, claiming that her father, William, a printer, was dead, and saying that she didn't know the date of her birthday but that she thought it was August 1851. This false story for a while misled researchers into thinking that she was only twelve when she married William Nichols. In reality it was her mother who was only twelve, the minimum age of consent, when she married eighteen-year-old Edward Walker on 17 February 1840.
4. The marriage was performed by Charles Marshall, vicar of Saint Bride's Parish Church, and witnessed by Seth George Havelly and Sarah Good, who were provided by the parish (see Neal Shelden (1999), *Jack the Ripper and His Victims* (Hornchurch, Essex: Neal Shelden).
5. The street was built about 1799 on the site of Whitefriars Priory (mentioned by Shakespeare in *Richard III*), a fourteenth-century vaulted crypt of great beauty from the monastery being preserved under the current number 30, built in the 1930s. *Punch*, which was to poke barbed comic fun at the Metropolitan Police and home secretary during the Ripper's Autumn of Terror, had its offices here.
6. This was a housing block, austere and architecturally uninspiring – Nikolaus Pevsner described a similar block at Wild Street as 'familiar but nonetheless detestable' – but designed to be 'cheap, cleanly, well-drained and healthful dwellings for the poor'. It was built with money provided by the American philanthropist George Peabody 'to ameliorate the condition of the poor and needy of the great metropolis and to promote their comfort and happiness'. The financing fund, called the Peabody

Donation Fund, which continues to this day, built its first development in Commercial Street, Spitalfields.

7. Holborn Board of Guardians, Mitcham Workhouse Record, 6 February 1888.

8. On 27 June 1876 Mary Ann left home and went to Lambeth Workhouse, where she stayed until 2 July. In December she gave birth to a girl, Eliza Sarah, at 3 J-Block and on 1 February the following year, when she registered the birth of the child, she gave her address as 3 D-Block, but William Nichols at that time appears to have been living at 6 D-Block. From all this it looks as if William Nichols had moved out of the family home in favour of Mary Ann, who may have moved into 3 J-Block for the delivery of her child.

9. Inquest testimony. For a short time in 1883 Mary Ann Nichols had lived with her father. He said that although she was not in the habit of staying out late at night and not, he thought, 'fast' with men, she had been a heavy drinker and this had led to friction and an argument. The following morning Mary had left.

10. *Daily Telegraph*, 10 September 1888.

11. At the inquest her husband was asked whether the man in question was 'the blacksmith' – a reference to Drew – and he said, 'No; it was not the same; it was another man. I had her watched. Witness further deposed that he did not leave his wife, but that she left him of her own accord. She had no occasion for so doing. If it had not been for her drinking habits they would have got on all right together' (*Daily Telegraph*, 4 September 1888).

12. *South London Chronicle*, 5 June 1886, carried a report of Edward Walker's death. He had been talking with his wife in the kitchen of their home in Camberwell and they were readying themselves for bed. Walker had been in the process of putting out a paraffin lamp when his hair caught alight. His wife screamed for help and their lodger rushed into the kitchen and extinguished the fire, but Walker had sustained severe burns, from which he died on 1 June 1886.

13. Nichols was the subject of an 'order of removal' from Holborn Union to Lambeth Union effected on 16 April 1888. This was under the provisions governing 'settlement'. Where a pauper had not acquired a settlement in a locality by the prerequisite period of residence without chargeability, the Board of Guardians might, after giving immediate relief, apply to the justices for an order removing the pauper to the authority with whom settlement had last been acquired.

14. Testimony of Mary Ann Monk (*The Times*, 1 September 1888).

15. £3 according to *The Times*, 1 September 1888.

16. *The Times*, 4 September 1888.

17. *Illustrated Police News*, 8 September 1888: 'She had a dark complexion, brown eyes, and brown hair, turning grey.' Also described as such on a form in the police files HO/144/221/A49301, fols. 129-134.
18. *East London Observer*, 1 September 1888.
19. Five teeth missing: variously reported as part of Dr Llewellyn's inquest testimony, but see *The Times*, 3 September 1888.
20. *East London Observer*, 8 September 1888.
21. Inquest testimony: *The Times*, 4 September 1888.
22. Inquest testimony: *Woodford Times*, 7 September 1888.
23. Inquest testimony: *East London Observer*, 8 September 1888.
24. *East London Observer*, 1 September 1888.
25. *East London Observer*, 8 September 1888.
26. *The Star*, 1 September 1888.
27. Called Ellen Holland in the police report – HO/144/221/A49301, fols. 129–134 – and some newspapers; Emily Holland in the *East London Observer* and the *Illustrated Police News*, 8 September 1888; Jane Hodden in the *Manchester Guardian*, 4 September 1888; and Jane Oram in *The Times*, 4 September 1888. She was described as the lodging house keeper in the *Woodford Times*, 7 September 1888, and in the *Daily Telegraph*, 4 September 1888. At the inquest she said that Nichols 'has not been in my house for the last ten days' (*East London Observer*, 8 September 1888).
28. A fire at London docks broke out shortly before 8.30 p.m. at one of the huge South Quay Warehouses, but delays notifying Whitechapel and other fire stations enabled the blaze to gain a hold. By 9 p.m. it was extremely fierce and visible for miles around. An enormous crowd gathered around the dockyard gates to watch as firemen, policemen and dock officers battled to extinguish the blaze, which had diminished by 11 o'clock but would not be finally extinguished until several hours later.
29. The original cottages and a small piece of land used for stabling had been demolished in 1875–6 when the East London Railway was put in. New Cottage was built in its place and was itself demolished sometime before 1948. For some time a garage-like structure replaced it, now also demolished but appearing in some of the more recent surviving photographs of the street.
30. Leonard Matters (1929), *The Mystery of Jack the Ripper* (London: Hutchinson); with a new introduction (1948) (London: W H Allen); n.d. (London: Pinnacle Books); original edition published as a paperback (1964) (London: Arrow).
31. *The Times*, 1 September 1888.
32. '[A] rough looking man', *Illustrated Police News*, 8 September 1888; 'a roughly dressed young fellow of low stature', *The Star*, 3 September 1888.

33. Wood's Buildings: *The Star*, 3 September 1888.

34. *The Times*, 4 September 1888.

35. *Illustrated Police News*, 8 September 1888.

36. *The Star*, 31 August 1888; *East London Advertiser*, 1 September 1888; *Weekly Herald*, 7 September 1888. The story seems to have had its origins with the Central News Agency.

37. *New York Times*, 1 September 1888. Also reported in *British Daily Whig* (Canada) on 1 September 1888.

38. *The Star*, 5 September 1888.

39. *Daily Telegraph*, 1 September 1888.

40. *The Star*, 5 September 1888.

41. *Daily Telegraph*, 1 September 1888.

42. *The Times*, 3 September 1888, spells the name 'Kerby', but the spelling is 'Kirby' in MEPO 3/140 fol. 242. Henry Kirby joined the Metropolitan Police on 4 May 1874 as PC 413 'S' (Warrant No. 57839), aged nineteen, the son of a policeman. He was elevated to second-class constable on 23 August 1878, first-class constable on 13 May 1882, and sergeant on 28 April 1884, being transferred to Bethnal Green police station. He was later severely reprimanded and demoted to first-class constable for 'improperly entering a public-house with a constable while on duty'. He was transferred to the Hampstead Division, and a twist of irony saw him moved back to the East End a week later to augment the men engaged in the hunt for the Ripper. In 1895 he was twice suspended with loss of pay for being drunk on duty. He managed to stay out of trouble thereafter and resigned on 7 May 1899 with a pension and took a job as a 'customs watcher' in the London Docks. See Bernard Brown (2003),'The Rise and Fall of Sergeant Kirby', *Ripperologist*, Issue 46, May.

43. Some sources gave his initial as 'G' or called him 'George' – see *The Star*, 3 September 1888, for example.

44. At the inquest PC Mizen testified that he had been approached by Cross and Paul, and that Cross had said to him, 'You are wanted in Buck's Row by a policeman; a woman is lying there.' Neither man, he maintained, had told him the woman was dead. This directly contradicted the testimony of Cross, who in any event hadn't seen a policeman in or near Buck's Row and therefore wouldn't have told PC Mizen that he was wanted by one. Cross was specifically questioned on this point at the inquest, and, asked if he'd told Constable Mizen that another policeman wanted him in Buck's Row, Cross had replied, 'No; because I did not see a policeman in Buck's Row.'

45. *Illustrated Police News*, 8 September 1888.

46. Or so he was reported to have said. At the inquest PC Neil said his words were, 'Here's a woman has cut her throat. Run at once for the doctor.'

47. *The Times*, 18 September 1888, which gives PC Thain the name 'Phail', gives the alternative testimony that 'he did not take his cape to the slaughterer's but sent it by a brother constable. When he was sent for the doctor he did not first go to the horse-slaughterer's and say that a murder had been committed he had better fetch his cape.' However, *Illustrated London News*, 22 September 1888, stated that at the inquest PC Thain said that 'he went to fetch his cape because he did not know where he would be sent by his inspector.'

48. *The Times*, 3 September 1888.

49. I do not know if this man was ever identified, but, though the expression 'old man' is a common one, it is interesting to note that Matthew Packer, who claimed to have sold some fruit to a later Ripper victim named Elizabeth Stride, said that a man had told him, 'Well, what's the price of the black grapes, old man?' And, on being told, had replied, 'Well, then, old man, give us a half a pound of the black.'

50. *East London Observer*, 8 September 1888.

51. *The Times*, 18 September 1888.

52. *The Star*, 31 August 1888; *East London Advertiser*, 1 September 1888.

53. *East London Observer*, 1 September 1888.

54. *The Times*, 1 September 1888.

55. The workhouse had an evil reputation of long standing. As far back as 1838 the *London Medical Gazette* (1837–8, vol. 21) recorded that a boy named Henry Bailey had been flogged to death there. At the inquest held at Norwood in Surrey on 26 January 1838 it was reported that Bailey, whose age was not given, had been flogged by Mr Rowe of the Lambeth Workhouse to a degree where the back, thighs, legs and arms were nearly covered with black marks. Still alive, he had then been taken from the Workhouse to the House of Industry at Norwood – used for the infant poor of the Parish of Lambeth – and died there six days later. It was stated that Mr Rowe apparently died on the morning the boy was taken to Norwood and was thus beyond punishment. How he'd died was not stated, but one hopes it was painfully. At the inquest it was debated whether Bailey had died from the severity of the whipping, from a disease of the lungs discovered during the postmortem examination or from the disease as exacerbated by the beating. Mr W Street, a surgeon giving evidence, sarcastically observed that the question was a 'very nice legal point'. Lambeth Workhouse achieved a degree of fame in much later years because in 1895 Charles Chaplin (then aged seven) became an inmate together with his mother and his younger brother Sydney. The

two children were later transferred to Hanwell School for Orphans and Destitute Children, while Charles's mother, who had suffered a mental breakdown, was sent to the Cane Hill Lunatic Asylum. In 1922, the workhouse and infirmary were amalgamated and renamed Lambeth Hospital and in 1930 its administration was taken over by the London County Council. The infirmary and most of the workhouse have now been demolished.

56. One was the 'Old Nichol gang', so called from the district around Old Nichol Street, Bethnal Green; another, which gained brief notoriety, was called 'the High-rip' from Hoxton.

57. *The Times*, 1 September 1888.

Chapter Five – Theories Abound, But Facts Are Scarce

1. *Leytonstone Express and Independent*, 8 September 1888.
2. *East London Observer*, 8 September 1888.
3. The Forester's story is variously reported and seems to have originated with the Central News Agency. See: *Manchester Guardian*, 4 September 1888; *Daily Telegraph*, 7 September 1888; *East London Advertiser*, 8 September 1888; *East London Observer*, 8 September 1888; and *Eastern Argus*, 8 September 1888. For an account of the attack by Hummerston see *Daily Telegraph*, 6 September 1888.
4. *The Star*, 1 September 1888.
5. Sir Robert Anderson (1910), *The Lighter Side of My Official Life* (London: Hodder and Stoughton), p. 128.
6. A department for plain-clothes detectives had been created at Scotland Yard in 1842 against a background of considerable opposition from people who believed it smacked of secret police and espionage. It was widely frowned upon until recent times, and the fears seemed to bear fruit in 1877, when three detective inspectors were convicted and jailed for accepting bribes. The scandal rocked the force and led to enquiries that, among other things, revealed that the uniformed police had better pay and promotion prospects. The detective branch therefore failed to attract the best men. The attitude towards detectives is also highly revealing and wholly bizarre to the modern observer because even within the force detective work was thought to be extremely distasteful and alien to the morally upright man. Superintendent (and later Chief Constable) Adolphus Williamson, who headed the detective branch until 1889, wrote in 1880 that the best men weren't attracted to detective work because the uncertain and irregular duties involved them in 'contact with the worst

classes, frequently cause unnecessary drinking, and compel them at times to resort to trickey [*sic*] practices', which he thought were 'very distasteful and repugnant to the better class of men' (Memorandum by F A Williamson, 22 October 1880, in MEPO 2/134). The enquiries resulted in improved pay and promotion prospects for detectives, reorganised and reborn on 8 April 1878 as the Criminal Investigation Department (CID), which in turn caused all the friction with the uniformed branch that Sir Charles Warren sought to resolve. Had he succeeded, rather than Monro, in the future the emphasis might have been placed on good general preventive policing rather than on catching criminals after the crime had been committed.

7. *The Penny Illustrated Paper and Illustrated Times*, 8 December 1888.
8. James Monro's memoirs, unpublished and discovered by Keith Skinner. Copy in the author's collection.
9. Ibid.
10. Commonly but erroneously believed to have evolved from Scotland Yard's Irish Branch, 'Section B'.
11. The policemen employed in the Secret Department were Chief Inspector Littlechild and Inspectors Pope, Melville and Burke.
12. Monro was probably justified, Chief Constable Frederick Adolphus ('Dolly') Williamson having become ill through overwork and who probably died prematurely as a consequence.
13. Monro to Warren, 15 February 1888: HO144/190/A46472B, sub. 9; and Bernard Porter (1987), *The Origins of the Vigilant State: The London Metropolitan Police Special Branch before the First World War* (London: Weidenfeld and Nicolson), p. 87.
14. Monro to Warren, 19 March 1888. HO144/190/A46472B, sub. 6.
15. This was embarrassing for Monro, who had already told Macnaghten that the job was his.
16. *The Star* reported the whole debacle without naming names: 'A gentleman of large Indian experience was recommended for the post, with the acquiescence of the Chief Commissioner, and the recommendation was formally made to the Secretary of State. But before the appointment had been actually made Sir Charles Warren withdrew his recommendation, on the ground that circumstances had come to his knowledge which made it undesirable that the gentleman in question should be appointed. The appointment was never made, and the question of creating the new post remains in abeyance. This did not improve the relations between Sir Charles Warren and Mr. Monro.'
17. *The Star*, 5 September 1888.
18. *East London Advertiser*, 13 October 1888.

19. Anderson, op. cit., p. 129.
20. Ibid., p. 134.
21. Porter, op. cit., p. 84.
22. Richard Southwell Bourke, sixth Earl of Mayo 1822–72, was appointed chief secretary for Ireland in Lord Derby's short-lived administration of 1858–9, and again during the administration of 1866–9. In 1869 he was appointed viceroy and governor-general of India, and was murdered while visiting the penal settlement of Port Blair on 8 February 1872 by a Pathan from Afghanistan named Shere Ali. A former Punjab mounted policeman, he had murdered an old enemy during a blood feud, but his death sentence had been commuted to life in prison. Killing a feuding enemy was not a crime in Shere Ali's opinion and he had resented being transported to Port Blair and resolved to kill 'some European of high rank'. Earl Mayo was the European. See Satadru Sen (2000), *Disciplining Punishment: Colonialism and Convict Society in the Andaman Islands* (Delhi: Oxford University Press), p. 68; and W W Hunter (1875), *A Life of the Earl of Mayo* (London: Smith Elder & Co.).
23. Troup memorandum, 8 April 1910: HO144/926/A49962, sub. 7; which may explain the blame Anderson laid at Lushington's door over the problems Warren had with Matthews, assuming Anderson ever knew of Lushington's objections.
24. Paul Begg, Martin Fido and Keith Skinner (1996), *The Jack the Ripper A to Z* (London: Headline) pp. 21–2.
25. J A Cole (1984), *Prince of Spies: Henri Le Caron* (London: Faber and Faber), p. 207.
26. Porter, op. cit., p. 70.
27. Cole, op. cit., p. 207.
28. Major Henri Le Caron (1895), *Twenty-Five Years in The Secret Service: The Recollections of a Spy* (London: William Heinemann), p. 271.
29. Anderson, op. cit., pp. 134–5. Anderson was referring to the murder of Mary Ann Nichols, the second, and Annie Chapman, the third. The first murder would therefore have been that of Martha Turner.
30. *East London Advertiser*, 8 September 1888.
31. *The Star*, 8 September 1888.
32. *East London Observer*, 8 September 1888.
33. *Eastern Argus*, 8 September 1888.
34. *East London Advertiser*, 8 September 1888.
35. *East London Advertiser*, 8 September 1888.
36. *East London Advertiser*, 8 September 1888.
37. *Manchester Guardian*, 5 September 1888.
38. *The Times*, 4 September 1888, said 'that it would be idle to refer to them'.

39. *Leytonstone Express and Independent*, 8 September 1888.
40. *The Mystery of Marie Roget* was the sequel to *Murders in the Rue Morgue* and was itself based on the real mystery surrounding the murder of Mary Rogers in New York in 1841.
41. *New York Times*, 4 September 1888.
42. *The Star*, 5 September 1888.
43. *The Star*, 8 September 1888.
44. *The Star*, 10 September 1888.
45. *The Star*, 12 September 1888.
46. Variously reported but see *East London Advertiser*, 8 September 1888.

Chapter Six – Annie Chapman

1. In 1660 the nucleus of the first standing army in English history was created from troops of cavalry now known as the First and Second Regiments of Life Guards. They fought in many military campaigns, notably the Peninsular War and Waterloo, after the latter not seeing active service until 1882. The whole period of George Smith's service was spent at barracks in London and Windsor, where the Life Guards alternated with the Blues, attending state ceremonials and providing escort duty.
2. Fontain Hamilton Smith married Edith Annie Lunn on 14 February 1886 at All Saints' Church. He became a stationer and lived at his mother's house. He later became a house decorator and by the end of his life he was living at 26 London Road, Chipping Norton. He died on 24 October 1933, aged 74, at the Radcliffe Infirmary, Oxford.
3. John Chapman was born on 11 August 1844 at Newmarket, Suffolk, the son of a brewer named George Chapman and his wife Ann.
4. Built in 1848–9, it was closed in 1955 and leased to the Russian Orthodox Church, who bought it in 1979, and it is now a Russian Orthodox cathedral. The Royal Gates, in the centre of an icon screen (iconostasis) at the eastern end, were rescued from the old Czarist embassy chapel.
5. Annie Georgina married a cowman, Edward William Pryke, on 10 February 1895, at St Saviour's Church, Croydon. She died in 1958.
6. This was on the estate of Leonard's Hill, Clewer, Windsor Forest, which was owned by Maria, dowager countess of Waldegrave, an illegitimate daughter of Sir Edward Walpole, and, according to the *Dictionary of National Biography*, 'the handsomest woman in England'. Her secret marriage to William Henry, Duke of Gloucester and brother of King George III led to the couple being banished from court and the validity of the marriage examined, but in June 1780 royal favour had been restored.

About 1782 the house had been bought by William Harcourt, a soldier who rose to be field marshal and as one of the two senior generals (the Marquis of Drogheda being the other) responsible for bearing the union standard at the coronation of George IV. Harcourt died at St Leonard's Hall in 1830 and the house was inherited by Dr Edward Harcourt, Archbishop of York, the grandfather of Sir William Harcourt, several times home secretary.

7. Probably best known as the home of Bray Studios, which in 1955 moved to Down Place. Next door was a large mansion, Oakley Court, now a hotel, and about two hundred movies were made in and around the building, including the St Trinians series, *Half a Sixpence*, *Murder by Death* and several Hammer productions, notably *Dracula*.

8. Neal Shelden (2001), *Annie Chapman, Jack the Ripper Victim. A Short Biography* (Hornchurch, Essex: Neal Shelden), p. 14.

9. 'While the deceased lived at Clewer she was in custody for drunkenness, but had not been charged before the magistrates' (*The Times*, 11 September 1888). Also see the *Windsor and Eton Gazette*, 15 September 1888: 'her dissolute habits made it imperatively necessary that she should reside elsewhere than on the gentleman's grounds.'

10. Ten shillings (or 50p in today's money) was a considerable amount of money and probably half a good labourer's weekly wage.

11. Variously reported, the *Woodford Times*, 14 September 1888, for example: 'There were two children of the marriage, a boy and a girl. The former lay ill for some time in a London hospital, while the latter lived at Windsor . . .'

12. Shelden, op. cit., p. 27.

13. For much of the biographical information about Annie Chapman, and, indeed, all the victims, I am indebted to Neal Shelden, whose small books – see bibliography – are warmly recommended.

14. Although this letter has so far been found quoted in full only in the *Manitoba Daily Free Press* (Winnipeg, Canada) on 9 January 1892, internal content suggests a date of composition in 1888 or 1889, and the same basic story, attributed to a letter, though said to be from a sister, was reported in the *Marion Daily Star* (Ohio) on 22 May 1889 and datelined London: 'The history of one of the Whitechapel victims of Jack the Ripper is a sad illustration of the fearful power of inherited alcoholism. It appears that there were four or five children in the family. The parents were intemperate. It is the sister of the poor creature who tells the rest. The unhappy woman had unfortunately inherited the craving, and before she was 14 had taken to drink. The others became converted, and did all in their power to cure their sister, but it was of no use. The sister at length married comfortably and children were born. But the craving for drink

grew greater and greater and at length she was sent to a home for enebriates [*sic*], where she stayed for a year. She left apparently, said the sister, a changed woman.

'Soon after, however, her husband caught a severe cold and before going out one morning drank a glass of hot whisky, taking care, however, not to do so in the presence of his wife. Then, as was his custom, before leaving he kissed his wife. At once the fumes of alcohol passed into her, and in an hour she was a drunk and roaring woman. She went from bad to worse, and at last left her husband and children, one of them a cripple through her drunkenness. The husband died two years ago a white-haired and broken-hearted man, though only 45 years of age. "Need I add," said the sister in a letter, "what became of her? Her story is that of Annie Chapman, one of the recent Whitechapel victims. That was my sister." '

15. This was a reference to the Belgrave Presbyterian Chapel in Halkin Street West, off Belgrave Square, built in 1830 and leased by the Presbyterian Church of Scotland. In 1866 the congregation merged with the Presbyterian Church of England congregation from Ranelagh Gardens, Chelsea, and the church addressed itself resolutely to evangelical reform, a Sabbath School and Mothers' Meetings. The building was expanded in 1882 at a cost of £5,000 to accommodate 500 worshippers at morning and evening services. An afternoon service was also held for the domestic servants of the area. The congregation dwindled following World War One and in 1923 the building was leased to Mrs Zoe Oakley Maund, who converted it into a private residence at a cost of £4,000. A devotee of spiritualism and the occult, she was renowned for the séances she held there in the early 1930s. In later years it became a club almost exclusively catering for officers and ex-officers of the Royal Air Force, was a dining club owned by renowned restaurateur Joseph Vecchi, and in 1987 became the Belfry, the restaurant of the esteemed chef Anton Mosimann.

16. *Manchester Guardian*, 10 September 1888, for example: 'she had two of her front teeth missing' – something they thought was in common with Mary Ann Nichols.

17. HO 144/221/A49301 C sub. 8a and MEPO 3/140, fols. 16, 18–20.

18. Called Amelia Farmer in the *Manchester Guardian* of 10 September 1888, and *The Times* of 11 September 1888, but Amelia Palmer in the *East London Advertiser* and *East London Observer*, 15 September. *The Star*, 10 September 1888, hedges its bets and gives both. She was described as 'a pale dark-haired woman' and 'poorly clad', the wife of Henry Palmer (or Farmer), who was a pensioned soldier, having served in the army reserve, and had been a foreman at the docks until suffering an accident at the beginning of 1888. Amelia supplemented the pension by charring for the

Jews (*East London Observer*, 15 September 1888).

19. According to Amelia Farmer, who told the inquest that she had last seen 'the sievemaker about 18 months ago in the City, when he had told her that he left the deceased, and that he was living in the neighbourhood of Notting Hill' (*East London Advertiser*, 15 September 1888).
20. *The Star*, 15 September 1888.
21. *East London Advertiser*, 22 September 1888, for example.
22. *Woodford Times*, 14 September 1888.
23. Ibid.
24. *East London Observer*, 15 September 1888.
25. *Woodford Times*, 14 September 1888.
26. *Manchester Guardian*, 10 September 1888.
27. *The Times*, 11 September 1888.
28. *East London Advertiser*, 15 September 1888.
29. *Woodford Times*, 14 September 1888.
30. *Manchester Guardian*, 10 September 1888.
31. *Weekly Herald*, 14 September 1888.
32. Fort Elson was one of five low-profile forts built on the western side of Gosport between 1853 and 1863 to protect Portsmouth harbour from a land attack. Elson, to the north, was one of the smaller forts, with only thirty guns. It is still Ministry of Defence property, but derelict and there is no access.
33. *The Times*, 20 September 1888.
34. *Woodford Times*, 14 September 1888.
35. *The Times*, 20 September 1888.
36. *Woodford Times*, 14 September 1888.
37. *East London Advertiser*, 15 September 1888.
38. *Woodford Times*, 14 September 1888.
39. MEPO 3/140, fols. 17–20. Report dated 15 September 1888 by Inspector Chandler, H Division.
40. 7 p.m. according to *The Times* of 11 September 1888.
41. Timothy Donovan, inquest testimony, *East London Observer*, 15 September 1888.
42. John Evans, inquest testimony, *East London Observer*, 15 September 1888.
43. *Woodford Times*, 14 September 1888.
44. As reported in *The Star*, 8 September 1888, calling him Frederick Stevens. To the police, on 15 September, however, he said that Chapman had said she had been to the hospital, and intended going into the Infirmary next day.
45. MEPO 3/140, fols. 17–20. Report dated 15 September 1888 by Inspector Chandler, H Division.
46. *The Times*, 20 September 1888.

47. Testimony of John Evans, *East London Observer*, 15 September 1888.

48. *East London Observer*, 15 September 1888. Curiously, Donovan, Evans and Stevens all described Chapman as being drunk, yet Dr George Bagster Phillips, who conducted the postmortem, testified at the inquest that Chapman's stomach had contained a little food – probably the potato – but no fluid. There was no appearance of alcohol and he was convinced that she had taken no strong alcohol for some hours before her death. We know that Chapman drank some beer with William Stevens and we know she had drunk more beer at the pub, but she can't have drunk much of it if a mere three hours later her stomach showed no sign of it. Amelia Farmer did say, however, that it didn't take much to make Chapman drunk. Alternatively, she was very ill, and this combined with fatigue and physical deprivation may have given her the appearance of being drunk.

49. *Eastern Post & City Chronicle*, 15 September 1888.

50. *The Star*, 8 September 1888.

51. *Manchester Guardian*, 10 September 1888.

52. Bud Flanagan (1961), *My Crazy Life* (London: Frederick Muller), p. 10.

53. Rudolf Rocker became the editor of *Arbeter Fraint* – see Chapter Nine: 'Elizabeth Stride' – and in 1905 was charged with being a German government spy at a meeting of anarchists held in the large rear room of a pub on the corner of Osborne Street and Old Montague Street called the Archers, one of the few surviving pubs off Commercial Road.

54. Among its more famous visitors were – or were said to be – Peter the Painter and 'a small, intense man who sat alone at a table in the corner. He had slant eyes, balding reddish hair, drank Russian tea and spoke little. He was Lenin.' Recalled by Millie Sabel, a volunteer worker there, in William J Fishman (1975), *East End Jewish Radicals 1875–1914* (London: Duckworth), p. 264.

55. Sheppard, F H W (1979), *Survey of London. Vol. XXVII. Spitalfields and Mile End New Town. The Parishes of Christ Church and All Saints and the liberties of Norton Folgate and the Old Artillery Ground* (London: The Athlone Press, Univ. of London), p. 192.

56. *East London Observer*, 15 September 1888.

57. *The Times*, 20 September 1888.

58. See *The Star*, 8 September 1888.

59. As the newspapers developed the story they often got names and other details wrong, so we find Annie Hardiman (*The Times*, 13 September 1888) and Mary Hardman (*The Times*, 10 September; *East London Observer*, 15 September 1888; *Eastern Post*, 29 September 1888). It is even possible that ages were given incorrectly, the people themselves not certain when they were born. A Harriet Hardiman is listed in the 1881

census as living at 27 Hanbury Street, a widowed slipper binder, aged 44, who lived there with a daughter also named Harriet.

60. Meat for cats, not meat of cats. She described herself in the 1891 census as a 'purveyor of horseflesh'.

61. Often given in the press as Emilia and in the 1891 census she seems to give her name as Ann.

62. Most of the newspapers referred to her as elderly and of advanced years – she was in fact 66 – and one newspaper observed that she was under examination at the inquest for half an hour, 'during which she was kept standing, evidently much to her distress. It would only have been common kindness to have offered her a chair, considering that she is now at an advanced age; but this little attention did not seem to strike the officials or the jurymen as being at all necessary' (*East London Advertiser*, 15 September 1888).

63. *Manchester Guardian*, 10 September 1888.

64. *East London Observer*, 15 September 1888.

65. Francis Tyler – *East London Advertiser*, 15 September 1888; John Tyler – *Eastern Post*, 15 September 1888; Taylor, *Woodford Times*, 14 September 1888.

66. *East London Observer*, 15 September 1888.

67. *The Times*, 10 September 1888.

68. Cooksley, *Eastern Post*, 15 September 1888.

69. Cooksly and Eliza, *Manchester Guardian*, 10 September 1888.

70. They are elsewhere called Mr and Mrs Copsey. And *The Star* of 8 September 1888 refers to a Charles Cooksley, whoever he may be.

71. *The Star*, 10 September 1888.

72. *East London Observer*, 15 September 1888.

73. The only reference to these young women in the passage so far found is in the *Boston Daily Globe*, 2 October 1888.

74. *East London Observer*, 15 September 1888.

75. *Eastern Post & City Chronicle*, 15 September 1888.

76. Various newspapers: *The Times*, 13 September 1888; *Eastern Post & City Chronicle*, 15 September 1888; *East London Observer*, 15 September 1888.

77. It would seem that he had died by the 1891 census, when a widow named Elizabeth Cadosch, aged 50, a china and glass dealer, with two daughters, Esther, 29, and Irene, 22, are listed. It is possible, however, that Albert Cadosch is the same man as is listed in the 1881 census, a 21-year-old glass cutter, who had been born in Paris, France, was married, and lived in the East End at 21 Finnis Street.

78. HO 144/221/A49301C, fols. 137–45. Report dated 19 October 1888 to the Home Office by Chief Inspector Swanson.

79. *The Times*, 20 September 1888.

80. Her address is variously given.
81. Various newspapers, but see *The Times*, 20 September 1888; *Woodford Times*, 21 September 1888; *East London Advertiser*, 22 September 1888. The same story was also attributed to a Mrs Durrell/Darrell, but several newspapers, including *The Star*, 12 and 13 September 1888, and *The Times*, 13 September 1888, which carry the same story, evidently derived from a news agency. That they were one and the same person is confirmed in the police papers, HO 144/221/A49301C, fol. 136, dated 25 October 1888.
82. *East London Observer*, 15 September 1888.
83. This now long-vanished hostelry featured once more in the Ripper saga when shortly before closing time on 10 October 1888 three men interrogated a stranger and searched him, taking away a large clasp knife. With the help of a constable, the man was then taken to the police station, where he was found to have two more knives, four rings, hairpins and money. He was able to satisfy enquiries and was liberated, but the story is one of many that illustrate the danger suspicious strangers ran at times in the area.
84. Mistakenly called James Cable in the *East London Observer*, 15 September 1888. He in fact lived in Cable Street.
85. The *East London Observer*, 15 September 1888, gave a graphic description of this young man describing his appearance at the inquest: '. . . he wore a long overcoat that had once been green, and into the pockets of which he persistently stuck his hands. He had a peculiar habit of lowering his neck into the blue and white spotted neckerchief which encased it when not under examination, and jerking it out suddenly whenever he was called upon to answer a question . . . A very demonstrative witness, too, was he, and his description of the finding of the body of Annie Chapman was a pantomimic repetition of the part which he enacted on being called to the scene by John Davis. When describing the wound to the throat of the murdered woman, too, he brought his neckerchief up to his throat and realistically described how the handkerchief found on the woman seemed "soaked into her throat." Then, unloosening his neckerchief, and extending his arms and fingers slightly upwards, he personified the position of the victim's hands on her discovery. When he had arrived at the discovery of the body, indeed, the hands of the witness were kept in constant motion – describing alternately, in pantomime show, how the intestines of the woman were thrown slightly over the left shoulder, and what position the body precisely occupied in the yard.'
86. Various newspapers but see *The Times*, 13 September 1888.
87. *The Times*, 13 September 1888; *Eastern Post & City Chronicle*, 15 September 1888.

88. The time is confirmed in MEPO 3/140 fols. 9–11, a report dated 8 September 1888 by Inspector Joseph Chandler of H Division.
89. Walter Dew (1938), *I Caught Crippen: Memoirs of Ex-Chief Inspector Walter Dew C.I.D.* (London: Blackie & Son), p. 116.
90. *Lancet*, 29 October 1888.
91. Ibid.
92. *The Star*, 8 September 1888: 'tied a handkerchief round it so as to keep it on . . .'
93. *The Times*, 14 September 1888.
94. HO 144/221/A49301C. fols. 137–45, report dated 19 October 1888 to the Home Office by Chief Inspector Swanson: 'Again if the evidence of Mrs Long is correct that she saw the deceased at 5.30 a.m. then the evidence of Dr Phillips as to probable time of death is incorrect. He was called and saw the body at 6.20 a.m. and he then gives it as his opinion that death occurred about two hours earlier, viz: 4.20 a.m. hence the evidence of Mrs Long which appeared to be so important to the Coroner, must be looked upon with some amount of doubt, which is to be regretted.'
95. Sergeant Venner took the body to the mortuary – *East London Observer*, 15 September 1888.
96. MEPO 3/140 fols. 17–20, report dated 15 September 1888 by Inspector Chandler, H Division.
97. HO 144/221/A49301C. fols. 137–45, report dated 19 October 1888 to the Home Office by Chief Inspector Swanson.
98. *The Star*, 8 September 1888.
99. *The Star*, 10 September 1888.
100. *The Times*, 10 September 1888.
101. *The Times*, 14 September 1888.
102. *East London Advertiser*, 15 September 1888.
103. *East London Observer*, 15 September 1888.
104. HO 144/221/A49301C. fols. 137–45, report dated 19 October 1888 to the Home Office by Chief Inspector Swanson.
105. *The Times*, 14 September 1888.

Chapter Seven – Leather Apron

1. *The Star*, 4 September 1888.
2. *The Star*, 5 September 1888.
3. *Austin Statesman*, 5 September 1888.
4. *The Star*, 25 September 1888.
5. *Lloyd's Weekly*, 30 September 1888.

6. *The Star*, 13 October 1888.
7. *The Star*, 20 October 1888.
8. *Eastern Post and City Chronicle*, 13 October 1888. Dr Saunders died under anaesthetic in January 1889 – he worked with prostitutes, was in the East End, and his death could explain the sudden cessation of the crimes. It is surprising nobody has advanced him as a suspect.
9. *Leytonstone Express and Independent*, 8 September 1888.
10. *Manchester Guardian*, 10 September 1888.
11. *Yorkshire Post*, 10 September 1888.
12. *Manchester Guardian*, 12 September 1888.
13. *The Referee*, 16 September 1888.
14. *The Star*, 6 September 1888.
15. *The Star*, 8 September 1888. The *Manchester Guardian*, 10 September 1888, said that, according to Donovan, Leather Apron had been at the lodging house about twelve months earlier with a woman who had screamed murder in the early hours of the morning, Leather Apron having knocked her down and torn her hair and clothes. He'd claimed the woman had been trying to rob him, but Donovan didn't believe him and threw him out. Leather Apron had been back several times since then, but had not been admitted.
16. MEPO 3/140, fol. 238.
17. MEPO 3/140, fols. 235–8.
18. *East London Observer*, 15 September 1888.
19. *The Star*, 12 September 1888.
20. Ibid.
21. 'John Piser, who was sworn after the Hebrew fashion, deposed: I am a shoemaker, and reside at 22, Mulberry-street, Commercial-road, East, I go by the nickname of "Leather Apron" ' (*East London Advertiser*, 15 September 1888). 'John Piser [Pizer], who admitted that his nickname was "Leather Apron", was brought in by Sergt. Thicke' (*East London Observer*, 15 September 1888). 'The Coroner asked, "Are you known by the nickname of "Leather Apron"? to which Piser answered, "Yes, sir" ' (*Eastern Post & City Chronicle*, 15 September 1888).
22. *East London Observer*, 15 September 1888.
23. Dew, op. cit., p. 89.
24. Jack London (1903; 1977), *The People of the Abyss* (London: Macmillan; London: Journeyman Press, with an introduction by Jack Lindsay).
25. *The Star*, 12 September 1888.
26. *Daily Telegraph*, 12 September 1888.
27. *The Star*, 6 September 1888.
28. *The Star*, 11 September 1888.

29. *The Star*, 12 September 1888.
30. *Manchester Guardian, The Times*, 10 September 1888.
31. *The Star*, 17 September 1888 – the suspect was Edward McKenna and Mrs Lyons said he wasn't the man she had seen.
32. *The Star*, 12 September 1888.
33. *The Times*, 12 September 1888.
34. *The Star*, 12 September 1888.
35. Charles Tempest Clarkson and J Hall Richardson (1889), *Police!* (London: Field and Tuer, The Leadenhall Press).
36. *The Star*, 13 September 1888.
37. *The Star*, 12 September 1888.
38. I have not been able to find any reports of Pizer actually receiving any large sums, only denials that such stories were true.
39. *East London Advertiser*, 13 October 1888.
40. As a 'curly-haired youth', Lincoln Springfield was chief reporter on *The Star*, and regarded as 'probably the best and keenest man of his day at a news story'. He went on to join the *Pall Mall Gazette* and afterwards became the first news editor of the *Daily Mail*.
41. The founder of *The Star* was T P O'Connor, who in his autobiography wrote, 'I was recommended by Sir John Robinson, of the *Daily News*, to a young man named Ernest Parke, then working in the office of a City newspaper. Ernest Parke was then a young, flossy-haired man, with a keen face, a lithe and agile body, a tremendous flair for news, and capable of twenty-four hours' work, if necessary, in a single day. He was, as he is, a singular mixture of shrewdness and ideals; an intense Radical, and at the same time a thoroughly practical journalist. He might be trusted to work up any sensational news of the day, and helped, with Jack the Ripper, to make gigantic circulations hitherto unparalleled in evening journalism.'
42. *The Star*, 5 October 1888.

Chapter Eight – Suspects

1. A rhyme called 'Hush' published in *The Referee*, 16 September 1888. In the same issue there was another poem by Sims about the detectives, in which was a reference to a 'Jack':

> *They took up a bishop, they took up a Bung,*
> *They arrested the old, they arrested the young;*
> *They ran in Bill, Thomas, and Harry and Jack,*
> *Yet still they remained on the murderer's track.*

2. Letter dated 28 August 1888 from Sir Charles Warren to Robert Anderson, held in a private collection but quoted in Stewart P Evans and Keith Skinner (2000), *The Ultimate Jack the Ripper Sourcebook* (London: Constable), p. 109.

3. MEPO 3/140 fols. 9–11. Note by Superintendent West appended to a report dated 8 September 1888 by Inspector Joseph Chandler of H Division on the finding of the body of Annie Chapman..

4. In *Jack the Ripper* (David Wickes, 1988) and in *From Hell* (Albert Hughes, Allen Hughes, 2001) respectively. He was also portrayed in a deservedly forgotten movie called *Love Lies Bleeding* (1999) by Wayne Rogers, best known as Trapper John in the TV series *M*A*S*H**.

5. Sir Melville Macnaghten (1914), *Days of My Years* (London: Longman, Green and Co.).

6. 'Dynamitard' was the name commonly applied to terrorists – mostly Irish-American Fenians, but also various anarchists – who planted dynamite and caused numerous explosions in late-Victorian London and elsewhere.

7. *The Penny Pictorial*, 19 February 1885.

8. *Pall Mall Gazette*, 24 March 1903.

9. See H L Adam (1930), *Trial of George Chapman*, Notable British Trials series (London: William Hodge and Co.); *Pall Mall Gazette*, 24, 31 March 1903; *The Referee*, 29 March, 5 April 1903.

10. Brief mention should be made of a claim by Nigel Morland (1905–86), one-time editor of *The Criminologist*, who wrote in the *Evening News* (28 June 1976) that he had visited Abberline in Bournemouth and questioned him about the Ripper. Abberline told him – and Morland said he was quoting the words exactly – 'you'd have to look for him not at the bottom of London society but a long way up.' In his introduction to Frank Spiering's (1975; 1980) *Prince Jack: The True Story of Jack the Ripper* (New York, NY: Doubleday; New York, NY: Jove Books), he recorded visiting Abberline at Bournemouth in the early 1920s and Abberline told him – and, again, Morland said he was quoting the words exactly – 'I cannot reveal anything except this – of course we knew who he was, one of the highest in the land.' What Abberline actually told Morland remains to be seen, as does whether Morland ever really met Abberline.

11. HO 144/221/A49301C. fols. 137–45, report dated 19 October 1888 to the Home Office by Chief Inspector Swanson. Although this report was dated 19 October 1888, it actually reflected the situation in mid-September because on 13 October 1888 Henry Matthews, the home secretary, had requested from Sir Charles Warren a report of all the investigations so far undertaken. Warren had passed the request over to

Chief Inspector Swanson, who copied and dated reports on each of the murders up to that time and these were submitted to Matthews. The position expressed in the report therefore pertains to the date when the original was written.

12. Charles S Murdoch was a Home Office clerk (third class) who in 1896 became assistant under-secretary. He retired in 1903.

13. C Stuart-Wortley, under-secretary, Home Office.

14. *East London Observer*, 21 April 1888.

15. Henry Shearly Sanders died on 5 February 1867 at Mount Aboo, near Deesa, Bombay.

16. Laura Tucker Sanders died on 26 February 1909 in Bath.

17. The Post Office London directories list Laura T Sandars at this address from 1874–96 inclusive.

18. Dr Edward Horatio Walker Swete (1827–1912) was a surgeon at Wrighton, Somerset, and a founder of the Cottage Hospital movement, on which he wrote a book (1870), *Handy Book of Cottage Hospitals* (Weston-Super-Mare: Hamilton, Adams and Co.).

19. Curiously, there was a patient at Holloway Sanatorium and Asylum, Virginia Water, named Newland Francis Forester Smith, who was admitted on 20 October 1891, who lived at 61 Trouville Road, Clapham Park, and had been a barrister. He had become insane, apparently, in consequence of an illness in India and overwork. His mind seems to have gone completely: he couldn't order his thoughts, his memory failed and he protested that he was accused of being Jack the Ripper (see case papers, Case 860, Male Patients' Casebook 1891).

20. West Malling Place, St Leonard's Street, West Malling, Kent, was established about 1770 by William Perfect and by 1875 was known as Malling Place Private Mental Nursing Home.

21. On the northern side of Brushfield Street – it does not exist today. Mrs Fiddymont was the wife of landlord Samuel Fiddymont.

22. *The Star*, 10 September 1888, stated that Mrs Chappell was a customer, not a friend of Mrs Fiddymont, this being important, apparently, as it lent weight to the independence of her account.

23. 'Four ale' was the common name for pale ale because it cost 4d. a quart. Other beers were bitter, which usually cost 2d. or less a pint – oh, those were the days! – and mild bitter, which cost 1d. a glass and was known as 'old six' because it cost 6d. a pot (two pints).

24. *The Times*, 19 September 1888.

25. *Illustrated Police News*, 22 September 1888.

26. *East London Observer*, 15 September 1888.

27. Ibid.

28. Ibid.
29. *The Star*, 13 September 1888.
30. *Eastern Argus*, 8 September 1888.
31. Letter from correspondent named 'ETA' in *The Times*, 22 September 1888.
32. *East London Advertiser*, 15 September 1888.
33. Ibid.
34. *New York Times*, 9 September 1888. The US election was won by the Republican Benjamin Harrison, who defeated Grover Cleveland to become the now largely forgotten 23rd president of the United States.
35. *The Referee*, 9 September 1888.
36. *East London Advertiser*, 15 September 1888.
37. Colonel Bolton James Alfred Monsell, 1840–1917. After the 'riots' of February 1886 a committee appointed to consider the reorganisation of the Metropolitan Police recommended that London be quartered and a chief constable be appointed to take responsibility for each quarter. Sir Charles Warren appointed Colonel Monsell, Colonel Roberts, Major Gilbert and Mr Howard. Monsell had jurisdiction over the East End.
38. *East London Advertiser*, 15 September 1888.
39. *Daily Colonist* (a Canadian newspaper), 11 September, 1888.
40. *Yorkshire Post*, 10 September 1888.
41. *East London Observer*, 15 September 1888.
42. *Daily Telegraph*, 10 September 1888.
43. *The Times*, 10 September 1888.
44. *The Star*, 10 September 1888.
45. This description was circulated *before* the police had Mrs Long's testimony and the author Philip Sugden suggested that the time of 2 a.m. was when Annie Chapman left the lodging house in Dorset Street. He has argued that the sentence should read, 'Description of a man who entered a passage of the house at which the murder was committed *of a* prostitute, *after* two a.m. the 8th.' It is a plausible and appealing idea, but one should be wary when theories involve changing the meaning of what the sources say. Sugden also suggested that the man in question was one who Mrs Richardson said had slept on the stairs between 3.30 and 4 a.m. and whom she described as speaking with a foreign accent (*Daily Telegraph*, 10 September 1888). But this incident had happened a month earlier. The man was not seen to enter the house but was found already inside and asleep on the stairs, and finding strangers in the house was not uncommon. Asked at the inquest if he'd found strangers in the house, John Richardson replied, 'Yes plenty. At all hours – both men and women. I have often turned them out.' It is therefore doubtful that the

police would have taken much interest in a man who had slept on the stairs a month earlier. And, if *The Star* is to be believed, the man *did* enter the passage with a woman on the day of the murder and the police duly identified him.

46. *The Star*, 12 September 1888.

47. *East London Advertiser*, 15 September 1888.

48. The names of the jury were Dawson, Knight, Upton, Gardiner, Wall, Hunt, Statham, Mead, Hawkins, Wood, Ford, Latier, Carter, Neville, Chamberlain, Kemp, Silvan and Birks. Mr Thorpe was unanimously selected as foreman.

49. *East London Observer*, 15 September 1888; *East London Advertiser*, 15 September 1888.

50. *East London Observer*, 15 September 1888.

51. *The Star*, 8 September 1888, carried a letter attributed to 'A Whitechapel Workman' in which he suggested that the police use bloodhounds, which the paper observed had been successfully used some years earlier – and, never able to resist a swipe, said, 'before our police force was presided over by Sir Charles Warren' – to trace a murderer named Fish. The suggestion was echoed a week later by the *Weekly Herald*, 14 September 1888. George Bagster Phillips at the inquest said that the police had asked him about both photographing the eyes and whether bloodhounds could be used with success, and that he had dismissed the first idea and ventured an opinion that the dogs would be useless because there was so much of the woman's blood in the yard that it would obscure the scent of the murderer (*The Times*, 20 September 1888; *Woodford Times*, 21 September 1888).

52. *The Star*, 13 September 1888.

53. *The Times*, 11 September 1888.

54. HO 144/221/A49301C, fols. 90–2, letter to E Ruggles Brise by Sir Charles Warren dated 19 September 1888.

55. Oswald Puckridge was born on 13 June 1838 at Burpham, near Arundel, in Sussex, the fourth of five children of John Puckridge, a farmer, and his wife Philadelphia (née Holmes). He became a chemist and on 3 October 1868 married Ellen Buddle, the daughter of a licensed victualler named Edward Buddle, at St Paul's parish church, Deptford. In 1870 at Deal they had a son, Edward Buddle Puckridge. He was admitted on 6 January 1888 to Hoxton House Lunatic Asylum – a famous establishment that had been a madhouse from 1695, among the more famous patients being Charles and Mary Lamb. Puckridge had been discharged on 4 August. On 9 August 1893, having been found wandering in Queen Victoria Street, London, he was admitted to Bow Infirmary, East

London. He was discharged on 18 August. He was readmitted on 5 February 1896 from Bridewell Police Station – at which time he gave his occupation as 'apothecary' – and was discharged on 14 February to the City of London Lunatic Asylum at Stone, Buckinghamshire. The Register of Lunatics record that he was a danger to others, but he seems to have recovered and was discharged on 9 July 1896. He made a will on 30 September 1896, giving his address at that time as 11 Saint James Street, Clerkenwell Green. He returned to the asylum on 19 August 1899, was discharged on 18 October, was admitted on 28 May 1900 to the Holborn Workhouse – giving his address as 34 St John's Lane, Clerkenwell, and his occupation as a general labourer – where he died on 1 June of 'Broncho Pneumonia'. He left effects of £300 to his son Edward Buddle Puckridge, grocer and provision dealer. See Philip Sugden (1993), 'Puckridge: A Cautionary Tale', *Ripperana*, issue 3, January, pp. 55–62; Philip Sugden (1994; 1995; 2001), *The Complete History of Jack the Ripper* (London: Robinson); in paperback (London: Robinson); with new introduction (London: Robinson). For a fuller account see Neal Shelden (2001), *Annie Chapman, Jack the Ripper Victim. A Short Biography* (Hornchurch, Essex: Neal Shelden).

56. *Lancet*, September 22, 1888.
57. *East End News*, 11 September 1888.
58. *The Star*, 13 September 1888.
59. *The Times*, 12 September 1888.
60. *The Times*, 11 September 1888.
61. Ibid.
62. *The Star*, 13 September 1888.
63. *The Star*, 14 September 1888.
64. *Daily Colonist*, 11 September, 1888.
65. *The Times*, 11 September 1888.
66. *Eastern Argus & Borough of Hackney Times*, 15 September 1888.
67. Ada Reeve (1874–1966), who explained in her autobiography that somehow she lost the 's' in her surname, was born into a minor show business family, became a child star and by the age of six was the family meal ticket. She became an adult star in the music hall and American vaudeville, touring the USA four times as a headliner. She graduated in musical comedy and in later years became a character on the stage and in several movies. She recalled in her autobiography: 'It used to be eleven at night before I got home, walking through the long, winding Hanbury Street, which led from the direction of Bishopsgate past the stage door of the Pavilion. Usually our maid was sent to fetch me, but on the night of September 29th, 1888, she could not come and I had to make the journey

alone. I have reason to remember that date – for next morning we heard that not one but two murders had been committed – the first in Berner Street, off the Commercial Road, and the second in Mitre Square, Aldgate. To get from one place to the other, the 'Ripper' must have passed along streets very close to my own route. I still feel cold when I realise that he may have been lurking in the shadows within reach of me that night.' In 1885 she had appeared at the Pavilion, Whitechapel, with Marie Kendall, the future daughter-in-law of a man named John McCarthy, landlord of a future victim of Jack the Ripper, Mary Kelly. In 1888, by the way, she played there in the pantomime *Babes in the Wood*. See Ada Reeve (1954), *Take It For a Fact* (London: William Heinemann).

68. *The Star*, 14 September 1888.
69. *The Star*, 15 September 1888.
70. Report dated 18 September 1888 by Inspector Abberline, MEPO 3/140 fols. 24–25.
71. *Yorkshire Post*, 13 September 1888.
72. *The Times*, 12 September 1888.
73. Ibid.
74. Ibid.
75. *Eastern Argus & Borough of Hackney Times*, 15 September 1888.
76. *The Star*, 12 September 1888.
77. *The Times*, 13 September 1888.
78. *Alderley and Wilmslow Advertiser*, 14 September, 1888.
79. *East London Advertiser*, 15 September 1888.
80. *Woodford Times*, 14 September 1888.
81. *Jewish Chronicle*, 14 September 1888.
82. The visit was widely reported – *The Times*, 14 September 1888; *The Star*, 14 September 1888; *East London Advertiser*, 15 September 1888 – and the story was the same in each paper, suggesting that this was possibly a piece given out by the police themselves.
83. *East London Advertiser*, 15 September 1888.
84. *The Star*, 15 September 1888.
85. In her controversial bestselling attempt to prove that the artist Walter Sickert was Jack the Ripper (see Chapter Twenty-two), the crime novelist Patricia Cornwell refers to 14 September 1888 being the day Annie Chapman was buried, then tells the story of the Tower Subway man yanking off false whiskers. This she for some reason associates with a letter dated 17 September 1888 received by the Metropolitan Police, which was the first use of the name 'Jack the Ripper', and to the appearance on the same day of an American at the Westminster Police Court who wanted legal advice about a problem he had with his landlady.

('Sickert was quite capable of faking an American accent,' says Cornwell, adding that the American claimed to be in London to study art at the National Gallery, which she evidently finds suspicious because, 'The National Gallery did not have an art school or students.') All of which seems to connect with a letter dated 27 November in which the author, the Ripper in Cornwell's view, wrote, 'I have got a jolly lot of false whiskers and mustaches.'

I'm not quite sure what it all added up to, although it could perhaps be observed that (a) the 27 November whiskers letter was written two months after the Tower Subway incident and, apart from the reference to whiskers, there is no known connection between them; (b) the 17 September 'Jack the Ripper' letter, which had no clear connection to whiskers, is almost beyond question a forgery of recent origin; and (c) the American said that he was studying art at the National Gallery, which then as now is what a lot of people visit the National Gallery to do, and did not say he was at school there.

All of which doesn't detract from the fact that a man ran through the Tower Subway wearing false whiskers. Why? One cannot sometimes escape the feeling that Victorian society was distinctly odd and that at least these days television keeps such people indoors.

86. *The Times*, 15 September 1888.
87. *The Star*, 15 September 1888.
88. *Illustrated Police News*, 22 September, 1888.
89. *The Star*, 14 September 1888.
90. By the writer and researcher Stewart P Evans.
91. On 7 May 1895 the *Pall Mall Gazette* reported apropos of the identity of Jack the Ripper, 'The theory entitled to the most respect, because it was presumably based upon the best knowledge, was that of Chief Inspector Swanson, the officer who was associated with the investigation of all the murders, and Mr Swanson believed the crimes were the work of a man who is now dead.' He was also credited by the *San Francisco Chronicle* (14 February 1891) with the absurd suggestion that the murderer of a woman named Frances Coles was a woman. This was based on the fact that Coles possessed two hats, an old one pinned beneath her dress and a new one purchased by a sailor customer. A Bristol newspaper, *Times and Mirror* (14 February 1891), reported that the suggestion had been made by 'one of the most experienced local police officers', and Swanson was not local, and the impression is that the hat clue was thought to pertain to the Coles case, not necessarily to the murders overall.
92. *East London Observer*, 15 September 1888.
93. *Illustrated Police News*, 22 September 1888.

94. *East London Observer*, 22 September 1888.
95. *East London Advertiser*, 29 September 1888.
96. *The Star*, 14 September 1888.
97. *Punch, or the London Charivari*, 29 September 1888.
98. *The Star*, 18 September 1888.
99. Ibid.
100. *The Star*, 2 October 1888.
101. Variously reported. See *The Star*, 27 September 1888; *The Times*, 28 September 1888; *The Eastern Post & City Chronicle*, 29 September 1888; *East London Advertiser*, 29 September 1888; *Macclesfield Courier and Herald*, 29 September 1888.
102. *Macclesfield Courier and Herald*, 29 September 1888.
103. *East London Advertiser*, 22 September 1888.
104. Reported succinctly but in some detail in *The Times*, 27 September 1888.
105. The *Law Journal* supported Baxter in this, saying that the summing-up 'on the whole promoted the true function of a coroner's inquest . . .' (quoted in *The Eastern Post & City Chronicle*, 29 September 1888).
106. *Law Journal* quoted in *The Eastern Post & City Chronicle*, 29 September 1888.
107. *Daily Telegraph*, 27 September 1888.
108. *Lancet*, 29 September 1888.
109. *The Star*, 29 September 1888.
110. *The Times*, 27 September 1888.
111. *East London Advertiser*, September 1888.
112. *Lancet*, 29 September 1888.
113. *The Times*, 2 October 1888.
114. *The Star*, 1 October 1888.

Chapter Nine – Elizabeth Stride

1. Despite being only five foot five (according to *The Times*, 1 October 1888) or five foot two (according to Detective Inspector Edmund Reid at the inquest). As Inspector Morse was informed in *The Wench Is Dead*, '. . . the Ripper's victims in the 1880s: four foot nine, four foot ten, four foot eleven – that sort of height: well, that's about what those dear ladies were. Except one. Stride. They called her "Long Liz" – so much taller . . . Five foot three . . .' (Colin Dexter (1989), The *Wench Is Dead* (London: Macmillan), pp. 163–4).
2. 'Epileptic Annie', *The Star*, 1 October 1888.
3. *The Star*, 1 October 1888.

4. *Boston Daily Globe*, 2 October 1888.
5. According to Mr North, probably the landlord of the Blackneys Head at 143 Polar High Street, who knew Elizabeth Stride and her husband when they owned a coffee shop nearby. She derived the nickname 'Mother Gum' as a result of 'a peculiarity of the top lip, which, when she laughed, showed the whole of the upper gum' (see Shelden, op. cit., p. 23).
6. On her marriage certificate in 1869 she gave her name as Elizabeth Gustifson and described her father as Augustus Gustifson, a labourer.
7. Lars Fredrik Olofsson (b. 9 August 1825) was not a widower, as often stated, but was married to Johanna Carlsdotter Nilsson (b. 21 April 1828) and they had a total of six children, although only three were alive when Elizabeth was in their employ. The eldest child, Johanna Elisabeth (b. 1853, d. 1860), died aged seven. Carl Otto (b. 1856), Johan Fredrik (b. 1857) and Anders Gustaf (b. 1863) were present when Elizabeth was there, and Augusta Theresa (b. 1865) and Hjalmar (b. 1867) were born after she left.
8. Research has failed to find any mention of Maria Wejsner in police records, for any crime whatsoever. She was born on 23 May 1845 in Valla, a small village on the west coast of Sweden, moved to Gothenburg in 1862 and two years later married a German named Carl Wenzel Wiesners (Wejsner). They had five children. Carl died in 1871 and Maria died a widow in 1907. The only anomaly is that while records show Carl Wejsner as the father of all five of Maria's children, the last two children were born over nine months after his death from scarlet fever! See Daniel Olsson (2004), 'Mrs Wenzel', *Ripperologist*, Issue 53, May.
9. Charles Preston, inquest testimony, *The Times*, 4 October 1888.
10. Michael Kidney, inquest testimony, *The Times*, 4 October 1888. He said he had 'seen the address of someone with the family she was living with at Hyde Park; but I cannot find it.' And he said that Stride had told him that when she lived in Hyde Park she used to see a policeman.
11. Biographical detail is provided by Klas Lithner in Donald Rumbelow (1975), *The Complete Jack the Ripper* (London: W H Allen; Boston, MA: New York Graphic Society, 1975; London: Star Books, 1976; New York, NY: Signet Books, 1976; London: Star Books, 1981; revised edition, London: W H Allen, 1987). Published in 1988 as *Jack the Ripper: The Complete Casebook* (Chicago: Contemporary Books). Published in 1988 as a revised edition with an addendum (London: Penguin Books). See also Birgitta Leufstadius (1994), *Jack the Rippers Tredje Offer* (Partille: Warne Förlag). This excellent biography of Elizabeth Stride deserves publication in English. My appreciation to Birgitta Leufstadius and translator Edwin R Nye. See also Daniel Olsson (2004), 'Elizabeth's Story', *Ripperologist*, Issue 52, March.

12. John Stride seems to have come from a well-to-do family, albeit one in which there may have been a rift. His parents were William Stride (b. 1784 in Plymouth, Devon; d. 1873) and Eleanor Monk (b. 1794), whom he married in Chatham, and they had nine children: William (1817–?), John Thomas, Edward (1823–81), Charles (1825–?), Susanah Eleanor (1827–?), Frederick Augustus (1829–58), George James (1832–1903), Daniel Elisha (1834–1900), and Sarah Ann (1837–1916). At some point most of the children moved to London and settled in the East End. William, who was deaf, went to Whitechapel and worked in the shipyards as a labourer. Charles lived in Mile End; George James lived in Stepney and although he'd trained as a schoolmaster he became a shipping clerk. Four of the children remained in Sheerness: Edward, who was a surgeon – a Fellow of the Royal College of Surgeons – and a dentist (Michael Kidney told the inquest that Stride had a brother-in-law practising as a surgeon in Kent, and it was reported that the police had contacted him); Frederick Augustus; Daniel Elisha, who was a bricklayer's labourer and would die in 1900 in the Kent County Asylum, Chatham; and Sarah Ann. The father, William Stride, was a substantial property owner and apparently built a street in Mile Town, Sheerness, called Stride's Row. When he died at 3 Stride's Row on 6 September 1873 he left number 4 to Edward, numbers 7 and 8 to the now married Sarah Anne, and the rest (1, 2, 3, 5 and 6) to Daniel Elisha, along with a stable, plots of ground, a coal shed, workshop and two tenements in Victory Street. Interestingly Daniel Elisha had a son, Daniel, who in 1901 was described on the census as a 'writer'. The children who moved to London, including John Thomas, appear to have received nothing.

13. The *Bywell Castle* sank without trace in the Mediterranean five years later.

14. *The Times*, 4 September 1878. For a full account of the disaster see Gavin Thurston (1965), *The Great Thames Disaster* (London: George Allen and Unwin).

15. *The Times*, 4 October 1888.

16. *Pall Mall Gazette*, 3 October 1888; *The Times*, 4 October 1888.

17. *The Times*, 4 October 1888.

18. *Manchester Guardian, Evening News*, 8 October 1888.

19. Elizabeth Tanner, inquest testimony. She said Elizabeth Stride had lodged there on and off for six years (*Daily Telegraph*, 4 October 1888).

20. Catherine Lane, a charwoman living at 32 Flower and Dean Street, said that Stride had told her that she had formerly lived in Devonshire Street.

21. *The Times*, 4 October 1888.

22. 'Payments to the Poor' book at the Swedish Church. Found by Klas Lithner.

23. *Te Aroha News*, 12 December 1888.

24. *The Times*, 4 October 1888.

25. Published in *The Times* of 9 October under the heading 'The Children of the Common Lodging Houses'.
26. *Daily Telegraph*, 4 October 1888.
27. Inquest testimony, *The Times*, 4 October 1888.
28. *The Times*, 4 October 1888.
29. Catherine Lane was married to a dock labourer named Patrick Lane and she had lived at 32 Flower and Dean Street since 11 February, but had known Stride for six or seven years. Charles Preston, a barber, had lived at that address for 18 months – see inquest testimony, *The Times*, 4 October 1888. Preston said that four or five months earlier Stride had been arrested one Saturday night for being drunk and disorderly at the Queen's Head public house and had been released on bail the following day.
30. Quoted in *The Star*, 1 October 1888.
31. *Evening News*, 1 October 1888.
32. A story Packer gave to the press, as quoted in the *East London Advertiser*, 6 October 1888.
33. 'In her right hand were tightly clasped some grapes, and in her left she held a number of sweetmeats' (*The Star* and *The Times*, 1 October 1888; that both newspapers used the same words indicates a common source, probably a news agency).
34. Louis Diemshutz, who discovered Stride's body, told a reporter that Stride's tightly clenched hands held sweets in one and grapes in the other (interview with the *Evening News*, 1 October 1888) and that 'She had a flower in the bosom of her dress. In one hand she had some grapes and in the other some sweets. She was grasping them tightly' (attributed to Louis Diemshutz, *Illustrated Police News*, 6 October 1888).
35. *East London Advertiser*, 6 October 1888.
36. *Daily Telegraph*, 6 October 1888.
37. *Manchester Guardian*, 9 October 1888.
38. Ibid.
39. *Daily Telegraph*, 15 November 1888.
40. *Daily Telegraph*, 16 November 1888.
41. *Manchester Guardian*, 19 November 1888.
42. Chief Inspector Swanson wrote in a report to the home secretary, '. . . Packer, who is an elderly man, has unfortunately made different statements so . . . any statement he made would be rendered almost valueless as evidence' (report by Chief Inspector Swanson to Home Office, HO144/221/A49301C).
43. *The Star*, 4 October 1888.
44. *The Star*, 5 October 1888.
45. *Yorkshire Post*, 1 October 1888.

46. *The Times*, 3 October 1888.
47. *The Times*, 6 October 1888.
48. *Daily Telegraph*, 6 October 1888.
49. *East London Advertiser*, 6 October 1888.
50. Report by Sergeant White, MEPO 3/140/221/A49301C, fols. 212–14.
51. There is an excellent analysis of the Packer story by Dave Yost in the 'Elizabeth Stride – Endnotes' in Alex Chisholm, Christopher Michael DiGrazia and Dave Yost (2002), *The News From Whitechapel: The Whitechapel Murders in the Daily Telegraph* (Jefferson, NC: McFarland and Company). For an account of Le Grand, see Gerry Nixon (1998), 'Le Grand of the Strand', *Ripperologist*, Issue 18, August, who provides full sourcing; *Newmarket Journal*, 17 October 1891, 24 October 1891; *The Times*, 12 July 1877, 8 June 1889, 27 June 1889, 29 September 1891, 7 October 1891, 13 October 1891.
52. Tom Cullen (1965), *Autumn of Terror: Jack the Ripper His Crimes and Times* (London: Bodley Head). Published as *When London Walked in Terror* (Boston: Houghton Mifflin 1965; London: Fontana Books, 1968). Published as *When London Walked in Terror* (New York, NY: Avon Books, 1968). Published as *The Crimes and Times of Jack the Ripper*, 1973.
53. The census records show that at this address there lived a bootmaker named William Marshall with his wife, May, a laundress, and their children, William and Janine. Since the witness was described as fifty years old, one assumes that it was the father, albeit that he is described in the press as a warehouseman rather than a tailor.
54. *The Star*, 6 October 1888.
55. Interpreted as five foot six by the *Manchester Guardian*, 6 October 1888.
56. *Manchester Guardian, The Star, The Times*, 6 October 1888; *East London Advertiser*, 27 October 1888.
57. Thomas B Eyges (1944), *Beyond The Horizon* (Boston, MA: Group Free Society), p. 79 – an unusual autobiography written in a singularly modest and pleasing style; well worth reading.
58. Attempts to close the newspaper ranged from bribing compositors – as when one was bribed to change the traditional last-page message 'Workers, do your duty. Spread the Arbeter Fraint!' to 'Workers, do your duty. Destroy the Arbeter Fraint!' – to paying printers not to print it. The wallet behind these efforts was widely believed to be that of Samuel Montagu, the Liberal MP for Whitechapel. The Club raised money from friends and supporters as far away as New York, and this enabled them to buy their own printing press, which was housed along with the editorial offices in a brick-built building in the yard behind the club.
59. It wasn't wooden.

60. It was in fact three storeys.

61. Eyges, op. cit., pp. 79–83.

62. John Henry Mackay (1891), *The Anarchists: A Picture of Civilisation at the Close of the 19th Century* (Boston: Benj. R Tucker). See also edition published by Autonomedia, New York, in 1999 (edited by Mark A Sullivan with essays by Hubert Kennedy, Edward Mornin, Sharon Presley and Peter Lamborn-Wilson), p. 113.

63. The 1891 census gives its name as Stable Yard.

64. *The Star*, 1 October 1888; *The Times*, 2 October 1888.

65. *The Times*, 1 October 1888; *Illustrated Police News*, 6 October 1888.

66. His beat went from the corner of Jower's Walk, off Commercial Road, to Christian Street, down Christian Street and Fairclough Street as far as Grove Street, then back along Fairclough Street as far as Backchurch Lane, then up Backchurch Lane to Commercial Road, taking in all the interior streets, including Berner Street and Batty Street. It took him 25–30 minutes to complete his beat.

67. *The Times, Manchester Guardian, The Star*, 6 October 1888.

68. *The Star, The Times*, 1 October 1888.

69. *The Times, Daily Telegraph*, 1 October 1888.

70. *Evening News*, 1 October 1888.

71. *Evening News*, 1 October 1888; report by Chief Inspector Donald Swanson, 19 October 1888, HO/144/221/A49301C 8a. It might also be worth observing that Charles Letchford said that his sister had been at the door of her home for ten minutes before 1 a.m. It is tempting to think that this woman was Mrs Mortimer, but Mrs Mortimer's maiden name was Skipp, which indicates that she was not Charles Letchford's sister and means that we have two women at their front doors for ten minutes prior to 1 a.m., neither presumably seeing the other or, more likely, being out at different times.

72. Walter Dew (1938), *I Caught Crippen: Memoirs of Ex-Chief Inspector Walter Dew C.I.D.* (London: Blackie and Son), p. 130.

73. HO 144/221/A49301C, fols. 148–59. Report to the Home Office by Chief Inspector Donald S Swanson dated 19 October 1888.

74. Correctly Ellen Street.

75. HO 144/221/A49301C, fols. 110–11. Home Office minute with attached letter initialled CW and counter-initialled GL, including appended note to Mr Murdoch initialled WTB dated 25 October 1888.

76. MEPO 3/140221A49301C, fols. 204–6. Report by Inspector Abberline dated 1 November 1888.

77. MEPO 3/140/221/A49301C, fol. 207. Draft letter from Robert Anderson to Sir Charles Warren dated 5 November 1888. Repeated

almost verbatim by Sir Charles Warren in a letter to the Home Office dated 6 November 1888 (HO 144/221/A49301C, fol. 199).

78. *The Star*, 1 October 1888.
79. *The Star*, 2 October 1888.
80. Or possibly the attacker, a consideration that arises from the possibility that Pipeman went to the aid of the woman and chased away her attacker, but the permutations and convolutions seem endless.
81. *New York Times*, 2 October 1888.
82. *East London Advertiser*, 6 October 1888.
83. *East London Observer*, 6 October 1888.
84. There is some confusion about what he did after discovering his wife safe downstairs. In one account he immediately got a candle and went outside (*East London Observer*, 6 October 1888), but the overwhelming testimony is that he went upstairs and informed people in the concert room, then got a candle and returned outside (even the *East London Observer* quotes him as saying, 'I then got a candle *and went down*' – my italics).
85. Mrs Mortimer was reported as saying that 'a young man and his sweetheart were standing at the corner of the street, about twenty yards away, before and after the time the woman must have been murdered, but they told me they did not hear a sound' (*Illustrated Police News*, 6 October 1888).
86. *The Times*, 3 October 1888.
87. On Saturday, 16 March 1889, a procession of Jewish unemployed marched from the club to the synagogue in Great Duke Street, Aldgate, but were refused admittance by the chief rabbi. The marchers then adjourned to the Mile End Waste, where they held a meeting before returning to the club. Here a crowd gathered and some boys and girls began knocking on the door. Either Diemshutz, described in one report as an unlicensed hawker, or Isaac Kozebrodsky came out of the door in his shirtsleeves, caught one of the lads and cuffed him. Hooting ensued, and then the two defendants, with a cap blocker named Samuel Friedman, struck out right and left among the crowd. They were arrested and charged with riotous conduct and with assaulting the delightfully named Israel Sunshine and Emanuel Snapper, along with Isaac Solomons, Emanuel Jacobs, Julius Barnett and PCs James Frost, 154 H, and George Harris, 269 H. A club member named Lewis Lyons in turn preferred charges against the police, which were dismissed. Those who were assaulted and who claimed to have been innocent passers-by said twenty or thirty men armed with sticks, broomsticks, walking sticks, umbrellas and other weapons, including a saucepan, had rushed out of the club and indiscriminately attacked anyone within reach, Samuel Friedman being overheard to say, 'I will do for someone to-night, and do not care if I get

12 months for it.' In their defence the defendants said that the crowd were creating a great disturbance and throwing stones, and the door of the club was broken open. The police, they maintained, were the aggressors, and none of the club members had assaulted anyone. The jury ultimately concluded that the defendants were guilty only of assault on the police. Kozebrodsky was 'recommended to mercy' and ordered to pay a fine of £4 or in default be given one month's imprisonment. Diemshutz, however, was sentenced to three months' imprisonment with hard labour, then to pay £40 and produce two sureties each willing to pay £20, to be forfeited if Diemshutz failed to be of good behaviour for twelve months (*The Times*, 9, 26 April 1889, *East London Advertiser*, 27 April 1889). Diemshutz stayed with the socialist movement and was a noted speaker, visiting Manchester in March 1891, where he was a speaker in memory of the Paris Commune along with the celebrated Benjamin Feigenbaum at a meeting in a crowded working men's club (*Freedom*, vol. 5, No. 53, April 1891).

88. *The Times*, 3 October 1888.
89. *The Times*, 6 October 1888.
90. *The Times*, 4 October 1888.
91. Conducted at St George's Mortuary by Drs Phillips and Blackwell in the presence of Dr Rygate and Mr Johnston.

Chapter Ten – Catherine Eddowes

1. The Old Hall Tin and Japan Works, sometimes known as Turton's Hall after Joseph Turton, was demolished in 1883 and stood on the site now occupied by Wolverhampton Central Library (see Dave Froggatt (1996), 'Catherine Eddowes: Wolverhampton and Birmingham', *Ripperologist*, No. 6, June).
2. Birth certificate.
3. Alfred, Harriet, Emma, Eliza, Elizabeth, Catherine (b. 1842), Thomas (b. 1844), George (b. 1846), John (b. 1849, d. 1849), Sarah Ann (b. 1850; she was admitted to Caterham Asylum for Imbeciles in 1870), Mary Ann (b. 1852), and William (b. 1854, d. 1854). Elizabeth married Thomas Charles Fisher in September 1857; Eliza married a butcher named James Gold in January 1859; she would by 1881 be living with a man named Charles Frost on the top floor of Thrawl Street, Spitalfields; Emma married James Jones in November 1860.
4. Harriet, Emma and Eliza.
5. Thomas, George, Sarah Ann, and Mary Ann.

6. According to another aunt, Sarah Croot.
7. Chapbooks were short and inexpensive booklets generally retelling traditional stories such as those of Jack the Giant Killer, Tom Thumb and Robinson Crusoe, and were so called because they were usually written (often very badly) by itinerant peddlers known as chapmen, who sold the 'books' from boxes on street corners in towns or to country folk. Among these chapbooks was a gallows ballad about Catherine's cousin, Christopher Charles Robinson, who was hanged in 1866 at Stafford Gaol for the murder of his fiancée Harriet Seager in Wolverhampton. Catherine and Thomas Conway were among the 4,000 people who attended the public hanging.
8. Catherine Ann Conway (b. Yarmouth Workhouse, Norfolk, 18 April 1863 – she would become known as Annie Conway).
9. According to her sisters Emma, who last saw Catherine at Christmas 1877, and Elizabeth.
10. Annie Philips, quoted in the *Wolverhampton Chronicle*, 10 October 1888. At the time of her mother's death Annie Philips was living at 12 Dilston Grove, Southwark Park Road. She was married to Louis Philips, a lamp-black packer. Two years earlier Eddowes had nursed her daughter through her confinement, but her overdrinking and appeals for money had led mother and daughter to part on bad terms. At that time Annie had been living in King Street, Bermondsey, but had soon left that address and had moved several times since. She had never left a forwarding address and her mother did not know where to find her.
11. Mrs Elizabeth Fisher, quoted in the *Wolverhampton Chronicle*, 10 October 1888.
12. *The Star*, 3 October 1888, published an interview with John Kelly in which he said: 'It is nigh on to seven years since I met Kate, and it was in this very lodging-house I first set eyes on her. We got throwed together a good bit, and the result was that we made a regular bargain. We have lived here ever since, as the people here will tell you, and have never left here except when we've gone to the country together hopping . . . Well, Kate and me lived on here as best we could. She got a job of charring now an then, and I picked up all the odd jobs I could in the Spitalfields Market. The people here were very kind to us.'
13. *Evening News*, 10 October 1888.
14. Frederick William Wilkinson, inquest testimony. *The Times*, 5 October 1888. Coroner's inquests (L) 1888. No. 135 Corporation of London Records Office.
15. John Kelly, inquest testimony. *The Times*, 5 October 1888. Coroner's Inquests (L) 1888. No. 135 Corporation of London Records Office.

16. Eliza Gold, inquest testimony. *The Times*, 5 October 1888. Coroner's Inquests (L) 1888. No. 135, Corporation of London Records Office.
17. *The Star*, 10 October 1888.
18. *East London Observer*, 13 October 1888.
19. The *Daily Telegraph* later reported that enquiries were made at 6 Dorset Street, and it was discovered that nobody named Jane Kelly lived there. The irony is that the next victim was a young woman who lived at 26 Dorset Street who was named Mary Jane Kelly. One wonders whether anyone would have directed the attention of the police to Mary Jane Kelly, who may have established that she was alive and may even have questioned her. Interestingly, a woman named Mary Price, who lived at 36 Flower and Dean Street, having seen the body, was of opinion that the woman was a certain Jane Kelly; but it's possible that she may have read about the pawn tickets in the newspaper. It was also reported that on the afternoon of 1 October two women said they were sure that Eddowes was a woman known as Annie who lived at a shop in a court near to Dorset Street. Mary Jane Kelly lived down a court next to a shop in Dorset Street. See *Daily Telegraph*, 2 October 1888.
20. *The Star*, 3 October 1888.
21. Tom Cullen, op. cit., claims that Eddowes had been standing in the street making the noise of a fire engine, but I have not been able to confirm this.
22. *The Star*, 1 October 1888. There is no further reference to James Blenkingsop and he did not appear at the inquest.
23. Kearley and Tonge was once a major player in the grocery business and even marketed products under the 'Mitre' brand, a clear allusion to Mitre Street and Square, but it has vanished under an extraordinary sequence of mergers and acquisitions. In 1876 Hudson Kearley founded a tea- and coffee-importing business called Heseltine & Kearley. He opened his first shop at Brentford in 1878, by now having expanded into groceries, and from 1880 onwards opened numerous branches around the country under the name of International Tea Company Stores. The company's expansion was great, and absorbed so many local grocery shops that it was even referred to by H G Wells in his novel *Tono Bungay*: ' "They'll have had the International Tea Company and all sorts of people cutting them up," I said.' G A Tonge joined the firm and on Heseltine's retirement in 1887 the business changed its name to Kearley and Tonge. Kearley sold his shares in Kearley and Tonge and International Stores in 1927 for £4,000,000.

   Meanwhile, in 1875 J H Mills had opened a family grocery shop in Bristol and like Kearley had soon opened numerous branches, becoming a limited company by 1900, and in 1950 changing their name to Gateway

Foodmarkets. In 1970 the company was taken over by Linfood Holdings Group, which changed its name to the Dee Corporation in 1983 and between then and 1987 merged with or acquired Keymarkets, Lennons, Fine Fare, the Carrefour Hypermarkets and International Stores. The whole lot was renamed the Gateway Corporation in 1988, all the stores by May 1994 being renamed Somerfield.

Turning to another strand, in far-off British Guiana (the present-day Republic of Guyana) the only possession Britain ever held on the mainland of South America, the Booker family, sugar and rum exporters, in 1834 founded Booker Brothers & Co. Over the next half-century or more the company gradually expanded its sugar plantation holdings until by the end of the nineteenth century Booker's owned most of the sugar plantations in the country and British Guiana was humorously known as 'Booker's Guiana'. In 1900 Booker's merged with another major company, John McConnell & Co., to become Booker Brothers, McConnell & Co. Limited, and in the years that followed expanded into a diverse range of businesses in several countries. In 1968 it changed its name to Booker McConnell, and in consequence of an approach that year by Tom Maschler of the publisher Jonathan Cape, sponsored a literary prize that soon became the most prestigious in Britain – the Booker Prize. About this time Booker acquired the Dee Corporation and changed its name to Booker Foodservice, adding it to a group that included Iceland Foods, Woodward Foodservices and Expert Logistics. Booker Foodservice was the largest cash & carry operator in the UK, with 177 branches serving more than 450,000 retailers and caterers across the country. Its divisions included the 3663 Contract Division, providing specialist logistics solutions for caterers such as Burger King and Prêt à Manger, and another division that supplied all the food requirements to her Majesty's Forces worldwide. In 1999 Booker Foodservice was acquired by BidVest, a South African-owned global conglomerate, and renamed 3663 First for Foodservice.

24. *The Star*, 1 October 1888.
25. *The Times*, 12 October 1888. See also HO 144/221/A49301C, fols. 184–94, report by Chief Inspector Donald S Swanson dated 6 November 1888.
26. *The Times*, 12 October 1888.
27. Lieutenant-Colonel Sir Henry Smith (1910), *From Constable to Commissioner: The Story of Sixty Years, Most of Them Misspent* (London: Chatto and Windus). Smith's description was wrong on several points: Lawende was not unable to fix the time, as Smith says; the man's jacket was pepper-and-salt, not navy serge; and he wore a cap with a peak, not a Sherlock Holmesian deerstalker. (Note that Smith was a major at the time

of the inquest, but his book was written later when he was a lieutenant-colonel.)

28. *The Star*, 1 October 1888.

29. A possible indication of Morris's character is provided by *The Star*, 12 September 1888, which reported the appearance of a shoemaker named Alexander Birke, who appeared before the magistrate charged with stealing an empty wooden champagne case from outside Kearley and Tonge at 4 Mitre Street. Morris was the complainant, but the magistrate pointed out that there was no proof that Birke took it, Birke had no prior convictions, and the case was worthless. On the last point Morris exclaimed, 'The value of the thing has nothing to do with it. I have known a person convicted for stealing a turnip.' The magistrate replied, 'Probably, but I never did convict for stealing a turnip, and I never will', and discharged Birke, reportedly to applause.

30. HO 144/221/A49301C, fols. 162–70, report to the Home Office by Inspector James McWilliam, City of London Police, dated 27 October 1888.

31. HO 144/221/A49301C, fols. 162–70, report to the Home Office by Inspector James McWilliam, City of London Police dated 27 October 1888.

32. Collard testimony: coroner's inquest (L), 1888, No. 135, Catherine Eddowes inquest, 1888, Corporation of London Records Office.

33. HO 144/221/A49301C, fols. 184–94, report by Chief Inspector Donald S Swanson dated 6 November 1888. It should be noted that neither Dr George William Sequeira of 34 Jewry Street, Aldgate, nor Dr William Sedgwick Saunders, of 13 Queen Street, Cheapside, the medical officer of health for the City of London, thought the murderer possessed of any great anatomical skill. See *The Times* 12 October 1888.

34. Variously reported in the press. See *The Times*, 5 October 1888; *Daily Telegraph*, 5 October 1888; *East London Advertiser*, 6 October 1888. Also the coroner's inquest (L), 1888, No. 135, Catherine Eddowes inquest, 1888, Corporation of London Records Office.

35. HO 144/221/A49301C, fols. 195–6, report by PC Alfred Long 254A; also cited in the *Manchester Guardian* and *The Times*, 12 October 1888.

36. HO 144/221/A49301C, fols. 197–8, report by Superintendent Thomas Arnold, H Division, dated 6 November 1888.

37. Probably Detective Baxter Hunt, who would in due course track down Thomas Conway (a.k.a. Patrick Quinn), Eddowes's husband.

38. PC Long reported in *The Times*, 12 October 1888.

39. HO 144/221/A49301C, fols. 173–81, report to Home Office from Sir Charles Warren dated 6 November 1888.

40. *Manchester Guardian,* 13 October 1888.

41. See HO 144/221/A49301C, fol. 171, Home Office minute sheet appended to McWilliam's report of 27 October 1888, HO 144/221/A49301C, fols. 162–70.

42. *The Star,* 12 October 1888.

43. Smith, op. cit.

44. *City Press,* 7 January 1905. This anecdote is told during a story about the retirement of a senior City detective named Robert Sagar, who it says was involved in the Ripper investigations, continuing: '. . . suspicion fell upon a man, who, without a doubt, was the murderer. Identification being impossible, he could not be charged. He was, however, placed in a lunatic asylum, and the series of atrocities came to an end.' The *City Press* then told the anecdote about the writing on the wall, prefacing the account by describing it as 'a peculiar incident . . . which may have been forgotten'. The anecdote about the writing has no direct relevance to what was said about Sagar and the lunatic patient and the juxtaposition could be entirely accidental, but it is also possible that the two incidents were in some sense connected. (See Chapter Twenty-two for possible further information about Sagar's suspect.)

45. Hiram Abiff, known as 'the widow's child', is mentioned in the Bible, where he is called Huram-Abi, described as the son of a widow of the tribe of Naphtali, and 'a man full of skill, intelligence, and knowledge in working bronze' (see 1 Kings 7: 13). The tribe of Naphtali was one of the twelve tribes of Israel and occupied a territory extending over 800 square miles of northern Canaan – the ancient name for the land of Israel and which in time would take the name Galilee from a Naphtali town called Galil.

In Masonic Ritual Hiram Abiff is Grand Master of the building of Solomon's temple, assigning the work for each day. Other workers are promised that once the work is completed they will be given the secrets that will allow them to become Master Masons, but three of them form a plot to get the information from Hiram ahead of time. Each waits at an assigned gate – the east gate, the south gate and the west gate – and in turn they accost Hiram, demanding that he reveal his secrets, and when he refuses each strikes him with one of the working tools, the last of them hitting Hiram on the head with a setting maul and killing him. The murderers then bury the body in temple rubble and at midnight return and rebury the body on a hill west of Mount Moriah. When Hiram is missed the next day, the plot is uncovered but it is fifteen days before the grave is found, at which time King Solomon raises Hiram Abiff from 'a dead level to a living perpendicular' using a grip known as the Lion's Paw (also called the Strong Grip), a secret handshake known only to Master

Masons. Basically the Masons interlace their thumbs and press the tops of their fingers against the other's wrist at the top of the hand. A Mason is shown the grip during initiation into the Third Degree and is told the words, Ma Ha Bone. Some people have interpreted the story of Hiram Abiff as told in Masonic ritual to parallel the story of Jesus – death, burial, resurrection – while others believe the origins are to be found in ancient pre-Christian religious beliefs.

Chapter Eleven – The Matter of Rewards

1. George R Sims, *The Referee*, 7 September 1888.
2. He was born Montagu Samuel to a Jewish watchmaking and silver-smithing family who had emigrated from northern Germany to Britain in the mid-1700s. For some reason his family changed his name to Samuel Montagu. In 1852, aged twenty, he borrowed £5,000 from his father and went into business with his elder brother, Edwin Samuel, a Liverpool bullion merchant, and what would become the successful banking firm of Samuel & Montagu was born. Soon Samuel Montagu was enormously wealthy. He was elected to Parliament in 1885 and was created Lord Swaythling in 1907. Very active in Jewish affairs, in 1887 he founded the Federation of Synagogues. He had ten children and one of his grand-children was Ewen Montagu, who wrote the wartime story *The Man Who Never Was*. The banking business remained independent until the 1950s. In 1974 it was acquired by Midland Bank, founded in Birmingham in 1836 to become through a series of mergers and amalgamations one of the major banks in Britain. In July 1992 it became part of HSBC – which retains its name from the founding company, The Hong Kong and Shanghai Banking Corporation Limited, founded in 1865.
3. *The Star*, 11 September 1888.
4. *The Star*, 1 October 1888.
5. *Manchester Guardian, Yorkshire Post*, 1 October 1888.
6. *Yorkshire Post*, 2 October 1888.
7. *Weekly Herald*, 7 September 1888.
8. *The Star*, 10 September 1888.
9. *Illustrated Police News*, 22 September 1888.
10. *The Star*, 19 September 1888.
11. *Daily Telegraph*, 1 October 1888.
12. *The Star*, 14 September 1888.
13. *The Star*, 18 September 1888.
14. *Daily Telegraph*, 19 September 1888.

15. *The Star*, 19 September 1888.
16. *Daily Telegraph*, 24 September 1888.
17. *Manchester Guardian*, 3 October 1888.
18. Shane Leslie (1921), 'Henry Matthews Lord Llandaff', *Dublin Review*, vol. 168, January, p. 6. I can find no confirmation of this. Salisbury, in a letter to Queen Victoria, said that Matthews was recommended by Lord Halsbury and Sir Henry James. The same source states that Matthews did not ask for the office of home secretary and 'was so flabbergasted by the offer . . . that he left Arlington House [Lord Salisbury's residence] under the impression that he had declined, but, finding himself gazetted Home Secretary the next day, accepted his fate'.
19. R H William (1889), *The Salisbury–Balfour Correspondence 1869–1892* (Hitchin: Hertfordshire Record Society), A J Balfour to Lord Salisbury, 28 January.
20. Sir Robert Ensor (1936), *England 1870–1914* (Oxford University Press).
21. Letter from Lord Salisbury to Queen Victoria dated 31 October 1888, in George Earle Buckle (ed.) (1930), *The Letters of Queen Victoria: Third Series: A Selection from Her Majesty's Correspondence and Journal between the years 1886 and 1901* (London: John Murray), Vol. I, p. 445.
22. Which is precisely what happened. Matthews was created Viscount Llandaff and thereafter travelled extensively and played no part in public life. His latter years were spent crippled by rheumatism and he died unmarried in 1913. There is an unpublished biography of Henry Matthews by W S Lilly.
23. The full import of this may be judged when one realises that Matthews had been 'a great favourite of the Queen', according to Leslie, op. cit.
24. MEPO 3/140, fols. 170–6, letter written by Samuel Montagu dated 10 September 1888 offering a reward.
25. HO 144/220/A49301B, fols. 184–5.
26. Ibid., fols. 180–1.
27. Watkin Wynn Williams (1941), *The Life of General Sir Charles Warren: By His Grandson* (Oxford: Blackwell).
28. HO 144/220/A49301B, fols. 182–3, letter by E Leigh Pemberton on behalf of Henry Matthews to Sir Charles Warren dated 13 September 1888 concerning his request for guidance concerning Samuel Montagu's offer of a reward. A copy also exists in MEPO 3/140, fols. 174–5.
29. HO 144/220/A49301B, fols. 172–3.
30. Ibid., fols. 170–1.
31. *The Star*, 11 September 1888.
32. HO 144/221/A49301C, fols. 173–81, report to Home Office from Sir Charles Warren dated 6 November 1888.

33. Rt Hon. John Satterfield Sandars (1853–1934), a lawyer who practised until 1886, when he was appointed private secretary to the home secretary.
34. *Morning Advertiser*, 4 October 1888. Interestingly, he met with James Monro to discuss rewards the next day.
35. J S Sandars's papers, MS. Eng. hist. c. 723. Bodleian Library, Department of Western Manuscripts, Oxford. Letter from Henry Matthews to Evelyn Ruggles Brise.
36. Ibid., letter dated 5 October 1888 from Henry Matthews to Evelyn Ruggles Brise.
37. HO 144/220/A49301B, fols. 246–52, letter from Sir Charles Warren to Henry Matthews dated 6 October 1888.

Chapter Twelve – Dear Boss

1. George R Sims, *The Referee*, 7 October 1888.
2. MEPO 3/3153, fols. 1–4, letter to the Metropolitan Police from Tom Bulling of the Central News Limited enclosing a letter received by them and signed 'Jack the Ripper', which the news agency had received on 27 September.
3. MEPO 3/142, fols. 2–3, postcard addressed to Central News Office, London City, EC.
4. *Daily Telegraph*, 1 October 1888.
5. *Daily Telegraph*, 4 October 1888.
6. *The Star*, 4 October 1888.
7. The Old Testament (Num. 35: 3–18) tells how the women of the countries of Moab and Midian literally seduced Israelite men into the worship of Baal-Peor, a fertility deity local to Peor, probably Mount Peor on the left bank of the River Jordan, in whose worship women prostituted themselves. The men of Israel were thus seduced into worshipping Baal themselves and incurred the wrath of God, who caused a plague to kill thousands of people. To end the plague, through Moses God instructed that the idolaters should be killed, and, on finding an Israelite chieftain named Zimri and a Midianite woman named Cozbi in the act of copulation, Phinehas, the grandson of Aaron the priest, drove a spear through the bellies of both and through this deed awakened the Israelites to their sins and brought the plague to an end. The letter writer, in saying that the divine power protected and helped him, evidently saw himself as Phinehas and hoped through the killing of prostitutes to awaken society to its ills and its salvation. There could even be a hint that the killer was a Jew, because the Moab and Midianite women were also encouraging the

Israelites to break the prohibition on intermarriage with foreign peoples and the feared consequent corruption of Israel's faith (Deut. 7: 1–5). Both Stride and Eddowes found employment among the Jews, both were prostitutes, and both may therefore have been perceived by a 'Phinehas Priest' in a very literal sense as 'women of Moab and Midian'. If so, perhaps the letter shows a greater understanding of scripture than might at first have been appreciated.

8. *The Star*, 8 October 1888.
9. Charles Tempest Clarkson and J Hall Richardson (1889), *Police!* (London: Field and Tuer), p. 278.
10. *The Referee*, 7 October 1888.
11. Sir Robert Anderson (1910), 'The Lighter Side of My Official Life. XI. At Scotland Yard', *Blackwood's Magazine*, March; later published as Sir Robert Anderson (1910), *The Lighter Side of My Official Life* (London: Hodder and Stoughton).
12. Sir Melville Macnaghten (1914), *Days of My Years* (London: Longman, Green and Co.), p. 58.
13. This is another little story requiring research. A life of William Palmer, who was hanged at Stafford on 14 June 1856, called *Palmer The Rugeley Poisoner* by Dudley Barker, was published by Duckworth in 1935. And a jockey named John Faulkner is apparently buried at Appleford, Berkshire. He apparently rode his first winner aged eight and his last at 74. The village of Culham on the Oxfordshire–Berkshire border, where the anonymous author says he and Best met Faulkner, is very close to Appleford.
14. Woodland *Daily Democrat*, 5 December 1890.
15. Lincoln Springfield (1924), *Some Piquant People* (London: T Fisher Unwin).
16. *Fresno Weekly Republican*, 21 November 1890.
17. 'Right from the opening chorus the audience went wild about *The Shop Girl*, a slight story of an attractive girl who serves in a store and charms all the customers and, after a few misunderstandings, agrees to marry her sweetheart, a young medical student . . .' Alan Hyman (1976), *Sullivan and His Satellites* (London: Chappell and Company).
18. The first of three plays written that year with Sims: *The Lights of Home*, *The Lost Paradise* and *The Black Domino*.
19. *Truth*, 11 October 1888.
20. George Scott (1968), *Reporter Anonymous: The Story of the Press Association* (London: Hutchinson), pp. 114–18.
21. Chris Moncrieff (2001), *Living on a Deadline: A History of the Press Association* (London: Virgin), pp. 53–8.

22. R Thurston Hopkins (1935), *Life and Death at the Old Bailey* (London: Herbert Jenkins), pp. 202–3.

23. *News of the World*, 7 October 1888.

24. *Eastern Post and Daily Chronicle*, 13 October 1888.

25. *The Times*, 15 October 1888.

26. 'Box of toys' is rhyming slang for 'noise', but here the writer seems to mean 'cowboys', suggesting that the Vigilance Committee were ineffectual.

27. *Daily Telegraph*, 19 October 1888.

28. *Daily Telegraph*, 20 October 1888.

29. Ibid.

30. *Daily Telegraph*, 19 October 1888.

31. HO 144/221/A49301C, fols. 184–94, report by Chief Inspector Donald S Swanson dated 6 November 1888.

32. *The Star*, 19 October 1888.

33. *The Star*, 20 October 1888.

34. Bright's disease – also known as acute glomerulonephritis, acute nephritic syndrome, acute nephritis – is a now obsolete term for a disease of the kidneys named after the British physician Richard Bright (1789–1858). At the inquest Dr Frederick Gordon Brown described Eddowes's 'right kidney pale bloodless with slight congestion of the base of the pyramids' (Coroner's inquest (L), 1888, No. 135, Catherine Eddowes inquest, 1888, Corporation of London Records Office), which would not be inconsistent with Bright's disease, but isn't evidence for the disease either, and no reason is given as to why the Lusk kidney suggested Bright's.

35. *Sunday Times*, 21 October 1888.

36. Lieutenant-Colonel Sir Henry Smith (1910), *From Constable to Commissioner: The Story of Sixty Years, Most of Them Misspent* (London: Chatto and Windus).

37. W Hale-White (1935), *Great Doctors of the Nineteenth Century* (London: E. Arnold).

38. London, 1891, vol. 1, p. 130.

39. London, 1891, vol. 1, p. 1408.

40. London, 1891/92, vol. 75, pp. 5–7.

41. Patricia Cornwell (2003), *Portrait of a Killer: Jack the Ripper – Case Closed* (London: Little, Brown); paperback (2003) (London: Time Warner). For a comprehensive account of all the Ripper correspondence see Stewart P Evans and Keith Skinner (2001), *Jack the Ripper: Letters From Hell* (Stroud, Gloucestershire: Sutton).

Chapter Thirteen – Are You One of Us?

1. *Daily Telegraph*, 1 October 1888.
2. *Boston Daily Globe*, 2 October 1888.
3. *East London Advertiser*, 6 October 1888.
4. *The Star*, 1 October 1888.
5. *Daily Telegraph*, 2 October 1888.
6. *Weekly Herald*, 5 October 1888.
7. *East London Observer*, 6 October 1888.
8. *The Star*, 1 October 1888.
9. *The Star*, 8 October 1888.
10. *Eastern Post & City Chronicle*, 13 October 1888.
11. *The Star*, 1 October 1888.
12. *Daily Telegraph*, 2 October 1888.
13. *The Star*, 1 October 1888.
14. *The Star*, 3 October 1888.
15. Ibid.
16. *Daily Telegraph*, 3 October 1888.
17. *The Star*, 1 October 1888.
18. *The Star*, 1 October 1888.
19. *Daily Telegraph*, 1 October 1888.
20. *The Star*, 1 October 1888.
21. *Daily Telegraph*, 2 October 1888.
22. *Daily Telegraph*, 4 October 1888; *East London Observer*, 6 October 1888.
23. The body *was* that of Elizabeth Stride, so either 'Annie Morris' was another of Stride's aliases or One-armed Liz's identification was wrong. What is curious is that One-armed Liz may have lived at 55 Flower and Dean Street, where Eddowes lived. The reason for this is that the *Daily Telegraph* (19 September 1888) stated that a woman who was threatened by Charles Ludwig had only one arm and was well known to the police (*Daily Telegraph*, 26 September 1888). *The Star* (2 October 1888) said her name was Elizabeth Burns, and that she was a prostitute who lived at 55 Flower and Dean Street.

    There cannot have been many one-armed prostitutes named Liz/ Elizabeth living in Flower and Dean Street, so it is a safe bet that One-armed Liz and Elizabeth Burns were one and the same, and it is therefore ironic that One-armed Liz therefore lived in the same lodging as Catherine Eddowes and yet identified the body of Elizabeth Stride, who lived on and off at 32 Flower and Dean Street. A *Star* reporter spoke to One-armed Liz in the crowded kitchen of the lodging house, where she was being fêted as if a heroine, and has left an account. The kitchen, he said, was large, with a very low ceiling, walls black with grime and filth, and the floor inches deep with dirt. The 'atmosphere could have been served up with a spoon' and at a huge fireplace a score of suppers were cooking under 'a halo of vile vapour' (*The Star*, 1 October 1888). He got little information from One-armed Liz and only a fraction more from a character known as Toby, although neither need have been discussing Stride.

24. *City Press*, 3 October 1888.
25. *The Times*, 2 October 1888.
26. Ibid.
27. *East London Advertiser*, 6 October 1888.
28. *New York Times*, 2 October 1888.
29. *Pall Mall Gazette*, 3 October 1888, reported 10,000.
30. *Daily Telegraph*, 4 October 1888.
31. HO 144/221/A49301C, fol. 147, 19 October 1888.
32. *Daily Telegraph*, 5 October 1888.
33. *Eastern Post & City Chronicle*, 13 October 1888.
34. *The Star*, 1 October 1888.
35. *The Star*, 5 October 1888.
36. *Daily Telegraph*, 2 October 1888.
37. *Daily Telegraph*, 3, 5 October 1888
38. *Atlanta Constitution*, 5 October 1888.
39. *The Star*, 4 October 1888.
40. *Daily Telegraph*, 4 October 1888; *The Star*, 4 October 1888.
41. Perhaps the same Frederick Jago who famously compiled two books about the Cornish language, *Ancient Language and Dialect of Cornwall*, which appeared in 1882, and *English–Cornish Dictionary* in 1887. In the latter he suggested that the word 'dowsing', which dates only from about 1831, came from the Cornish.
42. *The Times*, 3 October 1888.
43. The first suggestion that fingerprints could be used to identify criminals was made by Henry Faulds in the 28 October 1888 issue of *Nature*, but it failed to generate any interest. See Colin Beaven (2002), *Fingerprints, Murder and the Race to Uncover the Science of Identity* (London: Fourth Estate).
44. *The Star*, 3 October 1888; *Montreal Gazette*, 4 October 1888.
45. *Daily Telegraph*, 3 October 1888.
46. *Chicago Tribune*, 7 October 1888.
47. Leonard Gribble (1973), 'Was Jack the Ripper A Black Magician?', *True Detective*; Melvin Harris (1994, 1995), *The True Face of Jack the Ripper* (London: Michael O'Mara), Ivor J Edwards (2002), *Jack the Ripper's*

Black Magic Rituals: Satanism, The Occult, Murder, The Sinister Truth of the Doctor Who Was Jack the Ripper (London: Blake), completely revised and rewritten edition of a book privately published in 2001 (Lake, Isle of Wight: Penny Publishing).

48. *The Star*, 9 October 1888; *Illustrated Police News*, 20 October 1888.

49. *The Times*, 2 October 1888; *Jewish Chronicle*, 5 October 1888; *The Times*, 16 October 1888; *The Times* 25 October 1888.

50. *City Press*, 10 October 1888; *East London Observer*, 13 October 1888.

51. *Daily Telegraph*, 9 October 1888; *East London Observer*, 13 October 1888; *Eastern Post & City Chronicle* 13 October 1888.

52. *The Star*, 6 October 1888.

53. *Daily Telegraph*, 4 October 1888; 5 October 1888.

54. *The Star*, 6 October 1888.

55. *Daily Telegraph*, 2 October 1888.

56. *The Star*, 17 October 1888.

57. *Daily Telegraph*, 18 October 1888.

58. Sir Robert Anderson (1910), *The Lighter Side of My Official Life* (London: Hodder and Stoughton).

59. *Daily Telegraph*, 3 October 1888.

60. Philip Sugden says that this claim by Anderson can be 'categorically refuted' and that the house-to-house enquiry completed on 18 October 'did not persuade the police that the murders had been committed by a Jew'. Sugden gives three reasons for this claim. (1) That the police did not think the Ripper was a Jew is implicit in reports written on 6 November by Sir Charles Warren and Chief Inspector Donald Swanson, in which they say that the Goulston Street graffito was 'evidently written with the intention of inflaming the public mind against the Jews'. (2) Polish Jews were not reluctant to assist the police, numerous newspapers on 18 October carrying a statement of thanks by Sir Charles Warren to the people of all classes and creeds of the East End who 'with few exceptions' had cooperated with the house-to-house enquiry. And in a private memorandum written on 23 October 1888, Anderson had himself commented that 'the inhabitants of the East End have shown a marked desire to assist in every way, even at some sacrifice to themselves, as for example in permitting their houses to be searched . . .' (3) The house-to-house enquiry that finished on 18 October did not furnish *any* clues, as shown by Anderson's 23 October report, in which he frankly admitted failure when he referred to the CID as being without 'the slightest clue of any kind'. See Philip Sugden (1994), *The Complete History of Jack the Ripper* (London: Robinson); revised paperback edition (1995, London: Robinson; New York, NY: Carroll and Graf); paperback with new

introduction (2002, London: Robinson; New York, NY: Carroll and Graf), pp. 416–17.

But these arguments unacceptably stretch the context to achieve the author's desired interpretation. In the case of (1) the police were concerned to avert a violent reaction against the Jewish community that they feared sight of the writing would provoke, and their own opinions about who the murderer might have been didn't enter into it. But there was no certainty that the graffito had been written by the murderer, and reference in the reports to the writing as being blurred (old) and bearing no resemblance to the handwriting of the Jack the Ripper letter and postcard indicate that the graffito was not thought to have been written by the murderer. (2) Anderson's statement in 1910 does not contradict the comments. He did not say that Polish Jews were generally uncooperative, only specifically that they were reluctant to hand one of their own over to Gentile justice, a claim Anderson was not alone in making and one that was probably and understandably true. This said, the *Eastern Post and City Chronicle*, 17 November 1888, reported, 'It is understood that the police will not renew the house-to-house search, as it was found when last adopted to be a failure. The officers discovered nothing but poverty and vice, while a great number of the houses, if such they can be termed, they were resolutely refused admission.' (3) That the murderer was a low-class Polish Jew was a deduction, not a clue, but Anderson actually wrote, 'That a crime of this kind should have been committed without any clue being supplied by the criminal is unusual, but that five successive murders should have been committed without our having the slightest clue of any kind is extraordinary, if not unique, in the annals of crime.' From this it is clear that he was not admitting failure or suggesting that the police had no idea where to turn next, but was saying that a murderer usually left a clue, and the fact that no clue had been left after five successive murders was extraordinary. He went on to say that this had caused the police to follow up clues and suggestions from other sources.

Overall, there is nothing inherently unacceptable in what Anderson wrote, and the evidence from disparate sources suggests that the conclusion was indeed one they reached and reached for the reasons Anderson gave.

61. *Aftonbladet*, 26 October 1888.
62. *Daily News*, 16 October 1888.
63. *Daily Telegraph*, 16 October 1888.
64. *Manchester Guardian*, 16 October 1888.
65. *The Referee*, 18 November 1888.
66. *Daily Telegraph*, 2 October 1888.
67. Ibid.

68. *Daily Telegraph*, 3 October 1888.
69. *Daily Telegraph*, 4 October 1888; *The Star*, 5 October 1888.
70. Daily Telegraph, 2 October 1888; HO/144/221/A49301C, fols. 13–15, 71–5.

Chapter Fourteen – Francis Tumblety

1. *San Francisco Chronicle*, 23 November 1888; *New York Times*, 23 November 1888. The *San Francisco Chronicle* printed the reply: 'LONDON (England), Thursday, November 22 – P. Crowley, Chief of Police, San Francisco, Cal.: Thanks. Send handwriting and all details you can of Tumblety. ANDERSON, Scotland Yard.' That Scotland Yard took a month to respond to Chief Crowley's offer suggests that the need for the handwriting samples was not urgent.
2. Margaret died 27 May 1873, aged 87.
3. 1850 Federal Census, Rochester, NY, 8th Ward 25 28, where he is listed as Francis Tumathy, aged 19, occupation labourer, born Ireland. Tumblety told a young man named Martin McGarry that he was born in Dublin in 1835. He also claimed that he was the son of a wealthy Irish gentleman and had graduated from the University of Dublin (he produced a diploma as proof). He claimed to have studied medicine in Dublin (producing another diploma), and that he had left Ireland for America in 1853. Little of this was true, although he may have arrived in New York in 1853 – from Rochester.
4. Captain W C Streeter, Rochester *Democrat and Republican*, 3 December 1888. Attested by the 1851/52 Rochester City Directory.
5. Haywood said that one of Tumblety's brothers was a gardener for his uncle; this would have been Lawrence, whose occupation is given as gardener.
6. Captain W C Streeter, Rochester *Democrat and Republican*, 3 December 1888.
7. Edward Haywood, Rochester *Democrat and Republican*, 3 December 1888. The Brooklyn *Daily Eagle*, 10 May 1865, put a different slant on things, saying that Tumblety 'was employed at first as servant or errand boy in the office of Dr Lispenard, on Exchange place, a celebrated special practitioner. He afterwards studied medicine with Lispenard, and graduated in a short time, and it is stated left Rochester unceremoniously.'
8. This isn't confirmed.
9. *Evening Star* (Washington, DC), 11 May 1865, quoting the *Rochester Union* newspaper, 9 May 1865.

10. Ibid.
11. C S Gurnet to J G Bowes, mayor of Toronto, dated 8 February 1861, reprinted in *St John's Dispatch*, 28 March 1861.
12. Edward Haywood, Rochester *Democrat and Republican*, 3 December 1888.
13. *Le Courier du Canada*, 4 November 1857.
14. Thomas Darcy McGee was born in Ireland in 1825 and emigrated to the USA in 1842. He moved to Montreal in 1857, was elected to the House of Assembly in 1858, and is one of the Fathers of Confederation. He was assassinated on 7 April 1868 for his anti-Fenianism.
15. See the *Montreal Commercial Advertiser*, 7 December 1857.
16. *Brooklyn Daily Eagle* (New York), 10 May 1865.
17. *New York Times*, 23 November 1888.
18. C S Gurnet to J G Bowes, mayor of Toronto, dated 8 February 1861, reprinted in *St John's Dispatch*, 28 March 1861.
19. *Evening Star* (Washington, DC), 11 May 1865.
20. *Brandon Mail* (Manitoba, Canada), 22 November 1888.
21. *Evening Star* (Washington, DC), 27 November 1888, quoting the *New York World*.
22. *Daily Sun* (St John, New Brunswick, Canada), 22 November 1888.
23. *Eastport Sentinel*, as quoted in the *Morning Freeman* (New Brunswick, Canada), 29 September, 1860.
24. Ibid., 16 October 1860.
25. *New York World*, 27 November 1888.
26. 22 November 1888.
27. Tumblety moved to New York in 1864 from Nova Scotia, where he was known as Dr Sullivan – *New York Herald*, 19 November 1888.
28. *St John's Dispatch*, 28 March 1861.
29. *Daily Sun* (St John, New Brunswick, Canada), 22 November 1888.
30. *New York Herald*, 20 November 1888.
31. *New York Times*, 19 November 1888.
32. *Daily Sun* (St John, New Brunswick, Canada), 22 November 1888.
33. *Washington Star*, 20 November 1888; *New York Herald*, 21 November 1888.
34. Rochester *Democrat and Republican*, 3 December 1888.
35. *Evening Star* (Washington, DC), 11 May 1865.
36. Rochester *Democrat and Republican*, 3 December 1888.
37. Jacob Shall Golladay, born in Lebanon, Wilson County, Tennessee, 19 January 1819, died near Russellville, Logan County, Kentucky, 20 May 1887, represented Kentucky's 3rd District in the United States House of Representatives from 1867 to 1870. Edward Isaac Golladay, born in Lebanon, Wilson County, Tennessee, 9 September 1830, died Columbia, Richland County, South Carolina, 11 July 1897.

38. *Washington Star*, 21 November 1888.
39. *Evening Star* (Washington, DC), 4 December 1861.
40. Ibid.
41. *Brooklyn Daily Eagle* (New York), 6 and 10 May 1864.
42. *Hamilton Evening Times* (Hamilton, Ontario), 8 May 1865, quoting the *New York Tribune*, 5 May 1865.
43. Ibid.
44. Rochester *Democrat and Republican*, 3 December 1888; *Brooklyn Daily Eagle* (New York), 10 May 1865.
45. *Missouri Republican*, 7 May 1865; *New York Times*, 7 May 1865.
46. There is a biography of him by Nancy Disher Baird (1979), *Luke Pryor Blackburn: Physician, Reformer, Governor* (Lexington: University Press of Kentucky).
47. National Archives, War Department Records, File 'B', Doc. 261, JAO, quoted by Stuart Evans and Paul Gainey.
48. *New York Times*, 10 June 1865.
49. *Hamilton Evening Times* (Hamilton, Ontario), 29 May 1865.
50. Rochester *Democrat and Republican*, 3 December 1888.
51. *New York Times*, November 23, 1888.
52. *San Francisco Chronicle*, 20 November, 1888.
53. *Brooklyn Daily Eagle*, 2 February 1889. He also claimed that he went to London in 1863 with a letter of introduction from President Lincoln to the foreign secretary, Lord John Russell. This must be considered highly unlikely as relations with England at that time were very precarious. Britain's initial support of the Confederacy required the skilled diplomacy of Lincoln's minister in England, Charles Francis Adams, not an uneducated herbalist, no matter how successful. But the story illustrates how Tumblety seized news stories for his own publicity.
54. See Budd L Gambee (1964), *Frank Leslie and His Illustrated Newspaper, 1855–1860*, PhD dissertation, University of Michigan; and Madeleine B Stern (1953), *Purple Passage: The Life of Mrs Frank Leslie* (Norman: University of Oklahoma Press).
55. *New York Herald*, 4 December 1888.
56. *Irish Canadian*, 12 October 1875.
57. Holloway's Pills – which contained aloe, myrrh, and saffron – claimed to cure an astonishing range of diseases, though in reality they certainly didn't. They were the most famous patent medicine in the Empire and made Thomas Holloway a multimillionaire. He used some of his money to found Royal Holloway College in 1879. He was also responsible for the sanatorium at Virginia Water, opened in 1885.

58. Possibly the same person who was justice of the New York Supreme Court, 1st District, 1925–6, and justice of the Appellate Division of the New York Supreme Court, 1st Department, 1926.

59. Which prompts the question of who wrote his letters to Hall Caine.

60. In March 1880 she was stranded on Anglesey, North Wales, refloated but damaged so badly that she was scrapped.

61. Rochester *Democrat and Republican*, 3 December 1888, quoting the *New York World*.

62. *San Francisco Chronicle*, 20 November 1888.

63. Rochester *Democrat and Republican*, 3 December 1888, quoting the *New York World*.

64. *Atchison Daily Globe*, Kansas, 15 December 1888.

65. *New York World*, 4 December 1888.

66. Ibid.

67. *New York World*, 2 December 1888.

68. *New York World*, 4 December 1888.

69. Ibid.

70. Ibid.

71. Rochester *Democrat and Republican*, 3 December 1888.

72. *New York World*, 6 December 1888.

73. Thomas Byrnes was born in Ireland in 1842 and went to America as a child. He received very little education and began his working life as a gas fitter, but joined the New York police in 1863. Shrewd, brutal, the inventor of the 'third degree', he effectively ruled New York until the appointment of the young Theodore Roosevelt as president of the Board of Police Commissioners. Roosevelt thoroughly distrusted him and had him removed from office for 'selective enforcement', a web of corruption thereafter being revealed, although nothing specific seemed to attach itself to Byrnes, who in 1895 became an insurance investigator. He died of stomach cancer in New York on 7 May 1910.

74. *New York Herald*, 4 December 1888.

75. *New York Times*, 4 December 1888.

76. *St Louis Republican*, 22 December 1888.

77. *Pall Mall Gazette*, 31 December 1888.

78. Walter Dew (1938), *I Caught Crippen: Memoirs of Ex-Chief Inspector Walter Dew C.I.D.* (London: Blackie and Son). Walter Simon Andrews, his health failing him, retired from the police on 31 August 1889 and spent eight years as a private detective in London. His health then failed further and he developed mental problems, which in August 1899 caused him to hang himself from a tree.

79. Stewart Evans and Paul Gainey (1995), *The Lodger: The Arrest and Escape of Jack the Ripper* (London: Century); published (1996) as *Jack the Ripper: First American Serial Killer* (London: Arrow).

80. Leon OBroin (1971), *The Prime Informer: A Suppressed Scandal* (London: Sidgwick and Jackson), p. 66.

81. *Brooklyn Daily Eagle* (New York), 28 January 1889, 19 November 1890.

82. *Trenton Times*, 19 November 1890; *Washington Post*, 19 November 1890.

83. Chief Inspector Swanson, report dated 19 October 1888, HO 144/221/A49301C, fol. 147, date 19 October 1888.

84. *The Globe*, 10 October 1888.

85. *East Anglian Daily Times*, 11 October 1888.

86. *Suffolk Chronicle*, 13 October 1888.

87. *The Star*, quoting a Central News report, 19 October 1888.

88. *Daily Telegraph*, 23 November 1888.

89. 'Tumuelty' on the gravestone was one of the many spelling variations of this surname.

90. *Washington Post*, 18 November 1890.

Chapter Fifteen – Sir Charles Warren Resigns

1. George R Sims, *The Referee*, 18 November 1888.

2. Letter from Home Secretary Henry Matthews to Queen Victoria informing her of Sir Charles Warren's resignation, in George Earle Buckle (ed.) (1930), *The Letters of Queen Victoria: Third Series: A Selection from Her Majesty's Correspondence and Journal between the years 1886 and 1901* (London: John Murray).

3. Draft letter from Queen Victoria to Sir Henry Matthews commenting on Sir Charles Warren's resignation and police measures to catch the Ripper, in Buckle, op. cit.

4. *Alderley and Wilmslow Advertiser*, 26 November 1888.

5. *New York Herald*, 13 November 1888.

6. *Alderley and Wilmslow Advertiser*, 26 November 1888.

7. *The Times*, 13 November 1888.

8. Letter dated 24 November 1888 from Henry Matthews to Queen Victoria informing her of the appointment of James Monro as the new Metropolitan Police commissioner.

Chapter Sixteen – Mary Jane Kelly

1. *Boston Daily Globe*, 10 November 1888.
2. *Manchester Guardian, Western Mail*, 10 November 1888: Barnett 'at once identified the body as that of Kelly, of "Ginger," as she was called, owing to the colour of her hair.' (Other sources described her hair colour differently.)
3. Tom Cullen (1965), *Autumn of Terror: Jack the Ripper His Crimes and Times* (London: Bodley Head), reissued in paperback (1973) as *The Crimes and Times of Jack the Ripper* (London: Fontana). US title (1965): *When London Walked in Terror* (Boston, MA: Houghton Mifflin).
4. 'a blonde, of medium height', *East London Observer*, 17 November 1888.
5. *Manchester Guardian, Western Mail*, 10 November 1888.
6. *Daily Telegraph*, 10 November 1888.
7. 'She was short, stout and dark . . .' (Maurice Lewis as reported in the *Illustrated Police News*, 17 November 1888). One suspects that Morris Lewis thought someone else was Kelly.
8. *Daily Telegraph*, 10 November 1888. This description was possibly given by John McCarthy, Kelly's landlord at the time of her death, as it features in a paragraph in which he denied knowledge that she was a prostitute, her respectable appearance not indicating that she was.
9. Walter Dew (1938), *I Caught Crippen: Memoirs of Ex-Chief Inspector Walter Dew C.I.D.* (London: Blackie and Son).
10. Sir Melville Macnaghten (1914), *Days of My Years* (London: Arnold).
11. *Western Mail*, 12 November 1888.
12. Stephen Knight (1976), *Jack the Ripper: The Final Solution* (London: George G Harrap). Also published by Panther Books, London, in 1977; Treasure Press, London, in 1984; and by Chancellor Press, London, with a foreword by Nigel Cawthorne, in 2000.
13. The 1973 BBC six-part drama-documentary *Jack the Ripper* featured an elderly nun at the convent in Harewood Place, London W1, who said that in 1915 she had been a novice at the refuge and clearly remembered that an old nun who had been there in 1888 had told her, 'If it had not been for the Kelly woman, none of the murders would have happened.' It is obviously a very unreliable piece of testimony, but nevertheless a strange comment for a nun to have made.
14. This may be an incorrect spelling. There is nobody named Buki in the 1881 census.
15. *Evening Express*, 12 November 1888; *Western Mail*, 13 November 1888.
16. The name is incorrectly given as 'Mrs Carthy' in several newspaper reports, but as 'Mrs McCarthy' in the *Evening Express*, 12 November

1888. No Mrs Carthy has been found living in Breezer's Hill, but in his 2003 booklet, *Catherine Eddowes: Jack the Ripper Victim* (Hornchurch, Essex: Neal Shelden), Neal Shelden identified and described Mrs Mary McCarthy living at 1 Breezer's Hill, off Pennington Street, St George's-in-the-East. See also Paul Daniel (1996), 'McCarthy, Kelly and Breezer's Hill', *Ripperologist*, Issue 8, December.

17. This would put Kelly with Mrs McCarthy about 1885.
18. Mrs Carthy (née Brooks) of 1 Breezer's Hill had a sister named Elizabeth, but there is no record yet found of an Elizabeth Brooks marrying a man named Phoenix.
19. Three other residents listed in the 1891 census were, Ellen Forbes, Abey March and Emma Benton, all prostitutes.
20. Press Association report, *Western Mail*, 12 November 1888.
21. *Western Mail*, 12 November 1888.
22. Julia Venturney quoted in *The Times* and the *Western Mail*, 13 November 1888; MJ/SPC, NE1888, Box 3, Case Paper 19 (London Metropolitan Archives).
23. *Western Mail*, 10 November 1888.
24. Joseph Barnett told a newspaper reporter that he had met Kelly 'last Easter twelve month'. At the inquest he spoke of having met Kelly on a Friday night. Easter Sunday 1887 was 10 April, so Barnett and Kelly would have met on Good Friday, 8 April 1888. See *Observer*, 11 November 1888; *The Penny Illustrated Paper*, 17 November 1888, and others.
25. *Daily Telegraph*, 12 November 1888.
26. In an interview with Inspector Abberline on 9 November 1888 (MJ/SPC/NE 1888, Box 3, No. 19, Corporation of London, Greater London Archives, Coroner's Records), Barnett said that 'she had a brother named Henry serving in 2nd Battn. Scots Guards, and known amongst his comrades as Johnto, and I believe the Regiment is now in Ireland'. But the *Daily Telegraph*, 13 November 1888, reporting Joseph Barnett's testimony at the inquest, has him saying only that one of Kelly's brothers was named Henry, not that Henry was the brother in the army. This may simply be a minor slip, but Jonto or Johnto is an unusual nickname for someone named Henry, although I am aware that 'Jonto' was the nickname of a man named Samuel Holloway, who in the 1830s had been in jail nearly sixty times (*Windsor and Eton Express*, 21 January 1837), so it need not be a nickname for someone called John. However, one should perhaps allow for the possibility that Barnett confused the forenames of Kelly's father and brother, and that the father may have been named Henry and the brother named John.

27. *Daily Telegraph*, 12 November 1888.
28. John McCarthy in an interview with Central News reported in *The Times*, 10 November 1888.
29. *Yorkshire Post*, 2 October 1888.
30. *Daily Telegraph*, 10 November 1888.
31. *The Times*, 12 November 1888; that Kelly visited this pub nightly seems improbable and it may be a detail wrongly attributed to her.
32. *Daily Telegraph*, 12 November 1888.
33. Mrs McCarthy in a Press Association interview. *Western Mail*, 10 November 1888.
34. Press Association report in *Western Mail*, 13 November 1888.
35. Maria Harvey, 10 November 1888.
36. *Western Mail*, from Press Association, 10 November 1888.
37. Cullen, op. cit.
38. The London correspondent of the Philadelphia *Press* quoted in the *Evening Star* (Washington, DC), 10 November 1888.
39. *The Times*, 13 November 1888.
40. *Daily Telegraph*, *The Times*, 10 November 1888.
41. Inquest testimony, *Daily Telegraph*, 13 November 1888.
42. The address is given on his birth certificate.
43. Register of Billingsgate Porters' Licences 1877–1906, ref. MB/18/1/, held by the Corporation of London Records Office.
44. Inquest testimony of John McCarthy, MJ/SPC, NE1888, Box 3, Case Paper 19 (London Metropolitan Archives).
45. The old man may have been pointing to 35 Dorset Street, Crossingham's Lodging House, where Mary Ann Austin was murdered. In November 1898 two sisters, Elizabeth Roberts and Kate Marshall, returned to 26 Dorset Street, both drunk, and after an altercation Marshall fatally stabbed Roberts and after trial was sentenced to death. In July 1909, in the room above Mary Kelly's, occupied at the time of Kelly's murder by Elizabeth Prater, a young woman known as Kitty Ronan was murdered, her throat having been cut from ear to ear apparently while she was sleeping. As late as February 1960 murders were being committed in Duval Street: three men went into the Pen Club in Duval Street and shot a Soho club manager and a promising middleweight boxer.
46. In 1909 a young woman named Kitty Ronan (sometimes called Kitty Norman) was found dead in her room in Miller's Court on 2 July, her throat cut, apparently with a large pocket knife. She had taken a man home who looked like a sailor and he had left after staying with her for about half an hour. A Canadian journalist named Kathleen Blake Watkins misidentified the murder scene as the room above Mary Kelly's, occupied

in 1888 by Elizabeth Prater, but the room was upstairs in one of the houses in the Court, probably No. 12. The error has been repeated many times, but the correct location is made clear in several contemporary accounts of the crime, such as the *Illustrated Police News*, 10 July 1909, which said, 'Two doors away on the right hand side near the entrance, is the house in which one of the last "Jack the Ripper" murders was committed.'

47. The *Daily Telegraph*, 10 November 1888, reported that 'the walls are of thin match lining' and Elizabeth Prater, who lived in the room above Kelly's, said that 'on the stairs I could see a glimmer through the partition if there had been a light in the deceased's room' (MJ/SPC, NE1888, Box 3, Case Paper 19, London Metropolitan Archives).

48. *Daily Telegraph*, 12 November 1888.

49. *The Fisherman's Widow* is mentioned in a description of Kelly's room in the *Pall Mall Gazette*, 12 November 1888, and other sources that quoted it. A drawing of questionable accuracy of the interior of the room in *Reynolds News* shows a picture hanging on the wall. This painting has not been satisfactorily identified, although numerous candidates, none of them actually called *The Fisherman's Widow*, have been suggested.

50. *Daily Telegraph*, 10 November 1888. The *Evening Express*, 12 November 1888, says the front room was used to store 'barrows etc.' and adds that the room 'was formerly left open, and poor people often took shelter there for the night; but when the Whitechapel murders caused so much alarm the police thought the place offered too much temptation to the murderer, and so the front was securely boarded up.' The *Daily Telegraph*, 3 October 1888, reported a curious story to the effect that six woman and a man were taken to identify the body of Catharine Eddowes. Two women said the body was that of a woman they knew, but whose name they did not know. They said that the woman had frequently been without the money to obtain admission to the common lodging houses, and that she had, with the women who identified the body, slept in a shed off Dorset Street, which was 'the nightly refuge of some ten to twenty houseless creatures who are without the means of paying for their beds'. We do not know the location of any such shed, but there were no doubt numerous candidates. However, in view of the *Evening Express*'s comment that the front room of 26 Dorset Street was used by poor people, it is reasonable to speculate that the 'shed' in question was the front room of No. 26.

It would be ironic if Catherine Eddowes used 26 Dorset Street – and it cannot pass unobserved that Eddowes pawned John Kelly's boots in the name of Jane Kelly, giving the address 6 Dorset Street, and that a Mary

Price of 36 Flower and Dean Street viewed Eddowes's body and
identified her as someone she knew as Jane Kelly – whom subsequent
enquiries showed to be alive (*Daily Telegraph*, 2 October 1888). If
Eddowes did use the front room of 26 Dorset Street, could she have
known Mary Jane Kelly, who lived in the rear room?

It has long been speculated that the victims knew each other, and this
possibility is at the core of the overworked Royal Conspiracy theory, but
it has to be acknowledged that Dorset Street features prominently in the
story of most of the victims – Annie Chapman had lodged with Jack Sivvy
at 30 Dorset Street and when murdered was living at Crossingham's at 35
Dorset Street, and Elizabeth Stride lived at 38 Dorset Street with
Michael Kidney. If Eddowes also used 26 Dorset Street as an occasional
doss, the only victim without a known Dorset Street connection would
have been Mary Ann Nichols. John McCarthy's brother, Daniel, would
be running a business from there by 1890. He married Ann Susannah
Crossingham, the daughter of another big lodging house keeper in the
area, on 29 July 1890 at St Anne's Roman Catholic Church, Whitechapel.
Daniel eventually bought a shop at 36 Dorset Street, but he died on 29
August 1895.

51. *Daily Telegraph*, 3 October 1888.
52. *Daily Telegraph*, 10 November 1888.
53. 'I live at 20 Room, in Miller's-court, above the shed' (*Daily Telegraph*, 13
    November 1888). Elizabeth Prater in fact lived in the room above Kelly's,
    but it is interesting that she referred to 'the shed'.
54. Raphael Samuel (1981), *East End Underworld: Chapters in the Life of
    Arthur Harding* (London: Routledge and Kegan Paul), p. 100.
55. Ibid.
56. *Daily Telegraph*, 10 November 1888, and John McCarthy's inquest
    testimony as reported in the *Daily Telegraph*, 13 November 1888. *The
    Times*, 10 November, and the *East London Advertiser*, 17 November 1888,
    incorrectly gave the arrears as 35s. The amount of 29s. was an odd figure
    to have owed, it being an incomplete week's rent – six weeks' rent would
    have been 27s., seven weeks 31s. 6d.
57. That McCarthy was a pimp was suggested by the fact that the houses in
    Miller's Court were known as McCarthy's Rents. There is evidence that
    previously they had been known as Miller's Rents, so the name may have
    no significance.
58. Marie Lloyd (1870–1922) was born Matilda Victoria Wood, the eldest of
    nine children of John Wood, an artificial-flower maker and sometime
    waiter at the Royal Eagle Tavern, and his wife Matilda. She became
    immensely popular and was known as the Queen of the Music Hall.

59. Marie Kendall (1873–1964) was a doe-eyed singer of romantic songs, although she could put across a naughty song with the best of them, as she did at a benefit night for Marie Lloyd in 1899, when she sang 'If I Could See This For 1s. 6d., What Could I See For a Quid?'. She was a ruthless leader in the great strike by music hall performers. One who broke the picket lines was the pretentious Belle Elmore, the social-climbing treasurer of the Music Hall Ladies' Guild, who saw strike breaking as a chance to achieve a fame that her otherwise limited talents would not enable her to achieve. As some pickets tried to prevent her from crossing the lines, Marie Lloyd, who detested her, shouted, 'Don't be daft. Let her in. She'll empty the theatre.' Belle Ellmore would never achieve fame as an entertainer, but she did gain a dubious notoriety as a corpse when she was murdered by her long-suffering husband Hawley Harvey Crippen.

Marie Kendall is mentioned several times by James Joyce in Episode 10 of *Ulysses*: 'Then she stared at the large poster of Marie Kendall, charming soubrette . . .'; 'They passed Dan Lowry's music hall where Marie Kendall, charming soubrette, smiled on them from a poster a dauby smile'; and 'A charming soubrette, great Marie Kendall, with dauby cheeks and lifted skirt, smiled daubily from her poster upon William Humble . . .' She can be seen in two early movies, *Say It With Flowers* in 1934, in which she appears with several renowned music hall performers, and as a speciality act in *Happy Days Review* in 1936.

60. John Joseph McCarthy and Marie Kendall had two children, one of whom, Terrence Kendall-McCarthy, married Gladys Drewery and was the father of Kim and Kay Kendall-McCarthy. See Andy Aliffe (2002), 'The Kendall-McCarthys: A Showbusiness Dynasty', *Ripperologist*, 41, June, pp. 5–6; Eve Golden and Kim Kendall (2002), *The Brief, Madcap Life of Kay Kendall* (Lexington, KY: University Press of Kentucky), pp. 7–8.

61. Three or four months would date the loss of his job to July or August 1888, but this may be in error because, if he lost his job about the time Kelly went into arrears with her rent, the loss of his job would date from late September.

62. *Daily Telegraph*, 10 November 1888, reported that the window had been broken in the course of the quarrel, but a neighbour, Julia Venturney, said Kelly 'broke the windows a few weeks ago whilst she was drunk' (MJ/SPC, NE1888, Box 3, Case Paper 19, London Metropolitan Archives).

63. Following the murder of Kelly, Barnett lived with his sister at 21 Portpool Lane, off Gray's Inn Road.

64. MJ/SPC, NE1888, Box 3, Case Paper 19, London Metropolitan Archives.

65. *Daily Telegraph*, 10 November 1888.

66. *The Times*, 12 November 1888.

67. *Daily Telegraph*, 10 November 1888, *Penny Illustrated Paper*, 17 November 1888, which contains a sketch of Thomas Bowyer.

68. *Western Mail*, 12 November 1888. The fruiterer mentioned would have been Matthew Packer.

69. *Evening Express*, 12 November 1888.

70. In the early 1980s it was briefly renamed 'Jack the Ripper' and enjoyed celebrity as a tourist attraction. It survives today, has fine Victorian tiling, but otherwise totally eschews the fame bestowed by its limited Ripper connections.

71. *Evening Express*, 12 November 1888. The police had apparently been looking for Elizabeth Foster. A report in the *Yorkshire Post* on 12 November 1888 said, 'A woman who, it is alleged, would be able to give evidence, has not yet been found. Her name is Elizabeth Foster, and it is said she was seen drinking with the deceased the night before the murder.' Elizabeth Foster is hardly reported anywhere else.

72. Lizzie Albrook was not called to testify at the inquest, but gave her story to a Press Association reporter. She was reported in *The Observer*, 11 November 1888, and the *Western Mail*, 12 November 1888.

73. Her name is variously given as Julia Venturney (MJ/SPC, NE1888, Box 3, Case Paper 19, London Metropolitan Archives, Julia Vanturney (*Daily Telegraph*, 12 November 1888), Julia van Teurney (*The Times*, 13 November 1888), Julia Vanternie (*East London Advertiser*, 17 November 1888), for example.

74. *East London Advertiser*, 17 November 1888.

75. Ibid. contradicted this, reporting that she had said that during the night she had 'felt strange, thinking that she heard noises. The deceased was singing some Irish songs during the night.' But the *Daily Telegraph*, 13 November 1888, reported the coroner as asking, 'Did you hear any noises in the court?' – 'I did not. I heard no screams of "Murder," nor any one singing.' The coroner then asked, 'You must have heard deceased singing?' – 'Yes; I knew her songs. They were generally Irish.' From this is seems that she was actually saying that she had heard Kelly singing before, but not that night.

76. *Manchester Guardian*, 10 November 1888.

77. MJ/SPC, NE1888, Box 3, Case Paper 19, London Metropolitan Archives. Also, reports in the *Daily Telegraph* and *The Times*, 13 November 1888.

78. Walter Dew (1938), *I Caught Crippen: Memoirs of Ex-Chief Inspector Walter Dew C.I.D.* (London: Blackie and Son).

79. *Daily Telegraph*, 12 November 1888.
80. Cited in Elwyn Jones and Lloyd John (1975), *The Ripper File* (London: Arthur Barker). Picket doesn't appear to have been widely quoted, and doesn't appear in any of the more common newspapers.
81. This is indicated by the *Daily Telegraph*, 10 November 1888, which reported that Prater admitted that Kelly was 'one of her own class'.
82. *East London Advertiser*, 17 November 1888.
83. Sometimes called Pannier, as in the *Daily Telegraph*, 10 November 1888.
84. *Manchester Guardian, The Times*, 10 November 1888.
85. Hutchinson's military appearance was reported in *The Times*, 13 November 1888. His previous employment is given in the *Manchester Guardian*, 12 November 1888, among other newspapers, and his current unemployment was stated by Inspector Abberline in a report dated 12 November 1888. See HO 144/221/A49301C, fols. 42–6.
86. *The Times*, 14 November 1888 – by which Hutchinson presumably meant that he had been a client of Kelly's, which would explain his subsequent interest in the couple. It may have been in the hope of sharing the warmth of Kelly's room and bed that made him hang around for the man to leave.
87. *The Times*, 14 November 1888.
88. Ibid.
89. HO 144/221/A49301C, fols. 78–9. Statement given to the Metropolitan Police by George Hutchinson on 12 November 1888.
90. Ibid.
91. *Daily Telegraph*, 15 November 1888.
92. Unless otherwise indicated, Hutchinson's account is taken from his statement to the police: HO 144/221/A49301C, fols. 78–9, statement given to the Metropolitan Police by George Hutchinson on 12 November 1888.
93. *The Times*, 14 November 1888.
94. HO 144/221/A49301C, fols. 42–6. Hutchinson also said this in a statement to the press: 'My suspicions were aroused by seeing the man so well dressed, but I had no suspicion that he was the murderer . . .' (*East London Advertiser*, 17 November 1888). Hutchinson did not give his information to the police until 6 p.m. on 12 November 1888, by which time the inquest into Kelly's death had been concluded. He later told his story to a representative of a press agency, giving some additional details and claiming to have been out until 3 a.m. on 13 November looking for the man. He thought, but was not certain, that he had seen him in Petticoat Lane on the morning of 11 November.
95. A story matching that of Sarah Lewis in every respect was attributed by some newspapers to a Mrs Kennedy, who I have no doubt was the same person, and I have here combined the accounts.

96. *Daily Telegraph*, 12 November 1888; *East London Advertiser, Illustrated Police News*, 17 November 1888.

97. MJ/SPC, NE1888, Box 3, Case Paper 19, London Metropolitan Archives and various newspaper reports of her inquest testimony.

98. *East London Advertiser*, 17 November 1888.

99. *The Times*, 10 November 1888.

100. Her testimony, as reported in the *Daily Telegraph* on 12 November 1888, was: ' "We stay up all night, and yesterday (Friday) as I was going home, carrying my lantern and other things with me, I saw the woman Kelly standing at the entrance of the court. It was then half-past eight, and as it was unusual for her to be seen about at that hour, I said to her, 'Hallo! what are you doing up so early?' She said, 'Oh, I'm very bad this morning. I have had the horrors. I have been drinking so much lately.' I said to her, 'Why don't you go and have half a pint of beer. It will put you right.' She replied, 'I've just had one, but I'm so bad I couldn't keep it down.' I didn't know then that she had separated from the man she had been living with, and I thought he had been 'paying' her. I then went out in the direction of Bishopsgate to do some errands, and on my return I saw Kelly standing outside the public-house talking to a man. That was the last I saw of her." '

101. *Daily Telegraph*, 12 November 1888.

102. *The Times*, 12 November 1888.

103. *Daily Telegraph*, 13 November 1888.

104. Dew, op. cit.

105. *Illustrated Police News*, 17 November 1888.

106. McCarthy said that he sent Thomas Bowyer to collect the rent at 10.45 a.m., but the police recorded the time of the discovery as 10.30. A market porter leaving Miller's Court about 10.30 a.m. found the police already in charge of Miller's Court, and Dr Phillips received the summons to go to Miller's Court at 11 a.m.

107. *The Times*, 10 November 1888.

108. Dew, op. cit.

109. Ibid.

110. For almost complete error, the report in the *Eastern Post*, 10 November 1888, is an example. Under the heading ANOTHER HORRIBLE MURDER IN WHITECHAPEL. A WOMAN DECAPITATED, it reported, 'This morning (Friday) a horrible discovery was made in Spitalfields. Upon a person entering a room in one of the lodging-houses in Dorset Street, situated near to Spitalfields Church, a woman was discovered with her head entirely cut off from her body, and lying by her side. Alarm was at once given, and the police appeared on the scene. An arrest has been made; and it is so far satisfactory to learn that this is not supposed to be another of

the series of Whitechapel murders which have caused so much sensation in the past. It is reported that the cause of the dreadful crime was jealousy. First reports, however, are always more or less conflicting.'

111. Some reports also identified the second-floor room as being up an alley known as 'Cartin's Court', which apparently 'faces a small square with a narrow entrance, and is surrounded by squalid lodging-houses' (*Boston Daily Globe*, 10 November 1888).

112. See *The Times*, 10 November 1888, among other newspapers, for accounts of the child.

113. '[A]nd she had never had any children' – Joseph Barnett, reported in the *Daily Telegraph*, 10 November 1888.

114. *Western Mail*, 12 November 1888.

115. See MJ/SPC, NE1888, Box 3, Case Paper 19, London Metropolitan Archives. For Kelly's being named Lizzie Fisher see among others the *New York Times*, 10 November 1888. Curiously, and it is probably no more than coincidence, Elizabeth Fisher was the name of a sister of Catharine Eddowes; Catherine Eddowes used the name Kelly, of course, and she pawned John Kelly's boots in the name of Jane Kelly, giving the address 6 Dorset Street (26?).

116. On the recommendation of the home secretary, Henry Matthews, Sir Charles Warren had experimented with the use of bloodhounds and conducted trials to see how effective they could be. It was believed that they would be available for use, but this was incorrect.

117. *Daily Telegraph*, 10 November 1888.

118. *Daily Telegraph*, 13 November 1888.

119. *Daily Telegraph*, 10 November 1888.

120. *Daily Telegraph, Manchester Guardian*, 10 November 1888.

121. *The Times*, 10 November 1888; and Walter Dew wrote of 'the door which, if I remember rightly, had an automatic lock'.

122. *Daily Telegraph*, 10 November 1888.

123. *Manchester Guardian*, 10 November 1888.

124. *Daily Telegraph*, 10 November 1888.

125. *Daily Telegraph, The Times*, 10 November 1888, *Daily Telegraph, The Times*, 13 November 1888.

126. *The Times*, 10 November 1888.

127. This is an old term for what is today most often called hypersexuality or sex addiction, an abnormal compulsion to have sex, which isn't simply being oversexed but is a complex psychological condition that can lead to inappropriate and indiscriminate sexual activity, including excessive and public masturbation, exhibitionism, obsessive use of prostitutes, sexual assault and in extreme cases sexual savagery, and is a condition found in

serial killers. Although known for centuries, study and understanding of the illness has grown only in the last twenty years. Dr Bond's report clearly shows that, while they lacked the terms and understanding born from clinical trials and studies, the Victorian doctors – and through them the police, at least at a senior level – understood what they were dealing with, and it is interesting in this respect that Robert Anderson seems to have believed that Jack the Ripper was a man whose insanity was attributed to masturbation.

128. *Daily Telegraph*, *The Times*, 10 November 1888.

129. HO 144/221/A49301C, fols. 42–6, report by Inspector Abberline of statement made by George Hutchinson on 12 November 1888.

130. Walter Dew (1938), *I Caught Crippen: Memoirs of Ex-Chief Inspector Walter Dew C.I.D.* (London: Blackie and Son).

131. *Daily Telegraph*, 10 November 1888.

132. *Manchester Guardian*, 10 November 1888.

133. Letter from Henry Matthews to Evelyn Ruggles Brise dated 5 October 1888, J S Sandars papers, MS. Eng. hist c. 723, Bodleian Library, Department of Western Manuscripts, Oxford.

134. Sir Robert Anderson (1910), *The Lighter Side of My Official Life* (London: Hodder and Stoughton).

135. *Daily Telegraph*, 10 November 1888.

136. L Perry Curtis (2001), *Jack the Ripper & The London Press* (London & New Haven: Yale University Press).

137. RA VIC/A67/19 (Royal Archives), telegram from Queen Victoria to Lord Salisbury dated 10 November 1888.

138. *The Times*, 12, 13 November 1888.

139. *The Times*, 12 November 1888.

140. ALL-SPICE, a columnist in the *East and West Ham Gazette*, 17 November 1888.

141. *Daily Telegraph*, 12 November 1888.

142. *The Times*, 12 November 1888.

143. Twenty-seven-year-old Wolf Bendoff fought J R Couper in Johannesburg in July 1889 for the world heavyweight boxing championship. Couper won. The fight lasted 30 minutes and went 26 rounds.

144. *Daily Telegraph*, *Manchester Guardian*, 12 November 1888. *The Times*, 12 November 1888, reported that the incident happened near George Yard, which a woman named Humphreys was passing when a powerful-looking man wearing large spectacles confronted her. She asked what he wanted and he said nothing, just laughed. Policemen eventually found the man in a house and took him to the police station. He claimed to have been visiting a friend who lived in the house. He referred the police to a

well-known gentleman at the London Hospital and when his story was verified he was set at liberty.

145. *Daily Telegraph, The Times*, 13 November 1888

146. *Daily Telegraph*, 14 November 1888.

147. Ibid.

148. *The Times*, 15 November 1888.

149. Ibid.

150. *Daily Telegraph, Manchester Guardian, The Star, The Times*, 19 November 1888.

151. *New York World*, 18 November 1888, *San Francisco Chronicle*, 19 November 1888, *Ottawa Free Press*, 21 November 1888.

152. *Daily Telegraph*, 2 October 1888, 5 October 1888; a letter from Michael Mack, *The Times*, 6 October 1888; *New York Herald*, 13 November 1888. The newspaper said the story was based on several reports, among them a private letter from Paris received via the steamship *Saale* by the *New York World*. It was described as a very graphic letter from someone named H D'Altona, which was published in *Der Nene Yorker Herold*, and a late edition of the Paris *Temps*. The *New York Evening Star* of 14 November 1888 quoted a cablegram from Paris in the *New Yorker Zeitung*; it was also quoted, in different ways, in the *Montreal Daily Star*, 14 November 1888; *Manchester Guardian, Toronto Globe*, 15 November 1888; *The Star, Novosti*, 17 November 1888; *Daily Telegraph, Pall Mall Gazette, The Star*, 28 November 1888; *East London Observer*, 1 December 1888. See also Stepan Poberowski (2003), 'Nikolay Vasiliev: The Ripper From Russia', *Ripperologist*, No. 50, November.

153. *Daily Telegraph, The Star, The Times*, 19 November 1888.

154. *Daily Telegraph*, 14 November 1888.

155. *Walthamstow and Leyton Guardian*, 24 November 1888.

156. *East London Advertiser*, 24 November 1888.

157. *The Times*, 20 November 1888, *Barking and East Ham Advertiser, East London Advertiser, Walthamstow and Leyton Guardian*, 24 November 1888.

158. *East London Observer*, 24 November 1888.

159. *Daily Telegraph*, 22 November 1888.

160. Ibid.

161. *Manchester Guardian*, 22 November 1888, *The Times*, 23 November 1888, *East London Advertiser*, 24 November 1888.

162. See Chapter 21 for a full account of Anderson's theory and claim that the murderer was identified and fitted the police profile in every particular.

Chapter Seventeen – Murders After Mary Kelly

1. Report by Commissioner James Monro, 17 July 1889: HO 144/221/ A493011, fols. 5–6.
2. Sir Robert Anderson (1910), *The Lighter Side of My Official Life* (London: Hodder and Stoughton).

Chapter Eighteen – The Macnaghten Memorandum

1. Macnaghten Report, MEPO 3/141 fols. 177–83.
2. Aberconway papers, preserved in private collection.
3. Letter from Philip Loftus to Christabel, Lady Aberconway, dated 11 August 1972, preserved in private collection.
4. *Guardian*, 7 October 1972.

Chapter Nineteen – Montague John Druitt

1. *Blackheath Local Guide and District Advertiser*, 30 December 1893, 8 June 1912. George Valentine (1842–1912) retired in 1893 and died on 26 May 1912.
2. Blackheath Hockey Club Records.
3. C R Seymour, an Old Harrovian and barrister who played for MCC and Hampshire, and Vernon Royle, who played for Oxford, Lancashire and Gentlemen of England.
4. Malcolm Christopherson (1893), 'The Blackheath Cricket Club', *Blackheath Art Club Magazine and West Kent Review*, April/May. The article said M J Druitt was another keen and enthusiastic cricketer, who did 'many good feats with the ball'. For a detailed account of Druitt's cricketing career see Irving Rosenwater (1973), 'Jack the Ripper Sort of a Cricket Person', *The Cricketer*, January.
5. Call book for period 1875–94 (no details are given except the name), Library, Inner Temple.
6. Letters of Administration, 24 May 1891, Principal Registry, Family Division, Somerset House.
7. T H Escott (revised edition 1895), *England: Its People, Polity, and Pursuits* (London: Chapman Hall), p. 277. (First published 1885.)
8. Ann Druitt's case papers plus covering letter from Dr Gasquet to Dr T S Tuke of the Manor House Asylum, dated 6 June 1890; held at The

Wellcome Institute for the History of Medicine, Wellcome MS 6651, pp. 251–9, plus letter, 251* 251**. (The letter does not have a folio number. It is inserted between folios 250 and 251. It is two pages in length and designated as above.)

9. *Bournemouth Visitor's Directory*, 1 September 1888.
10. *The Times*, 29 November, 30 November, *Law Times*, 8 December 1888.
11. It is not clear whether 30 December is the date when Druitt was dismissed from the school – in which case it would be a mistake because we know that Druitt was dead by that time – whether it was the date when William Harvey Druitt visited Valentine's school, or whether it was a mistake for 30 November, when Druitt seems to have left the school.
12. Melville Macnaghten (1915), *Days of My Years* (London: Arnold).
13. Probably an article by George R Sims in *The Referee*, 29 March 1903, in which he wrote, ' "Jack the Ripper" committed suicide after his last murder – a murder so maniacal that it was accepted at once as the deed of a furious madman. It is perfectly well known at Scotland Yard who "Jack" was, and the reasons for the police conclusions were given in the report to the Home Office, which was considered by the authorities to be final and conclusive.'
14. *Pall Mall Gazette*, 31 March 1903.

Chapter Twenty – Michael Ostrog

1. Basil Thompson (1922), *Queer People* (London: Hodder and Stoughton).
2. *The Referee*, 22 September 1907.
3. *Oxford Chronicle and Berks Gazette*, 7 March 1863. *The Times*, 6 January 1874 says he used the name 'Max Grief, alias Gosler'.
4. *Herts and Essex Journal*, 6 February 1864, and *The Times*, 6 January 1874, refer to his activities in Bishop's Stortford and Cambridge.
5. *The Times*, 6 January 1874.
6. Ibid.
7. Ibid.
8. A 400-year-old coaching inn today called the Royal Victoria and Bull Hotel, and, indeed, known by that name in 1866, 'Royal Victoria' having been added to 'Bull' following a visit by Queen Victoria in 1836. Charles Dickens frequented the inn and it is mentioned in several of his novels.
9. Known as 'an amiable judge', he was born in 1838 and would try the Stratton brothers at the Old Bailey, the first murder case that relied on fingerprint evidence.
10. *Maidstone Telegraph*, 4 August 1866, gives an account of Ostrog's career until his sentence in August 1866. *The Times*, 6 January 1874.

11. Possibly the eminent pioneer gynaecological surgeon Dr Isaac Baker Brown (1812–1873), who became president of the respected Medical Society of London in 1865. Today he is primarily known for his advocacy about 1858 of clitoridectomy as a 'treatment' for masturbation in girls and women, which he claimed caused, among other things, hysteria, epilepsy, mania, insanity and death. His publication of *On the Curability of Certain Forms of Insanity, Epilepsy, Catalepsy, and Hysteria in Females* in 1866 caused a violent controversy. Few authorities disputed Brown's contention of what caused emotional disorders in women, but many opposed what the *British Medical Journal* in 1867 referred to as 'disgraceful mutilation', and the argument led to Brown's being expelled from the Council of the Obstetrical Society in 1867 and ostracism by the medical establishment. See Elizabeth Sheehan (1981), 'Victorian Clitoridectomy: Isaac Baker Brown and His Harmless Operative Procedure', *Medical Anthropological Newsletter*, August. Included in Roger N Lancaster and Micaela di Leonardo (eds) (1997), *The Gender/Sexuality Reader* (New York, NY: Routledge).
12. *Birmingham Daily Post*, reported in *The Times*, 3 October 1873.
13. *The Eton College Chronicle*, 9 October 1873.
14. Burton-on-Trent was the centre of brewing in Britain, more than thirty breweries being located there. The height of production was in 1888, when between them they produced 3 million barrels of beer. The Fox and Goose Inn was built in the late seventeenth century and was owned by the Marquis of Anglesey until sold early in the nineteenth century to the Bass brewery. It remained a Bass licensed house until it was closed in 1981. Delicenced and in a dilapidated condition, it was sold first to a solicitor and afterwards to Geoff Mumford and Bruce Wilkinson, who set up the small but respected Burton Bridge Brewery there.
15. *The Times*, 7 October 1873.
16. *Buckinghamshire Advertiser and Aylesbury News*, 10 January 1874.
17. Bucks CRO Q/AG/25, jail receiving books entries 5736 and 5767, quoted by Connell in a note below.
18. *Police Gazette*, 3 October 1883.
19. *Woolwich Gazette*, 29 July 1887.
20. *Woolwich Gazette*, 22, 29 July, 5, 12 August 1887.
21. *Bucks Herald*, 23 June 1894.
22. A good definition of mania as it seems to have been applied in the nineteenth century was given by Dr Alexander Morrison, the first visiting physician of the Surrey Pauper Lunatic Asylum, in the first volume of the Annual Reports of the Asylum Committee 1843–6. Insanity at that time was divided into mania and monomania, being general insanity and partial

insanity respectively. General insanity afflicted 'the different manifestations of mind, including attention, memory, imagination, judgement, and the affections and propensities'.

23. Surrey Pauper Lunatic Asylum, Register of Male Admissions 1880–88, Register of Discharges and Deaths, Males, Vol. IV, 1880–91.

24. *Police Gazette*, 26 October 1888, Register of Discharges and Deaths, Males, Vol. IV 1880–91.

25. *Bucks Herald*, 16 June, 23 June 1894.

26. *Bucks Herald*, 23 June 1894.

27. Ibid.

28. *Bucks Herald*, 16 June, 23 June 1894.

29. See also D S Goffee (1994), 'The Search for Michael Ostrog', *Ripperana*, No. 10, October; Nick Connell (1997), 'Ostrog – An Adventurer At Eton', *Ripperologist*, No. 10, April. For Ostrog's committal in France, see the new introduction in Philip Sugden (2002), *The Complete History of Jack the Ripper* (London: Robinson).

30. In 1891 Melville Macnaghten wrote to Banstead requesting that the Convict Supervision Office be informed if Ostrog was released. There is no suggestion that Banstead were informed that Ostrog was potentially dangerous, possibly a multiple murderer and perhaps Jack the Ripper. Nevertheless, it is this incarceration to which Macnaghten was presumably referring in the official version of the memorandum. At this time, 1891, Macnaghten clearly didn't know about Ostrog's detention in France during 1888, and he probably didn't learn about it until late in 1894. Ostrog is therefore to be distinguished from Druitt and Kosminski because the former was not disproved, in Macnaghten's eyes at least, and he continued to believe in his guilt until his death, and Kosminski was identified by an eyewitness and remained the leading suspect of Anderson and Swanson until 1910 and later.

Chapter Twenty-one – Kosminski

1. Macnaghten memorandum. A report by Sir Melville Macnaghten dated 23 February 1894 commenting on a story in the *Sun* newspaper of 13 February 1894 concerning Thomas Cutbush.

2. Perhaps needless to say, masturbation does not lead to insanity, but Victorian doctors and popular belief held that it led to all manner of ailments, including insanity and death. It may also be a case of confusing a symptom with a cause, as excessive or public masturbation and other inappropriate sexual behaviour can be associated with some mental disorders.

3. Many people, myself among them, misunderstood the words 'definitely ascertained fact' to mean that Jack the Ripper's identity was 'a definitely ascertained fact'. It has been forcibly pointed out, however, that a more sensible contextual interpretation is that Anderson meant it was 'a definitely ascertained fact' that the suspect was a Polish Jew. I now favour this interpretation, but acknowledge that ambiguity still exists. Believing that the suspect *was* Jack the Ripper, Anderson may still have intended his words to mean that it was 'a definitely ascertained fact' that Jack the Ripper was a Polish Jew.

4. According to the Trial of Lunatics Act, 1883, 'Where in any indictment or information any act or omission is charged against any person as an offence, and it is given in evidence on the trial of such a person for that offence that he was insane, so as not to be responsible, according to law, for his actions at the time when the act was done or the omission made, then, if it appears to the jury before whom such person is tried that he did the act or made the omission charged, but was insane as aforesaid at the time when he did or made the same, the jury shall return a special verdict to the effect that the accused was guilty of the act or omission charged against him, but was insane as aforesaid at the time when he did the act or made the omission.'

   Even if the suspect was manifestly insane, a trial could have taken place whereby the evidence against the suspect could be laid out and it would have been decided whether the suspect was sane enough to understand the charges and their implications and issue a plea, or whether he was insane and unable to stand trial. Either way, the police would have been able to demonstrate that they had got their man. But, if the suspect had already been certified insane, no trial to determine sanity would have been needed and the witness would never have been called to give evidence.

5. One cannot take a source on trust – that is an act of desperation – but when a source does not otherwise appear to be unreliable and was in a position to know the facts and distinguish between the likely and the unlikely, the historian has to accept that even the strangest story can be true. G R Elton's *The Practice of History* may have fallen a little out of favour in recent years, but he summed it up neatly when he wrote, 'The historian cannot but work on the assumption that whatever happened is capable of rational explanation and that evidence is the product of an act discoverable by reason' (G R Elton (1969), *The Practice of History* (London: Fontana), p. 105).

6. Hargrave Lee Adam (1911), *The Police Encyclopedia*, Vol. IV (London: The Waverley Book Company Ltd).

7. Robert Anderson (1907), *Criminals and Crime: Some Facts and Suggestions* (London: Nisbet), pp. 2–4.

8. It has been suggested that Anderson envied the powers of the French police but there is no evidence for this. In *Criminals and Crime* (op. cit.) he referred to their powers as 'despotic', which wasn't a term anyone would apply to powers one wished one possessed oneself, and in *The Lighter Side of My Official Life* (op. cit.) he tells an anecdote in which he says that the public were friends of and actively assisted the British police, whereas the French feared their police and did not assist them. Anderson clearly recognised that the strictures on the British police were for the public good.

9. Melvin Harris (1989), *The Ripper File* (London: W H Allen), p. 154: 'I cannot accept that the police allowed anyone to flout the law, refuse to testify, and then escape the consequence. Neither can I accept that the police needed to drag a reluctant suspect all the way from Whitechapel to Brighton simply to have him identified – the proposition is laughable.'

10. Philip Sugden (2002), *The Complete History of Jack the Ripper*, paperback with new introduction (London: Robinson; New York, NY: Carroll and Graf), in which the author cites two examples of Anderson's having a poor memory in later life. In 1931 the writer H L Adam quoted a letter in which Anderson confused cases of 1865 and 1877. The other example was an article in which Anderson wrongly attributed a clay pipe to the Kelly crime scene instead of that of Alice McKenzie and misidentified the home secretary in 1888 as Sir William Harcourt instead of Henry Matthews. 'Rational and fair-minded students may draw their own conclusions,' says Sugden (pp. xvi–xvii), but the significance, if there is any, is marginal. In the first example Anderson acknowledged his uncertainty and wrote, 'I am too tired tonight to recall it,' and, given the dominance of Harcourt in Anderson's life, it would have been an easy slip of the pen to have misnamed the home secretary – see, for example, the opening of Anderson's (1906) *Sidelights on the Home Rule Movement* (London: John Murray), and elsewhere. As for the clay pipe, as with all these examples, errors of memory over minor incidents and probable slips are not in the slightest degree comparable to falsely thinking that Jack the Ripper was identified (see H L Adam (1908), *C.I.D. Behind the Scenes at Scotland Yard* (London: Sampson, Low and Marston), and *Daily Chronicle*, 1 September 1908, for the Anderson errors).

11. Philip Sugden (1994), *The Complete History of Jack the Ripper* (London: Robinson); revised paperback edition (1995) (London: Robinson; New York, NY: Carroll and Graf); paperback with new introduction (2002) (London: Robinson; New York, NY: Carroll and Graf).

12. For example, Anderson said that the suspect had been released when the eyewitness refused to give evidence, and commentators have argued that the police would not have released the suspect but would have subpoenaed the witness and forced him to give evidence. Which is true – if they had charged the suspect and brought him to trial. The mystery is not why the police didn't subpoena the witness, but why they didn't charge the suspect, which is probably capable of an easy solution such as lack of evidence, or a decision to keep the suspect under surveillance while more evidence was found.

13. Martin Fido (1987), *The Crimes, Detection and Death of Jack the Ripper* (London: Weidenfeld and Nicolson); revised edition, 1989 (London: Weidenfeld and Nicolson); 1993 (New York, NY: Barnes and Noble). See also see http://www.casebook.org/dissertations/dst-cohen1.html, where Martin Fido explains at greater length the foundation of his assessment of Anderson.

14. J A Cole (1984), *Prince of Spies: Henri Le Caron* (London: Faber and Faber).

15. Sir Robert Anderson (1910), *The Lighter Side of My Official Life* (London: Hodder and Stoughton), p. 99.

16. Sugden, op. cit.

17. Phrases such as 'undiscovered crimes' illustrate the care we need to take when words such as 'find', 'discover' and so on are used. Griffiths obviously didn't mean 'undiscovered' in the sense of not known about, but meant that the criminal had not been detected, the crime remaining unsolved.

18. Alfred Aylmer (1895), 'The Detective In Real Life', *Windsor Magazine*, vol. no. 5, May.

19. Because Griffiths credits Anderson with a theory rather than actual knowledge, his remarks could be interpreted as diminishing Anderson's otherwise apparent certainty. But since Anderson all along made it clear that he had the moral not the legal proof, and as the suspect was never tried and found guilty, Anderson's thoughts about his suspect's guilt, no matter how firmly held, could not have been described as other than a 'theory'. It is also clear that Major Griffiths did not know the specifics of what Anderson thought. He believed Anderson thought the Ripper was an escaped lunatic whose murder spree ended when he was returned to the asylum, yet there is no hint of this in what Anderson or Swanson wrote. Mention should be made of a comment by Chief Inspector Littlechild in a letter to the journalist George R Sims, dated September 1913, which seems to endorse Griffiths. Littlechild wrote, 'I knew Major Griffiths for many years. He probably got his information from Anderson

who only thought he knew.' However, Littlechild probably meant Macnaghten rather than Anderson, as Littlechild was responding to a question from Sims about whether or not he had heard of a Ripper suspect called Dr D, probably M J Druitt. Druitt was Macnaghten's favoured suspect, and Macnaghten was most likely to have been Griffiths's source, rather than Anderson. Macnaghten also repeatedly acknowledged that he only thought he knew who the Ripper was, so he fits Littlechild's remark.

20. Anderson replied to 'Mentor's' initial criticism by saying, 'As for the suggestion that I intended to cast any reflection on the Jews anyone who has read my books on Biblical exegesis will know the high estimate I have of Jews religiously' (*The Globe*, 7 March 1910). And in a letter to the editor of the *Jewish Chronicle* he wrote, 'SIR, – With reference to "Mentor's" comments on my statements about the "Whitechapel murders" of 1888 in this month's *Blackwood* [*Blackwood's Magazine*], will you allow me to express the severe distress I feel that my words should be construed as "an aspersion upon Jews." For much that I have written in my various books gives proof of my sympathy with, and interest in, "the people of the Covenant"; and I am happy in reckoning members of the Jewish community in London among my personal friends' (*Jewish Chronicle*, 11 March 1910).

21. Leopold Jacob Greenberg was the most dominant force in the history of the *Jewish Chronicle*, which he took over in January 1907. He was an ardent Liberal and uncompromising Zionist, noted for his support of alien immigration and his polemics against Russian tyranny, and 'his style, if sometimes careless, was exceptionally forceful'. The column called 'In the Communal Armchair' was begun by the Reverend A A Green, the minister of the Hampstead Synagogue, in April 1907, but he resigned after a while and 'Mentor' took over. The character of the column changed. It was provocative and 'the style showed a considerable affinity to that of the editorial and leading articles from Greenberg's pen'. Although Greenberg's authorship was very strongly suspected, it was not admitted until his death and by order of his will. The attack on Anderson was not untypical of the emotive response 'Mentor' took to public figures when he fearlessly castigated their foibles and follies. See Anon (1949), *The Jewish Chronicle 1841–1941. A Century of Newspaper History* (London: Jewish Chronicle), pp. 124–40.

22. Lieutenant-Colonel Sir Henry Smith (1910), *From Constable to Commissioner: The Story of Sixty Years, Most of Them Misspent* (London: Chatto and Windus), p. 160. On the frontispiece of his copy of the memoirs, now held at the library of Scotland Yard, George H Edwards,

OBE, secretary to the Metropolitan Police, 1925–7, described Major Smith as 'a good raconteur and a good fellow, but not strictly veracious . . . when dealing with matters within his own knowledge he is often far from accurate . . .'

23. Harry Cox (1906), 'The Truth About the Whitechapel Murder', *Thompson's Weekly News*, 1 December.

24. Frederick Porter Wensley (1931), *Detective Days* (London: Cassell), p. 107.

25. Donald Rumbelow (1973; 1988), *The Houndsditch Murders and the Siege of Sidney Street* (London: Macmillan; revised edition, London: W H Allen), p. 99.

26. Chaim Bermant (1975), *Point of Arrival* (London: Macmillan), p. 118.

27. Lloyd P Gartner (1960), *The Jewish Immigrant in England 1870–1914* (London: Simon Publications), p. 167.

28. William J Fishman (1988; 2001), *East End 1888: A Year in a London Borough Among the Labouring Poor* (London: Duckworth; London: Hanbury).

29. *Jewish Chronicle*, 11 March 1910.

30. It is emphasised by Gartner, op. cit., p. 183: ' "Peaceful" and "law-abiding" were terms consistently applied to the immigrant community, but nevertheless, it had its criminal offenders. Among the varieties of criminality, Jews possessed certain distinctions of their own, such as the virtual absence of crimes of violence – murder, robbery and rape.'

31. Melvin Harris (1994; 1995), *The True Face of Jack the Ripper* (London: Michael O'Mara), pp. 31–2. The quoted report from Anderson is HO 144/221/A49301C, fols. 116–18.

32. The same author also misrepresented a report in the *Daily Chronicle* on 1 September 1908 in which Anderson said that he had 'told Sir William Harcourt, who was then Home Secretary, that I could not accept responsibility for the non-detection of the author of the Ripper crimes', an apparent admission in 1908 that the Ripper crimes had not been resolved, but Anderson was in fact referring to an exchange he had had with the home secretary in 1888 (Matthews, not Harcourt, who had been an earlier home secretary), which he described in his memoirs.

33. Melvin Harris (1989), *The Ripper File* (London: W H Allen), p. 146.

34. Leon OBroin (1971), *The Prime Informer: A Suppressed Scandal* (London: Sidgwick and Jackson), p. 118.

35. Subsequently published under that title as a penny pamphlet and in hard covers for one shilling.

36. Winston Spencer Churchill (1906), *Lord Randolph Churchill* (New York, NY: Macmillan), pp. 757–60.

37. Pigott's notoriety was such that he even became the subject of a poem by the brilliantly bad William McGonagall, which never fails to make me smile:

> *Richard Pigott, the forger, was a very bad man,*
> *And to gainsay it there's nobody can,*
> *Because for fifty years he pursued a career of deceit,*
> *And as a forger few men with him could compete.*
>
> *For by forged letters he tried to accuse Parnell*
> *For the Phoenix Park murders, but mark what befell.*
> *When his conscience smote him he confessed to the fraud,*
> *And the thought thereof no doubt drove him mad.*

38. Anderson was still having to correct misconceptions as late as 1913, and it was something that even warranted comment in some accounts of his death, as in the *News of the World*, 24 November 1918, which quoted a denial by Anderson: 'For reasons into which I cannot enter I wrote a letter to the "Times". The editor of that paper, it is true, headed my letter "Parnellism and Crime" but I had nothing whatever to do with that, nor had I anything to do with the writing of the series of articles published under that name.'

39. Monro received the CB in 1888, but otherwise no acknowledgement or recognition after he resigned in June 1890 following his support against the government for better pension rights for the police, an issue that at the time was propelling the police towards a national strike. As was so often the case, there was a deeper political issue about the role of the commissioner, effectively whether he was the ultimate advocate of the men under his command or the Queen's 'servant, bound as long as he held office, to consider the public service first', as Lord Salisbury nicely expressed what otherwise meant doing what the government wanted. *The Times* later saw Monro's resignation as self-sacrifice in the interest of his men (5 March 1903), but Lord Salisbury wrote to Queen Victoria that Monro 'posed not as your Majesty's servant . . . but as if he had been Captain of a band of Allied troops whom your Majesty had temporarily taken into your service . . . He was constantly threatening to resign unless this or that was done that he demanded. It was owing to his contrivance that first Mr Jenkinson, and afterwards, Sir Charles Warren, were induced to resign; and now it is evident that he would bear no control, and hoped to oust Mr. Matthews.' And in a later letter, when police dissatisfaction had reached boiling point, Salisbury informed the Queen that 'Mr Monro's evil practices are responsible for a great portion of it' (George Earle Buckle (ed.) (1930), *The Letters of*

*Queen Victoria: Third Series: A Selection from Her Majesty's Corres-
pondence and Journal between the years 1886 and 1901*, Vol. I (London:
John Murray), pp. 615–16, 623). From all this it seems that Monro was
rather more of a thorn than a simple advocate of his men would have
been. Anderson, when appointed assistant commissioner in 1888, had
his salary boosted by a special annuity of £800 for 'services rendered'
and against 'the abolition of Secret Service money by a rival government' (according to Salisbury's papers at Hatfield House) and in 1901
he received a knighthood.

40. F S L Lyons (1977), *Charles Stewart Parnell* (Oxford: Oxford University
    Press), p. 372.
41. Letters written by Henry Matthews in the archives of *The Times* dated 14
    February and 12 April 1887.
42. Andrew Roberts (1999), *Salisbury: Victorian Titan* (London: Weidenfeld
    and Nicolson).
43. Leon OBroin (1971), *The Prime Informer: A Suppressed Scandal* (London:
    Sidgwick and Jackson), p. 66; J A Cole (1984), *Prince of Spies: Henri Le
    Caron* (London: Faber and Faber), p. 154.
44. On 13 April 1910 James Monro wrote to Sir Edward Troup, a civil service
    junior of eight years in 1888 who was now permanent secretary of state at
    the Home Office: 'In 1887 I was Assistant Commissioner Metropolitan
    Police, under the Home Office, in charge of secret work. Mr Anderson
    was an agent of mine (as were others), chiefly on being a channel of
    information received from a man in America, who corresponded directly
    with him, and whose name I did not know. When *The Times*'s earlier
    articles appeared they certainly caused a sensation in London, and
    everybody was talking about them. I have no doubt that Mr Anderson and
    I talked about them, and I can quite imagine that I may have welcomed
    public interest being directed to the existence of a dangerous conspiracy.
    But such an expression of opinion was a very different thing from
    authorizing an agent of mine to give information to the public. Such a
    course would have been opposed to all my training in a service where
    communication on the part of officials with the Press was carefully
    limited. As a matter of fact, no such authority was asked by Mr Anderson
    and none was given to him by me. When subsequently articles appeared
    in *The Times* I was unaware of the name of the author, and naturally I
    made no report on the subject to the Home Office. A long time afterwards
    Mr Anderson informed me that he had written one or more of the articles,
    and I felt much annoyed. However, the evil, if such it was, was done, and
    nothing was to be gained by saying anything on the subject. I therefore
    observed silence. I may have mentioned the matter at the Home Office in

confidential talk, but as the incident had passed many months previously, and there was no object in reopening the question, I did not report it officially' (HO 144/926).

Given that Anderson stood accused of involving himself in the politics of the day without any authorisation whatsoever, it might be considered a trifle strange that, when informed about Anderson's authorship, Monro said nothing and 'observed silence' and 'did not convey his annoyance to Anderson'. It might be explicable if, as has been speculated, Monro was himself the author of a fourth article for *The Times* and that *The Star*, edited by pro-Home Ruler T P O'Connor, thought Monro had authored the whole lot.

Anderson clearly felt betrayed by his former colleague and friend, responding, 'During the debate a letter was read from the gentleman who had charge of the Secret Service in 1887, and in that letter he denied that he had had any knowledge of my *Times* disclosures until after the event. He is quite incapable of intentionally swerving from the truth; and I can only account for his letter by failure of memory. Our intercourse in relation to Secret Service matters at the period in question was characterised, not by official reserve, but by the confidence and freedom of a close and intimate friendship, which lasted until two years later. Our conferences on official matters were not confined to official hours. My diaries remind me of the many evenings I spent at his house, when all our work was discussed in tête-à-tête chats, as we sat together after dinner. I told him everything I was doing, frankly and fully, and without reserve; and neither then, nor at any time, did he express to me disapproval of my denunciation of the dynamiters in *The Times*' (Anderson, op. cit., p. 295).

It's easy to see what happened. Anderson said it was a good idea, Monro agreed, and Anderson took this as a sanction. That is if the whole thing wasn't done on behalf of and even at the behest of Lord Salisbury and Henry Matthews.

45. Sir Henry Smith's memoirs, published later in 1910, were likewise accused of being boastful, with hardly a single review of the book failing to remark on Smith's claim to know more about the Ripper crimes than anyone else alive. The *Yorkshire Post* even observed that the book's title was misleading, Smith never having been a constable, never proceeding by promotion through the ranks, and receiving the positions he obtained through 'favour'. The newspaper found some of Smith's remarks to be 'not in the best taste' and shared the view of other commentators such as the *Spectator*, which thought Major Smith's anecdotes 'marked by a sort of hot-tempered positiveness and a certain amount of prejudice'. The

Manchester Guardian felt that, when Smith talked about the blunders of the Metropolitan Police, he got 'a little incoherent'.

46. By which Anderson clearly meant a nuclear family, not the Jewish population as a whole. It is important to be clear about this, because as we have seen, 'Mentor' and Major Henry Smith mistakenly took him to task over the latter interpretation. All Anderson said was that the murderer had to be able to get rid of his bloodstains and therefore had the opportunity to do it secretly or could not otherwise have been able to hide them from 'his people', who in consequence had to have suspicions that they did not convey to the police.

47. This alone clinches the identification for me.

48. *The People*, 9 June 1912.

49. By which Major Griffiths can only have meant that 'homicidal tendencies' were not apparent at the time he was killing, but became obvious after the crimes had ceased.

50. Melville Macnaghten (1915), *Days of My Years* (London: Arnold). p. 20: 'my friends George R. Sims and Harry B. Irving'.

51. Admissions and Discharge Book, Mile End Old Town Workhouse, 12 July 1890, gives his date of birth as 1865.

52. Burial Record No. 399 CB fol. 263, United Synagogue. It says Aaron was born in Poland, had been in England for 37 years and was 54 years old when he died.

53. The Male Patients' Day Book, new series, No. 20, states that Aaron's nearest known relative was his brother, Woolf Kosminski, Sion Square, Commercial Road East.

54. Grave refers to a brother and sisters.

55. Admissions and Discharge Book, Mile End Old Town Workhouse, 12 July 1890, gives his profession as 'hairdresser'.

56. Ibid.

57. The 1891 census return shows that it was home to Woolfe Abrahams, aged thirty, a master tailor, born in Russia; Betsy (née Kosminsky – according to the birth certificate of her daughter Matilda), wife, aged 34, born in Russia, and presumably the sister of Aaron; Rebecca, daughter, aged nine, born in London; Millie, daughter, aged five, born in London; and Matilda, daughter, aged nine months, born in London on 26 May 1890. With so many women it cannot have been the most ideal household for a man suffering an extreme hatred of women.

58. Admissions and Discharge Book, Mile End Old Town Workhouse, 12 July 1890.

59. Ibid., 15 July 1890, calls him Aaron Kosorimski. The Religious Creed Register (GLRO x20/355) gives the following details:

Date of Admission 1890 July 12
Date of Discharge 1890 July 15
Christian Name Aaron
Surname Kosminski
Born in the year 1865
From where admitted 3 Sion Square
Religious creed Hebrew
Name if informant brother
Discharged or Dead To Brother

In 1889 Severin Klosowski (a.k.a. George Chapman) lived in Greenfield Street. He was also a hairdresser.

60. Ibid., 4 February 1891, says his first meal after admission was D, meaning dinner.
61. He was entered as 'Korominski', the name having been 'corrected' from 'Kosomonski'.
62. Admissions and Discharge Book, Mile End Old Town Workhouse, 4 February 1891.
63. Ibid., 7 February 1891, says the last meal before discharge was breakfast.
64. Under the name 'Kozominski'.
65. England's largest lunatic asylum, built in the hamlet of Colney Hatch, on the borders of Southgate and Friern Barnet. The foundation stone was laid on 8 May 1849. It would have more than two thousand patients, but only two directing physicians, each with one assistant. And there was one attendant for twelve patients.
66. Register of Admissions, Males No. 3, fol. 31.
67. The address is almost certainly wrong, because in April 1891, when the census was taken, a family named Greenwald was living at 8 Sion Square. It is possible that Woolf Kosminski moved out between February and April, but Woolf was living at 16 Greenfield Street when Aaron was admitted to Mile End Old Town Workhouse on 4 February 1891. The 1891 census shows 16 Greenfield Street empty, so Woolf certainly moved from there soon after Aaron's admission. He may have moved briefly to Sion Square, but it is more likely that 8 is a mistranscription for 3 and that either Woolf Abrahams is really Woolf Kosminski or Woolf Kosminski briefly moved in with his brother-in-law.
68. The 1891 census shows that 51 Carter Lane was a hotel/restaurant and pub with cooks, waitresses, barmaids and boarders. No Cohen was among them (see Scott Nelson (2002), 'Kosminski's Relatives', *Ripperologist*, No. 39, February). According to the 1891 census at 30 Greenfield Street there lived Jacob Cohen, tailor, aged 26, Poland; Sarah Cohen, wife, aged 23,

Poland; Amelia Cohen, daughter, aged 3, Commercial Road, London, born 1888; Sam, brother, machinist, aged 20, Poland. Number 16 Greenfield Street is given as the address of Aaron's brother.

69. Presumably meaning Yiddish.

70. Meaning his Parish Board of Guardians took all or some financial responsibility for Aaron Kosminksi's welfare and that he was transferred to the asylum at Leavesden.

71. Leavesden, at Leavesden Woodside, near Watford, Herts, was established under the provisions of the Metropolitan Poor Act of 1867 as the first asylum for the imbecile poor of London, and was built to contain 1,560 patients – 860 females and 700 males. A common mistake is that Leavesden catered only for imbeciles and harmless lunatics. As late as 1898 Medical Superintendent Elkins observed, 'It seems doubtful if many of the cases sent here are suitable for an asylum built and staffed as an institution for quiet imbeciles and chronic harmless lunatics, several patients have had to be secluded lately, and are much more suited to treatment in an ordinary asylum. In my opinion a case so bad as to need seclusion or restraint is not suitable for treatment here' (report of local government inspector and observations of medical superintendent, 1898, GLRO MAD 2403). Other statements make it clear that some violent cases were transferred to Leavesden. From 1896 'we saw a large number of feeble, helpless and degraded patients and quite a number of destructive cases' (report of medical superintendent, 1896, GLRO MAB 365, Vol. 15). During the month of November 1899 'no less than eleven of our cases have exhibited either suicidal or dangerous propensities' (GLRO MAB 368, Vol. 18). Leavesden apparently had no facilities for a person of the Jewish religion; the report of a visiting commissioner in lunacy dated November 1909 records the appeal of a male Jew who asked that he be returned to Colney Hatch because there were special provisions made there for a person of his religion (presumably diet, etc.). None of this means that Leavesden would have accommodated Jack the Ripper and there is no indication in the surviving papers of any particularly dangerous, notorious or otherwise distinguished inmate. But Kosminski's family are hardly likely to have admitted to the asylum authorities any suspicions they had that he was Jack the Ripper or even a murderer. One would have expected the police to have informed the asylum authorities, but if Aaron Kosminski was indeed their suspect then they presumably didn't do so. By a curious twist of coincidence, the 1910 census lists another inmate of Leavesden – Mary Kelly.

72. Now Newark Street.

73. Transferred from Vol. 9., 147, which is reported not to have survived.

74. The Trades Directory for 1919 shows that at the Dolphin, 99 Whitechapel Road, were Edward Cecil Moore and Mark Abrahams. The electoral roll for the pub in 1919 shows Florence Abrahams, Isaac Abrahams and Mark Abrahams, the last being publican with Edward Cecil Moore. Moore had two other public houses plus a restaurant at London Wall. Moore seems to have taken over the pub in 1919 from the previous landlord, John Levy, who died in 1918.

75. The meaning of 'brothers' is not known. It may mean brother or brother-in-law.

76. Burial record No. 399 CB, fol. 263, United Synagogue.

77. Aaron was committed from 16 Greenfield Street in February 1891, but by the time of the census in April 1891 the property was empty and the Lubnowskis had moved to New Street.

78. Police Seaside Home, and Southern Police Orphanage, 51 Clarendon Villas, West Brighton. First Annual Report 1890–1.

79. Major Arthur Griffiths (1898), *Mysteries of Police and Crime* (London: Cassell).

80. George R Sims (1907), 'Who Was Jack the Ripper?', *Lloyd's Weekly News*, 22 September.

81. Curiously, the description, which is quoted, does not match the description of the man given in a report by Chief Inspector Swanson (derived from City sources) and published in the *Police Gazette* (19 October 1888). The height and age are right, but the man described in the newspaper had a 'big moustache'; Lawende's man had a fair moustache, probably small; the newspaper's man was 'dressed respectably'; Lawende's man was of shabby appearance; the newspaper's man 'Wore pea jacket' (a short, warm, double-breasted coat of heavy wool, worn especially by sailors); Lawende's man wore a pepper-and-salt jacket (a strong, coarse fabric flecked with white); the newspaper's man had a muffler; Lawende's a 'reddish handkerchief tied in a knot'.

82. *Daily Telegraph*, 18 February 1891.

83. Philip Sugden (1994), *The Complete History of Jack the Ripper* (London: Robinson); revised paperback edition (1995) (London: Robinson; New York, NY: Carroll and Graf); paperback with new introduction (2002) (London: Robinson; New York, NY: Carroll and Graf), p. 410.

84. Objections to Schwartz are few. Philip Sugden dismissed Schwartz for seemingly good reasons: 'But Schwartz does not fit the bill anything like as well. If Schwartz was the witness then Macnaghten was completely wrong and the City Police would have had no business trespassing into Metropolitan Police territory in search of a man suspected of a crime (the Berner Street murder) committed within the jurisdiction of the

Metropolitan police force. Furthermore, if the man Schwartz claimed to have seen attacking Stride in Berner Street really did call out Lipski he is unlikely to have been, as Kosminski unquestionably was, a Jew.' (See Philip Sugden (1994), *The Complete History of Jack the Ripper* (London: Robinson); revised paperback edition (1995) (London: Robinson; New York, NY: Carroll and Graf); paperback with new introduction (2002) (London: Robinson; New York, NY: Carroll and Graf)).

However, the argument is unsound and based on a series of assumptions: for example, the assumption that the City Police were trespassing on Metropolitan Police territory and enquiring into a Metropolitan Police crime. The City Police might have been pursuing enquiries into a crime committed in their own jurisdiction, in which case they could have entered Metropolitan Police jurisdiction legitimately. And we don't know for certain that it was the attacker in Berner Street who called out 'Lipski', nor do we know if in this instance 'Lipski' was used as a term of abuse.

85. His case has the same minute number as three other cases, from which it would seem they were connected. Cases 22 and 23 were charges against Gertrude Smith and Mary Jones for keeping a brothel, and Case 24 was a charge against Ellen Hickey for assaulting N Cohen. Hickey was discharged. It is not known if Cohen was related to Aaron Davis Cohen in any way.

86. Whitechapel Workhouse Records, brought in by PC91H from the Thames Police Court, admitted 5.30 p.m., 7 December 1888, discharged 21 December to Colney Hatch.

87. Of course, the value of this topographical clue is negligible; any number of things could have dictated the route taken by the murderer when fleeing Mitre Square – people in conversation, someone walking down a street, night noises caused by animals such as cats, dogs or rats.

88. Thames Police Court, Register, Part 1, 1888.

89. Jerry White (1980), *Rothschild Buildings: Life In An East End Tenement Block 1887–1920* (London: Routledge and Kegan Paul), p. 77.

Chapter Twenty-two – Other Ripper Suspects

1. Harrison was the president of Harrison & Co., the San Francisco agents for the Liverpool-based insurance company Thames and Mersey Marine Insurance Co. A founder member of the Bohemian Club, whose members included Daniel O'Connell and Ambrose Bierce, he was later president of the Olympic Club and author of a book in 1915, *Making a Man – A Manual of Athletics* (San Francisco: H S Crocker Co.).

2. The Bohemian Club was formed in 1872 by five journalists on the *San Francisco Examiner* but today is an ultra-exclusive club for rich and powerful men – excluding journalists – which every year holds a gathering at Bohemian Grove, a 2,700-acre redwood forest on the Russian River near the hamlet of Monte Rio in Sonoma County, California, where national and international political and business policy decisions are reportedly made. It is even widely claimed that the Manhattan Project was conceived there. Its activities have been shrouded in mystery for decades, but assorted accusations have been levelled at it, among them claims of drunkenness, homosexuality and human sacrifice, and there is even a longstanding protest group, the Bohemian Grove Action Network, which seeks to draw international attention to the club.

3. This report was recently discovered by the indefatigable researcher Chris Scott.

4. And repeated elsewhere, such as the *Williamsport Sunday Grit* on 12 May 1895.

5. Neither of these men seems to have been identified; a Fred C Beckwith was the father of a Californian journalist named Loring Dumas Beckwith, but I know nothing further.

6. Letter from Dr Benjamin Howard to the editor of *The People*, 26 January 1896.

7. See obituary in *The Times*, 16 July 1900.

8. *Leicester Mercury*, 12 January 1931.

9. *Le Matin*, 21 and 22 March 1931.

10. D J West (1949), 'The Identity of "Jack the Ripper" ', *Journal for the Society for Psychical Research*, July–August.

11. Colin Wilson and Patricia Pitman (1961), *The Encyclopaedia of Murder* (London: Arthur Barker Limited), also published in paperback by Pan in 1964.

12. Castlereagh cut his throat with a penknife in his dressing room at North Cray Place in Kent and died almost immediately on 12 August 1822. He believed he was about to be exposed as a homosexual, but the facts are obscure. The most likely truth is that Castlereagh did accompany prostitutes who accosted him on his walk home from Parliament and that on one occasion he was recognised by a group of roughs. A short time later he accompanied a young woman to her rooms, where, to his horror, he discovered 'she' was a young man. At that moment the roughs burst into the room. Castlereagh handed over the money he had on him and paid up when he received a blackmail letter. Three years later, the receipt of a second blackmail letter at a time when he was under considerable strain turned Castlereagh's mind and he killed

himself. See also H Montgomery Hyde (1959), *The Strange Death of Lord Castlereagh* (London: Heinemann).

13. Philippe Jullian (1962), *Edouard VII* (Paris: Librarie Hachette), published in 1967 as *Edward and the Edwardians*, translated by Peter Dawney (London: Sidgwick and Jackson).

14. For what is probably the best account see H Montgomery Hyde (1976), *The Cleveland Street Scandal* (London: W H Allen), ch. 2. Hyde says that there is no evidence that Prince Albert Victor was homosexual, but is nevertheless persuaded that he visited the brothel, perhaps in the mistaken belief that it provided striptease or he was innocently taken there.

15. Thomas E A Stowell (1970), ' "Jack the Ripper' – A Solution?', *Criminologist*, Vol. 5, No. 18, pp. 40–51.

16. Theodore Dyke Acland (1896), *A Collection of the Published Writings of William Withey Gull* (London: New Sydenham Society).

17. In November 1970 he would write to *The Times* saying, 'I have at no time associated His Royal Highness, the late Duke of Clarence, with the Whitechapel murders or suggested that the murderer was of Royal blood' (Thomas Stowell (1970), 'Letters to the Editor: Jack the Ripper', *The Times*, 9 November). This was true. In fact at one point in his article in *The Criminologist* he wrote that Sir William Gull 'was physician to Guy's Hospital, Physician in Ordinary to Her Majesty, Queen Victoria, to H.R.H. The Prince of Wales, and physician to a large number of aristocracy and the wealthy including, if I am right in my deductions, the family of Jack the Ripper.' This would appear to suggest specifically that Prince Albert Victor was not 'S', but was one of the 'aristocracy and wealthy'. However, in 1960 Colin Wilson had written a series of articles for the *Evening Standard* ('My Search for Jack the Ripper', 8–12 August 1960) and in the mistaken belief that Wilson also thought the prince was the Ripper, Dr Stowell invited him to lunch at the Athenaeum and told him the substance of what appeared in his article a decade later. Colin Wilson told the story to several people, among them the German newspaper editor Frank Lynder, the writers Daniel Farson and Donald McCormick, the television journalist Kenneth Allsop and the editor of *The Criminologist* Nigel Morland. See Colin Wilson and Robin Odell (1987), *Jack the Ripper Summing Up and Verdict* (London: Bantam Press; also published in 1988 by Corgi Books), p. 200. All sources postdating 1960 could therefore be ultimately traceable back via Colin Wilson to Dr Stowell.

18. Cecil Roberts (1932), *Alfred Fripp* (London: Hutchinson).

19. Colin Kendall (1990), 'The Intentions of Thomas Eldon Stowell', *The Criminologist*, Summer.

20. Magnus Linklater (1970), 'Did Jack the Ripper Have Royal Blood?', *Sunday Times*, 1 November. Colin Wilson, who discussed the theory with Dr Stowell in 1960, thought Stowell had told him thirty years, which would have dated it about 1930, by which time Caroline Acland was dead. See Wilson and Odell, op. cit., p. 200.

21. Published in *The Times*, 9 November 1970.

22. Quoted in *The Times*, 14 November 1970.

23. John N Dalton (1886), *The Cruise of Her Majesty's Ship "Bacchante" 1879–1882. Compiled from the Private Journals, Letters, and Note-Books of Prince Albert Victor and Prince George of Wales* (London: Macmillan and Co.), 2 vols. Born in Margate, Kent, Canon John Neale Dalton was curate of Sandringham and tutor to Prince Albert Edward and his brother Prince George. Educated at Blackheath School, he was godfather to Sir Alfred Downing Fripp, among whose papers reference was made to Prince Albert Victor's having a gonorrhoeal infection.

24. See Michael Harrison (1972), *Clarence: The Life of H.R.H. The Duke of Clarence and Avondale 1864–1892* (London: W H Allen), published in 1974 as *Clarence: Was He Jack the Ripper?* (New York, NY: Drake); Dr David Abrahamson (1992), *Murder & Madness: The Secret Life of Jack the Ripper* (New York, NY: Donald I Fine), with new appendices: 1992, London: Robson Books; 1993, New York, NY: Avon Books. See also John Wilding (1993), *Jack the Ripper Revealed* (London: Constable). First proposed as a suspect by Michael Harrison, who in an interview in the *Listener* (17 August 1972) admitted that he didn't agree with the theory that the Ripper was Prince Albert Victor and had felt compelled to suggest an alternative candidate, settling on J K Stephen. Harrison suggested that the prince and Stephen had become lovers; Dr David Abrahamson suggested that J K Stephen *and* Prince Albert Victor committed the murders together, while John Wilding has argued that J K Stephen committed the murders with Montague Druitt. The arguments lack evidential support.

25. A contemporary account of which was published: see J D Rees (1891), *H.R.H. The Duke of Clarence & Avondale in Southern India, with a Narrative of Elephant Catching in Mysore by G. P. Sanderson* (London: Kegan Paul).

26. James Pope-Hennessy (1959), *Queen Mary* (London: George Allen and Unwin), p. 190.

27. As far as I am aware the BBC source has never been properly established. Paul Bonner and Ian Sharp of the BBC always claimed that it was G D Gregory, chief public relations officer at Scotland Yard, but Gregory subsequently denied it, apparently in front of Sir Robert Mark,

commissioner of the Metropolitan Police, and claimed that Paul Bonner obtained the information from documents at the Public Record Office.

28. Melvyn Fairclough (1991), *The Ripper and the Royals* (London: Duckworth), second edition (1992 and 2002) (London: Duckworth).

29. By coincidence an Elizabeth Cook moved into one of the flats built on the site and lived there between 1888 and 1893, but she wasn't the same person.

30. The Nancy Method was a technique of hypnosis introduced by Dr Ambroise-Auguste Liébeault of Nancy, where there is a street named after him and a bust in Olry park, and where in 1870 he was visited by Sigmund Freud.

31. Taken from an unpublished article by Frank Spiering found among papers purchased by the writer Paul Feldman in 1993.

32. Frank Spiering (1975), *Prince Jack: The True Story of Jack the Ripper* (New York, NY: Doubleday), also published in 1980 (New York, NY: Jove Books). See also Paul Begg, Martin Fido and Keith Skinner (1991), *The Jack the Ripper A to Z* (London: Headline). Revised editions (London: Headline), 1992, 1994, 1996.

33. Jean Overton Fuller (1990; 2001), *Sickert & the Ripper Crimes* (Oxford: Mandrake), revised edition: 2003.

34. Curiously the *Atlanta Constitution* reported on 1 December 1888, 'Artist Whistler, the eccentric American who is one of London's celebrities, is painting a horrible picture of one of the Whitechapel victims as her mutilated body appeared when it was discovered.'

35. On 12 September 1907 Emily Elizabeth Dimmock, known as Phyllis, was found dead in a flat she shared with her common-law husband Bertram Shaw at 29 St Paul's Road, north London. Her throat had been cut from left to right and the position of the body suggested that she had been sleeping at the time. She had last been seen in the company of a man named Robert Wood in the Eagle pub the previous evening, and Wood was arrested and charged. He was acquitted.

36. Virginia Woolf (1934), *Walter Sickert: A Conversation* (London: The Hogarth Press).

37. She discusses Jack the Ripper in her book *The Magical Dilemma of Victor Neuberg*, published in 1965, and says that she had done a good deal of research, which may in fact have amounted to little more than studying Donald McCormick's then recently republished book *The Secret Identity of Jack the Ripper*, which she mentions.

38. In *The Magical Dilemma of Victor Neuberg* she does not mention Florence Pash's story or intimate that she had any 'inside' information, and one might also observe that in January 1975 Stephen Knight actually contacted Jean Overton Fuller's friend and partner Timothy D'Arch

Smith, of Fuller D'Arch Smith Ltd Rare Books, referring to a book he was writing about Jack the Ripper, specifically mentioning Walter Sickert, and enquiring about a claim by Aleister Crowley that he possessed some compromising letters from Prince Albert Victor to a boy named Morgan of Cleveland Street. D'Arch Smith was helpful in his reply, but did not suggest that Knight contact Jean Overton Fuller, or, apparently, suggest that Fuller contact Knight, and Fuller states that she knew nothing of Joseph Sickert's story until a friend, Dr Margaret Little, sent her a paperback copy of Knight's book in 1977. This absence of pre-Knight corroboration of the story looks very suspicious. However, Fuller's mother was still alive at the time (she died on 12 September 1967) and may not have permitted her daughter to break the confidence she had sworn to Florence Pash all those years earlier. In any case Fuller has made it clear that Pash's story was rather nebulous, the details lacking any meaning and context until she read Knight's story.

39. Robert Emmons (1942), *The Life and Opinions of Walter Richard Sickert* (London: Faber and Faber). It is interesting to note how these little anecdotes change with retelling. By the time this story reaches Denys Sutton (Denys Sutton (1976), *Walter Sickert* (London: Michael Joseph), p. 51) we read, '. . . one night a party of girls, who came across him in Copenhagen Street, fled in terror when he said to them that he was "Jack the Ripper, Jack the Ripper".'

40. Osbert Sitwell (ed.) (1947) *A Free House! Or The Artist as Craftsman. Being the writings of Walter Richard Sickert* (London: Macmillan and Co.), pp. xxxviii–xxxix. Repeated verbatim (1950) in Osbert Sitwell's *Noble Essences: A Book of Characters* (London: Little, Brown and Company), pp. 211–13.

41. Keith Baynes (1887–1977) was a painter whose acquaintance Sickert made during World War One.

42. Marjorie Lilly (1971), *Sickert: The Painter and His Circle* (London: Elek).

43. A painting by Walter Sickert simply titled *One of Madame Villain's Sons* is thought to be of Maurice Villain.

44. A letter from Jacques-Emile Blanche to the writer Andre Gide, published in France and elsewhere. Whether or not Walter Sickert had in fact fathered 'a swarm of children', as Blanche claimed, it is clear that a close and intimate friend thought he was sexually promiscuous and capable of fathering children, a claim that runs contrary to Patricia Cornwell's belief that Sickert was impotent and had a stunted or perhaps amputated penis as a result of a childhood operation for a penile fistula.

45. *The Star*, 20, 23 October 1888; *The Times, Bradford Telegraph*, 22 October 1888; *The Star*, 23 October 1888; *Bradford Citizen*, 27 October 1888;

Bradford Telegraph, 26 October 1888. The others are Miriam Howells from Penrhiwceiber (*Cardiff Times*, 24 November, 1, 8 December 1888), and someone in Glasgow, who was too young to be charged (*Weekly Herald*, 26 October 1888).

46. Anna Gruetzner Robins (1996), *Walter Sickert. Theory and Practice: Word and Image* (London: Scolar Press), and (2003), *Walter Sickert. The Complete Writings on Art* (Oxford: Oxford University Press), among other writings.

47. Called 'the Sherlock Holmes of graphology', she was the author of two books: *The Art of Graphology* (ed. Jeanne M Reed), published in 1985 by the Whiston Publishing Company of Troy, New York, and *Sexual Deviations as seen in Handwriting*, from the same publisher in 1990.

48. *Daily Express*, 31 December 1993.

49. David Canter (2003), *Mapping Murder* (London: Virgin Books).

50. The story of the diary and the people involved, the defenders and detractors, and the sometimes heated (and occasionally overheated) claims and counterclaims is extremely complicated, so much so that it alone has been the subject of a coolly dispassionate book, by Keith Skinner, Seth Linder and Caroline Morris (1993): *Ripper Diary: The Inside Story* (Stroud, Gloucestershire: Sutton).

Bibliography

Aberconway, Christabel (1966), *A Wiser Woman? A Book of Memories* (London: Hutchinson).

Abrahamson, Dr David (1992), *Murder & Madness: The Secret Life of Jack the Ripper* (New York, NY: Donald I Fine), published with new appendices in 1992, London: Robson Books; and in 1993, New York, NY: Avon Books.

Ackroyd, Peter (2000), *London: The Biography* (London: Chatto and Windus).

Acland, Theodore Dyke (1896), *A Collection of the Published Writings of William Withey Gull* (London: New Sydenham Society).

Adam, H L (1908), *C.I.D. Behind the Scenes at Scotland Yard* (London: Sampson, Low and Marston).

Adam, H L (1911), *The Police Encyclopedia*, Vol. IV (London: Waverley Book Company Ltd).

Adam, H L (1930), *Trial of George Chapman*, Notable British Trials series (London: Wm Hodge and Co.).

Aliffe, Andy (2002), 'The Kendall-McCarthys: A Showbusiness Dynasty', *Ripperologist*, Issue 41, June.

Allen, Vivien (1997), *Hall Caine: Portrait of a Victorian Romancer* (Sheffield: Sheffield Academic Press).

Anderson, Robert (1907), *Criminals and Crime: Some Facts and Suggestions* (London: Nisbet).

Anderson, Sir Robert (1910), *The Lighter Side of My Official Life* (London: Hodder and Stoughton).

Anderson, Sir Robert (1910), 'The Lighter Side of My Official Life. Chapter XI At Scotland Yard', *Blackwood's Magazine*, March.

Anon (1949), *The Jewish Chronicle 1841–1941: A Century of Newspaper History* (London: *The Jewish Chronicle*).

Aylmer, Alfred (1895), 'The Detective In Real Life', *Windsor Magazine*, Vol. 1, No. 5, May.

Ball, Pamela (1998), *Jack the Ripper: A Psychic Investigation* (London: Arcturus).

Barnett, Henrietta Octavia (1918), *Canon Barnett: His Life, Work and Friends* (London: John Murray).

Barton, Margaret, and Sitwell, Osbert (1930), *Sober Truth, a Collection of Nineteenth-century Episodes, Fantastic, Grotesque and Mysterious* (London: Duckworth).

Beadle, William (1995), *Jack the Ripper: Anatomy of a Myth* (Dagenham, Essex: Wat Tyler Books).

Begg, Paul (1988), *Jack the Ripper, The Uncensored Facts* (London: Robson).

Begg, Paul (2002), *Jack the Ripper: The Definitive History* (London: Longman).

Begg, Paul, Fido, Martin, and Skinner, Keith (1991), *The Jack the Ripper A to Z* (London: Headline); revised editions, London: Headline, 1992, 1994, 1996.

Bentley, Michael (2001), *Lord Salisbury's World: Conservative Environments in Late-Victorian Britain* (London: Cambridge University Press).

Bermant, Chaim (1971), *The Cousinhood: The Anglo-Jewish Gentry* (London: Eyre & Spottiswoode).

Bermant, Chaim (1975), *Point of Arrival* (London: Macmillan).

Besant, Annie (1893), *An Autobiography* (London: T Fisher Unwin).

Booth, General (1890), *In Darkest England and the Way Out* (London: Salvation Army).

Bourgoin, Stéphane (1992), *Jack L'Eventreur* (Paris: Fleuve Noir).

Bourgoin, Stéphane (1998), *Le Livre Rouge De Jack L'Éventreur* (Paris: Bernard Grasset).

Briggs, Asa, and Macartney, Anne (1984), *Toynbee Hall: The First Hundred Years* (London: Routledge & Kegan Paul).

Buckle, George Earle (ed.) (1930), *The Letters of Queen Victoria: A Selection from Her Majesty's Correspondence and Journal Between the Years 1886 and 1901* (London: John Murray).

Campbell, Christy (2002), *Fenian Fire: The British Government Plot to Assassinate Queen Victoria* (London: HarperCollins).

Canter, David (2003), *Mapping Murder* (London: Virgin Books).

Caputi, Jane (1988), *The Age of the Sex Crime* (London: The Women's Press).

Caron, Major Henri Le (1895), *Twenty-five Years in The Secret Service: The Recollections of a Spy* (London: William Heinemann).

Cecil, Lady Gwendolen (1921; 1931; 1932), *Life of Robert, Marquis of Salisbury*, 4 vols (London: Hodder and Stoughton).

Chesney, Kellow (1972), *The Victorian Underworld* (London: Pelican Books).

Chisholm, Alex, DiGrazia, Christopher-Michael, and Yost, Dave (2002), *The News From Whitechapel* (Jefferson, NC: McFarland).

Christopherson, Malcolm (1893), 'The Blackheath Cricket Club', *Blackheath Art Club Magazine and West Kent Review*, April/May.

Churchill, Winston Spencer (1906), *Lord Randolph Churchill*, 2 vols (New York, NY: Macmillan).

Clarkson, Charles Tempest, and Richardson, J Hall (1889), *Police!* (London: Field and Tuer).

Cobb, Belton (1956), *Critical Years at the Yard* (London: Faber and Faber).

Cole, J A (1984), *Prince of Spies: Henri Le Caron* (London: Faber and Faber).

Connell, Nick (1997), 'Ostrog – An Adventurer At Eton', *Ripperologist*, No. 10, April 1997.

Connell, Nicholas, and Evans, Stewart P (2000), *The Man Who Hunted Jack the Ripper: Edmund Reid and the Police Perspective* (Cambridge: Rupert Books).

Cook, Chris, and Keith, Brendan (1975), *British Historical Facts 1830–1900* (London: Macmillan).

Corey, Melinda, and Ochoa, George (1996), *The Encyclopedia of the Victorian World: A Reader's Companion to the People, Places, Events, and Everyday Life of the Victorian Era* (New York, NY: Henry Holt).

Corfe, Tom (1968), *The Phoenix Park Murders: Conflict, Compromise and Tragedy in Ireland, 1879–1882* (London: Hodder and Stoughton).

Cornwell, Patricia (2002; 2003), *Portrait of a Killer: Jack the Ripper – Case Closed* (London: Little, Brown; London: Time Warner).

Cory, Patricia (1994), *An Eye to the Future: The Whitechapel Murders* (privately printed).

Coville, Gary, and Lucanio, Patrick (1999), *Jack the Ripper: His Life and Crimes in Popular Entertainment* (Jefferson, NC: McFarland).

Cox, Harry (1906), 'The Truth About the Whitechapel Murder', *Thompson's Weekly News*, 1 December.

Cullen, M J (1975), 'The 1887 Survey of the London Working Class', *International Review of Social History*, Vol. I, pp. 53, 55.

Cullen, Tom (1965), *Autumn of Terror: Jack the Ripper His Crimes and Times* (London: Bodley Head), published as *When London Walked in Terror* (Boston, MA: Houghton Mifflin (1965); London: Fontana Books (1968);

New York, NY: Avon Books (1968)), published as *The Crimes and Times of Jack the Ripper* (London: Fontana Books (1973); New York, NY: Avon Books (1973)).

Curtis, L Perry (1963), *Coercion and Conciliation in Ireland 1880–1892: A Study in Conservative Unionism* (Princeton, NJ: Princeton University Press).

Curtis, L Perry (2001), *Jack the Ripper & The London Press* (London & New Haven: Yale University Press).

Dalton, John N (1886), *The Cruise of Her Majesty's Ship 'Bacchante' 1879–1882. Compiled from the Private Journals, Letters, and Note-Books of Prince Albert Victor and Prince George of Wales*, 2 vols (London: Macmillan & Co.).

Daniel, Paul (1996), 'McCarthy, Kelly and Breezer's Hill', *Ripperologist*, Issue 8, June.

David, Saul (1997), *Military Blunders* (London: Constable Robinson).

Deacon, Richard (1965), *The Private Life of Mr Gladstone* (London: Frederick Muller).

'Defender' (Warren's pseudonym; 1902), *Sir Charles Warren and Spion Kop: A Vindication* (London: Smith Elder & Co.).

Dew, Walter (1938), *I Caught Crippen: Memoirs of Ex-Chief Inspector Walter Dew C.I.D.* (London: Blackie and Son).

Dilnot, George (1930), *The Story of Scotland Yard* (London: Geoffrey Bles).

Dorsenne, Jean (1935), *Jack L'Eventreur* (Paris: Les Editions De France); a translation is available by Molly Whittington-Egan (Malvern, Worcestershire: Cappella Archive).

Douglas, Arthur (1979), *Will the Real Jack the Ripper* (Chorley, Lancashire: Countryside Publications).

Douglas, John E., and Olshaker, Mark (2000), *The Cases That Haunt Us: From Jack the Ripper to Jonbenet Ramsey, the FBI's Legendary Mindhunter Sheds Light on the Mysteries That Won't Go Away* (New York, NY: Scribner).

Eddleston, John J (2001; 2002), *Jack the Ripper: An Encyclopedia* (Santa Barbara, CA, and London: ABC Clio; London: Metro Publishing).

Edwards, Ivor J (2002), *Jack the Ripper's Black Magic Rituals: Satanism, The Occult, Murder, The Sinister Truth of the Doctor Who Was Jack the Ripper* (London: Blake); paperback (2003) (London: John Blake). The Blake edition is a completely revised and rewritten edition of a book privately published in 2001 by Penny Publishing, Lake, Isle of Wight.

Elton, G R (1969), *The Practice of History* (London: Fontana).

Emmons, Robert (1942), *The Life and Opinions of Walter Richard Sickert* (London: Faber and Faber).

Ensor, Sir Robert (1936), *England 1870–1914*, Oxford History of England series (Oxford: Oxford University Press).

Escott, T H (1885), *England: Its People, Polity, and Pursuits* (London: Chapman Hall); revised edition (1895).

Evans, Stewart, and Gainey, Paul (1995), *The Lodger: The Arrest and Escape of Jack the Ripper* (London: Century); published (1996) as *Jack the Ripper: First American Serial Killer* (London: Arrow).

Evans, Stewart P., and Skinner, Keith (2000), *The Ultimate Jack the Ripper Sourcebook* (London: Robinson, 2000); published (2000; 2001) as *The Ultimate Jack the Ripper Companion* (New York, NY: Carroll and Graf; London: Robinson).

Evans, Stewart P, and Skinner, Keith (2001), *Jack the Ripper: Letters From Hell* (Stroud, Gloucestershire: Sutton).

Evans, Stewart P, and Skinner, Keith (2002), *Jack the Ripper and the Whitechapel Murders* (London: Public Record Office).

Eyges, Thomas B (1944), *Beyond The Horizon* (Boston, MA: Group Free Society).

Fairclough, Melvyn (1991), *The Ripper and the Royals* (London: Duckworth); second edition (1992; 2002) (London: Duckworth).

Farson, Daniel (1972; 1973), *Jack the Ripper* (London: Michael Joseph; London: Sphere Books).

Feldman, Paul H (1997; 1998; 2002), *Jack the Ripper: The Final Chapter* (London: Virgin).

Fido, Martin (1987), *The Crimes, Detection and Death of Jack the Ripper* (London: Weidenfeld and Nicolson); revised edition (1989; 1993) (London: Weidenfeld and Nicolson; New York, NY: Barnes and Noble).

Fido, Martin, and Skinner, Keith (1999), *The Official Encyclopedia of Scotland Yard* (London: Virgin).

Finch, Harold (1996), *The Tower Hamlets Connection: A Biographical Guide* (London: Tower Hamlets Library Services and Stepney Books).

Fisher, Peter (1996), *An Illustrated Guide to Jack the Ripper* (Runcorn, Cheshire: P and D Riley).

Fisher, Trevor (1995), *Scandal: The Sexual Politics of Late Victorian Britain* (Stroud, Gloucestershire: Sutton).

Fisher, Trevor (1997), *Prostitution and the Victorians* (Stroud, Gloucestershire: Sutton).

Fishman, William J (1988; 2001), *East End 1888: A Year in a London Borough Among the Labouring Poor* (London: Duckworth; London: Hanbury).

Fishman, William J (1975), *East End Jewish Radicals 1875–1914* (London: Duckworth).

Flanagan, Bud (1961), *My Crazy Life* (London: Frederick Muller).

Ford, Colin, and Harrison, Brian (1983), *A Hundred Years Ago: Britain in the 1880s in Words and Photographs* (Harmondsworth, Middlesex: Penguin Books).

Foster, R F (1981), *Lord Randolph Churchill, A Political Life* (Oxford: Clarendon Press).

Friedland, Martin L (1984), *The Trials of Israel Lipski: A True Story of Victorian Murder in the East End of London* (New York, NY: Beaufort Books).

Fuller, Jean Overton (1990; 2001), *Sickert & the Ripper Crimes* (Oxford: Mandrake); revised edition (2003), with material relative to Patricia Cornwell (q.v.) (Oxford: Mandrake).

Gardiner, A G (1923), *The Life of Sir William Harcourt*, 2 vols (London: Constable).

Gardiner, John (2002), *The Victorians: An Age in Retrospect* (London: Hambledon and London).

Gartner, Lloyd P (1960), *The Jewish Immigrant in England 1870–1914* (London: Simon Publications).

Goffee, D S (1994), 'The Search for Michael Ostrog', *Ripperana*, No. 10, October.

Golden, Eve, and Kendall, Kim (2002), *The Brief, Madcap Life of Kay Kendall* (Lexington, KY: University Press of Kentucky).

Gordon, R Michael (2001), *Alias Jack the Ripper, Beyond the Usual Whitechapel Suspects* (Jefferson, NC: McFarland).

Graham, Anne E, and Emmas, Carol (1999), *The Last Victim: The Extraordinary Life of Florence Maybrick, the Wife of Jack the Ripper* (London: Headline).

Gregory, Roy (1995), *Jack the Ripper and Victorian London* (King's Rippon, Huntingdonshire: ELM Publications).

Gretton, R H (1930), *A Modern History of the English People 1880–1922* (London: Martin Secker).

Griffiths, Major Arthur (1895), 'The Detective in Real Life', *Windsor Magazine*, Vol. 1, January–June.

Griffiths, Major Arthur (1898), *Mysteries of Police and Crime* (London: Cassell).

Hale-White W (1935), *Great Doctors of the Nineteenth Century* (London: E Arnold).

Han, Jeanette, and Han, Ann (2001), *Death of A Prince: Jack the Ripper and Other Souls* (Milsons Point, NSW: Arrow).

Harris, Jose (1972), *Unemployment and Politics: A Study in English Social Policy, 1886–1914* (London: Clarendon Press).

Harris, Melvin (1987), *Jack the Ripper: The Bloody Truth* (London: Columbus Books).

Harris, Melvin (1989), *The Ripper File* (London: W H Allen).

Harris, Melvin (1994; 1995), *The True Face of Jack the Ripper* (London: Michael O'Mara).

Harrison, Michael (1972), *Clarence: The Life of H.R.H. The Duke of Clarence and Avondale 1864–1892* (London: W H Allen); published (1974) as *Clarence: Was He Jack the Ripper?* (New York, NY: Drake).

Harrison, Paul (1991), *Jack the Ripper: The Mystery Solved* (London: Robert Hale).

Harrison, Shirley (1993), *The Diary of Jack the Ripper* (London: Smith Gryphon); including report on the diary by Kenneth W Rendell and a rebuttal by Robert Smith (1993) (New York, NY: Hyperion).

Hattersley, Roy (1999), *Blood & Fire: William and Catherine Booth and Their Salvation Army* (London: Little, Brown).

Haw, George (1907), *From Workhouse to Westminster: The Life Story of Will Crooks, M.P.* (London: Cassell and Co.).

Hayne, W J (1889), *Jack the Ripper: or The Crimes of London* (Chicago, IL: Utility Book and Novel Company).

Hinton, Bob (1998), *From Hell . . . The Jack the Ripper Mystery* (Abertillery, Gwent: Old Bakehouse Publications).

Hodgson, Peter (2002), *Jack the Ripper Through the Mists of Time* (Leicester: Minerva Press).

Hollingshed, John (1861), *Ragged London* (London: Smith, Elder and Co.).

Hopkins, R Thurston (1935), *Life and Death at the Old Bailey* (London: Herbert Jenkins).

Howells, Martin, and Skinner, Keith (1987; 1988), *The Ripper Legacy. The Life and Death of Jack the Ripper* (London: Sidgwick and Jackson; London: Sphere Books).

Humberstone, Thomas Lloyd (1948), *Commemoration of the Sixtieth Anniversary of the 'Battle of Trafalgar Square'* (London: Ridgill Trout).

Hyde, H Montgomery (1959), *The Strange Death of Lord Castlereagh* (London: Heinemann).

Hyde, H Montgomery (1976), *The Cleveland Street Scandal* (London: W H Allen).

Hyman, Alan (1976), *Sullivan and His Satellites* (London: Chappell and Company).

Jakubowski, Maxim, and Braund, Nathan (eds) (1999), *The Mammoth Book of Jack the Ripper* (London: Robinson).

James, Robert Rhodes (1959), *Lord Randolph Churchill* (London: Weidenfeld and Nicolson).

Jay, Rev. A Osborne (1896), *A Story of Shoreditch* (London).

Jenkins, Roy (1995; 1997), *Gladstone* (London: Macmillan; New York: Random House).

Jenkins, Roy (1998), *The Chancellors* (London: Macmillan).

Jenkins, Roy (2002), *Churchill* (London: Macmillan).

Jones, Elwyn, and Lloyd, John (1975; 1979), *The Ripper File: An Investigation by Detective Chief Superintendents Barlow and Watt* (London: Arthur Barker; London: Futura).

Jones, Gareth Stedman (1971; 1976), *Outcast London: A Study in the Relationships between Classes in Victorian Society* (Oxford: Oxford University Press; Harmondsworth, Middlesex: Penguin Books).

Jordan, Jane (2001), *Josephine Butler* (London: John Murray).

Jullian, Philippe (1962), *Edouard VII* (Paris: Librarie Hachette); published (1967) as *Edward and the Edwardians* (trans. Peter Dawney) (London: Sidgwick and Jackson; New York, NY: Viking Press).

Kee, Robert (1993), *The Laurel and the Ivy: The story of Charles Stewart Parnell and Irish Nationalism* (London: Hamish Hamilton).

Kelly, Alexander (1973), *Jack the Ripper: A Bibliography and Review of the Literature* (London: 1973); revised editions (1984; 1995) published by the Association of Assistant Librarians.

Kendall, Colin (1990), 'The Intentions of Thomas Eldon Stowell', *Criminologist*, Summer.

Knight, Stephen (1976; 1977; 1984), *Jack the Ripper: The Final Solution* (London: George G Harrap; London: Panther Books; London: Treasure Press); with a foreword by Nigel Cawthorne (2000) (London: Chancellor Press).

Leslie, Shane (1921), 'Henry Matthews Lord Llandaff', *Dublin Review*, Vol. 168, January.

Leufstadius, Birgitta (1994), *Jack the Rippers Tredje Offer (Jack the Ripper's Third Victim)* (Partille, Sweden: Warne Förlag).

Lilly, Marjorie (1971), *Sickert: The Painter and His Circle* (London: Elek).

Linemann, Albert S (2000), *Anti-Semitism Before the Holocaust*, Seminar Studies in History series (Harlow, Essex: Pearson Education).

Linklater, Magnus (1970), 'Did Jack the Ripper Have Royal Blood?', *Sunday Times*, 1 November.

Littlechild, John G (1894), *The Reminiscences of Chief-Inspector Littlechild* (London: The Leadenhall Press).

London, Jack (1903), *The People of the Abyss* (London: Macmillan); with an introduction by Jack Lindsay (1977) (London: Journeyman Press).

Longford, Elizabeth (1964; 2000), *Victoria R.I.* (London: Weidenfeld and Nicolson; London: Abacus).

Lynd, Helen Merrell (1945), *England in the Eighteen-Eighties: Toward a Social Basis for Freedom* (Oxford: Oxford University Press).

Lyons, F S L (1977), *Charles Stewart Parnell* (Oxford: Oxford University Press).

Macintyre, Ben (1997), *The Napoleon of Crime: The Life and Times of Adam Worth, the Real Moriarty* (London: HarperCollins).

Mackay, John Henry (1891), *The Anarchists: A Picture of Civilisation at the Close of the 19th Century* (Boston, MA: Benj. R Tucker); edited by Mark A Sullivan with essays by Hubert Kennedy, Edward Mornin, Sharon Presley and Peter Lamborn-Wilson (1999) (New York: Autonomedia).

Macnaghten, Sir Melville (1914), *Days of My Years* (London: Longman, Green & Co.).

Magnus, Philip (1954), *Gladstone: A Biography* (London: John Murray).

Mathias, Peter (1983), *The First Industrial Nation: Economic History of Britain, 1700–1914* (London: Routledge).

Matters, Leonard (1929), *The Mystery of Jack the Ripper* (London: Hutchinson); with a new introduction (1948) (London: W H Allen) and n.d. (London: Pinnacle Books); original edition published as a paperback (1964) (London: Arrow).

May, Trevor (2000), *The Victorian Workhouse* (Prince's Risborough, Buckinghamshire: Shire Publications).

Mayhew, Henry (1983), *London's Underworld* (London: Bracken Books). First published in 1875, this is the fourth volume in Mayhew's four-volume series *London Labour and the London Poor – Those That Will Not Work*; the previous three volumes were published in 1862 (London:

Griffin, Bohn). This 1983 edition, with an introduction by Peter Quennell, was first published in 1950, and has appeared in numerous editions since then.

McCormick, Donald (1959), *The Identity of Jack the Ripper* (London: Jarrolds); revised edition (1962) (London: Pan Books); second revised edition published simultaneously (1970) (London: John Long; London: Arrow).

Meikle, Denis (2002), *Jack the Ripper: The Murders and the Movies* (London: Reynolds and Hearn).

Menard, Peter (1903), *Certain Connections or Affinities with Jack the Ripper* (Edinburgh: Nimmo).

Mitchell, B R (1975), *European Historical Statistics 1750–1970* (London: Macmillan).

Moncrieff, Chris (2001), *Living on a Deadline: A History of the Press Association* (London: Virgin).

Morrison, Arthur (1894), *Tales of Mean Streets* (London: Methuen).

Morrison, Arthur (1896), *A Child of the Jago* (London: Methuen); edited with an introduction by Peter Miles (1996) (London: J M Dent).

Morton, James (2000), *East End Gangland* (London: Little, Brown).

Moylan, Sir John (1934), *Scotland Yard and the Metropolitan Police* (London: Putnam and Company).

Murray, Peter (1999), *Poverty and Welfare 1830–1914*, Access to History series (London: Hodder and Stoughton).

Muusmann, Carl (1908), *Hvem Var Jack the Ripper en dansk forhørsdommers undersølgelse* (Copenhagen: Hermann-Petersen); published privately in a limited edition by Adam Wood (1999) as *Who Was Jack the Ripper? A Danish Judge's Investigation* (trans. Rikke Skipper-Pederson with Adam Wood).

Nixon, Gerry (1998), 'Le Grand of the Strand', *Ripperologist*, Issue 18, August.

OBroin, Leon (1971), *The Prime Informer: A Suppressed Scandal* (London: Sidgwick and Jackson).

O'Connor, T P (1929), *Memoirs of an Old Parliamentarian*, 2 vols (London: Ernest Benn).

Odell, Robin (1965), *Jack the Ripper In Fact and Fiction* (London: Harrap); with additional material (1966) (London: Mayflower-Dell).

O'Donnell, Kevin, Parlour, Andy, and Parlour, Sue (1997), *The Jack the Ripper Whitechapel Murders* (St Osyth, Essex: Ten Bells Publishing).

Okey, Thomas (1938), *A Basketful of Memories. An Autobiographical Sketch* (London: J M Dent).

Olsson, Daniel (2004), 'Elizabeth's Story', *Ripperologist*, Issue 52, March.

Osher 583, Frater Aschad (1994), *Did Aleister Crowley Know the Identity of Jack the Ripper?* (Berkeley, CA: Pangenetor Lodge Publications).

Owen, Frank (1954), *Tempestuous Journey. Lloyd George His Life And Times* (London: Hutchinson).

Paley, Bruce (1995), *Jack the Ripper: The Simple Truth* (London: Headline).

Palmer, Alan (1989; revised 2000), *The East End: Four Centuries of London Life* (London: John Murray).

Palmer, Scott (1995), *Jack the Ripper: A Reference Guide* (Lanham, MD: The Scarecrow Press).

Partridge, Eric (1950; 1995), *Dictionary of the Underworld* (London: Routledge and Kegan Paul; Ware, Hertfordshire: Wordsworth Editions).

Pearsall, Ronald (1969), *The Worm in the Bud: The World of Victorian Sexuality* (London: Weidenfeld and Nicolson).

Pearson, Michael (1972), *The Age of Consent* (Newton Abbot: David and Charles).

Pope, Wilson (1938), *The Story of The Star 1888-1938* (London: The Star Publications Department).

Pope-Hennessy, James (1959), *Queen Mary* (London: George Allen and Unwin).

Porter, Bernard (1987), *The Origins of the Vigilant State: The London Metropolitan Police Special Branch before the First World War* (London: Weidenfeld and Nicolson).

Porter, Roy (1994), *London: A Social History* (London: Hamish Hamilton; London: Penguin Books).

Queux, William Le (1923), *Things I Know About Kings, Celebrities and Crooks* (London: Eveleigh Nash and Grayson).

Ransford, Oliver (1969), *The Battle of Spion Kop* (London: John Murray).

Rees, J D (1891), *H. R. H. The Duke of Clarence & Avondale in Southern India, with a Narrative of Elephant Catching in Mysore by G. P. Sanderson* (London, Kegan Paul).

Reeve, Ada (1954), *Take It For a Fact* (London: William Heinemann).

Richardson, J Hall (1927), *From the City to Fleet Street* (London: Stanley Paul & Co. Ltd).

Richter, Donald C (1981), *Riotous Victorians* (Athens, OH: Ohio University Press).

Riley, Peter (2001), *The Highways and Byways of Jack the Ripper* (Runcorn, Cheshire: P & D Riley).

Roberts, Andrew (1999), *Salisbury*: Victorian Titan (London: Weidenfeld and Nicolson).

Roberts, Cecil (1932), Alfred Fripp (London: Hutchinson).

Rose, Millicent (1951), The East End of London (London: Cresset Press).

Rosenwater, Irving (1973), 'Jack the Ripper Sort of a Cricket Person', Cricketer, January.

Rubinstein, W D (1998), Britain's Century: A Political and Social History 1815–1905 (London: Arnold).

Rumbelow, Donald (1975), The Complete Jack the Ripper (London: W H Allen; Boston, MA: New York Graphic Society, 1975; London: Star Books, 1976; New York, NY: Signet Books, 1976; London: Star Books, 1981; revised edition, London: W H Allen, 1987). Published in 1988 as Jack the Ripper: The Complete Casebook (Chicago: Contemporary Books). Published in 1988 as a revised edition with an addendum (London: Penguin Books).

Ryder, Stephen P (ed.) (1997), The First Fifty Years of Jack the Ripper, 2 vols (Paramus, NJ: Ripperological Preservation Society).

Samuel, Raphael (1981), East End Underworld: Chapters in the Life of Arthur Harding (London: Routledge and Kegan Paul).

Schults, Raymond L (1972), Crusader in Babylon: W.T. Stead and the Pall Mall Gazette (Lincoln, NB: University of Nebraska Press).

Scott, George (1968), Reporter Anonymous: The Story of the Press Association (London: Hutchinson).

Sharkey, Terence (1987; 1992), Jack the Ripper: 100 Years of Investigation (London: Ward Lock; New York, NY: Dorset Press).

Sheehan, Elizabeth (1981), 'Victorian Clitoridectomy: Isaac Baker Brown and His Harmless Operative Procedure', Medical Anthropological Newsletter, August; included in Lancaster, Roger N, and Leonardo, Micaela di (eds) (1997), The Gender/Sexuality Reader (New York, NY: Routledge).

Shelden, Neal (1999), Jack the Ripper and His Victims (Hornchurch, Essex: Neal Shelden).

Shelden, Neal (2001), Annie Chapman, Jack the Ripper Victim: A Short Biography (Hornchurch, Essex: Neal Shelden).

Sheppard, F H W (1979), Survey of London: Vol. XXVII: Spitalfields and Mile End New Town: The Parishes of Christ Church and All Saints and the Liberties of Norton Folgate and the Old Artillery Ground (London: The Athlone Press, University of London).

Sims, George R (1907), 'Who Was Jack the Ripper?', Lloyd's Weekly News, 22 September.

Sims, George R (1917), Glances Back (London: Jarrolds).

Sitwell, Osbert (ed.) (1947), A Free House! Or The Artist as Craftsman. Being the writings of Walter Richard Sickert (London: Macmillan and Co.).

Sitwell, Osbert (1950), Noble Essences: A Book of Characters (London: Little, Brown & Company).

Smith, Lieut.-Col. Sir Henry (1910), From Constable to Commissioner: The Story of Sixty Years, Most of Them Misspent (London: Chatto and Windus).

Smithkey, John (1998), Jack the Ripper, The Inquest of the Final Victim Mary Kelly (North Canton, OH: Key Publications).

Soltikow, Graf Michael Alexander (1944), Der Teufel von Whitechapel (Nürnberg: Willmy Verlag); published in 2001, retaining the German title, as a translation by Jesse Flowers (Paramus, NJ: Ripperological Preservation Society). (This book is a disgraceful but historically fascinating use of the Ripper in Nazi anti-Jewish propaganda.)

Spiering, Frank (1975; 1980), Prince Jack: The True Story of Jack the Ripper (New York, NY: Doubleday; New York, NY: Jove Books).

Springfield, Lincoln (1924), Some Piquant People (London: T Fisher Unwin).

Stewart, William (1939), Jack the Ripper: A New Theory (London: Quality Press).

Stow, John (1912), The Survey of London (London: J M Dent); Everyman edition (1987) with a new introduction by Valerie Pearl (London: J M Dent).

Stowell, Thomas E A (1970), ' "Jack the Ripper" – A Solution?', The Criminologist, Vol. 5, No. 18.

Strachan, Ross (1999), The Jack the Ripper Handbook: A Reader's Companion (Irvine, Scotland: Great Scot Services and Ross Strachan).

Sugden, Philip (1993), 'Puckridge: A Cautionary Tale', Ripperana, No. 3, January.

Sugden, Philip (1994), The Complete History of Jack the Ripper (London: Robinson); revised paperback edition, 1995 (London: Robinson); 1995 (New York, NY: Carroll and Graf); paperback with new introduction,

2002 (London: Robinson); 2002 (New York, NY: Carroll and Graf).

Sugden, Philip (1996), The Life and Times of Jack the Ripper (Avonmouth, Bristol: Sienna).

Sutton, Denys (1976), Walter Sickert (London: Michael Joseph).

Sweeney, John (1904), At Scotland Yard (London: Grant Richards).

Symons, J (1963), Buller's Campaign (London: Cresset Press).

Terrot, Charles (1959), The Maiden Tribute: A Study of the White Slave Traffic of the Nineteenth Century (London: Frederick Muller).

Thomas, Donald (1999), The Victorian Underworld (London: John Murray).

Thompson, Basil (1922), Queer People (London: Hodder and Stoughton).

Thorne, Guy (1913), The Great Acceptance: The Life Story of F.N. Charrington (London: Hodder and Stoughton).

Thurston, Gavin (1965), The Great Thames Disaster (London: George Allen and Unwin).

Tobias, J J (1967), Crime and Industrial Society in the 19th Century (London: Batsford).

Troup, Sir Edward (1925), The Home Office (London: G P Putnam and Sons).

Trow, M J (1997; 1998), The Many Faces of Jack the Ripper (Chichester, West Sussex: Summersdale).

Tully, James (1997; 1998), The Secret of Prisoner 1167. Was this man Jack the Ripper? (London: Robinson; New York, NY: Carroll and Graf); paperback (1998) (London: Robinson).

Turnbull, Peter (1996), The Killer Who Never Was (Hull: Clark, Lawrence Publishers).

Underwood, Peter (1987), Jack the Ripper: One Hundred Years of Mystery (London: Blandford Press).

Unsworth, Madge (1954), Maiden Tribute (London: Salvationist Publishing and Supplies Ltd).

Walkowitz, Judith R (1980), Prostitution and Victorian Society: Women, Class and the State (Cambridge: Cambridge University Press).

Walkowitz, Judith R (1992), City of Dreadful Delight: Narratives of Sexual Danger in Late Victorian London (London: Virago).

Wallace, Richard (1996), Jack the Ripper 'Light Hearted Friend' (Melrose, MA: Gemini Press).

Weinreb, Ben, and Hibbert, Christopher (1983), The London Encyclopedia (London: Macmillan).

Weintraub, Stanley (1987; 1988), Victoria: Biography of a Queen (London: Unwin Hyman); paperback (1988) (London: Unwin Paperbacks).

Wensley, Frederick Porter (1931), Detective Days (London: Cassell).

West, D J (1949), 'The Identity of "Jack the Ripper" ', Journal for the Society for Psychical Research, July–August.

White, Jerry (1980), Rothschild Buildings: Life In An East End Tenement Block 1887–1920 (London: Routledge and Kegan Paul).

Whitehead, Mark, and Rivett, Miriam (2001), Jack the Ripper (Harpenden, Hertfordshire: Pocket Essentials).

Whittington-Egan, Richard (1975), A Casebook on Jack the Ripper (London: Wildy and Sons).

Wilding, John (1993), Jack the Ripper Revealed (London: Constable).

William, R H (1988), The Salisbury–Balfour Correspondence 1869–1892 (Hitchin: Hertfordshire Record Society).

Williams, Montagu (1892), Round London: Down East and Up West (London: Macmillan and Co.).

Williams, Watkin Wynn (1941), The Life of General Sir Charles Warren: By His Grandson (Oxford: Blackwell).

Wilson, Colin (1960), 'My Search For Jack the Ripper', Evening Standard, 8–12 August.

Wilson, Colin, and Odell, Robin (1987; 1988), Jack the Ripper: Summing Up and Verdict (London: Bantam Press; London: Corgi Books).

Wintle, Justin (ed.) (1982), Makers of Nineteenth Century Culture 1800–1914: A Biographical Dictionary (London: Routledge and Kegan Paul).

Wohl, Anthony S (ed.) (1970), The Bitter Cry of Outcast London with leading articles from the Pall Mall Gazette of October 1883 and articles by Lord Salisbury, Joseph Chamberlain and Forster Crozier (London: Leicester University Press).

Wolf, A P (1993), Jack the Myth: A New Look At Jack the Ripper (London: Robert Hale).

Wolff, Camille (ed.) (1995), Who Was Jack the Ripper? (London: Grey House Books).

Woodhall, Edwin T (1937; 1997), Jack the Ripper or When London Walked in Terror (London: Mellifont Press; Runcorn, Cheshire: P&D Riley).

Wright, Stephen (1999), Jack the Ripper: An American View (New York, NY: Mystery Notebook Editions).

Index

533